HISTORY IN DISPUTE

ADVISORY BOARD

HISTORY IN DISPUTE

Volume 15

The Middle East Since 1945: Second Series

Edited by David W. Lesch

A MANLY, INC. BOOK

StJ

ST. JAMES
PRESS®

THOMSON
━━━✦━━━ ™
GALE

Detroit • New York • San Diego • San Francisco • Cleveland • New Haven, Conn. • Waterville, Maine • London • Munich

History in Dispute
Volume 15: The Middle East Since 1945, Second Series
David W. Lesch

Editorial Directors
Matthew J. Bruccoli and Richard Layman

Series Editor
Anthony J. Scotti Jr.

LIBRARY OF CONGRESS CONTROL NUMBER: 00-266495
ISBN 1-55862-478-3

Printed in the United States of America
10 9 8 7 6 5 4 3 2 1

CONTENTS

CONTENTS

CONTENTS

CONTENTS

CONTENTS

CONTENTS

ABOUT THE SERIES

History in Dispute is an ongoing series designed to present, in an informative and lively pro-con format, different perspectives on major historical events drawn from all time periods and from all parts of the globe. The series was developed in response to requests from librarians and educators for a history-reference source that will help students hone essential critical-thinking skills while serving as a valuable research tool for class assignments.

Individual volumes in the series concentrate on specific themes, eras, or subjects intended to correspond to the way history is studied at the academic level. For example, early volumes cover such topics as the Cold War, American Social and Political Movements, and World War II. Volume subtitles make it easy for users to identify contents at a glance and facilitate searching for specific subjects in library catalogues.

Each volume of *History in Dispute* includes up to fifty entries, centered on the overall theme of that volume and chosen by an advisory board of historians for their relevance to the curriculum. Entries are arranged alphabetically by the name of the event or issue in its most common form. (Thus,

in Volume 1, the issue "Was detente a success?" is presented under the chapter heading "Detente.")

Each entry begins with a brief statement of the opposing points of view on the topic, followed by a short essay summarizing the issue and outlining the controversy. At the heart of the entry, designed to engage students' interest while providing essential information, are the two or more lengthy essays, written specifically for this publication by experts in the field, each presenting one side of the dispute.

In addition to this substantial prose explication, entries also include excerpts from primary-source documents, other useful information typeset in easy-to-locate shaded boxes, detailed entry bibliographies, and photographs or illustrations appropriate to the issue.

Other features of *History in Dispute* volumes include: individual volume introductions by academic experts, tables of contents that identify both the issues and the controversies, chronologies of events, names and credentials of advisers, brief biographies of contributors, thorough volume bibliographies for more information on the topic, and a comprehensive subject index.

ACKNOWLEDGMENTS

James F. Tidd Jr., *Editorial associate.*

Philip B. Dematteis, *Production manager.*

Kathy Lawler Merlette, *Office manager.*

Ann M. Cheschi and Carol A. Cheschi, *Administrative support.*

Ann-Marie Holland, *Accounting.*

Sally R. Evans, *Copyediting supervisor.* Phyllis A. Avant, Caryl Brown, Melissa D. Hinton, Philip I. Jones, Rebecca Mayo, and Nancy E. Smith, *Copyediting staff.*

Zoe R. Cook, *Series team leader, layout and graphics.* Janet E. Hill, *Layout and graphics supervisor.* Sydney E. Hammock, *Graphics and prepress.*

Scott Nemzek and Paul Talbot, *Photography editors.*

Amber L. Coker, *Permissions editor and database manager.*

Joseph M. Bruccoli, *Digital photographic copy work.*

Donald K. Starling, *Systems manager.*

Kathleen M. Flanagan, *Typesetting supervisor.* Patricia Marie Flanagan, Mark J. McEwan, and Pamela D. Norton, *Typesetting staff.*

Walter W. Ross, *Library researcher.*

The staff of the Thomas Cooper Library, University of South Carolina are unfailingly helpful: Tucker Taylor, *Circulation department head, Thomas Cooper Library, University of South Carolina.* John Brunswick, *Interlibrary-loan department head.* Virginia W. Weathers, *Reference department head.* Brette Barclay, Marilee Birchfield, Paul Cammarata, Gary Geer, Michael Macan, Tom Marcil, and Sharon Verba, *Reference librarians.*

PERMISSIONS

ILLUSTRATIONS

Pp. 7, 36, 69, 99, 114, 145, 184, and 200: © AP/ Wide World Photos.

P. 17: Agence France Presse Photo.

P. 31: © Popperfoto.

Pp. 25, 47, 53, 118, 132, 162, 169, 224, and 272: © CORBIS/Bettmann.

P. 63: From Herbert Block, *Herblock's Special for Today* (New York: Simon & Schuster, 1958); © 1956 The Washington Post Co.

P. 74: Magnum Photo/Delahaye Luc.

P. 82: Eric Bouvet/Odyssey Matrix.

P. 94: Photograph by George Baramki Azar.

P. 136: Zahal, Israel Defense Forces.

P. 154: Magnum Photo/Eli Reed.

P. 178: Aramco.

P. 204: Photograph by Abbie Rowe.

P. 212: Topham.

P. 230: From Peter Chelkowski and Hamid Dabashi, *Staging a Revolution: The Art of Persuasion in the Islamic Republic of Iran* (New York: New York University Press, 1999).

P. 239: © CORBIS/David Rubinger.

P. 246: © CORBIS/BBC Hulton Picture Library.

P. 268: © CORBIS/AFP.

PREFACE

As I stated in *History in Dispute, Volume 14: The Middle East Since 1945, First Series,* few other areas of the world engender more debate and controversy than the Middle East. Most of the areas of dispute in the Middle East since 1945 can trace their origins to European colonialism in the nineteenth century. During this period the Ottoman Empire came under increasing pressure from the European powers. The resulting historical currents climaxed in the outbreak of World War I (1914–1918) and the secret agreements that in large part established the shape of the modern Middle East state system, introducing the problems that evolved into, inter alia, such notable events as the Arab-Israeli conflict, Arab nationalism, Islamic extremism, and the Algerian Revolution (1954–1962).

The Middle East in the nineteenth century comprised territories under direct Ottoman control (the Balkans, present-day Turkey, and the Levant), regions under nominal Ottoman sovereignty (some of the North African provinces), areas subject to direct European control (Algeria, Tunisia, and Egypt), independent empires such as Qajar Iran that were subject to constant European manipulation, and the so-called great game in south-central Asia (present-day Afghanistan, Pakistan, and India). Common to each of these regions was the actual or attempted extension of European influence and interference in the affairs of Middle Eastern peoples. This era was the heyday of European imperialism, when gunboat diplomacy was the norm rather than the exception. The Ottoman Empire as well as other Middle East entities desperately tried to stave off for as long as possible the deleterious effects of European encroachment.

The Ottomans throughout most of the nineteenth and early twentieth centuries launched a series of internal reforms in order to strengthen their Empire politically, militarily, and economically so that it could withstand the pressure emanating from a Europe that had long broken out of its economic dol-

drums and cultural lethargy with dramatic technological, industrial, and demographic growth. Despite attempts by Britain and France to maintain the integrity of the Ottoman Empire so that it could act as a buffer to Russian and European ambitions and keep the British lifeline to India intact (especially after the Suez Canal opened in 1869), the situation was a losing battle for the Ottomans. Overall, the programs of Westernizing reforms known as Nizam-i Jedid ("New Order," undertaken by Sultan Selim III in the 1790s) and the Tanzimat ("Reorganization," undertaken by sultans Abdulmecid I and Abdulaziz between the 1830s and 1870s) strengthened the Empire in some ways but weakened it in others. Britain and France, especially, came to follow a rather contradictory policy of attempting to maintain the integrity of the Empire, so demonstrably evident in the Crimean War of 1854–1856 (in which they helped the Ottomans push back the Russians), while at the same time picking away at the fringes of the realm and supporting independence movements in the Christian-dominated Balkan territories, such as occurred in Greece in 1830. The Europeans seemingly could not make up their minds whether they wanted the Ottoman Empire to survive or wither away. Certainly after the Russo-Turkish War (1877–1878), the so-called Eastern Question no longer focused on how to maintain the integrity of the Empire but instead on how to oversee its orderly breakup so that the dreaded imperialist landgrab did not occur—anything upsetting the balance of power in the Middle East could in turn upset the balance of power in Europe. Essentially, the Europeans and the Ottomans were unsuccessful in this endeavor. The results contributed mightily to the outbreak of World War I, which led to an even more direct European presence in the Middle East than ever before. Indeed, the Ottoman decision to enter the war, and to do so on the side of Germany, may be the single most important decision in modern Middle East history.

Since the Ottoman Empire sided with the Central Powers, the British no longer had to maintain even the pretense of supporting the Ottomans. As such, the British developed a three-pronged policy toward the Middle East: gain allies in the region to support the strategic objective of defeating the Ottoman Empire; create a pro-British buffer or bulwark in the region to protect the lifeline to India—essentially an Arab replacement for the Ottomans; and do both of these things without upsetting Britain's allies in the war, France and Russia, both of whom were bearing the brunt of the war in Europe. Achieving these goals was quite a tall task for the British, and in attempting to do so they would make what on the surface appeared to be contradictory promises to a variety of countries and groups regarding the dispensation of Ottoman lands in the Middle East following the anticipated victory in the war.

With strategic issues and European relations of paramount concern, the British and the French (Russia had withdrawn from World War I following the Bolshevik Revolution in 1917, and the new communist government renounced—and published—the secret wartime agreements) essentially created much of the Middle East nation-state system as it exists today, with all of its flaws, potentialities, and lingering controversy. Despite the desire of the indigenous peoples in the region for independence, spurred on by the promise of self-determination as espoused so publicly by U.S. president Woodrow Wilson, what was instituted for the most part throughout much of the Middle East was either the continuation of pre-war colonial control (especially in North Africa) or what was termed the *mandate system* (particularly in the Levant and Fertile Crescent) that promised eventual independence under the supervision of the mandatory powers—Great Britain and France—as ordained by the newly established League of Nations. To the Arabs living under the mandate system, the situation seemed more like an extension of colonialism by another name.

Iran, however, maintained its independence after the war, although the country was ravaged by the direct and indirect effects of the conflagration. This postwar scenario further weakened the Qajar dynasty, which had been in power since the late eighteenth century. In 1925 it was removed by the commander of the Cossack Brigade, Reza Khan, who then ascended to the "peacock throne" as Shah (king) and initiated the Pahlavi dynasty, which would continue under the auspices of his son, Muhammad Reza Pahlavi (otherwise known as the Shah of Iran), until the Iranian Revolution of 1979. Reza Shah attempted to modernize Iran, but he met with limited success.

Contrary to popular notion, World War I was not directly responsible for the end of the Ottoman Empire, although the conflict certainly weakened it. It was a secular Turkish nationalist movement led by Mustafa Kemal (who would later be accorded the title of *Ataturk* or "father of the Turks") that abolished the Ottoman sultanate and caliphate by 1923. Taking a dramatic step in the process of active reform along the European model present in the Ottoman Empire since the late eighteenth century, Ataturk tried, and to a significant degree succeeded in, forging a new secular Turkish Republic separated from its Ottoman past and taking it clearly in the direction of Europe by instituting a series of far-reaching Westernizing reforms; indeed, the policy priority today in Ankara of joining the European Union can be seen as the culmination of Ataturk's mission.

Throughout the Middle East the reaction to the continuation of European influence and control was generally hostile, spasmodically appearing in the shape of riots and rebellion, eventually leading to a series of revolutionary independence movements across the region after the European grip was further attenuated by the deleterious effects of World War II (1939–1945). At the level of ideology, there was also a variety of responses in the region spanning the spectrum of political culture, from socialism and fascism to Islamism (anything but liberal constitutionalism, the political ideology of the increasingly resented Western powers).

This combustible combination of the rise of nationalist movements across much of the region amid nascent state-building efforts, the decolonization process, the emerging superpower confrontation between the United States and the Soviet Union, and the creation of the State of Israel in 1948 has largely defined areas of conflict and dispute in the Middle East ever since. This volume endeavors to examine topics of dispute born out of the multidimensional Middle East matrix that came into being from the intermingling of these various historical forces since 1945 up to the end of the twentieth century.

As in any work, the sum total consists of its constituent parts. I would first like to thank the authors themselves for their commitment to the project and contributing a vast body of quality work. In addition, Manly, Inc., who initiated the project and oversaw the production of the volume, is a real pleasure to work with, and I greatly appreciate the high standards it has set and the help it has accorded me in my efforts. Finally, I want to thank Eunice Herrington in the Department of History at Trinity University, who, as always, has been of inestimable assistance in compiling the final product.

I have tried to maintain consistent spellings for the many terms, names, and places that have been transliterated in a variety of ways into English; indeed, some works have collected five or six distinct spellings over the years—hopefully, there are but a few occasions when one slipped by the multilayered editorial process. I have attempted to transliterate Arabic, Turkish, and Persian terms as accurately as possible into English; with several terms, however, I opted for the more popular version of the spelling even if it be somewhat inaccurate, simply because a specific spelling has become embedded into our collective memory more than an alternative spelling, thus facilitating recognition by the reader.

–DAVID W. LESCH,
TRINITY UNIVERSITY

CHRONOLOGY

1945

22 MARCH: The League of Arab States (Arab League) is formed. (*See* **League of Arab States**)

NOVEMBER: The Anglo-American Committee of Inquiry is formed to investigate Palestine's future and Jewish immigration to the region. (*See* **Birth of Israel**)

1946

JANUARY: The Democratic Party of Turkey is founded.

19 JANUARY: Iran appeals to the United Nations (UN) Security Council to have Soviet troops withdraw from Azerbaijan. (*See* **Superpower Cold War**)

22 MARCH: The Transjordan mandate ends, and the independent Kingdom of Transjordan is established with Abdullah as king.

1 MAY: The Anglo-American Committee of Inquiry issues a report on Palestine calling for a state divided between Palestinian and Jewish rule and allowing for greater Jewish immigration to the region. (*See* **Birth of Israel**)

6 MAY: Soviet troops are evacuated from Iran.

22 JULY: The Irgun (a splinter Jewish group in Palestine seeking independence for a Jewish state) blows up the King David Hotel in an attack on the British Headquarters there, killing eighty people.

1947

12 MARCH: The Truman Doctrine, which establishes the U.S. policy of blocking the spread of communism in the world, is announced; the United States provides financial assistance to Greece and Turkey. (*See* **Superpower Cold War**)

APRIL: The Baath Party (an Arab socialist, revolutionary, and nationalistic party) is formed at a conference in Damascus, Syria.

13 MAY: The UN Security Council on Palestine (UNSCOP) is created.

15 AUGUST: The state of Pakistan is created.

27 NOVEMBER: The UN partition plan for Palestine is passed by the UN General Assembly (Resolution 181); it calls for the establishment of a Jewish and Arab state in Palestine. (*See* **Birth of Israel**)

DECEMBER: Jewish-Arab communal warfare intensifies in Palestine.

1948

19 MARCH: The United States proposes UN trusteeship in Palestine.

9 APRIL: Jews attack Arabs at Deir Yassin; more than 140 Arabs are massacred. (*See* **Birth of Israel**)

14–15 MAY: The British mandate in Palestine ends; the State of Israel is proclaimed; and the first Arab-Israeli war begins when five Arab states (Transjordan, Egypt, Syria, Lebanon, and Iraq) invade Israel.

15 MAY: The United States recognizes Israel.

17 MAY: The Soviet Union recognizes Israel.

17 SEPTEMBER: UN mediator Count Folke Bernadotte, a supporter of Palestinian rights, is assassinated by the Jewish Stern Gang in Jerusalem; American Ralph Bunche is named as his successor.

1 DECEMBER: King Abdullah renames his state the Hashimite Kingdom of Jordan.

11 DECEMBER: The UN General Assembly adopts Resolution 194 dealing, inter alia, with the Palestinian refugee question.

1949

24 FEBRUARY: Israel and Egypt sign an armistice agreement at Rhodes.

23 MARCH: Israel and Lebanon sign an armistice agreement at Rhodes.

3 APRIL: Israel and Jordan sign an armistice agreement at Rhodes.

20 JULY: Israel and Syria sign an armistice agreement at Rhodes.

DECEMBER: King Abdullah of Jordan de facto annexes the West Bank and East Jerusalem (becomes formal 24 April 1950).

20 DECEMBER: In Syria the third coup d'état of the year occurs; this one, led by Colonel Adib al-Shishakli, succeeds in overthrowing the government.

1950

MARCH: Muhammad Musaddiq's National Front (an anti-Shah, pronationalist movement) makes significant gains in elections for the Iranian *majlis* (parliament). (*See* **Musaddiq Coup** *and* **Shah of Iran**)

9 MARCH: Turkey, which is the first Muslim state to do so, recognizes Israel.

15 MARCH: Iran recognizes Israel.

1 MAY: With the victory of the Democratic Party in Turkish elections, Adnan Menderes becomes prime minister.

25 MAY: Britain, France, and the United States issue the Tripartite Declaration, which regulates arms flow to the Middle East.

1951

7 MARCH: Iranian prime minister Ali Razmara is assassinated.

28 APRIL: Iran nationalizes the British-owned Anglo-Iranian Oil Company. (*See* **Oil Production**)

29 APRIL: Musaddiq becomes the Iranian prime minister. (*See* **Musaddiq Coup**)

20 JULY: King Abdullah of Jordan is assassinated by a Palestinian nationalist in Jerusalem at the al-Aqsa mosque (Prince Talal is crowned king on 6 September).

24 DECEMBER: Libya becomes independent, with Sidi Muhammad Idris (King Idris) as head of the nation.

1952

25 JANUARY: British troops battle Egyptian police in Ismailiya (astride the Suez Canal).

26 JANUARY: Anti-British riots erupt in Cairo on "Black Saturday."

18 FEBRUARY: Turkey joins the North Atlantic Treaty Organization (NATO). (*See* **Superpower Cold War**)

23 JULY: The Free Officers coup—led by Muhammad Neguib, Gamal Abd al-Nasser, and the Revolutionary Command Council (RCC)—overthrows the Egyptian monarchy (King Faruq abdicates on 26 July). (*See* **Free Officers Revolution**)

11 AUGUST: Hussein is crowned king of Jordan, replacing Talal.

1953

2 MAY: King Faisal II of Iraq is crowned on his eighteenth birthday, ending the regency of his uncle, Amir Abdullah.

13 AUGUST: The Shah of Iran dismisses Musaddiq, but he does not leave office; the Shah flees the country. (*See* **Musaddiq Coup** *and* **Shah of Iran**)

22 AUGUST: The Shah returns to power in Iran (the "Musaddiq Coup"), and Musaddiq is placed under house arrest.

3 NOVEMBER: Moshe Sharett becomes prime minister of Israel, replacing David Ben-Gurion, the first Israeli prime minister.

9 NOVEMBER: King Abd al-Aziz bin Abd al-Rahman bin Saud (known as Ibn Saud), founder of Saudi Arabia, dies; his son Saud becomes king.

1954

24 FEBRUARY: al-Shishakli is removed from power in Syria.

9 OCTOBER: The Anglo-Egyptian agreement (signed 27 July) on British evacuation of their Suez Canal base is activated.

26 OCTOBER: Members of the Muslim Brotherhood attempt to assassinate Nasser.

1 NOVEMBER: The Algerian rebellion against French rule begins. (*See* **Algerian Revolution**)

14 NOVEMBER: Egyptian president Naguib is deposed by a military junta, and Nasser is named president.

1955

24 FEBRUARY: Iraq and Turkey sign a mutual defense treaty, launching the Baghdad Pact (Great Britain joins on 3 April, Pakistan on 23 September, and Iran on 3 November). (*See* **Baghdad Pact**)

28 FEBRUARY: Israeli troops raid Gaza and kill 38 Egyptians.

27 SEPTEMBER: Nasser announces an arms deal with the Soviet Union (officially with Czechoslovakia). (*See* **Superpower Cold War**)

3 NOVEMBER: Ben-Gurion again becomes Israeli prime minister.

1956

1 JANUARY: Sudan proclaims its independence.

1 MARCH: King Hussein of Jordan dismisses British general John Bagot Glubb from command of the Arab Legion.

2 MARCH: Morocco gains its independence from France.

20 MARCH: Tunisia becomes independent from France.

16 MAY: Egypt recognizes the People's Republic of China.

19 JULY: U.S. secretary of state John Foster Dulles withdraws the U.S. offer of aid to Egypt to build the Aswan High Dam. (*See* **Superpower Cold War**)

26 JULY: Egypt nationalizes the Suez Canal Company. (*See* **Suez War**)

29 OCTOBER: Israel invades the Sinai Peninsula.

30 OCTOBER: The British and the French issue an ultimatum to Egypt and Israel to end hostilities in the Suez.

5 NOVEMBER: Anglo-French forces invade the Suez Canal zone.

6–7 NOVEMBER: Britain and France accept a cease-fire.

22 DECEMBER: British and French withdrawal from Egypt is completed; they are replaced by United Nations Emergency Force (UNEF) troops.

1957

5 JANUARY: The Eisenhower Doctrine, which authorizes U.S. funds to fight the spread of communism in the Middle East, is announced (it is approved by the U.S. Congress in March). (*See* **Eisenhower Doctrine** *and* **Superpower Cold War**)

7 MARCH: Israeli troops complete their withdrawal from the Sinai Peninsula.

25 JULY: The Tunisian monarchy is abolished, and Habib Bourguiba is named president of the new republic.

1958

1 FEBRUARY: Egypt and Syria formally merge to become the United Arab Republic. (*See* **United Arab Republic**)

14 FEBRUARY: Iraq and Jordan form the Arab Federation.

14 JULY: A revolution in Iraq overthrows the monarchy and ends the Arab Federation. (*See* **Iraqi Revolution**)

15 JULY: U.S. Marines land in Beirut, Lebanon; British forces land in Jordan on 17 July. (*See* **Eisenhower Doctrine**)

31 JULY: General Fuad Shihab (Chehab) is elected president of Lebanon.

25 OCTOBER: U.S. Marines complete their withdrawal from Beirut.

4 NOVEMBER: National Security Resolution 5820 ("U.S. Policy Toward the Middle East") is approved by President Dwight D. Eisenhower. It calls for the United States to work with Nasser to forestall Soviet influence in Egypt and to avoid being united with any one faction in Lebanon. (*See* **NSC 5820/1** *and* **Superpower Cold War**)

1959

18 AUGUST: The Baghdad Pact is renamed CENTO (Central Treaty Organization) following the departure of Iraq from the group on 24 March. (*See* **Baghdad Pact**)

1960

27 MAY: A Turkish military coup overthrows the government of Prime Minister Menderes, who, along with fourteen other leaders, is later executed.

16 AUGUST: Cyprus becomes an independent republic.

15 SEPTEMBER: The Organization of Petroleum Exporting Countries (OPEC) is formed. Saudi Arabia, Iran, Iraq, Kuwait, and Venezuela are its founding members. (*See* **Oil Production**)

1961

26 FEBRUARY: King Muhammad V of Morocco dies; he is succeeded by Hassan II.

19 JUNE: Kuwait becomes independent from Great Britain (and becomes a member of the Arab League on 20 July). (*See* **League of Arab States**)

25 JUNE: Iraq threatens a takeover of Kuwait, saying it is an "integral part" of Iraq; the attempt is thwarted by British troops.

JULY: Nasser issues a series of major socialization and nationalization decrees in Egypt.

28 SEPTEMBER: Syria secedes from the United Arab Republic (UAR) following a coup. (*See* **United Arab Republic**)

1962

18 MARCH: A cease-fire between France and the National Liberation Front (FLN) ends the guerrilla war in Algeria. (*See* **Algerian Revolution**)

3 JULY: Algeria becomes independent.

26 SEPTEMBER: The Yemeni civil war begins with the death of Imam Ahmad. Republican forces overthrow the regime of his replacement, Imam Muhammad al-Badr.

1963

8 FEBRUARY: A Baathist coup overthrows the government of Iraqi president Abd al-Karim Qassim, who is executed.

8 MARCH: A Baathist coup in Syria overthrows the government.

16 JUNE: Levi Eshkol becomes prime minister of Israel after Ben-Gurion resigns.

6 SEPTEMBER: A constitution is approved by voters in Algeria; Ahmed Ben Bella is elected president later in the month.

18 NOVEMBER: A countercoup in Iraq overthrows the Baathist regime.

DECEMBER: Water from the Jordan River is diverted into Israel, provoking a crisis with Syria and instigating an Arab summit in Cairo over the issue the following January.

1964

JANUARY: At the Arab League summit in Cairo it is agreed to establish the Palestine Liberation Organization (PLO), with Ahmed Shuqayri as its first chairman (formally comes into being on 28 May with meeting of first Palestine National Council). (*See* **League of Arab States** *and* **Palestine Liberation Organization**)

28 MARCH: King Saud of Saudi Arabia turns over his power to Crown Prince Faysal (Faisal), who officially becomes king on 2 November.

JUNE: Israel's National Water Carrier, a large-scale water distribution system, begins operations.

22 AUGUST: Libya announces that both Great Britain and the United States have agreed to give up their military bases in the country.

1965

1 JANUARY: The Palestinian group Fatah, an anti-Israeli guerrilla movement, is established. (*See* **Palestine Liberation Organization**)

19 JUNE: Colonel Houari Boumedienne replaces Ben Bella in a bloodless coup in Algeria.

27 OCTOBER: Sulayman Demiral becomes Turkish prime minister.

1966

23 FEBRUARY: An intra-Baath Party military coup in Syria is led by General Salah Jadid.

13 APRIL: President Abd al-Salam Arif of Iraq dies in a helicopter crash; his brother, Abd al-Rahman Arif, succeeds him.

29 AUGUST: Egyptian anti-Nasser activist Sayyid Qutb is executed.

4 NOVEMBER: Syria and Egypt sign a defense pact.

1967

7 APRIL: Israeli and Syrian fighters clash (six Syrian MIGs are shot down).

14 MAY: Nasser moves combat units into the Sinai Peninsula. (*See* **Arab-Israeli War of 1967** *and* **Israeli Victory in 1967**)

18 MAY: Egypt writes UN secretary-general U Thant informing him of its decision to remove UNEF troops from Egyptian territory.

22 MAY: Nasser announces blockade of the Strait of Tiran at the entrance of the Gulf of Aqaba to Israeli ships and ships carrying strategic material bound for Israel.

30 MAY: Jordan joins Egyptian-Syrian defense pact.

5 JUNE: The Arab-Israeli War (also known as the Six-Day War) begins with a preemptive Israeli air strike against Egyptian forces.

8 JUNE: A cease-fire is established on the Jordan-Israel front. An American intelligence vessel, the USS *Liberty,* sailing along the Mediterranean coast of Israel, is bombed and strafed by Israeli jets, resulting in the death of thirty-four sailors.

9 JUNE: A cease-fire is established on the Egypt-Israel front.

10 JUNE: Israel captures the Golan Heights.

11 JUNE: A cease-fire is established on the Syria-Israel front.

AUGUST: An Arab League summit meeting in Khartoum, Sudan, declares the three "nos": no recognition, no negotiation, and no peace with Israel. (*See* **League of Arab States**)

22 NOVEMBER: UN Security Council Resolution 242, calling for the withdrawal of Israel from the Occupied Territories (West Bank, Gaza Strip, and Golan Heights), is passed. (*See* **Resolution 242**)

28 NOVEMBER: Great Britain declares the independence of South Arabia (a British colony since 1839), which is renamed the People's Republic of South Yemen, with Aden as its capital.

1968

7 JULY: A coup in Iraq brings the Baath Party back to power, with Ahmad Hassan al-Bakr as president.

1969

3 FEBRUARY: Yasser Arafat becomes the head of the PLO. (*See* **Palestine Liberation Organization**)

8 MARCH: The War of Attrition begins between Egypt and Israel. (*See* **Black September**)

17 MARCH: Golda Meir becomes the Israeli prime minister, replacing Eshkol, who died 26 February.

MAY: General Jafar al-Numayri seizes power in Sudan.

21 AUGUST: Australian tourist Michael Rohan, a fanatical Christian, sets fire to the al-Aqsa mosque in Jerusalem, causing several million dollars worth of damage to the southeastern wing.

1 SEPTEMBER: In a coup, Muammar Qadhdhafi rises to power in Libya, overthrowing the monarchy of King Idris.

28 OCTOBER: Libya notifies the United States that it must evacuate the Wheelus Air Force base; the United States formally relinquishes it on 11 June 1970.

9 DECEMBER: U.S. secretary of state William Rogers outlines what becomes known as the Rogers Plan to bring about an Arab-Israeli peace agreement.

1970

14 APRIL: The Yemeni civil war ends.

5 JULY: Libya nationalizes the country's four oil distributors. (*See* **Oil Production**)

21 JULY: The Aswan High Dam is completed.

26 JULY: In a coup in the Sultanate of Oman, Qabus (Qaboos) bin Said overthrows his father, Said ibn Taymer.

7 AUGUST: Egypt and Israel agree to the Rogers Initiative limited cease-fire, ending the War of Attrition. (*See* **Black September**)

6–12 SEPTEMBER: The Popular Front for the Liberation of Palestine (PFLP) hijacks and blows up U.S. and Swiss airliners in Jordan, launching the Jordanian Civil War, or Black September (fought between Jordanian troops and the Palestinian Liberation Army).

28 SEPTEMBER: Nasser dies; he is succeeded by Anwar al-Sadat (sworn in on 17 October).

13 NOVEMBER: A coup in Syria is led by Hafiz al-Asad, who formally becomes president on 13 March 1971.

1 DECEMBER: Radical forces take over South Yemen and rename the country the People's Democratic Republic of Yemen.

1971

27 MAY: Egypt and the Soviet Union sign a Treaty of Friendship and Cooperation. (*See* **Superpower Cold War**)

10 JULY: Senior military officers unsuccessfully attempt to overthrow Moroccan king Hassan II.

14 AUGUST: Bahrain becomes independent.

1 SEPTEMBER: Qatar becomes independent.

30 NOVEMBER: Iranian troops occupy the islands of Abu Musa, Greater Tunb, and Lesser Tunb in the Persian Gulf.

2 DECEMBER: United Arab Emirates (UAE) becomes independent; it is formed from the seven states of Abu Dhabi, Dubai, Sharjah, Ajman, Umm al Qaiwain, Ras al Khaimah, and Fujairah.

1972

18 JULY: Sadat orders Soviet advisers to leave Egypt. (*See* **Superpower Cold War**)

11 SEPTEMBER: Eleven members of Israel's Olympic team are killed by Palestinian *fedayeen* (going by the name Black September) in Munich. Most of the victims, as well as a policeman and five terrorists, die in a botched rescue attempt at a military airport. Israel retaliates by bombing sites in Lebanon and Syria.

1973

MAY: Qadhdhafi publishes a tract that will become known as the "Green Book."

17 JULY: A military coup ousts King Muhammad Zahir Shah in Afghanistan; Sardar Muhammad Da`ud declares himself president of the new republic.

6 OCTOBER: The 1973 Arab-Israeli War begins as Egyptian and Syrian forces attack Israel.

18 OCTOBER: OAPEC (Organization of Arab Petroleum Exporting Countries—the Arab members of OPEC) announces a cutback on production and by 21 October establishes an embargo against the United States. (*See* **Oil Production**)

22 OCTOBER: UN Security Council Resolution 338 passes, calling for a cease-fire in the Arab-Israeli War.

28 OCTOBER: Egyptian-Israeli negotiations begin at kilometer 101 on the Suez-Cairo road.

22 NOVEMBER: Egypt and Israel sign a cease-fire accord; more than 3,000 Israelis and 8,500 Arabs perished in the war.

1974

18 JANUARY: Egypt and Israel sign a disengagement agreement (Sinai I). (*See* **Sinai I & II**)

FEBRUARY: The rightist Jewish party Gush Emunim (Bloc of the Faithful) is founded.

4 MARCH: Israel returns control of the Suez Canal to Egypt.

18 MARCH: OAPEC ends the U.S. oil embargo. (*See* **Oil Production**)

31 MAY: Israel and Syria sign a disengagement agreement.

2 JUNE: Yitzhak Rabin becomes the prime minister of Israel.

15 JULY: The Cypriot president is overthrown by Greek-supported forces; Turkish forces land on Cyprus five days later to block a union of the island with Greece.

16 AUGUST: Turkey declares a cease-fire on Cyprus after gaining control of one-third of the island.

28 OCTOBER: The Arab League at its summit meeting in Rabat, Morocco, declares the PLO the sole legitimate representative of the Palestinian people. (*See* **League of Arab States** *and* **Palestine Liberation Organization**)

13 NOVEMBER: PLO chairman Arafat speaks before the UN General Assembly.

1975

6 MARCH: Iraq and Iran settle their border dispute by signing the Algiers agreement.

25 MARCH: Saudi king Faysal is assassinated by a nephew; Khalid becomes the new Saudi monarch.

13 APRIL: A Phalangist (Christian Maronite militia) attack on a bus carrying Palestinian PFLP supporters sparks the beginning of the Lebanese Civil War. (*See* **Israel in Lebanon**)

5 JUNE: The Suez Canal is reopened.

4 SEPTEMBER: A second disengagement agreement (Sinai II) is signed by Egypt and Israel. (*See* **Sinai I & II**)

6 NOVEMBER: King Hassan II of Morocco claims the Spanish-held Western Sahara as thousands of Moroccans cross the border in the so-called Green March.

10 NOVEMBER: The UN General Assembly passes Resolution 3379, stating that "Zionism is a form of racism."

21 NOVEMBER: Spain withdraws from the Western Sahara; Morocco and Mauritania jointly administer the territory until 1979, when Mauritania abandons its claim.

1976

31 MAY: Syrian troops enter Lebanon. (*See* **Israel in Lebanon**)

4 JULY: A surprise Israeli raid frees 98 hostages, taken 28 June on an Air France flight by a Palestinian splinter group, at an airport in Entebbe, Uganda.

20 DECEMBER: Rabin resigns as prime minister of Israel.

1977

2 MARCH: Qadhdhafi renames Libya the People's Socialist Libyan Arab Jamahiriyya and replaces the Revolutionary Command Council with the General People's Congress.

17 MAY: The Likud Party wins Israeli elections for the first time, with Menachem Begin becoming prime minister.

JULY–AUGUST: A brief border war erupts between Egypt and Libya.

19 NOVEMBER: Sadat becomes the first Arab leader to visit Israel officially; he addresses the Israeli Knesset the next day. (*See* **Egyptian-Israeli Peace Treaty** *and* **Sadat Trip to Israel**)

1978

11 MARCH: Fatah militants launch raids out of southern Lebanon into Israel, killing nearly forty Israelis. (*See* **Israel in Lebanon**)

14 MARCH: Israel launches a large-scale military operation in southern Lebanon to clear out PLO positions. (*See* **Palestine Liberation Organization**)

27 APRIL: A Marxist coup in Afghanistan overthrows Daud, bringing to power Hafizullah Amin and Nur Muhammad Taraki.

8 SEPTEMBER: In Teheran, Iran, hundreds of student protesters die in demonstrations against the Shah's regime, in an uprising known as "Black Friday." (*See* **Iranian Revolution** *and* **Shah of Iran**)

17 SEPTEMBER: The Camp David accords are signed, following thirteen days of meetings among Sadat, Begin, and U.S. president Jimmy Carter. (*See* **Egyptian-Israeli Peace Treaty**)

31 OCTOBER: An Iranian oil strike begins.

29 DECEMBER: In Iran, the Shah appoints Shahpour Bakhtiar of the opposition National Front to head a new government.

1979

16 JANUARY: Muhammad Reza Pahlavi, the Shah of Iran, leaves Iran. (*See* **Iranian Revolution** *and* **Shah of Iran**)

1 FEBRUARY: Ayatollah Ruhollah Khomeini triumphantly returns to Iran; the Islamic

Republic of Iran is formally established on 31 March.

26 MARCH: The Egyptian-Israeli peace treaty is signed at the White House. (*See* **Egyptian-Israeli Peace Treaty**)

31 MARCH: Egypt is expelled from the Arab League; its headquarters is moved to Tunis. (*See* **League of Arab States**)

16 JULY: Saddam Hussein replaces Ahmad Hassan al-Bakr as president of Iraq.

16 SEPTEMBER: Hafizullah Amin takes control of the Afghanistan government from Taraki.

4 NOVEMBER: Iranian revolutionaries take over the U.S. embassy in Teheran, holding more than 50 Americans hostage for 444 days. (*See* **Iranian Revolution**)

20 NOVEMBER: Islamic militants take over the Grand Mosque in Mecca (Saudis regain control by 4 December); 63 captured militants are later put to death.

27 DECEMBER: The Soviets invade Afghanistan; Babrak Karmal is made president; and Amin is assassinated. (*See* **Superpower Cold War**)

1980

7 APRIL: The United States breaks diplomatic ties with Iran. (*See* **Iranian Revolution**)

20 APRIL: Berbers begin strikes in Algeria in response to the cancellation of a talk on Berber poetry by anthropologist Mouloud Mammeri, sparking the "Berber Spring," in which dozens of students are killed.

24–25 APRIL: A U.S. commando attempt (Desert One) is made to rescue hostages in Iran, but the effort fails; eight Americans are killed; Secretary of State Cyrus Vance resigns in protest over the rescue attempt.

27 JULY: The Shah of Iran dies in exile in Egypt. (*See* **Shah of Iran**)

30 JULY: The Knesset declares all of Jerusalem to be the united capital of Israel.

12 SEPTEMBER: A military coup ends the second Turkish republic.

17 SEPTEMBER: Iraq claims the Shatt al-Arab waterway. (*See* **Iran-Iraq War**)

22 SEPTEMBER: Iraq invades Iran, beginning the eight-year-long Iran-Iraq War.

8 OCTOBER: Syria and the Soviet Union sign a Treaty of Friendship and Cooperation.

1981

20 JANUARY: Iran releases the American hostages.

26 MAY: The Gulf Cooperation Council (GCC) is formed, consisting of Saudi Arabia, Kuwait, Qatar, Oman, Bahrain, and the United Arab Emirates.

7 JUNE: Israeli planes destroy the Osirak nuclear reactor outside Baghdad in Iraq.

22 JUNE: Abolhassan Bani-Sadr is dismissed as president of Iran by Khomeini.

8 AUGUST: Saudi Arabia's King Fahd announces an eight-point Middle East peace plan.

19 AUGUST: U.S. Navy F-14s shoot down two Libyan SU-22s in the Gulf of Sidra off the Libyan coast.

6 OCTOBER: Sadat is assassinated in Egypt by Islamic extremists; Hosni Mubarak becomes the new Egyptian president.

29 OCTOBER: The U.S. Senate upholds the sale of AWACS to Saudi Arabia.

14 DECEMBER: Israel extends its law and jurisdiction to the Golan Heights.

1982

22 MARCH: Iran launches an offensive that forces Iraqi troops from positions held inside Iran. (*See* **Iran-Iraq War**)

25 APRIL: Israel completes withdrawal from the Sinai Peninsula, per the 1979 Egyptian-Israeli peace treaty.

6 JUNE: Israel invades Lebanon. (*See* **Israel in Lebanon** *and* **Multinational Force in Lebanon**)

13 JUNE: King Khalid of Saudi Arabia dies; he is succeeded by Crown Prince Fahd.

19 AUGUST: The Israeli siege of Beirut ends.

23 AUGUST: Bashir Gemayel (Jumayyil) becomes president-elect of Lebanon.

25 AUGUST: The Multinational Force (MNF)—comprising American, French, and Italian forces—enters Beirut to escort PLO forces from Lebanon. (*See* **Palestine Liberation Organization**)

1 SEPTEMBER: The Reagan Middle East peace plan is announced; the last of 15,000 PLO and Syrian troops leave Beirut.

14 SEPTEMBER: Gemayel is assassinated in Beirut.

16–18 SEPTEMBER: Hundreds of Palestinians at the refugee camps of Sabra and Shatila are massacred by Christian Phalangist forces.

21 SEPTEMBER: Amin Gemayel (Bashir's brother) is elected president of Lebanon.

28 SEPTEMBER: The Kahan commission is established by the Israeli government to investigate the Sabra and Shatila massacres.

29 SEPTEMBER: MNF troops reenter Beirut in an attempt to restore order.

9 NOVEMBER: Kenan Evren is elected president of Turkey after a referendum on the new constitution on 7 November.

1983

8 FEBRUARY: The Kahan commission releases its report on the Sabra and Shatila massacres. (*See* **Israel in Lebanon**)

18 APRIL: The U.S. embassy in Beirut is destroyed by a bomb blast, killing 63 people; Islamic extremists claim responsibility. (*See* **Multinational Force in Lebanon**)

17 MAY: Lebanon and Israel sign an accord—Syria rejects it.

18 AUGUST: French reinforcements are sent to Chad in reaction to the buildup of Libyan forces along the Libya-Chad border.

15 SEPTEMBER: Begin resigns, citing his poor health; Yitzhak Shamir becomes the new Israeli prime minister.

23 OCTOBER: An attack against a U.S. Marine barracks in Beirut kills 241; a similar blast kills 58 French soldiers.

9 NOVEMBER: Turgut Ozal is elected prime minister of Turkey.

15 NOVEMBER: The Turkish Republic of Northern Cyprus is declared.

20 DECEMBER: Pro-Arafat PLO forces are evacuated from Tripoli, Lebanon. (*See* **Palestine Liberation Organization**)

1984

19 JANUARY: The Organization of the Islamic Conference readmits Egypt.

26 FEBRUARY: U.S. forces begin withdrawal from Lebanon. (*See* **Multinational Force in Lebanon**)

5 MARCH: Lebanon formally abrogates the 17 May 1983 agreement with Israel.

25 SEPTEMBER: Jordan reestablishes diplomatic ties with Egypt, the first Arab country to do so of the seventeen Arab nations that broke ties with Egypt following the 1979 Egyptian-Israeli peace treaty.

26 NOVEMBER: The United States and Iraq restore diplomatic ties, broken since the 1967 Arab-Israeli War.

1985

FEBRUARY: Hizbollah (Party of God) publishes its objectives, which focus on the establishment of an Islamic republic in Lebanon, based on the Iranian model.

6 APRIL: A military coup overthrows the government of Numayri in Sudan.

JULY: Israel completes its withdrawal from Lebanon, except for a security zone along the Israeli-Lebanese border.

7 OCTOBER: Palestinian gunmen hijack the Italian cruise ship *Achille Lauro;* four hijackers surrender on 9 October; U.S. warplanes intercept an Egyptian plane carrying the hijackers on 10 October and force it to land in Sicily.

21 NOVEMBER: Jonathan Jay Pollard, a civilian employee of the U.S. Naval Intelligence Service in Suitland, Maryland, is arrested and charged with selling classified information to Israel.

23 NOVEMBER: Ayatollah Hussein Ali Montazeri is named as the eventual successor to Khomeini in Iran.

8 DECEMBER: OPEC oil ministers decide to abandon their official pricing structure in an attempt to gain a larger share of the world's oil market. (*See* **Oil Production**)

1986

13 JANUARY: A civil war in South Yemen erupts.

11 FEBRUARY: In a major offensive, Iranians capture the Fao (Faw) Peninsula in Iraq. (*See* **Iran-Iraq War**)

5 APRIL: A bomb explodes in a nightclub in Berlin, killing 2 American soldiers and a Turkish woman and injuring more than 200 patrons; the Reagan administration suspects Libya is responsible.

15 APRIL: U.S. warplanes attack targets in Libya, including the residence and headquarters of Qadhdhafi.

22 JULY: Israeli prime minister Shimon Peres and Moroccan king Hassan II meet in Ifrane, Morocco.

11–12 SEPTEMBER: Mubarak and Peres meet in the first summit meeting between Israeli and Egyptian leaders in five years.

3 NOVEMBER: A Lebanese weekly magazine discloses secret U.S. visits and arms sales to Iran in an attempt to release U.S. hostages in Lebanon; this disclosure is the beginning of what will become known as the "Iran-Contra affair."

11 DECEMBER: Libyan troops launch a major offensive against Chad.

1987

17 MAY: An Iraqi warplane fires a missile that hits the frigate USS *Stark* in the Persian

Gulf, killing 37 crew members; Iraq claims it was an accident.

19 MAY: The United States and Kuwait sign an agreement for U.S. protection (reflagging) of Kuwaiti oil tankers in the Persian Gulf (escorts begin 22 July). (*See* **Iran-Iraq War**)

20 JULY: The UN Security Council passes Resolution 598, calling for a cease-fire in the Iran-Iraq War (Iraq accepts and Iran rejects it).

31 JULY: Rioting by pilgrims in Mecca kills more than 400 people.

8–11 NOVEMBER: At the Arab League summit meeting in Amman, Jordan, the focus of attention is on the Iran-Iraq War and not the Arab-Israeli situation. (*See* **League of Arab States**)

9 DECEMBER: The beginning of the Palestinian *intifada* (uprising). (*See* **Intifada 1987–1993** *and* **Palestine Liberation Organization**)

1988

FEBRUARY: The Palestinian Islamist group Hamas is created in the West Bank. (*See* **Intifada 1987–1993**)

16 MARCH: Iraq uses chemical weapons on the Kurdish town of Halabja. Approximately 5,000 people, mostly women and children, perish immediately in the attack, and as many as 12,000 die over the course of three days of attacks on the region. (*See* **Iran-Iraq War**)

14 APRIL: The Geneva accords are signed, arranging for the withdrawal of Soviet troops from Afghanistan. (*See* **Superpower Cold War**)

18 APRIL: Iraq recaptures the Fao Peninsula.

25 MAY: Libya recognizes Chad (diplomatic relations restored 3 October).

3 JULY: The USS *Vincennes* shoots a missile that destroys an Iranian Airbus over the Persian Gulf, killing all 290 passengers and crew.

31 JULY: Jordan's King Hussein renounces claims to the West Bank.

20 AUGUST: The Iran-Iraq War ends with mutual agreement to UN Security Council Resolution 598.

3 OCTOBER: Border hostilities between Chad and Libya end.

15 NOVEMBER: In Algiers, the Palestinian National Council (PNC) declares an independent Palestinian state. (*See* **Palestine Liberation Organization**)

14 DECEMBER: Following his speech addressing the UN in Geneva the previous day, Arafat reiterates his recognition of Israel's right to exist, accepts Resolutions 242 and 338, and renounces terrorism; the United States announces it will begin a dialogue with the PLO in Tunisia. (*See* **Resolution 242**)

21 DECEMBER: Pan American flight 103 is destroyed by a bomb over Lockerbie, Scotland, killing 270 people; Libya is suspected of being responsible.

1989

FEBRUARY: The Arab Maghrib Union (*Union du Maghreb Arabe,* UMA)—linking the North African states of Libya, Tunisia, Algeria, Morocco, and Mauritania in a cooperative organization—is formed.

9 FEBRUARY: The Soviet Union completes its withdrawal from Afghanistan. (*See* **Superpower Cold War**)

14 FEBRUARY: Khomeini calls on Muslims everywhere to kill British author Salman Rushdie for writing *The Satanic Verses,* which the Iranian leader calls blasphemous.

29 MAY: Egypt is readmitted into the Arab League. (*See* **League of Arab States**)

3 JULY: Khomeini dies.

13 JULY: Iranian Kurdish nationalist leader Abdul Rahman Ghassemlou is assassinated in Vienna by Iranian agents.

17 AUGUST: Ali Akhbar Hashemi Rafsanjani is inaugurated as Iranian president.

22 OCTOBER: The Taif Agreement is reached in Saudi Arabia among members of various Lebanese factions on national reconciliation that provides for equal representation between Muslims and Christians in the new Lebanese parliament (formally signed 24 October).

27 DECEMBER: Egypt and Syria restore diplomatic ties, broken since the 1979 Egyptian-Israeli peace treaty.

1990

22 MAY: The Republic of Yemen is created by the merger of the Yemen Arab Republic (North Yemen) and the People's Democratic Republic of Yemen (South Yemen).

20 JUNE: President George H. W. Bush suspends dialogue with the PLO. (*See* **Palestine Liberation Organization**)

2 JULY: A crowd stampede in Mecca kills 1,400 people during the pilgrimage.

2 AUGUST: Iraq invades Kuwait. (*See* **Gulf War 1991: Entry**)

7 AUGUST: U.S.-led coalition forces begin to assemble in Saudi Arabia.

28 AUGUST: The Iraqi regime declares Kuwait to be the nineteenth province of Iraq.

13 OCTOBER: Michel Aoun's Christian forces are defeated in Beirut, allowing Syria to exert its predominant position in Lebanon.

29 NOVEMBER: The UN Security Council passes Resolution 678, authorizing the U.S.-led coalition to use force to evict Iraq from Kuwait if Baghdad does not withdraw by 15 January 1991.

1991

17 JANUARY: Coalition forces begin an air attack against Iraq, launching Operation Desert Storm. (*See* **Gulf War 1991: Entry**)

24 FEBRUARY: Coalition forces launch the ground war against Iraqi forces.

27 FEBRUARY: Kuwait is liberated; Iraq agrees to a cease-fire offered by the United States on 28 February. (*See* **Gulf War 1991: Exit**)

3 APRIL: The UN Security Council adopts Resolution 687, setting the conditions for the lifting of international sanctions against Iraq.

22 MAY: The Lebanese-Syrian Treaty of Brotherhood, Cooperation and Coordination is signed.

30 OCTOBER: An Arab-Israeli peace conference begins in Madrid. (*See* **Syrian-Israeli Negotiations**)

14 NOVEMBER: The U.S. Justice Department links two Libyan operatives to the 1988 bombing of Pan American flight 103.

DECEMBER: The UN General Assembly repeals the "Zionism is racism" resolution.

1992

JANUARY: Parliamentary elections are canceled by the Algerian military; the assembly is dissolved; and a state of emergency is established by the ruling council. (*See* **Algerian Elections in 1992**)

28 APRIL: A coalition of Islamic groups takes power in Afghanistan from the communist government.

23 JUNE: The Labor Party wins Israeli elections; Yitzhak Rabin becomes prime minister and forms coalition government in July.

26 AUGUST: The United States and Britain establish no-fly zones in Iraq.

1993

14 JUNE: Tansu Ciller becomes the first female prime minister of Turkey.

13 SEPTEMBER: Israel and the PLO sign the Declaration of Principles on the White House lawn (Oslo accords). (*See* **Oslo Accords** *and* **Palestine Liberation Organization**)

26 NOVEMBER: Iraq accepts UN Security Council Resolution 715, which mandates UN inspections to prevent Iraq from developing weapons of mass destruction (WMD).

1994

4 MAY: An agreement on self-rule by Palestinians (Palestinian National Authority) in Jericho in the West Bank and in the Gaza Strip is signed by Rabin and Arafat. (*See* **Palestine Liberation Organization**)

1 JULY: Arafat returns to the Gaza Strip after twenty-seven years in exile.

7 JULY: A nine-week civil war ends in Yemen.

7 OCTOBER: Iraq deploys 20,000 troops toward the Kuwaiti border—U.S. troop response forces Baghdad to withdraw.

26 OCTOBER: Israeli-Jordanian peace treaty is signed.

10 NOVEMBER: Iraq recognizes sovereignty of Kuwait.

10 DECEMBER: Rabin, Peres, and Arafat receive the Nobel Peace Prize in Oslo, Norway.

1995

27 JUNE: Shaykh Hamad bin Khalifa Al Thani ousts his father in a coup in Qatar.

28 SEPTEMBER: The Oslo II accords are signed in Washington, D.C., expanding Palestinian self-rule in the West Bank. (*See* **Oslo Accords** *and* **Palestine Liberation Organization**)

4 NOVEMBER: Rabin is assassinated by a Jewish zealot in Israel; Peres succeeds Rabin as prime minister (he is formally sworn in on 22 November).

13 NOVEMBER: A car bomb in Riyadh, Saudi Arabia, kills five U.S. military personnel outside the headquarters of the Saudi National Guard; Islamic extremists claim responsibility.

27 DECEMBER: Syria and Israel resume peace negotiations at the Wye Conference Center in Maryland. (*See* **Syrian-Israeli Negotiations**)

1996

20 JANUARY: Arafat is elected president of the Palestinian National Authority. (*See* **Palestine Liberation Organization**)

FEBRUARY/MARCH: Three Hamas suicide bombings occur in Israel.

23 FEBRUARY: Hussein's two sons-in-law are executed upon their return from self-imposed exile.

4 MARCH: Israel suspends Wye negotiations with Syrians after Hamas suicide bombings. (*See* **Syrian-Israeli Negotiations**)

8–9 MAY: Israel launches Operation Grapes of Wrath in Lebanon against Hizbollah (a cease-fire is reached on 26 April).

20 MAY: The Oil-for-food program is established by the UN for Iraq (final agreement in the UN is reached on 25 November).

29 MAY: Likud Party leader Benjamin Netanyahu wins elections as the new Israeli prime minister.

25 JUNE: A truck bomb explodes in Khobar, Saudi Arabia, outside a base housing U.S. military personnel, killing 19 Americans and wounding 400 others.

SEPTEMBER: The Taliban takes control of Kabul in Afghanistan and soon controls 90 percent of the country.

1 SEPTEMBER: Libyan leader Qadhdhafi officially opens the Great Man-Made River (construction began in 1984), a giant water distribution system that takes water from the Sahara aquifer to drier coastal regions.

1 NOVEMBER : The al-Jazeera network (a television channel devoted to Islamic news and programs) is founded in Qatar.

1997

17 JANUARY: Israel withdraws from 80 percent of Hebron in the West Bank.

3 AUGUST: Muhammad Khatami, a reformist cleric, becomes president of the Islamic Republic of Iran.

17 NOVEMBER: Six gunmen from the Armed Islamic Group open fire near the Temple of Hatshepsut in Luxor, Egypt, killing 70 people, including 60 foreign tourists.

1998

23 FEBRUARY: Iraq and the UN sign an agreement regarding UNSCOM (UN Security Council Special Commission) inspections, ending the latest crisis concerning the level of Iraqi cooperation.

7 AUGUST: U.S. embassies in Nairobi, Kenya, and Dar al-Salaam, Tanzania, are bombed, killing more than 130 people, including 12 Americans; Osama bin Laden's al-Qaida is suspected as responsible.

20 AUGUST: The United States launches about 75 cruise missiles at suspected al-Qaida camps in Afghanistan.

22 SEPTEMBER: Iran renounces the death threat against British author Rushdie.

15 OCTOBER: Syria and Turkey sign an accord that stipulates that Syria will cease its support of the Kurdish Workers Party (PKK).

23 OCTOBER: The Wye interim agreement is signed by Arafat and Netanyahu at the White House. (*See* **Syrian-Israeli Negotiations**)

16–19 DECEMBER: A series of air strikes (Operation Desert Fox) is launched by the United States and Great Britain against Iraqi installations for what is claimed to be Iraq's continued defiance of UN resolutions and lack of cooperation with UNSCOM; Iraq formally ends UNSCOM inspections.

1999

7 FEBRUARY: King Hussein of Jordan dies; he is succeeded by his son Abdullah.

16 FEBRUARY: PKK leader Abdullah Ocalan is flown under custody to Turkey, and he is formally charged with treason by Turkish authorities on 23 February.

6 MARCH: Emir Isa bin Al Khalifa of Bahrain dies; he is succeeded by his son, Hamad bin Isa Al Khalifa.

5 APRIL: Libya hands over two suspects in the Lockerbie Pan Am bombing to a UN representative; they are eventually placed under Scottish custody; the UN suspends sanctions against Libya.

17 MAY: Labor Party leader Ehud Barak wins election as the Israeli prime minister.

23 JULY: King Hassan II of Morocco dies; he is succeeded by his son, Muhammad VI.

15 DECEMBER: Israel and Syria resume peace talks. (*See* **Syrian-Israeli Negotiations**)

2000

26 MARCH: U.S. president Bill Clinton and Syrian president Hafiz al-Asad meet in Geneva; they fail to reach an accord over Israeli return of the Golan Heights. (*See* **Syrian-Israeli Negotiations**)

11 MAY: Barak announces the decision to withdraw Israeli forces from positions in the South Lebanon security zone (withdrawal is completed in June).

10 JUNE: Hafiz al-Asad dies; he is succeeded by his son Bashar al-Asad as president of Syria.

11 JULY: The Camp David II summit meeting of Clinton, Arafat, and Barak begins; no agreement is reached.

28 SEPTEMBER: Sharon visits the Temple Mount in Jerusalem, though not the mosques, sparking Palestinian protests.

29 SEPTEMBER: The Palestinian al-Aqsa *intifada* (uprising) begins. (*See* **Palestine Liberation Organization**)

12 OCTOBER: A terrorist bombing of the USS *Cole* while it is on a refueling stop in Yemen kills 17 U.S. sailors; al-Qaida is held responsible by U.S. authorities.

2001

7 FEBRUARY: Likud Party leader Ariel Sharon wins a landslide election to become the Israeli prime minister.

MARCH: The Taliban regime orders the destruction of Afghanistan's celebrated Bamian Buddhas.

20 MAY: The Mitchell Report, named after former U.S. senator George Mitchell (formally the report of the Sharm al-Shaykh Fact Finding Committee), a device aimed at bringing a halt to the Israeli-Palestinian violence and restarting negotiations, is published.

9 SEPTEMBER: Ahmed Shah Massud, Afghan opposition leader and critic of bin Laden, is assassinated by two Arab terrorists posing as journalists.

11 SEPTEMBER: Al-Qaida carries out attacks against the World Trade Center in New York City and the Pentagon in Washington, D.C. One hijacked plane crashes in Pennsylvania. These attacks result in the deaths of more than three thousand people.

7 OCTOBER: A U.S.-led coalition begins a war in Afghanistan to overthrow the Taliban regime.

9 NOVEMBER: The northern Afghan city of Mazar-e Sharif falls to coalition forces.

11–14 NOVEMBER: Delegates to the first Arab women's summit meet in Cairo and establish the Arab Women's Organization (AWO).

6 DECEMBER: The fall of the Taliban stronghold in the southern Afghan city of Qandahar marks the collapse of the regime.

21 DECEMBER: An interim government in Afghanistan, headed by Hamid Kharzai, is sworn in.

2002

3 JANUARY: Israeli forces capture the *Karine A,* a ship with 50 tons of weapons report-edly en route from Iran to the Palestinians; in U.S. eyes, the event undermines Arafat's already diminishing credibility. (*See* **Palestine Liberation Organization**)

29 JANUARY: In his State of the Union address, President George W. Bush names Iraq, Iran, and North Korea as part of an "axis of evil."

13 MARCH: The UN Security Council passes Resolution 1397, calling for a two-state solution to the Israeli-Palestinian conflict, the end of violence and terrorism, and resumption of negotiations.

27 MARCH: A Hamas suicide bomber kills 27 Israelis at a Passover dinner in Netanya.

27–28 MARCH: At the Arab League summit meeting in Beirut, Crown Prince Abdullah of Saudi Arabia announces a comprehensive plan for Arab-Israeli peace. (*See* **League of Arab States**)

APRIL: Israel launches "Operation Defensive Shield" in the West Bank in response to a spate of suicide bombings.

18 APRIL: King Muhammad Zahir Shah returns to Afghanistan after twenty-seven years in exile; he is to serve in the role of an "elder statesman" to help unify the country.

13 JUNE: A *loya jirga* (meeting of tribal leaders) elects Kharzai as president of Afghanistan.

24 JUNE: In a major speech, President Bush calls for "a new and different Palestinian leadership" that will help bring about a Palestinian state—this call is taken to mean that the Bush administration will not deal with Arafat; he also announces his "vision" of "two states living side by side in peace and security." (*See* **Palestine Liberation Organization**)

8 NOVEMBER: The UN Security Council unanimously passes Resolution 1441, which outlines the parameters and conditions for the resumption of UN inspections in Iraq regarding weapons of mass destruction.

2003

28 JANUARY: Sharon is reelected prime minister of Israel.

19 MARCH: Operation Iraqi Freedom, the U.S.-led war against Iraq, commences with an air attack in Baghdad aimed at "decapitating" the Iraqi leadership.

29 APRIL: Mahmoud Abbas (Abu Mazen) ascends to the newly created office of prime minister of the Palestinian National Authority. (*See* **Palestine Liberation Organization**)

30 APRIL: The road map to peace in the Middle East authored by the "quartet"–the United

States, Russia, the European Union (EU), and the United Nations—is formally presented to Sharon and Abbas.

12 MAY: Suicide bombings at three residential complexes housing foreigners in Riyadh, Saudi Arabia, kill 34 people, including 9 attackers; Islamic extremists, particularly al-Qaida, are suspected as being responsible.

16 MAY: Forty-one people are killed and more than 100 wounded in a series of suicide bombings in Casablanca, Morocco; Islamic extremists are suspected as being responsible.

3 JUNE: In a U.S.-Arab summit meeting in Sharm al-Shaykh, Egypt, President Bush meets with the leaders of Saudi Arabia, Egypt, Bahrain, Jordan, and the Palestinian Authority to discuss the road map to peace; the next day he meets with Sharon and Abbas in Aqaba, Jordan.

CHRONOLOGY

ALGERIAN ELECTIONS OF 1992

Was the Islamist opposition in Algeria cheated out of a victory in the 1992 parliamentary elections?

Viewpoint: Yes. The Algerian regime, after in effect annulling the 1992 parliamentary elections, precipitated a brutal civil war while undermining the democratic alternative in the region.

Viewpoint: No. The Islamist opposition may not have had the genuine support of the Algerian people.

After gaining independence following the 1954–1962 revolution, the new Algerian government, dominated by members of the revolutionary movement *Front de Libération Nationale* (National Liberation Front, FLN), pursued a particularly rigid form of state socialism in its attempt to establish an industrial base from what had been a predominantly agrarian society. The result, typical of many other countries that implemented similar politico-economic policies (called import-substituting industrialization), was that Algeria built up a huge foreign debt by the late 1980s, especially as the worldwide oil glut severely reduced revenues from that sector for the government. (Algeria is a member of OPEC.)

Many countries in this economic predicament by the end of the 1980s attempted to alleviate the deteriorating conditions through rapid economic liberalization programs designed to integrate the country into the emerging global capitalist market. Such changes often do not occur smoothly, creating conditions that fuel opposition movements at times. The chances for instability multiply when political liberalization efforts lag far behind economic reforms, as the statist regimes that originally implemented the failed socialist-based economic programs desperately try to hold onto power through the ups and downs of the reform process. These regimes often became bloated, inefficient, and corrupt entities that were unable to manipulate the political process without public repercussions.

In Algeria, by the late 1980s, the ruling FLN admirably attempted to implement widespread political reforms to accompany the economic restructuring process. Included among the reforms were the authorization of new political parties, constitutional reform, and more freedom of the press. Indeed, to the outside observer, Algeria may have seemed at this moment the freest country in the Arab world. Among the new parties that formed was the *Front Islamique du Salut* (Islamic Salvation Front, FIS), an Islamist-based group that considered itself more of a populist party.

In elections for local and provincial assemblies in mid 1990, the FIS did remarkably well, garnering some 4.3 million votes out of an electorate of 12.8 million. Thus, almost all of the major towns came under FIS control, which began to implement Islamist policies, such as segregating education, rooting out corruption, and encouraging Muslim women to use the veil in public. Interestingly, there are some reports that claim clandestine support for the FIS from various elements within the FLN and/or the Algerian military who opposed the pace and depth of economic and political reform efforts of the government.

In the December 1991 parliamentary elections the FIS continued its show of strength, poised to become the majority in parliament after a second round of balloting in January 1992. Before that could happen, however, the military stepped in and canceled the second round of voting, removed President Chadli Benjedid from power, and established a *Haut Comité d'Etat* (High Council of State, HCE) to rule the country. While the silent majority of Algerians stood on the sidelines, the FIS and its supporters felt cheated—they had played by the rules of the democratic process and were prevented from taking power in an election they felt they had rightfully won. FIS leaders were eventually placed under arrest as tensions and violence increased following the military intercession. More radical Islamist groups, such as the *Groupe Islamique Armé* (Armed Islamic Group, GIA), emerged on the scene in opposition to a succession of military-dominated governments. Attacks and counterattacks became a common feature of Algerian society, and to date more than 100,000 Algerians have died in what has now been a ten-year-long civil war.

Viewpoint:
Yes. The Algerian regime, after in effect annulling the 1992 parliamentary elections, precipitated a brutal civil war while undermining the democratic alternative in the region.

In December 1991 Algeria held the first democratic parliamentary elections in the nation's history. The *Front Islamique du Salut* (Islamic Salvation Front, FIS), a mainstream Islamist party, took a commanding lead over its two main rivals, the ruling *Front de Libération Nationale* (National Liberation Front, FLN) and the Berber-based *Front des Forces Socialistes* (Socialist Forces Front, FFS). In the first round of voting on 26 December, the FIS gained 188 out of 430 seats in the National Popular Assembly and won 47 percent of all votes cast. The FLN and FFS combined won only 41 seats and 31 percent of the national vote. In the 199 electoral districts that were to be decided in a second round of voting in January 1992, the FIS had gained more votes in 143 of the districts in the first round than any other party. Had the military not staged a coup d'état in January 1992, the FIS would likely have gained more than two-thirds of the seats in the Assembly, which would have been enough to change the Constitution.

The Algerian military halted the most successful democratization experiment in the Arab world. Islamists had largely played by the regime rules and participated in free elections, only to have their popular victory stolen from them. By annulling the elections, outlawing the FIS, and appointing a collective ruling body called the *Haut Comité d'Etat* (High Council of State, HCE), the generals plunged the country into a bloody civil war that has lasted more than a decade. More than 150,000 people have died; tens of thousands have been injured; and at least 20,000 people have disap-

peared. Torture, rape, kidnapping, and extrajudicial killings have torn apart the social fabric. Since 1992, economic reforms have stalled and nearly 40 percent of the Algerian population lives below the poverty line. Much of the country's infrastructure has suffered damage. Unfair and rigged elections since 1992 have failed to reintroduce democratization. The actions of the military to deny a democratic victory to the Islamists precipitated one of the worst civil conflicts the Arab world has experienced since the 1950s.

An analysis of the FIS before and after the elections calls into question many of the claims advanced by regime defenders and apologists to justify the coup and the subsequent repression of the Islamists. Although it is impossible to know for sure what the FIS would have done had it been allowed to take power, the dire predictions of an Islamic revolution and a retrograde, Islamic regime imposing *sharia* (Islamic law) on a largely secular society were misguided.

The FIS emerged in 1988 after twenty-five years of single-party rule under the FLN, which, along with its military and technocratic allies, had lost its popular and revolutionary legitimacy. It was mired in corruption and proved incapable of transforming the economy. During riots in 1988 the army killed more than four hundred Algerians. Shortly thereafter, President Chadli Benjedid decided to liberalize the political system. The FIS rapidly emerged as the most important opposition party, espousing an Islamo-nationalist ideology and mobilizing successfully at the grassroots level throughout the country.

Detractors of the FIS have argued that the party never really believed in democracy and was utilizing the ballot box to gain power, after which its true intentions would be revealed. In reality, the party never had a monolithic ideology or a unified leadership. It was an amalgam of different voices and social forces. It was as much nationalist and populist as it was Islamist. While stressing the impor-

DISAPPEARANCES

The social upheaval as well as the disappearances of citizens in Algeria following the 1992 elections were addressed in a Human Rights Watch report:

Since 1992, Algeria has been riven by a conflict between security forces and armed opposition groups that call themselves Islamist. It has claimed at least 60,000 lives, many of them civilians. Under the guise of fighting "terrorism," security forces have engaged in systematic torture, summary executions, and arbitrary arrests with impunity. Armed groups have targeted for assassination individuals whom they viewed as hostile to their religious-political agenda or supportive of the present government, and have carried out a series of massacres of unarmed men, women and children in rural areas. In its reporting on the crisis in Algeria, Human Rights Watch has consistently condemned violations of human rights and of humanitarian law by all parties.

Among the many human rights tragedies in Algeria has been the "disappearance" of more than one thousand men and women since 1992, following their arrest by government forces.

Searching for their "disappeared" loved ones, families have made the rounds of police stations, jails and courthouses, filed missing-person complaints with official agencies, and sought help through informal channels such as freed prisoners or prison guards. When authorities have responded to their queries, it has generally been to deny that the person is in custody. Some of the relatives of the "disappeared" have recently taken to the streets, holding up photos of their missing fathers, sons, and brothers, demanding answers.

As with many acts of violence in Algeria, authorship of some cases of "disappearances" has been difficult to confirm. Persons have been seized at their homes, in their workplaces, or in public places, by men in plainclothes who refused to identify themselves or present a warrant, but who were later confirmed to be members of the security forces. There have also been instances of police-style actions by men in uniform—such as the staffing of checkpoints—where witnesses suspected the men of being members of armed groups who had disguised themselves as security force members.

In some cases, confirmation of security force responsibility was later confirmed when the person seized was located within the prison system or released after a period of detention. In other cases, such as the abductions of women that accompanied some of the gruesome massacres in villages southeast of Algiers during 1997, the circumstances of the abduction led families of victims to suspect the hand of armed opposition groups.

While abductions by armed opposition groups are a grave human rights problem in Algeria, there is overwhelming evidence that the security forces are responsible for many hundreds of unresolved cases of "disappearance." The phenomenon is of such proportions that it could only persist with the sanction of the highest levels of national authority. While high officials have admitted that persons have "gone missing" in state custody, we are aware of no high-level acknowledgment that the practice of forcible disappearance is rampant and ongoing, nor of any efforts by the Algerian authorities to bring to justice those responsible.

"Disappeared" persons come from a wide range of professions. They include government employees, physicians, businessmen, political activists, and journalists. Among the cases Human Rights Watch has investigated, the arrests took place mostly at night, and according to eyewitnesses, were carried out by mixed military and police forces who arrived in cars, generally with private license plates. Sometimes armored vehicles were also used. Some members of these forces wore uniforms and others were in plainclothes. When the police came wearing civilian clothes, they often wore jackets with a recognizable police insignia. When arresting someone at home or on the street, they rarely presented an arrest warrant or official identification. These were reportedly shown more often when the arrest was made at the person's workplace.

After a relative was seized, family members often visited nearby police stations to see if he or she was being held there. Some made inquiries with the state prosecutor's office after the twelve-day limit on garde à vue (pre-arraignment) detention had elapsed, and received a receipt acknowledging their complaint. Others reported locating their arrested relatives, only to lose track of them after being told they had been transferred to another place of detention whose location was not disclosed.

When detainees are held in unknown locations, they are invariably deprived of legal assistance and are at the mercy of the arresting authority, thereby making them more vulnerable to abuses such as torture or ill-treatment. A prisoner who was released in December 1996, after three and-a-half years in jail, told Human Rights Watch that he first obtained a lawyer only after he was charged and transferred to a prison, following three months in secret detention in police custody. Once in el-Harrache prison, he asked other detainees to have their visiting relatives inform his family of his whereabouts. When the former prisoner, who preferred to withhold his name, had earlier appeared before an investigating judge, he was not notified of his right to a lawyer or to contact his family. He also told us that he was tortured for three days while in police custody. The torture methods included beating with large sticks, the "chiffon" (or washrag) method in which a cloth soaked in dirty water and chemicals is stuffed down his mouth, and leaving him suspended by the arms for hours.

Source: *"Neither Among The Living Nor The Dead: State-Sponsored 'Disappearances' in Algeria,"* report, volume 10, February 1998, Human Rights Watch website <http://www.hrw.org/reports98/algeria2/>.

ALGERIAN ELECTIONS OF 1992

3

tance of Islamic values, many in the party emphasized the rule of law, the necessity of a government of popular legitimacy, and equal social opportunity for all Algerians. Abassi Madani and Ali Benhadj, the party's two main leaders, at various times made provocative remarks suggesting that they did not value democracy or believe in equal rights for women. Some of their pronouncements seemed to advocate violence and the imposition of Islamic restrictions on society. Benhadj expressed the most radical vision, while Madani mostly expressed moderate views that were consistent with a prodemocracy vision. Members of the FIS governing body, the Majlis al-Shura, held a variety of political beliefs. The widely divergent and often contradictory remarks of FIS leaders between 1988 and 1992 hardly prove that the party believed in "one-man, one-vote, one-time." Given the characteristics of the party and its leaders, one could argue that if it had taken power in 1992, it would likely have fragmented into several factions, making the domination of radical elements doubtful.

Many actions of the party leading up to the 1991 elections suggest it was generally committed to democratic practices. It performed many of the functions one would expect of a modern, mass-based party: mobilizing voters, campaigning, raising money, and distributing patronage. It had well-educated and competent cadres with significant administrative credentials. The party agreed to participate in local and provincial elections in June 1990, despite an unfair electoral code and fears that the FLN would manipulate the results. With 54 percent of the popular vote, the FIS won control of 853 communal assemblies and 31 regional councils. In the following year the FIS-controlled assemblies did not impose draconian social restrictions on the population. Isolated efforts to close cinemas, ban the sale of alcohol, discourage *rai* music and coeducation, and forbid the wearing of shorts were never particularly popular or successful. The party succeeded in collecting garbage, delivering social services, setting up low-cost local markets, and providing local administration despite financial restrictions and resistance from the central government.

When the government of Prime Minister Mouloud Hamrouche unveiled an unfair electoral code for the 1991 parliamentary elections that was full of gerrymandering, Madani had to work hard to get the Majlis al-Shura to support his call for a general strike in May. The originally peaceful strike, designed to produce a revision of the electoral code, turned into mass protests and demonstrations in the

streets of Algiers. The regime interpreted FIS actions as an uprising that threatened the security of the state, and the police and army crushed the protesters. The regime declared a state of siege; arrested Madani, Benhadj, and other top FIS leaders; and launched a crackdown on elected councils controlled by Islamists. Sid Ahmed Ghozali replaced Hamrouche as prime minister. He rescheduled parliamentary elections for December 1991 and revised the electoral code on terms fairer to the FIS. In retrospect, the strike was a strategic miscalculation by Madani that played into the hands of some radical Islamist elements bent on using force to bring down the government. Nevertheless, Abdelkader Hachani, a close associate of Madani, took over provisional leadership of the party and, with the help of other pragmatic moderates, convinced the divided party to stick to an electoral strategy. Despite the imprisonment of its leaders and repression by the regime, the FIS ran a successful and professional campaign resulting in the trouncing of the FLN in the first round of parliamentary elections. Despite their conflicting motives, the Islamists in the FIS largely played the democratic and constitutional game from 1989 to 1991.

President Chadli, the FLN, and many secularists had consistently underestimated the popularity of the FIS. The military elite believed that a coup was their last chance to preserve the integrity of the armed forces and prevent an Islamist takeover. Senior military leaders, supported by many workers, secularists, FLN cadres, and Berbers, feared that the FIS would use a victory to undermine the secular institutions of the government, end pluralism, and punish existing officeholders. They argued that democratization had to be halted in order to preserve long-term democracy, social peace, and the values inherited from the War of Liberation against France. Their fears often resulted from a misreading of the intentions and capabilities of Islamists. Many coup supporters simply wanted to preserve their own personal powers and privileges in the face of popular demands for social change. To justify their unconstitutional actions, they demonized the FIS and accused Chadli of having made a secret deal with its leaders that would have led to a purging of the military ranks after the elections. They also questioned the electoral popularity of the FIS by pointing out that if one factored in the number of defective ballots and a turnout rate of 59 percent, only 25 percent of Algerians had actually voted for the Islamists.

The coup and the actions of the army in the following months set in motion a dynamic of civil war that has foiled any return to democratic politics in Algeria. On 16 January 1992 Mohammed Boudiaf was installed as head of the HCE, the new collective presidency. Boudiaf, a respected figure from the war of liberation, had not even lived in Algeria for the previous twenty-eight years. Almost all of the leading FIS members not already in jail were arrested. Thousands of FIS militants were apprehended, and many were placed in detention camps in the Saharan desert. By 1995 the government admitted having arrested 34,000 people. Local and provincial assemblies controlled by the FIS were dissolved, and most of their members were imprisoned. Political activities at mosques were banned. In March 1992 the FIS was officially (and permanently) outlawed.

For several months following the coup, most FIS leaders urged party members to be steadfast and oppose the coup, but there were few calls for violence and armed struggle. Hachani sought cooperation with the FLN and the FFS, which also opposed the HCE as unconstitutional. Clashes between police and more-radical members of the FIS increased steadily. The regime had an important effect on the Islamist movement. By imprisoning so many, it prevented the largely moderate and pragmatic political leadership from controlling the most extreme members of the base. By dissolving the 1990 elected assemblies, annulling the 1991 elections, and banning the FIS, it undermined democratization and eliminated the possibility that the FIS could play a legal role in politics in the future. Decapitated and coerced, the party soon became radicalized. Extreme elements in and out of the party quickly organized for armed resistance and violence against the regime. By 1993 Algeria had been plunged into civil war. Many of the violent Islamists groups such as the *Groupe Islamique Armé* (Armed Islamic Group, GIA) that emerged were not controlled by the FIS, even though some drew their recruits from the party. It was not until July 1994 that the FIS formally constituted its armed wing, the Islamic Salvation Army (AIS), drawn largely from another loosely affiliated armed group, the *Mouvement Armé Islamique* (Armed Islamic Movement, MIA).

Since 1992 some former FIS leaders and a fair number of party supporters have entered the ranks of terrorist groups and committed atrocities that have prolonged Algeria's civil violence. However, these facts hardly serve as evidence that the FIS was always essentially radical, anti-democratic, and violence-prone, claims often used by the regime to justify the canceling of the elections. Some important actions of the FIS in the last ten years suggest that many FIS leaders remain pragmatists concerned with returning to a democratic process. That the FIS has not been legally reintegrated into the political system has less to do with the policies of its leaders than with the eradicationist and exclusionary attitudes of the military regime.

The FIS continually demanded the release from prison of Madani, Benhadj, and other leading members as a prerequisite for dialogue with the government. In late 1994 and early 1995, exiled FIS leaders Rabah Kébir and Anwar Haddam negotiated and signed an important accord with all of Algeria's major opposition parties, including the FLN and the FFS. In the Rome Platform, the party rejected violence, pledged to guarantee fundamental liberties, and supported multipartyism and alternation of power through free elections. With the apparent blessing of Madani and Benhadj, this important public commitment to democratic principles and a strategy for conflict resolution was summarily rejected by the military-backed government of President Liamine Zeroual. The regime staged presidential elections (1995, 1999) and parliamentary elections (1997, 2002). The outlawed FIS was barred from participating in any of them. In 1997 the AIS announced a unilateral truce and reached an agreement with the government to lay down its weapons and disband in exchange for amnesty. Many FIS leaders have called for dialogue with the government, release of prisoners, an end to violence, and free elections, only to be rebuffed by the regime. In 1997 Madani was released to house arrest, but after he called for an end to bloodshed and a role for the international community in resolving the conflict, he was put back in prison. During the 1999 presidential elections the FIS encouraged its supporters to vote for Ahmed Taleb Ibrahimi, a moderate Islamist-leaning candidate who appeared to be a strong rival to the military's choice, Abdelaziz Bouteflika. Claiming fraud at the last minute, Ibrahimi and all the other opposition candidates pulled out of the race. In 1999 Madani supported Bouteflika's referendum on an amnesty for Islamist fighters, and in January 2000 Kébir called for dialogue and praised Bouteflika for granting an amnesty to AIS fighters. Having completed their sentences, Madani and Benhadj were released from prison in June 2003, but the government banned them from political activity.

Despite these overtures to resolve the civil conflict, the military-backed regime has steadfastly resisted compromise with the FIS while it has sought to crush violent Islamist groups such as the GIA. Had the military not stolen the 1991 elections from the FIS, it is doubtful that a massive civil war would have occurred. While the party has often sent conflicting signals about its commitment to liberal politics, nonviolence, and women's rights, the bulk of the FIS leadership demonstrated a commitment to electoral politics from 1988 to 1992. It was a mainstream, Islamo-nationalist party with wide popular appeal. Had it come to power, it would likely have pursued its stated goals of introducing a rule of law, moralizing society, reducing corruption, making administration more effective, and reforming the economy. After a decade of conflict, Algeria is still faced with the task of reinstituting truly democratic and inclusive elections. Whether the regime can undo much of the damage resulting from its halting of democratization in 1992 will significantly depend on whether it allows a constructive and meaningful political role for the FIS.

–BRADFORD DILLMAN,
AMERICAN UNIVERSITY

Viewpoint:
No. The Islamist opposition may not have had the genuine support of the Algerian people.

According to one viewpoint, although not necessarily that of the author of this article, the cancellation of Algeria's parliamentary elections of December 1991/January 1992 was justified since it prevented a radical Islamist party from taking power. Algeria was unprepared politically, economically, socially, and culturally to proceed with its democratization after the first round held on 26 December 1991. The cancellation ended Algeria's rapid, though haphazard, democratization, but the process itself was terribly flawed. The decision even to have elections, given the eroding conditions of the country, was a tragic mistake. Before addressing the consequences of the cancellation, it is necessary to provide its historical context.

In November 1954 the *Front de Libération Nationale* (National Liberation Front, FLN) proclaimed its intention to fight for Algerian independence from France. Its War of Liberation ended in March 1962 with the signing of the Evian Accords. Algeria became officially independent that July. The FLN opted for a socialist direction and perceived itself as an avant-garde party entrusted to lead the fledgling nation in the postcolonial period. By that time, the FLN had jettisoned or co-opted liberals and *ulema* (Muslim clerics). A series of documents–the Tripoli Program (1962), the Algiers Charter (1964), and the National Char-

ters (1976, slightly revised or "enriched" in 1985)–defined the Algerian state as socialist and Muslim. Though the Constitutions of 1963 and 1976 included democratic articles stipulating political and civil rights, the reality was that the FLN and, beginning in June 1965, the army ruled in an authoritarian and exclusive manner. This power establishment composed of military officers, technocrats, and civilians–known as the Pouvoir (French for "power")–prohibited political dissent. Ahmed Ben Bella (premier, 1962–1963; president, 1963–1965), Houari Boumedienne (president of the revolutionary council, 1965–1976; president, 1976–1978), and Chadli Benjedid (president, 1979–1992) governed during these decades.

The early and mid 1980s signaled, however, portentous changes. First, Benjedid reoriented state planning from heavy industrialization to a more balanced approach to sector investment. Agriculture particularly received more attention. A tentative liberalization also occurred affecting the first sector (agriculture) and second sector (industry and manufacturing, primarily, hydrocarbons). This policy change shelved the traditional blueprint for Algeria's development and alienated technocrats from the Boumedienne period–many of whom had been removed after Benjedid assumed the presidency. Second, a populist and political Islamism arose that challenged the secular political culture of the country. Islam was used as a political instrument of protest. Benjedid's efforts to conciliate Islamists by releasing its imprisoned leaders and by passing the Family Law of 1984, which reinforced the *sharia* (Islamic law), failed. Indeed, by that time Mustapha Bouyali organized the *Mouvement [Algérien] Islamique Armé* (Algerian Islamic Armed Movement, M[A]IA). This activism caused another governmental crackdown against Islamists in 1985. Bouyali's telltale Islamist insurgency continued until his death in 1987. Nevertheless, it resonated in Algerian society. Third, Berbers–most notably the Kabyles–roiled over officially imposed Arabization and other threats to their culture. This anger incited violent disturbances in 1980, 1982, and 1986. Fourth, the continuing lack of economic, social, and economic opportunities exasperated the burgeoning youthful population. Fifth, hydrocarbon prices plunged in 1985 and 1986, compounding the distressful political, economic, social, and cultural condition of the country.

In early October 1988 widespread riots convulsed the country. This upheaval forced the government to inaugurate rapid reforms.

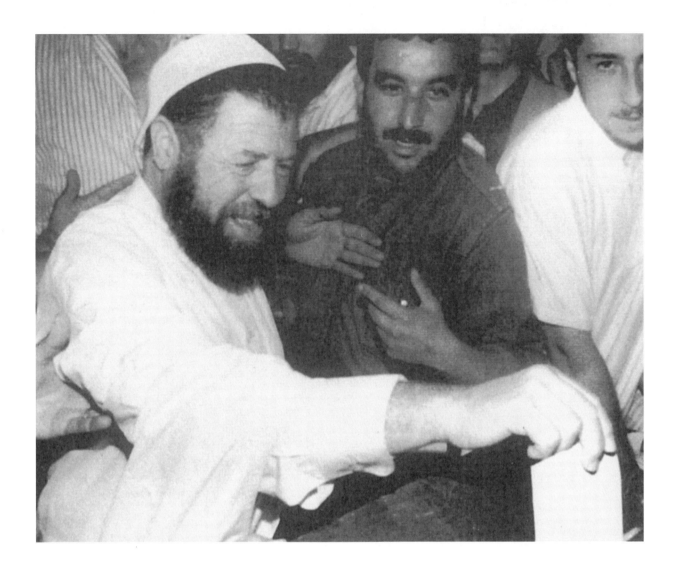

The amended constitution of February 1989 projected a multiparty state and ended the FLN's political monopoly. The *Front Islamique du Salut* (Islamic Salvation Front, FIS) received official recognition in September. Cofounders Shaykh Abbas Madani and Imam Ali Benhadj (Belhadj) attempted to unite the different Islamist tendencies—a difficult task. Prominent Islamists, notably Mahfoud Nahnah and Abdallah Djaballah, formed their own parties. The FIS itself fissured. The Algerianist faction—identified primarily with Madani—was interested in pursuing Islamism in an Algerian context. The Salafist group—associated with Benhadj—leaned toward linking with international Islamist movements. The Algerianists were regarded as more political and pragmatic, the Salafists as ideological and inflexible. The FIS also included a militant fringe—repatriated veterans of Afghan training and jihad. The very appearance of the FIS—and especially its being allowed by the government to exist—was in itself controversial (and arguably unconstitutional). On the one hand, the FLN may have thought that opposi-

tion to the FIS and its political ideal of an Islamist Algeria would restore the FLN's political fortunes or bond its fractured factions together. On the other hand, there is also the opinion that Benjedid authorized the FIS's legitimization as a means to weaken opponents and distance himself from the FLN. Recognition of the FIS deepened the Boumediennist faction's alienation. Former prime minister Kasdi Merbah resigned from the FLN and formed a separate party. Another former prime minister, Abdelhamid Brahimi, sacked after the October 1988 riots, claimed that the corrupt FLN and government officials accepted bribes and other kickbacks equal to the size of the foreign debt—$26 billion!

As the FIS fissured and the FLN fractured, Algeria experienced a remarkable political, social, and cultural fluorescence. Scores of newspapers, journals, and magazines appeared testifying to the political and ethnic diversity of the country—a pluralist historical identity. This change was radiated by the new media from 1989 to 1991 as Algeria attempted democratization. Tragically, the FLN and FIS

Sheikh Abassi Madani, a leader of the *Front Islamique du Salut* (Islamic Salvation Front, FIS) in Algeria, voting in municipal elections in 1990

(© AP/Wide World Photos)

relentlessly and recklessly pursued their own quests for power, regardless of the country's social realities and rising democratic expectations. The failure of democratization cannot be blamed on a single group or party. The culpability was shared as well for the ensuing catastrophe that has claimed 150,000 lives since the cancellation of the elections.

In June 1990 the first free elections occurred in Algeria's history. The FIS achieved stunning victories in regional and provincial races. It gained 32 regional assemblies (Assemblée Populaire de Wilaya, APW) out of 48 with 55 percent of the vote and 853 out of 1,539 local councils (Assemblée Populaire Comunale, APC) with 46 percent of the vote. How popular was the FIS? The FIS received 4.3 million votes. The FLN garnered 2.25 million votes. About 63 percent of the eligible voters participated; of them, 34 percent voted for the FIS. Many observers considered the FIS's success a consequence of protest voting against the political establishment. Nevertheless, the FIS's constituency spanned Algerian society. It ranged from middle-class Algerians, resentful of FLN party members' social and economic privileges, to disillusioned students with no employment opportunities to devout believers desirous of an Islamist order. FIS winners believed that they could now give Algeria an Islamist imprint. There were calls by Islamists for concurrent parliamentary and presidential elections.

The FLN still exercised national power, but it continued its blundering policy. Before the slated June 1991 parliamentary elections, the FLN-dominated *Assemblée Populaire Nationale* (National Popular [People's] Assembly, APN) enacted in March and April significant electoral law changes. This blatant gerrymandering would have given pro-FLN areas of the country (the far south) greater representation. The FIS responded by appealing for protests and strikes in May and June that provoked violence, a state of siege, and the postponement of the elections. Hamrouche was replaced by Sid Ahmed Ghozali. After threatening "holy war," the normally moderate Madani was arrested along with the more impulsive Benhadj. Abdelkader Hachani and Mohammed Said of the Algerianist faction provisionally took over the FIS leadership and effectively prepared for a new round of electoral confrontation.

Prime Minister Ghozali reformed the electoral laws—though the FIS still found them unsatisfactory—but abandoned the proportional system that would have changed the outcome of the rescheduled parliamentary elections. Instead, large parties would be over-

represented, which was an enormous mistake that benefited the FIS. A popular interpretation circulated that Ghozali hoped that the army would intervene in the election if the FIS gained significant representation. The first electoral round, held on 26 December, gave the FIS an astonishing 188 out of 232 seats won outright in the future 430-seat National Popular Assembly. The *Front des Forces Socialistes* (Socialist Forces Front, FFS), a Kabyle (Berber) party led by Algeria's most prominent democrat, Hocine Ait Ahmed, attained 25 seats. The FLN gained only 15. Out of the 13.3 million registered voters, 59 percent participated in the elections. The FIS received 3.3 million votes; one million less than in the June elections. This result signaled that the FIS—as reported by some observers—was losing its political momentum. The FLN, however, only received 1.6 million votes compared to 2.2 million in June, indicating its political collapse. Significantly, 40 percent abstained—illustrating the electorate's anxiety as well as apathy. There were also about one million blank or spoiled ballots. There were reports of irregularities in FIS-controlled municipalities impeding non-FIS voters. Nevertheless, there was no question that given the first round's results—no matter how flawed—the FIS was Algeria's dominant party.

It is argued that if the proportional system had been left in place, the FIS would have gained approximately one-third of the seats—a more accurate gauge of the FIS's political support. The anticipated second round (to be held on 16 January 1992) probably would not have given the FIS an absolute majority. The result would have been the necessity of a coalition government and, perhaps, an eleventh-hour reprieve of the democratic process, but it did not happen this way.

The specter of an FIS-controlled government alarmed members of the Pouvoir. Efforts toward some type of dialogue between Islamists and the military, in particular, failed. Rumors rampantly circulated. On 4 January a rally organized by Ait Ahmed's FFS attracted hundreds of thousands of demonstrators in Algiers, who called for a continuation of the democratic process but with "no police state, no fundamentalist republic." This protest represented the opinion of most Algerians. However, Pouvoir plotters, headed by General Khaled Nezzar, engineered the deposal of Benjedid, who was forced to resign on 11 January. A *Haut Comité d'Etat* (High Council of State, HCE) took power on 14 January and promptly canceled the elections.

While many Algerians condemned the intervention by the military and its civilian allies as undemocratic, others were relieved. The FIS failed to convince Algerians as a whole that it was democratic and tolerant. For example, the Algerianists and the Salafists projected different views toward democratic participation. Madani believed that an Islamist state could be achieved through democratic means, though his comment in June 1991 regarding "holy war" was disconcerting. The statement "there is no democracy in Islam"—usually attributed to Benhadj—contradicted a commitment to democratic process. Benhadj's fiery sermons and comments were often filled with menacing threats. The FIS usually pursued confrontation rather than compromise, thereby antagonizing its opposition. The FIS projected an unsettling uncertainty. The party's rhetorical ambiguity—perhaps necessary given its diverse membership—hardly fostered confidence. The Algerianist-Salafist rivalry compounded anxieties. How radical would the FIS be once in office?

Feminists strongly opposed the FIS. Professional and educated women dreaded the potential of gender subordination under a patriarchal FIS government. Disturbing accounts appeared, reporting of women being harassed in FIS-administered municipalities. Other Islamist parties feared for their own political and cultural voice and viability if the rival FIS took power. France, Algeria's most important economic partner, was concerned for the stability of moderate Morocco and Tunisia if an Islamist government took over in Algeria. In addition, it was haunted by the prospect of Algerian masses trying to emigrate, thereby fanning nativist movements such as the *Front National* (National Front, FN) of Jean-Marie Le Pen. France was hardly disinterested by events across the Mediterranean, especially when it was constantly targeted by the FIS rhetorically for its colonial exploitation of Algeria and its continued postcolonial technical, cultural, and economic presence.

The FIS willfully failed to appreciate Algerian pluralism. Its support of Arabization alienated 17 percent of the country's population—the Berbers, who cherished their own traditions and language (Tamazight). The Berbers not only opposed Islamist political presumptions but also resented those who implicitly questioned the depth of their own religious devotion. While Ait Ahmed's FFS wanted to work with the FIS democratically, the *Rassemblement pour la Culture et la Démocratie* (Rally for Culture and Democracy, RCD) of Said Saadi distrusted it and wanted it disbanded.

The cancellation of the elections is often couched in terms of selfish intentions—the Pouvoir desiring to protect and perpetuate its privileges. Certainly, this motive cannot be totally rejected. Yet, there is another side to this interpretation. The FIS constantly railed against the military as being part of the *hizb faransa* (French party) for its Francophone culture and often its training. Members of the military—especially field officers—were veterans of the *Armée de Libération Nationale* (National Army of Liberation, ALN) that struggled resolutely against the French to liberate Algeria. They remembered and profoundly resented aspersions that cast suspicion on their loyalty to the Algerian state and patriotism. The military leadership firmly believed that its mission was to save Algeria and its historic legacy.

The FIS identified with the historic, revolutionary FLN. Nevertheless, the FLN of 1955 was secularist and included liberals as well as the *ulema*. It initially aimed at including as many militants and nationalists under its umbrella as possible. The FIS was less a radical Islamist group than another exclusivist organization, like the FLN, in its scorned postcolonial configuration. It hardly appropriated the revolution. Indeed, its claims to have done so appalled the military and civilian elite, many of whom had fought and suffered during the revolution.

The argument that an FIS government would have avoided the civil war fails to take into account the historic determination of Algerians to live independently—including pursuing a secular life. Berbers would have soundly resisted if the FIS, as anticipated, moved toward establishing an Islamist, Arabized Algeria. Indeed, protests and violence in Kabylia since April 2001—that reportedly almost forced President Abdelaziz Bouteflika's resignation—illustrated the Berbers' destabilizing potential. If the FIS attempted to inaugurate an Islamist state, there would have been general resistance, given Algeria's strong ethnic and secular traditions. Furthermore, the Algerian community overseas, especially in France, questioned political Islamism. The FIS regarded that community's members (with its large percentage of Kabyles) as heretical—corrupted by French culture and language. Nevertheless, the manifold ties to and influence of the Algerian community in France would have been problematic for an FIS government bent on exercising morality with policy in creating an Islamist state.

Algeria imploded during this period. Its flawed democratic process produced an unrepresentative parliamentary election. Its parties were divided internally and ideologically. The economy floundered in spiraling debt compounded by an increasingly inflationary dinar. Algerian governments and certainly the FIS and other parties had little appreciation of the social, political, economic, and historical realities of the country. Certainly, the FIS sorely underestimated the political potential of the army. The FIS felt cheated by the cancellation of the elections, yet it is difficult to gauge its genuine popularity. It was the only effective political vehicle for Algerians to voice protest against the despised FLN establishment. When the civil war broke out, most Algerians tried to avoid the conflict rather than support the FIS's ideal of an Islamist Algeria. Fundamentally, democracy was pursued by people and parties who were inherently inexperienced in democratic process and more interested in achieving exclusive power. That ambition, shared by the FIS and the Pouvoir, drove Algeria toward its unremitting civil war.

–PHILLIP C. NAYLOR,
MARQUETTE UNIVERSITY

References

John P. Entelis and Phillip C. Naylor, eds., *State and Society in Algeria* (Boulder, Colo.: Westview Press, 1992).

Luis Martinez, *The Algerian Civil War, 1990–1998* (New York: Columbia University Press, 2000).

Robert Mortimer, "Islamists, Soldiers, and Democrats: The Second Algerian War," *Middle East Journal,* 50 (Winter 1996): 18–39.

William B. Quandt, *Between Ballots and Bullets: Algeria's Transition from Authoritarianism* (Washington, D.C.: Brookings Institution, 1998).

John Ruedy, ed., *Islamism and Secularism in North Africa* (New York: St. Martin's Press, 1994).

Benjamin Stora, *Algeria, 1830–2000: A Short History* (Ithaca, N.Y.: Cornell University Press, 2001).

Michael Willis, *The Islamist Challenge in Algeria: A Political History* (Washington Square, N.Y.: New York University Press, 1997).

ALGERIAN REVOLUTION

Were the military tactics employed by the French in the Algerian Revolution necessary?

Viewpoint: Yes. French actions in the Algerian Revolution were part of a wider Western crusade against communism at the height of the Cold War, and whatever abuses that did occur were justified by the overarching goal.

Viewpoint: No. French conduct in the Algerian Revolution was a shameful attempt by a declining empire to maintain some semblance of influence.

The necessity to protect trade routes prompted the French expedition to Algeria in 1830 (even more so than the protection of French honor following the Algerian dey's slapping of the French consul with a fly whisk in 1827!). By 1834 Algeria was made a colony of France; however, it took more than forty years for the French to subdue a series of opposition movements against colonial control, the most famous of which was that led by Amir Abd al-Qadir in the 1840s.

In 1848 Algeria was annexed, becoming an integral part of France, and a formal policy of colonization ensued. By 1881 there were more than 335,000 Europeans in Algeria, and it has often been said that Algeria was more profoundly affected by "Europeanization" than any other area of the Middle East. Nationalist opposition to the French began to rise again following World War I (1914–1918). It was urban based and, as scholar John Entelis states, reflected "a gradual shift from resignation to the French domination to a radical opposition that would lead to the struggle for independence."

Soon enough, questions of identity and a lack of full French citizenship became focal points of opposition by various groups of Algerians as the society as a whole, for good or bad, was being transformed, resembling more and more that of French culture and institutions. In early 1954 Algerian dissidents formed the *Comite Revolutionnaire d'Unite et d'Action* (CRUA), which by October evolved into the *Front de Libération Nationale* (National Liberation Front, FLN). On 1 November 1954 the FLN, which became the ruling party in the postindependence period, called on all Algerians to resist the French, thereby beginning the revolution. It was a violent war, with anywhere between 250,000 and 1.5 million (depending on the source) Algerians perishing, and more than 30,000 French killed. France committed an army of 500,000 to join 200,000 Algerian auxiliaries to combat the rebellion. Finally, a cease-fire was reached at Evian, France, in March 1962. The Evian accords stipulated a national referendum to decide the issue of Algerian independence. After more than 130 years of French rule, the Algerians voted in favor of independence on 1 July, and four days later the Democratic and Popular Republic of Algeria was proclaimed.

**Viewpoint:
Yes. French actions in the Algerian
Revolution were part of a wider
Western crusade against
communism at the height of
the Cold War, and whatever
abuses that did occur were justified
by the overarching goal.**

Through a protracted process of institution-alized amnesia, a view of the Algerian War (1954–1962) deliberately detrimental to the French military has emerged. Little of the impressive literature produced on this vexing topic sufficiently stresses the fact that the French Army was fighting its "battle of destiny," making a last bid to buttress its broken fortunes and to restore national honor within the framework of a Western alliance presumably united in its face-off with Marxism. More optimistically, many "crusaders" such as Jacques Allard, Antione Argoud, Pierre Château-Jobert, and other officers not only saw Algeria as the last Western bulwark in North Africa but also were holding out for a brighter future in a country rejuvenated by a newfound brotherhood between *pied noir* (liter-ally, "black feet," the colloquial term used to des-ignate North African–born Frenchmen) and Muslims, encapsulated in Colonel Maurice Big-eard's philosophy: "We are not here to defend colonialism. . . . We are defenders of freedom and a new order." True, this concept may have been construed a posteriori as a naive form of social-ism; nonetheless, as scholar Irwin M. Wall states, "The French presence there was regarded as pro-gressive and modernizing as against an indige-nous culture of obscurantist Islam and retrograde nationalism." The time seemed right, the cause a truly noble one.

Still smarting from a series of setbacks and supposed betrayals by politicians, the French Army had a clear notion of where its duty lay: defend Algeria, "one of the last Western outposts on African soil." Many young reserve officers, of whom the present writer was one, belonged to the World War II (1939–1945) generation nur-tured on heady ideals of honor, motherland, and empire, with distinguished military leaders from Louis-Hubert-Gonzalve Lyautey to Charles-Victor-Emmanuel Leclerc as role models. Disillu-sioned but defiant, officers returning from Indochina, who had been booed by crowds upon disembarking in Marseille, were determined there should be no "sell-out" in Algeria. A point was driven home by French commander in chief Gen-eral Raoul "Chinaman" Salan when, with unchar-acteristic candor, he warned that any suggestion of "abandonment" would be perceived by the

army as an affront and might trigger a desperate reaction. After four years of counterinsurgency operations, some French Army units had become ruthlessly efficient at crushing urban terrorists, chasing *fellaghas* (fighters) through the "djebel," or moving, according to scholar Alistair Horne, "like Mao's 'fish in water' among the uncommit-ted masses"—not to mention unexpectedly gener-ous and idealistic attempts to win the hearts and minds of Algerians by the *Sections Administratives Spéciales* (Special Administrative Sections, SAS), "a selflessly devoted and courageous band of men who were much loved by the local populace." The SAS was a politico-military bureau set up to administer any area that had been allowed to fall under the control of the *Front de Libération Natio-nale* (National Liberation Front, FLN) rebels, whose purpose was to bring the local population back into the loyalist camp. The politicians, for their part, behaved true to form: "Algeria is France," declared François Mitterand in 1954 upon the outbreak of the rebellion. Obviously, in the Cold War context, withdrawal remained unthinkable where Algeria was concerned.

What sort of case could the French military make for a possible Soviet threat? A fairly strong one, it would seem, with pride of place going to the much-publicized connection in Cairo between the FLN and Egyptian president Gamal Abd al-Nasser, who was seen as a Soviet surro-gate. Late in 1954 the French press harped on the theme of "revolt masterminded by Cairo" or encouraged by "foreign elements." All of which, according to scholar Martin Thomas, tended to blur the issue as "the French 'conflated' pan-Arabism with the Communist menace." The French gen-eral and commander in Algeria, Maurice Challe, and most of the "top brass" considered Algeria as a Cold War front line. The failure of some North Atlantic Treaty Organization (NATO) allies, especially the United States, to see eye to eye with the French, coupled with French misapprehen-sion of American aims, caused much disap-pointed Gallic shoulder shrugging, especially, according to Horne, "to men like Argoud (for whom) the war against Communism was a per-manent and unceasing phenomenon."

No wonder conventional French wisdom of the time visualized a strong Soviet threat to NATO's southern flank. As Horne noted: "Many a French para [paratrooper] gave his life heroically, assured that he was defending a bas-tion of Western civilisation, and the bogey slo-gan of the 'Soviet fleet at Mers El-Kébir' retained its force right until the last days of *présence française*."

It is all well for recent observers to belittle the actual extent of communist involvement in North Africa thanks to hindsight and access to archives, but elements of national decision-making

THEY WOULD EITHER TALK QUICKLY OR NEVER

In his memoirs of his activities in Algeria, French general Paul Aussaresses recalls the role of summary executions and torture of Algerian rebels:

During his private meeting with Max Lejeune, Massu told him that a group of terrorists had been arrested and that he was hesitating as to whether they should be handed over to the justice system or simply executed.

"Do you remember the DC-3 of *Air-Atlas,* the plane that was carrying Ben Bella, the head of the FLN, and his four companions last October 22?" asked Max Lejeune.

"Who wouldn't remember something like that, Mr. Minister?" answered Massu.

"It's a matter I'm well acquainted with because Premier Guy Mollet had me sort it out with General Lorillot. Once the government found out that those men were flying from Morocco to Tunisia, orders were given to the fighter planes based in Oran to shoot the plane down. The only reason we cancelled the order was that at the last minute we found out that the pilot and crew were French. It's regrettable for the French government that Ben Bella should still be alive. His arrest was a mistake. We intended to kill him."

Massu understood the message Max Lejeune was giving him. He summoned Trinquier and me immediately. When he told us that anecdote, the message was crystal clear for me as well: I would be executing twelve more men the following night. I could have left that unsavory task for Bigeard to finish but I preferred doing it myself with the NCOs of my first team. When we killed those prisoners there was no doubt in our minds that we were following direct orders of Max Lejeune, who was part of the government of Guy Mollet, and acting in the name of the French Republic.

Only rarely were the prisoners we had questioned during the night still alive the next morning. Whether they had talked or not they generally had been neutralized. It was impossible to send them back to the court system, there were too many of them and the machine of justice would have become clogged with cases and stopped working altogether. Furthermore, many of the prisoners would probably have managed to avoid any kind of punishment. . . .

Summary executions were therefore an inseparable part of the tasks associated with keeping law and order. That was the reason why the army had been called in. Counter-terrorism had been instituted, but obviously only unofficially. Clearly we had to wipe out the FLN and only the army had the tools for the task. It was so obvious that it became unnecessary to spell out such orders at any level. No one ever asked me openly to execute this one or that one. It was simply understood.

Regarding the use of torture, it was tolerated if not actually recommended. François Mitterrand, as minister of justice, had a de facto representative with General Massu in Judge Jean Bérard, who covered our actions and knew exactly what was going on during the night. I had an excellent relationship with him, with nothing to hide.

While torture was widely used in Algeria, it didn't mean that it was an ordinary occurrence. We didn't discuss it among officers and an interrogation didn't necessarily end up in torture. Some prisoners starting talking very easily. Others only needed some roughing up. It was only when a prisoner refused to talk or denied the obvious that torture was used. We did everything we possibly could to avoid having the youngest soldiers bloody their hands and many would have been unable to see it through anyway. The methods I used were always the same: beatings, electric shocks, and, in particular, water torture, which was the most dangerous technique for the prisoner. It never lasted more than one hour and the suspects would speak in the hopes of saving their own lives. They would either talk quickly or never.

Source: *Paul Aussaresses,* The Battle of the Casbah: Terrorism and Counter-Terrorism in Algeria, 1955–1957, *translated by Robert L. Miller (New York: Enigma, 2002), pp. 125–128.*

ALGERIAN REVOLUTION

vis-à-vis crises are to be sought as much in the contemporary appraisal of a situation, with perspective sharpened by eyewitness accounts, as by subsequent rummaging through dusty files in public record offices. As further evidence of Iron Curtain implication in North Africa, during the summer of 1956 Algeria received arms consignments from Moscow and Prague via Egypt. Although often labeled as Marxist by *pieds noirs,* the FLN stopped short of full satellite status vis-à-vis Soviet Russia. Amusingly though, FLN representatives visiting China in December 1958 were congratulated by Chairman Mao Tse-tung for tying down six hundred thousand NATO troops in North Africa. More seriously, in the second half of 1960, Algerian leader Ferhat Abbas pushed for and obtained more support from Moscow and Beijing.

There remained an abiding fear in Anglo-American circles, especially on the part of U.S. secretary of state John Foster Dulles with his "nightmare scenario" of a possible extension of the conflict, involving "volunteers perhaps from Egypt or farther east," tallying with reports of a communist plot with links to North Africa. Early in 1957 Foreign Minister Christian Pineau and other French officials presented Washington with documentation purportedly substantiating strong FLN links to international communism, coinciding with the enunciation of the Eisenhower Doctrine in January 1957, which committed the United States to assist countries in the Middle East that were under the threat of "international communism." As a matter of course, France's NATO allies—such as West Germany, Belgium, Holland, and especially Canada—tended, when the chips were down, to support it during policy debates. The British position, as noted by Michael Kettle, was "that the defence of Algeria by the French Army was vital to the NATO position in Europe. The FLN were not at the moment Communist inclined . . . but it was not safe to leave a vacuum." Support from the United States, however, was lukewarm and ambiguous at best, and it was dependent on French willingness to institute reform in Algeria. Apparently "torn between its need for France in Europe and its criticism of France in Africa," argued scholar Irwin M. Wall, America clearly wished to have its cake and eat it, to facilitate national emancipation and capitalist development in Arab countries while attempting to contain Marxist expansion.

True, the Algerian Communist Party (PCA) aided and abetted the rebellion, with one of their number, officer-cadet Henri Maillot, shipping a truckload of automatic weapons to the FLN, while others were involved in bombings. Simultaneously, in France, trade unionists and French Communist Party (PCF) stalwarts were causing disturbances at railway stations and generally seeking to undermine the morale of national servicemen leaving for Algeria. When changing trains in Lyons in January 1957, this writer, then in uniform, had to brush off an invitation to breakfast by a PCF cadre. In this connection one should not play down Anglo-American fears of a communist revolution in Paris "at the very heart of NATO," as a reaction to a possible coup engineered from Algiers by *Organisation Armée Secrète* (Secret Army Organization, OAS, which was an ultra-Right-wing group bent on keeping Algeria French, even through terrorist tactics—it was founded by Salan in 1961). All in all France's case for making a stand in Algeria against world communism would appear to have been based on fairly firm ground. Strangely, this particular mind-set survived for a long time. Recently, an elite unit of the Karen Liberation Army on the Burmese border, under a former captain of the Third RIMA, Michel Faulques, was named the *"Commando de chasse Lieutenant Degueldre."* Part villain, part hero, the former OAS Delta Commando leader, convinced he had ably defended *Algérie française* (French Algeria) by eliminating the Algiers *barbouzes* (special agents trained to combat the OAS in Algeria) in 1962, was arrested and subsequently faced a firing squad in France. Yet, Degueldre, so the former captain had told the Karens, was merely "a French soldier who had lost his life fighting against international communism."

France's resolve tended to harden around ideals such as *Eurafrique* (a concept of a European-African unity with its capital in Paris), central to its mission in Algeria, which was popular in 1956. This writer first heard the theme bandied about in February 1957 at Arzew during a "pep talk" by Colonel Fontès, then commanding the *Centre d'Instruction, Pacification et Contre-guérilla* (Instruction Center for Pacification and Counter-Guerilla Tactics, CIPCG), where young officers were taught the basic tenets of revolutionary war. A highly commendable plan, its success depended on genuine fraternization with Muslims, briefly conceived of as a reality on 16 May 1958, when some thirty thousand Muslims spontaneously linked hands with forty thousand *pieds noirs* in downtown Algiers. This demonstration was a highly emotional, heartwarming scene and, for a few days, proved a timely morale booster all across Algeria. *Intégration* (integration) had become a distinct possibility. There was real hope for a fresh start, hope in a renewed sense of purpose, dignity, and unity, coupled with confidence that French leaders would now take a firm stand against communism in the ongoing Algerian struggle.

It remained for French president Charles de Gaulle, on 29 August 1958, to spell out the philosophy behind this rationale. Later accompanied by the rabble-rousing cry "From Dunkirk to Tamanrasset—55 million Frenchmen!" *intégration* gave new life to the dream of *Eurafrique*, with a resurgent, oil-rich France spanning the Mediterranean, strangely reminiscent of Cecil Rhodes's 1890s vision of Africa colored red from Cape to Cairo. The mood became almost jingoistic, with *pieds noirs* in Tlemcen assuring this writer they would "eventually repossess Morocco and Tunisia," thereby giving substance to U.S. anxieties of an extension of the conflict. Surprisingly, support for *Eurafrique* was voiced by British junior minister Julian Amery, who saw de Gaulle's France as both an African power and a nuclear power, also "pinning great hopes on the Sahara."

However, for observers in the know, the writing was already on the wall. Attempts were being made in December 1959 by the French Fifth Bureau—in charge of psychological warfare—to promote a propaganda movie demonstrating to Muslims that victory in the field had eluded the FLN and the time had come to reconstruct Algeria in a spirit of generous intercommunal fellowship and goodwill. By the close of 1959, although it had proved an uphill task, thanks to "Operation Binoculars," Challe had as good as won the war, all rebel formations of *katiba* (company) size having been destroyed. At no time since the aftermath of the Battle of Algiers had FLN morale been so low, a situation that was sustained til the end of 1960, while a sizable segment of the Muslim population appeared to be swinging toward de Gaulle. A golden opportunity to capitalize on these assets, however, was lost. Once Challe had been posted back to France, the situation on the ground was allowed to deteriorate, thereby wrecking hopes of a just peace based on Saharan oil, "third force" Muslims, and economic reconstruction through application of the ambitious Constantine Plan.

Ultimately, *intégration* and *Eurafrique* proved impractical, their conceptualization and execution fatally flawed, while public opinion at home, not to mention worldwide diplomatic disapproval, began to turn the tide. France's failure to disengage satisfactorily from Algeria was perceived by observers such as Governor-General Paul Delouvrier in September 1959 as eventually leading to chaos in France with potential ripple effects for the whole of Western Europe. Hence, de Gaulle attempted (not without unprecedented prodding and prompting from the United States) to put out feelers for Algerian self-determination, simultaneously striving to hang on to the oil of the Sahara, while preparing to sell *Algérie française* down the river.

War is never pretty, and the "Dirty war" in Algeria was no exception. As the conflict unfurled, the FLN—initially a motley rabble of *bandits d'honneur*, small-time cutthroats, and deserters from the French Army—won itself an unenviable reputation for intimidation, torture, ghastly mutilation, and dog-pack tactics in sinister-sounding places such as El Halia, Palestro, and Melouza, which are infamous for the massacres perpetrated by the FLN. Most ignominious of all: at war's end, no fewer than 150,000 *harki* (Algerians who fought for France) paramilitaries were deliberately killed in an unprecedented orgy of medieval barbarity. There is little doubt that this callous, calculated savagery largely served as a catalyst for the abuses subsequently laid at France's door. Small wonder then that confronted with the grim reality of disemboweled and emasculated comrades, some French soldiers resorted to regrettable measures in "cold blood."

As a textbook exercise in selective amnesia, FLN implication in atrocities was conveniently glossed over, both during and after the war. It was certainly never aired at the United Nations (UN), overshadowed as it was by facile allegations of French torture, emanating mostly from the Left-wing press. The ruthless application of terror tactics by the FLN was, of course, aimed at unleashing a vicious cycle of repression and counterrepression that could only further the rebels' cause by driving a deeper wedge between the communities. Terror, according to Horne, "was to become accepted as a weapon of proven efficacy." Even such an impartial critic as journalist Edward Behr is forced to admit: "It is certain that without torture the FLN's terrorist network would never have been overcome." Even more revealing, FLN leader Ben M'Hidi acknowledged that the parachutists' counterterrorist's methods were efficient, while Battle of Algiers veteran Youcef Saadi declared on French television that "in revolutionary war, the end justifies the means." On the French side, Indochina veterans Argoud and Roger Trinquier decided that Algeria was the ideal test bed for *la guerre révolutionnaire* (revolutionary war). This doctrine was arguably, as French soldiers Claude Le Borgne and Pierre Debazies point out, "a pseudo-intellectual hotchpotch of over-simplifications and half-truths" and certainly a highly subversive mix that created an atmosphere conducive to the application of torture. Metropolitan France, however, never really understood what *la guerre révolutionnaire* was all about, wasting several golden opportunities in this field. Eventually, entrusted by an ailing civilian authority with a political mission for which it was inadequately prepared, and convinced that milder methods of intelligence gathering would not prevail, the French Army was trapped into committing certain abuses.

These abuses took the shape of more stern interrogation techniques, some involving electric shocks, especially during the Battle of Algiers. Such practices appeared totally justified in the contemporary context, given the situation of national emergency prevalent at the time, since vital, lifesaving intelligence could thus be gleaned from suspects and/or terrorists caught red-handed, some of whom were French communists and perceived as traitors to the "homeland." Accusations of torture leveled at the Army by the French Left, often emanating from pseudo-intellectuals who had condoned Stalinist purges or Budapest-style repression, were dismissed by Right-wing journalist Philippe Barrès as an attempt to undermine French morale.

It would be wrong to contend that torture was systematic and widespread. True, French governor-general Jacques Soustelle's February 1955 directive had banned its use. As for General Jacques Massu, victor of the Battle of Algiers, he once stated: "In an answer to the question 'Was there really torture?' I can only reply in the affirmative, although it was never either institutionalized nor codified."

Officialspeak at the Arzew CIPCG training center in February 1957 emphatically disallowed the use of torture, as this writer can attest. During a three-week crash course, a *képi bleu* (SAS officers who wore a blue-colored version of the typical French pillbox cap) attempted to instill into officer trainees the "softly-softly" approach for interrogation of suspects, strictly in accordance with the tactics of *nomadisation* (nomadising) as practiced by French units among "the Muslim populations in the *bled* [countryside]." Offstage remarks by fellow trainees, however, suggested that in Kabylia and the Aurès more-muscular methods were being employed. Nevertheless, back with his regiment, this writer never witnessed any atrocities. Likewise, a former paratrooper colonel, onetime commander of the elite Eleventh Shock commando unit, "knows countless comrades who never committed acts of torture," nor would he have brooked such conduct in his unit.

French involvement in Algeria, perceived as the last Western bastion in North Africa, was based on a love-hate relationship that brought out the best—and sometimes the worst—in men. As demonstrated by events in the Balkans, whatever his lofty ideals, the "defender of civilization" wears but a thin veneer of decency that easily wilts under the acid test of war. A further truism is that when both sides perpetrate atrocities the inevitable spiral of accusation and counteraccusation emerges, with propaganda and historical denial ultimately muddying the waters. Over and above the "gore and excreta" of the battlefield and torture chamber—whatever may have

been the latter's actual significance in Algeria—and however much the truth may have been subsequently distorted by Left-wing smear campaigns, at the time, and though this charge may now sound ludicrous, many high-minded French officers and gentlemen, according to Horne, "who had discovered sympathy at the predicament of the *pieds noirs,* coupled with repugnance at FLN atrocities," were convinced they were making a decisive stand for Western civilization. With the advantage of hindsight they feel they were right to do so but are likewise adamant that de Gaulle should have held out longer so as to guarantee a smoother path to decolonization.

–MICHAEL PEYRON,
AL AKHAWAYN UNIVERSITY

Viewpoint:
No. French conduct in the Algerian Revolution was a shameful attempt by a declining empire to maintain some semblance of influence.

The Algerian Revolution against French colonial rule erupted in 1954 and ended with the signing of the Evian accords in March 1962 and Algeria's declaration of independence the following July. For the French, the Algerian Revolution was a battle on three fronts. Most important, it was a tenacious effort to preserve French sovereignty within Algeria by crushing an armed rebellion spearheaded by the *Front de Libération Nationale* (National Liberation Front, FLN). The second front of the battle was within metropolitan France. The war directly contributed to the downfall of the Fourth Republic in 1958 and the reemergence of Charles de Gaulle as a dominant president in the 1960s under the Fifth Republic. It polarized French politics, drained the public budget, and produced a refugee population of nearly one million *colons* (European settlers, also known as *pieds noir*) and *harkis* (Algerians who fought for France) who fled to France after the war. The war was also fought on the international front. France doggedly tried to maintain the remnants of its colonial empire and use Algeria as a gateway to increased influence throughout Africa. However, the French eventually earned the enmity of the United States, Arab nationalists, and many of the nonaligned and newly independent Third World countries.

The war was a shameful period in French history, not only because of the unnecessary suffering of so many people but also because France

French soldiers and
onlookers standing over
an Algerian killed during
street fighting in 1957

(Agence France Presse Photo)

betrayed its national ideals of *liberté, égalité,* and *fraternité*. French actions in Algeria devastated the country and inflicted untold physical and psychological suffering on Algerians. France was humiliated as a global power and alienated many of its Cold War allies. Was the war necessary? Were French actions inevitable? Could France have prevented such an ignominious ending to its 132-year "civilizing mission" in Algeria? There were structural characteristics within Algeria and within French politics that made the early granting of independence, and therefore the avoidance of war, difficult. Weak French governments from 1954 to 1958 faced enormous pressure from *colons,* the colonial bureaucracy, and the military. They were dissuaded from granting significant autonomy, let alone independence, out of fear of civil conflict within metropolitan France and rebellion by *colons* in Algeria. De Gaulle needed several years to prepare the French population psychologically for loss of the colony in 1962. Moreover, by the mid 1950s most Algerians had become radicalized, and their overwhelming demands for independence made other potential settlements based on assimilation or self-determination under continued French tutelage entirely unrealistic. Despite factors on both the French and the Algerian sides making conflict likely, the out-

come could have been different, and much less bloody, had French decision makers adopted different policies.

By 1954 France had already laid the seeds for its subsequent humiliation. In May 1945 nationalist demonstrations in Setif had been crushed, resulting in the death of some five thousand to ten thousand Algerians. Since 1830 most valuable agricultural land had been brought under the control of *colons*. Muslim Algerians lacked citizenship rights and any meaningful role in decision making. Most Algerians lived in poverty, and only about 10 percent of Muslims had formal French education. More than one million European settlers completely dominated the economy and the administrative system, relegating the mass of nine million Algerians to permanent second-class status. Many Algerians, and certainly the founders of the FLN, determined that violent struggle was a necessary strategy in order to achieve their goal of self-determination.

Throughout the war, France never came up with a viable set of political reforms that would preserve the interests of *colons* while meeting the demands of Algerian nationalists. Various French proposals for political liberalization, administrative reform, legislative changes, and elections failed to provide Algerian Muslims full,

ALGERIAN REVOLUTION

democratic political rights or to separate Algeria from French domination. French political policies were anachronistic in an era in which the spread of Arab nationalism and the process of decolonization throughout the world made dismantling of an apartheid-type system seem both inevitable and morally imperative. Given the high population growth rate of Algerians, there was a completely unrealistic expectation that the *colon* minority could indefinitely suppress the political rights of Muslims, who clearly preferred independence.

As a substitute for meaningful political reform and negotiation with rebels, the French belatedly tried to earn the loyalty of Algerians by introducing a series of economic plans and educational reforms intended to ameliorate social conditions and bolster the middle strata of Algerian society. De Gaulle's Constantine Plan (1958) was a substantial program to establish industries, build more housing, and increase employment and schooling of Muslim Algerians. While the expensive plan met with some success, it bought the loyalty of few Algerians and failed to attract private capital from French investors who already foresaw the likelihood of independence.

Limited political and social reforms could not compensate for French military policies that inflicted great injustices on Algerians. In its shameful attempt to hold back the tide of Algerian nationalism, France killed more than 250,000 Algerians (some claim up to 1 million) and wounded hundreds of thousands. Torture and rape became institutionalized and common practices throughout Algeria, on a scale yet to be matched by any Western power since World War II (1939–1945). In the Battle of Algiers, General Jacques Massu crushed the FLN in Algiers through systematic torture, electric-shock treatments, and summary executions. Although France succeeded in sharply reducing urban terrorism after 1957, it did so through violation of the rules of war and through undermining its liberal democratic principles. In 1959 General Maurice Challe initiated a military strategy in the countryside to crush the Algerian mujahideen (holy warriors). By 1960, 25 percent of the Algerian population had been forcibly resettled to French-controlled villages and "regroupment centers" that resembled concentration camps. This devastating relocation of the rural population, who lost their livelihoods and were subjected to abuse and disease, was a precursor of the strategic hamlet program the United States would later adopt in Vietnam. In September 1959 de Gaulle publicly announced his recognition of Algeria's right to self-determination. While the Evian negotiations proceeded and independence became inevitable, a group of *colons* in early 1961 formed a terrorist group called the *Organisation Armée Secrète* (Secret Army Organization, OAS) to make a last-ditch effort to keep Algeria French. The group initially attempted a coup in Algiers and murdered French officials and carried out bombings. They soon began to terrorize the Algerian population. Once France had signed the Evian Accords in March 1962, the secretive OAS began a scorched-earth campaign causing large-scale destruction of Algerian infrastructure, including schools, power facilities, factories, the national library, and many public facilities. The wanton violence, occurring after independence was a foregone conclusion, was intended to make it difficult for future Algerian leaders to govern effectively and develop economically.

The Algerian Revolution also had a profound effect on metropolitan France. In 1958 dissident army factions supported by settlers challenged the weak French government and threatened to land paratroopers on the mainland. The Fourth Republic collapsed, and de Gaulle returned to power. In 1961, when de Gaulle had staged a referendum on Algerian self-determination and started negotiations at Evian, a handful of generals backed by mobs in Algeria staged a putsch that nearly sparked a coup d'état in Paris. The war precipitated significant threats of civil war and other political crises in France. French society was torn between holding on to *Algérie française* (French Algeria) or letting Algeria go independent. Debates raged over torture, terrorism, and the nature of democracy. The war also led to FLN-sponsored terrorism in France and considerable repression of Algerians living in France. In October 1961 Parisian police murdered nearly two hundred Algerians and arrested more than ten thousand following a peaceful demonstration.

Some two million French soldiers served in Algeria. Many witnessed atrocities that had a deep psychological impact on them when they returned home. Around thirty thousand French soldiers and civilians died in the conflict. The cruelty of the war affected not only soldiers and their families but also ordinary French citizens whose knowledge of the secrets of the undeclared war caused many to condemn colonialism and its "civilizing mission." The war experience also laid a foundation for the subsequent rise of anti-Maghrebi racism in France.

The costly war contributed to French economic problems such as budget deficits and inflation. It consumed public resources. In 1957 alone, some $1.1 billion was spent on military operations in Algeria. By the end of the war, France also had to absorb almost one million traumatized European refugees and *harkis*. Tens of thousands of other *harkis* were abandoned by the French in 1962 and killed by Algerian nationalists.

By the end of 1959 France had turned the tide militarily in Algeria through repression and construction of an electric fence along Algeria's border with Tunisia. On the ground, the war was essentially won as attacks by mujahideen steadily declined. Yet, France saw its international prestige diminish throughout the conflict. France felt that holding on to Algeria would help maintain its status as a great power and provide a bridgehead to the rest of Africa. Following its defeat in Indochina in 1954, France witnessed the steady erosion of its empire. Its invasion of the Suez Canal with Israel and Britain in 1956, designed to punish Egypt's Gamal Abd al-Nasser for his pan-Arabism and support of Algeria's rebels, was quickly reversed under American pressure. This Suez invasion and the bombing of the Tunisian border town of Sakiet in 1958 appeared as desperate actions by a declining colonial power. Both eroded France's support in the Arab world. By the late 1950s the emerging nonaligned movement turned against France in the United Nations. French policies in Algeria steadily increased tensions with the United States. Disagreements over Algeria crested following the election of U.S. president John F. Kennedy and contributed to de Gaulle's decision to withdraw France from the North Atlantic Treaty Organization (NATO) and pursue an independent foreign policy.

The Algerian Revolution was in many ways not a Cold War conflict. The FLN was fighting for independence, not for communism. France was not so much fighting for the West as it was struggling to preserve the power of *colons* and preserve a key role for itself in a postcolonial *Eurafrique*. French leaders, military officers, and *colons* made choices in the war under considerable structural constraints, but they often failed to seize opportunities to lessen the violence and achieve political resolution sooner. Even de Gaulle could probably have achieved a peace settlement earlier than 1961 had he not searched in vain for non-FLN Algerian negotiating partners and had he not insisted on detaching the Sahara from an independent Algeria (out of a desire to control Saharan oil fields, insure energy security for France, and continue using the desert for nuclear weapons testing). Even so, de Gaulle was able to end the conflict and reverse the French perception of humiliation by stimulating economic growth in the mainland and by pursuing an independent foreign policy. Several years after Algerian independence, France had recovered its standing in the Arab world. Moreover, France retained important economic interests in Algeria until 1971, and commercial relations with Algeria remain important to this day. Nevertheless, the Algerian conflict was a shameful period in French history. The wounds of the war remain, as evident in the political firestorm following the publication in 2001 of the memoirs of former general Paul Aussaresses, in which he described and defended the use of torture against Algerians from 1955 to 1957. France undermined its republican principles in the war, caused unnecessary death and destruction by delaying independence, and humiliated itself in the eyes of international public opinion as it lost its colonial empire.

–BRADFORD DILLMAN,
AMERICAN UNIVERSITY

References

Paul Aussaresses, *The Battle of the Casbah: Terrorism and Counter-Terrorism in Algeria, 1955–1957,* translated by Robert L. Miller (New York: Enigma, 2002).

Yves Courriere, *Les Fils de la Toussaint: La Guerre d'Algerie* (Paris: Fayard, 1968).

Courriere, *L'heure des Colonels: La Guerre d'Algerie* (Paris: Fayard, 1970).

Courriere, *Les temps des Leopards: La Guerre d'Algerie* (Paris: Fayard, 1969).

Alistair Horne, *A Savage War of Peace: Algeria, 1954–1962* (New York: Viking, 1977).

Henri Le Mire, *Histoire militaire de la guerre d'Algerie* (Paris: A. Michel, 1982).

John Ruedy, *Modern Algeria: The Origins and Development of a Nation* (Bloomington: University of Indiana Press, 1992).

Benjamin Stora, *Algeria, 1830–2000: A Short History* (Ithaca, N.Y.: Cornell University Press, 2001).

John Talbott, *The War without a Name: France in Algeria, 1954–1962* (New York: Knopf, 1980).

Martin Thomas, *The French North African Crisis: Colonial Breakdown and Anglo-French Relations, 1954–1962* (New York: St. Martin's Press, 2000).

Irwin M. Wall, *France, the United States, and the Algerian War* (Berkeley: University of California Press, 2001).

ARAB-ISRAELI WAR OF 1967

Was the Israeli preemptive strike in the Arab-Israeli War of 1967 a necessary and legitimate action?

Viewpoint: Yes. Given the nature of the Arab threat and the aggressive posture of Egyptian leader Gamal Abd al-Nasser, Israel was justified in its attack.

Viewpoint: No. Israel had wanted to acquire the West Bank and Gaza Strip since 1948, and it used the war rhetoric of Egyptian leader Gamal Abd al-Nasser as an excuse to launch a preemptive strike.

The Arab-Israeli War of 1967, often called the Six-Day War or the June War, was a singular event in the history of the modern Middle East. It represented a brilliant military victory for the State of Israel, which launched a preemptive strike and in just six days (5–11 June) defeated the combined Arab armies of Egypt, Syria, and Jordan. In the process, Israel acquired the Sinai Peninsula, Gaza Strip, West Bank (including East Jerusalem), and Golan Heights. These areas became known as the Occupied Territories (the Sinai Peninsula was returned to Egypt following the Egyptian-Israeli peace treaty in 1979).

Many observers would say that the war signaled the end of secular Arab nationalism, or at least Nasserist pan-Arabism, as an effective movement, and the birth of a more virulent form of Islamism. The superpowers, the United States and the Soviet Union, also, perforce, became more entrenched in the Arab-Israeli conflict, a dangerous situation that reached its climax during the Arab-Israeli War of 1973.

The 1967 conflict emerged from the heightened tensions in the inter-Arab arena in the early 1960s, or what noted Middle East scholar Malcolm Kerr termed the "Arab cold war." Inter-Arab rivalries, particularly among the so-called progressive Arab states of Egypt, Syria, and Iraq, compelled the acknowledged leader of the Arab world, Gamal Abd al-Nasser, to initiate a series of actions in response to what the Arabs viewed as Israeli provocations, primarily attempts to divert the headwaters of the Jordan River. Among these responses were the creation of the Palestine Liberation Organization (PLO) in 1964; the consummation of a Syrian-Egyptian defense treaty in 1966; and some rather feeble attempts by the Syrians to divert the tributaries that fed into the Jordan River (which only resulted in more-frequent Israeli-Syrian clashes leading up to the penultimate moments prior to the conflagration).

In response to a demonstrative display of Israeli air power against Syria, as well as what turned out to be Soviet disinformation that Israel was massing its forces along the Syrian border, Nasser engaged in a series of steps in May 1967 that, from the Israeli point of view, forced the Jewish state into a position of capitulating or choosing war. These steps included moving Egyptian forces into what had been since the Suez War of 1956 a demilitarized Sinai Peninsula; requesting the removal of United Nations Emergency Forces (UNEF) from the Sinai, which had been in place as a buffer between the two countries since the Suez conflict (the UN acceded to this request); and the closure of the Gulf of Aqaba (at the strategic entry point known as the Strait of Tiran) to Israeli shipping.

As the tension mounted, the Israelis launched a massive lightning air strike on 5 June, crippling Egyptian air capacity, and then in short order doing the same thing to the Jordanian and Syrian air forces. Bereft of air support, the Arab states quickly succumbed to Israeli ground offensives, resulting in Israel's acquisition of the aforementioned territories. UN-brokered cease-fires between the combatants were arranged on 8 June (Egypt), 9 June (Jordan), and 11 June (Syria), thus ending the 1967 war.

Viewpoint:
Yes. Given the nature of the Arab threat and the aggressive posture of Egyptian leader Gamal Abd al-Nasser, Israel was justified in its attack.

The 1967 Arab-Israeli War (also known as the Six-Day War) was a military masterpiece for Israel. Within a few hours, the Egyptian air force was destroyed on the ground, and in the following stages of the war *Tsahal* (the Israeli army) was close to both Cairo and Damascus. It was an unmitigated disaster for the Arab world, but it was an unprecedented triumph for the Israelis. Israel captured the Sinai Peninsula and Gaza Strip from Egypt, the Golan Heights from Syria, and the West Bank—including East Jerusalem and its holy sites—from Jordan. It was an overwhelming victory against those Arab countries that had not accepted the creation of the State of Israel and had continuously violated by force the United Nations (UN) resolution of 29 November 1947 that partitioned Palestine into two sovereign states. The Arab states sanctioned endless attacks and daily infiltrations by terrorists across Israel's borders causing Israeli civilian deaths and threatening the existence of the Jewish state itself.

The Suez War (1956) ended with a humiliating defeat for France and Great Britain, resulting in their unrelenting decline as colonial powers in the Middle East. Egyptian president Gamal Abd al-Nasser emerged from the conflict as the victor, and his prestige within the Arab world (and generally in the Third World) soared. Secular Arab nationalism, embodied by Nasser, seemed then to be the winning formula for Arab liberation from colonialism; Nasser's Arab neutralism was seen as a third way between capitalism and socialism, and Islamic fundamentalism appeared confined for the moment. The United States did not fully realize how to deal with Nasser: was he a real Arab leader and a potential friend of the West, or rather was his avowed neutralism the first step toward an alliance with Moscow? Actually, Nasser had been offended—he took offense easily—by the American refusal to fund the Aswan Dam, and he then went to the Soviets. Similarly, in September 1955 he received a large quantity of weapons from Moscow. Everything seemed to show that Egypt, together with the Arab nationalist movement, was shifting toward the Soviets. Exactly for this reason, Washington tried to reapproach the Arab leader and draw him away from the communist embrace.

The Suez War had not completely satisfied Nasser's ambitions; in fact, Israel, allied with France and Britain, had inflicted heavy defeats on the Egyptians in the Sinai Peninsula, occupying it for a while. This humiliation had hurt Nasser's pride and his presumption to be the triumphant leader of the Arab masses on the road to liberation. To Nasser, the Zionists had gone too far and they had to be punished. Hence, his prestige had to be restored and action taken toward Israel. Only by defeating the Jewish state could Nasser appear as the real leader of the Arab world. He wanted to take his revenge and remove the Jewish state from the Middle Eastern geographical map, but he failed.

The end of the Suez War brought the Israeli occupation of the Sinai to an end, without anything being required in return from Egypt. The Egyptian borders with Israel were partially demilitarized and put under the control of the UN; free passage through the Gulf of Aqaba and the Strait of Tiran was guaranteed. Also in this case, however, Nasser gained major political advantages, and he managed to flaunt the Israeli withdrawal from the Sinai as a great personal success. Hence, Nasserism achieved tremendous prestige within Egypt and throughout the Arab world. Anti-imperialism and anti-Zionism became the focus of Egyptian propaganda, and Israel was portrayed as the cause of a perceived injustice that had to be redressed. Israel's alliance with Britain and France during the Suez War was used as a proof that the Jewish state was a puppet of Western imperialism in the Arab and Islamic Middle East; this propaganda was supported by the Soviet Union, which, after the 1955 arms deal, was Egypt's superpower patron.

The Palestinian refugee question became an important factor in Nasser's policy against Israel. The Arabs realized that the refugees would be a useful weapon; moreover, through the creation of the refugee camps by Arab countries after the 1947–1949 war it was clear the latter would use the desperation of Palestinian refugees politically. On 11–12 July 1957 a refugee committee met in Syria and composed a document declaring that any solution to the refugee question that did not include the destruction of Israel would be unacceptable to the Arab people. Iraqi dictator Abd al-Karim Qassim, who was ostensibly pro-Nasser and was supported by Moscow, realized in the late 1950s

THE SCREAM OF LOW FLYING JETS

Kapil Bhargava, an Indian instructor who was training Egyptian pilots, was caught in the Israeli air raid on the base at Helwan on 5 June 1967:

At 11:10 am, I heard the scream of low flying jets. Running to the window, I saw four Mirage IIIC aircraft in a low run over our single runway. As they pulled up and turned left, two Vautours did a low pass on the runway and dropped thousand pound bombs. Two loud explosions followed after a short delay. We were truly under attack. Some Egyptian friends tried to pull me away from the window to go down with them to the ground floor, which was presumed to be safer if bombs fell over us. I refused to move and told them that the Israelis had come to destroy aeroplanes and would not waste ammo on people. I was proved right.

The four Mirages came into classic front gun attacks at the aircraft lined up on the tarmac and facing away from them. The leader went for the MiG-19. The others took the three MiG-17s. Seconds later, these four aircraft were on fire. The Vautours did not do a second run, but the Mirages came in for the second attack, as if they were on range practice. The leader and his number two took out the two HA-200s. The third pilot chose to fire at an An-12, which was the test bed for the E-300 engine. While the HA-200s caught fire, the An-12 leaked tons of fuel, which miraculously never ignited. The fourth pilot had no target left. He wasted a few rounds at the cement wall of the engine-test bed facility, making harmless pockmarks on it. One of the shells ricocheted and landed within inches of an officer visiting from HAL. The Mirages did one more low run over the airfield, presumably to photograph the damage, and headed home.

Soon after the Israeli had left, the air raid siren went off and several anti-aircraft guns opened fire! They kept going for forty-five minutes and the all-clear never came. I was getting impatient to see the damage for myself. I finally had to bully my way out of the building by explaining that no aircraft could stay around for more than a few seconds after it had completed its mission. I got into a jeep and drove out to the tarmac. The guns went silent on seeing the jeep. Burnt out skeletons of six aircraft and a damaged An-12 were grim reminders of the clinically precise Israeli action. One 19-year-old mechanic was the single casualty. He had been working on the MiG-19 and had chosen to hide under its wing when the attack came. No one else, Indian, Egyptian or European, was hurt. We had just witnessed a part of Operation Moked, and it sure had lived up to its title.

The runway had two craters and an unexploded thousand pound bomb. We had heard a lot about retro-bombs being developed by the Israelis to deactivate runways. But, this one had no parachute, or any other deceleration device, and no rocket to increase penetration. I knew there would be a fourth bomb somewhere. We finally found it buried in the sand two days later. It had skidded off the runway harmlessly. Not a single aircraft under tarpaulin cover had been fired at. Perhaps in their first run, the Israeli pilots recognised their shape as trainers and decided to leave them alone.

Source: Kapil Bhargava, "Eyewitness to the Six-Day War," Indian Air Force–Bharatiya Vayu Sena website <http://www.bharat-rakshak.com/IAF/History/1960s/Six-Day.html>.

---

the importance of this event and tried to appear as the champion and standard-bearer of the refugees' claims. King Hussein of Jordan soon followed him, and Nasser took the most important step by allowing the formation of a Palestinian radio program, the "Voice of Palestine." He also gave the Gaza territory a constitution, but with an Egyptian governor. Finally, the Palestinian refugees' policies alarmed Arab leaders, who tried various ways to channel this movement in line with their own agendas. Nasser took the lead in calling for the annihilation of Israel.

In 1958 the United Arab Republic (UAR) was founded with the merger of Egypt and Syria under the aegis of Nasser. It was contested by Jordan and Iraq. Nevertheless, the failure of the UAR in 1961 did not seem to tarnish Nasser's prestige; by then he was openly supported by Soviet premier Nikita Khrushchev in the struggle against American imperialism and Zionism. In May 1964 a Palestinian National Congress met in Jerusalem and gave rise to the Palestinian Liberation Organization (PLO). In March 1962 Nasser summoned a National Congress in Cairo in order to enact a charter claiming a permanent revolution of Arab peoples for the annihilation of Zionism. Although the project did not meet with great success, specifically among other Arab dictators who feared Nasser's supremacy, it escalated the activities of Palestinian guerrillas on the Golan Heights. On the contrary, the PLO Charter claimed the right to liberate Palestine from Zionism, condemning it as an intrinsically racist movement. These declarations together garnered a great deal of support among the Arab masses, all the while heightening regional tensions.

The Soviet Union took advantage of the escalation of anti-Israeli radicalism. Moscow appeared as an ideological and political backer of the anti-Zionist cause and supported Nasser in his campaign against Zionism. It is difficult to affirm that the Kremlin really wanted the annihilation of Israel, because this result would have provoked an American reaction leading to a direct conflict between the two superpowers; more likely, it backed the Arab cause in order to increase its presence in the Middle East. It is also likely that the Soviets wished for a local conflict that would cause a partial defeat of Israel, which would mean an American defeat. Nasser was willing to use Soviet support even beyond Moscow's intentions; that is, until Israel's ultimate defeat and annihilation. This maneuvering was a hide-and-seek game, obviously known to the Israeli government headed by Prime Minister Levi Eshkol.

In fact, after 1965 terrorist attacks intensified gradually and contributed to increased tension in the area. The first months of 1967 represented the zenith of the political and military situation before the outbreak of actual war. On 7 April, during a short air battle over Lake Tiberias, the Israeli Air Force shot down six Syrian MIG 21s (manufactured in the USSR). Moscow accused Israel of plotting the overthrow of the pro-Soviet Syrian regime. Soon after, Syria informed Nasser that Israel was massing a large number of troops on the Syrian border. In response, Eshkol invited Soviet ambassador Dimitri Shuvakhin to Israel to inspect the frontier for himself. Shuvakhin refused. The reports of foreign journalists and the denials of UN secretary-general U Thant, however, showed the information was, indeed, false. Nasser found the pretext to continue his political and military offensive. On 14 May Egyptian troops entered the Sinai, soon followed by Nasser's demand that the UN withdraw its contingents. With astonishing quickness, U Thant assented. On 22 May, Nasser announced the closing of the Strait of Tiran, through which Israeli ships passed to reach the Eilat harbor from the Red Sea. This act constituted a violation of the right of free navigation and was interpreted by Israel as a casus belli. Soon after, Egyptian contingents in the Sinai were increased to eighty thousand soldiers and nine hundred tanks.

The acquiescence of the UN and the indifference of the great powers made Israel realize that it was necessary to act preemptively. At the same time, the lack of reaction by the international community led Nasser and the Arabs to believe that they could win. Hence, on 30 May, Jordan negotiated a military agreement with Nasser, who was already allied with Syria. Iraq adhered to the pact, too, while Saudi Arabia, Kuwait, Algeria, Libya, and Sudan promised they would send troops. The pressure on Israel was immense. The political atmosphere in the Arab world became volcanic: calls for victory, great mass demonstrations, ardent prayers in mosques and squares, inflammatory statements on the radio and on television. Everything seemed to portend Israel's annihilation. Israel could not hesitate to act.

Israel, however, unlike the Arabs, could not afford either a long or expensive war. It could not let the Arabs attack first and gain the military advantage. Jerusalem's limited human and material resources, compared with those of Arab countries, forced them to utilize a preemptive, quick, successful, and decisive strike. At the political level, in Israel a government of national unity was formed: Moshe Dayan, the architect of the Suez campaign, became minister of defense; the right-wing opposition, with Menachem Begin (leader of the *Herut* Party) and Yosef Sapir (leader of the Liberal Party), joined the government. At a military level, Israel acted with quickness and efficiency. On 5 June 1967, within just three hours, the whole Egyptian air force was smashed on the ground; *Tsahal* broke into the Sinai and, on 7 June, in the greatest armored vehicle battle in military history, annihilated the Egyptian army, reached the Suez Canal, and occupied the Gaza Strip as well as Sharm al-Sheik on the Red Sea. The Egyptians lost six hundred of their one thousand tanks and suffered ten thousand dead and twelve thousand prisoners. On the Jordanian front, Hussein ignored Israel's warning to stay out of the conflict and launched an attack. The consequences were devastating: on 7 June the whole West Bank, including East Jerusalem, was in Israeli hands; Israeli soldiers reached the Wailing Wall, one of the greatest shrines for Judaism. On the Syrian front, the Jews showed greater hesitation in order not to strike Moscow's client state, but the military acted by 9 June and after a decisive battle the Golan Heights was occupied. *Tsahal* conquered the Syrian town of Quneitra and came to within sixty kilometers of Damascus.

On 11 June the war was essentially over. The UN Security Council imposed a cease-fire on all three fronts. Israel had conquered important territories, and the balance of power in the Middle East was shifted in favor of the Jewish state. Unlike 1956, the United States backed Israel in the fiery debate at the UN. Moscow proposed a resolution condemning Israel as an aggressive country, but this initiative was vetoed. Israel kept the Sinai until a peace agreement with Egypt in 1979, and it still has possession of the West Bank, Gaza Strip, and the Golan Heights. The advantages these conquests have brought to the Jewish state, however, is another matter. The

Six-Day War, if one analyzes the facts preceding it, was certainly a preemptive war, but above all it was a war of self-defense. As Israel could not afford to be attacked (as happened in 1973), it launched the first strike—and it is a fact that the Arabs were ready to attack. Relying on supposed Soviet support, Nasser wanted the conflict with Israel; hence, he prepared himself for this war, and everything was ready to launch the attack. Israel attacked for defensive reasons and prevented its defeat, winning an overwhelming victory on all fronts and security once and for all in the Middle East.

–ANTONIO DONNO,
UNIVERSITY OF LECCE

Viewpoint:
No. Israel had wanted to acquire the West Bank and Gaza Strip since 1948, and it used the war rhetoric of Egyptian leader Gamal Abd al-Nasser as an excuse to launch a preemptive strike.

For many Israeli politicians, among them the first prime minister of Israel, David Ben-Gurion, the 1948 war ended in an unsatisfactory manner. In retrospect, the war was viewed as a missed opportunity, as Israel could have determined the final borders of the state in a way that would have solved the Palestine question once and for all. It dawned upon the leadership that the balance of power at the end of the war could have enabled the Israeli forces to occupy, without much resistance, the West Bank and Gaza Strip, the only remaining 22 percent of Mandatory Palestine the Jewish state did not control. In the next years, politicians from within the Labor Party, which ruled Israel until 1977, urged the government whenever the circumstances seemed ripe to take over by force the West Bank or Gaza Strip.

The first opportunity was the 1956 war. The Israeli government colluded with France and Britain in the attempt to bring down Gamal Abd al-Nasser, the Egyptian leader, and took over the Gaza Strip, as well as the Sinai Peninsula, in a joint military operation. But Israel's lukewarm relationship with the United States and the American hopes of winning Nasser over to the pro-Western camp in the Cold War forced Israel to withdraw after a few months. In 1958 Israel filled a different role in the American perception of the Middle East after Nasser had allied himself with the Soviet Union and succeeded in inducing other Arab states to follow his lead. Western alarm grew particularly after the fall of the Hashemite regime in

Iraq and the emergence of pro-Nasserite movements in Lebanon and Jordan. However, U.S. support for Israel was limited to arms and did not extend, as the Israelis hoped, to providing an umbrella for taking over the West Bank as a reward for Israel's unconditional loyalty to the West in its own cold war against Nasser.

Many Israeli politicians and generals continued to contemplate the occupation of the West Bank, and the army was already geared in the late 1950s for such a task. An ideological consensus developed between the Right and Left in Israel that the West Bank was the heart of the ancient homeland; the question was how to acquire it. The chain of events that led to the 1967 war provided the coveted opportunity to fulfill the dream.

The immediate background to the June War of 1967 was the rising tension between Israel and Syria in 1966. Ever since 1949 the two countries competed for control over the "no-man's land" lying in the buffer zone between them. This friction escalated because of a fierce struggle in 1966 over the water sources of the Jordan River. This conflict by itself was not enough to provide the circumstances for taking more land in Palestine. It was the Egyptian leader who provided the pretext. Nasser, even before the tension grew in the north, had looked for a hegemonic role in the Arab world through the "Palestine" ticket. He wanted to unify the Arab states, under his leadership, allegedly for the purpose of liberating Palestine and repatriating its refugees. After the new tension between Israel and Syria broke out, he opted for a dangerous brinkmanship policy in the hope of triggering a diplomatic move that would reopen the debate over the Palestine issue and ease the pressure on Syria. He convened emergency Arab summits in an attempt to offer assistance to the Syrians against what he, and his Russian allies, deemed as a real Israeli threat to the regime in Damascus and for the sake of exerting military and economic pressure on Israel to accept the Palestinian demands. In that he played foolishly into Israeli hands. His war rhetoric came at an opportune moment, in 1966, when Israel underwent a deep economic crisis and looked for ways of extracting the country from the recession; there was no better way to accomplish this goal than going to war.

The more dovish members of the Israeli government, particularly Prime Minister Levi Eshkol, were pushed aside, and in their place hawkish members were recruited, such as Moshe Dayan and Menachem Begin. This new leadership started an overall Israeli offensive on 5 June 1967, which came in the middle of American diplomatic efforts to persuade Nasser to retract from two of his more-dangerous moves in the chess game he was playing: the removal of United Nations (UN) forces from the Sinai Peninsula and the closure of the Strait of Tiran—which meant the blocking of any ship move-

ment to Israel's southern harbor, Eilat. The eviction of the UN force was followed by the dispatch of many Egyptian troops into the peninsula.

The Israeli victory was swift and impressive; as a result Egypt lost the Sinai, and the Palestinians realized they could not rely on Nasser any more for furthering their struggle for liberation and independence. The young king, Hussein of Jordan, hoping to be absolved from any serious involvement in the war, limited his army's action to a symbolic bombardment of western Jerusalem, but this act led to a full-scale war with Israel—the West Bank was occupied in a premeditated and well-prepared Israeli operation. Syrian attempts to cease fire before it was too late for them were not reciprocated by Israel, and the Golan Heights was taken in two days and annexed to the Jewish state.

The dream of Greater Israel was now a fait accompli, long desired by many within the Israeli political system. This dream would become a nightmare for the Palestinians, as well as for quite a significant number of Israeli Jews. The 1967 war seemed to perpetuate the conflict and added new bones of contention that prevented the sides from reaching a comprehensive solution in the years to come.

–ILAN PAPPE,
HAIFA UNIVERSITY

References

Ibrahim Abu-Lughod, ed., *The Arab-Israeli Confrontation of June 1967: An Arab Perspective* (Evanston, Ill.: Northwestern University Press, 1970).

Robert J. Moskin, *Among Lions: The Battle for Jerusalem, June 5–7, 1967* (New York: Arbor House, 1982).

Donald Neff, *Warriors for Jerusalem: The Six Days that Changed the Middle East* (New York: Linden/Simon & Schuster, 1984).

Michael B. Oren, "Did Israel Want the Six Day War?" *Azure*, 7 (Spring 1999): 47–86.

Oren, *Six Days of War: June 1967 and the Making of the Modern Middle East* (New York & Oxford: Oxford University Press, 2002).

Richard B. Parker, *The Politics of Miscalculation in the Middle East* (Bloomington: Indiana University Press, 1993).

Nadav Safran, *Israel, The Embattled Ally* (Cambridge, Mass.: Belknap Press of Harvard University Press, 1981).

Israeli troops passing a truckload of Egyptian prisoners in 1967

(© CORBIS/Bettmann)

ARAB-ISRAELI WAR OF 1967

BAGHDAD PACT

Could the Baghdad Pact have been successful?

Viewpoint: Yes. The Baghdad Pact could have played a significant role in regional affairs had the United States followed a different policy, beginning with active participation.

Viewpoint: No. The Baghdad Pact was doomed from the beginning because of the failure in Washington and London to fully appreciate regional dynamics.

The Baghdad Pact is the name given to a Middle East–based defense alliance formed in March 1955. Among the signatories to the Pact were Iraq, Iran, Turkey, Pakistan, and Great Britain—conspicuous by its absence was the United States, which preferred to adopt an official observer status rather than join the alliance. The primary objective of the Pact was to contain the spread of Soviet/communist influence into the region. It essentially filled the gap in the containment belt between the already existing Cold War–based defense pacts of the North Atlantic Treaty Organization (NATO) and the Southeast Asian Treaty Organization (SEATO).

The Pact fell within the parameters of the New Look, the containment policy of the administration of President Dwight D. Eisenhower (1953–1961). As articulated by Secretary of State John Foster Dulles, the New Look envisioned a continuation of containment but at less cost. With more emphasis on a nuclear deterrent (rather than a high conventional-force posture), covert operations, and assistance from regional allies, the Eisenhower administration hoped to lessen the burden of containment on the American economy and taxpayers, thus constituting a fundamental shift in the implementation of containment policy in the Cold War.

Soon after the Eisenhower administration came to power, Dulles was sent on a tour of Middle Eastern and South Asian capitals to assess the feasibility of forming a Middle East defense pact. As U.S. and British officials discovered during earlier attempts to do so, as with the stillborn Middle East Command (MEC) and the Middle East Defense Organization, most of the Arab regimes had little appetite for joining a Western-inspired alliance so soon after ridding themselves of the last vestiges of European colonialism. Also complicating matters was the emerging Arab-Israeli dispute as well as the general feeling in Arab capitals that communism was not much of a threat. Accordingly, Dulles came up with an alternative plan, the Northern Tier approach, a defense pact composed of mostly non-Arab states along the northern edge of the region bordering the south-central parts of the Soviet Union. These states were presumed to understand the nature of the Soviet threat because of their proximity, and it was hoped that the envisioned defense pact would be detached from the complications of inter-Arab and Arab-Israeli rivalries.

Through a series of bilateral defense treaties among the constituent states, the Baghdad Pact incrementally came into being. The Pact came under a tremendous amount of criticism over the years, and it is generally considered to have failed; indeed, the Pact aggravated existing inter-Arab rivalries, particularly between Egypt and Iraq; it tended to split the region into pro-West and anti-West elements; and it accelerated the entry of the Soviet Union into the heartland of the Middle East, exemplified by the infamous Soviet-Egyptian arms deal of September 1955, exactly the type of coalition the Pact was intended to prevent. Could the Pact have succeeded if the United States had played a more active role, or was the Eisenhower administration insensitive to the dynamics of the regional environment in terms of the potential repercussions of the Pact?

Viewpoint:
Yes. The Baghdad Pact could have played a significant role in regional affairs had the United States followed a different policy, beginning with active participation.

The proposition that the Baghdad Pact did not accomplish its purpose, and that it failed because American policy was misguided, begs two questions: in what ways did the Baghdad Pact fail to play a significant regional role, and how did U.S. policy cause that failure? Of course, one could argue that since the Soviet Union never invaded the Middle East or gained control over the petroleum reserves of the region, and no Middle Eastern state turned communist, the Baghdad Pact in fact played a significant role in regional affairs and accomplished exactly the mission it was created for: preserving the territorial status quo and extending American influence and military power into the Middle East and South Asia as part of a global strategy to contain Soviet and communist influence. George McGhee, former ambassador to Turkey and Undersecretary of State for Near Eastern Affairs, has argued that the American alliance with Turkey, and the Turkish role of linking the North Atlantic Treaty Organization (NATO) to the Baghdad Pact/Central Treaty Organization (CENTO) countries, deterred Soviet expansion and saved the Middle East from communism.

However, who will celebrate the fiftieth anniversary of the Baghdad Pact in 2005? Beyond the narrow purpose of containment, the Baghdad Pact (1955–1958) and its successor, CENTO (1958–1979), were manifestations of a much larger Anglo-American mission to reshape the Middle East in the image of the West. Since the nineteenth century the British had encouraged political, economic, and cultural reforms in the Ottoman Empire and Egypt, and during the Cold War the Americans took over efforts to change both Middle East–West relations and regional dynamics within the Middle East. During the Cold War, American planners hoped a regional defense organization would encourage the spread of U.S.-style institutions and culture in Arab and non-Arab states of the Middle East, while promoting economic development and encouraging a sense of common interests and shared purpose, which was to be a joint defense against external Soviet aggression and internal communist subversion.

This project for the transformation of Middle Eastern states into "little Americas" was resurrected in 2001 with the "war on terrorism," which included plans for a regime change in Iraq and the rebirth of Iraq and other Arab states as liberal, democratic, pro-Western models of stability, moderation, and modernization. The current "war on terrorism," however, is directed against Islamist right-wing groups, whose popular influence in the Middle East owes much to the suppression of leftist discourse under the influence of the Baghdad Pact and CENTO.

The Baghdad Pact may have accomplished the narrow purpose of deterring Soviet conquest, but it failed in transforming the Middle East along Western lines. Beyond the small Western-oriented ruling elite, American influence in the region met with a mixed reception during and after the Cold War. In the 1950s the United States was still popularly viewed as a distant and benevolent power, willing to offer military and financial aid and technical assistance without having the territorial ambitions of Great Britain, France, and Russia. By the 1960s and 1970s, however, critics on both the Left and Right accused America of supplanting European imperialism with a new form of domination, a kind of "petro-imperialism" that favored authoritarian states and ignored the plight of the masses so long as local governments proved their anticommunist credentials. From beginning to end, the Baghdad Pact and CENTO were instruments of American power. Their regional impact was mainly in solidifying and magnifying U.S. power, and in this context the Baghdad Pact played a significant role, though not necessarily a positive one.

The Baghdad Pact could have played a more significant role, and not just as a conduit for American influence, but it did not, in part because it never gave the people of the Middle East a voice in either the project of national defense or the long-term, large-scale transformation. Without popular participation there was no popular support, and the demise of CENTO produced hardly a ripple in the Middle East. This failure is a lesson that seems to have been forgotten as the Americans push forward in their "war on terrorism," a diplomatic and military

BAGHDAD PACT

Whereas the friendly and brotherly relations existing between Iraq and Turkey are in constant progress, and in order to complement the contents of the Treaty of Friendship and Good Neighbourhood concluded between His Majesty the King of Iraq and his Excellency the President of the Turkish Republic signed in Ankara on March 29, 1946, which recognised the fact that peace and security between the two countries is an integral part of the peace and security of all the nations of the world and in particular the nations of the Middle East, and that it is the basis for their foreign policies;

Whereas article 11 of the Treaty of Joint Defence and Economic Co-operation between the Arab League States provides that no provision of that treaty shall in any way affect, or is designed to affect, any of the rights and obligations accruing to the Contracting Parties from the United Nations Charter;

And having realised the great responsibilities borne by them in their capacity as members of the United Nations concerned with the maintenance of peace and security in the Middle East region which necessitate taking the required measures in accordance with article 51 of the United Nations Charter;

They have been fully convinced of the necessity of concluding a pact fulfilling these aims, and for that purpose have appointed as their plenipotentiaries . . . who having communicated their full powers, found to be in good and due form, have agreed as follows:

ARTICLE 1

Consistent with article 51 of the United Nations Charter the High Contracting Parties will co-operate for their security and defence. Such measures as they agree to take to give effect to this co-operation may form the subject of special agreements with each other.

ARTICLE 2

In order to ensure the realization and effect application of the co-operation provided for in article 1 above, the competent authorities of the High Contracting Parties will determine the measures to be taken as soon as the present pact enters into force. These measures will become operative as soon as they have been approved by the Governments of the High Contracting Parties.

ARTICLE 3

The High Contracting Parties undertake to refrain from any interference whatsoever in each other's internal affairs. They will settle any dispute between themselves in a peaceful way in accordance with the United Nations Charter.

ARTICLE 4

The High Contracting Parties declare that the dispositions of the present pact are not in contradiction with any of the international obligations contracted by either of them with any third State or States. They do not derogate from and cannot be interpreted as derogating from, the said international obligations. The High Contracting Parties undertake not to enter into any international obligation incompatible with the present pact.

ARTICLE 5

This pact shall be open for accession to any member of the Arab League or any other State actively concerned with the security and peace in this region and which is fully recognized by both of the High Contracting Parties. Accession shall come into force from the date of which the instrument of accession of the State concerned is deposited with the Ministry for Foreign Affairs of Iraq.

Any acceding State party to the present pact may conclude special agreements, in accordance with article 1, with one or more States parties to the present pact. The competent authority of any acceding State may determine measures in accordance with article 2. These measures will become operative as soon as they have been approved by the Governments of the parties concerned.

ARTICLE 6

A Permanent Council at ministerial level will be set up to function within the framework of the purposes of this pact when at least four Powers become parties to the pact.

The Council will draw up its own rules of procedure.

ARTICLE 7

This pact remains in force for a period of five years, renewable for other five-year periods. Any Contracting Party may withdraw from the pact by notifying the other parties in writing of its desire to do so six months before the expiration of any of the above-mentioned periods, in which case the pact remains valid for the other parties.

ARTICLE 8

This pact shall be ratified by the contracting parties and ratifications shall be exchanged at Ankara as soon as possible. Thereafter it shall come into force from the date of the exchange of ratifications.

Source: "Pact of Mutual Cooperation Between the Kingdom of Iraq, the Republic of Turkey, the United Kingdom, the Dominion of Pakistan, and the Kingdom of Iran (Baghdad Pact), February 24, 1955," The Avalon Project at Yale Law School website <http://www.yale.edu/lawweb/avalon/mideast/baghdad.htm>.

offensive that has much in common with the Baghdad Pact.

In examining why the Baghdad Pact had so little positive impact on the societies of the Middle East, there are four considerations regarding American policy and the realities confronting the member states that must be discussed. First, this was a military pact, based narrowly on opposition to communism. At least until the Iranian Revolution (1979), which brought an end to CENTO, American policy makers consistently viewed Soviet expansion and influence as the most salient threat to the Middle East. Obsession with communism led American administrations one after the other to see the Middle East from the perspective of a bipolar worldview. American planners tended to see the Middle East as a chessboard and the various states and groups as pieces that were supposed to know and accept their role in a larger game of two players rather than trying to be players themselves. Thus, Americans considered the Baghdad Pact a tool to combat a global threat and to shape domestic and regional affairs to meet the needs of that threat. But statesmen of the Middle East viewed American proposals from the perspective of solving their own domestic and regional problems. Arab leaders rated the Soviet threat lower than the threat of Israel and the problem of Palestinian displacement, but they saw cooperation with the United States as a means to build up their militaries and internal security organizations in order to suppress political dissent.

For American planners, the logic of joint defense dictated close cooperation between the United States and each of its local allies, and close supervision to maximize efficiency, minimize waste, and maintain a steady focus on the shared enemy. Yet, American insistence on tight control reduced the Middle Eastern governments' abilities to use foreign aid for domestic purposes. Critics of the Baghdad Pact attacked the "servility" of signatory governments and America's apparent attempts to dictate domestic policy.

Second, the Baghdad Pact was not a force for the democratic transformation of member nations. The American obsession with fighting communism led to support for authoritarian regimes willing to mobilize resources for the struggle against communism, even at the expense of creating more just, free, equal, and democratic societies. American advisers perceived the economic development strategies of the Baghdad Pact states in terms of how effective they might be in diminishing the popular appeal of radicalism and in reducing the financial burden of Middle East defense on U.S. taxpayers. Since the Americans saw internal stability as essential to regional stability, the Baghdad Pact worked against bold reform of domestic institutions and social relations and against any transformation of the various Pact members' relations with each other, with other states in the region, or with the Western powers.

Third, the Baghdad Pact and CENTO also failed to encourage a significant increase in intra-alliance trade and investment, or to alter economic relations between the signatories and Western industrialized states. This failure, in turn, diminished the role of the Pact in strengthening regional ties and creating a sense of shared purpose or destiny. Planners in the Middle East saw their futures in stronger relations with the Western powers, not with each other. Since Iran, Iraq, Pakistan, and Turkey were all underdeveloped producers of agricultural commodities and exporters of raw materials, trade within the alliance remained restricted. Each country needed massive assistance from the United States to build up its own economy, a process that inevitably meant competition, not cooperation, among Pact members.

Fourth, in terms of promoting a sense of shared purpose or common identity, again the Baghdad Pact seems to have had little success. Iranians, Iraqis, Pakistanis, and Turks shared little in common besides predominantly Muslim populations. Different historical backgrounds, languages, cultures, levels of economic development, military capabilities, and popular aspirations made them ill suited to move beyond the basic level of interest in stronger relations with the United States. Once Iraq left the Pact in 1958, the only things the remaining states shared were non-Arab populations and borders with the Soviet Union—not enough to create or sustain any new identity that could challenge nationalism. As a result, the Pact engendered little cooperation beyond periodic joint military exercises.

Perhaps the most interesting aspect of the entire Baghdad Pact/CENTO experience was a series of technical conferences that brought specialists from the member states together to share technical expertise on a wide variety of matters of interest to scientists, academics, businessmen, policy makers, and soldiers. While the conferences often served as training seminars by American and British experts, a study of the programs reveals a fascinating process through which experts of developing countries shared not only technical expertise but also their understanding of how small states could succeed by cooperation in a world dominated by superpower competition. This effort continued even after the demise of CENTO in 1979, although to a lesser extent.

A final question remains: how might American policy toward the Baghdad Pact have been different and how might the Pact have affected the Middle East differently after World War II (1939–1945)? The most obvious possibility would have been the United States' joining the Baghdad Pact. Membership would have committed the Americans to fighting in the Middle East for the defense of states it had only limited relations with prior to 1955, and it could have led American planners to develop more sophisticated visions of regional concerns and local political relations. A second, and perhaps even more significant, possibility would have involved the abandonment of the bipolar vision of a struggle to the death with communism for global dominance in favor of a multipolar vision of diverse societies, divergent interests, and different perspectives on regional possibilities and problems. This change would have allowed American planners to pay more attention to the impact of U.S. policies on elite, as well as popular, opinion in the various states of the Middle East and increased their sensitivity to corrosive problems such as the dispossession of the Palestinians or continuing oppression and inequality. Over the long term the most significant impact of the Baghdad Pact was the suppression of communist sympathy and Left-oriented rhetoric in the Middle East. The political arena was left to those on the Right, including Islamists who viewed America in more-hostile terms than did the communists.

–JOHN M. VANDERLIPPE,
STATE UNIVERSITY OF NEW YORK,
NEW PALTZ

Viewpoint:
No. The Baghdad Pact was doomed from the beginning because of the failure in Washington and London to fully appreciate regional dynamics.

At the end of World War II (1939–1945) the Middle East appeared as a secondary theater where the superpowers confronted each other. Even if during the war Middle East oil had emerged as an important and strategic commodity, the Soviet Union and the United States were focused more on Europe. With more assertiveness than Moscow, Washington moved into the region to protect its interests. With little experience in the Middle East, and without help from Great Britain, the United States saw some of the local leaders as receptive to Soviet influence. In particular, both the Truman and Eisenhower administrations failed to understand the force of a new movement that was growing in the region: Arab nationalism. The colonial presence and influence of France and Great Britain in some of

the Middle East countries, the painful defeat by the new state of Israel in the Arab-Israeli War (1947–1949), and the Western use of oil facilities in the region frustrated the Arab masses, and some Arab leaders fostered relationships with the Soviet Union not so much because they sympathized with communist ideology but rather to cut Western ties.

President Harry S Truman and his aides failed to understand how far afield Arab leaders were from Soviet ideologies. Rather, the Arabs were tired of French and British imperialism. The first American initiative in the region was the Tripartite Declaration (1950), signed by the United States, France, and Great Britain. It was intended to safeguard existing state boundaries, prevent an arms race, and dampen a possible second round of conflict between the Arab states and Israel. This kind of initiative was weak from the beginning because by not involving the Soviet Union, it left Moscow free to sign agreements with the radical states of the Middle East. Moreover, only the United States decided to respect the prohibition against selling arms in the region. In fact, Great Britain continued to sell arms to Arab states, but it refused to do the same with Israel.

A new Western initiative began in 1950: creating a defensive and strategic alliance against the Soviet Union among the states of the Middle East. This alliance, called the Middle East Command (MEC), had to have its headquarters in Cairo because Egypt was seen by Anglo-American officials as the key state in the region. Even this initiative failed when Egyptian leaders—thanks to the mounting nationalist movement against the British presence in the country—refused to disregard the wishes of their own people. King Farouk and his advisers faced serious domestic difficulties (especially after the humiliating defeat by Israel in 1948), and they were in a weak position. Moreover, Great Britain, continuing its colonial policy, tried to erect the MEC in a heavy-handed fashion that did not sit well with the local populations. After three years of attempts and the changing of the name of MEC to the Middle East Defense Organization, the Truman administration decided to give up because of differences with London over the makeup of the proposed alliance and the beginning of the Korean War in June 1950.

The Eisenhower administration, with Secretary of State John Foster Dulles, brought to the fore new ideas about fighting communism and the Soviet Union. Considering the failed Middle East Defense Organization experience, and what it viewed as weak Truman administration actions against communism, Dulles, supported by President Dwight D. Eisenhower, brought into the Middle East the global strategy of the New

Look. Containing the Soviet Union was still paramount, but now it was time to confront Moscow in a more direct fashion.

After a fact-finding mission to the Middle East during May and June 1953, Dulles realized that Egypt could no longer be relied upon. President Muhammad Neguib, on one hand, and strongman Gamal Abd al-Nasser, on the other, stressed to Dulles that the real danger in the area was not the Soviet Union or communism but rather the British presence and Israel. Dulles, upset by the Egyptian stance, turned by 1954 to the Northern Tier approach, a proposed defense alliance composed of non-Arab countries along the northern perimeter of the Middle East—Iraq, Turkey, and Iran. Geographically, these states shared northern boundaries with the Soviet Union, so it was thought in Washington that they could better understand the need for containment and the establishment of a pro-West defense alliance.

After a series of talks with high-ranking officials in the administration, Eisenhower and Dulles decided to initiate a new military policy based on a North Atlantic Treaty Organization (NATO)-type alliance. The new strategy for the Middle East was presented by the National Security Council (NSC) in the fundamentally important and strategic document NSC 155/1 of 14 July 1953, which gave official voice to the Northern Tier approach. Emphasizing bilateral

military treaties among states of the region, the United States wanted to create a kind of cordon sanitaire around the Soviet Union to protect Middle East countries from communism. Even if the idea was directed toward the Northern Tier states, no Middle East country was officially excluded; however, Nasser's Egypt decided to boycott this strategy. The first step toward this alliance was the signing of the Turkish-Pakistani Treaty (April 1954), which became the basis of the so-called Baghdad Pact signed by Iraqi prime minister Nuri al-Said and Turkish prime minister Adnan Menderes on 23 February 1955. These treaties obliged the signatories to help each other in case of war.

The roots of the failure of the Baghdad Pact were present from the start. The Pact was based on the perception that the Soviet Union was the primary danger. Dulles did not understand and/ or digest contrary advice from Egypt, Jordan, and Israel: the Soviet Union was not a clear and present danger; Western colonialism and, above all, radical forces in the Arab states represented the greatest threat. When Dulles met with Israeli prime minister David Ben-Gurion, the prime minister reminded him that the social and economic situation of the Arab states was so bad that not communism but radical Islam and radical nationalism were the dangers that could cause instability for moderate regimes in the Middle East. Even Neguib and Nasser stressed how

Iraqi prime minister Nuri al-Said at a meeting of the Baghdad Pact in 1956

(© Popperfoto)

BAGHDAD PACT

strong the anti-British feeling was in Egypt and how this sentiment was more dangerous than the Arab-Israeli conflict. Dulles and his aides, however, preferred to see just the Soviet danger, believing that solving the Arab-Israeli conflict equated to preventing Soviet penetration.

One should add the continuing mistakes of Great Britain; in fact, London did not understand how dangerous its affiliation with the Baghdad Pact would be. The only Arab country among the signatories of the Pact was Iraq, and the Pact was affiliated with the most hated nation in the Middle East: Great Britain. It was easy for Nasser to discredit the Baghdad Pact, depicting it as a tool of Western imperialism and colonialism. To him, the Pact was just a means to break Arab unity and to subdue the whole Middle East. In fact, because the United States decided to support the Hashimite Kingdom of Iraq instead of Egypt, Nasser realized that his leadership within the Arab world could be in peril, which could be one of the reasons—along with the Gaza raid by the Israeli army in February 1955—that pushed Nasser and Egypt toward the Soviets. In fact, because of Nasser's feeling of insecurity he decided to buy heavy arms from the Soviets in September 1955—exactly what the Baghdad Pact was supposed to prevent.

The Eisenhower administration decided to stay out of the Pact, preferring to maintain an aloofness from the organization it had created largely in order not to be identified too closely with European designs. The Baghdad Pact, in fact, was now out of U.S. hands. It was no longer an alliance of local forces (as the Joint Chiefs of Staff suggested); instead, it brought together Arab countries against the Pact and enhanced the differences between moderate states (Jordan, Iraq, Saudi Arabia) and radical ones (Egypt, Syria). For the Eisenhower administration it was better not to participate in the Baghdad Pact and to try to look for a new strategy in the Middle East, especially considering the clear weakness of France and Great Britain after the Suez War (1956). In January 1957 the Eisenhower Doctrine was offered as something of a replacement for the Baghdad Pact—a clear indication that the Pact had failed.

–DANIELE DE LUCA,
UNIVERSITY OF LECCE

References

Michael Cohen, *Fighting World War Three from the Middle East: Allied Contingency Plans, 1945–1954* (London & Portland, Ore.: Frank Cass, 1997).

Saki Dockrill, *Eisenhower's New-Look National Security Policy, 1953–1961* (New York: St. Martin's Press, 1996).

Peter L. Hahn, *The United States, Great Britain, and Egypt, 1945–1956: Strategy and Diplomacy in the Early Cold War* (Chapel Hill: University of North Carolina Press, 1991).

Richard L. Jasse, "The Baghdad Pact: Cold War or Colonialism?" *Middle Eastern Studies,* 27 (January 1991): 140–156.

David W. Lesch, ed., *The Middle East and the United States: A Historical and Political Reassessment* (Boulder, Colo.: Westview Press, 1996, 1999, 2003).

William Roger Louis and Roger Owen, eds., *A Revolutionary Year: The Middle East in 1958* (Washington, D.C.: Woodrow Wilson Center Press, 2002).

George McGhee, *The US-Turkish-NATO Middle East Connection: How the Truman Doctrine Contained the Soviets in the Middle East* (New York: St. Martin's Press, 1990).

Magnus Persson, *Great Britain, the United States, and the Security of the Middle East: The Formation of the Baghdad Pact* (Lund, Sweden: Lund University Press, 1998).

Elie Podeh, *The Quest for Hegemony in the Arab World: The Struggle over the Baghdad Pact* (Leiden & New York: Brill, 1995).

BIRTH OF ISRAEL

Are the boundaries of Israel, which came into being as a result of the Arab-Israeli War of 1947–1949, legitimate?

Viewpoint: Yes. Israel comprises land acquired through legal purchases, owner abandonment, and the spoils of war.

Viewpoint: No. The State of Israel includes lands acquired in violation of UN Resolution 181.

The exact borders of the State of Israel have been a source of controversy ever since the Jewish state came into being in 1948 amid the Arab-Israeli War (1947–1949). The subject is awash in legalistic interpretations of boundary lines that hark back at least to World War I (1914–1918), religious and nationalistic emotions, legal and illegal land acquisitions, immigration and expulsion, and war and peace processes. Views on Israel run the gamut of extremes, from those who want its negation to those who believe in a "Greater Israel" that encompasses far more land than what is commonly accepted as Israel today. Sometimes the differences in interpretation cover many miles, sometimes a mere ten meters, as was the case in Syrian-Israeli negotiations in the late 1990s regarding Israel's withdrawal from the Golan Heights. Whatever version one accepts, there still remains a great deal of controversy about how Israel came into being and what the delineation of its borders at the time of its creation should have been.

Jewish immigration to what was called Palestine (as an administrative part of the Ottoman Empire) in the late 1800s resulted from heightened discrimination against and persecution of Jews, particularly in Eastern Europe and Russia, combined with the efforts of the embryonic secular nationalist movement called Zionism, led by Hungarian Jew Theodor Herzl, whose goal was to find safe refuge for persecuted Jews worldwide. After considering some other locales, such as Argentina and Kenya, the Zionist movement by the early 1900s settled on Palestine as the location for what was hoped to be a Jewish state in the near future. There were several migrations to Palestine, in Zionist lore called *aliyahs* (ascents) to the land, the second one (1904–1914) being of special importance because contained in it were many of the early leaders of Israel, including the first prime minister, David Ben-Gurion, as well as the socialist, agriculturally based, and self-sufficient ethos called labor Zionism.

The Balfour Declaration, issued by the British in November 1917, was a godsend for the Zionist movement, for while it did not establish a Jewish state, it provided the legal framework for Jewish immigration to Palestine by committing the most powerful internationalist country in the world to the establishment of "a national home for the Jews." The British had their own strategic reasons for taking what seemed to be a contradictory position in lieu of its relations with and various commitments toward Arab parties also fighting the Ottomans, who had aligned themselves with the Central Powers. Primarily London wanted to ensure that it had the support of at least one group of people in an important area that separated French-administered territory in Syria and Lebanon from the British protectorate in Egypt, particularly the Suez Canal. At least, indirect control of Palestine would also provide the much-sought-after land bridge across the heartland of the Middle East from the Mediterranean Sea to British possessions in the Persian Gulf region. Finally, the British hoped the Balfour Declaration would encourage worldwide Jewish support for the efforts of the Entente Powers, especially in Russia and in the United States, both of which were hesitant about their respective commitments to the war.

The mandate system that came into being after World War I reflected, for the most part, arrangements made by the Entente Powers during the conflict. Palestine became a British-mandated territory, first including the East Bank of the Jordan River. After the 1922 White Paper (issued by Secretary for the Colonies Winston Churchill) separated this territory from the West Bank, in the process essentially creating the present-day Hashemite Kingdom of Jordan, the Palestine mandate came to resemble what Israel, including the West Bank, geographically looks like today. The mandate years in Palestine between World War I and World War II (1939–1945) were characterized by increasing tensions and hostilities between the indigenous Arab population in Palestine and the growing Jewish population, who through land acquisition (particularly during the Great Depression when the *Yishuv,* or Jewish community, in Palestine essentially became the only viable financial element in the territory) and immigration (especially after Adolf Hitler was elected chancellor in Germany in 1933) became more of a threat to the Palestinians. The British attempted to maintain stability in the mandate, sometimes with success through objective arbitration and infrastructural investment, other times with less success from commission recommendations informed by on-site investigations following episodic eruptions of violence. Often in the process the British gained the enmity of both parties.

As World War II approached, the British started to adopt a more pro-Arab position regarding Palestine, realizing they needed the support, or at least the neutrality, of the Arab world. Exemplifying this new position was the 1939 White Paper, which, in essence, reversed the British commitment made to the Zionists in the Balfour Declaration, for it limited both Jewish immigration and land acquisition in Palestine (the twin pillars of the Zionist movement) and called for the creation of a Palestinian state within ten years. Obviously, Zionist leaders recognized that Britain could no longer be relied upon as a patron, and at the Biltmore Conference (6–11 May 1942) the Zionist movement for the first time officially called for the creation of a Jewish state in Palestine, and it worked tirelessly during and after World War II to achieve this goal, often directly against the British.

Weakened by war, London was forced to scale down commitments to its prewar colonial empire. With little support domestically, a hostile and costly environment in the mandate itself, the increasing realization that its interests lay more with the Arab world in the postwar alignment, and the desire not to directly confront the United States, the British government decided to unceremoniously dump the problem of Palestine into the hands of the newly formed United Nations (UN) in early 1947. After protracted deliberations and politicking throughout much of the remainder of the year, what resulted finally was UN Resolution 181, passed by the General Assembly on 29 November, which recommended the partitioning of Palestine into Jewish and Arab states, with Jerusalem under permanent trusteeship.

The First Arab-Israeli War can be said to have begun with the passage of the UN resolution. At first, the war was simply an intensification of the ongoing violence between Jews and Palestinians that was more characteristic of civil war; however, when the British mandate officially ended on 14 May 1948, upon which the State of Israel was officially declared, the second phase of the conflict ensued when five Arab armies from Egypt, Syria, Transjordan, Lebanon, and Iraq swooped down upon the new nation in a largely uncoordinated Arab League–mandated assault. Despite numerical inferiority, Israeli forces were able to turn back the Arab incursion and actually expand upon the land allotted them under UN Resolution 181. The fighting came to a close by early 1949, consecrated by a series of armistice agreements between Israel and the Arab nations.

Many issues arose from the ashes of this war, such as the Palestinian refugee problem, but the issue of Israel's borders remains a salient topic. In essence, the question is really over the legitimacy of the State of Israel itself. Some individuals feel that Israel was a manufactured state stemming from great-power intervention, illicit land acquisition, and other questionable activities; others believe that the State of Israel is as legitimate as any other country, formed out of legal land purchases and acquisition, UN covenants, and the strategic necessity that typically emerges from war.

Viewpoint:
Yes. Israel comprises land acquired through legal purchases, owner abandonment, and the spoils of war.

The First Arab-Israeli War (1947–1949), the so-called Israeli War of Independence, was caused by the Arabs with the consent of Palestinian leaders. The purpose was to "drive away the Jews into the sea." The war was preceded by a worldwide Arab propaganda campaign focused primarily at the United Nations (UN). Arab representatives openly declared that if the UN sanctioned the partition of Palestine and allowed Jews to have their own state, they (the Arabs) would reject such a partition and wage war on the Jews. On 29 November 1947 the UN-sanctioned partition of Palestine was announced. David Ben-Gurion, Israel's first prime minister, declared the birth of the State of Israel on 14 May 1948, whereupon the armies of five Arab countries, with the aid of Palestinian volunteers, violated the UN resolution, invaded Israeli territory, and attempted to destroy the newly created state. The war was caused by Arab countries who, therefore, are responsible for those Palestinian refugees forced to flee their homes in Israeli territory. Obviously, it is impossible to speculate what would have happened if the Arabs had not instigated the war, with respect to both the refugee problem and the attendant territorial, political, and military questions that persist to the present day. The problems of the Palestinian people took place not because of Israel but rather because of Arab policy.

In order to understand the dynamics of Arab-Zionist relations before the establishment of the State of Israel, one must look to the beginnings of the Zionist settlement of Palestine. First, one should distinguish between the words *settlement* and *colonialism*. Confusion exists because those who have challenged the settlements since the end of the nineteenth century have misused the latter term with the goal of discrediting Zionism. Colonialism is a precise historical period when the great European powers acquired and exploited vast territories in other continents. It was necessary to have almost unlimited political, military, and economic resources in order to conquer and establish colonies in the Americas, Asia, and Africa. Comparatively, Zionism was only an international political movement, with vague connections to the European centers of power, and it was economically subordinate to its affiliates and some philanthropists, who did not always agree with its policy. Zionism was a movement, not a country with precise territory and national sovereignty, and it was economically weak. In other words, it was lacking in all the features of a national state; hence, it could not pursue a colonial policy. Adopting the term *colonialism* in order to describe the Zionist purchase of territories in Palestine is historically inaccurate. In some recent historiographical revisions this term has been used inappropriately, showing the degree to which ideology has replaced responsible historical research.

In the last two decades of the nineteenth century, the Zionist purchase of Palestinian lands engendered the historical and political problems of Jewish settlements in Palestine. Zionist modernization efforts brought together two different civilizations and cultures. The purchase of huge territories from Arab landowners exacerbated the cultural differences between two worlds: Jewish land buyers were part of the European capitalistic mentality; Palestinian landowners, selling off abandoned and barren lands, were part of a mentality of accumulation of wealth. Finally, the conditions of Arab peasants, already desperate from endemic poverty, were made even worse by this massive transfer of land. Later, a religious element was grafted onto this economic scenario that widened the cultural conflict brought about, in part, when some Arab leaders urged the Arab-Palestinian population to liberate "Arab land" from the heathen. Strong doses of anti-Semitism were employed within this controversy, which intensified over the years. Therefore, until the First Arab-Israeli War, the Zionists continued to purchase land and to farm *kibbutzim* and *moshavim*—communities of Zionist Jews with different backgrounds—that established the *Yishuv* (Jewish community) in Palestine.

World War II (1939–1945) further solidified the opposing positions. While the Jews of Palestine supported the democracies against Nazi-Fascist totalitarianism, the Arab world, in its most radical, but also dominant, components, flirted with Adolf Hitler. The case of the Grand *Muftì* of Jerusalem, Haj Amin al-Hussein, is well known. Resorting to anti-Semitic rhetoric that the Nazis appreciated, he publicly encouraged Arabs to support Germany in order to do the same things to the Jews of Palestine that Hitler was undertaking in Europe. Certainly, this radical attitude did not help the Arab cause in its conflict with Zionism. This stance was the first of a series of mistakes made by the Arab world throughout the whole post–World War II period. The myth of the destruction of Israel is a nonproductive exercise for the Palestinian cause.

This Arab extremism culminated in the devastating Arab-Israeli War and in the *nakba* (catastrophe), as the Palestinians call their flight after the defeat experienced by the Arab countries. One consequence of the war gave Israel a modest territorial increase at the Palestinians' expense,

and, above all, it was a disaster for the Palestinian population.

Anti-Jewish activities in Palestine did not begin after the British withdrawal and the declaration of the birth of the State of Israel, but rather much earlier, soon after the UN resolution sanctioning the partition. In previous years, Arab uprisings tried to demolish Jewish Palestine. Nevertheless, the Arab violation of the UN resolution (a document that was supported by the Soviet Union as well) must be considered the starting point of the war. The Israelis rightly call it the "War of Independence," because it sanctioned the existence and the sovereignty of the Jewish state.

After 29 November, Arab irregular divisions trespassed into Jewish Palestine, often in implicit complicity with the British—whose army offered only a symbolic resistance to the invasion. The Jewish resistance was both stubborn and brave. Between November 1947 and May 1948 Jewish Palestine became a battlefield. It is instructive, although it is often omitted by certain ideological revisionist historians, that not only the Palestinian, but also the Jewish, population suffered. These communities often lived side by side. The war caused by the Arabs often forced peaceful and helpless populations to hate their own neighbors and to destroy them at all costs. With inflammatory rhetoric, the Arabs encouraged a

kind of "ethnic cleansing." As the Arabs began losing the war, those who had been obliged to hate and to annihilate their neighbors started fearing retaliation. So, thousands of Palestinian families not involved in the war began to panic in anticipation of a Zionist victory.

It is logical that the populations had two different and opposite reactions to these events. The Jewish population lived on its own land, officially assigned to it by the UN. That land had been cultivated with great sacrifices throughout the previous decades. The need for survival imposed a fierce and heroic resistance, a furious defense by the Israeli Army; the Palestinians were mindful that their properties were part of the State of Israel, and they knew that their survival was not brought to the forefront. Their fight beside the invading Arab armies was pointless. While some Palestinians escaped, others remained in Israel and represent the Arab minority of the Jewish state. On one side there was survival; on the other side there was an ideological fanaticism imposed from outside that did not consider the vital interests of Israel's Arab population. The drama of the flight was exasperated by the futility of the war waged by the Arab countries, which were indifferent toward the conditions of the Palestinians.

It is true that the flight of about eight hundred thousand Palestinians from their houses, and their lodging in the refugee camps prepared by the countries beyond the borders of Israel, was a collective tragedy, but this exodus was also the logical consequence of a war. For those who suffer, however, "a trouble shared is *not* a trouble halved." The Palestinian people are victims of a war waged by the Arab "brothers," who did not desire to give the Palestinians a homeland (as the long Jordanian occupation, from 1948 to 1967, of the West Bank and the Egyptian occupation of Gaza have widely shown: in fact, these were the territories assigned by the UN to the Palestinians). The Arabs wanted to destroy Israel, and therefore they exploited the Palestinians for an ideological war, molding European anti-Semitism to the peculiar necessities of Middle East politics.

The Arab Palestinian flight from the Israeli territories had more than one cause. Different reasons, objective and subjective, contributed to bring about its dramatic effect. While hundreds of thousands of Palestinians escaped beyond Israel's borders, many more remained in Israel, diminishing the argument that the Israeli government planned any expulsion of Arab Palestinians. Those who escaped did so for several reasons. The Arab armies thought they had already won (as Arab propaganda claimed); many families accepted the Arab leaders' advice to move temporarily beyond the borders in order not to obstruct the victorious advance and avoid the anticipated vengeful reactions of the defeated Jews. Other families were caught in the middle of combat and escaped panic-stricken, hoping to return to their land after the war. The first to escape, as happened in Haifa, were Palestinian leaders abandoning the population. In other areas, Palestinians were expelled at gunpoint.

The end of the First Arab-Israeli War resulted in some territorial expansion for Israel. While land purchased in the decades preceding the foundation of the Israeli state remained in Jewish hands, the evacuation during the feverish stages of the war allowed the Israelis to take possession of abandoned Arab properties. In the following decades, the Palestinians called for the restitution of their land, but by that time the war had established a new reality. Displacement is often the most painful result of war. After most conflicts, if peace is pursued, this situation is partially remedied, yet in the aftermath of the Arab-Israeli conflict no such possibility developed. With the passing of time and the reinforcement of new realities on the ground, it becomes extremely difficult, if not impossible, to turn back the clock. Indeed, claiming an impossible restitution after so many decades only delays the time for peace.

—ANTONIO DONNO,
UNIVERSITY OF LECCE

Viewpoint:
No. The State of Israel includes lands acquired in violation of UN Resolution 181.

Resolution 181 of the United Nations (UN) General Assembly was adopted on 29 November 1947. It ended thirty years of British rule in Palestine and was supposed to offer the basis for a comprehensive solution to the Jewish-Palestinian conflict. It called for the establishment of two states in Palestine: one Jewish and the other Arab. The area allocated to the Jewish state consisted of around 56 percent of Mandatory Palestine (much of the coastal plane, the Negev, and parts of the Galilee). Israel during the Arab-Israeli War of 1947–1949 occupied those parts and in addition annexed a sizable part of the area designated as the future Arab state. The war ended with Israel occupying 78 percent of historical Palestine. Thus, from an international point of view, Israel is built at least in part on an area it occupied illegitimately. Land taken in the war is considered in the Israeli laws, discourse, and collective memory as an integral and indisputable part of the Jewish state. Indeed, it is one of Israel's greatest successes that it persuaded the world at large that Palestine is only 22 percent of its original self—the West Bank and the Gaza Strip.

Despite the internal Israeli dispute over the fate of the West Bank and Gaza Strip, a consensus emerged to which all the Zionist parties in Israel subscribe, that greater Jerusalem (almost 30 percent of the West Bank) and areas adjacent to the Jordan valley (as well as the Golan Heights, which Israel captured from Syria in the June 1967 Arab-Israeli War) have a status similar to those areas that the state annexed in the 1947–1949 Arab-Israeli War.

Significant parts of the State of Israel do not belong to the state according to international law and UN resolutions. Does this occupation invalidate the legitimacy of the state as a whole? Among the Palestinians some of the most extreme opponents of Israel would accept Israel within the November 1947 borders (in control of over 56 percent of Palestine), and quite a few would allow for an Israel within the June 1967 borders (in control of 78 percent). In this case it can be argued that an Israeli withdrawal from all the areas it had taken by force in the past can relegitimize it in the eyes of international law and the international community.

There are also ethical problems involved in the question of legitimacy. One might employ a comparative paradigm. Had Algeria, or parts of it, still been occupied by French settlers, would it

RULES FOR JERUSALEM

In Resolution 181, the United Nations established rules for life in the city of Jerusalem, which had a diverse population:

The Administering Authority in discharging its administrative obligations shall pursue the following special objectives:

To protect and to preserve the unique spiritual and religious interests located in the city of the three great monotheistic faiths throughout the world, Christian, Jewish and Moslem; to this end to ensure that order and peace, and especially religious peace, reign in Jerusalem;

To foster cooperation among all the inhabitants of the city in their own interests as well as in order to encourage and support the peaceful development of the mutual relations between the two Palestinian peoples throughout the Holy Land; to promote the security, well-being and any constructive measures of development of the residents having regard to the special circumstances and customs of the various peoples and communities. . . .

Subject only to the requirements of public order and morals, the inhabitants of the City shall be ensured the enjoyment of human rights and fundamental freedoms, including freedom of conscience, religion and worship, language, education, speech and press, assembly and association, and petition.

No discrimination of any kind shall be made between the inhabitants on the grounds of race, religion, language or sex.

All persons within the City shall be entitled to equal protection of the laws.

The family law and personal status of the various persons and communities and their religious interests, including endowments, shall be respected.

Except as may be required for the maintenance of public order and good government, no measure shall be taken to obstruct or interfere with the enterprise of religious or charitable bodies of all faiths or to discriminate against any representative or member of these bodies on the ground of his religion or nationality.

The City shall ensure adequate primary and secondary education for the Arab and Jewish communities respectively, in their own languages and in accordance with their cultural traditions.

The right of each community to maintain its own schools for the education of its own members in its own language, while conforming to such educational requirements of a general nature as the City may impose, shall not be denied or impaired. Foreign educational establishments shall continue their activity on the basis of their existing rights.

No restriction shall be imposed on the free use by any inhabitant of the City of any language in private intercourse, in commerce, in religion, in the Press or in publications of any kind, or at public meetings.

Holy Places existing rights in respect of Holy Places and religious buildings or sites shall not be denied or impaired.

Free access to the Holy Places and religious buildings or sites and the free exercise of worship shall be secured in conformity with existing rights and subject to the requirements of public order and decorum.

Holy Places and religious buildings or sites shall be preserved. No act shall be permitted which may in any way impair their sacred character. If at any time it appears to the Governor that any particular Holy Place, religious building or site is in need of urgent repair, the Governor may call upon the community or communities concerned to carry out such repair. The Governor may carry it out himself at the expense of the community or communities concerned if no action is taken within a reasonable time.

No taxation shall be levied in respect of any Holy Place, religious building or site which was exempt from taxation on the date of the creation of the City. No change in the incidence of such taxation shall be made which would either discriminate between the owners or occupiers of Holy Places, religious buildings or sites or would place such owners or occupiers in a position less favourable in relation to the general incidence of taxation than existed at the time of the adoption of the Assembly's recommendations.

Special powers of the Governor in respect of the Holy Places, religious buildings and sites in the City and in any part of Palestine.

The protection of the Holy Places, religious buildings and sites located in the City of Jerusalem shall be a special concern of the Governor. With relation to such places, buildings and sites in Palestine outside the city, the Governor shall determine, on the ground of powers granted to him by the Constitution of both States, whether the provisions of the Constitution of the Arab and Jewish States in Palestine dealing therewith and the religious rights appertaining thereto are being properly applied and respected.

The Governor shall also be empowered to make decisions on the basis of existing rights in cases of disputes which may arise between the different religious communities or the rites of a religious community in respect of the Holy Places, religious buildings and sites in any part of Palestine.

In this task he may be assisted by a consultative council of representatives of different denominations acting in an advisory capacity.

Source: *"United Nations General Assembly Resolution 181, November 29, 1947," The Avalon Project at Yale Law School website <http://www.yale.edu/law-web/avalon/un/res181.htm>.*

be called a legitimate nation-state? Would South Africa be deemed legitimate as long as the apartheid system continued? From a different perspective, does the genocide of Native Americans in the United States or Aborigines in Australia cast doubt on the legitimacy of both countries as nation-states? From these four examples (one admittedly hypothetical) a mixed picture transpires. As Israel had not committed a genocide of the indigenous population, it was a legitimate settler state that turned into a nation-state as much as the United States and Australia had. On the other hand, it is the only colonial project in the Arab world that survived long after the process of decolonization ended in other parts of the world. From such a regional perspective it is difficult to comprehend its legitimacy.

Was and is Zionism a colonialist phenomenon? The movement of European people, Jewish by religion, into the inhabited land of Palestine in the late nineteenth century was motivated in part by national sentiment and ideology. The implementation of this ideology in a land where another people lived could only be achieved through colonization and active help from the colonialist British empire, but this aid was not enough to sustain the project, at least not in the eyes of the leaders of the Jewish community in Palestine, who as early as the 1930s regarded the transfer of the indigenous population as the only means of implementing the dream of creating a Jewish homeland in Palestine. This vision was translated into acts of mass expulsions in 1948 and further territorial expansion in 1967. Hence in the eyes of many Arabs, Israel is an illegitimate state because of the colonialist and military means it employed in its struggle against the Palestinians, in addition to the systematic abuse of human and civil rights inside and outside the Jewish state.

In summary, it seems that it is not only the historical circumstances in which the Jewish state came into being that raise severe questions about Israel's legitimacy in all, or some of, its territory. It is the continued oppression inflicted by Israel on the indigenous Palestinian population that raises grave questions about the state's claim to be a respectable member of the modern world of liberal democracies.

A nation-state can have several characteristics and should be examined according to its own definition of nationhood. Israel is self-defined as a "democratic Jewish state." It is not a democratic state by any definition, however, and because its founding fathers and successive leaders defined nationhood as depending on the state's democracy, it failed its own test of legitimacy.

As the question of legitimacy is connected to part of the land, or to certain characteristics of the regime as well as to past evils, there are ways of gaining or regaining legitimacy. One is withdrawal from occupied territories; another is the creation of a state for all its citizens instead of only the Jewish state; and the last is reinstituting the rights of those Palestinians evicted in 1948–by compensation, repatriation, or both. If some or all of these measures would be taken, the question of legitimacy would not arise.

–ILAN PAPPE,
HAIFA UNIVERSITY

References

Benny Morris, *1948 and After: Israel and the Palestinians* (New York: Oxford University Press, 1990).

Ritchie Ovendale, *Britain, the United States, and the End of the Palestine Mandate, 1942–1948* (London: Royal Historical Society, 1989).

Ilan Pappe, *The Making of the Arab-Israeli Conflict 1947–1951* (London & New York: I.B. Tauris, 1992).

Pappe, ed., *The Israel/Palestine Question* (New York: Routledge, 1999).

Eugene L. Rogan and Avi Shlaim, eds., *The War for Palestine: Rewriting the History of 1948* (New York: Cambridge University Press, 2001).

Howard Sachar, *A History of Israel: From the Rise of Zionism to Our Time* (New York: Knopf, 1996).

Tom Segev, *1949: The First Israelis* (New York: Free Press, 1986).

Anita Shapira, *Land and Power: The Zionist Resort to Force, 1881–1948*, translated by William Templar (New York: Oxford University Press, 1992).

Zeev Sternhell, *The Founding Myths of Israel: Nationalism, Socialism, and the Making of the Jewish State*, translated by David Maisel (Princeton: Princeton University Press, 1998).

BLACK SEPTEMBER

Did Black September, the Jordanian Civil War, represent a victory for King Hussein?

Viewpoint: Yes. King Hussein asserted control over his country and ousted the Palestine Liberation Organization infrastructure that was a destabilizing influence in Jordan.

Viewpoint: No. King Hussein of Jordan was a weak leader who had effectively abandoned the Palestinian cause, throwing in his lot with the West—and tacitly with Israel.

One cannot understand the Jordanian Civil War of 1970 (known as Black September by the Palestinians) without a basic knowledge of the War of Attrition that immediately preceded it. In March 1969 Egyptian president Gamal Abd al-Nasser initiated the War of Attrition against Israel, which was really just an intensification of the cross-border reprisals that had essentially existed since the Arab-Israeli War of 1967. Nasser had hoped that a drawn-out, low-level conflict would work to the advantage of Egypt because of its larger population and ready supply of weaponry (from the Soviet Union). Thus he could improve his bargaining position against Israel as well as restore some of the luster lost following his decisive defeat in 1967. (This strategy would actually be employed more effectively by Nasser's successor, Anwar Sadat, in the Arab-Israeli War of 1973.)

As the War of Attrition intensified, the superpowers attempted to ensure that it did not spiral out of control into a full-fledged conflict and also to protect their interests in the region. For the United States this involvement meant supporting a new diplomatic initiative based on United Nations (UN) Security Council Resolution 242, called the Rogers Plan after U.S. Secretary of State William Rogers; for Moscow, by spring 1970, it meant secretly placing its pilots in Egyptian uniforms in Soviet-supplied aircraft to help its client state fend off Israel, which at the time was gaining the upper hand in the war.

By the summer of 1970 both the Israelis and Egyptians seemed ready to accept a cease-fire, as both were becoming worn out by the conflict. Despite the failure of the Rogers Plan to be accepted by either Israel or Egypt, the intrepid U.S. secretary of state forged a cease-fire in August 1970 under the guise of the Rogers Initiative, a limited cease-fire agreement between the two antagonists that ended the War of Attrition—an agreement that Jordan's King Hussein also signed.

The Rogers Initiative was one of the last things the Palestine Liberation Organization (PLO) wanted to see. The PLO feared that any sort of an agreement between Israel and an Arab state (especially Egypt, the most powerful and populous Arab country) would weaken the Palestinian cause and might be a prelude to a formal peace arrangement. Most members of the PLO agreed that it was necessary to embroil the Arab world again in a war with Israel as soon as possible, something that could not be done without Egyptian participation—only with combined and coordinated Arab military action could Israel be defeated and the PLO hope to regain Palestine. Some factions of the PLO, particularly the Popular Front for the Liberation of Palestine

(PFLP), led by George Habash, and the Popular Democratic Front for the Liberation of Palestine (PDFLP), led by Nayef Hawatmah, called for Hussein's overthrow. PLO chairman Yasser Arafat's Fatah faction hesitated to go this far, as it had established its headquarters in the Jordanian capital of Amman.

The PFLP initiated the crisis when it hijacked, between 6 September and 9 September, four airliners, forcing three of them to land at an airfield outside Amman (the passengers were evacuated, but the planes were blown up soon thereafter). The hope was that this action might disrupt any momentum built up by the Rogers Initiative as well as compel Arafat to move more decisively. King Hussein, whose country was 60 percent Palestinian, undertook military action to oust the PLO from Jordan. The civil war ended by 25 September, with a clear victory for the Hashemite monarchy. One of the repercussions of this violent episode, which had effects far beyond the confines of Jordan, was the death only a few days later of Nasser, who, despite frail health, had desperately tried to diplomatically resolve the civil war.

Viewpoint:
Yes. King Hussein asserted control over his country and ousted the Palestine Liberation Organization infrastructure that was a destabilizing influence in Jordan.

During his forty-six-year reign, King Hussein of Jordan faced many threats to his person and to the survival of the Hashemite monarchy, including assassination attempts; failed coups d'état; ideological challenges from leftists, Arab nationalists, and Islamists; regional wars; economic crises; and domestic instability. Among these, the events that culminated in the 1970 civil war (known to Palestinians as Black September) were perhaps the gravest. During this time Hussein nearly lost his throne to the forces of radical Palestinian nationalism and foreign military intervention. For many reasons, the king was slow to take action against these threats, but when he finally did, he saved his kingdom, strengthened the identity of the state, and opened up the long process of peaceful accommodation with Israel.

The Arab-Israeli War of 1967 (also known as the Six-Day War or June War) was a catastrophe for Jordan. In just a few days of fighting, Jordan lost the West Bank and Jerusalem to Israeli control. Hussein had been aware that a military conflict would end in disaster, and he was even contacted by Israel with an offer to spare Jordan if it stayed out of the fighting. Yet, the pressure from Arab neighbors and domestic (particularly Palestinian) demands for action against Israel pushed the king to the fateful decision. Toward the end of his life, Hussein admitted that the war was a mistake and that his own domestic weakness determined his policy: "I had these options: either join the Arabs, or Jordan would have torn itself apart. A clash between Palestinians and Jordanians might have led to Jordan's destruction." As he had predicted, Jordan's

entry into the war came at a high price. Materially, the losses included vital water resources, arable land, and geostrategic territory. Approximately 40 percent of Jordan's gross national product was derived from the West Bank. Politically, the king had to bear the heavy burden of losing the old city of Jerusalem and its Muslim holy sites to the Jewish state.

Equally as important from the regime's perspective, the utter failure of the Arab states to advance the Palestinian cause led to the radicalization of Palestinian nationalism and the proliferation and rising power of *fedayeen* (guerrilla) movements. Frustrated by the military impotence and uncertain commitment of Arab states to their aspirations, Palestinians increasingly believed that they had to take matters into their own hands through an armed struggle against Israel. The militants were led by Yasser Arafat's Fatah faction, which gained control of the Palestine Liberation Organization (PLO) in 1969. While Fatah occupied the top leadership positions in the PLO, the organization was composed of many rivalrous groups and personalities. Particularly threatening for Jordan were leftist ideological movements that rejected the "reactionary" Hashemite monarchy. The most influential leftist factions were the Popular Front for the Liberation of Palestine (PFLP), the Popular Democratic Front for the Liberation of Palestine (PDFLP, later known as the DFLP), and groups associated with Syrian and Iraqi variants of the Baath Party.

Immediately following the June War, the *fedayeen* intensified their campaign of attacks against Israel, launching them mainly from the East Bank of Jordan, where they had set up bases of operations after the capture of the West Bank. Heightened *fedayeen* activism had mostly deleterious consequences for Hussein. The growing influence of the guerrillas and the "Palestinianization" of the Arab-Israeli conflict posed a direct challenge to the king's claims to the West Bank and undermined his legitimacy as the representative of the Palestinians. An important event in the rise of *fedayeen* power was the battle at Karamah (1968) in Jordan, in which Palestinian commandos, together with the Jordanian Army, fought off an Israeli military incursion. Although Jordanian tank and artillery fire was decisive in the fighting, the *fedayeen* were successful in characterizing the battle as a triumph of Palestinian resistance. On the one hand, the commandos' boldness in confronting Israel helped restore Arab pride wounded in the June War, but their widespread popularity came at the expense of Hussein's authority. In addition, Palestinian guerrilla attacks were invariably followed by harsh Israeli reprisals against targets in Jordan, damaging the country's infrastructure and jeopardizing Jordanian lives. On the other hand, Hussein's foremost goal after 1967 was to regain the West Bank and East Jerusalem, and the pain inflicted on Israel by the *fedayeen* potentially served Jordanian interests by pressuring Israel to negotiate the return of the captured territories.

A similarly contradictory relationship with the *fedayeen* existed for the other key player in the conflict, President Gamal Abd al-Nasser of Egypt. The reputation of Nasser as the leader of Arab nationalism was severely eroded by the failure in the 1967 war. Like Hussein, Nasser recognized the postwar influence of the *fedayeen* and sought to contain the movement and use it to his advantage. Also like Hussein, Nasser's primary goal was to regain territory lost in the war, in Egypt's case the Sinai Peninsula. Prior to the June War, Nasser was able to subsume the Palestinian national movement within pan-Arabism largely by the force of his own overwhelming popularity in the Arab world (indeed, the creation of the PLO in 1964 was under Nasser's auspices). After the war, the *fedayeen* catapulted the PLO into a formidable independent actor in its own right.

Partly because he was unwilling to stand against popular support for the *fedayeen* in the wake of the war and partly because their actions meshed with his own strategy vis-à-vis Israel, Nasser initially threw his weight behind the guerrilla factions. This support included diplomatic, financial, and military assistance and the use of Cairo radio for *fedayeen* broadcasts. After early attempts at a negotiated return of Egyptian territory following the June War failed, Nasser authorized in March 1969 the intensification of Egyptian military attacks on Israel in what became known as the War of Attrition. The aim of the War of Attrition was to wear down Israel through low-level conflict (and thereby raise the cost of its occupation of Sinai) and spark greater international engagement in resolving the dispute. Palestinian guerrilla operations magnified the pressure Egypt was able to apply to Israel.

Ultimately, however, the interests of both Nasser and Hussein diverged from those of the PLO. They both sought the return of their territories under Israeli occupation, and *raison d'état* took precedence over any commitment to a separate state of Palestine. Nasser and Hussein also realized that only a negotiated resolution to the conflict was possible given Israeli military might and its growing alliance with the United States. In Egypt's case, the War of Attrition was dangerously escalating in early 1970, with Israel attacking targets deep inside Egyptian territory and openly threatening to overthrow Nasser. Hussein had long before come to the conclusion that the return of the West Bank to Jordan could only result from an agreement that recognized Israel's right to exist, but Jordan's permeability to outside forces such as pan-Arabism, and its large Palestinian population that hoped for a state in all of Palestine, prevented the king from taking bold initiatives without broader Arab (particularly Egyptian) backing. It was in this context of deteriorating political and security conditions that Nasser accepted the Rogers Initiative in July 1970. This American plan called for a cease-fire in the War of Attrition between Israel and Egypt as the foundation for future comprehensive peace negotiations based on United Nations (UN) Security Council Resolution 242. Following in Nasser's footsteps, Hussein quickly signed on to the agreement.

The acceptance of the Rogers Initiative by Nasser and Hussein conflicted with the maximalist ambitions of the PLO. The organization worked to scuttle the plan by rallying Arab sentiment against it and by stepping up guerrilla operations against Israel. In response, Nasser cut off assistance and denied the *fedayeen* access to Cairo radio. It was during this time (June–September 1970) that the hostility between the *fedayeen* and the Hashemite regime boiled over into a full-scale civil war.

When Hussein unleashed the army on 16 September 1970 to expel the *fedayeen* from Jordan, it was the culmination of more than three years of growing tension. Hussein viewed the PLO as a rival to his authority over the West Bank. The explosion of the *fedayeen* onto the scene after the 1967 war transformed a political challenge into an immediate security threat. The danger posed by the guerrillas was multifaceted and called into question the survival of the monarchy.

By 1969 more than twelve thousand Palestinian guerrillas were operating in Jordan, virtually creating a state within a state. After repeated Israeli attacks on their positions in the Jordan River valley, the *fedayeen* moved their bases eastward into the Jordanian interior, with most of the factions eventually setting up their headquar-

SUCH WAS OUR POSITION

In a speech to his subjects on 12 October 1993, King Hussein of Jordan commented on Jordanian-Palestinian relations:

Looking back at the past, we have attempted with all we can, since the adoption of Security Council Resolution 242 in November 1967, to achieve progress towards the comprehensive implementation of that resolution. Then, in 1972 we announced that we were striving to remove the occupation from all the occupied lands in the West Bank, not to regain it for ourselves, but to place it under international auspices to enable the Palestinians in absolute freedom to decide on one of three options, one of which we had excluded right from the beginning, which was a return to the original union. This was in recognition of the fact of Palestinian adherence to the Palestinian identity and of Jordanian adherence to the Jordanian identity, despite the close ties between members of our one family. Only two options remained: a federal state or an independent Palestinian state—chosen in absolute freedom. This was also in response to the position of the Israeli leadership, which had refused to acknowledge any sovereign right by Jordan over the occupied West Bank and which had regarded the union between the two banks—held in trust until the resolution of the Palestinian issue in all its aspects—as Jordanian occupation terminated in 1967. Unfortunately, this position coincided with an acceptance by many of our Palestinian and Arab brethren of this interpretation. In addition to the above, we on our part called for the need for all Palestinians to come together under one Palestinian umbrella in the West Bank and Gaza once the occupation had come to an end. In other words, Israel had refused to recognize Jordan's right to strive to rescue the West Bank or to represent the Palestinians. . . .

Then the Arab summit of Rabat was held in 1974. After extensive discussions, we responded to the wish of our Palestinian brethren and the entire Arab nation to recognize the Palestine Liberation Organization as the sole, legitimate representative of the Palestinian Arab people. We committed ourselves to supporting it and to cooperating with it out of a desire to serve the struggle of the Palestinian Arab people in occupied Palestine. We regarded this position as one of rational honor to be fulfilled with our utmost capabilities until the occupation had been removed.

On the other hand, the course of Israeli politics underwent a radical shift immediately following the Rabat Summit. It began to tell the world that it recognized no other party but Jordan and would not deal with any other party as far as the future and fate of the occupied West Bank were concerned.

On our part, we had honored our direct political responsibilities—until the Rabat Summit—towards the occupied West Bank. We were committed to seeking its rescue and liberation to enable it to determine its own future. Then we adhered to the Rabat resolution with tenacity, sincerity and honor. This was done through the attempt, more than once, at Jordanian-Palestinian coordination and agreement; the decision to disengage legal and administrative ties with the West Bank, on the basis that it was an internal Jordanian-Palestinian affair not amenable to being relegated to any other party; through providing the umbrella to our Palestinian brethren at the Madrid, Moscow and Washington conferences enabling them to exercise their right to represent themselves; and up to the mutual Palestinian-Israeli recognition in Washington on September 13, 1993, and the start of the Palestinian-Israeli march towards peace—which we wish success, with God's help, in achieving its objectives.

Such was our position. No one may claim that while we shouldered our responsibilities—until we were relieved of their direct exercise in 1974—we had ceded an inch of Palestinian territory or an iota of the right of its people to their homeland. We then continued to support the people of Palestine and their right on their national soil—as an act of honor and a duty to be fulfilled until the need for it no longer exists. We also continued to provide assistance in the services of the common good as well as of peace.

Source: *King Hussein I, "Jordan and the Palestinian Cause: Consistent Support for the Palestinians," King Hussein I website <http://www.kinghussein.gov.jo/views_palestine1.html>.*

BLACK SEPTEMBER

ters in the capital city of Amman. The presence of the guerrillas in the cities was tremendously destabilizing because they acted with complete disregard for Jordanian law and authority. Such violations included wearing uniforms and bearing arms in the streets, breaking traffic laws with impunity, kidnapping and killing Palestinians suspected of collaborating with Israel or the Jordanian government, refusing to register their vehicles with the state, and extorting funds from foreigners and local merchants. As scholar Clinton Bailey noted, "it was as though the domain of the *fedayeen* was out of bounds for the Jordanian government." The *fedayeen* set up parallel institutions within Jordan, including their own court system, military police, media, information office, and civil society associations. They exempted their members from the Jordanian military draft and from Jordanian taxation. The heavily fortified *fedayeen* operational bases flew the Palestinian flag and were surrounded by Palestinian-run checkpoints. On separate occasions Hussein and his brother, Crown Prince Hassan, were denied access to areas around *fedayeen* bases in their own country.

Moreover, as tensions mounted, the *fedayeen* began to plot the elimination of the Hashemite regime. The leftist factions, especially the PFLP and PDFLP, openly discussed turning Amman into a "little Hanoi" and called for the replacement of the monarchy with a "revolutionary nationalist authority." There were at least two attempts on Hussein's life, in June and early September 1970, the latter attack occurring as the king's motorcade was on its way to the airport to pick up one of his children. Arafat and the Fatah faction, which had earlier tried to moderate the leftists, joined the antiregime camp in September 1970. A top Fatah official declared that Hussein was "a paper tiger, whom we can topple in half an hour." The PLO enjoyed considerable support within the Jordanian bureaucracy, and there were reports that Fatah had penetrated the army and security services. The king also risked alienating his Transjordanian loyalists in the army, who were enraged by the brazen lawlessness of the *fedayeen* and the king's hesitancy in addressing the challenge. As Hussein later recalled, "toward the end I felt I was losing control. The army began to rebel. I had to spend most of my time running from one unit to another. I think that the gamble [of the fedayeen] was that the army would fracture along Palestinian-Jordanian lines." The threat to the regime was further heightened by pledges from Syria and Iraq to assist the *fedayeen* should Jordan move against them.

Fedayeen activism also eroded the king's credibility in foreign relations, imposing constraints on his decision making. Not only did guerrilla attacks against Israel invite severe military retaliation against Jordan, but they also undermined the possibility of Hussein's reaching a peaceful settlement to the conflict. Because any deal with Israel was dependent on the king being able to stop the guerrilla attacks originating from his territory, and because a Jordanian-Israeli settlement would deprive the PLO of its essential cause, the *fedayeen* intentionally timed their activities to expose Hussein's weaknesses. Thus, for example, in April 1969 the *fedayeen* shelled the Israeli port city of Eilat on the day that Hussein arrived in the United States for an official visit. In April 1970 the PLO organized a massive demonstration in Amman against the impending visit of U.S. diplomat Joseph Sisco, who was in the region to discuss an American peace initiative. More than ten thousand people filled the streets, eventually attacking the U.S. embassy and burning down the United States Information Agency offices. Much to the embarrassment and frustration of the king, Sisco was forced to cancel his visit to Amman because of the chaos.

Most dramatically, the PFLP attempted to strike a deathblow to the Rogers Initiative by hijacking four Western airplanes (6–9 September 1970). Three of the planes were flown to a PFLP-controlled airstrip in Jordan. After releasing most of the passengers (but keeping fifty-four as hostages), they blew up the planes before the world's media. The hijacking was the final straw. Within the week, Hussein formed a military cabinet, declared martial law, and ordered the army to liquidate the *fedayeen*.

Clearly, the king had compelling justification for using force to restore order and protect the sovereignty of the kingdom. Indeed, given the magnitude of the threat to the regime, the question is not why Hussein took action against the *fedayeen* but rather why he waited so long to do so. For more than three years, the king sought compromise solutions to the challenges posed by the *fedayeen*. He repeatedly communicated his support for the right of Palestinians to resist Israeli occupation, declaring that "we are all fedayeen." His requests for coordination and prior consultation on guerrilla operations against Israel in order to prepare Jordanian defenses were to no avail. The king backed off enforcing regulations on the *fedayeen* presence in Jordan that were the result of an agreement reached in October 1968. After army units shelled two Palestinian refugee camps in June 1970 in response to an assassination attempt against the king, Hussein acquiesced to PLO demands to remove two members of the royal family from their leadership positions in the military. Hussein even offered Arafat the post of prime minister in June 1970.

The king's leniency and vacillation derived from his political vulnerabilities following the 1967 Arab-Israeli War. The popularity of the *fedayeen* with Jordan's Palestinian majority (and a sizable percentage of East Bankers) provided the movement with tremendous leverage against the king. The political strength of the *fedayeen* was enhanced by external diplomatic support from countries including Syria, Iraq, and (for a while) Egypt. Nasser's role was particularly critical. Only when the Egyptian president's relationship with the *fedayeen* ruptured following his acceptance of the Rogers Initiative did Hussein feel confident enough to move against the guerrillas. Additionally, although the balance of military forces favored the Jordanian army, the significant fighting capacity of the guerrillas contributed to the king's caution.

The other key factor in explaining Hussein's delay in reacting to the *fedayeen* threat was the long-term issue of Jordanian identity and the kingdom's claims to the West Bank. Since the merging of the East and West Banks in 1950, the Hashemites had attempted to forge an inclusive national identity. Jordan was the only Arab state to extend citizenship rights to Palestinians after the first Arab-Israeli War (1947–1949), and the West Bank was considered politically and economically integral to the kingdom. In the 1960s the Palestinian national movement, especially the rise of the *fedayeen,* called this relationship into question. The king hesitated to use force against the guerrilla factions in part because he worried that it would harm his relationship with Palestinians and jeopardize his legitimacy over the West Bank. As it turned out, his fears were well founded. West Bank Palestinians, especially the young and working class, became increasingly estranged from Jordan following the conflict, shifting their allegiance to the PLO. Nonetheless, the security threat eventually forced Hussein's hand and, in the end, the civil war opened a new era in the history of the Hashemite kingdom.

Once moved to action, the king's victory over the *fedayeen* was decisive. The Jordanian army inflicted heavy damage on the guerrilla forces in the first few weeks of fighting. At the urging of Nasser, the two sides signed a cease-fire agreement in Cairo on 27 September, but the truce did not hold. The army continued to push the *fedayeen* out of the cities throughout the late fall, eventually confining them to the Jerash/Ajlun area in the north of the country. Skirmishes occurred intermittently into the next year, culminating in a final showdown in the summer. On 13 July the Jordanian Army began an assault on *fedayeen* positions around Ajlun, Jerash, and the Jordan valley. Five days later, the PLO was evicted from its last strongholds in Jor-

dan, with more than two thousand *fedayeen* surrendering to the army. Most of the commandos accepted the king's offer to evacuate to Syria, and from there the PLO eventually reestablished itself in Lebanon.

The threatened intervention by Iraq, which had troops stationed in eastern Jordan, never occurred. The official Iraqi justification for abandoning the *fedayeen* was that the PLO had not requested direct military intervention. In reality, Iraq feared U.S. air strikes in defense of Jordan, with the Iraqi minister of interior admitting that "we can replace the [Palestinian] revolution with 100 others, but our regime is more important." Syria, on the other hand, sent an armored force of more than 200 tanks into Jordan to reinforce the PLO on 20 September 1970. Syrian troops took control of the northern town of Ramtha and advanced to Irbid, beating back Jordanian forces. However, because of an internal Syrian power struggle between President Salah al-Jadid and Defense Minister Hafiz al-Asad, combined with American and Israeli threats of intervention on behalf of the Hashemites, the Syrians did not provide air cover for their forces. By 22 September the Jordanian air force had destroyed 120 Syrian tanks and armored personnel carriers, and the surviving Syrian forces had retreated north of the border.

Despite Hussein's victory over the *fedayeen,* the conflict was costly for the regime. Libya and Kuwait, which had promised to provide Jordan with annual financial support in 1967, cut off their assistance. Algeria, Syria, and Iraq severed diplomatic relations with the kingdom. The radicalization of the PLO continued, and a new faction, calling itself Black September in memory of the civil war, assassinated Jordanian prime minister Wasfi al-Tal and carried out several international terrorist attacks. Most damaging for the Hashemites was the continued ability of the PLO to establish itself as the representative for Palestinians, a trend that culminated in the official recognition of the PLO as the "sole, legitimate representative of the Palestinian people" at the Arab League summit meeting in Rabat, Morocco (1974).

Nonetheless, given the enormous challenges to the regime, the outcome of the civil war was a success for Hussein. First and foremost, he survived the threat and gained control over the country. The years following the civil war were relatively stable for Jordan. The king had enough confidence in his political position to put forward his controversial "Federation Plan" in 1972 for two autonomous provinces (East and West Bank) in Jordan as part of a peace deal with Israel. Jordan's resistance to external Arab pressures during the civil war solidified the independence of the state, allowing the king, for example, to stay out of the 1973 Arab-Israeli War. The conflict also was a key factor in Jordan's strong alliance with the United States. The fragility of the king's position, his determination to fight to save the kingdom, his indications of a willingness to negotiate a settlement with Israel, and his stance against radicalism made Hussein a critical ally of the United States. After 1970 the United States became Jordan's primary source of economic and security support. In addition, Jordan's ties to the United States, its increased confidence in pursuing state interests, and the state's developing Transjordanian identity resulting from the civil war were among the factors that contributed to the long process of reaching a negotiated settlement with Israel in 1994.

Finally, the civil war marked a key juncture in Jordanian-Palestinian relations and the identity of the state. Without question, the conflict weakened the king's claims to the loyalty of Palestinians, but this dynamic was likely inevitable in any case. Palestinian nationalism was a cause, not a consequence, of hostility with the Hashemites. Within East Bank Jordan, the civil war led to a "Jordanization" process in which state identity was increasingly East Bank oriented. Transjordanians were given privileged positions in the military, security services, state bureaucracy, and top levels of government. Jordanian nationalism took on a distinctly Transjordanian character, despite the regime's commitment to "national unity." The question of identity remains open and fluid in Jordan, but at a minimum, the king emerged from the civil war with greater control over his country and a more clearly defined sense of the state and its interests.

–JEFFREY A. VANDENBERG,
DRURY UNIVERSITY

Viewpoint:
No. King Hussein of Jordan was a weak leader who had effectively abandoned the Palestinian cause, throwing in his lot with the West—and tacitly with Israel.

For the two decades that followed the Arab-Israeli War of 1947–1949, none of the Arab regimes allowed the Palestinians to establish their own independent national organizations. The task of restoring Palestinian claims was considered, at the time, the responsibility of the Arab armies and not the Palestinians themselves. Initially, Palestinians welcomed the Arab support, and many of their leaders became active members of pan-Arab organizations. However, after the collapse of the Egyptian-Syrian union (the United Arab Republic or UAR) in 1961, followed by the Arab armies' defeat in the 1967 Arab-Israeli War, Palestinian support for Arab regimes started to erode, and they instead began supporting the new factions known as the *fedayeen* (guerrilla), which in 1968 managed to take over and radicalize the Palestine Liberation Organization (PLO). While in Jordan, the *fedayeen* escalated their military raids against Israel and managed to highlight the centrality of the Palestine question in the region and, perhaps, around the world. This situation contributed to the "Palestinianization" of the Arab-Israeli conflict and complicated Palestinian relations with the Jordanian regime. The Arab-Israeli conflict also became more Palestinianized as a result of the *fedayeen*'s rejection of all Arab-Israeli peace efforts. Accordingly, the *fedayeen* were seen at the time as threatening, not only to Israel but also to certain Arab leaders, including Gamal Abd al-Nasser of Egypt on the left and King Hussein of Jordan on the right.

The Israeli victory over the Arab armies in 1967 had irreversibly undermined Nasser's legitimacy in the Arab world, removed his sponsorship of the Palestine issue, and discredited his pan-Arab ideology. Faced with these challenges, Nasser began searching for ways to enhance his prestige and preserve the old legacy of pan-Arabism. Consequently, in 1969 Nasser launched a low-intensity war against Israel in what became known as the War of Attrition. This war was not intended as a prelude to a larger war with Israel but rather as an attempt to regenerate Arab public support for Nasser while pressing Israel into giving up the territories it had acquired in the 1967 war. Contrary to Nasser's efforts, however, the war failed and Nasser had to abandon his hard-line policy toward Israel in ways that angered the *fedayeen*. The turning point for Nasser came in 1970 when he accepted the U.S. diplomatic peace mission, known as the Rogers Initiative, that called for a solution to the Middle East conflict on the basis of United Nations (UN) Security Council Resolution 242. The *fedayeen* criticized Nasser's acceptance of the Rogers Initiative, which they believed was damaging to the Palestinian cause. In response, Nasser decided to ban the *fedayeen*'s broadcasting centers in Egypt. Although the Rogers mission failed in the end, the *fedayeen* still considered Nasser's willingness to make peace with Israel as a betrayal to their cause and a factor that encouraged Hussein to also accept the plan, despite its negative effects on the Palestinians.

The conflict between Hussein's regime and the *fedayeen*, which culminated in a civil war in

1970 (known to the Palestinians as Black September), was rooted in various local and regional changes. Some of these changes were connected with the *fedayeen*'s rising popularity in the country, while others were related to more-controversial policies and tactics pursued by both parties, along with others in the region. For instance, the *fedayeen*'s successful showdown at the Karamah battlefield with Israel in 1968 was an event that empowered them and enhanced their popularity in Jordan. The Karamah battle, which was widely publicized in the Arab world, also made the *fedayeen* instant heroes and gave the Arabs a much needed boost in morale that had suffered immensely as a result of the 1967 defeat. At the same time, the *fedayeen*'s rising power was interpreted by the king as a threat to his authority and legitimacy, given that the *fedayeen* were also viewed as trying to create a PLO state inside Jordan. The *fedayeen* rejected such claims and insisted that their efforts were focused on confronting Israel, liberating their homeland, and preventing Arab leaders, including Hussein, from pursuing peace with the Jewish state.

Hussein was particularly threatened by extremist groups within the *fedayeen*'s factions that were not only interested in carrying out mil-

itant raids against Israel from within Jordanian territory but were also engaged in international acts of violence against U.S. interests. This situation placed the king under significant pressure to crack down on the *fedayeen*. The king was also fearful of the long-term effects of Israel's military attacks against the *fedayeen,* on Jordan's political stability and on the future of his own authority in the country. Hussein was troubled by the fact that the *fedayeen* continued to reject a cessation of attacks against Israel as well as the Rogers Initiative. In this regard, it was a matter of time before the king would find the proper justification to attack the *fedayeen* with the intent of annihilating them, and he would also satisfy Israel and the United States by creating better conditions for peacemaking.

Over the years, the *fedayeen* found it impossible to implement their militant strategy and pursue their uncompromising goals without having control over certain bases or areas bordering Israel, which would allow them to launch attacks against Israeli targets. When such bases became available, however, the *fedayeen* were either forced to become heavily dependent on host Arab countries or were subjected to attacks from such countries. In Jordan, the *fedayeen* indeed paid a heavy price, partly as a result of their

BLACK SEPTEMBER

refusal to comply with Hussein's demands and for objecting to his policies. Extremists within the *fedayeen*'s factions did not make the situation any easier, especially after they became involved in various international terror attacks and began calling for the overthrow of the king and the creation of a new revolutionary regime in Jordan.

In the initial phase of the civil war, the king was reluctant to call for an immediate elimination of the *fedayeen*, and instead he continued to provide lip-service support for the Palestinians. Aside from restoring his authority, the king's immediate concern was focused on preventing the *fedayeen* from carrying out militant raids against Israel. As for his long-term intentions, however, Hussein was more interested in eliminating the *fedayeen* altogether. Thus, in cooperation with the United States and Israel, he would have proceeded to finalize the Rogers Plan, which would have allowed the king to regain control over the West Bank. Aware of his general goals and tactics, the *fedayeen* generally believed the king was far more involved in preserving his own interests and satisfying U.S. and Israeli pressures rather than supporting Palestinians' claims.

The violent acts of terror in Jordan and in the region, mainly those carried out by the Popular Front for the Liberation of Palestine (PFLP), had given Hussein the opportunity and the compelling justification for launching his forceful military campaign against all the *fedayeen*, regardless of whether they were participants in terror. The PFLP's hijacking of civilian airliners in 1970, followed by its call along with the Popular Democratic Front for the Liberation of Palestine (PDFLP, later known as the DFLP) for the overthrow and replacement of the king, had escalated the conflict into a full-scale war. Hussein, supported by his loyal Bedouin army, used this situation as a pretext for dismantling the PLO. Placing confidence in his close advisers, who had assured him that the elimination of the PLO was possible within a few days, Hussein decided to attack the *fedayeen* in an attempt to achieve his goals. In a matter of a few weeks, rather than days, thousands of Palestinian fighters, along with an equal number of Palestinian civilians, were killed or injured.

The Black September civil war went through two main phases; in both phases, the balance of power was in the king's favor. The second stage of the fighting, following the signing of the Cairo Agreement sponsored by Nasser that led to the removal of PLO fighters from Amman into the wooded areas of Jerash and Ajlun, was particularly harsh. The evacuation of the *fedayeen* out of populated areas in and around Amman, as the Cairo Agreement had intended, only made it easier for the Bedouin army to dismantle the *fedayeen*. At the time the

PFLP was critical of Fatah's acceptance of the Cairo Agreement that, although signed by Hussein and the PLO, did not prevent the Bedouins from resuming the fighting following the completion of the evacuation of the *fedayeen* into new locations. In 1970 the total number of PLO fighters, most of whom were drawn into the fighting not by choice but in an attempt to resist the king's attacks on them, did not exceed ten thousand. Although Fatah, the largest *fedayeen* faction, had rejected the PFLP's and DFLP's call for the overthrow of the king and objected to the PFLP's hijackings, the Jordanian Army attacked all factions indiscriminately. By then, Fatah had changed its position from that which discouraged involvement in the internal affairs of the regime and adopted instead a new strategy calling for active resistance against the Bedouin army. Hussein's loyal Bedouin army was five times greater in number than that of the *fedayeen*. It was also far better trained, and it possessed heavy artillery and advanced equipment, none of which was available to the PLO. The first phase of the fighting was relatively limited in terms of its scale and intensity and was centered in the vicinity of the capital. The second phase, however, was more intense and lasted from 28 August until 17 September, when the Bedouins' military operation succeeded in liquidating most of the *fedayeen*'s fighters and many civilians. Those fighters who survived the onslaught were either imprisoned in Jordan or gradually expelled from the country into Lebanon during the period from September 1970 to July 1971.

At one point during the fighting, Syrian tanks had temporarily crossed into Jordan in a show of support for the *fedayeen*. Fearing the conflict might become more widespread with Syrian and/or Iraqi involvement, the United States and Israel had agreed, in consultation with the king, that they would intervene and rescue his regime. As events evolved, however, the Syrian army retreated, and the Iraqis never intervened, leaving the Bedouins to declare a full victory without any external help. As the fighting ended, most Palestinians, especially those living in Jordan (who had amounted to more than 55 percent of Jordan's population), felt betrayed and alienated. They believed that regardless of whatever justifications the king might have concerning his determination to exterminate the *fedayeen*, the attacks were too brutal and caused animosity between Palestinians and Jordanians for many years to come. On one occasion a PLO leader pointed to the savagery of the Bedouin soldiers and declared, "a sea of blood separates us from them." Others expressed similar resentment toward Hussein's plans to eliminate and contain Palestinian nationalism as a step toward serving his own, Israeli, and U.S. interests at the expense of the Palestinians. In succeeding years, the king would not abandon his claims to the West Bank, although he was forced to do so by 1988.

Obviously, through an excessive and disproportionate use of force against the PLO and the Palestinians in Jordan, the Bedouin army brought about a total dismantling of the *fedayeen*. The king had succeeded in calculating his risks carefully, and the crisis did not, as many had expected, generate major Arab or international outcries to rescue the *fedayeen*. Neither Iraq nor Syria honored its promise to prevent the Jordanian Army from destroying the *fedayeen*. Nasser's diplomatic plans also failed to deter the determined Hussein from eliminating the *fedayeen*. Perhaps the Cairo Agreement would have succeeded in redefining PLO relations with Jordan and spared much of the bloodshed had the king not anticipated certain political and territorial gains from his support for the Rogers Plan. It seemed, at least at the time, that it was not in the king's best interest to ignore the *fedayeen*.

To a certain degree, a large majority of Palestinians consider the Black September civil war as one of the consequences of Nasser's and Hussein's policies that supported the Rogers Initiative, which, according to the *fedayeen*, intended to serve Israeli and U.S. interests. *Fedayeen* opposition to the Rogers Plan, and to other peace plans at the time, was rooted in their belief that pursuing peace with Israel was not only a sign of weakness but was also counterproductive by legitimizing Israel's existence at the expense of the Palestinians. Having been committed to an all-or-nothing approach and a zero-sum strategy toward Israel, the *fedayeen* desperately needed to preserve their presence in Jordan as an essential base for the fulfillment of their goals. Most of the *fedayeen* factions were committed to ideologies inspired by the experiences of radical leaders and movements, including General Vo Nguyen Giap in Vietnam, Che Guevara in Cuba, Frantz Fanon in Algeria, and Mao Tse-tung in China; they were determined not to compromise, believing that they too would prevail in the end. In retrospect, it seemed also justifiable for the *fedayeen*'s extremist factions to consider their challenge to Hussein's regime as part of a larger war against colonial and reactionary regimes. Since their approaches, inspirations, and goals were incompatible, it seemed inevitable that the king and the *fedayeen* would clash at some point.

In assessing the causes of the civil war, observers often point to the provocative acts of violence and terror carried out by the PFLP, both inside and outside Jordan, along with other interferences in Jordanian political life by the *fedayeen*, as the primary causes for the clashes. Although these factors may have played a crucial role in escalating the fighting, they were,

however, not sufficient to explain the Black September tragedy. For its part, as a splinter group that came out of the Arab Nationalist Movement (ANM), the PFLP had indeed stressed the need for an Arab revolution to go hand in hand with the Palestinian revolution that would together create an Arab union capable of restoring Palestinian rights. Unlike Fatah, which had no coherent ideology and advocated a simplistic policy of noninterference in Jordan's political life, the PFLP's ideological belief system, rooted in Arabism and Marxist socialism, allowed it to interfere directly with the internal politics of Arab regimes. The PFLP's hijacking of TWA, Pan American, and Swissair passenger planes had finally brought the situation to the breaking point of confrontation.

Hussein's disapproval of the rising power of the *fedayeen* following the Karamah battle, along with the presence of Israeli and American pressures on him to confront them or face reprisals from Israel, as well as the rise of new possibilities for peacemaking with Israel, were the key factors that caused the civil war to erupt. With respect to the more immediate factors that escalated the war, it is unquestionably clear that the PFLP's hijacking activities, the PLO's raids against Israel, and the calls for the overthrow of the king all played crucial, but not sufficient, roles in forcing Hussein to dismantle the *fedayeen*. Since Hussein's attacks were indiscriminate and thus affected all *fedayeen* factions, instead of only the extremists among them, and showed no real concern toward civilian casualties, he may have been motivated more by his mutual interests with outsiders than by the presence of an imminent threat to his authority.

Since September 1970, Palestinians have generally reacted to Hussein's regime with anger and frustration. For example, in 1971 the Black September Organization assassinated the prime minister of Jordan, Wasfi al-Tal, who played a crucial role in dismantling the *fedayeen*. In terms of its political goals, the PLO also decided in 1972 to establish new guidelines for the formation of a united Palestinian-Jordanian front in order to overthrow Hussein's regime. On a more extremist level, the Black September Organization, which was expelled from the PLO soon after its creation, carried out major international terror attacks, including the Munich Olympics attack against Israeli athletes (1972).

The Black September Organization disappeared in the period that followed the 1973 Arab-Israeli War, which brought about other changes in Palestinian and regional politics. In 1974, for example, the Arab states decided at the Rabat Arab League summit meeting to recognize the PLO as the sole legitimate representative of the Palestinian people. Afterward, the

PLO began moderating its old militant strategy and formulated a more diplomatic approach that accepted negotiations as a means for settling the conflict with Israel. Since 1974, relations between Hussein and the leadership of the PLO, along with the Palestinian-Jordanian ties in general, have significantly improved.

–HUSAM MOHAMAD,
UNIVERSITY OF CENTRAL OKLAHOMA

References

Adnan Abu Odeh, *Jordanians, Palestinians and the Hashemite Kingdom in the Middle East Peace Process* (Washington, D.C.: United States Institute of Peace Press, 1999).

Clinton Bailey, *Jordan's Palestinian Challenge, 1948–1983: A Political History* (Boulder, Colo.: Westview Press, 1984).

Laurie A. Brand, "Palestinians and Jordanians: A Crisis of Identity," *Journal of Palestine Studies,* 24 (Summer 1995): 46–61.

Marc Lynch, *State Interests and Public Spheres: The International Politics of Jordan's Identity* (New York: Columbia University Press, 1999).

Joseph A. Massad, *Colonial Effects: The Making of National Identity in Jordan* (New York: Columbia University Press, 2001).

Kamal Salibi, *The Modern History of Jordan* (London & New York: I.B. Tauris, 1993).

Yezid Sayigh, *Armed Struggle and the Search for State: The Palestinian National Movement 1949–1993* (New York: Oxford University Press, 1997).

EGYPTIAN-ISRAELI PEACE TREATY

Was the Egyptian-Israeli peace treaty of 1979 flawed?

Viewpoint: Yes. The Egyptian-Israeli peace treaty upset the Arab balance of power and cleared the path for Israel's invasion of Lebanon in 1982.

Viewpoint: No. The Egyptian-Israeli peace treaty was a success because it provided the model for a diplomatic resolution to the Arab-Israeli conflict.

The outcome of the Arab-Israeli War of 1973 led to Egyptian-Israeli negotiations that resulted in two disengagement agreements (Sinai I in 1974 and Sinai II in 1975). When Egyptian president Anwar Sadat reinvigorated a stalled peace process with his dramatic visit to Israel in November 1977, the momentum toward an Egyptian-Israeli peace treaty began to build. After negotiations became stymied once again by the summer of 1978, U.S. president Jimmy Carter, who made a comprehensive Arab-Israeli agreement one of his foreign-policy priorities when he came to office, invited both Sadat and Israeli prime minister Menachem Begin to the presidential retreat located at Camp David, Maryland. The intent was to create a more conducive atmosphere for bargaining away from the limelight.

The thirteen days at Camp David were marked by intense and often acrimonious negotiations that included threatened walkouts by both sides and a panoply of arm-twisting and cajoling by Carter to keep the parties talking. What finally emerged was the Camp David accords, consisting of two frameworks for peace. One dealt primarily with bilateral Egyptian-Israeli issues, including, most importantly, a phased Israeli withdrawal from the remainder of the Sinai Peninsula in return for full normalization of relations with Egypt. The other framework dealt with issues related to a comprehensive Arab-Israeli peace, including the Palestinian problem. After some more diplomatic wrangling throughout late 1978 and early into the next year, the Camp David accords became the basis for the formal Egyptian-Israeli peace treaty signed in the White House in March 1979. The treaty went according to plan on the Egyptian-Israeli front, as the final portion of the Sinai Peninsula was returned to Egypt in April 1982 (although Sadat would not witness it, for he was assassinated in October 1981 by Islamists opposed to the peace treaty). Despite some serious bumps along the way and what many have described as a "cold peace" between the two former enemies, the Egyptian-Israeli peace treaty still stands; unfortunately, the broadening of the Camp David model to include other Arab states failed to materialize, and overall progress on a comprehensive Arab-Israeli accord faltered.

Viewpoint:
Yes. The Egyptian-Israeli peace treaty upset the Arab balance of power and cleared the path for Israel's invasion of Lebanon in 1982.

Only through the eyes of those with a superficial understanding of the facts and of the nature of power politics does the Egyptian-Israeli peace treaty of 1979 appear to be a step toward a broader peace in the Arab-Israeli arena. In reality, this separate peace between Israel and its heretofore main Arab opponent provided a major blow to the prospects for a comprehensive Arab-Israeli peace, particularly one embodying the degree of justice that realistically would make it viable. Those who say that it did more damage than the previous wars do not exaggerate. For Zionism, with its continuing colonialist strategy of dispossessing the indigenous people of Palestine, the Egyptian-Israeli treaty is one more in a series of achievements starting with the Balfour Declaration (1917): the British assertion that Jews should have a homeland in Palestine. Thus, it should not come as a surprise that this first peace treaty between Israel and an Arab state was concluded, not by Israelis representing the peace camp, but rather by the hawkish prime minister Menachem Begin and his Right-wing government dominated by the Likud Party.

The "divide-and-conquer" strategy of Israel that the treaty represents exemplifies the inevitable desire of aggressive, expansionist powers to weaken the forces aligned against them by making separate deals inducing major opponents to withdraw from the struggle. This arrangement is like a hypothetical situation in which the Soviet Union deserted its allies by concluding a separate peace with Germany in 1942, with the latter withdrawing from the former's territory and thus allowed to consolidate its other conquests. The marginalization of the Palestine issue in particular exemplifies the kind of peace process pushed by Washington (aside from the Carter administration's momentary call in 1977 for reconvening the Geneva Conference that Egyptian president Anwar Sadat derailed with his trip to Jerusalem shortly afterward) that thwarted the international consensus favoring an international conference that would bring about a two-state solution to the Palestine question and a complete termination of the post-1967 occupation. Instead, Washington's "peace process" allowed the effects of Israeli power not to be diluted by the involvement of other powers.

By accepting Egypt's demand for withdrawal from its territory, Israel was able to weaken the coalition opposing it so as to facilitate its consolidation of control over areas that, particularly to

Begin, were far more important. Begin was determined to keep all of historic Palestine (which to him was "Western Eretz Yisrael"), including the West Bank and Gaza Strip. While he would have preferred to retain parts of Sinai as well, particularly Israeli settlements there, he was willing, albeit reluctantly, to give up this territory in order to neutralize Egypt's role in the Arab-Israeli conflict and thus facilitate the annexation of the West Bank and Gaza. What Begin's government had in mind for the Palestinians under occupation (though not including Jerusalem) was only "autonomy"—not for the territories they lived in, whose water, land, and airspace would, according to his plans, be outside Palestinian control—but only for them personally. In effect, he envisaged an arrangement that would allow them to be kept under Israeli control but without citizenship and voting rights in Israel.

While the preamble to the peace treaty gave lip service to the need for a just and comprehensive peace and reaffirmed the "Framework for Peace in the Middle East Agreed at Camp David," and while a "side letter" promised further negotiations leading to a comprehensive settlement, the nature of such an agreement was not spelled out. Indeed, the Camp David framework invoked in the peace treaty seemed to transform Israel's obligation ultimately to relinquish its conquests into a commitment to negotiate a disputed territory. The call for a comprehensive settlement provided only a fig leaf for Sadat to enable him to make a case for the kind of bilateral treaty that he was concluding. That is, there was no linkage of the treaty to such goals as Sadat had called for in the period following the Camp David accords. If there had been an agreement in principle on eventual withdrawal from all occupied territories—with only the details left for later negotiations—and if the continuation of the Egyptian-Israeli peace had been contingent on this result, the separate peace would not have been so objectionable. Israel continually made clear, however, that it never would accept such terms—indeed, the peace with Egypt served to remove pressure for accepting this arrangement in the future.

After all, a decision by the Israelis to withdraw from additional territories would be expected to result only from the balance of power, not from the ability of their antagonists sitting across a negotiating table to convince them of the moral or legal imperatives involved. As long as the Israelis maintained military predominance over their enemies, a situation that the peace with Egypt was designed to perpetuate, the ultimate status of the occupied Palestinian territories would be one in which they in effect could—as someone put the matter in a later context—negotiate only with themselves, that is, determine what would be to their own advantage without being coerced by anybody else. In fact, Begin bluntly declared that after five years of the

Israeli prime minister
Menachem Begin, U.S.
president Jimmy Carter,
and Egyptian president
Anwar Sadat (l.-r.) at
Camp David, Maryland,
September 1978

(© CORBIS/Bettmann)

autonomy plan called for in the Camp David accords the Arabs would acquiesce in Israel's claim to sovereignty over the territories or else the existing arrangement would simply continue. According to scholar William B. Quandt, there were "few remaining incentives for Israel now to make concessions relating to the Palestinians."

Sadat's policies gave a stamp of legitimacy to Israel's illegal occupation of Arab territories. They even established peace between Egypt and Israel, with an exchange of ambassadors, before the occupation of Egyptian territory ended. Israel reached its long-term goal of formal recognition from an Arab state without having to give up Palestinian and Syrian territories. It is true that in international politics, as ancient Greek historian Thucydides quotes the conquering Athenians telling the people of Melos, "the weak suffer what they must" (although the United Nations Charter was supposed to change that). Sadat's path to the peace treaty, however, started in the aftermath of the 1973 war when he boasted with some truth about the Arabs' being the "sixth world power," disregarding the leverage the Arab world then enjoyed as well as the broader international support it could count on. In addition to putting Egypt outside the anti-Israel coalition, the peace treaty left the Arab world in disarray. Although this result was hardly predictable at the outset of Sadat's path to a separate peace, when he finally negotiated his treaty with the Jewish state the revolution in Iran (1979) had transformed that country from an ally

of Israel into its most ardent enemy. Except for Egypt's withdrawal from the ranks, the alliance facing Israel might have left it increasingly vulnerable to pressures for a comprehensive settlement.

Sadat's idea that the peace treaty and other attempts to ingratiate himself with Washington would enable him to compete with Israel for American favors—which he fancied as a kind of "strategic thinking" that others were incapable of understanding—had little foundation. He also seems naively to have taken U.S. statements calling for Israel ultimately to withdraw from almost all of the occupied territories to mean that Washington would insist on this policy in practice. Admittedly, the United States has the potential of dictating to Israel by threatening to cut off the massive economic, military, and political backing that makes its intransigence possible. Sadat apparently did not take into account the powerful forces in American politics that bolster the special relationship with Israel or the combination of racial and cultural prejudice and deeply ingrained misperceptions in the United States that militate against willingly supporting justice for the Arabs, particularly if that means using leverage against Israel.

It is hardly surprising that the process of excluding the main Arab state from the ranks of Israel's enemies coincided with the acceleration of another process, that is, the major expansion of Israeli settlements in the West Bank and Gaza. The difficulty of ever removing such settlements—what Israelis called "creating facts on the ground"—indicated that withdrawal would not be an option. Also, the conclusion of the peace treaty facilitated Israel's ability to launch air attacks on Arab states, including Lebanon and Iraq, to enact legislation "reunifying Jerusalem," and to annex the Golan Heights. Furthermore, the Israelis had barely completed their withdrawal from the Sinai in 1982 before they launched an aggressive invasion of Lebanon. The goal was to destroy the Palestine Liberation Organization (PLO) as a prelude to settling the Palestine issue on Israeli terms. It is doubtful that such acts would have been feasible in the absence of the peace treaty, for the Israelis would have had to worry about their southern front. In this and many other subsequent aggressive acts by Israel, Egypt found itself committed under the terms of the peace treaty not only to stand on the sidelines of any military conflict but also to maintain normal diplomatic, economic, and cultural relations with the perpetrator.

It is understandable that Egypt would tire of supporting the rights of other Arabs and would concentrate on liberating its own territory through diplomacy. The separate peace got every inch of Egypt's territory back (potentially an important precedent for the other occupied territories), although with the requirement that it be largely demilitarized. This demilitarization would not be onerous in the context of a just, comprehensive peace, but it further limits Egypt's ability to deter Israeli aggression against the Arab world.

A deeper look at the possible long-run costs of deserting the Arab and Islamic world leads one to conclude that the harm to purely Egyptian interests far overshadowed the gains. The Arab and Islamic identities of Egyptians run too deep for them to be content with the liberation of Egyptian territory while other Arabs and Muslims, notably the Palestinians, remain under Israeli apartheid. It is true that a diminution of Arab identity in favor of purely Egyptian nationalism accompanied the move toward peace with Israel, and perhaps that trend would have continued if the Palestine issue also had been resolved, something that the separate peace worked against. But the separate peace went against the grain of popular feeling, particularly after disillusionment set in with the initial notion that a broader peace would follow. For a regime to remain bound to such an arrangement and to an alliance with the United States (indeed, to a position of dependence that reeks of revived colonialism), when the latter remained committed to subsidizing and otherwise supporting Israel in the face of Egyptian popular resentment, necessitated a continuation—in some ways an intensification—of authoritarian rule. Even the path that led to the treaty was one in which Sadat carried authoritarian patterns to the extreme by not even consulting with others in his government, who often were aghast at the decisions he made (just as

his Israeli counterparts sometimes were pleasantly amazed with his eagerness to make concessions). As Sadat's approach came more into question, the preservation of an autocratic peace (fashionable theories of "democratic peace" notwithstanding) provided an underlying foundation for the failure of democratization to proceed, as both the regime committed to the separate peace and its American patron, which supports democratization in other parts of the world, do not dare allow the continuation of the peace with Israel and the alliance with Washington to be subject to free elections. The vacuum created by the decline of secular Arab nationalism came to be filled not so much by an Egyptian identity as by an Islamic millenarianism opposing the foreign-backed autocratic regime and its peace with Israel, the extreme manifestations of which have included the assassination of Sadat, Muslim-Coptic clashes, and the Egyptian al-Qaida terrorist Muhammad Atta's crash into the World Trade Center (11 September 2001).

One cannot exclude the possibility that unexpected consequences unfavorable to Israel will emerge in the long run from this short-term disaster for the Arabs. The trouble the Israelis got into in Lebanon following the invasion that the peace treaty emboldened them to carry out in 1982 already provides a case in point. If Israel—again, partly because of Egypt's absence from Arab ranks—holds on to the occupied Palestinian territories and resists the creation of a viable Palestinian state, which would have limited self-government in any case, the result may be the beginning of a long-term process whereby it is transformed into a democratic binational Israel/Palestine, a defeat for the idea of a Jewish state. Such long-term results, however, are still unpredictable.

—GLENN E. PERRY,
INDIANA STATE UNIVERSITY

Viewpoint:
No. The Egyptian-Israeli peace treaty was a success because it provided the model for a diplomatic resolution to the Arab-Israeli conflict.

The peace treaty signed on 26 March 1979 between Egypt and Israel resulted from the Arab-Israeli War of 1973. It also resulted from a reassessment by President Anwar Sadat of Egypt's geopolitical role in the Middle East and from his willingness to turn over a new leaf in order to lead his country to economic well-being.

If it had not been for the 1973 war, it is difficult to say what Sadat would have decided. Sadat

TODAY I TELL YOU

On 20 November 1977 Egyptian president Anwar Sadat made an historic speech before the Israeli Knesset (parliament), a portion of which appears here:

Yet today I tell you, and I declare it to the whole world, that we accept to live with you in permanent peace based on justice. We do not want to encircle you or be encircled ourselves by destructive missiles ready for launching, nor by the shells of grudges and hatreds.

I have announced on more than one occasion that Israel has become an established fact recognized by the world, and that the two superpowers have undertaken the responsibility for its security and the defense of its existence. As we really and truly seek peace we really and truly welcome you to live among us in peace and security.

There was a huge wall between us which you tried to build up over a quarter of a century, but it was destroyed in 1973. It was the wall of an implacable and escalating psychological warfare. It was a wall of the fear of the force that could sweep the entire Arab nation. It was a wall of propaganda that we were a nation reduced to immobility. Some of you had gone as far as to say that even for 50 years to come, the Arabs would not regain their strength. It was a wall that always threatened with a long arm that could reach and strike anywhere. It was a wall that warned us of extermination and annihilation if we tried to use our legitimate rights to liberate the occupied territories.

Together we have to admit that that wall fell and collapsed in 1973. Yet, there remains another wall. This wall constitutes a psychological barrier between us, a barrier of suspicion, a barrier of rejection; a barrier of fear, of deception, a barrier of hallucination without any action, deed or decision. A barrier of distorted and eroded interpretation of every event and statement. It is this psychological barrier which I described in official statements as constituting 70 percent of the whole problem. . . .

As for the Palestine cause—nobody could deny that it is the crux of the entire problem. Today nobody in the world could accept slogans propagated here in Israel, ignoring the existence of a Palestinian people and questioning even their whereabouts. The Palestinian people and their legitimate rights are no longer denied today by anybody; that is, nobody who has the ability of judgment, can deny or ignore it. It is an acknowledged fact, perceived by the world community, both in the East and in the West, with support and recognition in international documents and official statements. It is of no use to anybody to turn deaf ears to its resounding voice, which is being heard day and night, or to overlook its historical reality.

Even the United States of America, your first ally, which is absolutely committed to safeguard Israel's security and existence and which offered and still offers Israel every moral, material and military support—I say, even the United States has opted to face up to reality and admit that the Palestinian people are entitled to legitimate rights and

that the Palestinian problem is the cause and essence of the conflict and that so long as it continues to be unresolved, the conflict will continue to aggravate, reaching new dimensions.

In all sincerity I tell you that there can be no peace without the Palestinians. It is a grave error of unpredictable consequences to overlook or brush aside this cause.

I shall not indulge in past events such as the Balfour Declaration sixty years ago. You are well acquainted with the relevant text. If you have found the moral and legal justification to establish a national home on a land that did not all belong to you, it is incumbent upon you to show understanding of the insistence of the people of Palestine for the establishment of their state on their land. When some extremists ask the Palestinians to give up this sublime objective, this in fact means asking them to renounce their identity and every hope for the future.

I hail the Israeli voices that called for the recognition of the Palestinian people's right to achieve and safeguard peace.

Here I tell you, ladies and gentlemen, that it is no use to refrain from recognizing the Palestinian people and their right to statehood and their right of return. We the Arabs, have faced this experience before, with you, and with the reality of the Israeli existence, the struggle which took us from war to war, from victims to victims, until you and we have today reached the edge of a horrible abyss and a terrifying disaster unless, together, we seize this opportunity today of a durable peace based on justice.

You have to face reality bravely, as I have done. There would never be any solution to a problem by evading it or turning a deaf ear to it. Peace cannot last if attempts are made to impose fantasy concepts on which the world has turned its back and announced its unanimous call for the respect of rights and facts.

There is no need to enter a vicious circle as to Palestinian rights. It is useless to create obstacles. Otherwise the march of peace will be impeded or peace will be blown up. As I have told you, there is no happiness built on the detriment of others.

Direct confrontation and straightforwardness are the shortcuts and the most successful way to reach a clear objective. Direct confrontation concerning the Palestinian problem and tackling it in one single language with a view to achieving a durable and just peace lies in the establishment of a Palestinian state. With all the guarantees you demand, there should be no fear of a newly born state that needs the assistance of all countries of the world. . . .

Source: *"President Sadat's Address to the Knesset, 20 November 1977," Foreign Policy Positions & Documents, Egyptian Ministry of Foreign Affairs website <http://www.mfa.gov.eg/get-doc.asp?id=47&cat=030103>.*

EGYPTIAN-ISRAELI PEACE TREATY

had triggered the war against Israel, perhaps not to annihilate the Jewish state but rather to reactivate diplomacy at the international level. The Israeli occupation of the Sinai Peninsula in 1967 had provoked widespread popular discontent in Egypt, worsened by an economic crisis that Soviet support could not ameliorate. Hence, the Egyptian president's position was unstable, partly because the military pressed for revenge against Israel. Preparation for the war was elaborate, and initially the attack was successful. The Israelis were forced to retreat from the Suez Canal line, suffering heavy losses in the process, but Sadat did not count on defeating Israel once and for all. While the Syrian ally (always the most hostile toward the Jewish state) nursed this hope, Sadat's aim, in light of the following events, was more limited at a military level but politically critical for Egypt's future. It was a matter of recovering the Sinai and reestablishing the unity of the country, thus improving the bargaining leverage that would allow him to negotiate with Israel from a position of strength.

Sadat knew the United States would not allow an Arab victory. U.S. secretary of state Henry Kissinger could not compromise, at least on this point. It is possible to say, however, that the outcome of the Yom Kippur War was "arranged" by Sadat, Kissinger, and the Soviets—without Israel's involvement. The United States wanted Egypt to recover the Sinai, reestablishing national prestige for Sadat in order for Egypt to become a moderating factor in the Middle East. Of course, this conclusion meant the Soviet Union's alienation from Egypt and the alignment of the Arab country toward the West. Kissinger's aim (as well as Sadat's) was only partially executed: through the peace treaty, Egypt recovered the Sinai and national unity (and also a certain prestige), not after a partial victory but rather after a terrible military defeat.

The peace with Israel came after a humiliating military defeat; therefore, it was viewed by the military and the most radical Egyptian factions as a slackening stance toward the Zionists. Then, the peace treaty, along with the alienation of the Soviet Union and tilt toward the West, embittered Egyptian public opinion, which considered Sadat's policy an unacceptable reversal of the anti-West, anticolonialist, and nationalist policy adopted by his charismatic predecessor Gamal Abd al-Nasser. Hence, in October 1981 Sadat was assassinated by a group of Islamists in the Egyptian military. Finally, although the reacquisition of the Sinai had restored Egypt's lost prestige, the peace treaty proved less than fulfilling, especially since the humiliating defeat and the reversal of Egypt's international alliances subjected Sadat to a wave of criticism. Sadat's journey to Jerusalem and his historic speech at the Knesset (20 November 1977) was anathema to most Egyptians.

Despite these setbacks, the diplomatic process carried out by Sadat was both brave and fruitful. Contacts between Egyptian and Israeli diplomats had already begun in summer 1977. Surprisingly, the election of Israeli Right-wingers, headed by Menachem Begin, did not stop the communication between the two countries but rather accelerated it. Sadat was jolted by the 1 October 1977 U.S.-Soviet joint declaration on Israel's withdrawal from occupied territories and on Palestinians' rights. It was not the substance of the declaration that irritated Sadat but rather Moscow's involvement in the Middle East politico-diplomatic question. Sadat could not believe that the Soviet Union, after its alienation from Egypt, would play a role in the area; nevertheless, he was somewhat befuddled that his new American friends helped the Soviets return to center stage. On 9 November, before the Egyptian National Assembly, he solemnly declared that, in order to save his nation the tragedy of a new war, he would even be ready to go to Jerusalem. Begin did not want to miss this opportunity and invited Sadat to visit the Jewish capital. On 16 November, Sadat repeated his declaration during an interview with Walter Cronkite of CBS-TV. Three days later Sadat was in Jerusalem, and on the following day he delivered his historic speech at the Knesset.

Sadat's speech represented a revolutionary change in Arab-Israeli relations. For the first time an Arab head of state recognized the legitimacy of the Jewish state's existence and the necessity of a definitive and honorable peace. In fact, the following decades showed that Sadat's action unfortunately remained an isolated event, although it is still important. The Oslo accords (1993) seemed to open a new, maybe definitive age of peace between Arabs and Israelis, but they were later buried by the refusal of the most extremist part of the Arab world to participate. The Oslo process, as well as the Madrid process, which led to the Israeli-Jordanian treaty (1994), would not have been possible unless the acknowledged leader of the Arab world had already made peace with Israel.

The 1979 treaty came only after one and a half years of exhausting negotiations. It is convenient to summarize the events, since the contradictions implied in the final agreement gave extremist Arab factions the chance to criticize Sadat's presumptive "surrender" and to escalate the conflict with Israel. In his speech at the Knesset, Sadat declared himself ready to recognize Israel but asked in return for the total withdrawal from all the territories occupied in 1967 and the right of self-determination for the Palestinians. The Egyptian president's initial position was understandable for two reasons. First, the agreement, generally speaking, derived from a gradual convergence in the overall assessment of the Arab-Israeli situation. Second, and perhaps a much more important issue, by including references to the Palestinians, Sadat tried to assuage an Arab world that had condemned his initiative. In fact, the most radical Arab entities (Libya, Iraq, the extremist wing of the Palestine Liberation Organization [PLO], South Yemen, Algeria, and above all Syria) never accepted Sadat's steps, and, for this reason, Egypt was kicked out of the Arab League. On the home front, the most rabid opponents of Sadat's policy were the Egyptian political and intellectual communities. In Israel, meanwhile, Begin had to face the backers of "Greater Israel," in other words those who, after the 1973 victory, confirmed their idea to found a Jewish nation within its historical borders. At this point, U.S. president Jimmy Carter decided to support the initiative and help guide the negotiations toward a positive conclusion.

On 5 January 1978 in Aswan, Egypt, Sadat and Carter elaborated on a formula for the total and final solution of the Palestinian question. Begin did not support that formula. In Leeds, England, that same year in July, the foreign ministers of the United States, Israel, and Egypt moved toward a compromise solution that led to the difficult, but fruitful, thirteen-day meetings at Camp David in September. On 17 September Begin, Sadat, and Carter signed an historic document framing a peace treaty between Egypt and Israel. The main clause concerned "full autonomy and self-government" for the West Bank and Gaza for five years, throughout which the parties were supposed to negotiate the final status of the Palestinian territories. This clause was Israel's recognition of Palestinian rights. The following were the main principles of the agreement: the elimination of the use of force to solve disputes, mutual recognition, the normalization of relations, and the end of economic boycott. The agreement also decreed that Israel would return the Sinai to Egypt and that Egypt would definitively recognize Israel, sign a peace treaty within three months, and establish normal relations with the Jewish state.

In Washington, on 26 March 1979, the peace treaty between Egypt and Israel was signed. The repercussions of the treaty were significant. First of all, Egypt definitively broke away from the group of radical Arab countries that had confronted Israel. Therefore, Egypt placed itself in the moderate camp in a premier position from a geopolitical and diplomatic point of view for improving relations with the United States. The consequent readmission of Egypt to the Arab League allowed it to play a leading mediating role in the region. Egyptian mediation, closely connected with Washington, represented and still represents a prerequisite for peace, above all in times of major crisis. In fact, all the deals to date, although mostly partial, have seen Egypt play a prominent role at the negotiating table. It is true that the Egyptian example has not been followed by most Arab countries (except Jordan) and that the most extremist factions have condemned the Egyptian "betrayal" of the cause, but the fact remains that the most important Arab country chose to abandon confrontation, regarding it as detrimental to the Arab world (and particularly to the Palestinians), as a harbinger to war, and as creating fertile ground for the spread of Islamic terrorism. Although an anti-Israel (and often strongly anti-Semitic) mood is still rather widespread among Egyptian public opinion, it is fundamentally important for the Egyptian government to maintain an uncompromising and coherent position in the Middle East matrix, always placing itself in a mediating and moderating role in the Israeli-Palestinian conflict. Should Egypt, for the sake of argument, abandon the moderate front, the Middle Eastern crisis would worsen dramatically, possibly leading to the catastrophic war all hoped to avoid by embarking on the road to peace in the first place.

–ANTONIO DONNO,
UNIVERSITY OF LECCE

References

Naseer Aruri, *The Obstruction of Peace: The United States, Israel and the Palestinians* (Monroe, Me.: Common Courage, 1995).

Yaacov Bar-Simon-Tov, *Israel and the Peace Process, 1977–1982: In Search of Legitimacy for Peace* (Albany: State University of New York Press, 1994).

Boutros Boutros-Ghali, *Egypt's Road to Jerusalem: A Diplomat's Story of the Struggle for Peace in the Middle East* (New York: Random House, 1997).

Laura Zitrain Eisenberg and Neil Caplan, *Negotiating Arab-Israeli Peace: Patterns, Problems, Possibilities* (Bloomington: University of Indiana Press, 1998).

Burton I. Kaufman, *The Arab Middle East and the United States: Inter-Arab Rivalry and Superpower Diplomacy* (New York: Twayne, 1996).

David W. Lesch, *1979: The Year that Shaped the Modern Middle East* (Boulder, Colo.: Westview Press, 2001).

William B. Quandt, *Peace Process: American Diplomacy and the Arab-Israeli Conflict since 1967* (Berkeley: University of California Press, 2001).

Cheryl A. Rubenberg, *Israel and the American National Interest: A Critical Examination* (Urbana: University of Illinois Press, 1986).

Adel Safty, *From Camp David to the Gulf: Negotiations, Language & Propaganda, and War* (New York: Black Rose Books, 1992).

EISENHOWER DOCTRINE

Did the Eisenhower Doctrine work?

Viewpoint: Yes. The Eisenhower Doctrine was a legitimate alternative to the Baghdad Pact, and it was successfully applied in Jordan in 1957 and Lebanon in 1958.

Viewpoint: No. The Eisenhower Doctrine was a misapplied globalist policy that cast the United States in the position of taking over where the British and French had failed.

The Eisenhower Doctrine was announced by the Eisenhower administration in January 1957 and was passed by Congress the following March. In the aftermath of the Suez War (1956), the Eisenhower administration hastily formulated a policy to fill the perceived vacuum of power in the Middle East following the humiliation of the British and the French, who were forced by the United States to withdraw their forces from Egypt to end the conflict. The feeling was that the United States had to take a more assertive policy in the region before the Soviet Union took advantage of the situation to enhance its strategic position; in addition, administration officials believed the doctrine might act as something of a substitute for officially joining the Baghdad Pact (1955), which was now hopelessly delegitimized by its association with Great Britain.

The doctrine essentially offered economic and military aid to any country in the Middle East that requested it in order to fend off the advances of what the administration termed "international communism." It became the centerpiece of the new American policy in the region, and it was notably invoked on two occasions: during the Jordanian crisis (1957) and the Lebanese crisis (1958). It was also determined to be a way to "roll back" Nasserism, which was seen as a vehicle for Soviet expansionism, which had so markedly gained momentum as a result of Egyptian president Gamal Abd al-Nasser's stunning political victory in the Suez crisis and war.

Views of the efficacy of the Eisenhower doctrine have been mixed. Some see it as having been irredeemably misplaced, because it focused too much at the globalist level on the Soviet threat rather than adequately taking into account the concerns of the Arab states at the regional level, who saw Israel and Western imperialism as much greater threats to regional stability. Others, however, point to the successes in Jordan and Lebanon when the Eisenhower Doctrine provided the policy foundation to maintain two pro-Western regimes in power; it also indicated, at last, that the United States was inserting itself in a more direct way in the Middle East after having been less than committed to that point toward containing Soviet influence in the region, exemplified by Washington's decision not to formally join the Baghdad Pact.

Viewpoint:
Yes. The Eisenhower Doctrine was a legitimate alternative to the Baghdad Pact, and it was successfully applied in Jordan in 1957 and Lebanon in 1958.

The Baghdad Pact (1955) did not work. Signed in order to replace the unsuccessful Middle East Defense Organization (MEDO) formed in 1951, it divided the Arab world. The United States was unable to interact with Arab countries and win their friendship. The real difficulty facing the United States was Egyptian president Gamal Abd al-Nasser's rise in regional influence thanks to his concept of Arab nationalism. When U.S. president Dwight D. Eisenhower and his secretary of state John Foster Dulles started to plan a new U.S. strategy for the Middle East, they were unable to resolve the problems of establishing a Western presence in that area. MEDO was intended to be a military alliance between the Western countries and Egypt, in order to prevent Soviet intervention in the Middle East, but this proposal frittered away after King Farouq's monarchy was overthrown in a 1952 military seizure of power; the new regime was nationalistic and eventually anti-Western. Anticommunism was not considered necessary for the success of the Egyptian Revolution. The new regime wanted to end subordination toward France and Britain, and the United States was no exception. The fall of the pro-West Farouq and the nationalist military seizure of power was a watershed in modern Middle Eastern history, and hence, the United States began a painstaking search for a new policy in the Middle East able to challenge Soviet influence in the area. Washington regarded Arab nationalism as inimical to its interests and feared the Arab countries would side with the Soviet Union.

The idea of a Middle East defense system militarily and economically supported by the West was Eisenhower and Dulles's basic vision for U.S. Cold War strategy. At the beginning of 1953, Eisenhower and Dulles thought, quite ambitiously, that solving the Arab-Israeli conflict would open the way to the solution of the Middle East crisis. With American involvement, they argued, U.S. prestige in the Middle East would be reestablished, replacing the discredited Anglo-French policy. The American strategy dictated full U.S. political responsibility, marginalizing Britain and France's declining status in the Middle East. Indeed, Dulles believed that the Middle East Command (MEC)—MEDO's immediate forerunner—had failed on grounds of typical American disengagement and deference to

the British. Actually, Washington's relationship with London concerning the Middle East crisis had always been difficult. Washington resorted to a compromise on the question of British influence in the area, trying to disguise it behind the U.S. shield, but this ruse failed.

MEDO's failure and the American fear regarding the threat of Soviet expansion in the Middle East, coupled with the popular success of Arab nationalism, forced the U.S. government to formulate the Northern Tier approach—Arab or Islamic countries close to the southern borders of the Soviet Union that allied with and were friends of the United States would serve as a buffer against communist expansionism. The defense belt had to include Turkey, Iran, Pakistan, and Iraq. Nasser vehemently opposed the West, although he eventually wanted to exploit its money for his own purposes. Nasser tried to thwart the foundation of a unified command in Egypt (MEC and MEDO) because this type of alliance meant a decline in Egyptian sovereignty. Likewise, he opposed prospective alliances within other Middle East theaters, without Egypt's involvement, which could result in a decrease in his personal prestige in the eyes of other Arab peoples. For the Americans (and the West generally), Arab nationalism, and particularly Nasser's volatile policy, were tough nuts to crack. Irritated by Nasser's ambiguity, Dulles said that it was necessary to rely on loyal countries that were ready to cooperate with the West. Hence, the Northern Tier strategy was formulated and sanctioned on 14 July 1955 as National Security Council document 155/1. In April 1954 Turkey and Pakistan signed a cooperation agreement, followed by military-aid agreements between the United States and Pakistan and then between the United States and Iraq. Finally, on 23 February 1955, all these accords resulted in the Iraqi-Turkish treaty, called the Baghdad Pact. The problem was that everyone, especially Nasser, knew that the United States was behind the Baghdad Pact. Nasser's reaction was typically vehement, and some days later it was manifested in an economic and military cooperation pact between Egypt and Syria. Washington's plan was already beginning to backfire—in September 1955 Cairo received a large quantity of weapons from the Soviet Union. The last straw was London's attempt to return to the Middle East stage by officially adhering to the Baghdad Pact on 5 April 1955. The American strategy failed in little more than a year. Although Pakistan and Iran had adhered to the Baghdad Pact, the Arab nationalist reaction, headed by Nasser, roused the rest of the Middle East against the United States, considered the heir of British colonialism, thus condemning the Baghdad Pact to failure.

A GREATER RESPONSIBILITY

On 5 January 1957 President Dwight D. Eisenhower addressed Congress on his Middle East policy; a portion of his speech appears below:

Under all the circumstances I have laid before you, a greater responsibility now devolves upon the United States. We have shown, so that none can doubt, our dedication to the principle that force shall not be used internationally for any aggressive purpose and that the integrity and independence of the nations of the Middle East should be inviolate. Seldom in history has a nation's dedication to principle been tested as severely as ours during recent weeks.

There is general recognition in the Middle East, as elsewhere, that the United States does not seek either political or economic domination over any other people. Our desire is a world environment of freedom, not servitude. On the other hand many, if not all, of the nations of the Middle East are aware of the danger that stems from International Communism and welcome closer cooperation with the United States to realize for themselves the United Nations goals of independence, economic well-being and spiritual growth. . . .

The action which I propose would have the following features.

It would, first of all, authorize the United States to cooperate with and assist any nation or group of nations in the general area of the Middle East in the development of economic strength dedicated to the maintenance of national independence.

It would, in the second place, authorize the Executive to undertake in the same region programs of military assistance and cooperation with any nation or group of nations which desires such aid.

It would, in the third place, authorize such assistance and cooperation to include the employment of the armed forces of the United States to secure and protect the territorial integrity and political independence of such nations, requesting such aid, against overt armed aggression from any nation controlled by International Communism.

These measures would have to be consonant with the treaty obligations of the United States, including the Charter of the United Nations and with any action or recommendations of the United Nations. They would also, if armed attack occurs, be subject to the overriding authority of the United Nations Security Council in accordance with the Charter.

The present proposal would, in the fourth place, authorize the President to employ, for economic and defensive military purposes, sums available under the Mutual Security Act of 1954, as amended, without regard to existing limitations. . . .

Let me refer again to the requested authority to employ the armed forces of the United States to assist to defend the territorial integrity and the political independence of any nation in the area against Communist armed aggression. Such authority would not be exercised except at the desire of the nation attacked. Beyond this it is my profound hope that this authority would never have to be exercised at all.

In the situation now existing, the greatest risk, as is often the case, is that ambitious despots may miscalculate. If power-hungry Communists should either falsely or correctly estimate that the Middle East is inadequately defended, they might be tempted to use open measures of armed attack. If so, that would start a chain of circumstances which would almost surely involve the United States in military action. I am convinced that the best insurance against this dangerous contingency is to make clear now our readiness to cooperate fully and freely with our friends of the Middle East in ways consonant with the purposes and principles of the United Nations. I intend promptly to send a special mission to the Middle East to explain the cooperation we are prepared to give.

Source: *"President Eisenhower: The Eisenhower Doctrine on the Middle East, A Message to Congress, January 5, 1957," Modern History Source-Book <http://www.fordham.edu/halsall/mod/1957eisenhowerdoctrine.html>.*

EISENHOWER DOCTRINE

This background is necessary to explain the origin and the meaning of the Middle East Resolution (better known as the "Eisenhower Doctrine"), passed by the U.S. government after the Suez crisis, which was a lethal blow for Anglo-French supremacy in the Middle East. On 5 January 1957 President Eisenhower proclaimed to a joint session of Congress the contents of the Middle East resolution that recalled, through its guidelines, the objectives of the Truman Doctrine (1947). Essentially, in an even more unequivocal way than previous actions, the Eisenhower Doctrine committed itself to support militarily those Middle East countries that felt threatened by internal or international communism. Therefore, the Eisenhower Doctrine replaced the complex diplomacy of MEDO and the Baghdad Pact. The United States no longer sought the direct involvement of Arab countries in a system of political and military alliances. It now committed itself, directly and without diplomatic nuances, to intervene in a Middle East crisis considered threatening to American national interests, provoked by communism or not, simply by request.

The first tests came in Jordan in 1957 and in Lebanon in 1958. The October 1956 Jordanian elections produced unsuccessful results for the West, and King Hussein was forced to choose as prime minister Suleiman Nabulsi, who favored nonaligned positions and backed Nasser. Essentially, this anti-West policy alarmed the Americans, and it degenerated into a serious institutional crisis. Washington had always considered neutralist positions as leaning toward Moscow; therefore, the new Jordanian government was a confirmation for the Americans that Nasserism was spreading in Middle East countries that were traditional friends of the United States. Nabulsi asked Hussein to establish diplomatic relations with Moscow; soon after, he asked for the dismissal of many politicians and military officers from their posts and replaced them with elements backing the new government. Feverish activities followed, when it seemed, according to Central Intelligence Agency (CIA) director Allen Dulles, that the army was no longer loyal to the king. Nabulsi was removed from office, but the Jordanian public took to the streets to protest against the king's decision. The army was split between those who were loyal to the king and those who backed a Nasserist government. Hussein crushed the opposition, particularly the Nasserist leaders. These events showed, according to U.S. authorities, who was behind the Jordanian Free Officers movement: Syria, Egypt, and, therefore, the Soviet Union.

The crisis soon shifted from the military to the political sphere. Those who opposed the new royalist government met in Nablus and formulated a document calling for the dissolution of the government, formation of a new anti-monarchical coalition, a federation with Syria and Egypt, expulsion of the U.S. ambassador, and reintegration of the expelled officers. Faced with street protests in Jordan, Dulles and Eisenhower chose to implement the Eisenhower Doctrine. The president ordered the U.S. Navy's Sixth Fleet to move toward the eastern Mediterranean. The result was immediate and satisfactory. Hussein established a curfew in Amman and in almost the entire West Bank, while royalist Bedouin troops took up positions in the capital. Martial law was imposed and opposition parties were declared illegal. Hussein delivered a speech on television, saying that "international communism" had caused the Jordanian crisis. Through this declaration, the king endorsed the implementation of the Eisenhower Doctrine. As a direct consequence of this crisis, Washington launched an economic-aid program for Jordan and granted military aid for Hussein. In a 12 May 1957 letter the Jordanian king expressed gratitude to the Americans for helping him defeat communist intrigues. The Eisenhower Doctrine had been implemented without direct U.S. military intervention.

The Lebanese case was more serious and dangerous. President Camille Chamoun, a Maronite Christian elected in 1957, was accused of vote rigging and of intending to amend the constitution in order to gain a second term, which was clearly forbidden by the constitution. Behind this crisis was continuous Arab nationalist pressure, led by Nasser's Egypt and pro-Nasserist Syria. Chamoun intended to align with pro-West Iraq, but he was fiercely opposed by Islamic elements in Lebanon that contested his unconditional acceptance of the Eisenhower Doctrine. Chamoun thought he could gain American support for a second term, but Washington believed he was making a serious mistake. However, the United States decided to support him. Serious turmoil followed. In response, the White House declared itself ready to buttress, even militarily, the independence and integrity of Lebanon on the basis of the Eisenhower Doctrine. The United Nations (UN) sent the Observation Group in Lebanon (UNOGIL) to verify possible external interference in the Lebanese crisis. Their conclusion was negative, but Washington, confidentially, regarded the UNOGIL investigation as hurried and inaccurate.

On 14 July 1958 the situation came to a head in Baghdad. A group of young pro-Nasser officers, led by Abd al-Karim Qassim, took power, wiping out the royal family and assassinating Prime Minister Nuri as-Said. Therefore, Chamoun, regarding his country as vulnerable to the violence of Nasser's followers, had reason to ask once again for American intervention in Lebanon. At the same time, violent pro-Nasserist riots broke out in Jordan as well. Hussein asked for Western help, and Great Britain, through "Operation Fortitude," with Israeli permission to fly over its airspace, brought the Jordanian situation again under the king's control. Faced with these events, Washington decided to intervene militarily in Lebanon. On 15 July U.S. Marines landed on the Lebanese coast (Operation Blue Bat). American envoy Robert Murphy engaged in brilliant diplomatic work, negotiating an agreement for new elections, which, at the end of July, brought General Fuad Chebab to the presidency. By November 1958 the marines had left Lebanon.

The Eisenhower Doctrine was implemented successfully both in Jordan and in Lebanon. It was certainly a temporary success, but it did not generate a pro-U.S. alignment in the Middle East. Indeed, Nasserism remained particularly virulent in many important Middle East countries and a constant threat to Western interests in the area. Nevertheless, the Eisenhower Doctrine had a deterrent effect on Nasser's aggressiveness in the area. Nasser hoped that, being sheltered by the Soviet Union, he would be able to compel the United States to be more reluctant in applying the Eisenhower Doctrine. Instead, Washington considered that the presence of the Soviet Union alongside Nasser's Arab nationalism forced a firm action in those situations where Nasserism could spread. Nevertheless, even with the partial and temporary success of the Eisenhower Doctrine, the Middle East situation remained unstable.

–ANTONIO DONNO,
UNIVERSITY OF LECCE

Viewpoint:
No. The Eisenhower Doctrine was a misapplied globalist policy that cast the United States in the position of taking over where the British and French had failed.

With the end of the Suez War in November 1956 and the complete withdrawal of the Anglo-French-Israeli forces from Egypt, the Middle East entered a new era. The old colonial powers of France and Great Britain lost what remained of their influence and control in the region, and two new superpowers ascended in their place: the Soviet Union and the United States. The Eisenhower administration tried to

keep Moscow out of the area, but its failure to understand the intraregional dynamics, on one hand, and its failure to support the Anglo-French action in Egypt, on the other, enhanced the Soviet presence in the region.

Once Paris and London were effectively out of the Middle East, the United States filled the vacuum of power left by the colonial powers. The Eisenhower administration feared the Soviet Union's support of such radical countries as Egypt and Syria, as well as perceived attempts to overthrow moderate regimes in Jordan, Lebanon, Saudi Arabia, Iraq, and Iran. President Dwight D. Eisenhower and Secretary of State John Foster Dulles thought their actions opposing the tripartite invasion of Egypt during the Suez crisis could be leveraged to shape the future order in the Middle East. They were of the opinion that their pressure on Britain and France to withdraw from Egypt deserved to be rewarded by more support from the Arabs against the Soviet Union. Once again, however, the Eisenhower administration failed to clearly understand the real concerns of the individual states in the area. Jordan, Lebanon, and Iraq, for example, feared growing nationalism, such as the movement led by Gamal Abd al-Nasser in Egypt. Saudi Arabia was concerned by the increasing instability in Yemen paid for and supported by Nasser, who by 1962 would militarily intervene.

Reports from U.S. embassies in several Arab countries failed to state the importance of Arab nationalism; U.S. officials continued to consider it an instrument for Soviet penetration into the area rather than an independent movement and ideology. It is useful to remember that the Eisenhower administration failed to stop the Soviet-Egyptian arms deal of September 1955 and withdrew economic assistance for the construction of the Aswan Dam in Egypt, allowing Moscow to replace the Western money with their own.

After the failure of the Baghdad Pact, the administration chose another way to convince the Arab states to collaborate. At the beginning of 1957 a new strategic and economic doctrine was arranged. In fact, in the first days of January, President Eisenhower spoke to the most important senators and representatives. The new doctrine—then known as the Eisenhower Doctrine or Middle East Resolution—proposed, once again, that the Soviet Union and "international communism" were exclusive problems in the region. To address these issues, every country threatened or under a possible threat by "international communism" could ask the United States for economic or military aid or direct intervention by American forces.

Many U.S. politicians saw in the doctrine a "blank check" in the president's hands to use the

"How Do You Do"

PEACE

MIDDLE EAST SITUATION

ADMINISTRATION

HERBLOCK
©1956 THE WASHINGTON POST Co.

Political cartoon by Herbert L. Block portraying Dwight D. Eisenhower as a president who has no control over his foreign policy in the Middle East

(from Herblock's Special for Today, *Simon & Schuster, 1958)*

armed forces where he wanted. Others, rightly, realized the mistake of confusing Arab nationalism with communism. After the complete Israeli withdrawal from the Sinai Peninsula by March 1957, the Middle East Resolution passed the Senate with an important amendment: U.S. armed forces could intervene in case a country, fundamental for U.S. national security, was in peril. The Mansfield amendment was introduced by some senators who were worried about the Israeli position, since Israel could not call for the Eisenhower Doctrine because it was ostensibly not threatened by the Soviet Union. This amendment was fundamental for the direct application of the doctrine in Jordan and Lebanon.

In Jordan (1957) and Lebanon (1958) revolts broke out without the intervention of communist forces. In fact, in Jordan, King Hussein was threatened by a group of officers who had founded a movement based on the Egyptian Free Officers. The Jordan Free Officers were sponsored by Nasser, because he saw in the Jordanian regime a government too weak and too close to the West. The coup failed because, in that case, the U.S. Sixth Fleet sailed to the eastern Mediterranean. Moreover, American dollars supported the Jordanian kingdom and the weakened Hussein.

In Lebanon, a revolt broke out because President Camille Chamoun decided to remain in power, counter to the Lebanese constitution, causing clashes between Muslims and Christians. The revolt was, once again, supported by Nasser. Even in Lebanon, communism was not involved in the clashes directly or indirectly. It was a civil war based on internal causes. Nevertheless, the

EISENHOWER DOCTRINE

United States decided to intervene directly and invade Lebanon. Why?

One of the answers could be found in what happened in Baghdad just twenty-four hours before the American invasion of Lebanon, in other words, the so-called Iraqi Revolution. Without giving credit to many reports of a growing nationalist and Nasserist movement in Iraq, the Eisenhower administration decided not to intervene in Baghdad. The result was a bloody coup d'état with the extermination of the Iraqi royal family and Prime Minister Nuri as-Said. The Iraqi lesson pushed Eisenhower and Dulles to intervene in Lebanon. Without the Mansfield amendment, however, there was no legal basis for action in Jordan and Lebanon. In fact, because Jordan and Lebanon were declared vital for U.S. national security, the armed forces could act.

It is clear that the use of the Mansfield amendment to intervene revealed the complete and definitive failure of the Eisenhower Doctrine: to stop civil war and to support a weak government close to the West—neither Jordan nor Lebanon were threatened by communism. Moreover, after the strong stance of the Eisenhower administration against the Anglo-French-Israeli action at Suez, it lost almost immediately the merit points it had gained in the eyes of the Arab world. The Arab masses, in particular, saw the U.S. invasion as a new colonial action against Muslim brothers to help a Christian usurper. Moderate Arab leaders realized more and more that the real danger was radical Arab nationalism (Nasserism) that was able to win the broad support of the masses against their governments, which were seen as Western puppets.

After the Lebanon invasion and the withdrawal of U.S. troops starting in October 1958, the Eisenhower administration began to understand that it could not rely completely upon moderate Arab states (for example, Saudi Arabia denied the use of its air bases during the military campaign in Lebanon). Eisenhower and Dulles realized that they disregarded the only reliable and strategic ally in the Middle East region: Israel. The Jewish state—with its scientific know-how, its intelligence apparatus, and its military skill—could have been a real strategic asset for the United States in the region, much earlier than the 1970s, when Israel finally fulfilled that role for Washington. Eisenhower sowed the seeds of that friendship that would bear fruit with President John F. Kennedy and evolve into complete collaboration under Presidents Lyndon B. Johnson and Richard M. Nixon.

–DANIELE DE LUCA,
UNIVERSITY OF LECCE

References

Erika Alin, *The United States and the 1958 Lebanon Crisis: American Intervention in the Middle East* (Lanham, Md.: University Press of America, 1994).

Dwight D. Eisenhower, *Waging Peace, 1956–1961* (Garden City, N.Y.: Doubleday, 1965).

Steven Z. Freiberger, *Dawn over Suez: The Rise of American Power in the Middle East, 1953–1957* (Chicago: I. R. Dee, 1992).

Fawaz A. Gerges, *The Superpowers and the Middle East: Regional and International Politics, 1955–1967* (Boulder, Colo.: Westview Press, 1994).

David W. Lesch, "Prelude to the 1958 American Intervention in Lebanon," *Mediterranean Quarterly*, 3 (Summer 1996): 87–108.

Lesch, *Syria and the United States: Eisenhower's Cold War in the Middle East* (Boulder, Colo.: Westview Press, 1992).

Harold Macmillan, *Riding the Storm, 1956–1959* (New York: Harper & Row, 1971).

Robert Murphy, *Diplomat among the Warriors* (Garden City, N.Y.: Doubleday, 1964).

Ritchie Ovendale, *Britain, the United States and the Transfer of Power in the Middle East, 1945–1962* (London & New York: Leicester University Press, 1996).

Elie Podeh, *The Quest for Hegemony in the Arab World: The Struggle over the Baghdad Pact* (Leiden: Brill, 1995).

FREE OFFICERS REVOLUTION

Did the Free Officers Revolution of 1952 in Egypt signal revolutionary social change?

Viewpoint: Yes. The Free Officers Revolution was organized by a younger generation of Arabs frustrated by the inability of the older generation to deliver true independence and socio-economic justice.

Viewpoint: No. The Free Officers Revolution signaled the coming to power of a military dictatorship that imposed another form of authoritarianism.

On 23 July 1952 an event occurred in Egypt that has been variably described as the July Revolution, the Free Officers Revolution (Coup), and/or the Egyptian Revolution. Whether it was a true revolution depends upon one's definition of the word *revolution.* Was it, indeed, a transfer of power from one class to another accompanied by a completely different ideological foundation? Or was it simply the replacement of one type of authoritarian regime with another; in other words, a coup d'état? Does a revolution have to occur for there to be significant change? If not, did the Free Officers movement constitute a legitimate change from the previous regime?

To understand the July Revolution one has to understand the long history of colonial control in Egypt by the British, the internal politics in Egypt meshed with the growth of Arab nationalism in the years between World War I (1914–1918) and World War II (1939–1945), and, finally, the humiliating defeat in the First Arab-Israeli War (1947–1949). The British had essentially established a protectorate in Egypt in the 1880s to secure the all-important lifeline to the East represented by the Suez Canal (opened in 1869). As happened throughout the European colonial empires following World War I, nationalistic movements agitating against foreign control started to materialize—this transformation was certainly the case in the Middle East with the formalization of Arab nationalism. This younger generation of Arabs railed not only against colonial influence but also against those indigenous classes that seemed to be co-opted and manipulated by the colonial powers without providing the true independence or overall economic prosperity they had promised. It was within this milieu that the Free Officers movement, made up of disenchanted officers in the Egyptian military, formed in the 1930s. Among the initial members were Gamal Abd al-Nasser and Anwar Sadat. The accumulated frustration with a corrupt and aloof monarchy (a dynasty that had been in power since the early 1800s), as well as with the rich, landowning classes that dominated the rudimentary parliamentary system, was intensified by the ineptitude displayed by the armed forces in the First Arab-Israeli War. Within the next ten years all the Arab regimes that had participated in this conflict were cast aside, the war being something of a last straw for many disaffected elements of Arab society.

After a series of violent incidents between the Egyptians and the British in early 1952 and subsequent political turmoil gripping the monarchy and government, the environment seemed to turn more propitious for seditious activity. Recognizing the opportunity, the Free Officers surreptitiously planned and carried out their putsch, creating a Revolutionary Command Council (RCC) composed of eleven young officers and assuming supreme authority in the country. However one interprets the legacy of the event, one thing is certain: the strongman in the RCC, Nasser, became the most charismatic and important figure in the Arab world in the post–World War II era.

Viewpoint:
Yes. The Free Officers Revolution was organized by a younger generation of Arabs frustrated by the inability of the older generation to deliver true independence and socio-economic justice.

On 23 July 1952 Egyptian history changed. Tired of the corrupt regime of King Farouk I, some officers in the army began to organize a coup d'état to overthrow the ancien régime and give new life to the growing nationalist spirit. The leaders of the coup were General Muhammad Neguib and Colonel Gamal Abd al-Nasser.

The chain of events that led to the coup began with the failure of Arab armies in the First Arab-Israeli War (1947–1949). As Nasser remembered in *The Philosophy of the Revolution* (1959), the Egyptian Army was led by corrupt commanders. Moreover, in Cairo nobody really seemed to care about the war or wanted to defend the Arab world against "Zionist imperialism." Change was necessary.

Nasser and a few coconspirators convinced Neguib of the necessity to move against King Farouk and establish a new nationalist regime to achieve real independence. In fact, Great Britain still had some important facilities in Egypt: the Suez Canal (operated by the Suez Canal Company, which was 50 percent British owned) and a vitally strategic military base in the Canal Zone. Moreover, per the Anglo-Egyptian Treaty of 1936, London secured the right to intervene in the country in case of war. Egypt's legitimate sovereignty was infringed upon by the British presence on the most important and strategic Egyptian site. Britain's own position was anomalous, since it had to refrain from declaring a protectorate and regularly announced its intention of leaving. The so-called veiled protectorate looked to many like a typical manifestation of British hypocrisy and only served to increase resentment.

King Farouk and his regime were seen by the populace as subordinate to London and detached from the people, who suffered from the absence of real social, economic, and agrarian reform. Nasser and the Free Officers realized the growing frustration of the Egyptian masses. Nationalism was the new card on the Egyptian table. At a moment when Islamic radicalism and communism were increasing their influence in the country, Nasser understood that a new, strong, laical, and nationalist Egypt was necessary.

The Free Officers movement was composed of young elements of the Egyptian Army who were frustrated by the political attitude of the king and by the conduct of the war against Israel. Among the Free Officers were Abdul Hakim Amer, Abdul Latif al-Baghdadi, and Anwar al-Sadat, with Nasser as the unquestioned leader. To bring more legitimacy to the new regime, Nasser decided to involve Neguib, a well-known and respected officer. Neguib was a kind of puppet in the hands of the military junta, anyway. In fact, every important decision was taken by Nasser, and in 1954 he took complete power by exiling Neguib and assuming the office of president of the new Republic of Egypt.

When, on 26 July 1952, King Farouk signed the act of abdication in favor of his son, Ahmad Fuad II, it was clear that the century and a half of rule by the Muhammad Ali dynasty had come to an end. Though no one could be sure at the time, this act was much more than a mere coup d'état. It was a true revolution that would affect, in varying degrees, all Egyptian classes and institutions and change the course of history.

The Free Officers had been planning this revolt for years in secret and against all odds. They had a clear idea of what they wanted to eliminate in Egypt: the monarchy, the power of the landlords, foreign influence, and the corruption of political life. They had a vision of a new kind of society. The great majority of the revolutionaries, including Nasser, were Egyptian nationalists.

One of the first acts taken by the new regime was land reform. In fact, in September the Revolutionary Command Council (RCC), as the military junta now called itself, took what was the most important domestic measure of the early years of the Revolution. The decree limited land holdings to 200 *feddans* (1 *feddan* = 1.038 acres), with an extra 100 if the owner had two or more children, and provided for the redistribution of confiscated land to *fellahin* (peasants) in lots of between 2 and 5 *feddans*. The significance of agrarian reform was that it sharply reduced, though it did not destroy, the political influence of big landowners. It was

FATE DOES NOT PLAY JOKES

In The Philosophy of the Revolution *(1959), Gamal Abd al-Nasser explained the position of Egypt:*

I survey our conditions and find out we are in a group of circles which should be the theatre of our activity and in which we try to move as much as we can.

Fate does not play jokes. Events are not produced haphazardly. Existence cannot come out of nothing.

We cannot look stupidly at a map of the world not realizing our place therein and the role determined to us by that place. Neither can we ignore that there is an Arab circle surrounding us and that this circle is as much a part of us as we are a part of it, that our history has been mixed with it and that its interests are linked with ours. These are actual facts and not mere words.

Can we ignore that there is a continent of Africa in which fate has placed us and which is destined today to witness a terrible struggle on its future? This struggle will affect us whether we want or not.

Can we ignore that there is a Muslim world with which we are tied by bonds which are not only forged by religious faith but also tightened by the facts of history? I said once that fate plays no jokes. It is not in vain that our country lies to the Southwest of Asia close to the Arab world, whose life is intermingled with ours. It is not in vain that our country lies in the Northeast of Africa, a position from which it gives upon the dark continent wherein rages today the most violent struggle between the white colonizers and black natives for the possession of its inexhaustible resources. It is not in vain that Islamic civilization and Islamic heritage, which the Mongols ravaged in their conquest of the old Islamic Capitals, retreated and sought refuge in Egypt where they found shelter and safety as a result of the counterattack with which Egypt repelled the invasion of the Tartars at Ein Galout. . . .

There is no doubt that the Arab circle is the most important and the most closely connected with us. Its history merges with ours. We have suffered the same hardships, lived the same crises and when we fell prostrate under the spikes of the horses of conquerors they lay with us.

Religion also fused this circle with us. The centres of religious enlightenment radiated from Mecca, from Koufa and later from Cairo.

These were also collected in an environment in which all these historic, spiritual and material factors are closely knitted. As far as I am concerned I remember that the first elements of Arab consciousness began to filter into my mind as a student in secondary schools, wherefrom I went out with my fellow schoolboys on strike on December 2nd of every year as a protest against the Balfour Declaration whereby England gave the Jews a national home usurped unjustly from its legal owners.

When I asked myself at that time why I left my school enthusiastically and why I was angry for this land which I never saw I could not find an answer except the echoes of sentiment. Later a form of comprehension of this subject began when I was a cadet in the Military College studying the Palestine campaigns in particular and the history and conditions of this region in general which rendered it, throughout the last century, as easy prey ravaged by the claws of a pack of hungry beasts.

. . . The Arab nations entered the Palestine War with the same degree of enthusiasm. They all shared the same feelings and had known quite well the limits of their security. They came out of the war with the same bitterness and frustration. Every one of them was thus exposed, in its own country, to the same factors and was governed by the same forces, that caused their defeat and made them bow their heads low with shame and humiliation.

Source: *Gamal Abd al-Nasser,* The Philosophy of the Revolution *(Buffalo, N.Y.: Smith, Keynes & Marshall, 1959), pp. 59–64.*

largely because of its domination by the landowning class that the Wafd Party had consistently failed to carry through reforms when it was in power at various times after World War I (1914–1918).

The foreign policy of the revolutionary movement was quite clear. The emphasis was neutralism. In particular, nonalignment with either of the two superpower blocs in the Cold War was fundamental to Nasser's political outlook. This stance was an inevitable development of his passionate Egyptian and Arab nationalism that compelled him to want to rid the Middle East of all foreign influence, but this goal was not immediately evident when he came to power. Indeed, in the early years of the Revolution, he was regarded as pro-American. The only important aim in the foreign policy of the young revolutionaries was to get rid of the British, and the United States seemed to show at least an understanding of their desire to make Egypt truly independent. This pro-Americanism did not last through 1954, however, largely because the United States misjudged its dealings with Egypt. American diplomacy had helped to bring about the 1954 Anglo-Egyptian settlement for the withdrawal of British troops from the Suez Canal; American experts came to Egypt in increasing numbers and development credits were raised to $40 million. These advances were nullified, however, by the efforts of the Eisenhower administration to bring Egypt into a Middle East defense pact against the Soviet Union and to push Egypt to adhere to the so-called Alpha Plan sponsored by the United States with the aim of settling the Arab-Israeli conflict.

Nasser's neutralism acquired a new dimension during the Bandung conference (April 1955). Meeting on equal terms with Indian leader Motilal Nehru, Chinese premier Chou En-lai, and other senior Asian statesmen, Nasser's forecast about Egypt's potential role in the world seemed to be coming to pass. At the same time, he was more convinced than ever that to play this role, Egypt ought not to be tied by any pact with the West. President Tito of Yugoslavia, who had defied the Communist bloc and had gotten away with it, proved to be a successful model for Nasser.

After Bandung, Nasser engaged in several defiant initiatives that further alarmed and angered the Western powers. In September 1955 he arranged a large-scale purchase of heavy Soviet arms through Czechoslovakia. In addition, Nasser's decision to recognize communist China in 1956 further separated Egypt from the West. Yet, even his decision to approach the Soviet government to buy arms was primarily a

question of business and security and not because he sympathized with the Soviet Union.

Nasser was never a communist or a Western tool but just an Egyptian nationalist who always encouraged Arab unity. Nasser had always worked for real Egyptian independence with no ties to the West or the East. What was important was the realization of a new, free, autonomous Egyptian state as part of the great dream of a strong and united Arab nation. In *The Philosophy of the Revolution* Nasser remarked rather enigmatically that history was full of great roles that had never found anyone to play them and that the Middle East was in search of a hero. Undoubtedly he had already come to the conclusion that he and Egypt were to fulfill this role and the Free Officers Revolution was the means to achieve it. This different class of rulers initiated new domestic policies and pursued drastically different foreign policies—it was, indeed, a revolutionary time.

–DANIELE DE LUCA,
UNIVERSITY OF LECCE

Viewpoint:
No. The Free Officers Revolution signaled the coming to power of a military dictatorship that imposed another form of authoritarianism.

The military putsch, led by the Free Officers secret organization within the Egyptian Army that resulted in the overthrow of the monarchical government headed by King Farouk I, was not a revolution. Although the Supreme Command Council, which assumed control of the government after 23 July 1952, differed drastically from the Palace and the popularly elected parliament that had hitherto governed Egypt, it had no distinct ideology, no plan of action, and no long-term goals for the nation. Only later did it rename itself the Revolutionary Command Council (RCC), after the term *revolution* became acceptable to Egypt's new rulers. Gamal Abd al-Nasser and his fellow officers were in their thirties and wanted mainly to oust Farouk, preserving the monarchy under a regency for his infant son, Ahmad Fuad II. The Free Officers turned the government over to a veteran politician, Ali Mahir, whom they viewed as untainted with the dishonesty commonly ascribed to pre-Revolutionary politicians. When Ali Mahir resigned in protest against their land reform program, they conferred the position of prime minister upon General Muhammad Neguib and, ultimately, upon themselves.

Egypt had been convulsed by a popular revolution following World War I (1914–1918), and the people naturally expected a sequel in 1945, but there was none. The defeat of the Egyptian Army at the hands of the Israelis in 1948–1949 was a national humiliation, but the repressive policies of the government led by Ibrahim Abd al-Hadi cowed the dissidents. The Wafd Party was swept back into power by a relatively free and fair election in January 1950. Its leader, Mustafa al-Nahhas, was unquestionably popular, and he appointed some reformers to his cabinet, including Taha Husayn as his education minister and Ahmad Husayn (the two men were not related) with the portfolio for social affairs. The Wafd, as Egypt's nationalist party, contained politicians from many points on the political spectrum, including a Wafdist vanguard that was starting to advocate socialism. Its leaders, though, were big landowners and wealthy businessmen. Nahhas, from a humble background, tended to defer to his ambitious young wife, Zaynab al-Wakil, whose family ranked higher than his in the pecking order. The Wafd in 1950 did pass legislation mandating free and compulsory educa-

tion, as guaranteed in Egypt's 1923 constitution, but it balked at land reform and other social issues. Neither the Party nor its vanguard faction could lead a popular revolution comparable to that of 1919, when the Wafd began.

The most revolutionary movements in Egyptian society were the communists and the Muslim Brothers (*al-Ikhwan al-Muslimin*). The first socialist was elected to Egypt's parliament in 1950, but the socialists' cautious approach to revolution led to their eclipse by the communists, who called for a radical restructuring of Egyptian society. There were two major Marxist movements, the Egyptian Communist Party and Hadeto (*al-Haraka al-dimuqratiyya li al-tahrir al-watani*, or Democratic Movement for National Liberation), as well as several splinter parties. Egyptian Muslims viewed communism as alien and atheistic and would have nothing to do with it; most Marxists were Jews, Greeks, and Egyptians who had been educated abroad. The stronger threat came from the Muslim Brothers, who had amassed widespread support from middle- and lower-class Muslims who resented the Westernization

Gamal Abd al-Nasser (seated left) and Muhammad Neguib (seated center) with other members of the Free Officers movement, July 1952

(© AP/Wide World Photos)

of Egyptian society and militantly resisted British imperialism, Israel, and manifestations of European and American culture. The Muslim Brothers were suppressed after they assassinated a prime minister in 1948 and lost their charismatic leader, Hasan al-Banna, in 1949. Extreme Egyptian nationalists had formerly gravitated to Young Egypt, but its fascist tendencies had blunted its appeal when Germany was defeated in World War II (1939–1945). Most informed Egyptians dismissed the officers in the army as upper class, apolitical, and loyal to King Farouk.

The pervasive sense of hopelessness in Egypt between 1949 and 1952 discredited the king and the status quo, and many Egyptian and foreign observers thought that some kind of a revolution was imminent. Farouk himself expected one. A murkier issue was how the British might react to a movement hostile to their occupation of Egypt. They still had eighty thousand troops in the Suez Canal region, in the largest military base in the noncommunist world; in the past, the British had intervened to quell overly ardent nationalists. Many groups of disgruntled army officers were known to exist, but no one expected that any were capable of organizing a revolution in the face of British and Egyptian intelligence. That the Free Officers, numbering less than a hundred, successfully took over the main army bases and government buildings on the night of 22–23 July 1952 was a notable achievement.

The Free Officers had no plan to govern Egypt. Their stated goals were to oust the British, clean up corruption, and then return to their barracks. Nasser had hoped that the people would rally behind them and that a leader would emerge to implement reforms. The people held back, however, and no leader materialized. Everyone who aspired to lead the country talked of keeping his rivals out of power. Factory laborers seeking higher wages and better working conditions went on strike at Kafr al-Dawwar three weeks after the military putsch and were promptly jailed and tried by the new leaders. The RCC did promulgate an agrarian reform program that limited the amount one person could own to 200 *feddans* (about 205 acres), though he could also retain up to 100 *feddans* for each of his sons. The RCC also began trying, jailing, and sometimes exiling leaders of the ancien régime. It abolished the ancient honorific titles of pasha and bey and discouraged men from wearing the fez. Some years were to pass before the new regime turned against foreigners and minorities. The government even relaxed an earlier requirement that at least 51 percent of the directors of any corporation in Egypt must be Egyptian. Both Neguib and Nasser hinted that they might make peace with Israel, mainly for foreign—not domestic—consumption.

The true Egyptian Revolution, however, occurred well after 1952. It was punctuated by the triumph of Nasser over Neguib (1954), the agreement to purchase arms from communist Czechoslovakia (1955), nationalization of the Suez Canal Company (1956), the aborted Anglo-French-Israeli attack later in that year, Egypt's union with Syria (1958), the building of the Aswan High Dam (1960–1971), and the nationalization of foreign- and Egyptian-owned firms in the name of Arab socialism. The July Laws of 1961 heralded the rise of Arab socialism, a doctrine that promised to better the lot of Egyptian workers and peasants and to weaken landowners and capitalists by further limiting landholdings and sequestering or nationalizing industrial, commercial, and financial firms. The creation of the Arab Socialist Union was supposed to inculcate socialism in the workers and peasants and to empower them to enter the political arena. By 1964 Egypt's government, economy, and society had become far more revolutionary than in the months following the 1952 coup.

These historic changes affirmed Egypt's independence; the triumphs were nationalist and political. The economic and social changes were short-lived, in part the result of the defeat of Egypt in the Arab-Israeli War of 1967 and later Anwar Sadat's "de-Nasserizing" policies during his presidency (1970–1981). Since 1952 Egypt has undergone few intellectual or cultural changes that could be termed revolutionary, and it is now apparent that the life of the mind has dimmed under the authoritarian rule of the Free Officers. Nasser was a popular leader who evolved as president toward leading an ongoing revolution in Egypt, but his policies proved costly and evanescent. The Egyptian people are more united now than they were a half century ago, no foreign military occupation curtails their freedom of action, and their government enjoys more foreign respect than it did under Farouk. The idea of revolution has faded, however, and most people act as if it had never really happened.

–ARTHUR GOLDSCHMIDT,
PENNSYLVANIA STATE UNIVERSITY

References

Anouar Abdel-Malek, *Egypt: Military Society* (New York: Random House, 1968).

FREE OFFICERS REVOLUTION

Kirk J. Beattie, *Egypt during the Nasser Years: Ideology, Politics, and Civil Society* (Boulder, Colo.: Westview Press, 1994).

Miles Copeland, *The Game of Nations* (London: Weidenfeld & Nicolson, 1970).

Arthur Goldschmidt, *Modern Egypt: The Formation of a Nation-State* (Boulder, Colo.: Westview Press, 1988).

Joel Gordon, *Nasser's Blessed Movement: Egypt's Free Officers and the July Revolution* (New York: Oxford University Press, 1992).

Derek Hopwood, *Egypt: Politics and Society 1945–1990* (London & New York: Routledge, 1993).

Peter Mansfield, *Nasser's Egypt* (Baltimore: Penguin, 1965).

Khaled Mohi El Din, *Memories of a Revolution: Egypt, 1952* (Cairo: American University in Cairo Press, 1995).

Mohammed Naguib, *Egypt's Destiny: A Personal Statement* (Garden City, N.Y.: Doubleday, 1955).

Gamal Abd al-Nasser, *Egypt's Liberation: The Philosophy of the Revolution* (Cairo: Information Department, 1954).

Anwar El Sadat, *Revolt on the Nile* (New York: John Day, 1957).

P. J. Vatikiotis, *Nasser and His Generation* (New York: St. Martin's Press, 1978).

GULF WAR 1991: ENTRY

Did the United States enter the Persian Gulf War to deter Iraq from developing weapons of mass destruction?

Viewpoint: Yes. The United States entered the Persian Gulf War primarily to oppose military aggression against Kuwait and to halt the proliferation of weapons of mass destruction.

Viewpoint: No. The United States entered the Persian Gulf War for less-than-altruistic reasons, including the protection of oil and business investments.

Iraq invaded and took over the Persian Gulf sheikhdom of Kuwait on 2 August 1990, thus initiating what came to be known in the West as the Persian Gulf Crisis and War (1990–1991). It was a shocking move that took the world by surprise despite knowledge of Iraqi president Saddam Hussein's troop buildup along the Kuwaiti border to the south during the previous month. In many ways the Iran-Iraq War (1980–1988), or what is known in the region as the First Gulf War (the 1990–1991 episode thus termed the Second Gulf War), set the stage for Iraq's invasion. After an initial advance during the First Gulf War, Iraqi forces suffered several setbacks, and Iran advanced into Iraqi territory; following a prolonged stalemate, a cease-fire was reached in August 1988. Hussein claimed victory in the Iran-Iraq War, creating heightened expectations within the military and among the populace for some sort of victory dividend. The problem was that Iraq was severely in debt, having gone from a more than $60 billion surplus before the Iran-Iraq War to a $40 billion debt after the war ended, with billions of dollars of reconstruction left to be done because of the damage inflicted by Iran. Dictators need money. Hussein saw the "bank" to the south called Kuwait, with its lucrative oil fields (which would give Iraq, in addition to its own substantial oil reserves, control over 21 percent of the world's proven oil reserves), and wanted to initiate his own type of merger and acquisition. A significant portion of the Iraqi national debt was owed to Kuwait, which supported Iraq against Iran; however, the Iraqis felt that the Kuwaitis should just erase the debt since they had, in essence, protected Kuwait with their blood and incurred the cost of the physical destruction of a good part of Iraq—surely that was worth more than what they owed the Kuwaitis; however, Kuwait declined to forgive the debt.

In addition, Iraq had some outstanding territorial issues with the Kuwaitis that had not been satisfactorily put to rest, including ownership rights to the Rumaylah oil field that sat astride the border and the Bubiyan and Warba islands belonging to Kuwait just off its northern coast. The Iranian conquest of the Faw Peninsula in 1986 had indicated to the Iraqis just how easily they could be cut off from the Persian Gulf—and how crippling this situation was to its oil industry. Iraqi control of the islands (and Baghdad had repeatedly tried to negotiate a lease arrangement with Kuwait) would provide it with better access to the Gulf; indeed, taking Kuwait would expand the Iraqi coastline, thus making it less vulnerable in the future to any Iranian thrust across the Shatt al-Arab waterway, the confluence of the Tigris and Euphrates Rivers in southern Iraq that flows into the Persian Gulf.

Officially, the Iraqis declared that they were just taking back what was rightfully theirs, in other words, that Kuwait was the "19th province" of Iraq. This assertion was a rather specious claim that pointed to the fact that during the days of the Ottoman Empire, Kuwait had been a district within the province of Basra, modern Iraq's second-largest city; the Iraqi government failed to acknowledge, however, that during Ottoman times there was nothing administratively known as "Iraq," the country being rather artificially formed following the breakup of the empire after World War I (1914–1918).

Perhaps the main reason Hussein invaded Kuwait was that he thought he could get away with it. In fact, he came close to doing just that. Why he felt this way, and why it was a legitimate thought process, stems in part from the Iran-Iraq War, particularly the strong strategic and commercial relationship Baghdad built up with the United States during the course of the conflict, brought together by the mutual priority of preventing an Iranian victory. Washington and Baghdad reestablished diplomatic relations in 1984 (which had been broken ever since the 1967 Arab-Israeli War), and the Reagan and Bush administrations believed Iraq could be a useful surrogate in both the Persian Gulf and Arab-Israeli arenas, filling the empty shoes of both the Shah of Iran, who had been the policeman of the Gulf for the United States until his overthrow in 1979, and Egypt's Anwar Sadat, who was assassinated by Islamist extremists in 1981 for having made peace with Israel. Bush officials, inheriting previous policy, tended to overlook the excesses of Hussein's actions in the latter part of the war with Iran, in the interim period after the war, and preceding the invasion of Kuwait. Indeed, President George H. W. Bush and Secretary of State James Baker admitted in the aftermath of the Gulf War that they "stayed" with Saddam too long, hoping to moderate his behavior so that he might become Washington's new gendarme of the Gulf region and even a moderating influence in the Arab-Israeli arena.

The Iraqi president, on the other hand, possibly in a case of hearing only what he wanted to hear, also failed to read Washington's signals indicating its opposition to many of his policies, not least of which was the buildup of troops along the Kuwaiti border. Instead, he focused on ambiguous statements from a host of U.S. officials regarding the Kuwaiti situation during the summer of 1990 as proof of American disinterest in protecting a nondemocratic regime with which Washington had not previously had a particularly close relationship—especially if the oil kept flowing at reasonable prices. Hussein also apparently concluded that the United States was still hampered by the Vietnam War syndrome, and it had as a result little stomach to engage in another conflict so far from home. Furthermore, with the end of the superpower Cold War, it was obvious that the invasion, even though Iraq was considered a Soviet client state, was not directed by the Kremlin; therefore, there was no rationale, and there would be little public or congressional support, for the United States to send half a million troops halfway across the globe as it had done in Korea (1950–1953) and Vietnam (ending 1975) during the height of the Cold War.

Hussein obviously miscalculated. The Bush administration began a six-month buildup of forces in the Persian Gulf region and put together an impressive array of twenty-nine countries in a United Nations (UN)-mandated coalition with the express purpose of evicting Iraq from Kuwait. The U.S.-led forces began the air campaign in mid January 1991, with the ground offensive beginning in February, the latter taking only about one hundred hours to liberate Kuwait.

Viewpoint:
Yes. The United States entered the Persian Gulf War primarily to oppose military aggression against Kuwait and to halt the proliferation of weapons of mass destruction.

The Bush administration's decision to lead a coalition to attack Iraq in January 1991 was the result of several factors: the need to force Iraq to leave Kuwait and return to the international border; unwillingness to allow Iraq to dominate the region and threaten Saudi Arabia and other U.S. allies; concern regarding the impact of Iraqi control over a large portion of Middle Eastern oil production; and the implications of Iraqi efforts

to acquire weapons of mass destruction (WMD) and long-range ballistic missiles.

The Persian Gulf War (1990–1991) took place against the backdrop of the end of the Cold War, the collapse of the Soviet Union, and the emergence of the United States as the world's only superpower. In this political environment, the Bush administration was determined to preserve international stability and pursue a "new world order," which would increase security and prevent the growth of new strategic threats to the United States and the world. The Iraqi invasion of Kuwait was the first international crisis of the post–Cold War era, and the United States was aware of the degree to which its response would be carefully examined. If allowed to stand, Iraq's blatant aggression and the violation of the sovereignty of a member of

U.S. troops after disembarking from a civilian airliner in Kuwait, 1990

(Magnum Photo/Delahaye Luc)

the United Nations (UN) would set a dangerous precedent, particularly in the troubled and unstable Middle East.

In addition, Iraq under Saddam Hussein had become a troublesome source of regional instability, threatening to engulf the entire area in a series of bitter wars. Although the United States had provided some support to the Iraqi dictator during the Iran-Iraq War (1980–1988), this balance-of-power policy was understood to be highly problematic. Hussein's increasing extremism, including threats to use chemical weapons against Israel, added to the concerns. Despite the economic costs of the long war with Iran, Iraq continued to pour oil revenues into the acquisition of a large army (maintained long after the cease-fire with Iran) and to purchase combat aircraft, tanks, tank transporters, missiles, and other weapons. More than fifty combat divisions were created; mobile weapons systems could be transferred quickly to the Saudi border or, in seventy-two hours, through Jordan to a confrontation with Israel. The quick Iraqi conquest of Kuwait showed that his capability could and would be used to advance Hussein's often-stated goal of dominating the Middle East. In this environment, America's primary interests were challenged, and a military response became necessary when diplomacy failed to dislodge the Iraqi army.

The greatest source of concern to the United States was the arsenal of WMD being developed and acquired by Hussein. The importance of this capability, and the willingness to use such weapons, was demonstrated during the war with Iran, when Iraqi forces attacked civilians in the Kurdish regions with chemical weapons, as well as repelled Iranian attacks. Iraq also fired hundreds of SCUD missiles at Iranian cities, eventually leading to their evacuation. The chemical attacks and conventional missile bombardments were considered essential in preventing an Iranian victory.

In addition to the tons of chemical weapons (mustard gas, sarin, and VX) known to be in the Iraqi inventory, the continued pursuit of nuclear weapons added an even greater cause for concern in Washington. Iraq had been known to be seeking nuclear weapons for many years. In 1981 the Israeli Air Force destroyed the French-supplied reactor that was to be the primary source of fissile material, but Iraq resumed these efforts after the cease-fire agreement with Iran. At first, as U.S. intelligence assets were still largely focused on the Soviet Union, the Iraqi nuclear program received little attention, but after the invasion of Kuwait, American and Israeli security officials began to see more signs of activity. In November 1990 the goal of destroying Iraq's nuclear program became a central theme in the justifications offered by President George H. W. Bush and other officials with respect to the planned coalition attack against Iraq.

Indeed, following the war, UN weapons inspectors were surprised to discover a highly advanced Iraqi nuclear-weapons program that had been hidden from the International Atomic Energy Agency (IAEA) verification system, in violation of the Nuclear Non-Proliferation Treaty (1968). Iraq had begun to produce enriched uranium using electromagnetic separation technology (a process dating from the 1940s) and was also holding a significant amount of uranium obtained for use in a reactor, but available for bomb making as well. An Iraqi team of nuclear scientists was also found to have completed design and testing of a bomb casing for use once the required amount of fissile material had been obtained.

In addition, Iraq was pursuing biological agents, including anthrax and smallpox, for use in attacks and to threaten opposing forces and their home countries. At the same time, the range of Hussein's arsenal of SCUD missiles, which were used with great effectiveness against Iran, was being extended. In 1988 Iraq even attempted to place a satellite in orbit, demonstrating at least a first-generation ability to produce an intercontinental ballistic missile (ICBM) capable of striking both Europe and the United States. During the war, dozens of extended-range SCUDs, fired from mobile launchers and carefully hidden from coalition aircraft, were fired at Israel and Saudi Arabia.

Thus, in the course of the crisis triggered by the Iraqi invasion of Kuwait in August 1990, the focus of U.S. concern and policy shifted from deterring further aggression and blocking instability in the Middle East to the prevention of acquisition of WMD by Hussein. The Americans recognized the dangers posed by a tyrannical leader, willing to take huge risks and sacrifice the lives of millions, including citizens of his own country, and armed with WMD and long-range missiles. The centrality of these goals was highlighted after the Iraqi withdrawal from Kuwait and the acceptance of the terms for a cease-fire. In the postwar environment, the United States continued to place primary emphasis on destroying the remaining WMD facilities and materials hidden throughout Iraq. This goal was clearly indicated in UN Security Council Resolution 687, the maintenance of sanctions to try to prevent further acquisition of these weapons and related dual-use technology, and the establishment of the UN Special Commission (UNSCOM) to implement the disarmament of Iraq. Indeed, the Iraqi efforts to impede the work of UNSCOM in completing and verifying this process, as well as the failure of the sanctions

efforts, led to a continuing dispute between the United States and Iraq, which erupted again in 2001 and resulted in the American invasion of Iraq two years later.

–GERALD STEINBERG,
BAR ILAN UNIVERSITY

Viewpoint:
No. The United States entered the Persian Gulf War for less-than-altruistic reasons, including the protection of oil and business investments.

Iraq invaded Kuwait, in what became known as the Persian Gulf War (1990–1991), because the latter was drilling oil that belonged to the former. Yet, Iraq did not rush to war. It first tried to assess the position of the United States. On 25 July 1990, when Iraqi president Saddam Hussein asked the U.S. ambassador to Iraq, April Glaspie, the U.S. position on the escalating Iraq-Kuwait conflict, she replied that the United States would not become involved in Arab-Arab conflicts "such as your dispute with Kuwait." Within days after getting that green light, Iraq invaded Kuwait. A more difficult question is why the United States went to war against Iraq.

With the end of the Cold War, the United States needed a new enemy, especially if the Pentagon were going to be able to keep the military at Cold War levels in regard to personnel and equipment. Without a new adversary, major military contractors such as Boeing, Lockheed Martin, McDonnell Douglas, General Dynamics, Northrop Grumman, and Veridian (to name a few) just might be so adversely impacted by a sudden termination of orders that their inevitable layoffs would severely impact American unemployment levels, which were already on the rise in the late 1980s.

Military and political experts could not agree upon one singular threat to take the place of the Soviet Union, or what President Ronald Reagan referred to as the "evil empire." Instead, American theorists envisioned that a future threat would come from not one but from multiple countries. As no one country was powerful enough to successfully threaten the United States or its interests, several countries were expected to gang up, attacking U.S. interests simultaneously. One of the new theories, called the rogue-state doctrine, stated that countries such as Libya, Syria, Iraq, and North Korea would attack the United States or its interests in different parts of the world.

President George H. W. Bush envisioned that the United States, as the sole superpower,

NEW WORLD ORDER

On 11 September 1990 President George H. W. Bush went before a joint session of Congress and explained his reasons for pursuing war in the Middle East:

Our objectives in the Persian Gulf are clear, our goals defined and familiar: Iraq must withdraw from Kuwait completely, immediately, and without condition. Kuwait's legitimate government must be restored. The security and stability of the Persian Gulf must be assured. And American citizens abroad must be protected. These goals are not ours alone. They've been endorsed by the United Nations Security Council five times in as many weeks. Most countries share our concern for principle. And many have a stake in the stability of the Persian Gulf. This is not, as Saddam Hussein would have it, the United States against Iraq. It is Iraq against the world.

As you know, I've just returned from a very productive meeting with Soviet President Gorbachev. And I am pleased that we are working together to build a new relationship. In Helsinki, our joint statement affirmed to the world our shared resolve to counter Iraq's threat to peace. Let me quote: "We are united in the belief that Iraq's aggression must not be tolerated. No peaceful international order is possible if larger states can devour their smaller neighbors." Clearly, no longer can a dictator count on East-West confrontation to stymie concerted United Nations action against aggression. A new partnership of nations has begun.

We stand today at a unique and extraordinary moment. The crisis in the Persian Gulf, as grave as it is, also offers a rare opportunity to move toward an historic period of cooperation. Out of these troubled times, our fifth objective—a new world order—can emerge: a new era—freer from the threat of terror, stronger in the pursuit of justice, and more secure in the quest for peace. An era in which the nations of the world, East and West, North and South, can prosper and live in harmony. A hundred generations have

searched for this elusive path to peace, while a thousand wars raged across the span of human endeavor. Today that new world is struggling to be born, a world quite different from the one we've known. A world where the rule of law supplants the rule of the jungle. A world in which nations recognize the shared responsibility for freedom and justice. A world where the strong respect the rights of the weak. This is the vision that I shared with President Gorbachev in Helsinki. He and other leaders from Europe, the Gulf, and around the world understand that how we manage this crisis today could shape the future for generations to come.

The test we face is great, and so are the stakes. This is the first assault on the new world that we seek, the first test of our mettle. Had we not responded to this first provocation with clarity of purpose, if we do not continue to demonstrate our determination, it would be a signal to actual and potential despots around the world. America and the world must defend common vital interests—and we will. America and the world must support the rule of law—and we will. America and the world must stand up to aggression—and we will. And one thing more: In the pursuit of these goals America will not be intimidated.

Vital issues of principle are at stake. Saddam Hussein is literally trying to wipe a country off the face of the Earth. We do not exaggerate. Nor do we exaggerate when we say Saddam Hussein will fail. Vital economic interests are at risk as well. Iraq itself controls some 10 percent of the world's proven oil reserves. Iraq plus Kuwait controls twice that. An Iraq permitted to swallow Kuwait would have the economic and military power, as well as the arrogance, to intimidate and coerce its neighbors—neighbors who control the lion's share of the world's remaining oil reserves. We cannot permit a resource so vital to be dominated by one so ruthless. And we won't.

would become the linchpin from which the world would turn, but Hussein upset Bush's plan by invading Kuwait. Thus, to prove to the world that the United States would dominate Bush's new world order, and in the absence of the Soviet Union—in other words, there was no country to counter the United States in the Middle East—the Americans invaded Iraq in order to prove the veracity of this new-world-order thesis.

During the waning years of the Reagan administration, the United States recognized the Palestine Liberation Organization (PLO) as the legitimate representative of the Palestinian people and thus began a series of discussions between American and PLO representatives in Tunis. By 1990 it became apparent to U.S. decision makers that Yasser Arafat, head of the PLO, was either unwilling or unable to meet American requests,

Recent events have surely proven that there is no substitute for American leadership. In the face of tyranny, let no one doubt American credibility and reliability. Let no one doubt our staying power. We will stand by our friends. One way or another, the leader of Iraq must learn this fundamental truth. From the outset, acting hand in hand with others, we've sought to fashion the broadest possible international response to Iraq's aggression. The level of world cooperation and condemnation of Iraq is unprecedented. Armed forces from countries spanning four continents are there at the request of King Fahd of Saudi Arabia to deter and, if need be, to defend against attack. Moslems and non-Moslems, Arabs and non-Arabs, soldiers from many nations stand shoulder to shoulder, resolute against Saddam Hussein's ambitions.

We can now point to five United Nations Security Council resolutions that condemn Iraq's aggression. They call for Iraq's immediate and unconditional withdrawal, the restoration of Kuwait's legitimate government, and categorically reject Iraq's cynical and self-serving attempt to annex Kuwait. Finally, the United Nations has demanded the release of all foreign nationals held hostage against their will and in contravention of international law. It is a mockery of human decency to call these people "guests." They are hostages, and the whole world knows it.

Prime Minister Margaret Thatcher, a dependable ally, said it all: "We do not bargain over hostages. We will not stoop to the level of using human beings as bargaining chips ever." Of course, of course, our hearts go out to the hostages and to their families. But our policy cannot change, and it will not change. America and the world will not be blackmailed by this ruthless policy.

We're now in sight of a United Nations that performs as envisioned by its founders. We owe much to the outstanding leadership of Secretary-General Javier Perez de Cuellar. The United Nations is backing up its words with action. The Security Council has imposed mandatory economic sanctions on Iraq, designed to force Iraq to relinquish the spoils of its illegal conquest. The Security Council has also taken the decisive step of authorizing the use of all means necessary to ensure compliance with these sanctions. Together with our friends and allies, ships of the United States Navy are today patrolling Mideast waters. They've already intercepted more than 700 ships to enforce the sanctions. Three regional leaders I spoke with just yesterday told me that these sanctions are working. Iraq is feeling the heat. We continue to hope that Iraq's leaders will recalculate just what their aggression has cost them. They are cut off from world trade, unable to sell their oil. And only a tiny fraction of goods gets through. . . .

I cannot predict just how long it will take to convince Iraq to withdraw from Kuwait. Sanctions will take time to have their full intended effect. We will continue to review all options with our allies, but let it be clear: we will not let this aggression stand.

Our interest, our involvement in the Gulf is not transitory. It predated Saddam Hussein's aggression and will survive it. Long after all our troops come home—and we all hope it's soon, very soon—there will be a lasting role for the United States in assisting the nations of the Persian Gulf. Our role then: to deter future aggression. Our role is to help our friends in their own self-defense. And something else: to curb the proliferation of chemical, biological, ballistic missiles and, above all, nuclear technologies.

Let me also make clear that the United States has no quarrel with the Iraqi people. Our quarrel is with Iraq's dictator and with his aggression. Iraq will not be permitted to annex Kuwait. That's not a threat, that's not a boast, that's just the way it's going to be.

Source: *"Toward a New World Order: A Transcript of Former President George Herbert Walker Bush's Address to a Joint Session of Congress and the Nation," Council on Domestic Relations <http://www.sweetliberty.org/issues/war/bushsr.htm>.*

such as the Bush administration's instruction to the PLO to discipline Abu Abbas and members of the Palestinian Liberation Front for the attack on the Italian cruise ship *Achille Lauro* (1985). In addition, it appeared to the United States that Arafat was possibly cultivating new sources of financial, political, and logistical support.

According to scholar William B. Quandt, Arafat was spending "increasing amounts of time in Baghdad, and reports were received that he was thinking of moving his political headquarters there from Tunis." Furthermore, Salah Khalaf, also known as Abu Iyad, one of Arafat's advisers, noted that "Arafat was coming under Saddam's influence" and further reported that an earlier attempt by Abbas's organization to infiltrate and attack targets in and around Tel Aviv was an Iraqi operation. Thus, for the first time it appeared that the Palestinian-Israeli conflict could become even more deadly if Iraq continued to offer aid and support to Palestinian attackers operating in Israel and the Occupied Territories (West Bank, Gaza Strip, and Golan Heights). Moreover, some in Israel feared that the end of the Cold War would decrease Israel's value to the United States, while at the same time Israel would fall under increased pan-Arab threats, especially if one Arab leader with enough oil wealth and a sizable military were able to use either a carrot or a stick to develop a pan-Arab/anti-Israeli military front. The United States thus also went to war against Iraq in order to sever Palestinian-Iraqi relations and to prevent the development of a pan-Arab/anti-Israeli nexus by Hussein through the use of the combined oil wealth of Iraq and Kuwait.

It is no surprise that U.S. decision makers were concerned about Iraqi control over Kuwaiti oil. As Quandt noted, "If Saddam controlled Iraqi and Kuwaiti oil supplies directly, and if he kept troops on the Saudi border, he would in fact dominate the Gulf's vast reserves of oil and would become a one-man OPEC, able to manipulate the supply of oil and to achieve whatever price he wanted." In fact, President Bush noted the "vital economic interests" of oil in his 11 September 1990 address to the joint session of Congress.

American companies controlled nearly three-quarters of Iraqi oil production prior to Iraq's nationalization of its oil industry in 1973. As scholar Khalil al-Anani points out, the American loss resulted in gains for France and Russia. Maybe the United States saw the Iraqi invasion of Kuwait as a pretext to regain its position in the international oil community. Joe Stork, editor of the *Middle East Report*, concluded, "the fact that Japan and Europe are more dependent on oil imports from the Persian Gulf than the US has led some to conclude that the US used this crisis as an opportunity to position itself to control the access of its chief competitors to this vital resource."

Iraq needed money as a result of the Iran-Iraq War (1980–1988); Baghdad's debt was approximately $40 billion (other estimates range as high as $100 billion); and Japan had cut off Iraq's credit. The Soviet Union put increasing pressure upon Iraq to pay its loans, and even European airlines stopped paying the Iraqi tax on airline tickets. Of course, the biggest holders of notes were Saudi Arabia and Kuwait. Sandra Mackey estimates that Iraq owed approximately $35 billion to those two oil kingdoms. There was little chance for these countries to recover their loans without going to war.

The United States had also loaned much money to Iraq. In 1989 the Bush administration forwarded $1 billion in loan guarantees to Iraq, even against the advice of the Treasury Department. Iraq had been a good trading partner, especially for American wheat (particularly from states such as Kansas). In 1989 the Department of State said that Iraq was "key to maintaining stability in the region, offering great trade opportunities for U.S. companies." If the United States were ever to get its money back, it could not allow Iraq to become a "one-man OPEC." Senator Robert Dole (R–Kansas) and other influential Republican senators traveled to Baghdad to shore up Iraqi wheat purchases. In addition, if Midwestern politicians were to continue to enjoy the support of their grain farmers, then the United States would have to attack in order to assure future U.S.-Iraqi trade.

In fact, the war helped American companies. For example, Kuwait declined to purchase British-made Challenger tanks and instead bought M-1A tanks made by General Dynamics. As Stork noted, American companies, such as Bechtel, "have done very well in the post-war reconstruction contracts." An article in *International Politics Journal* reported that "Iraq purchased millions of dollars worth of grain and other commodities from the US on favourable credit and financing terms. This trading relationship was actively supported by several influential Republican senators, such as Robert Dole and Alan Simpson." The United States was not going to get a return from its investment unless it went to war. In other words, the United States went to war against Iraq in order to force Iraq to pay its loans, to shore up U.S. trade, and to create even more markets for its companies in postwar Iraq.

The United States cultivated close ties with the Hussein regime for several decades. In the 1980s, long before George W. Bush, Donald Rumsfeld, Dick Cheney, and Colin Powell asserted in 2003 that Iraq controlled weapons of mass destruction (WMD), George H. W. Bush, Rumsfeld, Cheney, and Powell were actively involved in providing, and then allowing the Hussein regime to construct and use, WMD against Iran and against his own people, primarily the Kurds.

During the Bush administration, more than $1.5 billion worth of U.S. technology was sent to Iraq. American companies such as Hewlett-Packard, Honeywell, Unisys, International Computer Systems, Rockwell, and Tetronix all signed trade agreements with the Iraqi Atomic Energy Commission. Furthermore, U.S. companies such as the American Type Culture Collection provided Iraq with anthrax, botulinum, and *E. coli* to establish biological weapons. According to Representative Sam Gejdenson (D–Conn.), "From 1985 to 1990, the United States Government approved 771 licenses for the export to Iraq of $1.5 billion worth of biological agents and high-tech equipment with military application."

The United States not only supplied Iraq with the necessary technology and supplies to develop their own chemical and biological weapons programs, it also never registered a complaint when Iraq used those agents. As M. Cherif Bassiouni points out, "the US turned a blind eye to Iraq's use of chemical weapons in 1983 against Iranian civilians in two border regions. This included such internationally prohibited weaponising of mustard gas, sarin, and VX poisonous agents." Americans provided not only the ability for Iraq to develop its own WMD program, but it also provided Iraq with the necessary intelligence (such as satellite targeting information) to ensure proper delivery of its poisons during the Iran-Iraq War.

U.S. support continued even in the face of Iraq's most hideous chemical attack against a civilian population. In 1988 an estimated 100,000 Kurds were killed by poison gas during the Anfal campaign—5,000 alone in the town of Halabja. According to the *Christian Science Monitor*, "During the Anfal campaign, [human] rights groups say more than 100,000 men disappeared, 4,000 villages were destroyed, and 60 more villages were subject to chemical weapons attack."

The sin that Hussein committed on 2 August 1990 was not one of naked aggression. Rather, the Iraqi government seemed no longer appreciative of all the things the United States did to build and support its military complex when it no longer answered to U.S. decision makers. In other words, Iraq's sin was to evolve into a country with foreign and domestic policies that the United States could no longer control. As philosopher Noam Chomsky said, "the problem is not crimes, but insubordination." Thus, the United States invaded Iraq in order to discipline it for acting outside the command and control of U.S. policy makers.

The United States did not go to war against Iraq in order to protect the Kuwaiti people from a brutal invasion and an illegal occupation. As Middle East specialist Phyllis Bennis points out, "Iraq was not, after all, the first Middle East country to invade and occupy a neighbor. Morocco remained occupying Western Sahara; Turkey had invaded Northern Cyprus and maintained a rump 'Turkish Republic' there since 1974; and Israel continued its internationally-condemned occupation of the Palestinian West Bank, Gaza, East Jerusalem, as well as the Syrian Golan Heights."

The United States did not go to war against Iraq in order to protect the rich democratic history of and long tradition of gender equality in Kuwait. Instead, the United States attacked Iraq for a plethora of less-than-altruistic reasons, which included testing its newest theory on how the world should be ordered, the Palestinian-Israeli conflict, money, oil, trade, and the ultimate sin of insubordination.

Maybe the United States invaded because President Bush, who along with his predecessor believed that the War Powers Act (1973) was unconstitutional, wanted to test his thesis and thus committed troops in what he believed to be a popular war. Bush's attempt to challenge the War Powers Act ran into trouble. Senator Henry B. Gonzales (D–Texas) sought to have President Bush impeached in 1991, charging that Bush had violated the Hague Convention, the Geneva Conventions, the Nuremberg Charter, the Genocide Convention, the United Nations (UN) Declaration of Human Rights, and the War Powers Act. Gonzales also levied lesser charges against Bush, such as bribery when he promised aid to several members of the UN (such as Egypt, Russia, Germany, Colombia, Zaire, and Saudi Arabia) if they voted in support of the U.S. resolution against Iraq in 1990. There is no singular, or clear, reason for why the United States invaded Iraq; however, these many theories dovetail rather nicely to better facilitate our understanding as to the less-than-altruistic reasons behind the U.S. attack on Iraq.

–JIM ROSS-NAZZAL,
MONTGOMERY COLLEGE

References

Phyllis Bennis and Michel Moushabeck, eds., *Altered States: A Reader in the New World Order* (New York: Olive Branch Press, 1993).

Lawrence Freedman and Efraim Karsh, *The Gulf Conflict, 1990–1991: Diplomacy and War in the New World Order* (Princeton: Princeton University Press, 1993).

Majid Khadduri and Edmund Ghareeb, *War in the Gulf, 1990–1991: The Iraq-Kuwait Conflict and its Implications* (New York: Oxford University Press, 1997).

Michael Klare, *Rogue States and Nuclear Outlaws: America's Search for a New Foreign Policy* (New York: Hill & Wang, 1995).

David W. Lesch, ed., *The Middle East and the United States: A Historical and Political Reassessment* (Boulder, Colo.: Westview Press, 1996, 1999, 2003).

Micah L. Sifry and Christopher Cerf, eds., *The Gulf War Reader* (New York: Times Books, 1991).

U.S. News & World Report, *Triumph without Victory: The History of the Persian Gulf War* (New York: Times Books, 1993).

GULF WAR 1991: EXIT

Was the Bush administration wise to terminate the Persian Gulf War before forcibly ousting Saddam Hussein?

Viewpoint: Yes. If coalition forces had gone further into Iraq, international support for the war effort would have dissipated, negating chances for the Madrid peace process and leading to a heavy U.S. investment in lives and matériel.

Viewpoint: No. The United States ended the Persian Gulf War (1990–1991) prematurely; it should have removed Saddam Hussein from power when it had the opportunity to do so with broad international support.

The Persian Gulf War (1990–1991) ended on 28 February following a one-hundred-hour ground offensive by U.S.-led coalition forces that succeeded in expelling Iraqi forces from Kuwait. At the time, most observers expected the regime of Iraqi president Saddam Hussein to fall either from the pressure of elements within the regime itself or from opposition forces in the Kurdish north or the Shiite-dominated southern regions of the country. It was only as Hussein hung onto power after the war, seemingly ignoring United Nations (UN) resolutions and inspection teams attempting to monitor and destroy Iraq's weapons of mass destruction (WMD) program, that the question of whether the administration of George H. W. Bush ended the war too soon became an issue of debate and conjecture. In other words, should the Bush administration have ensured the fall of Hussein in 1991 when it clearly had the upper hand, when it had coalition forces in the area, and when Iraqi forces were in considerable disarray following their defeat?

This issue had become especially pertinent by 2003 because of the course of events that preceded the second Persian Gulf War waged by Bush's son, President George W. Bush, that removed the Baathist regime of Hussein from power. The implication surrounding the issue (and outright charge in some cases) is that Saddam's removal should have been done correctly the first time around, thus negating the impetus to go to war again in 2003 as well as the decade of frustration that enveloped the relationships between Iraq, the United States, and the UN.

**Viewpoint:
Yes. If coalition forces had gone
further into Iraq, international
support for the war effort would
have dissipated, negating chances
for the Madrid peace process and
leading to a heavy U.S. investment
in lives and matériel.**

When the administration of George H. W.
Bush ended the Persian Gulf War (1990–1991)
on 28 February by declaring a cease-fire, it did so
at the appropriate time. Over the past decade or
so, however, Bush has been relentlessly admonished by critics from both the Left and Right of
the political spectrum for having ended the war
too soon, thus allowing Iraqi president Saddam
Hussein and his repressive regime to remain in
power. Because Hussein remained in Baghdad
and continued to be a thorn in the side of the
United States as well as the international community, the chorus of those who believed Bush
stopped the war too soon grew proportionately.
This discontent was especially the case as the
United States in 2003 was poised to engage Iraq
in another Gulf War, with or without the United
Nations (UN) and this time, according to many,
not only to disarm Iraq of weapons of mass
destruction (WMD) but also to effect regime
change in Baghdad; in other words, to finish off
a job that should have been completed in 1991.

The general rationale behind the decision of
the Bush administration to terminate the first Persian Gulf War when it did was generally lauded the
world over at the time on strategic, legal, and
humanitarian grounds. President Bush and Secretary of State James Baker had worked assiduously
to piece together what came to be called the Gulf
War coalition. It was a UN-mandated coalition
led, of course, by the United States. It included
many countries from all over the globe, providing
various military services. Most important, it
comprised several Arab states as well, including
Syria, which had been at the forefront of the
Arab countries arrayed against Israel over the
years. In other words, the Arab contingent in the
coalition was made up of not just the usual
American allies in the region, such as Egypt,
Morocco, and Saudi Arabia, but also countries
that traditionally had, at best, strained relations
with Washington, D.C. This support was a tremendous achievement in American diplomacy.

Now, the cynic would say that garnering the
UN resolution that provided for the use of force
to evict Iraq from Kuwait was as much a domestic maneuver to bludgeon a skeptical Congress
into granting such authority as it was an act of
international diplomacy—and this argument is

partly true. (The Joint Congressional Resolution
authorizing the use of force was passed on 12
January 1991.) One could also argue that the
timing for such UN Security Council support
(or at least the lack of opposition) was never so
perfect, coming as it did on the heels of the end
of the Cold War and with a reeling Soviet Union
only about a year from disintegrating and in dire
need of economic support from the West—this
contention is also true. Regardless of whether
the Bush administration would have acted unilaterally if it had not acquired UN authorization to
use force, it in fact went through the UN, and it
was, therefore, for the sake of international legitimacy and UN viability, bound to abide by the
strictures set forth in UN Security Council Resolution 678, passed on 29 November 1990. (Cuba
and Yemen voted against, China abstained, and
the other twelve members of the Security Council voted in favor.) The resolution called on Iraq
to comply with the previous eleven resolutions
passed since Iraq invaded Kuwait, including,
most importantly, the call for its withdrawal
from the country. If it had not done so by 15
January 1991, the member states were authorized "to use all necessary means to uphold and
implement" the resolutions and "restore international peace and security in the area." The use of
"all necessary means" is diplomatic code for the
use of force, which President Bush made clear in
subsequent statements.

The collective will of the United Nations—
and the international community—as expressed
in UN resolutions was for the liberation of
Kuwait; in other words, to push Iraqi forces out
of the Persian Gulf emirate. It was not to effect
regime change in Baghdad by bringing the war
into Iraq in an offensive strategic manner. Yes,
U.S.-led coalition forces entered Iraq on the
ground, and a good portion of Iraq was bom-
barded during the air campaign that began on 17
January, but this activity was for the sole purpose of facilitating the coalition's military
actions and gaining strategic advantage in successfully attempting to oust Iraqi forces from
Kuwait, thereby fulfilling the UN mandate. Few
people, of course, would have shed a tear if Hussein's regime fell in the process of liberating
Kuwait and decimating Iraq's military capability,
but despite possible unofficial attempts to kill
Hussein through precision air attacks, this overthrow was not the stated purpose of the U.S.-led
coalition. Since President Bush saw the Gulf crisis and war in the wake of the end of the superpower Cold War as auguring a "New World
Order" of international cooperation toward the
negation of the type of "naked aggression" perpetrated by Hussein, exceeding the mandate by
overtly effecting regime change and moving
troops deep into Iraq would have undermined

the very framework of international relations he was trying to create.

If the United States had "taken care of business" in 1991 by getting rid of Hussein, the UN coalition would have broken apart. Certainly the Arab states would have cried foul and accused the United States of using the situation in the Persian Gulf as an excuse to establish an imperium in the region, which had actually been the mantra of those few states who were outwardly opposed to the U.S.-led military riposte–they would have been proven correct. Also, several European states would have probably split from the coalition at a time when U.S.-European solidarity and cooperation were vitally necessary in managing the breakup of the Soviet Union and the emerging democracies of Eastern Europe. Support from the international community is important not only in carrying out a war but even more so to assist in political and economic activities in the postwar environment. If countries such as Saudi Arabia, Germany, and Japan could not operate under the cover of a UN resolution, they may not have financially supported the UN coalition in the war and in the postwar reconstruction as much as they did; indeed, the war was virtually cost free in economic terms for the United States. If the United States exceeded the UN mandate, not only would it have been

guilty of setting a terrible international legal precedent but it also would have alienated most of the countries that had at least grudgingly supported the war effort.

In addition, there existed serious concerns at the time, and in 2003 as the United States contemplated a renewed war with Iraq, about the contiguity of Iraq if military action were taken in it and/or extended toward it. Iraq is an artificial country, having been essentially stitched together by the British following World War I (1914–1918); indeed, there had not been an official entity known as "Iraq" prior to Britain's patchwork. The Ottoman Empire, which had basically ruled over the territory known today as Iraq since the early 1500s, correctly recognized that the three distinct regions of Mesopotamia/Iraq–the province of Mosul in the north, composed of primarily Sunni Kurds; the province of Baghdad in the center, primarily made up of Sunni Arabs; and the province of Basra in the south, predominantly populated by Shiite Arabs–should be administered separately. It seems that British power and the relative stability that could be provided by a repressive military dictatorship (such as Hussein's regime) were the only things that could keep this artificial creation together for any length of time. It was feared in 1991 by a host of experts and officials in and outside of the Middle East that if the Baghdad regime was forcibly removed, Iraq might devolve once again into its constituent parts. If this unraveling were to happen, it could immeasurably destabilize a region that contains two-thirds of the world's proven oil reserves, as, inter alia, Turkey, Syria, and Iran could be drawn into a regional free-for-all in terms of enhancing strategic security, gaining allies, and/or acquiring territory in a broken-up Iraq. To prevent this upheaval, the United States would have been beholden to occupy and rebuild Iraq—an occupation that would have been tremendously costly for the U.S. taxpayer as well as dangerous, since U.S. forces could have increasingly been seen as imperialist occupiers and become a target for guerrilla and terrorist opposition groups (as U.S. forces had experienced in Lebanon in 1983 and in the post–Iraq War environment in 2003). Arab allies such as Egypt and Saudi Arabia were clamoring for the Bush administration not to go further into Iraq for fear of the potential instability it could cause in the region—Hussein might or might not leave or be overthrown, but the Sunni Arab ruling authority was the only element in Iraq capable of providing indigenous leadership at the time; the hope was that a more amenable Sunni Arab leader would come to power, but, obviously, it did not happen. This desire may have been wishful thinking, and Hussein's longevity has provided grist for the mill, but the regional and international risks at the time were deemed too high—since it did not happen, one will never know if this supposition was correct, but President Bush made the right decision.

Maybe the most important reason for not going further into Iraq and eliminating Hussein in the 1991 Gulf War (and all that decision entailed) was that the postwar regional balance of power that produced the Madrid peace process would never have come into being. Combined with the end of the superpower Cold War, the Gulf War realigned the regional dynamics in the Middle East that made the embarkation of a comprehensive peace process possible. It began with the meeting in Madrid in October 1991 sponsored by the United States and the Soviet Union, and it comprised Israel and the remaining Arab states bordering Israel that were still officially at war with the Jewish state (Syria, Lebanon, and a joint Jordanian-Palestinian delegation)—it was the first time that representatives from Israel and these Arab states had officially sat in the same room across from one another in order to negotiate peace. Syria's participation in the Gulf War coalition was the key to getting the Madrid peace process off the ground. In effect, those Arab states that participated in the U.S.-led coalition were on the same side as Israel, even though through heavy U.S. pressure Tel

Aviv decided not to enter the conflict despite the fact that Iraq had been lobbing SCUD missiles into Israeli territory. This partnership broke a tremendous psychological barrier. There were obviously some practical reasons why a country such as Syria joined the Gulf War coalition (such as enmity toward Iraq; need for U.S. and Western economic assistance now that the Cold War was over and its superpower patron, the Soviet Union, was falling apart; and financial grants and aid from grateful Persian Gulf states for the ailing economy), but by doing so it had, as Syrian president Hafiz al-Asad stated, made a strategic decision to pursue peace with Israel.

The Madrid peace process produced some direct and indirect successes, such as the Israeli-Jordanian peace treaty (1994); serious peace negotiations between Israel and Syria on several occasions in the 1990s; and, indirectly, the Oslo accords (1993) between Israel and the Palestine Liberation Organization (PLO), consummated in the Declaration of Principles signed on the White House lawn in September 1993. In the post al-Aqsa *intifada* (uprising) and World Trade Center attack (11 September 2001) atmosphere in the Middle East, however, it is perhaps too easy to dismiss the Madrid peace process as a failure. In the end it did not result in a Syrian-Israeli peace treaty; it did not end the Arab-Israeli conflict and produce in its wake a Middle East common market; and, with the failure of the Oslo process, it did not resolve the Israeli-Palestinian problem lying at the heart of the Arab-Israeli imbroglio. But this result does not mean it should not have been tried. One can legitimately label the Madrid process a failure, but one can state with equal authority that it should have succeeded, and if it had, the world would be quite different: an Israeli-Syrian peace treaty; a viable independent Palestinian state; no al-Aqsa *intifada;* an isolated and less powerful Iraq; Arab states, indeed the world, supporting the United States if it decided to enforce UN resolutions in Iraq; no more Arab-Israeli conflict per se; economic development across the region through economic integration and cooperative enterprises and investment; shrinking extremist Islamist opposition; and possibly even no terrorist attacks against the United States. Historians might be unkind to those who failed to take advantage of the windows of opportunity begun by the Madrid peace process. Who could have known that Israeli prime minister Yitzhak Rabin would be assassinated in 1995? Who could have calculated the seemingly innumerable errors of judgment by a constellation of leaders regarding the peace processes in the Middle East?

Even though the Madrid process and everything that emanated from it has been considered a failure and new peace-process paradigms are being constructed, it was not a totally meaningless effort. A great deal of progress was made on several fronts that inevitably in some form or fashion will be included in new paradigms, even if it is only utilized as a point of reference. Just because popular perception concludes that it did not work does not mean it should not have been tried, and the Madrid process would not have been possible in the first place had the Bush administration abandoned the UN mandate vis-à-vis Iraq in 1991.

The world is now assessing the aftermath of the 2003 U.S. war against Iraq and the overthrow of Hussein. Those who support the 2003 version are generally also those who condemned the decision by the Bush administration in 1991 to halt the war when it did; those who at least have serious reservations about the resort to war against Iraq in 2003 generally support the timing of the 1991 cessation of the conflict. Current events are often used to justify past actions, but this orientation takes for granted that historical events could only have produced the timeline now observed as history without taking into account the myriad of variables that could have changed that history—for better or worse. President Bush's decision in 1991 was the right decision at the time, and it almost produced earth-shattering results; indeed, it should have.

–DAVID W. LESCH,
TRINITY UNIVERSITY

Viewpoint:
No. The United States ended the Persian Gulf War (1990–1991) prematurely; it should have removed Saddam Hussein from power when it had the opportunity to do so with broad international support.

When the United Nations (UN) coalition had successfully liberated Kuwait from the Iraqi forces in 1991, a decision had to be made. Should the U.S.-led forces take available steps to remove Saddam Hussein from power in Iraq or should they consider their job done? History has proven that the Bush administration ended the Persian Gulf War (1990–1991) prematurely and that the United States should have finished the job when it had the chance to remove Hussein from power.

Much of the discussion in retrospect argues that the removal of Saddam from power, although welcome, was never a stated objective

of U.S. policy. Former Secretary of State James A. Baker III recalls,

> We were always very careful to negate it as a war aim or political objective. At the same time, we never really expected him to survive a defeat of such magnitude. Perhaps we should have remembered that Saddam had always been a wily survivor, somehow finding a way to confound his enemies. To this day he remains in control of his country, while the administration that defeated him in a textbook case of diplomatic and military skill is no longer in power. In occasionally reflecting on this perverse twist of history, I'm reminded of something Tariq Aziz [currently Iraqi Deputy Prime Minister] said to me in Geneva: "We will be here long after you're gone." It was one of the few things he said that proved to be true.

Despite the administrative certainty about Saddam, *Washington Post* writer Rick Atkinson argued, "No American military decision since the Vietnam War provoked more controversy, more debate, more caustic commentary, than the choice to offer Iraq a merciful clemency." No later than eight months after the war, two-thirds of Americans polled said that the war had ended too soon. President George H. W. Bush's decision on 28 February 1991 to order a cease-fire enabled Hussein's army to survive the war with many units intact and helped keep the regime in power. Bush's justification for stopping the war was that if the Americans had gone to Baghdad, they would have had to occupy the place for months afterward. He also argued that the UN resolutions under which he had launched the war authorized only the liberation of Kuwait, and he could not legally have gone further.

Similarly, Baker argued that "We never adopted as a war aim or a political aim the elimination of Saddam Hussein's leadership and if you weren't focusing on that as an aim, for what purpose would you occupy?" Baker also argued that, as much as Saddam's neighbors wanted to see him gone, they feared that Iraq might fragment in unpredictable ways that would play into the hands of the mullahs in Iran, who could export their brand of Islamic fundamentalism with the help of Iraq's Shiites and quickly transform themselves into a dominant regional power.

Later, in 1997, Paul Wolfowitz, the former undersecretary of defense for policy, stated that the Bush administration was slow to recognize the importance of removing Saddam from power. He stated several reasons for this failure: "One reason was the nature of the consensus regarding war objectives. The United Nations resolution and, more importantly, the U.S. Congressional resolutions that gave president Bush his political mandate, focused almost exclusively

HIGHWAYS OF DEATH

Lebanese American journalist Joyce Chediac wrote the following report about an American air assault on an Iraqi motorized column leaving Kuwait in late February 1991:

I want to give testimony on what are called the "highways of death." These are the two Kuwaiti roadways, littered with remains of 2,000 mangled Iraqi military vehicles, and the charred and dismembered bodies of tens of thousands of Iraqi soldiers, who were withdrawing from Kuwait on February 26th and 27th 1991 in compliance with UN resolutions.

U.S. planes trapped the long convoys by disabling vehicles in the front, and at the rear, and then pounded the resulting traffic jams for hours. "It was like shooting fish in a barrel," said one U.S. pilot. The horror is still there to see.

On the inland highway to Basra is mile after mile of burned, smashed, shattered vehicles of every description—tanks, armored cars, trucks, autos, fire trucks, according to the March 18, 1991, *Time* magazine. On the sixty miles of coastal highway, Iraqi military units sit in gruesome repose, scorched skeletons of vehicles and men alike, black and awful under the sun, says the *Los Angeles Times* of March 11, 1991. While 450 people survived the inland road bombing to surrender, this was not the case with the 60 miles of the coastal road. There for 60 miles every vehicle was strafed or bombed, every windshield is shattered, every tank is burned, every truck is riddled with shell fragments. No survivors are known or likely. The cabs of trucks were bombed so much that they were pushed into the ground, and it's impossible to see if they contain drivers or not. Windshields were melted away, and huge tanks were reduced to shrapnel.

"Even in Vietnam I didn't see anything like this. It's pathetic," said Major Bob Nugent, an Army intelligence officer. This one-sided carnage, this racist mass murder of Arab people, occurred while White House spokesman Marlin Fitzwater promised that the U.S. and its coalition partners would not attack Iraqi forces leaving Kuwait. This is surely one of the most heinous war crimes in contemporary history.

The Iraqi troops were not being driven out of Kuwait by U.S. troops as the Bush administration maintains. They were not retreating in order to regroup and fight again. In fact, they were withdrawing, they were going home, responding to orders issued by Baghdad, announcing that it was complying with Resolution 660 and leaving Kuwait. At 5:35 p.m. (Eastern Standard Time) Baghdad radio announced that Iraq's Foreign Minister had accepted the Soviet cease-fire proposal and had issued the order for all Iraqi troops to withdraw to positions held before August 2, 1990 in compliance with UN Resolution 660. President Bush responded immediately from the White House saying (through spokesman Marlin Fitzwater) that "there was no evidence to suggest the Iraqi army is withdrawing. In fact, Iraqi units are continuing to fight. . . . We continue to prosecute the war." On the next day, February 26, 1991, Saddam Hussein announced on Baghdad radio that Iraqi troops had, indeed, begun to withdraw from Kuwait and that the withdrawal would be complete that day. Again, Bush reacted, calling Hussein's announcement "an outrage" and "a cruel hoax."

Eyewitness Kuwaitis attest that the withdrawal began the afternoon of February 26, 1991 and Baghdad radio announced at 2:00 a.m. (local time) that morning that the government had ordered all troops to withdraw.

The massacre of withdrawing Iraqi soldiers violates the Geneva Conventions of 1949, Common Article III, which outlaws the killing of soldiers who are out of combat. The point of contention involves the Bush administration's claim that the Iraqi troops were retreating to regroup and fight again. Such a claim is the only way that the massacre which occurred could be considered legal under international law. But in fact the claim is false and obviously so. The troops were withdrawing and removing themselves from combat under direct orders from Baghdad that the war was over and that Iraq had quit and would fully comply with UN resolutions. To attack the soldiers returning home under these circumstances is a war crime. . . .

The victims were not offering resistance. They weren't being driven back in fierce battle, or trying to regroup to join another battle. They were just sitting ducks, according to Commander Frank Swiggert, the Ranger Bomb Squadron leader. According to an article in the March 11, 1991 *Washington Post,* headlined "U.S. Scrambles to Shape View of Highway of Death," the U.S. government then conspired and in fact did all it could to hide this war crime from the people of this country and the world. What the U.S. government did became the focus of the public relations campaign managed by the U.S. Central Command in Riyad, according to that same issue of the *Washington Post.* The typical line has been that the convoys were engaged in "classic tank battles," as if to suggest that Iraqi troops tried to fight back or even had a chance of fighting back. The truth is that it was simply a one-sided massacre of tens of thousands of people who had no ability to fight back or defend themselves.

The *Washington Post* says that senior officers with the U.S. Central Command in Riyad became worried that what they saw was a growing public perception that Iraqi forces were leaving Kuwait voluntarily, and that the U.S. pilots were bombing them mercilessly, which was the truth. So the U.S. government, says the *Post,* played down the evidence that Iraqi troops were actually leaving Kuwait.

Source: Joyce Chediac, "The Massacre of Withdrawing Soldiers on 'The Highway of Death'," submitted on 11 May 1991, in "War Crimes: A Report on United States War Crimes Against Iraq to the Commission of Inquiry for the International War Crimes Tribunal," by Ramsey Clark and others, The Commission of Inquiry for the International War Crimes Tribunal <http://www.deoxy.org/wc/wc-death.htm>.

on the goal of ejecting Iraqi forces from Kuwait."

Wolfowitz argued that, because of the narrow margin by which President Bush prevailed in Congress, it was extremely doubtful that he would have received the necessary support had he declared that the objective of the war was Hussein's removal from power. Therefore, according to Wolfowitz, the major responsibility for the failure to finish the job and remove Hussein from power rests with those who opposed the use of force even for more limited goals.

Contrary to the above arguments, former Bush national security adviser Brent Scowcroft conceded publicly on national television in an interview with Peter Jennings that the U.S. had targeted Hussein and tried to kill him but failed. Scowcroft admitted, "Yes, we targeted him and deliberately set out to kill him and we did not get him." According to Atkinson, the targeting was scheduled in August 1990 when U.S. Air Force planners wrote, "Saddam is the main priority in the first bombing plan."

Michael R. Gordon stated that the Bush administration was not willing to take the risk of sending its troops to Baghdad. Instead, the administration sought to undermine Hussein through air and ground attacks. The goal was the replacement of one Iraqi dictator by another strongman committed to holding Iraq together. Atkinson asserted that many American officers believed that Iraqi survivors in the military would likely join a coup; sufficient combat power existed in the south, according to one intelligence assessment, to ensure an orderly transfer of power when Saddam fell. The analysts in all U.S. agencies believed without a doubt that Hussein was going to fall. Based upon such intelligence, the United States allowed Saddam to withdraw his Republic Guard force from the Kuwait Theater of Operations (KTO) intact. Atkinson stated,

> The Defense Intelligence Agency later concluded that seventy to eighty thousand Iraqi troops had fled into Basrah. An army analysis estimated that as many as one third of the Republican Guard's R-72s made it out of the KTO. Other intelligence analysis calculated that roughly eight hundred tanks and fourteen hundred armored personnel carriers escaped destruction. Within days of the cease-fire, Iraqis would use dozens of Hind and Hip helicopters—part of a surviving fleet of several hundred—to terrorize rebels in the Shiite south and Kurdish north.

At the same time, the U.S. military killed thousands of ordinary Iraqi solders. These solders were forced by Saddam to go to the front. According to Seymour M. Hersh in *The New Yorker,* these Iraqi solders offered only disorganized and ragged opposition to the American

forces. The so-called Highway of Death, the road between Kuwait and Basra in southern Iraq, was littered with blackened tanks, trucks, and bodies, and became a symbol of the extent of Iraqi losses and pain. Army historian Colonel Richard M. Swain (Ret.) noted in *Lucky War: Third Army in Desert War* (1994) the troubling fact "that most of the Iraqi killed seem to have been headed north or simply milling around—and not into the defender's lines." Swain added: "only a small number of Iraqis seem to have acted with hostility."

One other crucial piece of this puzzle was the public message President Bush sent in February 1991 to encourage the Iraqi people to revolt against Saddam's regime. Immediately after the cease-fire, the Iraqi people did exactly what Bush asked. For a few days, progress was made: fourteen of the eighteen Iraqi states were taken out of Saddam's control, and for the first time since he became president, the Iraqis were getting close to freedom. However, instead of helping them to overthrow Saddam's regime, the White House gave Hussein the green light to suppress the uprisings by announcing that U.S. forces would not shoot down Iraqi helicopters. Saddam's forces came down hard on the rebels, whom Saddam called "enemies of the state," and, instead of the promised support from the United States, the Iraqi rebels saw the American planes flying over Saddam's helicopters, witnessing their demise but doing nothing. In addition to not making any move to assist the rebels, the United States actually gave tacit assistance to Saddam's forces by blowing up the few arms caches the rebels had in southern Iraq, thus depriving the rebels of one of their few means of obtaining weapons.

President Bush in 1994 justified such action as a concern "that the uprisings would sidetrack the overthrow of Saddam, by causing the Iraqi military to rally around him to prevent the breakup of the country. That may have been what actually happened." Even the Saudis were unhappy that Hussein had survived in power and wanted to launch a covert program of weapons deliveries to the Iraqi people, but the Americans still preferred a coup to an uprising. Also, the Americans were concerned that the rebels were Shiites, pro-Iranian, and anti-American. All of these ill-timed actions by the United States not only allowed Saddam to destroy the rebel forces but also were used and continue to be used by Saddam to convince the Iraqi people that the United States was not serious about removing him from power. In essence, that decision strengthened Saddam's position and contributed to his survival.

A year and a half after the Bush administration decided not to help the Iraqi revolt against

Saddam, the United States found that, while the war in the desert was over, the confrontation between Hussein and the United States persisted. The United States recognized its mistake, reversed itself, and imposed a no-flight zone in the south similar to the one it had established in the north immediately after the war to protect the Iraqi Kurds from Hussein.

So how do we explain the failure of the Bush administration to finish the job and remove Hussein from power? The answer lies in the fact that the United States did not want him to be overthrown by the Iraqi people. The United States never believed the rise of democracy in Iraq would safely lead to the fall of Saddam; they preferred something more predictable. They wanted "some element within the military," a general next to him, to stage a coup; it really did not matter if the general was like Saddam or worse. This overthrow, of course, did not happen, and thus the United States missed a golden opportunity to get rid of him.

This decision is regarded by many analysts as one of the most significant foreign policy mistakes by a U.S. administration since World War II (1939–1945). From a military perspective the United States had been able to mobilize the most tremendous resources seen since World War II. The U.S. army corps was on the ground in Iraq, it had command of the skies, and the Iraqi military was in a state of disarray: American forces would never again be in such a strong position to press their demands. However, the Bush administration let the moment pass, and by 2003 it became necessary to go back in and finish the job.

In spite of repeated claims from U.S. officials that the problem was Saddam, not the Iraqi people, the economic embargo that was put in place after the Gulf War targeted the Iraqi people and not Saddam. In May 1991 former deputy national security adviser Robert Gates stated, "Saddam is discredited and cannot be redeemed. His leadership will never be accepted by the world community. Therefore, Iraqis will pay the price while he remains in power. All possible sanctions will be maintained until he is gone . . . any easing of sanctions will be considered only when there is a new government." The UN economic embargo proved to be highly problematic, far more so than the administration publicly admitted. Not only did the embargo have severe and damaging effects on the lives of the Iraqi people, but it also forced them to be more dependent than ever on Saddam's regime for shrinking food rations and limited opportunities for employment. People were forced to spend most of their time securing their basic needs, no matter how much they may have resented the regime. This dependency, coupled with Sad-dam's brutal repression of political opposition within Iraq, meant that the effects of the embargo had not only economic but also political repercussions.

A decade after the Persian Gulf War, in the first year of the new millennium, there was a new president in the White House, George W. Bush. The same dilemmas returned, and once again a Bush called on the Iraqi people to rise up and remove their dictator, and again there were promises of support. This time, however, Bush sent his own army and a few allies to "liberate them." With a few "lead role" changes, the majority of the participants', the victims', and the dictator's roles were left intact. There were some significant differences, however. In 1991 the first President Bush received full backing and support from the UN, many Arab and Muslim countries, and the rest of the world. The war was legitimized and backed by UN resolutions. Arab and Muslim armies participated in the war, and American forces were seen as the liberator. This time the United States was seen as the aggressor and went in without the support or participation of Arab and Muslim countries.

A second major change was that in 1991 the oil-producing Arab countries, along with the rest of the world, committed financially to sponsor the war, so the conflict did not cost the United States much. In 2003 the United States paid most of the cost itself. According to *The New York Times* of 30 November 2002, the bill to the American taxpayers for the 1991 war was about $7 billion; the cost for the 2003 conflict may range between $100 and 200 billion. In addition, William Nordhaus, a professor of economics at Yale University, estimates the indirect cost of the war could be as high as $1 trillion.

The credibility of the United States was also challenged by the failure to remove Saddam in 1991. Three months after the Gulf War, President Bush signed an authorization for the Central Intelligence Agency (CIA) to mount a covert operation to create conditions for the removal of Hussein from power. However, twelve years later Saddam was still in power, and the United States was still trying to oust him.

Much suffering and pain continued for the people of Iraq after the 1991 Gulf War. They believe that the United States let them down when they needed help to get rid of Hussein's dictatorship. The tragedy, Gordon argued, is that "The United States might have used its occupation of southern Iraq to press for further demands. It might have insisted that the Iraqis reach a new political accommodation with the Shiites and Kurds, or at least not attack them. It might even have pressed for the removal of the Saddam Hussein regime. But it did none of this." Wolfowitz has rightly described the cease-fire agreement that led to the preservation of Hussein's hold on power in Iraq as a lost opportunity.

—ABBAS MEHDI,
ST. CLOUD UNIVERSITY

References

Rick Atkinson, *Crusade: The Untold Story of the Persian Gulf War* (New York: Houghton Mifflin, 1993).

James A. Baker III, *The Politics of Diplomacy: Revolution, War, and Peace, 1989–1992* (New York: Putnam, 1995).

Lawrence Freedman and Efraim Karsh, *The Gulf Conflict, 1990–1991: Diplomacy and War in the New World Order* (Princeton: Princeton University Press, 1993).

Michael R. Gordon and General Bernard E. Trainer, *The Generals' War: The Inside Story of the Conflict in the Gulf* (Boston: Little, Brown, 1995).

Majid Khadduri and Edmund Ghareeb, *War in the Gulf, 1990–1991: The Iraq-Kuwait Conflict and Its Implications* (New York: Oxford University Press, 1997).

Abbas Mehdi, "Towards a New Policy Framework," in *The Future of Iraq,* edited by John Calabrese (Washington, D.C.: Middle East Institute, 1997).

U.S. News & World Report, *Triumph without Victory: The History of the Persian Gulf War* (New York: Times Books, 1993).

INTIFADA 1987–1993

Was the Palestinian *intifada* of 1987–1993 a spontaneous uprising in the Occupied Territories?

Viewpoint: Yes. The *intifada* of 1987–1993 was a result of Palestinian frustration with the failed leadership of the Palestine Liberation Organization.

Viewpoint: No. The *intifada* of 1987–1993 was a long-simmering intensification of existing animosity toward Israeli policies in the Occupied Territories.

The Palestinian *intifada* (uprising) is considered to have officially begun on 8 December 1987, when an Israeli tank-transport truck crashed into several Arabs in Gaza, killing four of them. The funerals of the deceased Palestinians erupted into widespread demonstrations against Israeli occupation and signaled a heightened level of resistance. This *intifada* has often been compared to the Arab Revolt in Palestine (1936–1939) against the British mandate. As in the Arab Revolt, the vanguard of the uprising that began half a century later consisted primarily of a younger generation of Arabs who had known only occupation and were becoming frustrated by the relative docility and impotence of the older generation.

The *intifada* was initiated and carried out by Palestinians actually living in the Occupied Territories (West Bank, Gaza Strip, and Golan Heights). Some claim that the uprising stemmed primarily from their frustration with the relative weakness of the Palestine Liberation Organization (PLO) after it had been expelled from Lebanon following the Israeli invasion in 1982. The fact that the PLO leadership was far afield in Tunisia gave the impression that it had become disassociated from the everyday travails of the Palestinians living under occupation. That the Arab League summit meeting in Amman, Jordan (November 1987), relegated for the first time the Palestinian issue to a secondary priority in lieu of the Iran-Iraq War (1980–1988) confirmed these fears. Others believe that this *intifada* was primarily a cathartic reaction to years of creeping Israeli control over the Occupied Territories, especially since the right-wing Likud governments in Israel beginning in 1977 had accelerated the settlement process. The situation only needed a spark to explode, such as the one that occurred in December 1987.

Whatever the causes, the *intifada* transformed the Arab-Israeli dispute into more of a Palestinian-Israeli issue for the time being, as world opinion, even in the United States, began to sympathize with the Palestinians, who were seen over the global airwaves as fighting desperately against overwhelming military force. The chairman of the PLO, Yasser Arafat, indeed the PLO itself, was in a sense rehabilitated by the *intifada*. So that it would not be marginalized, the PLO began to adopt the more moderate position of a two-state solution to the conflict, one that the vast majority of Palestinians in the Occupied Territories had adhered to for quite some time. By December 1988 Arafat had satisfied U.S. conditions for bilateral negotiations by publicly accepting United Nations (UN) Security Council Resolution 242, thereby accepting the two-state solution and renouncing terrorism.

The *intifada* had lost much of its steam by August 1990, when the Iraqi invasion of Kuwait and subsequent UN response overshadowed the ongoing resistance. The PLO's tacit support of Iraq's Saddam Hussein during the Persian Gulf crisis and war (1990–1991) negated much of the international sympathy the Palestinian resistance had garnered in the previous couple of years (in addition to the enmity of the Arab Gulf sheikhdoms such as Kuwait and Saudi Arabia, which decided to cut off their significant funding of the PLO). Despite this setback, however, the uprising adjusted the politics of the Palestinian-Israeli situation, which, in turn, laid the foundation for the resumption of negotiations following the Gulf War and eventually the Oslo accords (1993). One other important consequence of the *intifada* was the increased level of popularity garnered by Palestinian Islamist groups in the Occupied Territories that never wavered from their commitment to the destruction of Israel and that rejected Arafat's two-state solution. Groups such as Islamic Jihad and Hamas (acronym for *Harakat al-Muqawama al-Islamiya,* or Islamic Resistance Movement) became more prominent, and although they constituted a minority of Palestinians in the Territories, they enhanced their power at the expense of the PLO and local authorities whenever these secular entities faltered—a trend that continued into the so-called al-Aqsa *intifada,* which began in September 2000.

Viewpoint:
Yes. The *intifada* of 1987–1993 was a result of Palestinian frustration with the failed leadership of the Palestine Liberation Organization.

Shortly after the initiation of the Palestinian *intifada* (uprising, 1987–1993), a spontaneous eruption by Palestinians in the Occupied Territories, Yasser Arafat, head of the Palestine Liberation Organization (PLO) and Fatah, did two things. First, he claimed responsibility for initiating the civil and not-so-civil disobedience toward the Israeli occupation. Second, he tried to direct the course of the *intifada.* Interestingly enough, the *intifada* arose as a result of the frustration among Palestinians with the ineptitude and irrelevancy of the PLO.

First, it is important to note that the PLO was not a monolithic entity. Scholar William B. Quandt said of the *intifada:* "the previously quiescent Palestinians of the West Bank and Gaza were coming of political age." Long before the Palestinians in the Occupied Territories added their voices of frustration and protest against the PLO, individuals broke away from Fatah and the PLO to form their own organizations, such as the Popular Front for the Liberation of Palestine (PFLP). There were many other splinter Palestinian organizations such as the Popular Democratic Front for the Liberation of Palestine (PDFLP), which was a Marxist group led by Nayef Hawatmah; the Palestine Liberation Front, headed by Abu Abbas; and of course, Islamic movements such as Hamas (Islamic Resistance Movement) and Islamic Jihad.

One characteristic of the *intifada* was the distribution of a series of numbered leaflets that instructed citizens in the Occupied Territories to close their shops and build roadblocks, while demanding that the occupiers withdraw from Palestinian territories. The first of these leaflets

was issued by the PFLP, a Marxist group started by George Habash in January 1988. In fact, many (often conflicting) political and religious Palestinian groups were issuing instructions and can thus be seen as attempting to command and control the *intifada,* or at least challenge Arafat's hegemony (real or imagined) over the *intifada.* Groups such as the PLO-controlled Fatah and non-PLO-controlled groups such as PFLP, PDFLP, Islamic Jihad, and Hamas all laid claim to the mantle of initiating the *intifada,* and all, at one time or another, attempted to control the *intifada* through the distribution of these leaflets—a sign that many of the groups acted out of frustration with the failed policies of the PLO.

Many of these splinter groups were antithetical to Arafat himself or to the seemingly failed policies of the PLO. For example, in 1983 the Syrian-backed al-Saiqa (Pioneers of the Popular War for Liberation) and the PFLP withdrew from the PLO. During the Israeli invasion of Lebanon, some of those anti-PLO factions even turned their weapons against the PLO, such as al-Saiqa, which actually fought against Fatah in Lebanon in 1976. According to Baruch Kimmerling and Joel S. Migdal, the main reason for mutiny among the PLO cadre in the early 1980s was "the PLO's treasonous appeasement of its enemies—and its gradual abandonment of the claim to total repatriation, its acceptance in theory of an independent state limited to the West Bank and Gaza." Islamist groups such as Hamas, Islamic Jihad, and others tried to steer the *intifada* away from PLO control, who they believed wanted to establish a secular state. The movement against the PLO and its alleged secular ways was led most tenaciously by Sheikh Ahmad Ismail Yasin, who gained control of the Islamic University in Gaza and in the process removed the pro-PLO factions from the school.

Kimmerling and Migdal noted that by the early 1980s Palestinians living under Israeli occupation developed an "economic hopelessness" as well as "flagging hopes that international diplomacy, the PLO, or outside Arab armies would bring an end to the occupation." Believing that no one would or could come to their rescue, and experiencing increased economic hardships, the Palestinians of the Gaza Strip and West Bank just might have been catapulted to write their own Horatio Alger story in the form of the *intifada*. That sense of hopelessness may have come, at least in part, from the decline of the PLO and their inability to keep the question of Palestine at the top of the agendas of the United Nations (UN), the Arab League, and other international organizations. At the 1987 Arab League meeting, for example, the main point of discussion was the Iran-Iraq War (1980–1988), much to the disappointment of Arafat and adding to the frustration of Palestinians in the Occupied Territories who, after two decades of occupation, came to the conclusion that even fellow Arabs were no longer interested in spearheading Palestinian independence.

Second, the PLO in general and Arafat in particular failed to alleviate the pressures and stresses that the Israeli occupation manifested in the daily lives of Palestinians. In some cases, Arafat and the PLO leadership failed to prevent the extension of Israeli brutality to Arabs outside the geographic limits of Israel and the Occupied Territories. They failed to protect Palestinians from attacks from Syria, Lebanon, other Arab governments, and, of course, the Israelis. In 1976, for example, Lebanese opponents of the PLO attacked two Palestinian refugee camps in and around Beirut, in which nearly three thousand Palestinians were killed by Phalangists (Lebanese Christian forces). Similarly, the Israeli occupiers failed to prevent the Phalangists from entering and slaughtering thousands of Palestinian men, women, and children in the Beirut refugee camps of Sabra and Shatilla in September 1982.

Needless to say, the PLO failed to protect Palestinians, and its policies did not end Israeli occupation and human rights abuses in the Occupied Territories. As William Cleveland points out, Israeli troops shot at unarmed Palestinians and utilized collective punishments against entire villages—such as mass arrests, curfews, house demolitions, the cutting off of water and electricity, and the closing of schools and universities.

Furthermore, the PLO had limited control over most aspects of Palestinian lives under occupation, such as the Israeli economy; oil prices; donations from Saudi Arabia, Kuwait, and other wealthy Arab nations to the PLO; and the salaries paid to Palestinian civil servants by the government of Jordan. Nevertheless, the *intifada* can be seen as a reaction against the PLO's inability to end the occupation. Cleveland wrote

that "The intifada began as a purely local Palestinian response to unbearable local conditions." The PLO leadership and its policies were simply unable to alleviate the suffering, thus the people took matters into their own hands.

Overall, Edward Said notes, "alone in the territories occupied by Israel since 1967, the West Bank and Gaza remained in an unforgiving limbo of local repression and frozen political process." The PLO was unable to stop Israel from expropriating more Palestinian land and from building more apartheid-like "settlements" in the Occupied Territories in which only Israeli Jews were allowed to live. In 1976 Israel allowed the Palestinians to hold municipal elections. After the population returned an overwhelming number of pro-PLO candidates to office, Israel simply dismissed them. Israel arrested, jailed, or exiled Palestinian leaders (usually without trials or even evidence). Palestinian books were banned, and the Palestinian flag was outlawed. Israel used several tactics to humiliate and terrorize the Palestinian population such as administrative detentions, the dynamiting of houses, torture, collective punishments, mass arrests, and exile. The occupied population was forced to pay Israeli taxes and had "to submit to the increasingly cruel whims of settlers who did what they wanted with impunity."

Interestingly enough, the *intifada* resulted in elevating local Palestinian leaders onto the national stage. Palestinian leaders in the West Bank and Gaza began to pressure the exiled leadership in Tunis "to engage in peace talks with Israel, to advocate a two-state solution, and to renounce terrorism." By the end of 1988 Arafat renounced terrorism and accepted UN Security Council resolutions 181 and 242, thus recognizing Israel's right to exist. In other words, Palestinians within the Occupied Territories began to chart the course of the external PLO organization as a result of the *intifada*. Palestinians established their own political organizations, such as the *lijan shaa biya* (popular committee), which became responsible for daily social-service activities such as food distribution, judicial matters, and education. According to some historians, such as Glenn E. Robinson, initially the PLO tried to "undermine this alternative leadership" and did not accept the situation inside the territories until 1991 when the PLO succeeded in replacing the new, local leadership with established (albeit splinter) leaders such as Zuhara Kamal of the DFLP and Ghassan Khatib of the Communist Party.

Third, the *intifada* started outside the scope of Arafat's or the PLO's control, which suggests that it was indeed a reaction against the failed direction of Arafat and the lack of

THE BANNER OF PALESTINE

On 15 November 1988 the Palestine Liberation Organization issued the Palestinian Declaration of Independence, a portion of which appears here:

The State of Palestine is the state of Palestinians wherever they may be. The state is for them to enjoy in it their collective national and cultural identity, theirs to pursue in it a complete equality of rights. In it will be safeguarded their political and religious convictions and their human dignity by means of a parliamentary democratic system of governance, itself based on freedom of expression and the freedom to form parties. The rights of minorities will duly be respected by the majority, as minorities must abide by decisions of the majority. Governance will be based on principles of social justice, equality and non-discrimination in public rights of men or women, on grounds of race, religion, color or sex, and the aegis of a constitution which ensures the rule of law and an independent judiciary. Thus shall these principles allow no departure from Palestine's age-old spiritual and civilizational heritage of tolerance and religious coexistence.

The State of Palestine is an Arab state, an integral and indivisible part of the Arab nation, at one with that nation in heritage and civilization, with it also in its aspiration for liberation, progress, democracy and unity. The State of Palestine affirms its obligation to abide by the Charter of the League of Arab States, whereby the coordination of the Arab states with each other shall be strengthened. It calls upon Arab compatriots to consolidate and enhance the . . . reality of state, to mobilize potential, and to intensify efforts whose goal is to end Israeli occupation.

The State of Palestine proclaims its commitment to the principles and purposes of the United Nations, and to the Universal Declaration of Human Rights. It proclaims its commitment as well to the principles and policies of the Non-Aligned Movement.

It further announces itself to be a peace-loving State, in adherence to the principles of peaceful co-existence. It will join with all states and peoples in order to assure a permanent peace based upon justice and the respect of rights so that humanity's potential for well-being may be assured, an earnest competition for excellence may be maintained, and in which confidence in the future will eliminate fear for those who are just and for whom justice is the only recourse.

In the context of its struggle for peace in the land of Love and Peace, the State of Palestine calls upon the United Nations to bear special responsibility for the Palestinian Arab people and its homeland. It calls upon all peace and freedom-loving peoples and states to assist it in the attainment of its objectives, to provide it with security, to alleviate the tragedy of its people, and to help it terminate Israel's occupation of the Palestinian territories.

The State of Palestine herewith declares that it believes in the settlement of regional and international disputes by peaceful means, in accordance with the U.N. Charter and resolutions. With prejudice to its natural right to defend its territorial integrity and independence, it therefore rejects the threat or use of force, violence and terrorism against its territorial integrity or political independence, as it also rejects their use against territorial integrity of other states.

Therefore, on this day unlike all others, November 15, 1988, as we stand at the threshold of a new dawn, in all honor and modesty we humbly bow to the sacred spirits of our fallen ones, Palestinian and Arab, by the purity of whose sacrifice for the homeland our sky has been illuminated and our Land given life. Our hearts are lifted up and irradiated by the light emanating from the much blessed intifada, from those who have endured and have fought the fight of the camps, of dispersion, of exile, from those who have borne the standard for freedom, our children, our aged, our youth, our prisoners, detainees and wounded, all those ties to our sacred soil are confirmed in camp, village, and town. We render special tribute to that brave Palestinian Woman, guardian of sustenance and Life, keeper of our people's perennial flame. To the souls of our sainted martyrs, the whole of our Palestinian Arab people that our struggle shall be continued until the occupation ends, and the foundation of our sovereignty and independence shall be fortified accordingly.

Therefore, we call upon our great people to rally to the banner of Palestine, to cherish and defend it, so that it may forever be the symbol of our freedom and dignity in that homeland, which is a homeland for the free, now and always.

Source: *"Declaration of Independence," Palestine-Net website <http://www.palestine-net.com/politics/indep.html>.*

social, political, and economic success of the PLO. The Middle East Research and Information Project (MERIP) noted the *intifada* "was not started or orchestrated by the PLO leadership in Tunis. Rather, it was a popular mobilization that drew on the organizations and institutions that developed under occupation." Quandt notes that the PLO leadership was "caught by surprise by the timing of the uprising and by how quickly it spread." Kimmerling and Migdal argue that the PLO was taken so off guard by the tenacity of the *intifada* that Palestinians residing in the Occupied Territories began to shape the decisions being made by the PLO leadership (which was in Tunis). Overall, because the *intifada* was an indigenous uprising outside the context and control of the established Palestinian "leadership," and even though participants in the *intifada* were a threat to the command and control of Arafat within the Territories, the Palestinians living in the territories began "to play a major role in determining the national political agenda, and to transform the accepted national tactics." For example, the PLO Executive were forced to give up their idea of massive, organized, and unified armed struggle against Israel as the only means to end the occupation. According to Joshua Teitelbaum and Joseph Kostiner, "Not only had the Palestinian movement become a mass movement, but its political center of gravity had shifted" from the established leadership in exile to the "new men" who established and led the popular committees and who lived, worked, and died in the Occupied Territories.

Overall, the *intifada* can be seen as a reaction against failure. It might have started because, as Kimmerling and Migdal point out, "A sense of hopelessness had pervaded the territories in November, 1987—a feeling that all the diplomatic jet-setting by PLO Executive members and Arab statesmen would not bring an end to occupation." Yet, the Fatah had been calling for a massive armed rebellion against the Israeli occupation by Palestinians living in the Occupied Territories as well as Israel proper. Instead, the *intifada* was more of a widespread series of acts of resistance, driven initially by economic weapons such as boycotts and store closings and symbolic acts such as boys throwing stones. Kimmerling and Migdal wrote, "the PLO, at the end of the 1980s and the beginning of the 1990s, was unable to show tangible gains . . . Along with its other difficulties, the organization's want of definition left its leadership vulnerable to challenges from within and to the rising tide of Islamic movements." The *intifada* can be seen as a formidable challenge to Arafat and two decades of failed PLO polices.

—JIM ROSS-NAZZAL,
MONTGOMERY COLLEGE

Viewpoint:
No. The *intifada* of 1987–1993 was a long-simmering intensification of existing animosity toward Israeli policies in the Occupied Territories.

Scholars have long recognized that revolutions and sustained rebellions do not arise simply because a people's anger finally boils over. This "volcano" approach to studying events such as the Palestinian *intifada* (uprising, 1987–1993) is almost always tautological, as there is no way of knowing when there is "enough" anger directed against the ruling elite short of the revolution actually happening. While Palestinians had plenty to be angry over, given life under a harsh Israeli military occupation, one has to look deeper at the structural changes wrought in Palestinian society since 1967 to understand why the *intifada* occurred and how it could be sustained for so many years. Four such changes stand out: the transformation of Palestine's peasants, who provided a mass base for revolt; the opening of Palestinian universities, which created a new political elite; large confiscations of land, which undermined the old landed Palestinian elite; and the Israeli invasion of Lebanon (1982), which prompted a mass mobilization campaign in the West Bank and Gaza. Thus, while Israeli repression and Palestine Liberation Organization (PLO) ineptitude certainly played a role in shaping the environment that led to the *intifada*, it was internal changes in Palestinian society that enabled anger to be sustained into a mass rebellion over a six-year period.

The most important structural change in Palestinian society since the 1967 Arab-Israeli War was the virtual elimination of the peasantry in the West Bank and the Gaza Strip. Peasants became Palestinian nationalists as they left their farms to work inside Israel. Following the war, in which Israel captured the West Bank and Gaza Strip (along with the Golan Heights and Sinai peninsula) from its Arab neighbors, Israel opened its labor markets to Palestinians from the Occupied Territories. Employing Palestinian labor (in the agricultural and construction sectors primarily) served both communities. For Israel, the plentiful supply of cheap labor helped fuel an economic boom; for Palestine even the discriminatory wage rates provided an income well above what could be made at home. Within a few short years 40 percent of the total Palestinian labor force was employed in Israel. The Gaza Strip became completely dependent on jobs over the "Green Line" in Israel to sustain its population.

Masked Palestinian youths near Bethlehem, West Bank, December 1988

(Photograph by George Baramki Azar)

Opening Israel's labor market to the "lower rungs" of Palestinian society had profound social and political consequences. The most immediate and important consequence was to disrupt and even destroy the traditional patron-client networks that linked the urban-based Palestinian landed elite to rural communities and, to a lesser degree, refugee camps. It also exposed working-class Palestinians in a direct way to the everyday humiliations of being a conquered people. In short, to borrow a phrase from France's historical experience, Israel's labor policies had the unintended consequence of making peasants into Palestinians. These Palestinians provided fertile grounds for recruitment into the mobilization efforts that began in the late 1970s and 1980s.

The second consequential structural change was the creation of a new and much broader political class formed in the newly opened Palestinian universities in the West Bank and Gaza. The first to open, in 1972, was Birzeit University, a transformed teacher's college. It was followed in the subsequent fourteen years by universities in Bethlehem, Hebron, Nablus, Jerusalem, and Gaza and was joined further by many community colleges.

Prior to 1972 only the sons of the local elite could afford to acquire a university education either in the Arab world or abroad; by the fall of 1987 nearly twenty thousand Palestinians were enrolled in Palestinian universities and colleges in the West Bank and Gaza.

The opening of Palestinian universities created a large local elite distinct from traditional Palestinian landowners. This new elite based its position on educational achievement and broadly reflected the society from which it emerged: 70 percent of Palestinian university students came from refugee camps, villages, and small towns. This new elite—educated, nonlanded, and less urban—built the institutions of civil society in the 1980s and subtly mobilized disaffected Palestinians against both the Israeli military occupation and the old Palestinian landowning elite; and they sustained the Palestinian *intifada*.

Most of these cadres were tied to one of the major factions of the PLO. Thus, it is incorrect to say that this new elite was hostile to the PLO. It would be correct, however, to note that sociologically and politically, this new elite was quite distinctive from its counterparts living in Tunis and elsewhere. They were better educated but poorer, more "modern" but more radical, and more democratic and institutional in their politics.

The eclipse of the Palestinian landowning elite was helped along directly by the Israeli policy of land confiscation. Begun under Labor Party rule, land confiscation accelerated dramatically when the conservative Likud Party came to power in Israel in 1977. Land confiscations took many forms, from direct and legal expropriation to (more commonly) the use of land for "security" reasons. A common ploy was to declare land as "state lands" unless proved otherwise beyond a shadow of a doubt. The burden of proof was not on the state to show that these were indeed state lands but on Palestinians to prove private ownership. Most Jewish settlements in the occupied territories today (and they are specifically for use by *Jews,* not *Israelis,* per se) are built on lands taken for security purposes or declared state lands by Israel. By the start of the first Palestinian *intifada,* about two-thirds of the West Bank and half of the Gaza Strip had been confiscated from or otherwise declared off-limits to Palestinians.

The biggest political loser in the land confiscations was the Palestinian landowning elite, which sometimes lost land directly and in any case showed that it could no longer control or influence the fate of Palestinian lands. Unable to control the land—a key source of power and patronage—the landowning elite was further marginalized. As a result, Israel lost the key element of social control in the West Bank and Gaza, as this elite historically had acted as the intermediary between the Israeli state and Palestinian society.

Thus, on the eve of the *intifada,* Palestinian society was greatly different than it had been a mere two decades earlier. In a short twenty years, Palestine had witnessed the rise of a new elite through Palestinian universities, the eclipse of the old elite (which, like landowning elites everywhere, was anathema to institutional politics and social transformation) through land confiscation, and the creation, through Israel's labor policies, of a Palestinian population open to new forms of social organization and mobilization. These three elements combined to make possible the building of new social institutions upon which to base organized economic, social, and (ultimately) political activity.

Israel's invasion of Lebanon (1982) had the unintended consequence of rapidly accelerating the recently started grassroots mobilization campaign in the West Bank and Gaza. Israel invaded Lebanon in order to destroy the PLO as a political—not military—force and thereby create the circumstances for permanent Israeli dominion over the West Bank. What happened instead was to energize the local PLO cadres—members of the new elite—and push the mobilization campaign in order to prevent the permanent absorption of the Occupied Territories by Israel. Put another way, a war designed by Ariel Sharon to make Israeli control and annexation of the West Bank easier in fact had the opposite consequence of making the occupation harder and more costly than ever before.

The mobilization campaign, which consisted primarily of building institutions of civil society and recruiting like-minded members into them, impacted all segments of Palestinian society. The defining feature of the mobilization campaign was the competition among four major factions within the PLO: the Fatah, the Palestine Communist Party (PCP), the Popular Front for the Liberation of Palestine (PFLP), and the Democratic Front for the Liberation of Palestine (DFLP). During the late 1970s and early 1980s each faction created its own federation of labor unions to organize workers, committee to integrate women into the national struggle, relief committee to increase agricultural production and minimize land confiscations (fallow lands were particularly vulnerable to confiscation), medical relief committee to improve health standards through primary health care, bloc to organize university students politically, and voluntary works program to cement ties between secondary and university students on the one hand and rural Palestinians on the other through a national service program.

Throughout the 1980s, and especially during the Palestinian uprising, the individuals and institutions active in civil society formed what can only be called a protostate, organizing its members and providing an (incomplete) network of social services. Authority in this nascent state structure had three defining characteristics. First, authority devolved into lower strata of society both reflecting the changing social structure of Palestinian society and making Israeli attempts to capture or disrupt this authority more difficult—devolved authority points out the grassroots nature of the politics of the new elite. Second, authority was practiced institutionally as opposed to residing in individual personalities. Institutional politics and authority distinguished the new elite from the political practice and authority of the old landowning families who relied on personal ties to govern. Third, authority was pluralistic, and even democratic, in its decision making. Given the grassroots nature of authority in the new structure, the new elite had little choice but to incorporate multiple voices and inputs into the making and implementing of decisions.

INTIFADA 1987–1993

Like all rebellions, the first Palestinian *intifada* started with an unforeseen and unpredictable spark: a traffic accident in the Gaza Strip involving an Israeli and a Palestinian vehicle that left a handful of Palestinian laborers dead. Similar potential sparks had happened every day for twenty years under a harsh military occupation, yet without the same consequence. The reason for this difference was not the nature of the spark but the preparedness of Palestinian society to sustain such a revolt. Palestinian society in 1967 was not structured in a way that could sustain a revolt against a powerful Israel. By 1987 Palestinian society had been so transformed that it could pull off what is anywhere a most difficult accomplishment: to sustain a revolt for six years against an enemy far more powerful militarily and economically than itself.

-GLENN E. ROBINSON,
NAVAL POSTGRADUATE SCHOOL

References

Robert O. Freedman, ed., *The Intifada: Its Impact on Israel, the Arab World, and the Superpowers* (Miami: Florida International University Press, 1991).

Baruch Kimmerling and Joel S. Migdal, *Palestinians: The Making of a People* (New York: Free Press, 1993).

Zachary Lockman and Joel Beinin, eds., *Intifada: The Palestinian Uprising against Israeli Occupation* (Boston: South End, 1989).

William B. Quandt, *Peace Process: American Diplomacy and the Arab-Israeli Conflict since 1967*, revised edition (Berkeley: University of California Press, 2001).

Zeev Schiff and Ehud Yaari, *Intifada: The Palestinian Uprising—Israel's Third Front* (New York: Simon & Schuster, 1990).

IRAN-IRAQ WAR

Did Iraqi leader Saddam Hussein attack Iran in 1980 in order to achieve domination in the Persian Gulf region?

Viewpoint: Yes. With the overthrow of the Shah in Iran and the decline of Egyptian influence, Saddam Hussein saw an opportunity to fill the power vacuum in the Arab world.

Viewpoint: No. Saddam Hussein attacked for defensive reasons, because he feared that Iran was intent on exporting its Revolution.

On 22 September 1980 Iraq launched an invasion of its neighbor to the east, Iran. It was a devastating war in both matériel and human terms (with more than one million casualties), lasting eight years, until both sides reluctantly accepted a United Nations (UN) resolution declaring a cease-fire in August 1988. There were many reasons why the war lasted so long. The advantages of one country were offset by the advantages of the other. Iran's population at the time was approximately three times larger than Iraq's (55–60 million to 17–20 million), which tended to be offset by Baghdad's technological advantage in terms of the amount and quality of military hardware. This latter assertion seems inconsistent with the fact that Iran under the Shah had been the largest recipient of U.S. military aid. Yet, following the fall of the Shah with the culmination of the Iranian Revolution in February 1979 and, especially, the taking hostage of U.S. embassy personnel by Iranian revolutionary guards in November, Washington and Teheran severed diplomatic relations. As a result, Iran was bereft of U.S. ammunition, spare parts, and training while Iraq continued to receive matériel from France and the Soviet Union, its traditional suppliers.

The international community, and even countries in the region, were not terribly motivated to end the war. Indeed, Washington and Moscow were primarily interested in making sure the conflict remained insulated and did not escalate into a superpower confrontation (especially with the Soviets mired in Afghanistan following their invasion in December 1979). Reflecting this posture, the UN Security Council did not meet to discuss the crisis for several days, which is unusual because two-thirds of the world's known oil reserves are located in the Persian Gulf area. It seems that Iran's isolation, accelerated internationally by the hostage crisis, was coming home to haunt Teheran; having the regime of Ayatollah Ruhollah Khomeini humbled was not inconsistent with the wishes of many countries, including the Persian Gulf states, who, for the most part, felt compelled to support Iraq during the war.

A host of miscalculations on both sides also prolonged the conflict. Iraq first attacked southwestern Iran—the Khuzistan province—not only for geographical and strategic reasons but because that part of the country is home to the majority of Iran's Arab minority. Iraqi president Saddam Hussein hoped that the Arabs in Iran would support his invasion, making his offensive that much more effective and depleting Iran's ability to counterattack. Unfortunately for Baghdad, the Arabs in Khuzistan were largely ambivalent to the outcome, making any chance of a swift knockout punch of Iran all but impossible. Similarly, after Iran had turned back Iraq's initial foray and went on the offensive in 1982, eschewing a possible diplomatic resolution at a propitious

97

moment, it too thought that the majority Shiite Muslim population in southern Iraq (Iran is a Shiite Islamic Republic, whereas Iraq has a Shiite majority ruled by a Sunni Muslim minority) would support its cause. Again, however, it was another bad miscalculation. Although there were certainly some groups of Shiite Iraqis that supported Teheran actively, the expected en masse Shiite uprising never materialized, primarily because of the effective repressive apparatus in Baghdad and the distaste many of the mostly secularized Iraqi Shiites had for Khomeini's brand of Shiism and theocratic regime. The ideological opposition of the regimes (secular Arab of Iraq versus Islamist Persian of Iran) and the personal animus and mutual recriminations and boasts invested in the war by the two respective leaders greatly complicated attempts at diplomatic resolution throughout the conflagration.

Most of the war was characterized by static trench warfare reminiscent of World War I (1914–1918), which contributed to the high casualty count. By 1982 Teheran, trying to take advantage of its superior numbers, established multiple fronts against the Iraqis, hoping to extend Iraqi forces beyond their defensive capacity and to wear them down through attrition. To the extent that Iraq had a strategy after 1982, Baghdad wanted to internationalize the conflict by bringing in the superpowers, especially the United States, so that it could exert pressure on Iran to cease and desist. Iraq eventually accomplished this goal through its initiation of the so-called tanker war, targeting ships carrying Iranian oil, a tactic that was sure to draw the attention of the international community. Iran, likewise, targeted tankers carrying Iraqi oil. The embarrassment of the Iran-Contra affair, revealed in late 1986, compelled the United States to side more openly with Iraq than it had up to that point. As such, the United States militarily intervened in the Persian Gulf to protect Kuwaiti tankers transporting oil from Iraq.

It was American military aid to Iran throughout 1985 and 1986 (contrary to a U.S.-implemented arms embargo against Iran called Operation Staunch) that constituted the Iran-Contra affair, the objective of which was to persuade moderate elements within the Iranian hierarchy to use their influence with the Iranian-funded and -influenced Shiite Muslim group called Hizbollah (Party of God) in Lebanon to release American hostages taken there. This aid actually helped the Islamist regime launch a successful offensive in early 1986 that cut Iraq off from the Persian Gulf (by taking the Faw Peninsula) and that came close to taking Iraq's second-largest city, Basra. It was this desperate state of affairs that led Iraq to engage in the tanker war, and following the uncovering of the Iran-Contra affair, the United States saw the reflagging of Kuwaiti tankers as a way to shore up its relations with Iraq and other Persian Gulf states.

With Iran more and more isolated and with the United States openly supporting Iraq, by the summer of 1988 Khomeini decided to cut his losses. In a decision that he said was more "bitter than taking poison," Khomeini accepted a UN-brokered cease-fire, ending the Iran-Iraq war. Claiming victory, Saddam then embarked on a path over the next two years that led to a fateful direct confrontation with his former ally, the United States, when he invaded Kuwait in August 1990. Since Saddam has often been in the headlines since this series of events, it is interesting to postulate why he actually invaded Iran back in 1980. Was it primarily for offensive reasons, in other words, to attain his ambitious objectives, or was it mainly for defensive reasons, especially in reaction to the threat emanating from the new regime in Teheran?

Viewpoint:
Yes. With the overthrow of the Shah in Iran and the decline of Egyptian influence, Saddam Hussein saw an opportunity to fill the power vacuum in the Arab world.

On 22 September 1980 Iraqi president Saddam Hussein ordered his troops to invade Iran. Iraqi jets attacked air bases in nine locations throughout Iran. Iranian defenses were caught by surprise. Iraq sent six divisions across the border, occupying one thousand square kilometers of Iranian territory and several towns. A major southern city, Khurramshahr, was seized. Iran refused

to accept defeat and slowly began a series of counteroffensives in 1981. The Iran-Iraq War, which lasted eight years, cost hundreds of thousands of lives and millions of injured in both countries, devastated both Iraq's and Iran's economies, and destroyed many cities and economic projects. Many considered the outcome of the war to be a cause of the Iraqi invasion of Kuwait (1990).

Tension between Iran and Iraq has deep roots. Just as in any war, there were general and specific causes. History, religion, ethnicity, ideology, territory, and ambition were all underlying causes for the war. Long-standing major problems included rivalries between the minority Sunni Muslims who dominated Iraq and the majority Shiite Muslim population. Kurdish aspirations to autonomy in northern Iraq were supported by

IRAN-IRAQ WAR

Iran to weaken Iraq's regime. There were disputes over borders that confined Iraq to its narrow access to the Persian Gulf by way of the Shatt al-Arab waterway. Iraq also perceived revolutionary Iran's Islamic agenda as threatening to its pan-Arabism. Specifically, Saddam tried to assert his rule and to dominate the region, mainly after the death of Arab nationalist Egyptian president Gamal Abd al-Nasser in 1970; the dramatic policy changes in Egypt that followed his death; and the deposition of the Shah of Iran, Mohammad Reza Pahlavi, in 1979, who had dominated the Persian Gulf region for many years.

Iraqi authorities often cited the prospect of expansion of the Shiite Islamic revolution in Iran to Iraq, the majority of whose people adhere to Shiism, as a reason to go to war. The foreign policy of the new regime in Iran was considered simply an extension of the expansionist policy of the deposed Shah, whose policies before the Revolution were supported by the United States and Britain. They saw the Shah as a guarantor of oil supplies in the Persian Gulf to the West.

Iraq, led by the pan-Arab Baath Party, protested against the Shah's policies. Baghdad presented itself as a protector of the Arab world's interests. It protested the Iranian seizure of three Gulf islands (1971) that had belonged to the United Arab Emirates (UAE) and retaliated by restricting access to Iran's oil refinery at Abadan, which is located on the eastern bank of the Shatt al-Arab waterway. Iran began to develop alternative ports along the Gulf and gave considerable support to Kurdish fighters in northern Iraq. Despite their differences, Iran and Iraq signed the landmark Algiers agreement (1975), which settled the border dispute over the Shatt al-Arab waterway in Iran's favor and ended the Shah's support of the Kurdish insurgency in Iraq. It was a major victory for Iran; the Baath regime felt compelled to accept it in order to survive.

To weaken Iran after the 1979 Revolution, Iraqi secret services engaged in failed activities to promote rebellion in the southern Iranian province of Khuzistan (called Arabistan by Iraq), which contains a majority Arab population in largely Persian Iran. Border incidents multiplied, and Saddam reacted to military clashes along the border by terminating the Algiers agreement and demanding restoration of Iraq's eastern bank of Shatt al-Arab in an effort to maximize Iraqi power. Five days later, Iraq launched a full-scale invasion of Iran, a decision taken at a moment of perceived Iranian weakness, especially since Tehran was clearly bereft of U.S. military aid following the taking of American hostages in November 1979.

To reach its goals, Iraq relied on the uprising of the Arab population at Khuzistan, the collapse of the Iranian army, and the overthrow of the Aya-

tollah Ruhollah Khomeini's regime once the southern oil fields had been separated from the rest of Iran. Iranian political leaders were engaged in an intensive power struggle. The economy was deteriorating rapidly, and the Kurds and various tribal groups in Iran were in a state of revolt. Despite these developments, Iraq failed to fulfill any of its objectives.

An important Iraqi goal was to topple the new regime in Iran, put down the Islamic revolution, and prevent its spread to Iraq. Prior to Khomeini's triumphant return to Iran on 1 February 1979, the Iraqis had opposed change in Iran by expelling Khomeini from Iraq (he was living in al-Najaf) and supporting Prime Minister Shahpour Bakhtiar.

The Iraqi government tried to justify its invasion of Iran by claiming it was a defensive or preventative war, ignoring the United Nations (UN) charter and international law that prohibited the use of force to settle disputes between states. Iraq took the offensive role without going to the UN to complain that there was an "imminent threat" from Iran. Other facilitating factors that spurred Iraq to attack were Iran's ill-equipped armed forces, an Iranian population exhausted by the new policies of the Islamic regime, and the disintegration of military leadership as most of Iran's highest ranking officers were executed or forced into exile.

Iraqi foreign policy regarding Iran was in many ways an extension of its internal politics, reflecting a policy of domination and power. Saddam desired to contain internal opposition and the Kurdish people's struggle for their national rights. In part, he wanted to divert people's attention away from Iraq's internal problems. In this way the war was a mere continuation of Saddam's policy by other means, a normal instrument of state policy.

In order to confront Iran and to build strong regional relationships, Iraq initially tried to normalize its relations with what it used to call "the reactionary regimes," such as Saudi Arabia, Jordan, Oman, and other Persian Gulf states. Iraq also sought to strengthen its relations with the West, including the United States.

To implement his hegemonic policy in the region, Saddam expanded Iraq's military capabilities by adding more naval warships and by building ports to defend the "Arabism" of the Gulf. He sought to develop military technology, hoping also to acquire nuclear weapons, in order to dominate the entire Arab world. By building such a powerful state, Saddam would be in a better position to maintain an Arab leadership role. Saddam wanted his power to be acknowledged—he was not a subtle hegemon.

Iraq sought to acquire for itself the role as guarantor of Arabian security, heretofore provided by the United States. A few months before the war, Saddam declared that he was prepared to defend Saudi Arabia from any foreign invasion and even to fight the Soviets if they attempted to occupy Saudi territory. The Iraqis spoke frequently about their opposition to the Soviet invasion of Afghanistan. Saddam, in the National Charter (1980), emphasized that the presence in the "Arab homeland of any foreign troops or military forces shall be rejected" and that no facilities for the use of Arab territory "shall be extended to them in any form or under any pretext of cover." The Charter stated that Iraq "reaffirms its readiness to assume the commitments . . . toward all Arab states or any party that adheres to it."

Saddam was imitating the Arab nationalist policy of Egyptian president Gamal Abd al-Nasser. Nassersim was the rallying cry of Arab aspirations against imperialism and Zionism and for the creation of a giant unified Arab nation. Nasser inspired the majority of Arabs to think of themselves as one nation that had to restore its glorious past. Many Arabs looked to Nasser as a symbol of Arab dignity and pride. Saddam believed in Arab nationalism, and he took refuge in Egypt during Nasser's rule when he fled Iraq in the late 1950s and early 1960s. Arab nationalism influenced Saddam's decision to invade Iran, and he used it to rally both the Iraqi and Arab people and to justify his actions.

Within Iraq the Arab nationalist faction was strengthened after the Egyptian Revolution (1952), which brought Nasser to power. One Arab nationalist group, the Baath Party, played a crucial role in Iraqi politics after the 1958 Revolution. Its official name is the Arab Baath (Renaissance) Socialist Party, with its main feature being pan-Arabism. Saddam became a prominent leader of the Baath Party and dreamed of taking over Nasser's nationalist leadership role. There is little doubt that Saddam dominated Iraqi decision making to the degree that no important decision was made without his initial approval. The Iran-Iraq War was officially called "Saddam's Qadisiyya," a reference to the location of a battle that took place between Arabs and Persians in the early days of Islam in the seventh century.

When Nasser died and Anwar Sadat became president, Sadat changed Egyptian politics dramatically by opening up to the West and embracing Israel in a peace treaty (1979) that removed Egypt from the Arab fold. The majority of Arab states opposed Sadat's appeasement policy toward Israel. Saddam presented himself as the main Arab leader who opposed the Egyptian-Israeli peace treaty.

An Iraqi victory over Iran would have made Saddam the undisputed master of the Gulf and an important leader in the Arab world, a position to which he had long aspired. Given his high self-esteem and his belief in his nation's economic might, the temptation to launch the war seems to have been irresistible. Saddam wanted to play a role similar to that of Otto von Bismarck in Prussia, and he tried to convince Arabs that he was fighting Iran to protect the eastern gate of the Arab nation and to defend the security of the Persian Gulf region.

The Iraqi defense minister, Saddam's cousin and brother-in-law Adnan Talfah, reflected this point in a speech by stating that Iraq's role is to help its Arab brothers, "many of whom are very rich, but weak militarily." He said, referring to the Persian Gulf states, that "we [the Iraqis] want them to enjoy their wealth peacefully." Saudi Arabia was too weak to confront the perceived threat of Iran. Iraq, with its pan-Arab slogans, could play a role that defended the Gulf states and served American interests in the region. The United States could then depend on Saddam as it had depended on the Shah for regional security and for the free flow of oil from the region.

The outbreak of the Iran-Iraq war was one attempt to contain and defeat Islamic Shiite radicalism in Iran, which best benefited Western interests and objectives. Iraq, aided and supported by the West and the Persian Gulf states, was successful in containing Iran. Iraq emerged as the undisputed political and military regional power, but it was also financially and politically weak.

Whatever Saddam's claims, the Iran-Iraq War was the result of many factors, internal and external, but the most important factor was Saddam's desire to be an heir to Nasser in his leadership of the Arab world and to replace the Shah as a policeman of the Gulf, with the approval of the Western world. Iraq used the war to transform its strategic position in an attempt to impose its domination over the region, as became so readily apparent with its invasion of Kuwait in August 1990.

–SHAK HANISH,
NATIONAL UNIVERSITY

Viewpoint:
No. Saddam Hussein attacked for defensive reasons, because he feared that Iran was intent on exporting its Revolution.

Because of the outright hostility between Saddam Hussein and the United States since the Persian Gulf War (1990–1991), in retrospect it is inviting to conclude that Iraq's president invaded Iran in September 1980 for purely offensive reasons; surely, this act fits the pattern that has since become commonly accepted and so flagrantly observed when Iraq invaded and occupied Kuwait in 1990, thus initiating the chain of events leading to the Gulf War. Other than possibly Osama bin Laden, there is no other single international figure as vilified in the United States and most of the rest of the world as Saddam. He launched two wars against his neighbors in the last two decades of the twentieth century; he used chemical weapons against domestic and foreign enemies alike; he flouted United Nations (UN) sanctions put into place following the Gulf War; and he ruthlessly ruled over a captive population in Stalinist fashion—he was a supreme thug, and it is almost distasteful to defend his motivations and objectives when he attacked Iran. Yet, what results after the fact should not necessarily be used to confirm current popular perception.

In 1979 the Iranian Revolution occurred, culminating in the return of the exiled Ayatollah Ruhollah Khomeini in February, upon which he proclaimed the Islamic Republic of Iran. Later that year, in November, forces loyal to Khomeini, in what was more of an internal power play than a swipe at the United States, took U.S. embassy personnel hostage for 444 days, finally releasing them in January 1981. The United States was labeled by Khomeini as the "Great Satan"—an evil that must be resisted and opposed at all costs. The United States had propped up and supported the repressive, unjust, and sacrilegious regime of Reza Shah Pahlavi. One must remember that as much as Saddam is lambasted and denounced in Western circles today, Khomeini was at least as reviled and berated while he was in power—so much so, in fact, that apart from the events surrounding the Iran-Contra affair (1985–1986), the United States, at first tacitly and then openly, supported Iraq in the Iran-Iraq War. Saddam was envisioned by both the administrations of President Ronald Reagan and President George H. W. Bush as a potential successor to the Shah of Iran as the U.S. "policeman of the Gulf," protecting and securing U.S. interests in the oil-rich Persian Gulf region; indeed, there were some important officials who even saw Saddam as a potential successor to Egyptian president Anwar Sadat, leading moderate Arab states into a comprehensive settlement of the Arab-Israeli conflict. The United States restored diplomatic relations with Iraq (broken since the 1967 Arab-Israeli War) in November 1984, and it supplied critical logistical, strategic, and material support for Iraq throughout the remainder of the conflict with Iran; indeed, the United States reflagged Kuwaiti oil tankers that were transporting Iraqi oil through the Persian

Gulf, coming into direct conflict with Iranian forces on several occasions while doing so. So at least from the perspective of Washington the immediate threat in the Persian Gulf at the time was Iran, not Iraq.

The threat from Iran following its Revolution was also apparently high in the calculations of Saddam when he decided to invade his neighbor to the east. Even though the Iranian Revolution was a Shiite Muslim revolution, Muslims across the Middle East, both Sunni and Shiite, who had become disaffected with secular pan-Arab nationalism and state building since the effectual death of Nasserist pan-Arabism in the 1967 Arab-Israeli War, hailed the event as a true harbinger of things to come. No longer would the Islamic world have to kowtow to the West and accept the inevitability of Israel. Islam's cultural identity and heritage need not be replaced by Western cultural and economic imperialism. Islamists could point with pride to a successful example of religious revolution and Islamic rule in the modern era to combat the internal and external threats to their societies. With a charismatic and firebrand demagogue such as Khomeini calling for the export of the Islamic revolution, the liberation of Jerusalem, and a confrontation with the Great Satan, the Middle East was immediately transformed. To Khomeini and his followers, the Revolution was an Islamic and not just an Iranian one; the zeal and ardor of the Revolution's supporters and the righteousness of their religious ideology would not cease at the borders of Iran. As Khomeini stated in a speech delivered on 21 March 1980, "We must strive to export our Revolution throughout the world, and must abandon all ideas of not doing so, for not only does Islam refuse to recognize any difference between Muslim countries, it is the champion of all oppressed people. Moreover, all the powers are intent on destroying us, and if we remain surrounded in a closed circle, we shall certainly be defeated." Iraq was the first target.

Iraq has a majority Shiite Arab population (about 55 percent) that is ruled by a minority Sunni Arab regime (Iraq is about 20–25 percent Sunni Arabs, and the remainder is mostly Sunni Kurds). Even though the Shiite population in Iraq is, for the most part, secularized, there was still a great deal of concern in Baghdad that the Iranian Revolution could easily spread to Shiite parts of Iraq, especially in southern Iraq—and Khomeini was publicly calling for the overthrow of the secular Baathist Iraqi regime. The Algiers accord, negotiated between the two countries in 1975, dramatically improved relations between Baghdad and Teheran and consisted of a host of agreements

UN RESOLUTION 598

In 1987 the United Nations issued the following resolution concerning the Iran-Iraq War:

Adopted by the Security Council at its 2750th meeting on 20 July 1987

The Security Council,

Reaffirming its resolution 582 (1986)

Deeply concerned that, despite its calls for a cease-fire, the conflict between Iran and Iraq continues unabated, with further heavy loss of human life and material destruction,

Deploring the initiation and continuation of the conflict,

Deploring also the bombing of purely civilian population centers, attacks on neutral shipping or civilian aircraft, the violation of international humanitarian law and other laws of armed conflict, and, in particular, the use of chemical weapons contrary to obligations under the 1925 Geneva Protocol,

Deeply concerned that further escalation and widening of the conflict may take place,

Determined to bring to an end all military actions between Iran and Iraq,

Convinced that a comprehensive, just, honourable and durable settlement should be achieved between Iran and Iraq,

Recalling the provisions of the Charter of the United Nations and in particular the obligation of all member states to settle their international disputes by peaceful means in such a manner that international peace and security and justice are not endangered,

Determining that there exists a breach of the peace as regards the conflict between Iran and Iraq,

Acting under Articles 39 and 40 of the Charter of the United Nations,

1. Demands that, as a first step towards a negotiated settlement, Iran and Iraq observe an immediate cease-fire, discontinue all military actions on land, at sea and in the air, and withdraw all forces to the internationally recognized boundaries without delay;

2. Requests the Secretary-General to dispatch a team of United Nations Observers to verify, confirm and supervise the cease-fire and withdrawal and further requests the Secretary-General to make the necessary arrangements in consultation with the Parties and to submit a report thereon to the Security Council;

3. Urges that prisoners of war be released and repatriated without delay after the cessation of active hostilities in accordance with the Third Geneva Convention of 12 August 1949;

4. Calls upon Iran and Iraq to cooperate with the Secretary-General in implementing this resolution and in mediation efforts to achieve a comprehensive, just and honourable settlement, acceptable to both sides, of all outstanding issues in accordance with the principles contained in the Charter of the United Nations;

5. Calls upon all other States to exercise the utmost restraint and to refrain from any act which may lead to further escalation and widening of the conflict and thus to facilitate the implementation of the present resolution;

6. Requests the Secretary-General to explore, in consultation with Iran and Iraq, the question of entrusting an impartial body with inquiring into responsibility for the conflict and to report to the Security Council as soon as possible;

7. Recognizes the magnitude of the damage inflicted during the conflict and the need for reconstruction efforts, with appropriate international assistance, once the conflict is ended and, in this regard, requests the Secretary-General to assign a team of experts to study the question of reconstruction and to report to the Security Council;

8. Further requests the Secretary-General to examine in consultation with Iran and Iraq and with other states of the region measures to enhance the security and stability of the region;

9. Requests the Secretary-General to keep the Security Council informed on the implementation of this resolution;

10. Decides to meet again as necessary to consider further steps to insure compliance with this resolution.

Source: *Resolution 598 (1987), United Nations, UN Documents: A Selection of Official UN Documents regarding IRAQ website <http://home.achilles.net/~sal/un-ros/un_ros_0598_(1987).html>.*

IRAN-IRAQ WAR

on issues that divided them (it was abrogated soon after the Revolution). From Saddam's perspective it seemed as if it was just a matter of time before Iran would be able to match deeds with words and seek to remove the Baathist regime from power.

In the short period of time following the Revolution the Iraqi regime also had ample evidence of the destabilizing effects of Khomeini's rise to power. Not only was there the American hostage crisis in early November, but later that month a group of Islamists in Saudi Arabia took over the Grand Mosque in Mecca, Islam's holiest site. Even though the militants were by and large Sunni, they had been galvanized and energized by the success of the Iranian Revolution. This episode was embarrassing for the Saudi monarchy, since the Al Saud are officially the Guardians of the Two Holy Places (Mecca and Medina), and a significant part of their legitimacy stems from the family's control and upkeep of the shrines as well as the annual *hajj* (pilgrimage). The apparent inability of the Saudi monarchy to protect the Grand Mosque in the face of continuing accusations from the militants of corruption and subservience to the United States amounted to a serious moment of vulnerability for the Saudi regime. The Saudis authorized force to be used in expelling the militants from the mosque, but the resulting bloodshed in Islam's holiest site almost shook the monarchy to the ground. Saddam observed this shocking episode closely.

The Iraqi president witnessed another disturbance in December 1979 that also threatened the stability of the Saudi regime, suggesting to Saddam that reverberations from the Iranian Revolution would be more than just fitful. The Shiite minority in Saudi Arabia lives, for the most part, in the northeast portion of the country in the al-Hasa region, where most of the active oil fields in the country are located. The relationship is not coincidental; the Shiite population constitutes the lion's share of oil field laborers. Overworked, underpaid, and underprivileged, the Shiites needed only a spark to cathartically unleash their frustration against the monarchy. That spark was the annual *ashura* celebration during the Islamic month of Muharram. This event, or passion play to be more precise, commemorates the martyrdom of the Imam Hussein, grandson of the Prophet Muhammad and one of the central figures in Shiite Islam, who was killed by "godless" forces on the plains outside Karbala in present-day Iraq in 680 C.E. It is a highly emotional affair, as many Shiite youths flagellate and bloody themselves in order to empathize with the suffering of the Imam Hussein. With the Iranian Revolution still burning in the hearts of many Shiites and with the Grand Mosque epi-sode still fresh in their minds, the emotional atmosphere normally present at such commemorations intensified, leading to destructive riots amid vocal support for Khomeini. Again, the Saudi regime had to use force to put down the disturbances—and Saddam looked on with increasing consternation.

There were also pro-Khomeini demonstrations and some disturbances in the island country of Bahrain, located in the Persian Gulf. Bahrain, like Iraq, is a majority Shiite Arab country ruled by a Sunni Arab minority. Taking into account all of these occurrences, Saddam obviously felt endangered by the turn of events in Iran. In addition, Saddam knew that the Ayatollah held him personally responsible for the assassination of his son in Iraq, probably at the behest of the Shah, so to the ideological and geostrategic factors weighed against Iraq can be added personal animus.

In this threatening atmosphere Saddam probably believed that the best defense was a good offense—hit Iran while it was still experiencing the destabilizing aftershocks of the Revolution. Teheran had alienated the United States, and therefore its once formidable American-supplied military no longer had direct access to U.S. spare parts, ammunition, and training. By breaking international law with the taking of American hostages, Iran had also alienated much of the international community, so Saddam most likely felt (and he was correct) that the United Nations would not be terribly interested in jumping to the aid of Iran in the event of war—and that most of the Arab states, especially those in the Persian Gulf, also felt threatened by the specter of Khomeinism and would support Iraq in its stated policy to protect the Arab world from Persian expansionism. There was also a good deal of internal political turmoil in Iran, as the various components of the coalition that overthrew the Shah jockeyed for power; the hostage crisis not only provided additional proof of the domestic instability in Iran, but it was also the crowning blow to U.S.-Iranian relations. The Iraqi invasion served to consolidate Khomeini's hold on power, as the country rallied to the defense of the homeland and allowed the theocratic regime to purge its opponents.

Undoubtedly this apparent Iranian vulnerability appeared to Saddam as an exceptional opportunity to expand his influence in the Middle East. The two Arab League summit meetings held in Baghdad (1978 and 1979) in response to the Egyptian-Israeli peace talks at Camp David overtly displayed Saddam's hegemonic ambitions. What initially elicited Iraqi thoughts of invading Iran was, indeed, the perceived imminent threat the Iranian Revolution posed. Would Saddam have invaded Iran if the Revolution had not occurred? The answer is obviously no; in fact, Iraq actually improved relations with Iran under the Shah. What changed the situation was the Iranian Revolution, which provided the opportunity that Saddam possibly had been looking for, but it is also logical to assume that he invaded Iran for primarily defensive reasons, and much of the rest of the world agreed with him.

–DAVID W. LESCH,
TRINITY UNIVERSITY

References

Christine Moss Helms, *Iraq: Eastern Flank of the Arab World* (Washington, D.C.: Brookings Institution, 1984).

Ralph King, "The Iran-Iraq War: The Political Implications," *Adelphi Papers,* 219 (Spring 1987).

David W. Lesch, *1979: The Year That Shaped the Modern Middle East* (Boulder, Colo.: Westview Press, 2001).

Phebe Marr, *The Modern History of Iraq* (Boulder, Colo.: Westview Press, 1985).

Gerd Nonneman, *Iraq, the Gulf States, and the War: A Changing Relationship, 1980–1986 and Beyond* (London & Atlantic Highlands, N.J.: Ithaca Press, 1986).

Farhang Rajaee, ed., *The Iran-Iraq War: The Politics of Aggression* (Gainesville: University Press of Florida, 1993).

Gary Sick, "Trial by Error: Reflections on the Iran-Iraq War," in *Iran's Revolution: The Search for Consensus,* edited by R. K. Ramazani (Bloomington: Indiana University Press, 1990).

IRANIAN REVOLUTION

Did the 1977–1979 Revolution in Iran rid the country of a repressive tyrant?

Viewpoint: Yes. Despite the negative publicity the Revolution received, it was mostly a positive development that set the stage for a democratic society in Iran.

Viewpoint: No. The Revolution led to an even more repressive regime coming to power that had a negative impact on Iran over the long term.

The culmination of the Iranian Revolution was marked by the return of the Ayatollah Ruhollah Khomeini to Teheran on 1 February 1979, effectively signaling the end of the reign of Muhammad Reza Pahlavi, otherwise known as the Shah of Iran, and the beginning of the Islamic Republic of Iran. Various explanations of the Iranian Revolution draw from the historical experience of Iran dating back to the Safavid empire of the sixteenth and seventeenth centuries, when Shiite Islam became the state religion; the Qajar period in the nineteenth century, when Iran encountered Russian and British imperialism; and World War I (1914–1918), which paved the way for the Pahlavi dynasty to come to power in 1925 with the ascension to the peacock throne of Muhammad Reza Shah's father, known simply as Reza Shah. Other explanations focus on World War II (1939–1945), when Reza Shah was removed by the British in 1941 because of his perceived pro-German sympathies. His young and untested teenage son was then placed on the throne in 1945, beholden to the British and soon to the Americans, facing a host of challenges, particularly one emanating from an austere intellectual liberal constitutionalist named Muhammad Musaddiq, whose overthrow in 1953 was engineered in Washington and London.

Virtually all of the explanations for the Iranian Revolution, however, touch at least to some degree on the subject of change resulting from the overly rapid modernization process the Shah had embarked upon in earnest in the early 1960s. This change had economic, political, and social repercussions, accelerating what scholar Nikki R. Keddie called the "dual culture" nature of Iranian society, which had in effect begun when the Shah's father implemented his own modernization program in the 1920s and 1930s. Whenever there is change of a significant order brought on by regime policy, there are those who benefit from it, and there are those who do not. The environment for revolutions tends to become much more propitious when the bulk of the population considers itself in the latter category.

In the 1960s and especially in the 1970s, with the available capital from increased revenues resulting from the oil price hike following the Arab-Israeli War (1973), the Shah implemented an economic program that many other countries, particularly in the developing world, also attempted: import-substituting industrialization (ISI). The idea behind ISI was to move nations that were traditionally dependent upon imports for primary and secondary products to an industrial footing. In essence, ISI, riding the crest of the wave of nationalism that had been sweeping across the post-British and post-French colonial world, was supposed to create economically independent countries that would no longer be subject to the economic, and thus political, whims of the developed world. In Iran, ISI was intended to establish a solid economic foundation for the Shah's dream of making his nation a regional power that also, with the growing dependence of the West upon Middle East oil and at the height of the Organization of Petroleum Exporting Countries (OPEC)'s influence, would be a player of global significance.

Even though ISI resulted in a growing gross national product (GNP) in the immediate term, internally the economic, political, and social gaps between classes only widened. With ISI's emphasis on heavy industry, the agricultural sector was typically neglected, which directly affected a significant portion of the population since the vast majority of workers were still farmers. Therefore, incomes in the agricultural sector tended to decrease (or at least not increase at nearly as high a rate as bourgeois and upper-class incomes). The so-called *bazaaris* (small merchants) also tended to suffer from economic policies designed to the advantage of large-scale manufacturers. In other words, no adequate consumer base was developed that could keep the factories operating at full capacity. As a result, economies of scale subsequently drove up the price of products, which, subsequently, could only be purchased by the upper classes, exacerbating the separation of classes. It was this disenchantment that Ayatollah Khomeini and others tapped into and that generated the revolutionary period of 1977–1979.

The Shah also enacted policies and adopted measures of a noneconomic nature that further alienated Iranians from the regime and created more fodder for revolutionary propaganda. The event singled out most often as an indication of the Shah's megalomania and how out of touch he was with the vast majority of his subjects was the $300 million "party" he hosted in 1971 to commemorate the 2,500th anniversary of the Achmaenid dynasty, held at the ancient site of Persepolis. Not only was the lavishness and prodigality an affront to many Iranians living in poverty, but the celebration of a pre-Islamic entity or event was offensive to the religious classes and to a deeply traditional society as a whole. Other aspects of the Shah's reign that added to the opposition's ranks were the repressive activities of his security apparatus, known by its Persian acronym SAVAK, and his close relationship, especially in terms of military cooperation, with the United States, as well as his strategic relationship with Israel.

A series of events in the 1977–1979 period coalesced elements of the opposition and fueled the revolutionary fervor that bridges the oftentimes large gap between a vocal opposition and actually taking the actions necessary to overthrow the regime. These flash points also brought to the fore various groups or individuals, in this case the Ayatollah, who seized the moment and rose to leadership positions within the movement. One particular event in September 1978 became the turning point in the Revolution. An apparent misunderstanding about the timing of a curfew announcement following a peaceful opposition march of more than one million people in Teheran led to the deaths of up to one thousand Iranians killed in a follow-up demonstration. This tragic event, known in Iran as Black Friday, essentially ended any hope of accommodation between most elements of the opposition and the regime. It was also when many Iranians began to see the value of Khomeini's uncompromising stand, which he had been enunciating for years: the Shah had to go, and an Islamic republic had to be formed.

More-moderate alternative solutions, such as the constitutional monarchy advocated by some opposition groups, had little chance of succeeding because of the virulent anti-Shah hostility that had been building, which was vividly displayed in huge demonstrations and widespread strikes. The Shah effectively abdicated by leaving the country on 16 January 1979, weak from the cancer that would take his life shortly thereafter. All that was left was for Khomeini to triumphantly return from his fifteen-year exile on 1 February.

Viewpoint:
Yes. Despite the negative publicity the Revolution received, it was mostly a positive development that set the stage for a democratic society in Iran.

Almost twenty-five years after the Iranian Revolution (1977–1979), Iran is still struggling to build the just and prosperous "Islamic" society Ayatollah Ruhollah Khomeini and the Shiite *ulema* (Muslim clerics) had envisioned. The takeover of the state ideology and apparatus by the *ulema* and their allies, however, has led to the creation of an expanded network of personalities and institutions, united by their common "Islamic" ideology and privileged economic and political positions in society. Society in Iran in the meantime has gone through drastic socioeconomic and cultural changes, much of it because of the ideology and policies of the state itself. Iranian society today is dynamic and burgeoning, with an energetic young generation that is more concerned with sociopolitical freedom and tangible material gains than spiritual fulfillment through living an "Islamic" life. State-society relations in Iran, although currently stigmatized with persistent economic problems, political polarization, and state repressiveness, is heading toward a more balanced position. Iran for the first time in its long history is on the verge of political democracy and possibly a more mature and prosperous economy, something that would not have emerged as such without the Revolution. The removal of the monarchy and the entrance of the *ulema* to the center stage of politics have drastically changed the historical and modern forces of Iranian society, setting the stage for a democratic Iran. The harsh years following the Revolution are the price millions of Iranians are paying in the realization of a free society.

The history of modern Iran coincides with the rise of the Reza Shah Pahlavi to the throne in 1925, itself the consequence of years of the persistent political ineptitude of the last monarchs of the Qajar dynasty, constitutional revolution, foreign occupation and control, and overall political instability in the first quarter of the twentieth century. Reza Shah's ascendance to power was facilitated by the British colonial influence interested in a new oil-rich, united, and stable Persia under strong leadership to counter the Soviets' ambitions in expanding southward toward the Persian Gulf. Reza Shah proved himself to be much like his admired counterpart in neighboring Turkey, Mustafa Kemal Ataturk, a secular nationalist. Reza Shah's drive for modernization in Iran resulted in a strong centralized government and somewhat successful attempts at building the foundation of a modern economy and society. Reza Shah, although a dictator, created, inter alia, Iran's first modern army, a more cohesive tax system, an education system, an expanded network of roads, and a railroad system. Reza Shah's attempt at laying the industrial foundation of Iran through close cooperation with Germany for building Iran's first steel mill was, however, interrupted by European colonial rivalry vying for influence in Iran, the advent of World War II (1939–1945), and his eventual abdication from power in September 1941 when invading Soviet and British forces ignored Iran's neutrality.

The landed elite and the religious *ulema* challenged Reza Shah's attempts at socio-economic reforms. The *ulema* continued losing their hold on society in the areas of education, administration of justice, and control of religious or Waqf land that was also a source of income. The Uniform Dress Law of December 1928 introduced Iranians to Western dress and the so-called Pahlavi cap, followed later by a ban on the wearing of the *chador*, the long head-to-toe cloth that covers women's bodies. The *ulema*, although weakened by Reza Shah's reforms, maintained their

hold on society and coexisted with, and sometimes rivaled, the state as a major source of social power, culminating in their taking over the state in 1979. The landed elite continued, however, to resist reforms, and by 1946 peasants still constituted 75 percent of the labor force.

Reza Shah's patrimonial style of leadership did not attempt political institutionalization and reform. Political opposition remained either nonexistent or oppressed; political parties, organized labor, and agents of civil society were not allowed to function, and the state's overwhelming presence left no public space for ordinary people to have a voice in the affairs of the state. Intellectual and professional opposition were similarly suffocated.

The reign of Muhammad Reza Shah began with his ascension to power in 1941 and Iran's occupation by the Soviet and British "allied" powers. The young Shah continued his father's mission of modernization, but he remained heavily dependent on American power and largesse for his survival and continued rule. At the conclusion of World War II, the Shah relied on the United States to force Soviet troops out of northern Iran, but he also had to tolerate political opposition from Iranian nationalists and the Left. The post–World War II relative political freedom led to the coming to power in 1951 of Prime Minister Muhammad Mussadiq, whose nationalist fervor put the young insecure Shah on the defensive on the issue of nationalization of Iran's oil industry. Mussadiq's drive for nationalization challenged British control of the Iranian oil industry and made the Eisenhower administration in the United States nervous about the seeming rise of popularity of the leftist Tudeh Party. Mussadiq successfully challenged the young Shah, forcing him to leave the country for exile, but the oil-dependent Iranian economy after months of boycotts by the Anglo-Iranian Oil Company (later called British Petroleum) was in trouble by 1953, resulting in scattered demonstrations against Mussadiq's administration. It took the Central Intelligence Agency (CIA) relatively little finance and effort to convince the Iranian military, in the absence of religious leadership support for the Mussadiq government, to overthrow the regime.

The return of His Majesty to the throne in 1953 was the beginning of a long and close relationship between the Shah and the United States. The CIA took the responsibility for training Iran's notorious SAVAK as well as training and arming the Iranian armed forces. American support for the Shah remained strong: Iran became a regional ally to the United States, received the latest weaponry in the U.S. arsenals, and, upon the departure of the British naval forces from the Persian Gulf in 1971, was entrusted by the United States to safeguard the security of the Persian Gulf region. The Shah served his purpose by taking a pro-Israeli posture in the Arab-Israeli conflict. He supplied Israel with its fuel needs and, when asked, sent Iranian troops to Oman and successfully defended the conservative monarch, Sultan Qaboos, against leftist insurgents. Iran under the Shah, along with Saudi Arabia and other conservative Persian Gulf states, also had an overall moderate approach toward setting oil-export quotas in the Organization of Petroleum Exporting Countries (OPEC).

The Shah embarked upon some crucial socio-economic reforms, but his rush for Westernization left most Iranian people deprived of real economic benefits and confused with the speed of change and the assault on traditional Islamic values. The Shah, like his father, had little respect for the *ulema* and their role in society in maintaining social cohesion. The Shah's insistence on secularization of Iranian society, combined with imbalanced and uneven economic development, favor shown urban centers at the expense of the rural population, and almost total negligence of political development, set Iran on its path toward revolution. The impressive economic growth in the 1960s later accelerated in the 1970s with the rise in oil prices, but it still left the bulk of the population deprived of basic necessities such as fresh water, electricity, access to public baths, and decent roads. The rising middle class, professionals, and intellectuals also had to contend with His Majesty's absolutist rule, not having any avenues— such as legitimate political parties, labor unions, and civic associations—to participate in politics. For example, as Reza Baraheni recalled in *The Crowned Cannibals: Writings on Repression in Iran* (1977), "in Quri-Chai, the northern slums of Tabriz, there is only one school for 100,000 schoolchildren. In most of the cities of Baluchestan, there is only one bath for the entire population (in the city of Bampour, for instance), but since people are so poor that they cannot afford to pay the nickel required to go to the bath, it has fallen in ruins. People have frozen to death in winter in this great oil-producing country."

In the political arena, the Shah became increasingly authoritarian, and by 1975 he declared Iran a one-party system, although the two existing (mostly ceremonial) parties in Iran were merely legitimating tools for the regime and had no real power. According to Amnesty International's Annual Report 1974/1975, "the total number of political prisoners was in 1975 between 25,000 to 100,000." The Secretary General of Amnesty International, Martin Ennals, wrote in the report, "The Shah of Iran retains his benevolent image despite the highest rate of death penalties in the world, no valid system of civilian courts and a history of torture which is beyond belief." Moreover, "Ninety-five percent of all the available press in Iran was in the hands of two families, the Mesbahzadeh and Mas'udi families who ran Kayhan and Etteleat publications, who took their orders from the Shah and the police." The Shah's intolerance for minorities also was evident in his policy of "Persianization" of Iran, practically trying to assimilate, but not integrate, the Turkish, Kurdish, Arab, and other minorities into the dominant Persian culture. Baraheni in 1977 wrote:

> Shah also pursued racist policies to Persianize the Azerbaijanis and the Kurds and the Arabs and the Baluchis. For example, the 3,000 American children brought to Iran by their parents working for Grumman can go to an English-speaking school. Yet millions of native Iranian children born to Azerbaijani, Kurdish and Arab parents do not have even one school in which they can study everything in their native languages. This is only one aspect of the Shah's racism.

The Iranian society's experiences in the post-Revolution era have also been intense, violent, and widespread. The revolutionary upheaval, antigovernment armed insurgencies by opposition groups, eight-year-long war with Iraq (1980–1988), rapid population growth and urbanization, flood of Afghani and Iraqi refugees, U.S. economic sanctions, and most of all, the persistent economic crisis have had an enduring impact. These events, along with the deliberate state policy of "Islamization" and populist economic policies to give priority to rural development and an overall more balanced approach to development, have reshaped Iran's socio-economic and political structure. Despite all the shortcomings of the Revolution, Iranian society's outlook on the state and its own self-image has fundamentally changed.

The power distribution in state-society relations until the Revolution had been structured by a complex relationship among the monarchy and its supporters, the *ulema* and the religious establishment, and the traditional *bazaaris* (small merchants). The politically powerless middle and working classes did not play central roles in setting the national agenda. Similarly, the intellectuals' influence over the masses in the national struggle for freedom—which since the Constitutional Revolution (1906) had focused against anticolonialism and foreign domination and not democracy per se—remained marginal for the most part.

Intellectuals, professionals, the media, filmmakers, and artists are now among the forerunners in the national struggle for democracy and freedom. It is only in the past twenty years that

DELIBERATE AND DREADFUL SLAUGHTER

Sattareh Farman Farmaian describes some of the revolutionary events that occurred in Iran in 1979:

On September 4, in observance of a religious holiday, a series of peaceful demonstrations began in the capital, larger than any in the past. The crowds were gigantic, composed of men and women from every class and political viewpoint, with tens of thousands of people chanting in unison the best-known slogan of the opposition movement: "*Allahu akbar, Khomeini rahbar*": "God is Great, Khomeini is our leader." Over the next three days, despite the calls of the National Front and the moderate religious opposition for restraint, these peaceful demonstrations became larger and more radical-sounding, until over half a million people were shouting slogans calling for the downfall of the Shah, an end to America's presence in our country, the return of Ayatollah Khomeini from exile—and, for the first time, an Islamic republic. Scrawled messages appeared on walls, in doorways, and on banners that the crowds waved: "Death to the Shah and the Imperialists," "Bring back Ayatollah Khomeini," "We want an Islamic republic."

On Friday, September 8, unaware that on the previous evening the Shah had forced the cabinet to declare martial law, an enormous crowd estimated to be somewhere between five and twenty thousand people staged a sit-down protest in Jaleh Square in South Tehran. Ordered to leave by the troops of the general who had just been appointed governor of the capital—the same man who had ordered the shooting of protestors in June 1963—they refused, and with that the soldiers began pumping round after round into the defenseless crowd. Soon Jaleh Square looked like a slaughterhouse, with blood running on the pavement and prone bodies piled up one on top of the other, wherever they had been sitting or standing. The killing went on all day. Army helicopter gunships hunted down demonstrators who fled. Not even the riots of 1963 had seen such deliberate and dreadful slaughter. September 8 became known to Iranians as "Black Friday.". . .

This horrible event shattered any hope of gradual political progress, or even of a return to normal life. . . .

On November fourth, the worst violence Tehran had seen yet began when the army fired into a crowd of students at the University who, to mark the fourteenth anniversary of Ayatollah Khomeini's exile to Iraq, were trying to pull down a statue of the Shah. The next day, hundreds of thousands of people demonstrated in the center of the city, and smoke rose from the European shops on the Avenue Lalezar and every other business associated with the West, luxury, and imperialism. Foreign banks and the British Embassy were set ablaze and barricades of tires, rubble from construction sites, and abandoned cars were erected to block the way of the tanks that ground along the streets, and from which soldiers fired on unarmed demonstrators.

Late that afternoon, the Shah flew over the city in his helicopter to view the charred husks of high-rise hotels, cinemas, stores, and the Embassy building. He was reported to be distraught, close to a nervous breakdown, because the Americans would not tell him what to do about the demonstrators. The next day, however, the government announced that the Shah would take decisive measures to deal with the crisis. Once again, people felt relieved, expecting that at last the Shah understood that he must relinquish power.

That evening, November sixth, the king went on television. Weeping and in a breaking voice, he declared that the wave of strikes was justified. The people, he said, had risen against oppression and corruption, and he, their king—before he had always referred to himself as Iran's "emperor"—had heard their "revolutionary message" and supported it. The monarchy was "a gift entrusted to him by the constitution and the people," and he, our king, would rectify "past mistakes."

Source: *Sattareh Farman Farmaian, with Dona Munker,* Daughter of Persia: A Woman's Journey From Her Father's Harem Through the Islamic Revolution *(New York: Crown, 1992), pp. 296–297, 303–304.*

the monarchy disappeared as a central contender for power, and the *ulema* was weakened as the legitimate heir to Allah's rule on earth in the absence of a *Mahdi* (Messiah). The rise of the *ulema* to political power, moreover, exposed their vulnerabilities to trappings of power, thereby raising doubt about their ability and sincerity to act simultaneously as political and religious leaders. The *ulema,* now contenders for power, are no longer perceived as sincere men of God and immune from corruption. When Reporters Without Borders published its first worldwide press-freedom index on 23 October 2002, Iran was ranked 122 out of 139. The index measures how much freedom journalists and the media have and what efforts the government makes to ensure press freedom. Overall, according to Naser Momayesi, "the clergy's direct involvement in state affairs has made it the main target of blame for the ills of society and the state. The cleric's mismanagement of the economy, totalitarian control over the country's cultural life, and above all, abuse of power, have severely undermined their once untarnished moral authority."

Nevertheless, Iran is making progress toward its Millennium Development Goals. It is "on track" in the following areas: halving the proportion of people suffering from hunger and undernourishment, eliminating gender disparity in education, reducing by two-thirds the under-five and infant mortality rates, and halving the proportion of people without access to improved water resources. It is slipping back, however, in ensuring that all children complete primary education, in terms of the net primary-school enrollment ratio. Iranians remain concerned with their future, and like people elsewhere they mostly care about their families and their economic well-being. A poll has found that the greatest public concerns are inflation and unemployment. Of the people surveyed, 74.6 percent said that economic issues are the biggest societal problem. Almost 50 percent said that inflation is their biggest concern; 18 percent complained about unemployment; and 10 percent mentioned corruption. When asked to prioritize their concerns, unemployment came out ahead of inflation and high prices.

The polarization of politics has intensified and must come to a resolution, since the survival of the Islamic Republic depends on it. Ayatollah Hussein Ali Montazeri, the most prominent critic of Ayatollah Khamenei (the Supreme Guide in Iran and ultimate authority), with millions of supporters has called for changes to the Iranian constitution so that the concentration of power in the hands of a single person does not continue. Montazeri also has suggested that "either the post of president and spiritual leader

should be combined to create a powerful elected leader or the president should be given more powers and the spiritual leader should just fill an advisory role." Montazeri subsequently sent a written message to the legislature in which he stated his support for legislation that would limit the Guardian Council's power. Montazeri wrote, "The Guardian Council has denied people's rights and restricted their freedom in vetting hopefuls standing for elections." Montazeri said the council has deviated from its mandate and abused its authority in the vetting process.

Given the socio-economic and political problems of Iran, it is hard to conceive of a better Iran anytime soon. There are still severe economic and social problems in Iran, and the polarization of politics in the past twenty-four years is likely to continue for some time to come. However, the cultural, social, and political fabric of Iran has fundamentally changed, and with the eventual resolution of political stagnation the path to renewed economic, social, and political vibrancy will occur. For the moment, the biggest challenge is to find the appropriate place of Islam in society and politics, where it will remain a dominant social force but without overwhelming all social, political, and economic activities. The removal of the institution of monarchy, the rise and now seeming decline of the "absolutist version of Shiite clerical rule," and the overall social and economic changes have left Iran a place totally different from its past under the Shah and indeed since the early 1500s when Shiite Islam became the state ideology that united Persia under the Safavid dynasty. True, the human-rights record of the Islamic Republic as well as its economic performance leaves one wondering about the future of Iranian society and politics, but the turbulent years of the postrevolutionary period is the price Iranians are paying for a more civil society and polity and hopefully a more prosperous economy in the future.

–ALI ABOOTALEBI,
UNIVERSITY OF WISCONSIN–EAU CLAIRE

Viewpoint:
No. The Revolution led to an even more repressive regime coming to power that had a negative impact on Iran over the long term.

The Iranian Revolution (1977–1979), which replaced the monarchical regime with a millenarian Islamist tradition in Iran, was a significant event in the twentieth century. After the departure of Muhammad Reza Shah, the Shiite clergy gathered around Ayatollah Ruhollah Khomeini, who emerged as the new power and achieved his aim: the establishment of an Islamic government. In order to accomplish this goal, the clergy did not hesitate to use every means available. Censorship, repression, purges, and mass demonstrations were used by the religious leaders to silence or exile those liberals, nationalists, progressives, and other Left-wingers who had formed part of their coalition that opposed the Shah's regime. The clergy, however, claimed exclusive responsibility for the Revolution. According to Khomeini, "it was the clergy that carried out the uprising," and the monopoly of power rested with it. The new leadership gave birth to a despotic and authoritarian regime, bringing the Persian country as much repression as that which had existed under the Shah, as well as international isolation. Khomeini's aim was to replace the Pahlavi monarchy with a theocracy, where absolute authority was supposed to be in religious *faqih* (jurist) hands, but in reality it was in his own hands. In fact, his state theory was implemented in Iran soon after the Revolution, based solely on the concept of *velayat-e faqih* (religious jurists' government), upon which is based the constitution of the Islamic Republic of Iran.

The modernization program imposed by the Shah, which, according to the clergy, had poisoned Iranian society through materialism and cultural influence from abroad, had been superficial and had not benefited the population. The Shah seemed committed to destroying Islam, the source of national spirituality. He had exiled Khomeini, reduced the power of *ulema* (Muslim clergy), killed theology students, and introduced Western-based reforms, such as women's emancipation.

Khomeini's goal was to create a just society, ruled according to *sharia* (Islamic law). In November 1978, Khomeini declared that the purpose of the Revolution was to found an Islamic Republic and protect the independence and democracy of the Iranian state, but the problem of uniting popular sovereignty (democracy) with the religious jurists' government proved to be an impossible task. Resorting to the concept of democracy, however, was useful for the Ayatollah to attract as wide a coalition as possible against the Shah's regime. His political skill was utilized to unify the different factions of a movement: the clergy, Marxists, nationalists, and socialist Shiites. Actually, Khomeini was not interested in democratic developments in the Revolution, as was shown in the process that led to the constitution of the Islamic Republic and by the wave of purges following his seizure of power. In fact, in the name of religion, the rights of the population were sacrificed and any hope for democracy was destroyed.

The Islamic character of the Iranian state was already specified in the constitution's preamble: "In the view of Islam, government does not derive from the interests of a class, nor does it serve the domination of an individual or a group. Rather, it represents the fulfilment of the political ideal of a people who bear a common faith and common outlook, taking an organized form in order to initiate the process of intellectual and ideological evolution towards the final goal, i.e., movement towards Allah." Actually, the writing of the Iranian constitution was a complex and tricky process, above all the introduction of the concept of *velayat-e faqih*. It was a process that was always completely controlled by Khomeini. In fact, the Iranian clergy as a whole was not in favor of the introduction of this concept into the constitution, believing it would lead to a religious dictatorship and a clerical tyranny. The foundation of the new Islamic Republic had to be built on an "exemplary society" with the assistance of "Islamic ideals," the realization of the "movement's religious principles," not only for the Iranians but for Muslims all over the world, in other words, for any *mostaz'afin* (those deprived of rights). The preamble of the constitution states:

> With due attention to the Islamic content of the Iranian Revolution, which has been a movement aimed at the triumph of all the *mostaz'fin* over the *mostakbirun* [oppressors], the Constitution provides the necessary basis for ensuring the continuation of the Revolution at home and abroad. In particular, in the development of international relations, the Constitution will strive with other Islamic and popular movements to prepare the way for the formation of a single world community.

In order to create an Islamic community, it was necessary to fight against the heathen.

Khomeini regarded war as "an essential element in the Islamic Revolution" and as "its philosophy of human experience." The decision to continue the war (1980–1988) against Iraq (even after the withdrawal of Iraqi troops from Iranian territory) was taken by Khomeini, the only political figure in Iran with the power to decide in favor of war or peace. According to Khomeini, "our war is not aimed solely against Saddam, but against all unbelief." The war against evil, against Satan's followers, according to Khomeinist ideology, represented the exclusive task of Allah's partisans. To fight against Satan meant fighting against the world powers, first of all the United States (Great Satan), considered as "devils of varying degrees of evil." In this context, it is necessary to analyze the famous slogans "Neither West Nor East," "Export the Revolution and the Islamic

Republic," and "War, War until Victory," from which the Khomeinist conception of the Islamic state and its role in global politics emerged. Asserting the universality of Islam, the new Islamic state was obliged to pursue its aims, such as spreading the faith. This goal is represented in a desire not only to be independent from the two superpower blocs but also to achieve an even more ambitious aim—to establish an Islamic society all over the globe. It was an Islamic, not just an Iranian, revolution. The state was employed for this purpose. The ideologically oriented army of Revolutionary Guards was not only responsible for the defense of the state, but it could also take on "the burden of the ideological mission, i.e., the holy war (jihad) to spread the rule of God's law throughout the world." In fact, soon after the Revolution, several agencies were established with the task of spreading the revolutionary message to Muslims all over the world.

The founding of the Hizbollah (Party of God) movement in Lebanon represents the most important and successful example of the Iranian intent to export the Revolution beyond its borders. Khomeini's Iran turned the Lebanese movement into a viable terrorist organization, sending to Lebanon not only weapons and ammunition but also Revolutionary Guard officers in order to instruct Shiite volunteers. Iranian foreign policy has tried to unite state interests and the ideal of exporting the Revolution. Khomeini's Iran became a leader of the Islamic radical movement, culturally, economically, and politically supporting those groups engaged in the struggle against the United States. The consequences of Iran's foreign policy have been striking: the long and exhausting war against Iraq resulted in more than one million casualties and economically destroyed the two countries, and the support for Islamic radical groups brought on international isolation and economic sanctions promoted by the United States that further crushed the already deteriorating Iranian economy.

The preamble to the Iranian constitution states that, while founding the political structures at the heart of this new society, "the righteous will assume the responsibility of governing and administering the country (in accordance with the Koranic verse 'Verily My righteous servants shall inherit the earth' [21:105]). Legislation setting forth regulations for the administration of society will revolve around the Koran and the Sunnah. Accordingly, the exercise of meticulous and earnest supervision by just, pious, and committed scholars of Islam is an absolute necessity."

According to Khomeini's state theory, described in his writings ten years before the Revolution, the religious jurists' powers had to be absolute and the leader's power had to be even more absolute. He had to fulfill the function of a guardian of law, a protector, and a liberator. People were not active subjects of the state, but rather they were its object. From 1979 to when Khomeini died in 1989 a period of autocracy existed. The absolute power of the velayat-e faqih, theorized by Khomeini, had to be similar to the total authority the Prophet wielded in his role as God's deputy on earth. The introduction of this concept into the constitution allowed the Ayatollah to wield an unlimited amount of power in every aspect of public administration. On the basis of this concept, Khomeini wielded dictatorial power in every political field, imposed his will in all government bodies, and made important decisions without consulting anyone. It was the restoration of a dictatorship, but this time under the Ayatollah's turban. The utopian ideals of the Revolution were acted on by an exclusive group of revolutionaries, who soon adopted intolerant positions toward every kind of criticism or dissent. Political parties were banned; freedom was denied; and certain mannerisms were regarded as immoral.

Khomeini often acted in violation of established procedures. Much of his power was derived from his qualities as a charismatic leader. His absolute powers, sanctioned by the constitution, nullified popular sovereignty, which was constitutionally recognized (articles 56–61). In fact, the powers of the institutions representing the people (the parliament, the president of the republic, and the Assembly of Leadership Experts) are extremely limited. The Majlis (parliament) is elected by the people and empowered to make laws, but it is not the only source of law in Iran. It shares its decision-making power with eleven members of the Council of Guardians who, according to the constitution, have the right to review and therefore to reject those laws produced by the parliament that they do not regard as compatible with the principles of Islam. The Council of Guardians can also interfere with the Council of Ministers' decrees, statutes, and treaties. The president of the republic is the highest-ranking public official in the country. It is his responsibility to implement the constitution and act as the head of the executive, "except in matters directly concerned with the office of the Leadership" (Article 113). In a republican regime, the most powerful official of the state should be the head of government. In Iran the president is not the highest authority of the state. According to Article 112 of the constitution, the religious figure of the velayat-e faqih, guardian of religious law and leader of the revolution, is the supreme source of authority and power. Article 110 describes his "power to determine the general policies of the system of the Islamic Republic of Iran, supervise the good performance of the regime's general policies, hold

the supreme command of the armed forces, declare war or peace, dismiss the President of the Republic." Therefore the final decision on important domestic or foreign policy questions rests exclusively with the Supreme Guide of the Revolution. Power is distributed in a hierarchical and inequitable way among the institutions of the state. Religious bodies constitutionally hold the power to portray the public policies of the Islamic republic as infallible.

The Islamic community prevails over the Iranian nation; Islamic principles and rules limit the rights of people; the Council of Guardians deprives the parliament of its power and ultimately controls the president of the republic. The concept of *velayat-e faqih* contradicts the very idea of republicanism. Although rights are sanctioned by the constitution, they are immediately limited in the name of Islamic principles. For example, if Article 26 says that the "formation of parties, societies, political or professional associations, as well as religious societies, whether Islamic or pertaining to one of the recognized religious minorities, is permitted," this right is recognized provided that "they do not

violate the principles of independence, freedom, national unity, the criteria of Islam, or the basis of the Islamic Republic." Thus, in the name of the Revolution such freedom is suppressed. Every opposition party was banned officially because an Islamic society was moving together toward a common goal, led by only one leader, who was God's representative on earth; therefore, no reason to divide it into opposite political forces existed. No kind of opposition was tolerated. During a speech in November 1979, Khomeini announced the suppression of freedom of the press, too. Less than half of the 444 newspapers and magazines remained open. In 1988 only 121 were still active and all of them were controlled, although in different ways, by the Islamic government.

Despite the existence of democratic elements and the role Iranians want to play in political life, voting for parliamentary candidates and the president of the republic remains significantly restricted. Candidates must be judged suitable by Islamic jurists, and there are no institutions safeguarding the political and civil rights of citizens. A man, a clergyman, or a politi-

Ayatollah Ruhollah Khomeini, Supreme Leader of the Islamic Republic of Iran (center with hand raised), in 1979

(© AP/Wide World Photos)

IRANIAN REVOLUTION

cal personality may be elected president but only after declaring himself loyal to the principles of the Islamic Republic and the state religion (this excludes, for example, Sunni Muslims and those who belong to other religions). He must be subject to the Supreme Guide's will.

This repressive policy and the atrocities committed in the name of the Revolution have had devastating effects on Iranian society. Discrimination and violations of the people's rights have severely affected Iranians' lives. Religious leaders have preferred to continue using violence and terror in order to wield every political and economic lever of power. Nevertheless, their inability to create a dynamic economy, to guarantee the well-being of the population, and to encourage freedom has not only caused a legitimacy crisis for the Revolution, but it has also ironically produced a revolutionary atmosphere against it.

–VALENTINA VANTAGGIO,
UNIVERSITY OF LECCE

References

Mohammed Amjad, *Iran: From Royal Dictatorship to Theocracy* (New York & London: Greenwood Press, 1989).

Said Amir Arjomand, *The Turban for the Crown: The Islamic Revolution in Iran* (New York: Oxford University Press, 1988).

Mehrzad Boroujerdi, *Iranian Intellectuals and the West: The Tormented Triumph of Nativism* (Syracuse, N.Y.: Syracuse University Press, 1996).

Eric Hooglund, ed., *Twenty Years of Islamic Revolution: Political and Social Transition in Iran since 1979* (Syracuse, N.Y.: Syracuse University Press, 2002).

Homa Katouzian, *The Political Economy of Modern Iran: Despotism and Pseudo-Modernism, 1926–1979* (London: Macmillan, 1981).

Nikki R. Keddie, *Roots of Revolution: An Interpretive History of Modern Iran* (New Haven: Yale University Press, 1981).

Ayatollah Ruhollah Khomeini, *Islam and Revolution: Writings and Declarations of Imam Khomeini,* translated and annotated by Hamid Algar (London: KPI, 1981).

George Lenczowski, ed., *Iran under the Pahlavis* (Stanford, Cal.: Hoover Institution Press, 1979).

David Menashri, *Post-Revolutionary Politics in Iran: Religion, Society and Power* (London & Portland, Ore.: Frank Cass, 2001).

IRANIAN REVOLUTION

IRAQI REVOLUTION

Was the Iraqi Revolution of 1958 a step forward in the political development of Iraq?

Viewpoint: Yes. The Iraqi Revolution expanded the political base in Iraq, removing the ancien régime and opening the door for independent socio-economic development.

Viewpoint: No. The Iraqi Revolution was a violent event that established a precedent for future political developments in the country.

The Iraqi Revolution occurred on 14 July 1958. The Hashemite monarchy that had ruled over Iraq since the country was artificially formed by the victorious European powers following World War I (1914–1918) was swept aside by a new regime led by General Abd al-Karim Qassim. Both the young King Faisal II and his regent (and uncle) Crown Prince Abd al-Ilah were executed, along with the oft-serving and powerful pro-Western prime minister, Nuri al-Said.

Until this time Iraq had generally established a working, if not close, relationship with Great Britain, which was assigned as the mandate power over Iraq in the post–World War I agreements. Even though Iraq had formally achieved independence as well as entrance into the League of Nations by the early 1930s, London still retained control over Iraq's defense and foreign policies and the wherewithal to influence domestic politics. As such, Iraq became a linchpin of Western Cold War defense schemes after World War II (1939–1945), exemplified by the consummation of the Baghdad Pact (1955).

The Suez War (1956) really sealed the fate of the Iraqi monarchy. The immense popularity accruing to Egyptian president Gamal Abd al-Nasser after withstanding the tripartite invasion by the British, French, and Israelis cast the British-supported Hashemite regime in an increasingly negative light in the region. Egypt was clearly winning the inter-Arab rivalry with Iraq as the latter became more isolated in the Arab world. Nasserism was reaching its climax, crowned by the formation of the United Arab Republic (the merger of Syria and Egypt) in February 1958. The pan-Arab Nasserist tide was building in and outside of Iraq, and it only seemed a matter of time before the ancien régime fell to a combination of forces that had opposed the monarchy.

Viewpoint:
Yes. The Iraqi Revolution expanded the political base in Iraq, removing the ancien régime and opening the door for independent socio-economic development.

The Iraqi Revolution (14 July 1958) affected not only Iraq but the whole Middle East region. The Revolution, as with any great event, may be viewed as having positive achievements as well as negative effects. There is no doubt that the Iraqi people, who received news of the Revolution with relief, benefited tremendously from the new government. The significant achievements and the socio-economic development that followed outweighed the many failures of the Revolution in achieving its stated goals.

To understand the significance of the Revolution, one has to examine its time span in the course of another—that of the pro-British monarchy; the Revolution spanned a course of about four and a half years, compared to the pro-British monarchy that lasted about four decades. One can even compare it to the events that follow the bloody coup on 8 February 1963, which brought the Baath Party and other Arab nationalists to power, and to the tragic events in Iraq's modern politics.

Modern Iraq was created at the end of World War I (1914–1918) to serve the interests of British imperial power. With the discovery of oil fields in Iraq, the country became an even more important interest to the British; thus, a monarchic regime was installed when they realized that indirect rule served best the British interests, especially after the 1920 Iraqi revolt against the British.

The British exerted their power and consolidated the tribal leaders' rights to land and power over their subjects as an initial step in eventually consolidating their position in Iraq. These tribal leaders, the sheikhs, became legal landowners of communal land. Common tribal members were reduced to sharecroppers, who were obliged to serve their new economic lords.

The effects of the consolidation of tribal leaders' rights also led to the widening of class divisions and disparities. Approximately 2 percent of the landlords controlled more than two-thirds of Iraq's agricultural land. A great majority of Iraqis were peasants who were poor, had no land, and worked as sharecroppers in terrible conditions. They lived and worked under the mercy of the few landlords. These class divisions and disparities helped to foment the Revolution.

The period preceding the Revolution could be described as authoritarian at best. The monarchic system was oppressive, and it relied solely on army and security forces to suppress opponents and dissenters. The monarchic regime deprived people of their democratic freedoms and imposed severe sentences upon dissenters. Many opposition leaders were executed and thousands imprisoned. Kurdish uprisings were suppressed. Therefore, there was a broad spectrum of national liberation movements calling for real change and for resistance to the Anglo-Iraqi Treaty (1930) and to the mutual defense treaty (1948).

Iraq's foreign policy was pro-British. In 1955 Iraq joined the Baghdad Pact, which was organized by Britain and included Iran, Turkey, and Pakistan; the aim of this pact was to fight communism and Arab nationalist inspirations. This organization reaffirmed to many that Britain was the real power behind the royal palace. Against such background and as a result of the combined efforts of the National Union Front—consisting of the National Democratic Party, the Independence Party, the Communist Party, and the Baath (Rebirth) Party, with collaboration from the Free Officers Movement—the stage was set for the 1958 Revolution.

The Revolution was enthusiastically welcomed by the Iraqi people. To the poor it offered hope for the future. From the first hours of the Revolution there was an active support from Iraqis, who took to the streets celebrating and vowing to defend it. The monarchic regime fell, and Iraq was proclaimed an independent republic. Abd al-Karim Qassim, head of the Free Officers Movement, became prime minister and the true ruler of Iraq.

On 26 July 1958 the Interim Constitution was adopted, proclaiming the equality of all Iraqi citizens under the law and granting them freedom without regard to race, nationality, language, or religion. The government freed political prisoners and granted amnesty to the Kurds who participated in the Kurdish uprisings (1943–1945). Exiled Kurds returned home and were welcomed by the republican regime.

The objective of the Revolution, as defined by its leaders, was to liberate Iraq from the oligarchic monarchy and British imperialism and to rebuild and reconstruct Iraq by adapting social and economic measures to improve peoples' living standards. The three-man sovereignty council, announced in the beginning of the Revolution, represented the main sectors of Iraq's nationalities and religious sects. It contained a Sunni Arab, a Shiite Arab, and a Kurd. This council was to collectively carry out the ceremonial tasks of president. Qassim represented its unity. His mother was a Shiite and his father a

Royal possessions on the lawn of the Royal Palace after the assassination of Iraqi king Faisal II and his ministers in July 1958

(© CORBIS/Bettmann)

Sunni Muslim. Almost all members of the central organization of the Free Officers came from relatively poor or low-income families, and the officers depended on their salaries. They were part of the great majority of Iraqi people, or the discontented classes, and they spoke on behalf of the ordinary citizen. The leader of the Revolution was influenced by liberal ideas and was a moderate Iraqi nationalist. Theoretically, he favored democracy and supported the views of the National Democratic Party.

The Iraqi people loved Qassim, who associated himself with them. He was humble and tolerant. Most of his speeches carried phrases such as "sons of my homeland and my people. I am the son of the people. I shall offer my life for the

Iraqi people. Corruption, tyranny, and exploitation shall not return. We shall always be tolerant, even toward the evil-doer of the past regime."

One goal of the Revolution was to abolish oppressive acts passed by the old regime. The Revolution freed political prisoners and reduced the sentences of others. The Revolution granted freedom to teachers and students who were dismissed by the old regime because of their political activism. For the first time ever, Iraqis felt they were masters in their homeland. The Revolution galvanized the population, and simple people were subsequently attracted to politics. They organized and held meetings to celebrate major events and achievements and to push the Revolution to serve their interests. One new change was freedom of the press. In Baghdad alone about forty-five newspapers and magazines were allowed to be published. Outside of Baghdad another twenty newspapers and magazines were also published.

Many steps were taken to modernize Iraqi society. The new regime abolished tribal jurisdictions. By such measures the legal basis for the feudal system in Iraq was dismantled. The names of Iraqi provinces referring to tribal designations were changed.

The Revolution improved the status of the peasants and the economic conditions of the rural areas. It started the process of land reform within the first few months of the Revolution. This agrarian reform was modeled after the Egyptian agrarian reform following the 1952 Revolution that brought Gamal Abd al-Nasser and the Free Officers to power. The law put a maximum limit on land owned by landowners, who could retain up to 1,000 dunums (100 hectares) of irrigated land or twice the amount of land that depended on rainfall. Any land in excess of such amount would be expropriated by the government. The expropriated land would be distributed to landless peasants. Each peasant would get 7 or 15 hectares of land, depending on whether the land was irrigated or depended on rainfall. The recipients would pay the government the price of the land over a twenty-year period. This law, despite its deficiencies, was able to break the large landowners' political power.

Another measure implemented by the new regime was the rent-control law. It restricted the landlord's power to evict tenants and placed a ceiling on how much could be charged to rent a dwelling. The government also started to build public housing projects. These buildings were given to poor people, who were looking for jobs and had migrated from the countryside to the outskirts of cities during the monarchic era. A popular measure was the construction of Madinat al-Thawra (The Revolution's City), which was a low-cost housing complex for the poor who dwelled in the outskirts of Baghdad. For better-off segments of the population, the government encouraged housing associations to provide low-interest loans for civil servants, engineers, teachers, and others to own their own houses at affordable prices. Among other government measures was control of the price of foodstuffs. Salaries of government employees were raised. Institutions caring for orphaned, destitute, and disabled children were also established.

Labor laws were revised in May 1959. The working day was reduced from nine hours to eight hours. This measure covered all workers without exception. All employees working in establishments of 30 or more workers were to be covered by social security law in all Iraqi provinces. In the past only five provinces had been covered. The law granted workers the right to organize themselves into trade unions. One month after the issuance of the law 275,000 workers organized themselves into workers' unions.

The leaders of the Revolution fought for Iraq's national interests. Negotiations over Iraqi oil prices between Iraqi authorities and representatives of the British-owned Iraqi Petroleum Company (IPC) took place in Baghdad between August and October of 1961. When the company failed to meet Iraqi demands, the government passed law number 80, which gave the Iraqis control of 99.5 percent of the unexploited areas of oil in Iraq. An Iraqi National Oil Company was created to exploit oil in the new territory.

In addition to workers' rights and economic development, women also received rights equal to men for the first time in modern Iraq. Women engaged in politics, and Iraq got its first woman minister. The Revolution issued the social conditions law, setting the minimum marriage age to eighteen years, except for certain conditions. It outlawed polygamy unless authorized by a civil-law judge. It set harsh conditions for granting divorces and had many clauses to protect the wife, giving her the same right to divorce. The law also equalized inheritance rights between males and females. This law was a progressive step toward liberating women. It is therefore no wonder that conservatives and religious circles attacked the law as un-Islamic.

The new regime also paid special attention to the Kurdish problem. The Arabs and the Kurds were considered to be partners in the Iraqi homeland, and the constitution affirmed their national rights within Iraq. Nationalist Kurdish leader Mustafa al-Barzani was allowed to return to Iraq from exile in the Soviet Union and was granted a privileged political position. Many Kurdish newspapers were allowed to publish in the Kurdish language. The national Kurdish day, *Nawroz*, was declared a national holiday each 21 March. The Revolution allowed Kurds to study in Kurdish and allowed thousands of immigrant Kurds to return to Iraq with their full rights.

The national culture in Iraq also flourished during the Revolution. The Iraqi book market was filled with thousands of scientific and cultural publications from Arab and international sources. Many prominent international and humanistic stories and novels were translated into Arabic and published in Iraq. In one year during the revolutionary period the number of books published exceeded that which had been published in the preceding thirty years.

Foreign policy that resulted from the Revolution reflected the wishes and struggles of the Iraqi people toward genuine independence. It was a policy that opposed colonialism and tilted toward liberation and anti-imperialistic objectives. Thus, one of the first acts as a result of the Revolution was to pull Iraq out from the pro-British Arab Federation with Jordan. In addition, all Iraqi ties with the Baghdad Pact were severed. As a result of Iraq's withdrawal the headquarters was moved from Iraq to Turkey and the pact was renamed the Central Treaty Organization. After its withdrawal from the Baghdad Pact, Iraq abolished its treaty of mutual security and bilateral relations with Britain. Also, Iraq withdrew from an agreement with the United States that was signed by the monarchy regarding military aid. On 30 May 1959 the last British soldiers and military officers departed the al-Habaniyya base in Iraq.

The new Iraqi regime was quickly recognized by the Soviet Union, China, and other progressive regimes. Therefore, the Revolutionary leaders established normal diplomatic relations with many socialist countries—the Soviet Union, Peoples' Republic of China, United Arab Republic, Bulgaria, Romania, Poland, Hungary, Czechoslovakia, Albania, and Yugoslavia.

The Soviet Union helped to arm and train the Iraqi Army to strengthen its defense capabilities. The monopoly of arms by the imperialistic countries was broken by Iraq. The imperialistic countries used to control not only the quality and quantity of the exported arms but also their use. The goal of Iraq's new relations was to build and develop a foreign policy based on mutual assistance, respect, and equality. Iraq declared its belief in a positive, mutually beneficial policy that did not depend on the capitalist-imperialist market economy.

The imperialistic powers quickly tried to threaten or eliminate the effects of the Revolution. The U.S. Navy was sent to Lebanon, and the British Army was sent to Jordan. There were military movements in Turkey. The Soviet Union warned the imperialist powers about interfering with Iraq, and the outpouring of support from the Iraqi people helped to eliminate direct imperialist intervention in Iraq.

The new regime declared on many occasions that Iraq was fighting all manifestations of colonization and its associated aggressive alliances or plans. Iraq believed in the principles of peaceful coexistence, positive neutrality, and in adhering to the principles of the United Nations and the Bandung conference of the nonaligned movement held in Indonesia in 1955. The dinar, Iraq's currency, was liberated from the British pound. This change was a step toward economic independence for Iraq and the development of its political independence.

The Revolution helped Iraq assert its brotherly relations with other Arab states. Iraq's temporary constitution declared its inclusion as part of the Arab world. In addition, Iraq supported the Algerian people's struggle against French colonization and helped the Palestinian people strive for their national rights. Two million Iraqi dinars were allocated to help the Algerian peoples' struggle for independence. Iraq severed its relations with France and formally recognized the free Algerian government established in September 1958. Iraq's policy was to help people fight colonization, including aiding the people of Oman against British colonization.

There is no doubt that the Revolution, despite its achievements, faced problems and obstacles and fell short of establishing a democracy. In less than five years the Revolution did much to help the Iraqi people strive for an independent Iraq. It was a real revolution in the sense that power was transferred from the monarchy and the large landlords to the national bourgeoisie class in the new republic. It was also a real revolution in that it had tremendous popular support. For the first time in modern Iraq the president was considered the son of the people and not a stranger or a member of an alien monarchic family.

The struggle among Iraq's political parties after the Revolution limited its effect and was the main cause for its later downfall. One can understand clearly how beneficial the Revolution was to common Iraqis by comparing their situation from 1958 to 1963 with what happened after the February 1963 coup when the Baathists and other Arab nationalists staged a bloody takeover—and certainly with what existed in Iraq for more than two decades under the rule of Saddam Hussein.

–SHAK HANISH,
NATIONAL UNIVERSITY

Viewpoint:
No. The Iraqi Revolution was a violent event that established a precedent for future political developments in the country.

The Iraqi Revolution was a violent episode befitting the political culture of Iraq. I served in the British embassy in Baghdad from November 1957 until March 1961, as Oriental Counsellor, that is to say, political advisor and interpreter. I spoke and wrote Arabic. When I arrived in Baghdad on 1 November 1957, the situation was unsettled. I would put it that the Iraqi regime was in a precarious, but not entirely hopeless, situation.

My first task was to see for myself and form my own opinion. The Iraqis, who, in spite of all that has happened in that unfortunate country, are a friendly, warmhearted, hospitable people, and they were kind to me. On my first evening in Baghdad I was invited to a middle-class nationalist's home on the Tigris. There were some twelve professional, educated Iraqis present. I was given an historical lecture in familiar terms to one who had studied that history—the betrayal of the Arabs after World War I (1914–1918), the installation in Iraq of the British puppet Hashemites from the Hejaz, the Balfour Declaration (1917), Israel, Nuri al-Said, and Suez. This lecture was a wonderful introduction to Iraq, delivered with great courtesy and confirmed by all my later contacts in the opposition.

Iraqis of all persuasions were keen to talk to me and were remarkably open and frank. This openness, in itself, said something positive about the government, in that it allowed such extremely critical views to be aired freely. To my knowledge I was not followed, and none of my interlocutors got into trouble with the authorities. Prerevolution Iraq was not a police state. I felt the difference sharply after the Revolution, and one can only imagine what it was like under Saddam Hussein.

The civilized and intelligent Iraqis to whom I spoke really believed that Great Britain controlled the Iraqi government, which can explain their readiness to give so much time to a sympathetic British listener. They hoped that I could help to change what they saw as a misguided policy. In fact, the British government had much less influence over Nuri than was popularly supposed. He was our ally, not our stooge; he had a strong mind of his own, saw communism as his enemy, and the West, the enemy of his enemy, as his friend. But he was not going to let the British run his country. Furthermore, he had grown old and careless. He said, "I know my people, they trust me; you should not believe these extremist lawyers; it is all hot air." The nationalist opposition stressed that Iraq had gotten out of the mainstream of resurgent Arab nationalism, led and inspired by Egyptian president Gamal Abd al-Nasser. There were other factors in this opposition. From a long-term point of view Iraq's oil revenues were being wisely administered for the development of the country. But there was at that time little to show for it, and so the Iraqis thought that the authorities were using the money for themselves. This fraudulent behavior was not the case, as the government was, by Middle Eastern standards, honest and not corrupt.

Then there was no counter to Nasser's "Voice of the Arabs" radio broadcasts, no effective "Voice of Iraq." So Nasser's propaganda screamed night and day from every little transistor radio in every field, shed, or urban apartment. It was basic, crude, violent, and effective. Everything was the fault of the imperialists and their lackeys, who ruled Iraq. It was the big Goebbels type lie, repeated over and over again.

In my trips round the country I saw the transistors and heard the endless propaganda. It fell on fertile ground, for the conditions of the peasants were still bad and the tribal sheikhs enjoyed too much power. After my trip to southern Iraq I wrote, inter alia, the following:

> Kut—This is a depressed area and looks it. According to the Mutasarif (local Governor) and others I spoke to, there is considerable unemployment, widespread poverty and actual hunger. The area is quiet at the moment, but there is constant potential for serious trouble. The main cause of the trouble is the large feudal landlords.
>
> Amara—the sarifah (mud and palm huts) dwellers seemed to be simple people, who would be satisfied with little, but that little needs to be much more than their present lot. They asked me to do something for them, because the British were their "Father." On the other hand one of the local officials told me that Nasser was "Allah" to these people. In Mosul, in the North, I was told that he was merely "the Prophet."
>
> Conclusions:—The Kut and Amara Liwas (provinces) are neglected and the standard of living is shamefully low. The basis is present for both communism and anarchic nationalism. In Kut I was told that the communists would win a free election. Serious unrest could be whipped up either by political events outside Iraq, or by continued Government refusal to take action against the sheikhs, or a combination of both.

The story was the same everywhere. The government and the monarchy were in mortal peril. But what could the British do? We were not, contrary to popular belief, the real rulers of Iraq. We could only advise, and Nuri did not take advice he did not like. He had a couple of puppet prime ministers at this time, but he continued to rule together with the crown prince. Our ambassador tried to convey tactfully to the government the urgent need for reforms and the vital importance of curbing the power of the sheikhs. Nothing was done, and it seemed to me that radical action was required to save Iraq from violent revolution. To this end I devised a plan, which owed much to the views of thoughtful and patriotic nationalist Iraqis who were interested in saving the monarchy and avoiding bloodshed. The plan was as follows: Nuri should resign and the crown prince be exiled. Then a certain able army officer, Nuruddin Mahmoud, acceptable to the Crown, the military, and the nationalist opposition, should be asked by the

THE EVENTS AT THE PALACE

On 14 July 1958 members of the Iraqi royal family and several government leaders were murdered during a military coup; a portion of an account published by Life *appears here:*

Nothing but fire-blackened ruin and debris today testify to the events at the Palace of Spaciousness. The occupants died—17 in all, it is said, including King Faisal and Crown Prince Abdul Illah. Those who, with a leer, point out that the crown prince's bedroom still smells of perfume despite the fire are the same people who delight in saying that the corpses included three foreign party girls, one killed in the nude. The government speaks vaguely and variously of resistance, ascribing it to trigger-happy palace guards or to the reckless crown prince.

In any event it was all over at the palace before 6 a.m., the hour by which Kassem had planned to be in full control of Baghdad. By this time the radio was already announcing not only the success of the revolution but also a full roster of names for the revolutionary government, including civilian ministers. Kassem had forgotten nothing.

. . .The dead crown prince was hanged at least twice that day. Between hangings, his body suffered indignities: stoning, knifing, gradual attrition of parts as eager knives stripped away grisly souvenirs.

That afternoon Nuri's turn came. In Baghdad's future "Liberty Street" appeared three veiled, shapeless figures of *umm el aba* (grandmothers in black coats). Someone noticed men's shoes and the bottoms of pajama pants below the folds of one black *abaya*.

A man jerked open the *abaya* and, seeing the pale face, the arrogant high-bridged nose, the pouched eyes, yelled, "Nuri!" Unmasked, it is said, Nuri wearily confessed, "I am the pasha. I am sick."

One version insists that Nuri drew a pistol and fired first. This conforms to the thesis that force was used only to meet resistance. Another version has it that Nuri turned to run but that the hue and cry of the mob alerted a passing driver who hurdled the curb with his car and pinned Nuri against a wall.

The government will not say exactly what happened. But it realizes, and a few frank Baghdadi will admit, that if either Nuri or Faisal or Abdul Illah had been left alive, the new regime would have been in endless danger. Once before Nuri had come back from exile to smash revolutionaries. Such an eagle of a man could not be allowed to live.

Nuri's body was attacked long after death. The mob had at him for a time where he died. Then the army arrived, rescued what remained, loaded it on a taxi's baggage rack and took it to a hospital.

Source: *Keith Wheeler, "First Full Story of a Coup that Set Off World Crisis,"* Life *(18 August 1958): 25.*

king to form a government. This government would have contained, inter alia, Muhammad Hadid, later Abd al-Karim Qassim's finance minister, and Abdul Rahman Bazzaz, later prime minister under Abdul Salaam Arif. I discussed this plan with my ambassador. He did not dismiss it out of hand and at least discussed the general dangerous state of the country with the chief of the palace, Abdullah Bakr, an influential and rational man. I discussed my plan with him, and it is reported to have gotten to the crown prince. This may sound like terrible hindsight, but it is confirmed in a book, *Republican Iraq: A Study in Iraqi Politics since the Revolution of 1958* (1969), by an Iraqi intellectual, Majid Khadduri.

On another historical note of interest, I have given talks in recent years about how the Iraqi Revolution might have been prevented. At one of these talks an Iraqi lady asked to meet me after the talk. She was the daughter of General Ghazi Daghestani, deputy chief of staff before the Revolution. She told me that he had the same ideas as my nationalist friends: to save the king and the regime and avoid bloodshed, the Crown Prince had to leave Iran and Nuri had to resign. What is remarkable about this is that Crown Prince Abd al-Ilah and Nuri also saw the wisdom of this course; Abd al-Ilah had even gone to Turkey for a "holiday" (according to the same lady, Nuri would have resigned upon the abdication of Abd al-Ilah). King Faisal pleaded with him to return, however, as he felt he would be unable to deal with the situation without his uncle's advice. With tragic results, Abd al-Ilah returned to Baghdad reluctantly.

The long hot summer of 1958 scorched relentlessly on. It was clear that something unpleasant was going to happen. My wife even heard talk of impending revolution in a bus traveling between Baghdad and Teheran. The crown prince, Nuri, the minister of interior, and the chief of general staff were warned of the likelihood of an army coup, and they were even given Qassim's name. They disregarded these warnings. Diplomatic life went on, and I remember remarking after a particularly lavish party: "1789."

On 9 July I had a long talk with the minister of interior, Said Qazzaz, later murdered by the revolutionaries after a mock trial. He told me—I knew him well and do not think he was trying to pull the wool over my eyes—that the situation in Iraq was less tense than it had been at the time of the Suez crisis. Iraq had come through Suez virtually unscathed and would therefore survive the present tensions!

On 12 July the ambassador took me to call on Nuri, the king, and the crown prince to introduce me as chargé d'affaires. Neither Nuri nor the king seemed the least bit concerned.

Abd al-Ilah, on the other hand, was in a terrible state. He paced up and down the room muttering, "These dreadful things, these dreadful things." Then he explained that he was expecting a Nasserist coup to depose King Hussein of Jordan. Odd, this might have been in the wind, but he was also afraid of and had been warned about a coup in his own country. There is no room in this short essay to describe the revolution. I have done so in my autobiography, *My Lucky Life in War, Revolution, Peace and Diplomacy* (1996).

On 15 July I accompanied the ambassador to call on the new head of state, Brigadier General Qassim, at the Ministry of Defense. We called not to congratulate the head of state but to protest the burning of our embassy and the murder of a member of our staff. On behalf of the British government the ambassador demanded an apology and compensation for the loss of life and destruction of diplomatic property. We got some compensation later but no apology. Qassim took note of our protest. He was soft-spoken and relatively courteous and, in spite of the circumstances, did not make such a bad impression. Colonel Abdul Salaam Arif, Qassim's deputy, on the other hand, was aggressive and offensive. We deserved all that we had gotten. We had oppressed the Iraqi people through our puppets and lackeys for years. A peaceful crowd had surrounded the embassy to express their joy at their newfound freedom. The British embassy had opened fire on the crowd and wounded a soldier. We told Arif what really happened, but of course he was not prepared to believe us. A nationalist friend of mine, Muhammad Hadid, was at the meeting, and I arranged to call on him the same afternoon.

We took a route to Hadid's home along the bund, or embankment, that surrounded Baghdad. The poorest of the poor lived there. They were mostly from the countryside, seeking work in the city, some quarter of a million of them living in poverty and squalor, with little fresh water or sanitation. They were overjoyed at the revolution and had huge green Islamic flags outside their huts. The sarifah dwellers had come out of their huts in the thousands and danced up and down chanting, "Qutila el kha'en Nuri es Said" (The traitor Nuri al-Said has been killed). We had inadvertently come close to the mob that had killed Nuri, which was, to say the least, an uncomfortable moment. We left the area unnoticed and arrived safely at Hadid's home.

Less than a day after a convulsion that shook the Middle East, I found myself being welcomed with traditional courtesy by the minister of finance, the senior civilian minister in the revolutionary government. Hadid was very cultured, and he had frequently visited Britain. Before 14 July, he had been a successful businessman and deputy leader of the National Democratic Party, based on British Labor. They were not allowed to function properly before the Revolution, and their leader, Kamil Chaderchi, had been put in jail as a communist, which he was not. Hadid was relaxed and friendly. This conversation was probably the first substantial one between a member of the new government and a representative of the West. There is no space for a full account of this intriguing interview. Hadid was polite. He deeply regretted the excesses of the mob and the murder of the crown prince and Nuri. We did not at that time know what had happened to the king. I asked Hadid to use his considerable influence to prevent further killing.

Discussing the future, Hadid told me that the oil industry would not be nationalized and that the government was not communist, although the communists were well-disposed toward them. He also told me that the government would be neutral in the Cold War and wanted good relations with all states, especially in the Arab and Muslim world. Iraq would neither leave the Baghdad Pact nor join the United Arab Republic. Hadid hoped that Britain would recognize the new government, which was intent on having friendly relations with the West. This positive discussion gave me the chance to talk of mercy. Recognition would be difficult if the killing continued. Hadid mentioned that U.S. Marines landing in Beirut did not help matters—Iraqi public opinion was angry about this situation. He reiterated that the country was secure and that the armed forces were solidly behind the government. The Iraqi people would be dangerously aroused if there were an attack from abroad. But he assured me that foreign nationals would be safe. We then parted on the best of terms and remained in close contact as long as I was in Iraq (until March 1961). This was invaluable because Hadid was the only constant member of Qassim's government. He remained a member of the government, at great danger to himself, to try and prevent Qassim going completely crazy.

The coup was initially accompanied by genuine popular jubilation. This joy was not only to celebrate the passing of the ancien régime but to augur in the beginning of a new era. The British masters and their alien Hashemite puppets were gone for good, and freedom had dawned. Capturing this euphoric mood, a popular Iraqi poet by the name of Abdul Wahab al-Batati wrote the following poem called "14 Tammuz" (14 July):

The sun shines in my city
The bells ring out for the heroes
Awake, my beloved, we are free!

As in most revolutions, it was a panorama of unrealizable dreams that offered a brief moment of freedom from tyranny and the opportunity to express desires, orientations, and political ambitions. Yet, this dream eventually turned into a nightmare, ending in unbelievable death and destruction and a tyrant, Saddam Hussein, who made the ancien régime look like a bunch of kindergarten school teachers and Qassim an angel of mercy.

We did not know then what was to happen. I was sick at heart that no one had heeded the warnings of many, including myself. I took some chilly comfort in the fact that the new government, most of whose members I knew, would be good for Iraq and not too hostile to the West. I had talked at length with the finance minister, Hadid, and the government was not unlike the one I had dreamed up before the Revolution: multiparty, moderate nationalist. Unfortunately, the new rulers had come to power by a military coup aided by mob violence: the murder of the royal family and the dragging of the mutilated bodies of Nuri and the crown prince through the streets of Baghdad, the corpses then strung up as a spectacle for the mob. The military held the key posts in the government, except Hadid at finance. Qassim took the offices of prime minister and minister of defense, while Arif was second in command of the armed forces and interior minister. Communist influence began to show itself, spreading rapidly through the population and, to a lesser extent, the armed forces.

Qassim was regarded as the "sole leader" by the communists, something he yearned for, and he received their vociferous support. Interestingly, it was the anticommunist Arab nationalists, Arif and Rashid Ali, who first threatened Qassim. Ali had gained fame as vigorously anti-British during World War II, going so far as collaborating with the Nazis—he became something of a national hero. Both were suspected, with reason, of plotting against Qassim with Nasser and anticommunists. They were arrested and condemned to death but never executed. Qassim lapped up all of this adulation, realizing that the communists could help him outflank the Nasserist-nationalist opponents who were determined to oust him from power. As a result of Qassim's apparent attachment to the communists, his anticommunist ministers, except for Hadid, soon resigned, and by February 1959 the communists were well placed in the government while their opponents grew anxious.

This activity led to the Mosul Revolt, led by the anticommunist Colonel Shawaf, in March, which failed. After the revolt there was a period of violent anarchy in Mosul and the communists really took off. By early summer of 1959, the government seemed to have neither the will nor the means to control the communist thugs (the so-called People's Resistance Force) who terrified large portions of the population. The period has been called the Red Terror or Red Flood. This weakness looked bad, but in June Qassim realized they were going too far too fast and becoming a danger to his regime. In brief Qassim checked the communists, while continuing to use them in his power balancing act. Slowly the peril lessened, but this did not diminish one of the most disagreeable features of the Qassim regime, the People's Court. This kangaroo court started off by trying members of the ancien régime and then moved on to Arab nationalists. It was Qassim's main propaganda outlet and was on TV for hours every evening. It was horrifying, but its bark was worse than its bite. It condemned almost all the accused to death, but of the ancien régime only three were actually executed.

The next excitement was when Baath Party members attempted to assassinate Qassim on 7 October 1959. His car was riddled with bullet holes. Qassim was hit three times, but he was not seriously hurt. He had always been a bit odd, but his little adventure sent him completely round the bend. Qassim preserved the car as a monument, while the bloodstained shirts he had been wearing were kept in a glass case in his office and displayed to visitors, including on one occasion, my ambassador and myself. He believed that Allah had saved him, that his narrow escape from the assassination attempt (in which, by the way, a young Saddam Hussein played a role) was some sort of divine miracle. Qassim was not up to the job. He was a good conspirator, but he was no executive president. By plotting and playing his myriad opponents off against each other, he survived until 8 February 1963, when the Baath got him. They installed Arif as president and hoped he would be their puppet. Arif and his presidency was Iraq's last best hope. He appointed Bazzaz as prime minister in 1965, and they made a good team. Arif was tough and could control the army, while Bazzaz was a competent administrator with a human face. The beginning of the end came when Arif was tragically killed in a helicopter crash on 13 April 1966. His weaker brother, Abdul Rahman, took power, but he could not control the army, which four months later forced Bazzaz to resign. Ahmed Hassan al-Bakr and his right-hand man, Saddam Hussein, led the Baathists to power in another coup on 17 July 1968. Saddam would later push al-Bakr aside, overtly assuming the full reins of power in July 1979. What followed was over two decades of misery for the Iraqi people, highlighted by the Iran-Iraq War (1980–1988) and the Gulf Crisis and War of 1990–1991. This story is indeed tragic and could have been avoided if Nuri had listened to advice and resigned in 1958, which he almost did. It haunts me to this day. Like many others I saw what was about to happen, but I could not persuade anyone to listen and take the necessary action.

–SIR SAMUEL FALLE,
MARIANNELUND, SWEDEN

References

Hanna Batatu, *The Old Social Classes and the Revolutionary Movements of Iraq* (Princeton: Princeton University Press, 1978).

Uriel Dann, *Iraq under Qassem: A Political History 1958–1963* (New York: Praeger, 1969).

Sir Samuel Falle, *My Lucky Life in War, Revolution, Peace and Diplomacy* (Sussex: Book Guild, 1996).

Marion Farouk-Sluglett and Peter Sluglett, *Iraq since 1958: From Revolution to Dictatorship* (London & New York: KPI, 1987).

Samira Haj, *The Making of Iraq, 1900–1963: Capital, Power and Ideology* (New York: State University of New York Press, 1997).

Majid Khadduri, *Republican Iraq: A Study in Iraqi Politics since the Revolution of 1958* (London: Oxford University Press, 1969).

Phebe Marr, *The Modern History of Iraq* (Boulder, Colo.: Westview Press, 1985).

ISRAEL IN LEBANON

Was the failure of Israel's Peace for Galilee campaign in 1982 a result of the attempt to install a government in Beirut friendly to the Jewish state?

Viewpoint: Yes. Once invading Israeli military forces moved beyond PLO strongholds and occupied Beirut, Syrian opposition in Lebanon stiffened, public support in Israel weakened, and Israeli casualties rose to intolerable levels.

Viewpoint: No. The hard-line policy of destroying the PLO, adopted by the Likud Party when it came to power in 1977, was doomed from the start, causing moderate Islamic leaders to be replaced by militants determined to resist Israeli threats at all costs.

Lebanon could have been the "Switzerland of the Middle East" had it not been located in the midst of the Arab-Israeli conflict. Obtaining independence during World War II (1939–1945) from the French mandate, Lebanon quickly became a financial center and tourist mecca for Arabs and Europeans alike—it was a modernized, secular nation; indeed, the capital city of Beirut was known as the "Paris of the Middle East." Upon Lebanon's independence in 1943, the National Pact affirmed that political power and representation would be based on a confessional system of government; in other words, power would be apportioned according to the population figures for each of the vast array of religious groups in the country. The agreement was based on a census taken in the 1930s under French supervision during the mandatory period. Census results indicated that the Maronite Christians were by a slight margin the largest confessional grouping, with Sunni Muslims the second largest and Shiite Muslims third. As such, the president of Lebanon would be Maronite (as long as the population figures remained constant); the prime minister would be Sunni; the speaker of the parliament would be Shiite; and so on, with proportional representation making up parliament as well.

The first problems in Lebanon began to emerge in the 1950s and 1960s when the power positions in the country continued to be in the hands of the Maronites despite the fact that they were no longer the most numerous religious grouping; by the 1970s, Shiites were probably the largest group, followed by the Sunnis and then the Maronites. In essence, the internal disruptions that occurred from time to time were based more on the issue of political representation than religious differences, although the confessional system made it seem otherwise to outside observers. At its simplest, it was a struggle between those who wanted a greater share of power due them in a democratically based system and those who did not want to relinquish power and all the benefits that accrue from it because of their dominant political position.

Left to themselves, the Lebanese might have eventually resolved the internal political problems that had beset them; however, when one adds to the already volatile mix in Lebanon a plethora of malignant external influences and interventions emanating from the international superpower arena, the inter-Arab arena, the Arab-Israeli conflict, and even the Iran-Iraq War (1980–1988), it is little wonder that civil war eventually broke out in 1975 and lasted essentially until 1990, in the process of which most of Lebanon was razed.

This destructive path was jump-started in the early 1970s when the Palestine Liberation Organization (PLO) relocated its headquarters to Beirut after being expelled from Jordan during the Jordanian Civil War (1970), or what the Palestinians called Black September. This situation did two things to Lebanon that accelerated the drift toward civil war: it intimately involved the country in the Arab-Israeli conflict as the PLO launched attacks against northern Israel, thus subjecting Lebanon to forceful Israeli reprisals, highlighted by an Israeli military sweep of southern Lebanon in 1978; and it upset the already tenuous balance among various factions in the country and opened the door for external forces to extend their influence with one group or another—particularly characterized by the increasing cooperation between Israel and the Maronites on the one hand and Syria and the Muslim factions on the other hand. All of this upheaval blew up into civil war in 1975, and as a result Lebanon could no longer divorce itself from regional tensions.

Syria had actually received permission from the Arab League in 1976 to deploy troops in Lebanon in an attempt to stabilize the situation. Damascus sent in approximately thirty thousand soldiers, supporting a variety of factions in the immediate stages of the conflict in order to prevent one side from emerging clearly victorious, especially if it meant Israeli intervention to protect its Maronite allies. Syrian troops remain in Lebanon to this day. Because of this troop deployment, Lebanon became more and more a proxy battleground between Syria and Israel and subject to the influence of Damascus.

The 1982 Israeli invasion of Lebanon began in June, only a couple of months following the return by Israel of the final portion of the Sinai Peninsula to Egypt per the Egyptian-Israeli peace treaty (1979). Detractors of the treaty in the Arab world feared that once Egypt was removed from the Arab-Israeli dispute, Israel would have then a free hand to move militarily to the north. The timing of the Israeli invasion did nothing to dispel these assertions.

The immediate casus belli of the invasion was the attempted assassination of an Israeli diplomat in London earlier in June by a PLO splinter group. The objectives of the invasion were many, but at the least it was an opportunity to destroy the PLO infrastructure in South Lebanon and get rid of the deadly PLO attacks against northern Israeli towns. Most believed the invasion would resemble the Israeli incursion of 1978, but within a month Israeli military forces had gone well beyond that earlier strike, to the outskirts of Beirut itself, in the process of which the war had gained the attention of the international community.

Many scholars have termed the Lebanese episode as Israel's "Vietnam"—in other words, that Israel involved itself in an unwinnable quagmire from which it was difficult to extricate itself. Others, however, point to certain limited objectives achieved as well as the fact that with more foresight it could have been much more successful. Whatever the case, the Israeli military withdrew from their forward position in 1985 to establish a cordon sanitaire in South Lebanon (assisted by an allied militia called the South Lebanon Army), and in May 2000 Israel unilaterally withdrew from all of Lebanon. The Taif Agreement (1989), negotiated at the mountain resort city in Saudi Arabia, laid the basis for the reapportionment of political power in Lebanon. By 1991 the Lebanese government had come to an agreement with Damascus that made Syria the unquestioned power broker in the country. With relative stability restored in most of the country throughout the 1990s, Lebanon has been struggling to recover some of what has been lost.

Viewpoint:
Yes. Once invading Israeli military forces moved beyond PLO strongholds and occupied Beirut, Syrian opposition in Lebanon stiffened, public support in Israel weakened, and Israeli casualties rose to intolerable levels.

On 6 June 1982 the Israel Defense Forces (IDF) mounted Operation "Peace for Galilee." Its aim, as explained to the Israeli public, was the removal of the terrorist threat posed by the Palestine Liberation Organization (PLO) to the civilian population in northern Israel. This declared objective enjoyed wide support within the Israel public in view of the long period of repeated terrorist attacks along the northern border, beginning in the 1970s when the PLO established and strengthened its stronghold in Lebanon.

The immediate background to the campaign was the attempt on the life of Israel's ambassador in London, Shlomo Argov. This assassination attempt provided Israel with the excuse it needed to breach a cease-fire agreement with the PLO, indirectly brokered by the Americans, that had been in force since July 1981. However, it should be noted that the man who shot Argov in London belonged to the Abu Nidal (Sabri al-Bana) faction, which was identified with Iraqi president Saddam Hussein and known to be PLO chairman Yasser Arafat's bitter rival. Arafat

SABRA AND SHATILA

Dutch physician Ben Alofs was working in Sabra and Shatila during the 1982 Israeli invasion of Lebanon; he witnessed the horrific events of 16–18 September when the Phalangists (Lebanese Christian militiamen) occupied the two refugee camps:

One Palestinian nurse, who thought he would be safe with us, was identified. He was led away at gunpoint, out of sight. A moment later we heard the shots. . . .

We had almost reached the Kuwaiti Embassy roundabout, when we were told to stop and line up in front of a wall. Phil McKennon, a female Irish anaesthetist, expressed our feelings when she called out: "OK, it's the firing squad!," certainly when we were ordered to take off our white hospital clothes. I took off my white coat and stood there, my torso bare. Others did the same, but for the women among us it was difficult to strip, because they didn't wear anything under their white T-shirts. They refused to strip and the militiamen didn't react to it.

With armed militiamen lined up in front of us the whole situation was extremely threatening. We waited and waited. Trucks with benches on them passed by. A few meters away, on a hillock, stood an Israeli army half-track, affording excellent views of Shatila. Then came the order to start walking again. We crossed the roundabout in the direction of a badly damaged UN-building. An army vehicle with an Israeli officer approached us. He asked us, what the militiamen intended to do with us. We told him, that we had been taken out of Gaza hospital and that the militiamen were taking us with them. The Israeli asked the "officer" what they intended to do with us. The "officer" told the Israeli to mind his own business. One of the Norwegian doctors told the Israeli officer to go and get help. "Don't worry", he answered. When the "officer" heard this, he said, loud enough for everybody to hear: "Don't think he will remember you, you won't see him back again."

After crossing the roundabout we were led to a courtyard behind the UN-building. There was broken glass and rubble, the walls pockmarked with shrapnel holes. It seemed like a good place for an execution. New faces awaited us. The Phalangists appeared to have some kind of command post there. We were told to sit down and hand in our passports. They asked us, who among us spoke French. Several of us did. And then again the question if we knew we were working in a "terrorist hospital". We replied truthfully, that we also worked in Lebanese government

hospitals in Zahle (christian), Saida and Baalbek. They were surprised to hear this and also, that we worked for the MECC. Then they began to preach about murderous and bloodthirsty Palestinians and about the justness of the Phalangists. The "officer" declared with a straight face, that they honored the Geneva Conventions and to illustrate this, a macabre spectacle ensued. They brought in a Palestinian boy with injuries to his throat. "See how we treat Palestinians." After the boy's injuries were examined and dressed in an ambulance in the courtyard he was carried away in a landrover. We feared the worst for this poor chap.

The "officer" and the menacing man with his black beard and beret, who had been very aggressive, were now kept in the background. Most of us took turns to be interrogated. Had we ever looked after injured Palestinian fighters? Had we seen any fedayeen in the hospital? We had not. Had we ever been praised for our work by Palestinian leaders?

While I waited to be interrogated I heard the sound of explosions and automatic rifle fire coming from the camps.

At about 9.30 or 10 a.m. we were handed over to the Israeli military. The Phalangists—it seemed—followed orders. The Israeli forward command post, in a building with 7 floors, was about a hundred meters away from the Phalangist headquarters. It was situated on the edge of Shatila. Weeks later I returned to this building and from the top I had an excellent view of Shatila, especially the part where most of the slaughter had taken place.

The Israeli soldiers looked uncomfortable, being confronted with about 20 Europeans and Americans. They asked us what we wanted. We told them that we wanted to go back to the hospital, but we were told it was too dangerous. Eventually three of us were allowed to go back to Gaza hospital with a laissez-passer in arabic and hebrew. One of my colleagues who went back, Dr. David Gray, still has this laissez-passer. He told me, that he is prepared to give testimony. He, Dr. Egon and Philip, the British nurse was dropped by an Israeli officer at the Sports Stadium. He refused to go into the camp. . . .

I was deeply shocked when—as Saturday passed—the extent of the massacre became apparent.

On Sunday I accompanied a Dutch journalist and his Danish colleagues back to the camps. Sometime during Saturday morning the Phalangists had left and Sabra and Shatila were now closed off by the Lebanese Army. Journalists were not allowed in, but we found a way in via the back of Akka-hospital. Members of the Lebanese Civil Defense who had begun to collect the bodies, that had not been buried by the bulldozers, offered to show us around. We entered Shatila, where I had left it on Saturday morning. I saw at once that after we had left there had been an awful lot more killing and destruction. People had been killed in their houses, which were subsequently bulldozed. I saw a woman in a little field. She was lying face down and had been shot in the back as she tried to flee. Her body had swelled up terribly in the heat. All over Sabra and Shatila there was the sickly sweet stench of decomposition. It was terrible to walk between all those dead people, many of whom had been tortured and hacked to death. Whole families slaughtered together. Young men lined in front of a wall and killed. Pieces of body, charred remains. All the animals had been killed as well. I never forget the huge mound of red earth in the southern part of Shatila with arms and legs sticking out. Next to it sat a father crying unconsolably with the pictures of his murdered children in his hands. We walked over freshly dug mass graves. The large group of people we had passed in Sabra Street had vanished. So many people simply disappeared.

We will never know how many people were exactly butchered during those terrible days of the 16th, 17th and 18th of September 1982. 784 or so bodies were recovered by the Civil Defense and were buried in the official mass grave near the southern exit of Shatila. Others were buried by relatives. A large mass grave at a nearby golf course and others were not to be opened. Prohibited by the Lebanese government and its new president Amin Gemayel, Bashir's brother.

When the autumn rains began to fall at the end of November, congested sewers flooded Sabra and Shatila. The congestion was caused in part by bodies that had been dumped in the sewers. The estimates are that at least 1500, but more likely 2000 people were murdered.

Source: *"Eyewitness-account of the Massacres in Sabra and Shatila, September 1982,"* Palestine Chronicle, *17 September 2001 <http:// www.palestinechronicle.com/article. php?story=20010917035111888>.*

---

actually wanted at that time to maintain quiet along the Israeli-Lebanese border, even if only temporarily. When Israeli intelligence, known for its opposition to deeper Israeli involvement in internal Lebanese politics, tried to explain to Israeli prime minister Menachem Begin that it was Abu Nidal who was responsible, he fobbed them off with a shrug and the quip, "All of them are Abus" (reference is to the accepted name *Abu–father of*–which most Arab men are called along with the name of their firstborn son).

Thus, the Israeli government decided to mount a military campaign. However, it quickly transpired that the aim of the operation was not only to protect the settlements along Israel's northern border but to create new realities in the region. Within a week Israeli army forces arrived at the outskirts of Beirut and subsequently took over the Lebanese capital for a short time. Under pressure from the Israeli forces the PLO was forced to withdraw from Beirut, ultimately settling in Tunis. The PLO's departure brought an end to its foothold in, to say nothing of its con-

trol of, Lebanon. At the same time the Israeli Army confronted the Syrian Army, forcing it to withdraw from South Lebanon and Beirut. All of these moves allowed Israel to bring about the election of its ally Bashir Gemayel as president of Lebanon in August 1982, although he did not serve in this office for even one day, because he was assassinated on 14 September by a Lebanese Christian working for the Syrians.

Thus, it would appear that Israel's long-term aims, which became clear with the passage of time, went beyond ensuring quiet on its northern border and included destroying the PLO's ground base in Lebanon. There are even those (such as then Minister of Defense Ariel Sharon, architect behind the "Peace for Galilee" campaign) who claimed that eliminating the PLO would marginalize or minimize the Palestinian problem.

Second, Israel would strike a blow at the Syrian Army, which at that time was undergoing a military buildup. Such a strike, many in Israel hoped, would force Syria to leave Lebanon in Israeli hands. It should be mentioned that in the wake of the Israeli-Egyptian peace agreement (1979), Syria remained the only immediate threat facing Israel at that time. Thus, defeating the Syrian Army strengthened Israel's strategic position. In December 1981 Israeli law was applied to the Golan Heights, which Israel had captured from Syria in the June 1967 Arab-Israeli War. The Israeli operation in Lebanon was part of an assertive policy adopted by the Israeli government under Begin aimed at minimizing the threat Syria posed. Finally, Israel hoped to make Lebanon a protectorate under the leadership of its friend and ally, Christian Phalangist leader Gemayel.

It should be noted that Israel's objectives in mounting the Peace for Galilee campaign fit in with the strategy of Sharon, who wished to see Israel as a kind of regional power able to maintain its hegemony over at least parts of the Middle East. He drew up the plans that brought the Israeli Army for the first time into a capital of an Arab country and to interfere in internal Lebanese politics by bringing about the election of a regime friendly to Israel.

Sharon's belief that it would be possible to establish in Lebanon a Christian pro-Israel regime was an outgrowth of a concept that had taken root in the Israeli defense establishment in the 1950s, according to which the Christians, members of the Maronite sect in Lebanon, were Israel's natural allies, and that if only given the chance, they would turn their backs on the Arab world and join up with Israel. David Ben-Gurion, while in self-imposed political exile in his Negev retreat at Sde Boker (1954–1955), presented to Prime Minister Moshe Sharret a plan in which the Jewish state would encourage a military coup in Lebanon to bring to power a Christian president friendly toward Israel. Sharret, however, did not support the proposal, and when Ben-Gurion returned in the autumn of 1955 to serve as prime minister, he never did anything to promote the plan or implement it, and he may well have come to understand its impracticability. After all, the Maronites were only a small part of the Lebanese population, about 29 percent, and even among them, to say nothing of other Christian factions in Lebanon, there were those who believed in the importance of maintaining close relations with the Muslim population in Lebanon and also with the Arab world. However, in the 1980s the idea of bringing the Maronites to power in Lebanon again took hold among some decision makers in Israel.

The objectives of the Peace for Galilee operation were kept from most of the Israeli public, from most of the government ministers, and even from most of the army commanders. For example, the northern commander at that time, Amir Drori, testified that he was not made party to the war's strategic planning. He claimed that he had been prepared for a military campaign focused on striking a blow at the PLO in South Lebanon, but he found himself suddenly in confrontation with the Syrian Army along the Beirut-Damascus road and in the outskirts of Beirut.

Indeed, even though the campaign had been planned for many months, the basic assumption of the junior military echelons and most of the ministers who approved it was that it was to be a limited operation against PLO bases along the Israeli Lebanese border. Therefore, Begin promised his ministers that it was to be limited to forty-eight hours at most, and he assured the Knesset (Israeli parliament) that Israel was not interested in a confrontation with the Syrians. To this day the reasons for the operation having been turned from a limited to a full-scale war have not been properly explained, especially regarding who kept the government in the dark about the campaign's ambitious aims—Sharon or Chief of the General Staff Raphael Eitan. Or had Begin been a party to the secret?

Israel found itself embroiled in an ambitious strategic plan in Lebanon, documented by two leading Israel journalists, Zeev Schiff and Ehud Yaari. The title of the Hebrew version of their book, *Milhemet sholel* (The War of Deceit), bears witness, of course, to the manner in which its authors viewed this war, although the English title was more muted and cautious: *Israel's Lebanon War* (1984). Some details of this involvement eventually became a subject of litigation between some Israeli journalists who claimed that Sharon had hoodwinked the ministers of the Israeli government and the man who headed it, Begin. Sharon quickly denied this charge and sued the journalists.

As the dimensions of Israel's involvement in Lebanon became clear, and as the crossbar of the goals Israel had set for itself in this campaign was ratcheted progressively higher, Israel moved farther away from achieving them. Begin had promised a forty-eight-hour campaign at whose end the Israeli Army would leave Lebanon, but after several weeks of fighting had passed, the army found itself in the heart of Beirut and far from accomplishing its aims. In this respect the assassination of Gemayel on 14 September 1982 dashed Israeli goals in Lebanon, since it suddenly became clear just how unrealistic the hope of establishing a Christian pro-Israeli regime in Lebanon was. It will be recalled that after his election and prior to his assassination, Gemayel was quick to disassociate himself from Israel, and in response to a demand by Begin, whom he met several days after he was elected, he denied making promises to reach a peace agreement with Israel— he favored "friendship under the table," which would not complicate his relations with the Muslim population in Lebanon and with the Arab world, mainly Syria.

Meanwhile, Israel's casualties grew, and it quickly became clear that Israel was unable to bear the extent of the loss of life that it would have to suffer in order to realize its goals in Lebanon. The Syrians, however, were prepared to do so and, in fact, paid the price to ensure their interests in Lebanon, ultimately leading to their takeover of that country.

Moreover, the sight of the battles raging in the heart of civilian residential areas, mainly in Beirut, in addition to the massacre carried out by Phalangist forces in the Sabra and Shatila refugee camps in September 1982, left a blot on Israel's ethical image. In the wake of the massacre a mass demonstration was held in Tel Aviv in which hundreds of thousands protested against Israel's involvement in Lebanon. A State Commission of Inquiry was subsequently set up to investigate the circumstances of the massacre. Sharon was forced to step down in the wake of this inquiry. While the commission did not hold Sharon directly responsible for the incident, it concluded that he had not done enough to prevent it as he had ignored the possibility that Phalangist forces would carry out revenge in the wake of the assassination of Gemayel.

In the wake of this upheaval, public support in Israel for the Peace for Galilee campaign began to wane. The heavy price that Israel was forced to pay, emerging in part from the unrealistic aims of the campaign as well as from the lack of a clear definition of the objectives, forced Israel once more to focus on the defense of northern Galilee and to disassociate itself from what was going on in the corridors of power in Beirut. The Israeli Army's separation and withdrawal from Lebanon was also influenced by the change in regime in Israel in the summer of 1984 and rise of the Labor Party under Shimon Peres as part of the government of National Unity. Nevertheless, after the withdrawal from most of Lebanon the Israeli Army remained in a narrow strip along the Israeli-Lebanese border. It was only in May 2000 that Israel withdrew its forces completely from Lebanon.

In this connection it is worth stressing that mounting the Peace for Galilee campaign was a serious deviation—in practical terms—from Israel's traditional policy regarding Lebanon. For years Israel was prepared to grant military assistance, mainly training and weapons, to various elements in Lebanon, mostly in the Christian camp, but under no circumstances was it prepared to fight their war. This policy was expressed well by Prime Minister Yitzhak Rabin in 1976 when he explained to the Christian leaders who had approached him after the outbreak of civil war in Lebanon asking for assistance that Israel would "help the Lebanese to help themselves." Following that response and for other reasons, these leaders

turned to Syria, which exploited the opportunity to send its forces into Lebanon as a preliminary step toward gaining control over the country.

A comparison to Vietnam is perhaps not necessarily appropriate in the Lebanese context; after all, Lebanon is located on Israel's northern border and had been a departure base for many terrorist attacks against its citizens. Nevertheless, for an entire generation of Israelis, Lebanon has been viewed as an example of an unnecessary intervention, accompanied by great bloodshed, in a distant land; an intervention that accomplished nothing, leaving behind many casualties.

Nevertheless, the United States left Vietnam. The Lebanese case is different, and proof of this assertion is in the fact that even after its withdrawal from Lebanon, Israel is still grappling with the implications of its presence there. Many feel the activities of Hizbollah (Party of God) arose out of Israel's activities in Lebanon. After all, Israel released the Shiites from the yoke of the PLO, thus creating a vacuum in South Lebanon that Hizbollah filled. The United States returned to Vietnam as a partner in economic cooperation, but Israel is liable to return to Lebanon only as a fighting army answering the challenge from Hizbollah, a challenge that is more, not less, serious than that posed by the PLO.

–EYAL ZISSER,
TEL AVIV UNIVERSITY

Viewpoint:
No. The hard-line policy of destroying the PLO, adopted by the Likud Party when it came to power in 1977, was doomed from the start, causing moderate Islamic leaders to be replaced by militants determined to resist Israeli threats at all costs.

As long as the Israeli Labor Party was in power (1948–1977), the overall strategy in the struggle against the Palestinian war of liberation was focused on reaching an understanding with the Jordanians over the division of the West Bank as the best means of achieving an end to the conflict. This policy was replaced by a different strategy in 1977 when a Likud government, headed by Menachem Begin and Ariel Sharon, came to power. The new policy was to destroy the Palestine Liberation Organization (PLO) strongholds wherever they were: in the West Bank and in Lebanon. As the West Bank was under direct Israeli occupation, there was no need to look for an excuse or pretext, and indeed, soon after the new government was sworn in, a brutal clampdown on the Palestinian leadership in the

Medical workers preparing to remove the corpses of Palestinians from a street in Sabra, Lebanon, in September 1982

(© CORBIS/Bettmann)

occupied territories began, which led eventually to the rise of extreme political Islamic forces replacing the more moderate politicians.

Already, in the municipal elections in the West Bank and Gaza Strip in 1976, it had become clear that the population's allegiance was to the PLO and not to any other political actor, namely Israel or Jordan. Sharon, as minister of defense, tried to crush the PLO's influence and prestige within the Occupied Territories (West Bank, Gaza Strip, and Golan Heights) by first arresting, expelling, and killing the young pro-PLO leadership that emerged in the late 1970s, and then when this policy failed, by inventing a pro-Israeli leadership, called the "village leagues," which were totally unacceptable to the Palestinians and were regarded as collaborators.

He was then convinced that there was a need to destroy the PLO at its headquarters in Lebanon. He had quite easily swayed the rest of the Likud government into adopting similar notions. Israel did not have a free hand in Lebanon as it did with the Occupied Territories. Sharon and the rest of the ministers were eagerly looking for an excuse that would allow them to invade Lebanon and destroy the PLO. In Sharon's mind what was needed was not just the expulsion of the PLO from Lebanon but a restructuring of Lebanon, or rather its remaking as a Christian pro-Israeli state that would challenge Syria and the rest of Israel's immediate neighbors.

A terror attack near Tel Aviv provided an excuse for occupying southern Lebanon in 1978, while at the same time Israel got involved in the Lebanese Civil War by establishing its own Chris-

tian militia, the South Lebanon Army (SLA). This incursion, however, was not enough for Sharon. The PLO still controlled extensive areas adjacent to South Lebanon and enjoyed political autonomy in Beirut itself. It is also noteworthy that by 1978 the PLO became internationally recognized as the sole and legitimate representative of the Palestinian people; in fact, it had more legations and mini-embassies than Israel had in the world at large. It was also adopting a pragmatic approach to the conflict, abandoning the "secular democratic state" solution for the sake of the two-states solution.

Sharon was looking for a pretext in order to deepen the Israeli presence in Lebanon so as to undermine the PLO existential basis as well as its legitimacy, but these aspirations were hindered by a pragmatic PLO policy vis-à-vis Israel. After long months of escalation between the PLO and Israel on the northern border a cease-fire was obtained with the help of American mediation (through the services of the ambassador at large, Philip Habib). The PLO maintained the peace throughout 1981. The attempted murder of Israel's ambassador to Britain, Shlomo Argov, provided the rationale for a wide-scale Israeli invasion of Lebanon, despite the 1981 cease-fire. The Israelis, and quite surprisingly the international media as well, ignored the fact it was the Abu Nidal group that tried to assassinate the ambassador. Abu Nidal was a renegade from the PLO, not its emissary, and had acted in order to undermine the Fatah's hegemonic position within the PLO. These facts, however, did not deter the Israeli government from declaring a clear link between the attempted assassination and the PLO.

The web of contacts Israel had established before the invasion, such as the strong alliance with the Christian Phalanges (Lebanese Kataeb Social Democratic Party), the extremist Maronite militia, increased the appetite of Sharon, who wished to turn the invasion from a punitive mission against the PLO, which is how Prime Minister Begin understood it, into a tour de force that would change beyond recognition the political identity of Lebanon. Sharon was planning not only the annihilation of the PLO in Lebanon but also the establishment of a pro-Israeli government in Beirut, so as to limit and eventually annul the Syrian presence in the country (that had begun in 1976). He had to trick the prime minister. It is no wonder Begin felt betrayed by him when the fiasco in Lebanon became his personal and political demise. Begin regarded the whole war as a failure, took sanctuary at home, resigned, and died embittered by this crisis, instead of rejoicing at the achievements such as the bilateral peace treaty he had signed with Egypt in 1979.

The invasion began in June 1982. The Syrian forces were provoked into action. They were in Lebanon as part of a pan-Arab emergency force sent by the Arab League to pacify the civil war that had raged since 1975. The pan-Arab intervention turned into direct occupation. It was quite clear that the regime in Damascus hoped to avoid participation in the campaign, but it could not stand still when it was shot at and attacked. Drawing the Syrians into the campaign widened the battlefield and increased the number of Lebanese and Israeli casualties. The Israeli Army occupied Beirut and other major towns with the help of carpet bombing and massive ground forces. The Israeli operation, euphemistically called "Peace for Galilee," namely providing defense for northern Israel against PLO attacks, turned into an occupation of much of Lebanon, with no peace for Galilee.

The Israeli attempt to seat in Babda, the Lebanese presidential palace, a local Maronite collaborator ended in disaster for the candidate and his family. This particular attempt increased tensions between Maronites and Palestinians in Greater Beirut. With the encouragement of Israeli officers, the Phalangists massacred hundreds of Palestinians in Sabra and Shatila, two refugee camps in southern Beirut in the autumn of 1982. Although this massacre opened a public discussion in Israel about the validity of the whole invasion, it did not end the Israeli occupation.

An efficient guerilla campaign by the newly founded Shiite militia groups, headed by Hizbollah (Party of God) and Amal, forced the Israelis to withdraw from Lebanon. The large number of Israeli casualties during the years following the invasion drove the civil society in Israel to organize its own campaign for the unilateral withdrawal from Lebanon. Prominent among the nongovernment organizations active in such demands was the "Four Mothers" association, mothers to soldiers serving in Lebanon, and *Yesh Gevul* (There Is a Limit), an association of soldiers refusing to serve in Lebanon. This internal pressure and the continued guerilla warfare led Prime Minister Ehud Barak in the summer of 2000 to declare a unilateral withdrawal. In the next years peace returned to the Galilee once more, but the military occupation of more than a decade had left hundreds dead, thousands wounded, and tens of thousands of people imprisoned without trials in infamous and brutal prisons, such as the Hiyam prison, which added to the overall animosity in the area against the Jewish state and devastated the south of Lebanon in a way that would take years to rebuild and rehabilitate.

Indeed, Lebanon became for a while Israel's Vietnam, resembling in more than one way the unhappy episode of America's war in Southeast Asia (ended 1975). Unlike the U.S. experience in Vietnam, however, Israel still holds a large number of Lebanese citizens it had kidnapped and imprisoned, and as the south of Lebanon is still the home for many Palestinian refugees, the crisis of southern Lebanon is far from being solved. The long years of ruthless occupation, destruction, imprisonment, and torture pushed the majority of the people living in the south, who are Shiite Muslims, to support the Hizbollah, an organization that is connected to Iran and Syria and hence to the struggle against Israel. The real Vietnam for Israel is still the Occupied Territories; Lebanon is more of a kind of a Laos or Cambodia to the Israelis, an extended arena for policies of aggression and occupation disguised in the name of self-defense. The trauma of Lebanon will be solved when peace returns to Palestine. Even then, Lebanon will still have its own particular problems to deal with before moving toward peace.

–ILAN PAPPE,
HAIFA UNIVERSITY

References

Walid Khalidi, *Conflict and Violence in Lebanon: A Confrontation in the Middle East* (Cambridge, Mass.: Harvard University Center for International Affairs, 1979).

Itamar Rabinovich, *The War for Lebanon, 1970–1983* (Ithaca, N.Y.: Cornell University Press, 1984).

Kamal Salibi, *A House of Many Mansions: The History of Lebanon Reconsidered* (Berkeley: University of California Press, 1988).

Zeev Schiff and Ehud Yaari, *Israel's Lebanon War* (New York: Simon & Schuster, 1984).

Kirsten E. Schulze, *Israel's Covert Diplomacy in Lebanon* (New York: St. Martin's Press, 1998).

ISRAEL IN LEBANON

ISRAELI VICTORY IN 1967

Was the outcome of the Arab-Israeli War of 1967 an unmitigated triumph for Israel?

Viewpoint: Yes. Victory in the 1967 War secured Israel's presence in the region and gave it bargaining leverage with neighboring Arab countries.

Viewpoint: No. Victory in the 1967 War created many problems for the State of Israel, such as the issue of Palestinian refugees and security in the Occupied Territories.

Few would deny that Israel's victory in the 1967 Arab-Israeli War (also known as the Six-Day War or the June War) was a tremendous military feat. In six days Israel defeated the combined armies of Egypt, Syria, Jordan, and a host of other Arab nations that sent military contingents into the fighting. The Israel Defense Forces (IDF) displayed audacious tactics in the lightning initial air assault that crippled the air power of the Arab combatants, leaving their ground forces at the mercy of Israeli air and land units. Over the course of time, however, a current of opinion has emerged that postulates that the victory may have created as many or more problems for Israel over the long term than it solved.

As a result of the war Israel acquired the Sinai Peninsula and the Gaza Strip from Egypt (the Sinai has since been returned to Egypt following the 1979 Egyptian-Israeli peace treaty), the West Bank and East Jerusalem from Jordan, and the Golan Heights from Syria. There were/are several strategic, geopolitical, and religious benefits for Israel as a result of the acquisition of these territories; in addition, the one-sided nature of the victory convinced most Arabs that Israel was here to stay, that there was no longer any reasonable hope of vanquishing and eliminating the Jewish state. By acquiring these lands, Israel also had bargaining leverage that it could utilize in return for peace with its Arab neighbors, a land-for-peace formula codified in United Nations (UN) Security Resolution 242 passed in November 1967.

However, many view the victory as generating strategic, demographic, legal, and religious problems for Israel. The lands obtained in the war are now known collectively as the Occupied Territories, which have become the object of a wrenching domestic, regional, and international debate regarding their disposition, one that at times has torn apart the Israeli political environment. In addition, with these lands came a great many more Palestinians. Israel all of a sudden had a much more complex Palestinian problem on its hands, a conundrum that a host of countries are still fruitlessly trying to resolve amid spasms of violence. So, ultimately, did the benefits outweigh the costs?

Viewpoint:
Yes. Victory in the 1967 War secured Israel's presence in the region and gave it bargaining leverage with neighboring Arab countries.

Between 1947 and 1982 Israel engaged in six wars, and the central question, "Should Israel still exist?," remains an issue in the Middle East. Included in this count is the so-called War of Attrition that was started by Egyptian president Gamal Abd al-Nasser on 8 March 1969 and ended on 7 August 1970, thanks to the mediation of U.S. secretary of state William Rogers. This war caused as many Israeli casualties as the 1967 Arab-Israeli War (also known as the Six-Day War or the June War) and thousands of dead among Egyptian military and civilians as well. Furthermore, it suspended the Jarring mission (named after Swedish ambassador to the Soviet Union Gunnar Jarring) to negotiate an Arab-Israeli peace set by the United Nations (UN) Security Council Resolution 242, issued on 22 November 1967.

The genesis for the Six-Day War, in fact, lay in the long-term policy of raids carried out by the Fatah movement, led by Yasser Arafat, from Syria, where it enjoyed the support of both the Syrian Baath Party and the Syrian Army. On 7 April 1967, during an air battle above Lake Tiberias, the Israelis shot down six Russian-supplied Syrian MiG-21s. This event enabled the Soviet government to justify its claims of a possible Israeli strike against Damascus. Secretary-General of the United Nations U Thant reassured Nasser that there was not a deployment of Israeli troops along the Israeli-Syrian border, and the Egyptian president, instead of dispatching forces to Syria, concentrated the bulk of his army in the Sinai Peninsula. Then, on 16 May, Nasser asked U Thant to close down the United Nations Emergency Force (UNEF) operation, the troops of which "had been stationed both at Sharm el Sheikh and in the Gaza Strip since 1956." As former Israeli prime minister Golda Meir states in her autobiography, Nasser had the right to ask for such a closing. In fact, only Egypt had given consent for the international police force to be stationed on Egyptian soil. What was really surprising was U Thant's reaction; he agreed immediately to Nasser's request on 19 May. Because of U Thant's move, Nasser announced on 21 May the Egyptian blockade of the Strait of Tiran to Israeli shipping. Nasser's decision was considered by the Israeli government to be a casus belli. The blockade, which precluded navigation through the Gulf of Aqaba, was illegal considering the "secret under-

taking he [Nasser] had given Israel in 1957 that the Strait of Tiran would remain an international waterway," according to scholar Thomas G. Fraser. The secret agreement was supported by nations such as the United States, France, Great Britain, and Canada.

In the meantime, Washington was trying to cope with President Dwight D. Eisenhower's declaration of 1 March 1957, in which the United States "endorsed the right of free and innocent passage through the Strait of Tiran by dispatching an American warship through the Gulf of Aqaba to Eilat." As recorded by scholar Howard M. Sachar, Israeli foreign minister Abba Eban was informed that the Department of State had warned Moscow with the following message: "The United States will regard any impingement of freedom of navigation in the Strait of Tiran, whether under the Israeli flag or another, as an act of aggression, against which Israel, in the opinion of the United States, is justified in taking defensive measures." On 23 May President Lyndon B. Johnson issued a statement in which he reaffirmed the American commitment "to the support of the political independence and territorial integrity of all the nations of the area. The United States strongly opposes aggression by anyone in the area, in any form, overt or clandestine." President Johnson wanted on one hand for Israel not to react to the Egyptian blockade, and on the other hand he looked for support from France and Great Britain.

On 24 May 1967 Eban met first with French president Charles De Gaulle, who frankly stated: "Do not make war! Do not make war! In any event, do not be the first to fire!" Then in the afternoon the Israeli foreign minister met with British prime minister Harold Wilson, who spoke of an international naval task force to police the Strait of Tiran. The outcome of the meeting was not satisfactory to anyone. At home, in fact, as Fraser underlines, the moderate Israeli government of Prime Minister Levi Eshkol and Foreign Minister Eban was held in check by the supporters of David Ben-Gurion and Menachem Begin, who sponsored the hard line.

Finally, on 25–26 May, President Johnson received Eban. The dream of unconditional support from the United States was shattered by Johnson's decision to restrain Israel from taking the first step toward war. It was the opinion of the U.S. Congress and of the Senate Foreign Relations Committee that the matter should be put before the U.N. Security Council. However, the Security Council did not succeed in ameliorating the situation. In a letter to Eshkol, who was also the minister of defense, Johnson admitted that "the United States

An Israeli soldier praying at the West Wall in Jerusalem, 1967

(Zahal, Israel Defense Forces)

could not act without congressional approval, and in any case our leadership is unanimous that the United States should not act alone." War, however, was imminent. The Syrian-Egyptian coalition was joined by Jordan (on 30 May) and Iraq (on 3 June), the latter signing a mutual-defense pact with Egypt the day before the conflict began. Nasser was also offered assistance and support by King Hassan of Morocco, President Habib Bourguiba of Tunisia, King Faisal of Saudi Arabia, and by other Arab countries such as Algeria and Kuwait.

At the same time Israel too was reorganizing its government and military forces. On 1 June, Gahal (Gush Herut-Liberalim, or Freedom Liberal Bloc) and Rafi (Israel Labor List), the two major opposition parties, joined the coalition in a government of national unity, and Eshkol gave up his position as minister of defense to Lieutenant-General Moshe Dayan. The war started at 7:10 A.M. on 5 June with an aerial attack on Egypt's key bases in the Sinai Peninsula, the Suez rectangle, and the Nile Valley. Then a ground attack at 8:15 A.M. opened the way to al-Arish, the administrative capital of Sinai. After three days of fighting, Sinai and the Gaza Strip had fallen to Israel. The West Bank and East Jerusalem as well had been conquered between 5–7 June. The first UN Security Council cease-fire resolution passed unanimously on 8 June. It was accepted by both Nasser and Jordan's King Hussein.

The attack against the Syrians took place on 9–10 June, when the Israelis conquered the Golan Heights, but on 9 June the Syrian representative to the Security Council stated that his government accepted the UN cease-fire resolution. During the first five days two important phone calls were made between Soviet prime minister Alexei Kosygin and President Johnson. During the first one, on 5 June, the former asked the latter "to use his influence on the Israeli government to withdraw its forces." In the second one, on 10 June, Kosygin asked Johnson to stop the Israeli advance toward Damascus. In such an awkward situation the American president acted in a much more incisive way. In fact, notwithstanding the regrettable "Liberty incident," during which the electronic-surveillance vessel USS *Liberty* was attacked by Israeli Mirage and Mystère aircraft (although it was in international waters and was well recognizable), Johnson decided to dispatch three Sixth Fleet task forces in the direction of the Syrian coast. The war ended at 6:30 P.M. on 10 June.

The June conflict had put to the test everyone inside and outside the Middle East.

Israel, although a young country, immediately understood that it could count only on its own forces. The conflict, in fact, was not meant to establish a new state but to reinforce its existence. The war demonstrated the Arab countries' weakness and absolute incapacity to carry out their design: Israel's extirpation from the Middle East. Israel had experienced an internal crisis, quickly solved thanks to the appointment of Dayan as minister of defense. As Sachar argues, Israel's strength rested on analysts and intelligence. It was not the superiority in weapons but the human element that was the successful factor. To put it in Meir's words, "the price," in the aftermath of the Six-Day War, "would be peace, permanent peace, peace by treaty based on agreed and secure borders."

France, an ally of Israel, tried to limit U.S. and Soviet influence in the Middle East, and even though the "French arms shipments to Israel had continued unabated in recent wars," its government was ready to shift to a new policy toward Israel. On the contrary, no shift was contemplated on Great Britain's part. Her Majesty's government had no more interests in Palestine, or, more precisely, the only interests it had were economic and related to oil resources located in the Persian Gulf.

Washington for its part, though stating once more that it opposed aggression by anyone in the area, which had been the policy of the United States under four presidents—Harry S Truman, Eisenhower, John F. Kennedy, and Johnson—involved itself only near the end of the conflict. Moreover, Johnson had already entered the Vietnam quagmire (ended 1975), concentrating all of his energies on a war that would end his presidency in 1969.

Certainly, Israel's victory generated many still unsolved problems such as the issue of a Palestinian homeland. Nonetheless, it once and for all secured Israel's presence in the region and gave it bargaining leverage, because that war, though a preventive one, frustrated Nasser's plans to destroy the Jewish state first through diplomacy, by closing down the UNEF operation with U Thant's immediate support, and then economically, with the blockade of the Strait of Tiran, precluding Israeli navigation through the Gulf of Aqaba. Nasser's moves aimed at testing the international community, and in that difficult situation no one seemed to be terribly interested in dealing with the crisis but Israel. Israel did not want another Suez crisis, with the same outcome, so it chose war—and it won.

—PAOLA OLIMPO,
UNIVERSITY OF LECCE

Viewpoint:
No. Victory in the 1967 War created many problems for the State of Israel, such as the issue of Palestinian refugees and security in the Occupied Territories.

In order to fully understand the strategic complications and burdens generated for Israel by the 1967 Arab-Israeli War (also known as the Six-Day War or the June War), one has to reconsider its origins. It began as a result of a deterioration of relations between Israel and Syria in the 1960s. Israel tried to grab more land in the buffer area between the two countries, the demilitarized zone, and was resisted by force. The Israeli government quite clearly stated, a few months before the war started, that it would attack Syria if these skirmishes continued. For many in the Arab world an Israeli attack on Syria was imminent. In order to deter Israel, and as well as for the purpose of obtaining a hegemonic role in the Arab world, Egyptian leader Gamal Abd al-Nasser took several steps to exert pressure on the Jewish state, which included the concentration of troops near Israel's border, a military alliance with King Hussein of Jordan, and the takeover of two islands in the Strait of Tiran (connecting the Gulf of Aqaba with the Red Sea) that, according to international law, belonged to Egypt and strategically and effectively controlled the sea routes to the Israeli seaport of Eilat at the northern end of the Gulf of Aqaba.

The Israeli government launched an attack on 5 June 1967, while the international community was still seeking a diplomatic resolution to the crisis. In two days the Israelis reopened the way to Eilat and expelled the Egyptian and Jordanian forces on its border. However, a hawkish government, which included the leader of the right-wing Revisionist movement, Menachem Begin, extended the war into a campaign for the occupation of those parts of Palestine that Israel had not seized in the 1948 war, as well as for the sake of building a miniempire stretching from the Suez Canal in the south to the Hermon Mountains on the border with Lebanon and Syria in the north. As Begin himself later explained, this war was meant to create a Greater Israel. This dramatic expansion of the Jewish state beyond its internationally recognized borders wreaked havoc not only on the Jewish state and the Palestinians but on the area as a whole.

In the wake of the 1967 War, Israel annexed four different areas: the Sinai, the Golan Heights, the West Bank, and the Gaza Strip. The Sinai Peninsula was returned to Egypt by 1982. One cannot say that during that period of Israeli occupation the situation deteriorated in any way, although the occupation of the Sinai was the cause for the 1973

USS *LIBERTY*

In a letter to President Bill Clinton, Captain William L. McGonagle, former commander of the USS Liberty, an intelligence-gathering vessel that was attacked by Israeli forces during the 1967 Arab-Israeli War, asked for a better accounting of the incident:

Israeli aircraft conducted surveillance of the ship within moments of our arrival on station off the coast of the Sinai on the morning of June 8, 1967. The ship was soon identified as USS LIBERTY by Israeli Naval Headquarters, by referring to "JANE'S FIGHTING SHIPS" 1966 or 1967 issue, which showed a photograph of the ship and listed in detail its characteristics. In fact, an identification "tower" was placed on their Battle Plot with an "A" on the tower to identify the ship as an American ship. The plot was not kept up to date, and was removed when the watch changed at noon that day. The ship was overflown on several occasions before the attack commenced. An Israeli Naval Officer went to the American Embassy Naval Attaché to obtain information that the ship was indeed USS LIBERTY, but the US Naval Attaché did not have our operating schedule, so he could neither confirm nor deny that the ship was the USS LIBERTY.

When the attack began about 2:00 p.m. (local time) the ship was subjected to relentless and repeated murderous fire from the attacking aircraft (which were unmarked—a violation of international law). The gun crews of the two (2) bow .50 cal. machine guns were killed during the initial strike on the ship. We could not man the starboard bridge level .50 cal. machine gun, because our life boat was burning (1) deck below and the heat did not allow anyone to approach the gun. We could not man the port bridge level .50 cal. machine gun, because two (2) 55 gallon gasoline drums were burning furiously one (1) deck below. Again the heat of the flames prevented anyone from approaching the gun. WE WERE DEFENSELESS against the onslaught of eight (8) or more firing passes by at least four (4) aircraft, and the strafing and launching of five (5) torpedoes by three (3) motor torpedo boats. That a larger number of casualties was not reported is a tribute to the fighting spirit of the officers, crew, civilians, and Marines, when they had nothing to defend themselves with, during our awesome hours of peril.

USS LIBERTY (AGTR-5), a Technical Research ship was sailing legally and peacefully, in international waters in the Eastern Mediterranean Sea, twelve and one-half (12.5) nautical miles from the nearest land off the coast of Sinai, during the Arab-Israeli Six Day war, when it was attacked, without warning or provocation, by four (4) unidentified jet fighter aircraft, firing rockets, machine guns, and napalm. The ship was then strafed and torpedoed by three (3) Israeli motor torpedo boats. One (1) torpedo exploded in the Research spaces of the ship, where it caused the majority of the fatalities. The Government of Israel shortly after the attack acknowledged that their armed forces conducted the assault. The apology for the attack was accepted, but the reason for the attack as "misidentification" was never accepted by the US Government.

Thirty-four (34) officers, sailors, a civilian, and a US Marine were killed or died of their wounds as a result of the attack. One hundred seventy-one (171) additional crew members received wounds as a result of the attack. The Government of Israel did compensate the families of those killed, the individuals that were wounded, and eventually paid reparations for the damage done to the ship and its equipment. . . .

Except for a few high ranking naval officers, no one has felt our pain of not knowing exactly why the ship was attacked. Over thirty-one (31) years after the attack, the crew is entitled to know the details concerning the attack by the Government of Israel and also the details of the role the US Government in the entire affair. Why were our aircraft recalled to their carriers on two (2) occasions before they reached our location to assess the situation, and what official ordered the recall after "Hot Line" communication was established with Moscow to alert Nasser that the planes were being sent to see what the condition of USS LIBERTY was? None of the planes ever reached our location. For over seventeen (17) hours we received no assistance from US forces in the Mediterranean.

This is the only US Navy ship attacked by a foreign nation, involving a large loss of life and so many personnel injured that has never been accorded a full Congressional hearing.

Source: *Captain William L. McGonagle, USN (Ret.), to President Bill Clinton, 24 October 1998, Arlington National Cemetery website <http://www.arlington-cemetery.net/wlmcgon.htm>.*

Arab-Israeli War, which ended with a large number of casualties on both the Israeli and the Egyptian sides. The return of this area to Egypt facilitated a bilateral agreement that holds until today.

In the Golan Heights the Israelis cleansed dozens of villages, emptied the land of its original population, and resettled a relatively small number of its own citizens there. As in the case of the Sinai for Egypt, it was the cause for Syria's participation in the 1973 war against Israel, but it did not lead to a peace agreement between the two countries; instead, the Golan Heights were de facto annexed to Israel in 1981, and the small Druze community remaining on the land was forced to show loyalty to the state of Israel or suffer from an oppressive policy of discrimination. The continued Israeli occupation of Syrian territory disabled a comprehensive peace between Israel and the Arab world at large, and without such a comprehensive peace the bilateral peace agreements Israel concluded with Egypt in 1979 and Jordan in 1994 remain precarious diplomatic arrangements that could be reversed if current conditions continue to deteriorate.

Furthermore, the absence of peace with Syria, and as a result with most of the Arab world, led to a strong alliance between Israel and the United States. Since Syria was considered the front base of the Soviet Union in the area, it was easy to form a coalition that would raise the American military and financial commitment to Israel to the level of Washington's North Atlantic Treaty Organization (NATO) allies, if not beyond. This "special relationship"—translated into supplying Israel, quite often for free, with the most updated and best American weapons in abundance—continues to this day, long after the collapse of the Soviet Union. The American-Israeli alliance resulted in turning the Israeli Army into the strongest military force in the region and allowed Israel to develop nuclear and nonconventional capabilities, reciprocated unsuccessfully by similar attempts in several Arab countries. While the rest of the world was trying to disarm, the Middle East was drawn into an accelerated arms race, even after the end of the Cold War. The almost total identification with Israel by the United States not only prevented Washington from being an honest broker in the conflict, it also seriously damaged America's image and prestige in the Arab world to the point where today it may be at the lowest possible level. America became not only the enemy of the Palestinians and the Arabs but of the Muslim world as a whole.

It is mainly the misery experienced by the residents of the West Bank and the Gaza Strip after the war that accentuates how ill-fated and destructive this military achievement was in the long run. From its first day the Israeli occupation of these two areas was a horror story for its inhabitants. Expulsions of a large number of Palestinians from refugee camps in the area of Jericho, from the Old City of Jerusalem, and from Qalqilya were just the beginning of a callous military occupation. Curfews, closures, and collective punishments were frequently imposed and inflicted on the local population, whether as retaliation to a developing resistance movement or just as part of a policy aimed at turning life under occupation into an impossibility.

The occupation bred two kinds of fanaticism on both sides of the divide and defeated the best intentions of moderates and peace seekers in Israel and in Palestine. The first was a Jewish messianic movement, Gush Emunim, which with the help of successive Israeli governments, established settlers in the Occupied Territories, quite often on land confiscated from the local population. They are still at it in 2003, some harboring dreams of taking over Haram al-Sharif, the holy place for Islam on the Temple Mount at the heart of Jerusalem—a move that could infuriate and antagonize the Muslim world as a whole. These fanatics were also directing their destructive energies into Jewish society against those whom they regarded as traitors, namely those who were willing to withdraw from the Occupied Territories. One such "traitor" was the late prime minister Yitzhak Rabin, who was assassinated by a Gush Emunim sympathizer in 1995. This movement transformed the whole political scene in Israel toward ethnocentrism and nationalist extremism and away from moderation and peace-seeking activities.

The economic deprivation in the West Bank and the Gaza Strip and the Israeli clampdown on the national secular forces of the Palestinians has allowed a fanatic Islamist movement to rise in the Occupied Territories. This movement led the Palestinians to a desperate and abortive attempt to end the occupation by force, resulting in the employment of suicide bombs in the 1990s. The rise of Palestinian extremism was reciprocated by an even harsher Israeli policy of oppression leading in the beginning of the twenty-first century to the destruction of the Palestinian social fabric and threatening its existence in the Occupied Territories.

The evil wreaked by the 1967 War on the life of the Palestinians in the Occupied Territories can be best exemplified in two economic phases. Initially, the Palestinians were allowed, indeed invited, to work as a cheap labor force in Israel—they were underpaid, without any basic rights as employees, and lived an economic existence characterized by daily humiliation in checkpoints and "slave markets." After the so-called al-Aqsa *intifada* (uprising) burst out in September 2000, Israel barred the movement of Palestinian workers into its territories. As a result, unemployment in the Occupied Territories soared, reaching 70 to 75 percent in most places, leading to widespread malnutrition and hunger among those who lost their source of living.

The 1967 War was both another chapter of Israeli expansionism and a clumsy pan-Arab attempt to navigate between war rhetoric and military incompetence. The victims, as in 1948, were first and foremost the Palestinians, although quite a few Israelis felt they lost the country they dreamed of—once it became a mini-empire, occupying another people's land—and it was rejected by the countries around it.

In strategic terms the war and its consequences illustrated that the gigantic Israeli arsenal built with the exclusive help of the United States and the secret services employed to control the Occupied Territories did not bring security to Israel but, on the contrary, brought war into the Jewish state itself. None of the mighty military apparatuses Israel possessed was able to crush the Palestinian demand for independence and self-determination. Wherever they were after the 1967 war—in the Occupied Territories, in Israel, or in foreign refugee camps—Palestinians reminded the Israelis that they had the potential of undermining the personal security, if not the existence, of Jews living in Palestine and Israel. The bitter fruits of the 1967 War have increased the mutual hatred, deepened the suspicions on both sides, and rendered even practical solutions—such as the division of Palestine into two states—unattainable as long as the Israeli occupation and colonization of the West Bank and the Gaza Strip continues.

–ILAN PAPPE,
HAIFA UNIVERSITY

References

Eli Barnavi, *Une Histoire Moderne d'Israel* (Paris: Flammarion, 1988).

Moshe Dayan, *Moshe Dayan: Story of My Life* (New York: Morrow, 1976).

Herbert Druks, *The Uncertain Alliance: The U.S. and Israel from Kennedy to the Peace Process* (Westport, Conn.: Greenwood Press, 2001).

Michael Oren, *Six Days of War: June 1967 and the Making of the Modern Middle East* (New York: Oxford University Press, 2002).

William B. Quandt, *Peace Process: American Diplomacy and the Arab-Israeli Conflict since 1967*, revised edition (Berkeley: University of California Press, 2001).

Howard M. Sachar, *A History of Israel: From the Rise of Zionism to Our Time* (New York: Knopf, 1976).

LEAGUE OF ARAB STATES

Has the League of Arab States been a successful organization?

Viewpoint: Yes. The League of Arab States has been a relatively effective regional organization, helping to unify the Arab world.

Viewpoint: No. The League of Arab States is more of a sign of Arab disunity than unity, as it is a loose coalition of independent states that have acted separately on many occasions.

The League of Arab States, or what has become simply known as the Arab League, was established on 22 March 1945, months prior to the establishment of the United Nations (UN) in San Francisco. The charter of the League was based on the Arab unity consultations held in Alexandria, Egypt, in the summer of 1944, the documentation of which became known as the Alexandria Protocol (7 October 1944), which laid down the political, legal, and institutional frameworks as well as the overall objectives of the proposed organization. Comprising twenty-two states by the end of the twentieth century, the League originally included the following founding members: Egypt, Iraq, Jordan, Lebanon, Saudi Arabia, Syria, and Yemen. The most recent member, the Comoros Islands, was admitted in 1993. For most of the League's existence the headquarters has been located in Cairo, except for the period in the late 1970s through the late 1980s when it was moved to Tunis, Tunisia, in protest of Egypt's 1979 peace treaty with Israel. The Arab League defines itself as a "national and regional organization that seeks to promote closer ties among member-states and coordinate their policies and their economic, cultural and security plans with a view to developing collective cooperation, protecting national security and maintaining the independence and sovereignty of member-states, thereby enhancing the potential for joint Arab action in all fields."

The formation of the League emanated from a confluence of sources: the crest of Arab nationalist ideology that crystallized during the mandate period in the Middle East between World War I (1914–1918) and World War II (1939–1945) that had as its ultimate goal the unification of the Arab peoples in the region; the power void in the region amid the beginning of the end of European colonialism and the postcolonial resurgence of Third World nationalism; and the realization that the international organization that would soon become the UN did not adequately reflect the regional concerns of its constituent parts and was skewed more toward the agendas of the great powers (the Latin American states also shared this concern).

Some individuals have viewed the Arab League as a failed organization; indeed, the mere fact that the League was composed of separate, independent nations contradicted the intended goal of Arab nationalism. It is simply a loose conglomeration of states whose representatives consult at various summit meetings, the resolutions and declarations of which are not binding on any member state. These same people would say that the Arab League can be characterized more by division than cooperation, which has hamstrung its effectiveness throughout its history, and that it has, in fact, been overtaken in many ways by subregional organizations, such as the Gulf

Cooperation Council (GCC), which more adequately reflects the concern of its smaller and less diverse group of members.

Still others view the Arab League as, while not the perfect model of a regional grouping, a relatively successful organization that has accomplished a great many practical achievements in the Arab world, such as the formation of the Arab Bank for Economic Development in Africa (ABEDA) and the Arab Fund for Technical Assistance (AFTA). In addition, it has been instrumental in coordinating Arab responses to crises, especially in the Arab-Israeli arena. If one strips away the veneer of the impossibly lofty goals that surrounded the creation of the League and sees it for what it is, compared to other similar regional organizations it has, indeed, been more effective than not.

Viewpoint:
Yes. The League of Arab States has been a relatively effective regional organization, helping to unify the Arab world.

In March 2002, during a summit meeting in Beirut, the League of Arab States (Arab League) adopted a peace initiative proposed by Crown Prince Abdallah of Saudi Arabia, thus making it an all-Arab peace initiative enjoying broad support (at least outwardly) from even the most radical Arab leaders such as Syria's President Bachar el-Assad and representatives of Libya and Iraq. It is still too early to assess whether this initiative is destined to be a turning point in the history of the Arab-Israeli conflict. Nevertheless, even those in Israel who had their reservations about the initiative—for example, the unequivocal demand it includes for Israeli withdrawal to the 4 June 1967 borders—found it difficult to criticize its historical importance. After all, this was the first time that the Arab world had expressed a commitment to a vision of peace with Israel, even if this pledge was somewhat reserved and conditional on Israel acceding to Arab demands.

Even though the Arab League summit meeting did not conform to the line set down by radical elements in the Arab world, it encouraged moderate Arab states to seek peace and reconciliation with Israel. No wonder Hasan Nasrallah, secretary general of Hizbollah (Party of God), who had over the past decade cast himself as the antithesis to those in the Arab world who expressed their readiness to come to terms with Israel, claimed that these leaders did not represent the common Arab in their readiness to make peace with Israel. Nasrallah might have been right, but the important fact remained that the Arab leaders were not deterred by public opinion from adopting the policy that they felt was proper and even mandatory in promoting the interests of their countries. This episode dem-

onstrated that, contrary to accepted opinion, the Arab League and its institutions were capable of fulfilling a positive role as a body able to gather the Arab states behind effective policy designed to promote the interests of individual states and the entire region.

The Arab League, founded in 1945, was formed to serve as a guiding and coordinating body for the regional states and to help promote the idea of Arab unity. However, its organizational structure as well as its charter, designed to preserve the independence of its member states and therefore the political division of the Arab world, actually was an obstacle in the path of any attempt to unite the Arab states.

The establishment of the League grew out of the balance of power existing between two factions of Arab states in the 1940s—a balance of tension and animosity between the Hashemite axis (Transjordan and Iraq) on the one hand and Egypt and Saudi Arabia on the other. Each of these actors had conflicting desires and wishes. The Hashemites wanted either the annexation of Palestine, Syria, and Lebanon to the Hashemite-controlled region, thus creating "Greater Syria" according to Jordanian king Abdullah's vision, or the creation of a "Fertile Crescent" envisioned by Iraqi prime minister Nuri al-Said. Both concepts aroused the opposition of Egypt and Saudi Arabia. The result was the establishment of the Arab League as a body whose interests lay in maintaining the existing political status quo in the Arab world. In the meantime, the Hashemite monarchy in Iraq (1958) and the monarchy in Egypt (1953) disappeared. Nevertheless, the basic conflicting interests of the member states and of their leaders, and thus a delicate balance of power between them, have remained unchanged.

Thus, it transpired that Arab unity in the practical sense was not a real or practical objective in the Arab world of the 1940s and 1950s, and this situation in essence has remained the case. There is no doubt, however, that the common Arab was deeply committed to the idea of Arab unity, thus forcing the Arab regimes to pay lip service to this idea and to try to appear to be

ALEXANDRIA PROTOCOL

On 7 October 1944 representatives from five Arab nations issued the following protocol:

1. League of Arab States

A League will be formed of the independent Arab States which consent to join the League. It will have a council which will be known as the "Council of the League of Arab States" in which all participating states will be represented on an equal footing.

The object of the League will be to control the execution of the agreements which the above states will conclude; to hold periodic meetings which will strengthen the relations between those states; to coordinate their political plans so as to insure their cooperation, and protect their independence and sovereignty against every aggression by suitable means; and to supervise in a general way the affairs and interests of the Arab countries.

The decisions of the Council will be binding on those who have accepted them except in cases where a disagreement arises between two member states of the League in which the two parties shall refer their dispute to the Council for solution. In this case the decision of the Council of the League will be binding.

In no case will resort to force to settle a dispute between any two member states of the League be allowed. But every state shall be free to conclude with any other member state of the League, or other powers, special agreements which do not contradict the text or the present dispositions.

In no case will the adoption of a foreign policy which may be prejudicial to the policy of the League or an individual member state be allowed.

The Council will intervene in every dispute which may lead to war between a member state of the League and any other member state or power, so as to reconcile them.

A subcommittee will be formed of the members of the Preliminary Committee to prepare a draft of the statutes of the Council of the League and to examine the political questions which may be the object of agreement among Arab States.

2. Cooperation in Economic, Cultural, Social, and Other Matters

A. The Arab States represented on the Preliminary Committee shall closely cooperate in the following matters:

(1) Economic and financial matters, i.e., commercial exchange, customs, currency, agriculture, and industry.

(2) Communications, i.e., railways, roads, aviation, negation, posts and telegraphs.

(3) Cultural matters.

(4) Questions of nationality, passports, visas, execution of Judgments, extradition of criminals, etc.

(5) Social questions.

(6) Questions of public health.

B. A subcommittee of experts for each of the above subjects will be formed in which the states which have participated in the Preliminary Committee will be represented. This subcommittee will prepare draft regulations or cooperation in the above matters, describing the extent and means of that collaboration.

C. A committee for coordination and editing will be formed whose object will be to control the work of the subcommittees, to coordinate that part of the work which is accomplished, and to prepare drafts of agreement which will be submitted to the various governments.

D. When all the subcommittees have accomplished their work, the Preliminary Committee will meet to examine the work of the subcommittees as a preliminary step toward the holding of the General Arab Conference.

3. Consolidation of These Ties In the Future

While expressing its satisfaction at such a happy step, the Committee hopes that Arab States will be able in the future to consolidate that step by other steps, especially if post-war world events should result in institutions which will bind various Powers more closely together.

4. Special Resolution Concerning Lebanon

The Arab States represented on the Preliminary Committee emphasize their respect of the independence and sovereignty of Lebanon in its present frontiers, which the governments of the above States have already recognized in consequence of Lebanon's adoption of an independent policy, which the Government of that country announced in its program of October 7, 1943, unanimously approved by the Lebanese Chamber of Deputies.

5. Special Resolution Concerning Palestine

A. The Committee is of the opinion that Palestine constitutes an important part of the Arab World and that the rights of the Arabs in Palestine cannot be touched without prejudice to peace and stability in the Arab World.

The Committee also is of the opinion that the pledges binding the British Government and providing for the cessation of Jewish immigration, the preservation of Arab lands, and the achievement of independence for Palestine are permanent Arab rights whose prompt implementation would constitute a step toward the desired goal and toward the stabilization of peace and security.

The Committee declares its support of the cause of the Arabs of Palestine and its willingness to work for the achievement of their legitimate aims and the safeguarding of their Just rights.

The Committee also declares that it is second to none in regretting the woes which have been inflicted upon the Jews of Europe by European dictatorial states. But the question of these Jews should not be confused with Zionism, for there can be no greater injustice and aggression than solving the problem of the Jews of Europe by another injustice, i.e., by inflicting injustice on the Arabs of Palestine of various religions and denominations.

B. The special proposal concerning the participation Of the Arab Governments and peoples in the "Arab National Fund" to safeguard the lands of the Arabs of Palestine shall be referred to the committee of financial and economic affairs to examine it from all its angles and to submit the result of that examination to the Preliminary Committee in its next meeting.

Source: *"The Alexandria Protocol; October 7, 1944," The Avalon Project at Yale Law School <http://www.yale.edu/lawweb/avalon/mideast/alex.htm>.*

LEAGUE OF ARAB STATES

working toward its realization. In actual fact, these regimes wanted to preserve the independence and sovereignty of their countries.

In view of the conflicting interests of the League's member states and rising tensions, it is little wonder that in its early days the League appeared to be ineffective and lacking power. The image it projected was one of a platform for squabbling, not for making practical decisions. Moreover, there were many who argued at the time, and to a considerable extent still claim, that divisions among member states of the Arab League and, more important, the weakness of Arab regimes, could lead to a situation where the League might actually create the dynamics that would increase factionalism and rifts in the ranks of the Arab world. Even worse, this reality might drag the Arab world to adopt radical policies (adopting the line of its most radical elements or influenced by the Arab street). After all, it appeared that in view of the structural weaknesses of the Arab states, most of which are ruled by authoritarian regimes, they might be forced unwillingly to fall into line with popular sentiment in order not to arouse the displeasure of the populace; in other words, they might be forced to adopt policies that no Arab regime really wants and that are inimical to their political interests.

The manner in which the Arab world conducted itself during the First Arab-Israeli War (1947–1949) is ostensibly an excellent example of how the entire Arab collective, as well as individual states, were dragged along by popular sentiment toward adopting radical policies on the question of Palestine. Most of the Arab states wanted to refrain from any deep involvement in the Palestine conflict; however, public opinion in those countries alongside the animosity and suspicion among the states, especially between Jordan and Egypt, created the dynamics that in early 1948 sparked the decision to invade Palestine. Transjordan, followed by Egypt—and after that, Iraq, Syria, and Lebanon—were drawn into the maelstrom.

The League's subsequent path did not bode well for unity either. In many cases, especially in the 1950s and 1960s, it played no effective or constructive role; in some cases it played a negative role, as it lacked any real power and was guided by the emotions of the radical elements in the Arab world. One example was its rejection of a Western proposal at the beginning of the 1950s to establish a Middle Eastern Defense Command. Other problems were the continuous inter-Arab tensions, the so-called Arab "cold war" throughout the 1950s and 1960s, the Iraqi-Egyptian conflict in the early 1960s, the Syrian-Egyptian confrontation in September 1961 (in the wake of Syria's withdrawal from the United Arab Republic), the Saudi-Egypt war in Yemen from 1962, and finally the eruption of the Six-Day War in June 1967. In each of these instances the League did nothing to moderate the situation. Moreover, during most of these episodes it was claimed that the League had become a tool in the hands of Egyptian president Gamal Abd al-Nasser, thus inciting divisiveness in the Arab world by serving Egypt's aims rather than serving the Arabs as a whole.

Similar examples can be found after the Six-Day War at the Khartoum summit in September 1967, which sent the message of the "three no's" to Israel (no reconciliation, no recognition, and no negotiations), or at the summits of the late 1970s at which Egypt was ousted from the Arab League for having signed a peace agreement with Israel. Nevertheless, despite its undeniably problematic past, one must admit that in retrospect the League was revealed as having been more effective than might have been expected at its inception. Over the years it made a certain contribution to the promotion of a comprehensive regional Arab policy that might even be considered pragmatic and moderate.

For example, the Arab summits in the early 1960s were used by Nasser to moderate and rein in the radical Baath Party regime in Syria and to prevent deteriorating Arab-Israeli relations from turning into a regional conflict with Israel. Only toward the end of 1966, when Nasser—for domestic and regional considerations—withdrew from the summit policy and formed an Egyptian-Syrian alliance, did momentum toward war increase.

Other achievements from the Arab point of view include recognition of the Palestine Liberation Organization (PLO) as the sole legitimate representative of the Palestinian people, at the Rabat Arab summit of 1974. One must also mention the efforts of the League's institutions to contain the crisis in the Arab world in 1958 following the outbreak of civil war in Lebanon and the July Revolution in Iraq. However, special attention should be paid to the role played by the League and its institutions during the Gulf crisis and war beginning in the summer of 1990. Most Arab states decided to join the United States in its war against Iraq. It may be argued that had there not been a body such as the Arab League that supported the U.S.-led coalition and granted legitimacy to the joint inter-Arab mobilization against Iraq, it is doubtful whether most of the Arab states could have allowed themselves to join the coalition.

The Arab League did not play an active or constructive role throughout the Arab-Israeli peace process for most of the 1990s. The summit

meeting in Beirut in March 2002 might be considered a turning point in this regard. In addition, following the terrorist attacks of 11 September 2001 against the United States, the League is facing a real challenge in having to present the Arab world to the West. This challenge will provide it with a golden opportunity to play an active and leading role in the international struggle against terrorism under U.S. leadership. However, at the same time the League's other face may come into view, revealing its ineffectiveness.

On more than one occasion the League served a unifying function in the Arab world, as an effective element in facilitating an Arab consensus, thus promoting moderate and pragmatic policies. While it is true that one should not overstate the significance and importance of the League as an effective regional body, it should not be dismissed altogether. The truth apparently lies somewhere in the middle. After all, the League is the sum of all its members—in other words, an expression of the desires of its members, mainly that of Egypt as well as Saudi Arabia, Syria, and Iraq. Since 1945 these member states have grown stronger and as a result have grown more determined and better able to promote their national interests. On more than one occasion these interests ran completely counter to the concerns of the Arab man on the street. It is here in particular that the contribution of the Arab League is clearly seen, since it served as an instrument in the hands of Arab rulers in circumventing public opinion and promoting more moderate and balanced policies, taking into consideration domestic, regional, and international constraints. Indeed, it may be said in the final analysis that the League has revealed itself as an effective element only in those cases where its consensus enjoyed the support of its members, mainly Egypt and Saudi Arabia. Where that consensus, and thus the desire to support it, was lacking, its effectiveness was minimal.

—EYAL ZISSER,
TEL AVIV UNIVERSITY

Meeting at the Arab League headquarters in Cairo in 1964

(© AP/Wide World Photos)

LEAGUE OF ARAB STATES

Viewpoint:
No. The League of Arab States is more of a sign of Arab disunity than unity, as it is a loose coalition of independent states that have acted separately on many occasions.

From its inception the League of Arab States (Arab League) has been an organization of independent states acting according to their own interests rather than a manifestation of Arab unity. While pan-Arabism—the aspiration to establish a unified Arab state—was a powerful ideological force in the interwar years in the Middle East, the newly formed Arab League that largely reflected state interests, though its establishment was couched in pan-Arab terminology. In fact, this ideology reflected the existing zeitgeist, serving as a springboard for launching various political schemes. Indeed, an analysis of the interests and motivation of the players concerned, the text of the Arab League Charter, and the organization's historical experience will substantiate the assertion that the fundamental idea of the Arab League was in reality far removed from "union."

Scholars usually regard British foreign secretary Anthony Eden's "Mansion Speech" (29 May 1941) as the starting point of a chain of events that culminated in the formation of the Arab League in March 1945. Eden declared Britain's willingness to support any scheme aimed at strengthening political, cultural, and economic relations that the Arabs might agree upon. Eden repeated this declaration in Parliament in February 1943. These statements were intended to harness Arab support for Allied efforts in World War II (1939–1945) as well as offer an Arab umbrella to the solution of the Palestine conflict. Instead, they unwittingly propelled the Hashemite rulers of Iraq and Transjordan to embark upon pan-Arab schemes, which in essence reflected their regional aggrandizement ambitions. In fact, the two branches of the Hashemite dynasty constituted revisionist forces in the emerging Arab system, attempting to redress the territorial mistakes that, in their opinion, the British made after World War I (1914–1918). Iraq's quest for expansion was motivated by three other considerations as well: first, a desire to acquire access to the Mediterranean, mainly for exporting its oil; second, a need for stronger protection from its non-Arab neighbors (Iran and Turkey); and, finally, a desire to encompass a larger Sunni Muslim population within the Iraqi state. This move would change the demographic balance in favor of the Sunni minority vis-à-vis the Shiite majority in Iraq.

In December 1942 Jordanian king Abdullah submitted to the British his "Greater Syria" plan, which was followed by the submission of Iraqi premier Nuri al-Said's "Fertile Crescent" plan in February 1943. These two plans, under the guise of Arab unity, essentially attempted to promote their respective interests in what they considered to be their own spheres of influence. Pan-Arabism was used to promote state interests since it became a popular ideological force of the *effendiyya* (educated middle class), and subsequently of the elite, in their struggle against the foreign powers (Britain and France). Although the British rejected both plans, Nuri al-Said initiated a round of consultations with fellow Arab leaders concerning possible avenues for bringing about Arab unity.

Nuri's initiative, however, was adopted by Egyptian prime minister Mustafa Nahhas. It was a move intended to forestall a change in the balance of power in favor of the Hashemites but which resulted from other considerations as well. First, the domestic pressure on the government to revise its 1936 treaty with Britain led to a growing Egyptian involvement in Arab affairs—a trend reinforced by the Arab Revolt in Palestine (1936–1939). Second, with its "discovery" of the Arab world and taking into account its political and military capabilities, Egypt sought leadership of—if not hegemony with—the emerging Arab system. Indeed, the 1943–1945 consultations can be viewed as "a contest for Arab primacy between Iraq and Egypt." As it turned out, Egypt led the Arab dialogue from March 1943 and hosted the conference that resulted in the signing of the Alexandria Protocol in October 1944. Eventually, Cairo became the center of the Arab League, and an Egyptian was nominated as its first Secretary-General. These developments largely institutionalized Egypt's leading role within the Arab state system.

The loose form of the Arab association that emerged in March 1945 owed much to the lukewarm Saudi and Lebanese attitude toward pan-Arabism. Since this ideology was largely associated with the Hashemites, the Saudis were apprehensive lest Iraq and/or Transjordan exploit their state to regain their forefather's territory of the Hijaz, if not the entire Arabian Peninsula. Consequently, the Saudis joined the Arab League only after Egypt and Britain reassured them that the new enterprise would constitute no threat to their sovereignty. Similarly, the Lebanese Christian Maronites feared being marginalized in a Sunni Arab–Muslim dominated union. Only when a special annex was added to the Alexandria Protocol assuring its independence was Lebanon willing to commit itself to the new organization. None of the other Arab actors—Syria, Yemen, the Palestinians, and the North African states—joined the Arab League for ideological reasons; all were prompted by their own selfish motives.

A textual analysis of both the Alexandria Protocol and the League's Charter clearly validates the assertion that attainment of all-Arab unity was not the main goal of negotiators during their deliberations. In the preamble of the Protocol the delegates pledged their desire "to strengthen and consolidate the ties which bind all Arab countries and to direct them toward the welfare of the Arab world, to improve its conditions, insure its future, and realize its hopes and aspirations." Though vaguely phrased, this declaration was clearly not supportive of Arab unity. The Charter preamble was even more diluted, emphasizing that the strengthening of relations would be on "a basis of respect for the independence and sovereignty" of the member states.

Indeed, the first Article of the Charter stated that the Arab League "is composed of the independent Arab states which have signed the Pact." Article 2 mentioned the strengthening of relations among the Arab states and coordination of their policies to achieve cooperation and safeguard their independence among the League's major objectives. It particularly emphasized cooperation in the following spheres: economy, communication, culture, and health. In addition, Article 9 stipulated that states "which desire to establish closer cooperation and stronger bonds than are provided by this Pact may conclude agreements to that end." In other words, the term "Arab unity" did not appear in the text of the Charter. The only indirect reference to this goal appeared in Article 9, which allowed member states to conclude other agreements in order to attain higher degrees of cooperation (or integration).

The Arab League's relatively long historical experience allows several generalizations concerning its role in Arab politics. First, the interests of the *wataniyya* (territorial state) always prevailed over all *qawmiyya* (pan-Arab interests). The Arab League has never been successful in promoting and achieving unity; even the one-time, short-lived Egyptian-Syrian union (1958–1961) was formed outside its framework and then largely in response to state interests. Second, in most of the disputes among the member states the League was paralyzed, reflecting Arab divisions, and thus unable to offer viable solutions. Though Article 5 of the Arab League Charter speaks of the arbitration and mediation mission of the League, in reality only a handful of inter-Arab conflicts were resolved as a result of its mediation (the Iraqi-Kuwaiti 1961 crisis and the 1975–1990 Lebanese Civil War are two cases in point). The League's impotence largely stemmed from the absence of a binding mechanism to enforce its resolutions. Third, Egyptian president Gamal Abd al-Nasser's decision to hold an Arab summit in January 1964, and subsequently to turn this institution into the highest Arab forum, attested to the failure of the League as a conflict-resolution mechanism as well as a possible vehicle for Arab unity. Fourth, the establishment of three subregional organizations in the 1980s–the Gulf Cooperation Council (GCC, 1981), the Arab Maghreb Union (AMU, 1989), and the Arab Cooperation Council (ACC, 1989)–was a clear indication that the Arab League's functioning was far from satisfactory. Based on geographical proximity, mutual security, and economic interests, these organizations represented viable alternatives to the League.

An analysis of the interests and motivations of the various Arab actors, the texts of both the Alexandria Protocol and the Arab League's Charter, as well as its legacy in Arab politics, validates the assertion that its establishment only served to institutionalize a system of independent Arab states. Thus, scholar Elie Kedourie was right to conclude that the Arab League "proved to be a device designed not so much to bring Arab unity, as to keep the . . . Arab states at arm's length from one another." Moreover, according to historian Ahmed M. Gomaa, it seems that even the modest aim of providing "a useful forum within which grievances could be aired, and direct contacts between high-level Arab delegates could be made more easily" was rarely met by the Arab League. Predictably, only significant amendments to the Charter and a strict enforcement of its resolutions by its members would turn the institution into a more effective device in regulating Arab policies, perhaps even leading to some form of integration among the Arab states.

–ELIE PODEH,
HEBREW UNIVERSITY

References

Israel Gershoni and James Jankowski, *Redefining the Egyptian Nation, 1930–1945* (Cambridge, U.K. & New York: Cambridge University Press, 1995).

Ahmed M. Gomaa, *The Foundation of the League of Arab States: Wartime Diplomacy and Inter-Arab Politics, 1941 to 1945* (London & New York: Longman, 1977).

Robert W. MacDonald, *The League of Arab States: A Study in the Dynamics of Regional Organization* (Princeton: Princeton University Press, 1965).

Bruce Maddy-Weitzman, *The Crystallization of the Arab State System, 1945-1954* (Syracuse, N.Y.: Syracuse University Press, 1993).

Elie Podeh, *The Decline of Arab Unity: The Rise and Fall of the United Arab Republic* (Brighton, U.K. & Portland, Ore.: Sussex Academic Press, 1999).

Porath Yeshoshua, *In Seach of Arab Unity, 1930–1945* (London: Frank Cass, 1986).

MULTINATIONAL FORCE IN LEBANON

Was the Multinational Force (MNF) in Lebanon a success?

Viewpoint: Partly. The first contingent of the MNF achieved its objective of escorting the Palestine Liberation Organization out of Beirut, but the second contingent failed to help the Lebanese government restore its authority.

Viewpoint: No. The MNF was a total failure because it had no autonomous political authority, the troop contingents were too small to be effective, and none of the combatants was willing to respect the cease-fire.

The Multinational Force (MNF) in Lebanon was composed of soldiers from the United States, Great Britain, France, and Italy. The forces were put into the middle of the war in Beirut in August 1982 following the Israeli invasion of Lebanon the preceding June. Resisting the invasion were Syrian armed forces that had been stationed in Lebanon since the beginning of its civil war in 1975 as well as the Palestine Liberation Organization (PLO), the elimination of which in Lebanon was one of the Israeli objectives. As the Israel Defense Forces (IDF) approached Beirut, the attention of the international community was aroused, especially as the shelling of the city produced more and more civilian casualties. The PLO and Syrian forces hunkered down in Beirut preparing for a last showdown with the Israelis, who, fearing the human costs of an urban battle if they entered the heart of the city, paused along the outskirts for strategic reasons as well as in response to international pressure.

From the Reagan administration's point of view the United Nations (UN) could not be utilized since the Security Council would be prevented from acting by an expected veto from the Soviet Union. During the height of what many have called the second Cold War between the superpowers, the United States also could not allow Soviet participation in a UN peacekeeping force; therefore, in order to mobilize and intervene in the quickest and least politically complex manner, a multinational force composed of North Atlantic Treaty Organization (NATO) allies with interests in the region was formed in the hopes of restoring some semblance of order and preventing the situation from escalating into an all-out regional, and possibly even superpower, conflagration.

The MNF's initial objectives were to escort PLO forces out of Beirut—amid the international outcry over the televised mayhem, death, and destruction occurring in and around the city—as well as to safeguard the lives of those Palestinians left behind in the refugee camps. By 1 September 1982 the PLO forces had left Beirut en route to establishing a new headquarters in Tunis, Tunisia. The MNF was summarily withdrawn to its ships anchored offshore. A Middle East peace plan, called the Reagan Plan, was also proffered on 1 September, attempting to take advantage of the situation on the ground by drawing moderate Arab states into a Camp David–like peace process. Both the Arab states and Israel rejected the Reagan Plan for different reasons, but ending all hope for a quick resolution of either the Lebanese situation or the Arab-Israeli conflict was the assassination of Maronite Christian president Bashir Gemayel on 14 September by anti-Israeli and pro-Syrian elements; Gemayel's militia supporters subsequently took their revenge two days later when they entered the Palestinian refugee camps of Sabra and Shatila in south Beirut, massacring more than eight hundred Palestinians, most of them women, children, and elderly men (since most able-bodied males had been fighting the Israelis and had been escorted out of Beirut).

In an almost convulsive response to this destabilizing situation, the MNF forces were ordered back into Beirut to prevent the whole thing from spiraling out of control altogether. After experiencing a series of blows over the next year and a half, highlighted by the bombing of the Marine barracks at Beirut International Airport that served as the headquarters for the American MNF contingent, killing 241 soldiers, the MNF withdrew totally from Lebanon by February 1984, the country still in chaos.

Viewpoint:
Partly. The first contingent of the MNF achieved its objective of escorting the Palestine Liberation Organization out of Beirut, but the second contingent failed to help the Lebanese government restore its authority.

The involvement of Lebanon in the Arab-Israeli conflict began with the 1967 War, when the already considerable Palestinian community in Lebanon became an important reference point for those Palestinians who, expelled from the other Arab countries, had decided to undertake the armed struggle against Israel for the liberation of Palestine. This new militancy caused a gradual deterioration in the already unstable domestic political balance inherent in the confessional state of Lebanon. In fact, the National Pact, signed soon after independence (1943), assigned every religious community the role it had to play in the political life of the country, but it was not able to establish a national identity and consciousness.

Starting in 1952 there was a series of crises leading to the outbreak of the civil war in 1975, during which central authority crumbled and the National Pact lost its legitimacy. The enhanced Palestinian presence in Lebanon, following the expulsion of the Palestine Liberation Organization (PLO) in the Jordanian crisis of 1970 (or what the Palestinians refer to as Black September), modified the regional context and the relations among several states of the area. In a short span of time PLO militants, involved in the struggle against Israel; Syrian troops, backing the Lebanese Muslim component with an anti-Israeli bent; and Israeli troops, in cooperation with the Lebanese Christians, began to gather in Lebanon. The Palestinian struggle against the "Zionist occupant" enjoyed a large consensus among the Muslim community and those pan-Arab political groups who felt bound to support the claims of the Palestinian people. Rapidly, this struggle became the symbol of the popular uprising against the political class and the Christian ruling community in Lebanon.

During the 1970s, the PLO presence in Lebanon had become problematic. In southern Lebanon, militias headed by Yasser Arafat created a state within the state, controlling the territory between West Beirut and the border with Israel. Arafat's men controlled the political and economic life of a country shattered by the civil war. From an administrative and military point of view the PLO proved to be an organization able to replace the weak Lebanese government apparatus and carry out its actions against Israel, massing its own guerrilla forces at the border between the two countries. Quickly, Lebanon became the ideal field for a political and military conflict between the two major regional powers: Israel and Syria. Syria has always defended its presence in Lebanon, claiming the role of peace-keeper. It regards Lebanese territory as indissolubly bound to Syria for historical and strategic reasons. The two regional powers joined in the Lebanese Civil War (1975–1990): Syria backed the Muslim component, particularly the most radical groups, such as the PLO, while Israel cooperated with the dominant Christian community, with which it had good relations. The position the PLO had achieved in Lebanon in the early 1980s, combined with the murder of Egyptian president Anwar Sadat, which threatened the Egyptian-Israeli peace treaty (1979), exacerbated the situation, compelling Israel to intervene. Similarly, as the Shah in Iran had been overthrown by an Islamic Revolution (1979), there were repercussions across the Middle East.

In early 1982, considering the chaos in Lebanon and the continuing threat of Palestinian raids, Israel launched the "Peace in Galilee" plan: specifically, to form a 45-kilometer demilitarized strip in southern Lebanon as a security belt to defend Israel from the almost constant Palestinian attacks. The Israel Defense Forces attack was quick, and in four days Israeli troops entered West Beirut, thanks in part to the cooperation of the Christian Phalangist militias. In a short span of time the Israeli Army and Syrian troops settled in Lebanon and were entangled in a fierce struggle that resulted in the intervention of the international community, and the United States in particular. In fact, on 11 June the Americans imposed a cease-fire and at the same time engendered an initiative to resolve the situation.

Thenceforth, the Lebanese question became of strategic interest to the U.S. government, which gradually increased its political and military involvement in the affairs of that Middle Eastern country. President Ronald Reagan's "strategic consensus" policy gave a boost to American policy in the Middle East. It was necessary to create a consensus in the Middle East for a globally based strategy, appealing to the most moderate countries in the area, such as Egypt, Israel, and Saudi Arabia. The American plan to resolve the Lebanese question included the withdrawal of PLO combat forces under the supervision of an ad hoc international military contingent. The United States wanted to prevent Lebanon from becoming a battlefield between Israelis and Syrians, to safeguard the concepts of political pluralism and cultural freedom, and above all to use the crisis atmosphere to champion a regional peace process, which became the primary goal of American policy in the Middle East.

Therefore, in August 1982 diplomacy intensified. The United Nations (UN) Security Council passed a Franco-Egyptian plan, including the decision to send in observers, in order to monitor the situation in and around Beirut. At the same time American diplomacy managed to gain Israel's approval for the evacuation of the PLO from Lebanon. The final agreement on evacuation terms was reached on 18 August, and the Lebanese government formally asked the United States, France, and Italy to contribute contingents to the Multinational Force (MNF). The MNF's aim was to give proper assistance to the Lebanese Armed Forces (LAF) and to facilitate the withdrawal of Palestinian leaders and fighters, with special attention for the security of Beirut's civilian population. Every contingent had to form a command exclusively responsible for the sector it was assigned, coordinating their activities with the LAF, especially with regard to the evacuation of PLO forces. The first French MNF contingent arrived in Beirut on 21 August 1982. On 25 August the MNF had 850 French, 820 American, and 530 Italian soldiers and, assisted by the Lebanese Army, began the evacuation of the Palestinians.

It was one of the most complex peacekeeping operations in modern history. The basic difference from later peacekeeping efforts was the presence of an independent command for every military contingent, subordinate to its own state—in other words, not the UN. Therefore, the MNF did not possess either a unified general staff or common installations. Rather, it was a coalition force—a temporary military association among states—with a specific purpose. The only coordinated command dealt with the use of political forces. This command had political and military tasks: it oversaw the evacuation plan, and it was responsible for the relations between the Israeli soldiers and the Palestinian forces still in Lebanon. The whole mission was not supposed to last longer than thirty days.

The evacuation of the Palestinian fighters from Lebanon was carried out successfully. According to President Reagan, the first step toward a long-lasting peace in the Middle East had been taken, thanks to the American intervention. However, the Lebanese quagmire was only a portion of the more general Middle Eastern situation, where not only the Arab-Israeli conflict continued but also Lebanon's domestic situation needed attention. In fact, the Lebanese government, even after the Palestinian fighters withdrew, was unable to restore order and control over the country. On 14 September, the day following the withdrawal of the MNF contingents, Lebanese president Bashir Gemayel was murdered, and Israel, under the rubric of keeping order, reentered West Beirut, where its Phalangist allies broke into the refugee camps of Sabra and Shatila, slaughtering the Palestinian refugees. Yet, the Israelis were not the only force in Lebanon. Syrian troops were also in Lebanese territory. Syrian president Hafiz al-Asad, worried by undue American interference in the country and wanting to ward off an agreement between Lebanon and Israel, decided to strengthen the Syrian military presence in the country. It was exactly in this context that it was decided to send the MNF again into Lebanon.

Once again, the basic agreements on MNF were carried out through an exchange of notes between the Lebanese government and each country taking part in the multinational force. On 24 and 25 September 1982 the American, French, and Italian contingents arrived. In January 1983 another contingent from Great Britain was added to those already in Lebanon. The aim of this second multinational force was to assist the Lebanese government and armed forces in restoring their sovereignty and authority in and around Beirut. More particularly, the MNF II goals involved overseeing the withdrawal from Lebanon of all foreign forces; restoring Lebanese government control over all its territory; assisting the Lebanese government in stabilizing authority, independence, and territorial integrity; and encouraging a national reconciliation.

American involvement in this second mission was greater both on military and diplomatic levels. In fact, the U.S. Navy was later empowered to implement an assistance and training program for the Lebanese regular army. The task of this operation was to build an effective local army, able to guarantee the security of Beirut and

A SUNDAY MORNING

In a televised speech from the White House on 27 October 1983 President Ronald Reagan spoke about the terrorist bombing of a U.S. Marines barracks in Beirut:

In Lebanon, we have some 1,600 Marines, part of a multinational force that's trying to help the people of Lebanon restore order and stability to that troubled land. Our Marines are assigned to the south of the city of Beirut, near the only airport operating in Lebanon. Just a mile or so to the north is the Italian contingent and not far from them, the French and a company of British soldiers.

This past Sunday, at 22 minutes after 6 Beirut time, with dawn just breaking a truck, looking like a lot of other vehicles in the city, approached the airport on a busy, main road. There was nothing in its appearance to suggest it was any different than the trucks or cars that were normally seen on and around the airport. But this one was different. At the wheel was a young man on a suicide mission.

The truck carried some 2,000 pounds of explosives, but there was no way our Marine guards could know this. Their first warning that something was wrong came when the truck crashed through a series of barriers, including a chain-link fence and barbed wire entanglements. The guards opened fire, but it was too late. The truck smashed through the doors of the headquarters building in which our Marines were sleeping and instantly exploded. The four-story concrete building collapsed in a pile of rubble.

More than 200 of the sleeping men were killed in that one hideous, insane attack. Many others suffered injury and are hospitalized here or in Europe. This was not the end of the horror. At almost the same instant, another vehicle on a suicide and murder mission crashed into the headquarters of the French peacekeeping force, an eight-story building, destroying it and killing more than 50 French soldiers.

Prior to this day of horror, there had been several tragedies for our men in the multinational force. Attacks by snipers and mortar fire had taken their toll.

I called bereaved parents and/or widows of the victims to express on behalf of all of us our sorrow and sympathy. Sometimes there were questions. And now many of you are asking: Why should our young men be dying in Lebanon? Why is Lebanon important to us?

Well, it's true, Lebanon is a small country, more than five-and-a-half thousand miles from our shores on the edge of what we call the Middle East. But every President who has occupied this office in recent years has recognized that peace in the Middle East is of vital concern to our nation and, indeed, to our allies in Western Europe and Japan. We've been concerned because the Middle East is a powderkeg; four times in the last 30 years, the Arabs and Israelis have gone to war. And each time, the world has teetered near the edge of catastrophe.

The area is key to the economic and political life of the West. Its strategic importance, its energy resources, the Suez Canal, and the well-being of the nearly 200 million people living there—all are vital to us and to world peace. If that key should fall into the hands of a power or powers hostile to the free world, there would be a direct threat to the United States and to our allies.

We have another reason to be involved. Since 1948 our Nation has recognized and accepted a moral obligation to assure the continued existence of Israel as a nation. Israel shares our democratic values and is a formidable force an invader of the Middle East would have to reckon with.

For several years, Lebanon has been torn by internal strife. Once a prosperous, peaceful nation, its government had become ineffective in controlling the militias that warred on each other. Sixteen months ago, we were watching on our TV screens the shelling and bombing of Beirut which was being used as a fortress by PLO bands. Hundreds and hundreds of civilians were being killed and wounded in the daily battles.

Syria, which makes no secret of its claim that Lebanon should be a part of a Greater Syria, was occupying a large part of Lebanon. Today, Syria has become a home for 7,000 Soviet advisers and technicians who man a massive amount of Soviet weaponry, including SS-21 ground-to-ground missiles capable of reaching vital areas of Israel.

. . . We have strong circumstantial evidence that the attack on the Marines was directed by terrorists who used the same method to destroy our Embassy in Beirut. Those who directed this atrocity must be dealt justice, and they will be. The obvious purpose behind the sniping and, now, this attack was to weaken American will and force the withdrawal of U.S. and French forces from Lebanon. The clear intent of the terrorists was to eliminate our support of the Lebanese Government and to destroy the ability of the Lebanese people to determine their own destiny.

Source: Ronald Reagan, televised speech, 27 October 1983, Washington, D.C., The Beirut Memorial On-Line <http://www.beirut-memorial.org/history/reagan.html>.

MULTINATIONAL FORCE IN LEBANON

subsequently of the whole Lebanese territory. In this way the MNF II tasks changed: from a mere "presence" force, the mission turned into an "assistance" force, causing not only an alteration of the mission role but also a change of perception by the Lebanese population toward the mission itself. American assistance for the Lebanese Army was seen as domestic interference, above all by the Lebanese Muslim community, which began to doubt the neutrality of the MNF.

It was evident that the success of the mission depended on the capability to arrange, on a political and diplomatic level, the withdrawal of Israeli and Syrian troops from Lebanon and to gain a new consensus in the country. It was no simple task. The negotiations, always under American aegis, continued until May 1983, when an agreement was reached between Israel and Lebanon, which sanctioned a cease-fire between the two countries and granted Israel a security zone in southern Lebanon. Even in this case, however, American efforts exacerbated the situation. Syrian opposition to the agreement had serious consequences. The government of President Amin Gemayel stalled before the ratification of the agreement with Israel, and, once the Israeli troops began to withdraw (3–4 September) from the Awali River, the Lebanese Army was not able to control the domestic situation. Syria decided not to support the Lebanese government but rather the Shiite Muslim community, which opposed both the central government and the MNF. These internal struggles involved MNF II as well; in fact, they led to the gradual entanglement of the MNF II contingents in the hostilities between the Lebanese factions.

MNF II contingents, particularly the French and American, became a target for terrorist attacks. On 23 October, while the French contingent was being attacked, an explosion in the Beirut airport zone of American concern killed 241 Marines. The escalation of violence forced the United States to launch an offensive against Syrian positions, clearly jettisoning the supposedly peaceful mission of its military presence in Lebanon. By the end of 1983 Lebanon was declared a vital area for American interests, and the Lebanese question became directly linked to the superpower Cold War. In the meantime the UN intervened in an attempt to solve the situation, suggesting it send observers to Lebanon to replace the MNF.

While MNF I had managed to achieve its aims, liberating Lebanon from the Palestinian fighters, MNF II encountered many more complex problems. It was mainly the political and military interference of Asad's Syria that exacerbated the Lebanese internal environment. Its support for the Lebanese Shiite community prevented the United States and the international

forces from achieving their goals. Syria was clever to entangle the United States militarily in Lebanon, thus smashing to pieces the pacific and neutral aspect of the MNF mission. Amin Gemayel's decision (5 March 1984) to cancel the agreement with Israel gave clear indication of the failure of MNF II. In late March the last French and U.S. contingents withdrew, leaving Lebanon at the mercy of a bloody civil war.

—VALENTINA VANTAGGIO,
UNIVERSITY OF LECCE

Viewpoint:
No. The MNF was a total failure because it had no autonomous political authority, the troop contingents were too small to be effective, and none of the combatants was willing to respect the cease-fire.

Lebanon was regarded as the "Switzerland of the Middle East." After the 1958 crisis, however, the country gradually slid into an institutional crisis that nearly led, within three decades, to its total collapse as a sovereign state. Today, Lebanon can be considered a Syrian province. Actually, since the formation of Middle Eastern nation-states after the end of World War I (1914–1918) Syria has always regarded Lebanon as an historical part of its territory. The collapse of Lebanese sovereignty is no longer the result of a domestic institutional crisis but rather of the presence of external factors that have strongly influenced Lebanon's social and political life.

Lebanese social relations, after the 1958 institutional crisis, were no longer positive. The lower classes' discontent and the southern Shiites' protest, complaining about poor representation in the political system, soon became intertwined. Domestic social turmoil combined with another destabilizing element in Lebanon—the arrival of Palestinians by 1971. Palestinian terrorists regarded the southern Lebanese border as its most useful base from which to attack Israel's Upper Galilee region. Because of the domestic turmoil in South Lebanon, primarily caused by the Shiites' poor living standards, it was more easily exploitable by external forces, such as the Palestinians, who were able to establish their own power base. Furthermore, Upper Galilee did not have effective Israeli defensive lines. Hence, South Lebanon became the focus of terrorist action by the Palestinian *al-Fatah*, pro-Syrian armed groups of the Popular Front for the Liberation of Palestine (PFLP), and several pro-Iraqi terrorist groups—a tangle of armed factions cooperating with one another in terrorist actions against Jewish civilian towns in Upper Galilee and frequently fighting against one another for supremacy in the struggle against Israel. After the creation of the Palestine Liberation Organization (PLO) the situation became clearer. This organization took control of the movement and imposed its domination. In November 1969, under Egypt's auspices, an agreement between representatives of Lebanon and Yasser Arafat was signed, giving the Palestinians free rein in the refugee camps and in the outskirts of Lebanese main towns in return for recognition of the Lebanese armed forces' authority. The agreement was never respected by Arafat, who soon created a kind of state within the Lebanese state, thus contributing to the final collapse of the country. Consequently, Israeli reprisals became more and more frequent, and the Lebanese front became the most important one in the struggle against terrorism.

From 1975 to 1982 Lebanon was a theater of mutually destructive struggles among countless armed groups, bound to other Arab countries, to the nationalities settled in the country, or even to local warlords, often fighting against one another merely for personal interests. In summary, the final result was that Lebanese sovereignty evaporated; Syria became the master of the country (and today it still is); and Palestinian terrorist groups gained unqualified control of the southern part of Lebanon, turning it into a logistics base for their terrorist attacks against Israel. Later, they were replaced by the Hizbollah (Party of God), a pro-Iranian terrorist group, which is still well settled in that territory. However, in 1978, following an Israeli military incursion in South Lebanon to clear out the PLO, the United Nations (UN) sent in a force—the UN Interim Force in Lebanon (UNIFIL)—whose purpose was to pacify the country, force Israel to withdraw from South Lebanon, and help the Lebanese government restore its authority: a noble aim, but impossible to achieve considering the political chaos faced by Lebanon. UNIFIL failed, but there was little if any chance for success to begin with.

The failure of the international community to restore peace and order in Lebanon again energized the internecine struggle and above all heightened terrorism against Israeli northern enclaves. In 1982, when the situation became unbearable for Israel, the Jewish state decided to intervene massively in South Lebanon through operation "Peace in Galilee." At first, the operation was regarded as a "clean-up" of a 40-kilometer-wide territory beyond the frontier, but Ariel Sharon, minister of defense, soon brought the Israeli Army to Beirut, defeating Palestinian groups and

the Syrians repeatedly. Military success, however, did not translate into political success. There were too many actors on the stage, and the Lebanese political situation was too complex to be resolved through a traditional military operation. Therefore, international diplomacy intervened. On 11 June 1982 the United States, backed by Moscow, imposed a cease-fire. The first stage of operation "Peace in Galilee" was over, with the armies and the armed groups still in the positions they held, but a few days later, breaking the cease-fire, the Israel Defense Forces (IDF) entered Beirut with the purpose of finishing the job.

The renewal of hostilities resulted in chaos again. At this point the United States intervened through special envoy Philip Habib's mediation. Habib, after exhausting negotiations, managed to persuade the Israelis to suspend fighting. At this point the UNIFIL action was over, as the UN Charter forbade the use of military force to resolve the problem, but above all because the UN contingent had not been able to handle the situation at the border between Israel and Lebanon, which is why the first MNF sent to Lebanon failed. It was established on the basis of three distinct and bilateral agreements between the United States, France, Italy, and Lebanon. MNF tasks were the cessation of hostilities; peaceful evacuation of the Palestinians from Beirut, where they were besieged by the Israeli army; Palestinian civilian respect of the laws of Lebanon; protection, with the support of the Lebanese Army, of the Palestinian civilians living in West Beirut; and the restoration of the sovereignty and the authority of the Lebanese government in all zones of Beirut. Every contingent was supposed to have its own independent headquarters responsible for a particular zone. Apart from the lack of a coordinated command, and different perspectives of the situation by every contingent, the failure of the first MNF was caused by one simple reason: none of the parties was really determined to respect the cease-fire and emphasize diplomacy in lieu of force. Considering this roadblock, the MNF action was pathetically inadequate to carry out its task. It had no real autonomous political authority, relied on a nonexistent Lebanese government that was protected by the Syrian army, whose intervention in Lebanon had been one of the most serious causes of the Lebanese mess, and was too small to carry out the task. The parties on the ground knew well how inadequate MNF was, accepting it for a time only to assuage the international community.

After the slaughter of Palestinians in the refugee camps of Sabra and Shatila, carried out by Lebanese Christians (16–18 September 1982), with the compliance of the IDF (which was

An American military
helicopter lifting off near
a group of Lebanese
civilians in West Beirut,
1982

(Magnum Photo/Eli Reed)

unable to handle the security with which they were invested by the clauses of the MNF I agreement), and after the assassination of Lebanese president Bashir Gemayel, it was decided to send in a second MNF, made up of Americans, French, Italians, and British. Actually, MNF II's task was not altogether different from that of MNF I, but the ultimate objective was to draw both the Israeli and Syrian forces away from Lebanon. For Israel it was then time to withdraw from its most advanced positions; Syria—as it would soon become apparent—had no intention of withdrawing, but rather its purpose was to strengthen its presence in the country. Hence, while Israel came to an agreement with Lebanon, by virtue of which the IDF was supposed to withdraw from Beirut and the Chouf Mountains, the Syrians never accepted a withdrawal since it would be contrary to its objectives in Lebanon; instead, Syrian President Hafiz al-Asad strengthened the Syrian military presence in the country.

On 23 October a Syrian-sponsored terrorist attack killed three hundred U.S. and French soldiers, and soon after the Syrians started a violent campaign to acquire better positions on the ground. Syria openly showed the ultimate goal of its involvement in Lebanon—to subjugate the country and make it one of its provinces. Months of unsuccessful peacemaking attempts followed, above all by the Americans, when everybody already knew that "peacemaking" would have been executed only if Lebanon had been placed in Syria's hands. On 7 February 1984 U.S. president Ronald Reagan ordered the Marines' withdrawal from Lebanon; the other contingents did the same by 29 March. Israel controlled a southern strip along its frontier in order to prevent terrorist attacks on its northern territories; the Lebanese government vanished, and Syria was the undisputed master of the country. The West acquiesced in Syria's takeover of the country in Pontius Pilate-like hypocritical fashion. MNF I and MNF II had completely failed.

—ANTONIO DONNO,
UNIVERSITY OF LECCE

References

Trevor N. Dupuy and Paul Martell, *Flawed Victory: The Arab-Israeli Conflict and the 1982 War in Lebanon* (Fairfax, Va.: Hero, 1986).

Robert Fisk, *Pity the Nation: Lebanon at War* (Oxford: Oxford University Press, 1991).

John Mackinlay, *The Peacekeepers: An Assessment of Peacekeeping Operations at the Arab-Israeli Interface* (London & Boston: Unwin Hyman, 1989).

Anthony McDermott and Kjell Skjelsbaek, eds., *The Multinational Force in Beirut, 1982–1984* (Miami: Florida International University Press, 1991).

Istvan S. Pogany, *The Arab League and Peacekeeping in the Lebanon* (New York: St. Martin's Press, 1987).

Ramesh C. Thakur, *International Peacekeeping in Lebanon: United Nations Authority and Multinational Force* (Boulder, Colo.: Westview Press, 1987).

MULTINATIONAL FORCE IN LEBANON

MUSADDIQ COUP

Did the United States and Great Britain make a mistake in orchestrating the overthrow of Iranian prime minister Muhammad Musaddiq in 1953?

Viewpoint: Yes. The coup removed opposition to the repressive regime of the Shah and thus presaged the Iranian Revolution of 1979.

Viewpoint: No. The coup was necessary given the Cold War environment and the genuine threat of Muhammad Musaddiq succumbing to communist control in such a vital geostrategic region.

Muhammad Musaddiq was appointed prime minister of Iran by its reigning monarch, Shah Muhammad Reza Pahlavi (the son of Reza Shah Pahlavi), in April 1951 following the assassination of the preceding prime minister by an Islamist group. Musaddiq led the National Front, a secular, nationalist party that had formed in Iran soon after World War I (1914–1918), which was primarily interested in reducing the British presence in Iran as well as implementing true liberal constitutionalist reform. His overall domestic popularity was based not only on his reformist and anti-imperialist posture but also on his austere, humble, and intellectual demeanor. It was this popular base that translated into strong support in the Majlis (Iranian parliament) that essentially compelled the Shah to appoint Musaddiq.

One of the lightning rods of discontent over British influence in Iran was the position of the Anglo-Iranian Oil Company (AIOC, later British Petroleum). In the first decade of the twentieth century, Iran became the first Middle Eastern country to produce oil. Lacking technology and equipment, the Iranian monarchy (the Qajar dynasty) relied on the British to produce the oil, which became a strategic necessity to London after it had shifted its navy from coal to oil shortly before World War I. Obviously, the AIOC dominated the oil industry in Iran, to the point that by World War II (1939–1945) the AIOC was actually paying more in taxes on its Iranian oil profits to the British government than it was in royalties to the Iranian government for exploitation of the oil concessions. The general post–World War II nationalist sentiment across the former European colonial territories fed into the already existing resentment in Iran of the lack of control over its own resources and the strong belief that it was not getting its fair share. As a condition for becoming prime minister, Musaddiq insisted that a nationalization act against the AIOC be passed first; as such, the government implemented the rallying cry of the National Front by nationalizing the oil industry in Iran just prior to his assumption of power.

Regardless of the legality of the act, the British government was disturbed lest a precedent be set in other British spheres of interest; indeed, for the same reason, the large Western-based multinational oil companies that controlled most of the oil industry at the time also opposed nationalization, and an oil boycott of Iran was instituted (in this case a boycott by consumers against a producer, which is the opposite of what has been experienced since the early 1970s). The initial U.S. outlook on Musaddiq was actually somewhat positive based on the fact that he was a liberal constitutionalist and was not beholden to the British. This assessment began to change, however, especially after the Eisenhower administration came to power in January 1953 with a more forward attitude toward regime change as the Cold War heated up. Musaddiq's perceived alliance with and reliance upon the communist Tudeh (masses) Party for support in the increasingly politically and economically chaotic situation in Iran probably was his downfall, as domestic and regional elements of the crisis became subsumed in a Cold War atmosphere. The end came in August 1953, when the United States and Great Britain covertly arranged a coup d'état that ousted Musaddiq and brought the Shah back firmly into power.

Viewpoint:
Yes. The coup removed opposition to the repressive regime of the Shah and thus presaged the Iranian Revolution of 1979.

After decades of denial by the U.S. government, there is no longer any doubt that the Eisenhower administration used the Central Intelligence Agency (CIA) to orchestrate the overthrow of Iranian prime minister Muhammad Musaddiq in August 1953. Historians now recognize this event as a model for subsequent plots in Guatemala (1954), Syria (1957), and Cuba (1960). Westerners often criticize the people of the Middle East for too easily accepting conspiracy theories; in Iran the theory became reality.

Musaddiq had a long history of selfless devotion to his country before he became prime minister in May 1951. In a variety of positions—governor, minister, and member of Parliament—he had repeatedly shown himself to be honest, hardworking, and patriotic. His opposition to the rise of Reza Shah Pahlavi in the early 1920s, however, had cost him dearly. After establishment of the Pahlavi dynasty (1925–1979) Reza Shah sentenced him to internal exile, where he spent most of the interwar years. He was able to return to public life only after the forced abdication of the Shah in September 1941. He soon led a coalition of groups, the National Front, in opposition to foreign control over Iran's oil resources.

Although Musaddiq was in many ways an admirable individual, one should not glamorize him. He would surely have rejected such treatment. He had many fine qualities but also weaknesses. One can say without hesitation, however, that he offered a much-welcomed leadership alternative, refusing to ally with either the Soviets or the West in the Cold War world of the 1950s.

On matters of principle he could be rigid, even stubborn, and this characteristic did not always serve him well. British and American leaders lost patience with him for dragging out the dispute over the nationalization of Iran's oil. They rationalized their decision to move against him by arguing that at seventy-plus years he was too old and naive to maintain a firm stand against the Soviet Union and his own internal communists, the Tudeh (masses) Party. He would, they reasoned, destabi-

lize Iran, opening the way for Soviet gains. Yet, Musaddiq had steadfastly kept the Tudeh Party at arm's length, repeatedly refusing to enter into any popular front alliance with them. Some of his closest advisers, such as Khalil Maliki, were among the staunchest of anticommunists. Even on the eve of his overthrow, with a CIA-funded mob running riot in the streets of Teheran, he refused to distribute arms to his supporters, fearing the bloodshed that would follow.

Despite the claims of his enemies, he was no demagogue. He allowed his bitterest opponents, several of whom were newspaper editors plotting secretly for his destruction, to continue publishing their venomous attacks on his government. Nor did he ever consider establishing a secret police force, such as the Shah's SAVAK, which ran counter to his principles.

Others charged that he wished to overthrow the Shah and make himself dictator, when his real objective was to create the limited monarchy envisaged in the 1906 constitution. Perhaps he was unrealistic, given the previous twenty-five years of centralization under the Pahlavis, but it was ironic that his adoption of the British model of limited monarchy should have brought him into such disrepute. Muhammad Reza Pahlavi resisted Musaddiq's reforms and plotted against him, finally fleeing the country on 16 August 1953, when the scheme appeared to have failed.

Most American journalists accepted uncritically the Eisenhower administration's view of Musaddiq as a menace who threatened U.S. security by weakening containment of the Soviet Union. Cartoonists lampooned him, and their images have persisted. Only the articles of *New York Times* correspondent Albion Ross showed any understanding of what Musaddiq intended. These articles proved that even in 1952 an enlightened attitude was not impossible.

Musaddiq likened Iran's struggle with Britain to the colonists' campaign against the tyranny of George III in the 1770s, and he drew examples from early American history to make this point. When a visiting U.S. official urged him to compromise with Britain over oil, for example, he asked how colonial Americans would have responded had Iranian mediators shown up at Boston in 1773, urging them not to throw chests of tea into the harbor. Later, from his prison cell, he suggested that the cultural affairs officer at the U.S. embassy broadcast to Iranians the history of the American

Revolutionary War (1775–1783) and urge them to become the Washingtons and Franklins of their generation in order to preserve their freedom.

Not all American officials agreed that the United States should become involved in the plot to overthrow Musaddiq. An American military officer in Teheran pointed out to Ambassador Loy Henderson (1951–1955), in the wake of an earlier failed attempt, that Musaddiq seemed to represent just the kind of leader the United States ought to support, for he was popular with his people and an anticommunist, a rare combination. Another embassy officer had noted that the Iranians had their own national interests and that the crusade against communism was an American, not an Iranian, priority. Ambassador Henry F. Grady (1950–1951) became one of Musaddiq's strongest supporters. In Washington, too, there were those who cautioned against supporting Britain's anti-Musaddiq policies, including Assistant Secretaries of State for the Near East George McGhee and Henry Byroade, and Secretary of Defense Robert Lovett. Unfortunately, early in the Eisenhower administration the balance shifted to the hard-liners: Henderson, Secretary of State John Foster Dulles, and his brother Allen, director of the CIA.

Historians continue to debate how consequential was CIA involvement. After all, some argue, Musaddiq faced a rising chorus of opposition months before August 1953. Although one can identify several sources contributing to the success of the coup, among them disgruntled officers whom the prime minister had dismissed for incompetency and prominent royalist politicians, these elements had been present for some time. Without American money and support for the plotters—the CIA had arranged for the evacuation of General Fazlollah Zahedi, leader of the coup, should it fail—Musaddiq could have maintained control indefinitely. The Iranian economy was in better shape than the Western media could admit, for prices of Iranian exports such as cotton had risen sharply as a result of the Korean War (1950–1953).

One unexpected result of the successful coup d'état of 19 August 1953 was that it seemed to have brought about a transformation in the Shah, who returned from his self-imposed exile in Rome three days later. He came to believe, against all the evidence, that the Iranian people out of regard for their monarch had risen up to overthrow Musaddiq and bring their beloved sovereign back to his throne. This conviction grew in the Shah's mind. He repeated it to visitors and in several written accounts in subsequent decades. If the Americans had assumed that a grateful Shah would now follow their directions or be content to reign and not rule, they were badly mistaken. In fact, in subsequent years the Shah took more authority into his own hands, often against the better judgment of U.S. officials. Occasionally, as during the early

Kennedy administration, Washington would try to redirect the Shah toward a more open, liberal regime, but mainly they acquiesced in whatever he proposed, increasingly concerned not to anger him.

In May 1972 President Richard M. Nixon and National Security Adviser Henry Kissinger visited Teheran briefly and gave the Shah carte blanche to purchase any nonnuclear weapon in the American arsenal, without being subjected to the usual screening procedures. As the Shah's megalomania became more pronounced, he delighted in lecturing the Americans about the evils of Western society, disparaging what he considered its crass materialism. To assurances of continued U.S. support from President Gerald R. Ford the Shah responded that given what was at stake he did not expect the president's response to be otherwise.

Throughout these years American officials forgot the details about Musaddiq, who died under house arrest in March 1967. National Security Council expert Gary Sick admitted that by 1978 "the events of 1953 had all the relevance of a pressed flower." When officials thought of him at all, it was as a figure of ridicule, for all they remembered were his tearful and emotional speeches or his meetings with foreign dignitaries at his bedside, with the chronically ill prime minister dressed in striped pajamas. Or they dismissed him as a naive and dangerous leader, who would have so weakened Iran that without its Shah the country would have fallen under Soviet control.

Sadly, they transferred this aversion to his associates as well, and for decades they refused to consider any of them, even the most capable, worthy of high office in Iran. They railed against the "Musaddiqists," who, they charged, had never given up their extreme views and plans to subvert the Shah's regime. The Shah made the most of this American myopia to justify excluding the leaders of Musaddiq's National Front from power. Only in the final months before the collapse of the Shah's regime did the Americans finally reconcile themselves to the idea of Musaddiq's associates—men such as Shahpour Bakhtiar, Mehdi Bazargan, or Karim Sanjabi—wielding power in Iran. By then, of course, it was too late, for control had passed into the hands of the clerics, men such as Ayatollah Ruhollah Khomeini, who had no goal of creating a liberal Iran. The secular middle class assisted the Revolution of 1979, but having failed in its mission in 1953 under Musaddiq, its members now had to assume a subordinate role.

Interestingly, Khomeini had no time for Musaddiq either, and his regime did all it could to disparage the memory of the still-popular nationalist. After a huge march to Musaddiq's grave on the twelfth anniversary of his death, the government of the Islamic Republic forbade such gatherings and began a propaganda campaign to vilify him. They had no more success, however, than

A MAN OF STRENGTHS
AND WEAKNESSES

In a 1973 interview, Loy W. Henderson, former ambassador to Iran (1951–1955), recalled Muhammad Musaddiq:

Mossadegh was an attractive man although he was neither handsome nor elegant. He was tall and lanky; his long horse like face topped with rather disheveled gray hair was expressive like that of an actor. He had a large mouth and when he smiled, his whole face lit up and one felt drawn toward him. He liked jokes and liked to laugh at them—a trait which is always helpful, particularly when one is engaged in serious conversation. He was troubled with dizzy spells so he would remain in bed much of the time. In general I found our conversations interesting and even agreeable. During most of them he was in bed and I was sitting beside him. He was quite frank, at times, without being offensive in criticizing our policies, and I was equally frank with him. So we got along quite well, each pointing out where he felt the other was wrong.

Mossadegh's weakness, in my opinion, was that he still felt that he was living in an era of about 1910–1912, when Iran's basic foreign policy consisted of playing the Russian Empire off against the British Empire. He did not seem to realize that the Soviet Empire was quite a different entity from that of the Czars, and was using different tactics and different methods in its endeavor to extend its power and its territories, and that the British Empire was gradually evaporating. The British were no longer the threat to Iran that they were when they controlled South Asia and much of the Middle East.

Mossadegh was not a Communist, and I was convinced that he was opposed to communism as an ideology. Nevertheless, he was willing to accept Communists and their fellow-travelers as allies. He had, I understood, a princely background and was related to the ruling family of the regime which had been overthrown by the father of the Shah. I thought that one of his ambitions was to be the Regent or a member of a Board of Regents which would replace the Shah and rule the country until an appropriate successor could be found. He did not understand that the Communists and their allies had no use for him and that they would get rid of him just as soon as he had served their purpose.

One of his ambitions was to make Iran completely independent. He had been one of the leaders in opposing the Soviet efforts in the middle 1940s to obtain oil concessions in Iran, and at that time he had intimated that the British concessions should also get out of the southern part of the country. He hoped to be able to play the Americans as well as the Russians off against the British. For that reason he tried hard to get my personal support. I tried to make him understand that in the Middle East it was important for the Americans, so far as possible, to cooperate with the British; that unless we could cooperate the Soviet Union would take advantage of our disunity and that could be disastrous to Iran.

. . . Early on the following morning, Wednesday, August 19, 1953, an important date, I received word while I was having breakfast that an uprising was taking place in the lower part of the city. I hurried across the Embassy garden to the chancery where I learned that a group of members of a well-known athletic club had suddenly emerged from the club with various kinds of arms calling upon the people to help them overthrow the Mossadegh regime and restore the Shah. In this club its members were accustomed to work hard developing their torsos in accordance with certain Iranian traditional exercises, which included the swinging of heavy clubs. The leaders of the demonstration, therefore, were men with almost frightening physiques, and they were rapidly joined by people on the street. Members of my staff whom I had sent out to find what was going on kept us informed by telephone. Within an hour the demonstrators reached the building which houses one of the leading pro-Mossadegh newspapers and destroyed the plant. I was confident that when the crowd would come into contact with the military, it would disperse, but to my surprise the military joined it. By noon the demonstrators had taken over the Foreign Office and a little later the area surrounding our Embassy compound was full of cheering people. General Zahedi, whom the Shah had appointed to succeed Mossadegh, and who had been in hiding, came out and seated on a tank moved through the applauding, waving crowds.

Late in the evening Ardeshir Zahedi, the son of the new Prime Minister, came to see me. He said that the leading cities of the country and most of the countryside were now under the control of the army, which had come out for the Shah and his father. He added that his father had asked him to inquire if I had any suggestions to offer. After a minute's thought I said, "Yes, I have three suggestions. In the first place, I think every effort should be made to prevent Mossadegh from being harmed or killed. If he is taken prisoner, care should be exercised to make sure he is not physically abused. The question of his punishment, if any, should be left to the courts. In the second place, a circular telegram might be sent out at once to all the Iranian diplomatic missions and consular offices informing them that the new Prime Minister appointed by the Shah has taken over and they should continue to transact their business as usual. No revolution has taken place, merely a change in government. My third suggestion is that a similar announcement might be made for the benefit of the civil servants. They should be told by radio that they should report to work tomorrow as usual."

During the next twenty-four hours, Mossadegh was captured and imprisoned pending a trial. Most of the Iranian diplomatic and consular offices carried on as usual. On the following day the governmental machinery was for the most part functioning. Zahedi proceeded to set up a new cabinet for the Shah's approval. The Shah, who was in Rome on the day that Zahedi took office, returned to Tehran on August 22. I have never seen Tehran so happy as it was when it greeted him back.

Source: *"Oral History Interview with Loy W. Henderson," 5 July 1973, Truman Presidential Museum & Library <http://www.trumanlibrary.org/oralhist/hendrson.htm>.*

MUSADDIQ COUP

had the Shah, and by all accounts his memory is widely revered today.

Iranians knew well the story of Musaddiq's overthrow long before it became common knowledge in the United States, and to them "it was as fresh as if it had happened only the week before." The Americans had intervened once to remove a popular leader, and they might do it again. Thus, when the Shah came to the United States in October 1979 for medical treatment, Iranians believed that this move was a pretext so that the deposed monarch could plot with the CIA to return him to power. To forestall such an event, Iranian students seized the American embassy and held its occupants hostage for more than a year. U.S.-Iranian relations have made little improvement since that time.

In 1980 Chargé D'Affaires Bruce Laingen, then a hostage at the Iranian Foreign Ministry in Teheran, reflected on the course of bilateral relations since the coup of 1953. In a letter home he cited the words of Undersecretary of State Joseph Cisco to the effect that removing Musaddiq had gained twenty-five years of stability in U.S.-Iranian relations and that seemed a pretty good exchange. Today, following a quarter century of turmoil in U.S.-Iranian relations with no end in sight, one suspects that those officials would have welcomed the opportunity to modify their earlier, hasty remarks.

–JAMES GOODE,
GRAND VALLEY STATE UNIVERSITY

Viewpoint:
No. The coup was necessary given the Cold War environment and the genuine threat of Muhammad Musaddiq succumbing to communist control in such a vital geostrategic region.

My qualification for doing this essay is that I served in the British embassy in Teheran in 1952 as acting Oriental Counsellor, that is to say, political adviser and interpreter to the Chargé d'Affaires, George Middleton. With hindsight there is possibly a case against the coup in 1953. In my view it was essential. Nobody could then have foreseen that Shah Muhammad Reza Pahlavi would become such a disagreeable tyrant and provoke his people, particularly the religious fraternity, to the 1979 revolt. Then, while Ayatollah Ruhollah Khomeini was tiresome and regarded the United States as the "Great Satan" (the British were a "little Satan"), he was not a serious menace in the Cold War context. He had no love for the Soviet Union.

Let us recall the immediate post–World War II world. The Soviet Union had occupied Iranian Azerbaijan in 1946 and then reluctantly withdrawn, but remained a considerable threat. Joseph Stalin was still alive, and the Soviet Union further demonstrated its aggressiveness by the Berlin blockade in 1948. I was stationed in the British Zone of Germany at that time, and World War III was believed to be close. Then, we had just had the Korean War (1950–1953) to keep us on our toes.

The facts of history are well known, and I shall mention them only briefly. My object is to show why the liberal Middleton; Monty Woodhouse, our brilliant and experienced Head of Intelligence; and I all came to the conclusion that Musaddiq must go. We later helped the U.S. government and an initially reluctant British Foreign Secretary Anthony Eden to accept this course of action.

The oil crisis started off this conspiracy. The Anglo-Iranian Oil Company (AIOC) failed to match the American company ARAMCO's 50/50 deal with the Saudi government, while the British government did not bring pressure on the AIOC, who tried to get Iran to accept their own so-called Supplemental Agreement, which was somewhat less favorable to Iran and much less simple to understand than a clear-cut 50/50. General Ali Razmara, the Iranian prime minister, tried to get the Supplemental Agreement through the *Majlis* (Iranian parliament) and was assassinated for his pains. Dr. Muhammad Musaddiq came to power on a wave of popular emotion and nationalized the AIOC, which was heralded by the majority of the Iranian people as a great victory over imperialism.

During 1951 there were several attempts by the British, the distinguished American diplomat Averell Harriman, and the World Bank to reach an oil settlement with Iran. All were technically good for Iran, but that is not essentially the point. Musaddiq would not settle; his whole position, power, and popularity were based on his nationalization of the British oil company, and it was politically impossible for him to allow them to return, certainly not openly, probably not even in disguise. In his excellent book, *The British Empire in the Middle East, 1945–1951: Arab Nationalism, the United States, and Postwar Imperialism* (1984), William Roger Louis states that "It is debatable whether any Englishman, even of the stature of Mountbatten could have successfully negotiated with Musaddiq."

But it was more complex than that; Musaddiq had rejected the offer from the World Bank on the grounds that it would compromise Iranian sovereignty. Even though Musaddiq had the best interests of his country at heart, it seemed unwise not to consider an American-sponsored deal, since the Americans were well disposed toward him. Their great hope was that a patriotic, honest, noncorrupt nationalist could bring Iran peace, prosperity, and democracy, while keeping the Tudeh Party (communists) at bay. The Americans now came to know how difficult it was to negotiate with Musaddiq. And even though President Harry S Truman found him charming upon the Iranian prime minister's visit to Washington in summer 1951, the rejection of the World Bank report gave the Americans pause.

In early 1952, when I came to Teheran, Middleton was, despite the frustrations of 1951, determined to do everything possible to come to terms with Musaddiq, with whom he was personally friendly. He found him a most civilized human being. Both men spoke fluent French and conversed easily together. The U.S. ambassador, Loy Henderson, a wise and experienced diplomat, held similar views to Middleton, and they got on well.

Despite Musaddiq's popularity and his anti-imperialist stance, many educated Iranians, including some important clerics, began to doubt his capacity to rule. This was my job—to talk to as many Iranians as I could to assess their views—and I was somewhat surprised at discovering these sentiments. It seemed that the emotion of the initial stages of the Musaddiq revolution were dissipating as fast as the economy was deteriorating, damaged as it was by the oil embargo. My contacts told me that they doubted that we would ever be able to reach an agreement with Musaddiq. Nevertheless, Middleton was a more supple and subtle negotiator than his predecessors, and he was determined to succeed.

Nineteen fifty-two was an exciting time to be in Iran. History was being made, and both the American and British embassies hoped and worked for a just solution. Middleton had many, as he put it, delightful meetings with Musaddiq. One day he returned elated from a marathon session. "I think we have done it this time, Sam." He sent his telegram to London describing what appeared to be a sensible and equitable settlement. Two days later Musaddiq rejected the proposed settlement and came back with some impossible demands.

This style of diplomacy was typical and happened many times. But Middleton was persistent and kept on trying. Eventually, around midsummer 1952, even Middleton came to the sad conclusion that his dear old friend was not able, or possibly was not permitted by his own extremists or even the Tudeh Party, to reach any sort of settlement that would be acceptable to the British or even the Americans. Musaddiq initially dealt bravely and firmly with the British—the AIOC deserved what they got. He was, however,

unwise not to negotiate with the Americans. Also, for the sake of relations with the international oil business, he should have been more forthcoming and rational on compensation for the AIOC.

It is generally believed that the Qavam al-Sultaneh interlude in July 1952 was a failed British coup, partly because Qavam had met the British right-wing politician, Julian Amery, in London. This period of rule was not our coup, perhaps unfortunately; all Qavam got from Great Britain was moral support and general encouragement. Musaddiq's resignation on 16 July 1952 was precipitated by the Shah's refusal to agree to his prime minister's request for control of the armed forces, which was the Shah's principal source of influence.

Qavam was rational and able. I had several talks with him and found him as much of a nationalist as Musaddiq, but he, from experience, especially in 1946, regarded the Soviet Union, rather than Britain, as the principal threat to Iran's independence.

Qavam fell after only five days because the Shah failed to provide him support. He lost his nerve and was intimidated by the Tudeh-controlled mob. Many, including Middleton and Henderson, believed that had the Shah held fast, Qavam could have stayed on because he did enjoy considerable support among the *Majlis* and thinking Iranians. Middleton wrote to the Foreign Office: "The Shah was in the grip of fear, fear of taking a decision that might expose him to the fury of the populace, should Qavam not, in the event, remain in control. This attitude of the Shah is one of the central features of this crisis. We had long known that he was indecisive and timid, but we had not thought that his fear would so overcome his reason as to make him blind to the consequences of NOT supporting Qavam."

One more quote from Middleton from my own personal records sews up his view at the time:

Mussadiq's strength lies in his power of Demagogy and he has so flattered the mob as the source of his power that he has, I fear, made it impossible for a successor to oust him by normal constitutional methods. His followers, and principally Ayatollah Kashani, have probably gone further than he intended in enlisting the support of the Tudeh for Monday's trial of strength. The chief question now facing us is whether Mussadiq's Government, or any other short of a military dictatorship, can avoid the "kiss of death," which is the well known consequence of flirting with communists.

These words were written in July 1952, not by U.S. Senator Joseph McCarthy but by an experienced and forward-looking diplomat who knew Musaddiq well and liked him as a person. I do not

Former Iranian prime minister Muhammad Musaddiq signing documents sentencing him to three years of solitary confinement for treason, December 1953

(© CORBIS/Bettmann)

apologize for repeating this statement, as it is one of the strongest justifications for the coup. The Shah succumbed to all Musaddiq's demands as the latter returned in triumph with the support of the mob and the Tudeh Party. The Shah, meanwhile, became more and more of a feeble, terrified shadow of a ruler. Now we had to think seriously about the future. I tended to sympathize with decolonization and the new nationalism. From the beginning I had been in complete agreement with Middleton and Henderson that we must pull out all the stops to reach agreement. Now the world situation was such that we had to consider covert action. This activity was not "my part of the ship," as we say in the navy, but at that time I spoke fluent Iranian, then known as "Farsi" or "Persian." It was thought that I might be useful through my contacts.

This was "my finest hour," as I saw it. I was being asked to participate in what others

wiser than me considered an operation to prevent World War III. My grandchildren's generation will doubtless consider this activity to be absurd and old-fashioned imperialism. It was not; the threat was urgent and real. Part of my task was to discover if there were any potential successors to Musaddiq who could command enough popular support to run the country, crush the Tudeh, and reach a tolerable oil settlement. Would such a candidate need "assistance" from the West? If so, what form should it take?

My first and principal contacts were three notorious brothers. When I first wrote, some years ago, their names were confidential and I shall continue to call them "the brothers," although they have become well-known. They were successful businessmen and Iranian patriots, who no longer worked for money since they had plenty. They were convinced that Musaddiq was a disaster who would hand over Iran to the Tudeh. They had wide connections in the government, *Majlis*, bazaar, armed forces, and throughout all levels of society. They were long-standing friends of the British, in spite of our oil folly. They had a great contempt for the Shah but admitted that he was a necessary evil. They used to say, "*Bichareh mesleh sag, mitarseh*" (Poor bastard, he is scared as a dog!)—the dog is considered an unclean and unloved animal in Iran. I used to breakfast with the brothers. Their breadth of knowledge was amazing, and they were charming and amusing company, even at breakfast. We discussed possible prime ministers; their favorite was a fascinating old gentleman, Sayid Zia-al-Din Tabataba'tai. He had been prime minister briefly in 1921 but had been deposed by Reza Khan, the Shah's father. He was still in good shape and widely respected in Iran. We discussed his eventual premiership, and the brothers reluctantly agreed that he was too pro-British in the present atmosphere.

So I took a little trip to a pleasant house in the hills north of Teheran to visit the next candidate, General Fazlollah Zahedi. He was a retired general with a seat in the senate and with political ambitions. The British had imprisoned him during World War II for pro-Nazi activities, and therefore he could not be accused of being a British stooge. He was apparently pleased to see me, and politics demanded that he should bear no grudge. After all, there was a decent job at stake, and Zahedi had no doubt that he should succeed Musaddiq, support the Shah, and clobber the Tudeh. Zahedi made a good impression on me, although I was young and probably easily flattered. In my report at the time I described him as "tough and clear headed." I doubt if our American allies, who ran the coup itself, would agree. I think they found him rather wet, but where was the alternative? To excuse myself, I may have been the first plotter to approach Zahedi, but I was certainly not the last. On our side both Middleton and Woodhouse visited the general and, to the best of my knowledge, approved of him as the best available, even if not ideal. I attended the visits as interpreter.

Of course, our visits to Zahedi were not secret. Embassy officials had every right to visit a distinguished senator. There was, as far as I know, no plot at that time, and Zahedi was not paid. But Musaddiq felt instinctively that we had ceased to favor him and broke off diplomatic relations with Britain on the pretext of an attempted coup. And so in October 1952 Middleton, my embassy colleagues, and I left Teheran for Beirut. The Iranians bade us a most friendly farewell and hoped we would soon return—no violence, no unpleasantness. Musad-

diq gave Middleton a warm and tearful farewell and wished him luck in his future career.

We had only been in Beirut a few days when I received an order to accompany Woodhouse to Washington, D.C., to meet with State Department and Central Intelligence Agency (CIA) officials. It was an interesting time in Washington. The Republican Eisenhower administration had replaced the Truman administration. The Eisenhower administration considered the Musaddiq situation to be much more of a threat, and it was known that Secretary of State John Foster Dulles's brother (Allen Dulles), as head of the CIA, thought that more direct action was a possibility. The State Department was listening to our arguments, but even as late as November 1952 they were still convinced that Musaddiq was the last best hope to save Iran from communism. We disagreed, and with my field knowledge of the brothers and our acquaintance with Zahedi, we made a persuasive argument. Even though State was impressed, they did not change their policy, but with Allen Dulles and Kermit Roosevelt the CIA was much more receptive. Roosevelt is well known as the executor of the coup and the author of the book that described his exploits, *Countercoup: The Struggle for the Control of Iran* (1979).

Thus ended my personal involvement with the famous or infamous coup of 19 August 1953. Britain is said to have played a minor part in the coup. In its execution, yes, we were not in Iran. As for the planning, our role was important. We certainly made an impression on the CIA in November 1952, and they took over "the brothers" from us. We drafted the original plan. I feel honored to have been involved at the start, and I think I was the first to meet Zahedi.

In conclusion, I would like to quote Sir Winston Churchill's wonderful remark to Roosevelt: "Young man, if I had been but a few years younger, I would have loved nothing better than to serve under your command in this great venture." This essay spells out the case that favored the deposing of Musaddiq. Clearly, it would have been more desirable and in the interests of the United States, Iran, and, indeed, Britain if we could have made a reasonably satisfactory deal with Musaddiq. It might even, with the benefit of hindsight, have been better to make a poor deal than no deal at all. There were, however, limits beyond which it would have been impossible to go without upsetting the global oil business. Maybe it would have been worth it, and the cost to the United States might have been less than that of the Khomeini Revolution. It is difficult to say, but, in my opinion, Musaddiq turned down some good offers that might have prevented the crisis.

In 1952 we were very worried about the Soviet, Chinese, and world communist threats, with extremely good reason: Tensions were high and real. There was the Korean War, and Stalin was still alive in all his psychopathic and dangerous malevolence. At the time the prospect of a communist Iran was alarming and, we thought, could have led to World War III. To this day I remain utterly convinced that the communist danger was too great to ignore and would have produced knee-jerk reactions that could have led to global catastrophe. Not only our intelligence services but also an enlightened liberal of the caliber of Middleton, who tried desperately to reach an agreement with Musaddiq, were in no doubt that the lovable old man had to go.

To finish on a personal note: In the British Foreign Service I was known as "Red Sam." This name was given because I believed in liberal causes, resurgent nationalism, and the like. Later I was a fervent supporter of both Egyptian president Gamal Abd al-Nasser and the Iraqi nationalists. Thus, Musaddiq was initially a man after my own heart, and I am on record as a remorseless critic of the AIOC. The fact that even I eventually became convinced that he had to be replaced says something; all my beliefs, or, if you like, prejudices, were in the other direction—on his side. Sadly, he could not control the communists, and they would have removed him from power and replaced him with one of their own.

–SIR SAMUEL FALLE,
MARIANNELUND, SWEDEN

References

James A. Bill, *The Eagle and the Lion: The Tragedy of American-Iranian Relations* (New Haven: Yale University Press, 1988).

Farhad Diba, *Mohammad Mossadegh: A Political Biography* (London & Dover, N.H.: Croom Helm, 1986).

Mostafa Elm, *Oil, Power, and Principle: Iran's Oil Nationalization and Its Aftermath* (Syracuse, N.Y.: Syracuse University Press, 1992).

Sir Samuel Falle, *My Lucky Life in War, Revolution, Peace and Diplomacy* (Sussex: Book Guild, 1996).

James Goode, "A Liberal Iran: Casualty of the Cold War," in *Paths Not Taken: Speculations on American Foreign Policy and Diplomatic History, Interests, Ideals, and Power,* edited by Jonathan M. Nielson (Westport, Conn.: Praeger, 2000), pp. 161–173.

Goode, *The United States and Iran: In the Shadow of Musaddiq* (London: Macmillan, 1997).

Homa Katouzian, *Musaddiq and the Struggle for Power in Iran* (London & New York: I. B. Tauris, 1990).

Kermit Roosevelt, *Countercoup: The Struggle for the Control of Iran* (New York: McGraw-Hill, 1979).

Gary Sick, *All Fall Down: America's Tragic Encounter with Iran* (New York: Random House, 1985).

MUSADDIQ COUP

NSC 5820/1

Was the National Security Council (NSC) directive 5820/1 of November 1958 a positive policy shift for the Eisenhower administration?

Viewpoint: Yes. Recognizing the influence of Arab nationalism, the Eisenhower administration began a process, culminated during the Kennedy administration, of working with Arab nationalists against the spread of communism in the region.

Viewpoint: No. NSC 5820/1 represented a step backward in U.S. Middle Eastern policy because the Eisenhower administration did not differentiate between communism and Arab nationalism and failed to contain radical Arabs and their demands on Israel.

National Security Council (NSC) policy directive 5820/1 of 4 November 1958 was titled "U.S. Policy Toward the Near East," and it was subsequently approved by President Dwight D. Eisenhower, who ordered it to be implemented "by all appropriate Executive departments and agencies of the U.S. government." The introductory statement in NSC 5820/1 captures the thrust of the policy:

> The most dangerous challenge to Western interests arises not from Arab nationalism per se but from the coincidence of many of its objectives with many of those of the USSR. . . . It has become increasingly apparent that the prevention of further Soviet penetration of the Near East and progress in solving Near Eastern problems depends on the degree to which the United States is able to work more closely with Arab nationalism and associate itself more closely with such aims and aspirations of the Arab people as are not contrary to the basic interests of the United States.

NSC 5820/1 further stated as an operational item that the United States should "endeavor to establish an effective working relationship with Arab nationalism while at the same time seeking constructively to influence and stabilize the movement and to contain its outward thrust, and recognizing that a policy of U.S. accommodation to radical pan-Arab nationalism as symbolized by Nasser would include many elements contrary to U.S. interests."

U.S. policy prior to this directive had been criticized and, for the most part, hampered by Washington's tendency to lump left-wing Arab nationalists with communists as a monolithic bloc whose objectives were to undermine Western influence and advance the interests of the Soviet Union. What Washington failed to realize was that, more often than not, Arab nationalists and communists had ultimately divergent goals. While both groups professed anti-imperialism, the communists, to the distaste of neutralist, nonaligned pan-Arabists, were subordinate to Moscow and, like the class of capitalists and landed aristocrats who had been co-opted and manipulated by the European powers and whom they had just overcome, would lead the Arab world into a colonial relationship with another external power. The fact that the communists and Arab nationalists often joined forces to combat imperialism and/or Israel tended to reinforce the connection between the two in Washington.

After experiencing crises throughout 1957 and 1958 in the Middle East (Jordanian crisis, American-Syrian crisis, the Iraqi Revolution, and the Lebanese crisis), the Eisenhower administration seemed to begin to grasp that Arab nationalism and communism in the region could be (and were) separate entities. As such, Washington concluded that while the United States would not be able to establish the level of ingress that it would with outright pro-West, capitalist-based regimes, by default, leftist/socialist Arab nationalism could act as an effective bulwark against Soviet expansionism. NSC 5820/1 was the manifestation of this foreign policy shift toward the Middle East.

Viewpoint:
Yes. Recognizing the influence of Arab nationalism, the Eisenhower administration began a process, culminated during the Kennedy administration, of working with Arab nationalists against the spread of communism in the region.

To understand the nature of U.S. foreign-policy shifts toward the Middle East in 1958, one must go back to National Security Council (NSC) policy paper 5428 of 23 July 1954. The General Considerations of the document stated:

> The Near East is of great strategic, political and economic importance to the free world. The area contains the greatest petroleum resources in the world; essential locations for strategic military bases in any world conflict against Communism; the Suez Canal; and natural defensive barriers. It also contains Holy Places of the Christian, Jewish, and Moslem worlds, and thereby exerts religious and cultural influences affecting people everywhere. The security interests of the United States would be critically endangered if the Near East should fall under Soviet influence or control.

Four years later a new document, NSC 5820, titled "Long Range U.S. Policy Toward the Near East," replaced NSC 5428 considering "the many changes which have taken place in the area." The emergence of radical pan-Arab nationalism, as demonstrated by both the Jordanian and Syrian crises in 1957, alarmed Washington. The internal instability in the area and the knowledge that the Eisenhower Doctrine was not viable in the long term caused the Republican administration to formulate a new document. The new policy recognized the importance of Arab nationalism free from Soviet influence and separate and distinct from Nasserism.

NSC 5801 was amended by NSC Action No. 1845-c, approved by President Dwight D. Eisenhower on 24 January 1958 and was presented as NSC 5801/1. Later in October, while the Lebanese crisis was almost resolved (April–October 1958) and the Iraqi military coup on 14 July 1958 forced the Eisenhower administration to send fifteen thousand U.S. marines into Leba-

non, the NSC Planning Board revised the new basic paper NSC 5801/1, designating it NSC 5820. This latest document contained much of the same language as NSC 5801/1 but, in addition, pointed out that Washington's deteriorating position in the Near East had been accelerated by "the emergence of radical pan-Arab nationalism as the predominant force in the area with Nasser as its symbol and de facto spokesman and the Soviet Union's identification with and continuing exploitation of this movement."

To understand how Arab nationalism was perceived by the U.S. government, one should analyze a crucial document issued by the Special National Intelligence Estimate (SNIE) on 12 August 1958. After lengthy discussions were held on the aforementioned crises, the document refocused on Arab nationalism's aims and objectives, pointing out its desire to create a "centralized and unitary empire" of Arab states. Though the document concluded that this empire was far from being created because of the many incompatibilities between Egypt and the states in the Fertile Crescent, and with the Arabian Peninsula and the states on the Mediterranean seaboard, two critical uniting factors emerged: Egyptian president Gamal Abd al-Nasser and the existence of Israel.

Nasser's acquisition of Soviet arms (1955), nationalization of the Suez Canal (1956), and establishment of the United Arab Republic (UAR) on 1 February 1958 with Syria (and its enlargement to Yemen in May, forming the United Arab States or UAS) represented a danger to the United States because of the Egyptian leader's appeal and skillfulness in utilizing subversive methods and propaganda. Thus, the United States had to redefine radical pan-Arab nationalism in order to make it compatible with Western interests in the Middle East.

U.S. interests revolved around Israel's existence and "the maintenance of Western control over (as distinguished from access to) the oil of the area, and the use of military bases." The policy statement in NSC 5820 was approved by President Eisenhower on 4 November 1958 and adopted by the National Security Council as NSC 5820/1.

The fact that Arab nationalism was not necessarily seen as a danger and the recommendation

THE COMMON PURPOSE

In a 31 July 1958 letter to his friend Reverend Edward L. R. Elson, U.S. president Dwight D. Eisenhower commented on U.S. foreign policy in the Middle East:

I concur in the advice, "Keep Israel out of this crisis completely. If possible do not mention the word." The difficulty here is that in any conversation with an Arab, he is the one that brings up the subject of Israel. Underlying all Arab thought is resentment toward the existence of Israel and an underlying determination, some day, to get rid of it. So while I agree that in this crisis we should try to prevent Israel from being a principal subject in our discussions and planning, yet it is necessary to remember that it is antipathy against that State, practically universal among all Arabs, that provides fertile ground for Nasser's hate propaganda.

I assure you that I never fail in any communication with Arab leaders, oral or written, to stress the importance of the spiritual factor in our relationships. I have argued that belief in God should create between them and us the common purpose of opposing atheistic communism. However, in a conversation of this kind with King Saud, he remarked that while it was well to remember that the Communists are no friends of ours, yet Arabs are forced to realize that Communism is a long ways off, Israel is a bitter enemy in our own back yard. But the religious approach offers, I agree, a direct path to Arab interest.

Next, this Administration has never been antagonistic to Arab nationalism. Our own history as well as our sense of justice impel us to support peoples to achieve their own legitimate nationalistic aspirations. I think that possibly we have failed to make this clearly apparent to our Arab friends. The Cairo and Moscow radios have too long been falsely drumming in their ears the charge of Western imperialism and the clear purpose of Western nations, including the United States, to dominate all Arabs.

This brings to mind the need for a better and more consistent operation of our information services throughout the Arab region and indeed, through all the Muslim countries. George V. Allen, now in charge of our information services, is the most capable and knowledgeable man we have yet had in that post. He is struggling hard to find the facilities and the techniques whereby we, through friendly Arab spokesmen, can reach over good communications, the entire populations with the message of truth and fact about the West.

Source: *"Document 133: United States. White House Letter from Dwight D. Eisenhower to Edward L. R. Elson. [Response to Letter on the Middle East], July 31, 1958," The National Security Archive <http://www.gwu.edu/~nsarchiv/NSAEBB/NSAEBB78/propaganda%20133.pdf>.*

---

that the United States work more closely with it was at least a tentative change in the U.S. approach to the Middle East after the Harry S Truman era. The Eisenhower administration had already demonstrated it would neither endorse the special relationship with Israel established by the previous administration nor try to work with radical pan-Arab nationalism not identified with Nasser, which could mean to "include many elements contrary to U.S. interests." According to the Joint Chiefs of Staff, characteristics of these nationalist elements included "unscrupulous expansionist tendencies; interference, including incitement to violence in the affairs of neighboring nations; and, unfriendly propaganda activities directed against other nations of the Near East, the West in general, and the United States in particular." Quite certainly, if the Eisenhower administration's foreign-policy makers had evaluated Nasser's strategy in light of his participation in the Bandung nonalignment conference in April 1955, U.S. behavior toward Arab nationalism would have changed some years before. At Bandung, Nasser was the youngest leader, but not the least experienced. On the one hand, his meeting with leaders such as Jawaharlal Nehru (India), Chou En-lai (China), and Marshall Tito (Yugoslavia) confirmed, as Peter Woodward states, that it was possible "to come together to create a new movement, helping each other towards a more neutral international perspective, and a freer, fairer world." On the other hand, that meeting gave Nasser the opportunity to arrange arms deals with the Soviets through Chou En-lai, and inspired awareness that "links with the Soviet Union could be developed without the latter [the Soviet Union] becoming the dominant partner in the relationship."

State Department efforts to carry out shifts in the U.S. attitude toward radical pan-Arab nationalism were not in vain, but there was serious disagreement with the Departments of Defense and Treasury, who argued that "Washington should merely accept pan-Arab nationalism, of which Nasser is the symbol, and seek to normalize relations with him only as head of the UAR." The differences were soon healed by the approval of NSC 5820/1. Certainly, as Malik Mufti states, the document remained a controversial one, and the two departments cited above put their dissenting opinions on record (as Secretary of State John Foster Dulles did), pointing out that to appease Nasser would have meant a move away from Great Britain as an ally. The decision was made, and when, in late 1958, Eisenhower met with Egyptian ambassador Mustapha Kamel, they agreed on the "icebox approach." Cooperation between the two countries led Eisenhower to authorize $153 million in food aid in 1959–1960 and also "consigned to the icebox . . . the Eisenhower Doctrine."

President Eisenhower fully understood the nature and scope of radical pan-Arab nationalism. Beyond Nasser's and Egypt's desire to keep the Arab world united, there was a kind of grand design of steering a separate path, ideologically speaking, from that of the superpowers, while at the same time enjoying American loans/grants and Soviet arms. Nasser's policy toward his Egypt superpower benefactors turned out to be the only way he could "have his cake and eat it too." He wanted Egypt to progress economically and politically, and he charted his path by nationalizing the Suez Canal Company. In that particular episode Nasser succeeded in pushing aside France's and Great Britain's hopes, frustrating Israel's aggressive action, and gaining unconditional U.S. support.

Nevertheless, the Eisenhower administration was aware that it could not count exclusively on the moderate Arab countries and that its collaboration with them, based above all on oil-resources management, depended on the American approach toward Nasser. It was all a diplomatic game: U.S. recognition of radical pan-Arab nationalist strength and Nasser's leadership in exchange for keeping that nationalism free from Soviet and communist influence.

Of course, Egypt's arms deal with the Soviet Union in 1955 was of tremendous importance, but for the moment the clash between the two superpowers was on the ideological plane, and the military buildup could wait. Yet, the Eisenhower administration had recognized the influence of Arab nationalism and was ready to negotiate, thanks to the collaboration and common perspective shared between the White House and the Department of State, whose choice between Israel and the Arab states had already been made. The shift toward radical pan-Arab nationalism was not

gradual. In effect, the administration jumped onto a moving train whose direction was not yet established. On the contrary, President John F. Kennedy's approach to Nasser and his movement aimed "to restore a friendly working relationship with all the states in the area regardless of their systems and ideological proclivities." Kennedy's targets, George Lenczowski continues, were "respect for nationalism, acceptance of neutrality, and help in the modernization process." If Nasser had concentrated on progress, he would have produced a change at home without looking for adventures abroad. The American president always informed Nasser of "certain major policy moves by the United States, whether or not they affected Egypt directly," extended aid to Egypt through the PL-480 Food Program, and was sympathetic toward Nasser in the aftermath of crises such as Syria's defection from the UAR and Iraq's volte-face toward the pan-Arab program following the Iraqi Revolution (1958). The Kennedy administration adjusted itself to the new Middle Eastern realities.

–PAOLA OLIMPO,
UNIVERSITY OF LECCE

Viewpoint:
No. NSC 5820/1 represented a step backward in U.S. Middle Eastern policy because the Eisenhower administration did not differentiate between communism and Arab nationalism and failed to contain radical Arabs and their demands on Israel.

Between 1956 and 1958 the Middle East experienced crises, internal clashes, and a war, all of which led to direct and indirect superpower intervention. After the Suez crisis (1956) and the perceived enhanced likelihood of Soviet penetration in the region, the United States decided to enter more directly into the Middle East. Ever since the Eisenhower administration took power in 1953, it considered regional problems through an East-West prism. President Dwight D. Eisenhower and Secretary of State John Foster Dulles did not fully appreciate the intra-regional dynamics, the strong force of nationalism, the weakness of communist parties in the area, and Soviet astuteness, which took advantage of every opportunity presented to Moscow.

At the end of the Suez crisis the United States—convinced that, after the war, a vacuum of power eventually had to be filled—decided to

defend its interests in the Middle East. It is within this political framework that one should read the Eisenhower Doctrine (1957), which was designed to help those countries under Soviet pressure or communist threat, but which neglected the real concern of most states in the Middle East: radical Arab nationalism led by Egyptian president Gamal Abd al-Nasser, whose influence and popularity had skyrocketed after his political victory in the Suez War.

In 1957 and 1958 three important crises inflamed the Middle East. In 1957 the young Jordanian king Hussein resolved an internal crisis caused by the local pro-Nasserist Free Officers Movement. King Hussein was also helped by timely and direct U.S. intervention with strong economic assistance and the threat of employing American forces. In 1958 a nationalist coup d'état overthrew the pro-Western Iraqi government—with the extermination of the royal family and of Prime Minister Nuri al-Said. Simultaneously in Lebanon, President Camille Chamoun tried to remain in power by subverting the Lebanese constitution. For this reason a civil war broke out between Muslims and Christians, indirectly caused by the Arab nationalist movement.

Neither in Jordan, nor in Iraq and Lebanon, was the communist movement or the Soviet Union involved in any significant fashion. Every problem, one should emphasize, was caused by internal discontent and by frustration with the Western powers.

Notwithstanding some analyses by high-ranking State Department officials (such as Undersecretary of State Robert Murphy), President Eisenhower and Secretary Dulles were always convinced that communism and the Soviet Union were the real dangers in the Middle East and that radical Arab nationalism was just a Soviet means to enter the area. With this concern in mind, Eisenhower ordered, per the Eisenhower Doctrine, U. S. military intervention in Lebanon in July 1958. U.S. Marines remained in Lebanon until October, just enough time to see the retreat of Chamoun from his position and the election of a new Lebanese president.

After the Suez War, the Iraqi coup, and the Jordanian and Lebanese crises, the U.S. mindset changed. The result of this change was one of the most important but controversial strategic documents prepared by the National Security Council: NSC 5820/1 of 4 November 1958.

U.S. president Dwight D. Eisenhower (left) and King Hussein of Jordan, March 1959

(© CORBIS/Bettmann)

NSC 5820/1

In the introduction to the document, U.S. analysts recognized the growing force of the pan-Arab nationalist movement, even if they still stressed the importance of the Soviet threat in the area. These two parallel threats were clear in the document: "The most dangerous challenge to Western interests arises not from the Arab nationalism per se but from the coincidence of many of its objectives with many of those of the U.S.S.R. . . . Soviet policy in the Near East is aimed at weakening and ultimately eliminating Western influence, using Arab nationalism as an instrument." Once again, Arab nationalism did not have not its own independent life but was just a puppet of Moscow: two heads of the same monster. Yet, the "nationalist monster," to the U.S. administration, seemed easier to handle. In fact, NSC advisers were convinced that "the prevention of further Soviet penetration of the Near East and progress in solving Near Eastern problems depends on the degree to which the United States is able to work more closely with Arab nationalism and associate itself more closely with such aims and aspirations of the Arab people as are not contrary to the basic interests of the United States." The problems were: how to achieve these results; how to confront Nasser; how to help the conservative and moderate Arab countries experiencing Nasserist pressure; and how to defend Western interests, such as oil resources, in the region. In the document there are no clear answers to these questions.

The Eisenhower administration focused on two primary objectives: denial of the Middle East to the Soviets and continued availability of sufficient Near Eastern oil to meet vital Western European requirements on reasonable terms. Yet, the administration was quite confused about how to achieve both objectives. As such, it was important to "demonstrate to the peoples and governments of the area that primary U.S. objectives are fundamentally compatible with the goals of Arab Nationalism, whereas the objectives of international Communism are incompatible with the aims of true nationalism." Peoples and governments of the Middle East saw in that year, however, American soldiers invade an Arab country and threaten to do the same with another. The Soviet Union was out of the region; its policy was just to support the Arabs economically and militarily. Arab peoples did not care whether Arab nationalism was compatible or incompatible with communism. Moreover, according to the document, the United States should support "leadership groups which offer the best prospect of progress toward U.S. objectives in this area . . . [and] seek to discredit groups which promote pro-Soviet thinking." How could the United States deal with an Egyptian president who was the most important and popular leader in the

region? NSC 5820/1 never answered this question.

It is easy to find further incongruities in NSC 5820/1. On one hand, the administration recognized the necessity to encourage the resistance of Arab nationalism to "Soviet imperialism," avoiding "for the present any active efforts to enlist Arab nations in regional collective security arrangements" and realizing the uselessness of the "dying" Baghdad Pact (1955). Yet, on the other hand, regarding the possible resolution of the Arab-Israeli dispute, the NSC proposed the already dead and buried Alpha Plan, stressing again the "limitation on annual immigration into Israel." In fact, no major supply of arms had gone to Israel, but, above all, the United States had to make clear that "while U.S. policy embraces the preservation of the State of Israel in its essentials, we believe that Israel's continued existence as a sovereign state depends on its willingness to become a finite and accepted part of the Near East nation-state system." Again, the United States should "be prepared to support Israel's legal right to use the Suez Canal when it is at issue, but, recognizing the intransigent UAR [United Arab Republic] attitude on this matter and its connection with the Arab-Israeli dispute and the Gulf of Aqaba question, discourage Israel for the time being from asserting the right of Israeli flag vessels to use the Canal." This plan is the most ambiguous part of the whole document. Since its creation, Israel had tried to be part of "the Near East nation-state system," but this objective only encouraged Arab rejection—so how could the United States now ask Israel to be more willing? How could there arise in the region a new Middle East by accepting the radical ideas of Arab nationalism and neglecting the only democracy in the region—Israel?

In short, the Eisenhower administration, with NSC 5820/1, decided to repeat the same mistakes of the previous year: it saw few differences between international communism and Arab nationalism; it put pressure on Israel to accept Arab demands; and it failed to contain the radical Arab countries. NSC 5820/1 represented a further step backward in American Middle East policy, leaving more room for the Soviets to maneuver and less U.S. capacity to develop and adopt a clear and strong position. New problems were continuing to arrive on the table of U.S. foreign policy in the Middle East, and the Eisenhower administration failed to find real solutions to these problems; it only passed relatively worthless NSC resolutions that did not address the root causes of the disturbances in the region that so deleteriously affected Washington's objectives in the region.

–DANIELE DE LUCA,
UNIVERSITY OF LECCE

NSC 5820/1

References

Erika Alin, *The United States and the 1958 Lebanon Crisis: American Intervention in the Middle East* (Lanham, Md.: University Press of America, 1994).

Uriel Dann, *King Hussein and the Challenge of Arab Radicalism: Jordan, 1955–1967* (New York: Oxford University Press, 1989).

Fawaz A. Gerges, *The Superpowers and the Middle East: Regional and International Politics, 1955–1967* (Boulder, Colo.: Westview Press, 1994).

George Lenczowski, *American Presidents and the Middle East* (Durham, N.C.: Duke University Press, 1990).

Wm. Roger Louis and Roger Owen, eds., *A Revolutionary Year: The Middle East in 1958* (Washington, D.C.: Woodrow Wilson Center Press, 2002).

Malik Mufti, "The United States and Nasserist Pan-Arabism," in *The Middle East and the United States: A Historical and Political Reassessment*, edited by David W. Lesch (Boulder, Colo.: Westview Press, 1996, 1999, 2003), pp. 167–186.

Roger Owen, *State, Power and Politics in the Making of the Modern Middle East* (London & New York: Routledge, 1992).

Chester J. Pach and Elmo Richardson, *The Presidency of Dwight D. Eisenhower* (Lawrence: University Press of Kansas, 1991).

Robert B. Satloff, "The Jekyll-and-Hyde Origins of the U.S.-Jordanian Strategic Relationship," in *The Middle East and the United States: A Historical and Political Reassessment*, edited by Lesch (Boulder, Colo.: Westview Press, 1996, 1999, 2003).

Peter Woodward, *Nasser* (London & New York: Longman, 1992).

OIL PRODUCTION

Were the multinational oil companies needlessly exploitative in developing the Middle Eastern oil fields?

Viewpoint: Yes. The deals engineered by the multinational oil companies sowed the seeds of the OPEC-led revolt against corporate control and the oil crises of the 1970s.

Viewpoint: No. The multinational oil companies successfully introduced Middle Eastern oil into the world market without lowering prices or sparking corporate battles over market shares.

The oil industry has since World War II (1939–1945) been most often associated with the Middle East. This connection, of course, stands to reason since two-thirds of the world's proven oil reserves are located there in addition to the fact that predominant forces in the Organization of Petroleum Exporting Countries (OPEC)—most notably Saudi Arabia—can be found in the region. Most people, however, forget that by the time the British first discovered oil in the Middle East in Iran (1908), the oil industry already had about a half century behind it. It effectively began in the western Pennsylvania town of Titusville, where a group of investors established the Rock Oil Company in the 1850s. (John D. Rockefeller acquired this company as well as others, incorporating his various interests as Standard Oil Company in 1870.) The United States quickly became the primary producer and exporter of oil in the world; indeed, by the end of World War I (1914–1918), the United States was supplying approximately 70 percent of the world's oil supply. As Daniel Yergin noted in his seminal book, *The Prize: The Epic Quest for Oil, Money, and Power* (1990), which surveyed and examined the development of the global oil industry, it is with some irony that in the late nineteenth century the kerosene in the lamps that lit the tomb of the Prophet Muhammad in Medina (in present-day Saudi Arabia) most likely came from the United States.

American and British multinational oil companies began to intensify their search for Middle East oil in the 1920s and 1930s, establishing the framework for the post-1945 expansion of oil production in the region; indeed, by 1939, before the postwar economic boom and reconstruction efforts, Middle East oil contributed only 5 percent of total world oil production. Until the late 1960s and early 1970s, the multinational oil corporations dominated the chain of activities that composed the global oil industry, from production, transportation, and refining to marketing and distribution all the way to the gas pump. In his famous work, *The Seven Sisters: The Great Oil Companies and the World They Shaped* (1975), Anthony Sampson points out how the seven major oil companies—Standard Oil of California (Socal, later Chevron),Texaco, Standard Oil of New Jersey (later Exxon), Standard Oil of New York (Socony, later Mobil), Gulf Oil Company, British Petroleum, and Royal Dutch Shell—actually formed something of an oil cartel themselves until the host countries wrested away control of production and pricing decisions by 1970–1971. To a greater or lesser degree, all of these companies participated in the development of the oil industry in the Middle East. Considering the tug-of-war relationship between the multinationals and the host countries for much of this period, especially heating up in the 1950s, these corporations have often been viewed as needlessly exploitative in a classic colonial sense, thereby exacerbating already existing nationalist fervor that coalesced into the formation of OPEC and led to the oil shocks of the 1970s. Yet, there are those who assert that one must look past more recent history and examine the important role multinationals played in developing the industry in the region from virtually nothing and in a manner that did not disrupt the already existing oil market nor create internecine corporate warfare.

Viewpoint:
Yes. The deals engineered by the multinational oil companies sowed the seeds of the OPEC-led revolt against corporate control and the oil crises of the 1970s.

In the twentieth century no other raw material has matched the strategic importance of oil. It has been at the center of foreign-policy objectives, national and international security concerns, and local and world economic strategies. The British government quickly understood such strategic importance, when, on the eve of World War I (1914–1918), it purchased the majority of shares in the Anglo-Iranian Oil Company (AIOC, later British Petroleum, BP) that ran an oil concession in Iran. In fact, the Royal Navy had supported the modernization project, based on the usage of oil instead of coal for the supply of the British fleet. Such a process was fundamental for victory in the war. Therefore, for the first, and certainly not the last, time, oil became an instrument of national policy. The oil companies and governments of the great powers were involved in a struggle for control of the world's oil resources. The Middle East was the main battlefield. In fact, after the great oil discoveries in Iran in the early twentieth century, and in Saudi Arabia and Kuwait in the 1930s, this area stood out as containing the world's largest proven oil reserves, and it became, after World War II (1939–1945), the undisputed leader in the world oil market.

Since the mid 1940s, the oil industry has become the basic element for global economic growth. An exclusive group of multinational oil companies, the so-called Seven Sisters—composed of Standard Oil of California (Socal, later Chevron), Texaco, Standard Oil of New Jersey (later Exxon), Standard Oil of New York (Socony, later Mobil), Gulf Oil Company, British Petroleum, and Royal Dutch Shell—dominated the international oil market. Between 1950 and 1970, these seven companies controlled 80 percent of the world's resources (outside of the United States, Canada, and the Soviet-bloc countries) and nearly all Middle Eastern oil. Taking advantage of a true international monopoly, they were able to decide the international oil price.

Such a price, set by the same companies according to each country's crude oil supply and demand forecasts, was reported to the producing countries and publicized. Once the prices were set, the producing countries' profits were estimated, and the companies were able to manipulate production and price levels. Such actions were possible thanks to the Seven Sisters' control of the Middle Eastern oil concessions and also to their capability to control the entire oil cycle, from extraction of crude oil to the final selling of the product.

When oil demand quintupled and coal was replaced by oil as an energy source, the multinational oil companies were supported by the governments—first of all the United States, by that time mindful of the strategic importance of oil resources. In fact, at the end of World War II, with the first signs of the Cold War, the U.S. government understood the necessity to gain international oil supremacy and to maintain control of most world oil resources. Above all, it was necessary to prevent this control from falling into the hands of the Soviet Union. Besides the financial issues, the United States was concerned with another question: crude oil availability. For the United States, 1947 had meant the beginning of a period of oil importing. Therefore, on approving the main features of the Marshall Plan (1948), the U.S. Congress recognized the necessity to find alternative oil sources in order to provide Europe the crude oil supply necessary for the reconstruction program.

The plentiful Middle Eastern stocks seemed the right choice for that purpose, but soon after the war the Middle East area was rocked by political tension. The resentment toward the colonial powers and the founding of the State of Israel had strengthened Arab nationalism, which managed to destabilize the whole area and to turn it into a fertile ground for Soviet expansionism. Therefore, a series of specific events soon after the war—from the 50–50 profit-sharing agreement in Saudi Arabia to the nationalization of the oil industry in Iran, from the Marshall Plan to the Arab-Israeli question—forced Washington to try to solve the oil questions. The strategic importance of oil led the United States to abandon its traditional anticolonialist policy in favor of a new political and military interventionist strategy in the Middle East. An integral feature of this new policy was the role played by the

OIL PRODUCTION

A FATEFUL, BUT SURPRISINGLY CORDIAL, PARTNERSHIP

In 1998 former U.S. ambassador and Foreign Service officer Parker T. Hart commented on the Saudi-American relationship in producing oil and gaining concessions:

From 1940 to 1942, Standard Oil of California (SOCAL) waged a campaign at high levels in the Department of State to have a resident minister stationed in Saudi Arabia to lend support to the American presence following the 1938 oil discovery. On June 30, 1939, Secretary Hull was sufficiently impressed by a report from the American consulate in Cairo on the growth of the American oil community to 325 in the Dhahran area and by reports of German and Japanese diplomatic efforts to win oil concessions from Ibn Saud to recommend, with FDR's immediate acceptance, that American ministers to Egypt be co-accredited to Saudi Arabia, without incurring the cost of the rental or building of a legation structure or hiring a resident staff. On August 10, 1939, he appointed Bert Fish, US minister to Egypt, to carry out the mission. Fish made a single journey to Jeddah on February 4, 1940, and met with the king, after which he resigned both positions and left Cairo. So much for the earliest of face-to-face contacts of American officials with Ibn Saud.

These penny-pinching, arm's-length contacts between rulers and presidents contrasted with the live-together-work-together melding of Americans and Arabs in the Dhahran area and with the inherent need they recognized each had for the other. Ibn Saud's selection of SOCAL for a sixty-year concession over what was then believed to represent virtually all of the oil-bearing structures of the country placed the two peoples in fateful, but surprisingly cordial, partnership. The concession document had been signed May 29, 1933, and ratified on July 7, 1933. It covered 360,000 square miles of thinly populated area. Geology finally won over State's penny-pinching myopia, but not easily. By early 1938, Max Steineke, CASOC's head geologist, and his men had found no oil in commercial quantities. Six dry holes had been drilled in the Bahrain Zone, a formation in eastern Saudi Arabia that had earlier yielded success in Awali. Failures in drill tests were costly, and CASOC had spent $50 million already. Though the cost of trying for a still deeper deposit—then estimated at an average $1 million per hole—was great, Steineke nonetheless wired his strong recommendation to CASOC headquarters in San Francisco urging authority to drill for a deeper zone (henceforth called the Arab Zone). Dammam Number 7 rewarded the gamble, yielding commercial grade oil at 4,727 feet in March 1938.

In later years Ibn Saud enjoyed entertaining American visitors with the following reasons for choosing an American firm over one from Great Britain, France, Germany, or Japan, despite the offer of much better terms for a smaller concession. "First," he said, "because you are good oil men. You found it in Bahrain when others said it was not there. Second," said the king, "you treat your Arab employees as equals. Bahrainis are our brothers. We like what we hear. Third," said the king, "yours is a big and powerful country with lots of space and a democratic system; and furthermore, you are more interested in business than in acquiring political advantage. Fourth and lastly," concluded the king, "you are very far away!"

Source: *Parker T. Hart,* Saudi Arabia and the United States: Birth of a Security Partnership *(Bloomington & Indianapolis: Indiana University Press, 1998), pp. 37–38.*

multinational oil companies, which became an additional instrument at the disposal of the U.S. government for the achievement of foreign-policy goals. The oil companies influenced the U.S. government in order to achieve a solution in their favor on several occasions. After backing the Aramco agreement and promoting the birth of the Iranian consortium, the United States had practically handed over its oil policy to the multinational oil companies, both for practical and political reasons. Relying on its expertise within the oil industry allowed the U.S. government to avoid discussing serious questions regarding the Arab-Israeli arena. However, if on one side this situation allowed the multinational oil companies to gain an international monopoly, on the other side it provoked dangerous resentment among the oil-producing countries. This situation led to the foundation of the Organization of Petroleum Exporting Countries (OPEC) in 1960, the first international oil crisis in 1973, and the definitive realization by the oil-producing countries of the political importance of oil in international political events.

The strength of nationalism soon involved the oil sector: concessions were renegotiated according to the 50–50 formula, on which basis the royalties and taxes paid to the Middle East governments were equal to the net incomes of the Western companies. This new system, quite complex, satisfied both the producing countries, whose oil profits no longer fluctuated, and the oil companies, whose incomes remained unaltered. The new system, which spread quickly all over the area, partially caused the first oil crisis. Because AIOC refused to implement the 50–50 formula, the Iranian government, headed by nationalist leader and prime minister Muhammad Musaddiq, decided to nationalize the company, provoking an international crisis and the immediate boycott of Iranian oil exports. With the Cold War escalating, after the outbreak of the Korean conflict (1950–1953), the geographical position of Iran and its large oil production—40 percent of the whole Middle East—made it a vital resource. After American pressure on Great Britain for a quick solution to the controversy, the United States decided to intervene definitively in order to end the 1951–1953 oil crisis through a Central Intelligence Agency (CIA)–led coup, which removed Musaddiq from office. The oil situation in Iran was then solved through the institution of a Western companies consortium. Iranian oil continued to belong to the National Iranian Oil Company (NIOC), but its operations were carried out by the international consortium made up of five American and two British companies. In this way, the United States became a primary actor in Middle East political and oil questions. Although the supply interruption during the crisis had been weathered quite easily, the United States was still concerned over the increasing dependency on Middle East oil.

In the late 1950s, after the Soviet Union's reentry into the international oil market, there was oil overproduction. The U.S. government, partly as a result of competition from small oil producers, was forced to limit oil imports from the Middle East. Domestically produced oil was cheaper. Similarly, reduced oil self-sufficiency threatened to make the United States and the whole West dependent on distant and politically unstable countries. The 1959 oil import limitation program penalized the Seven Sisters, which reacted through a posted price reduction in order to pay fewer taxes to the producing countries. This action was unilateral, through which the oil companies cut the resources of Middle Eastern countries, whose total incomes were 80 percent dependent on oil profits. The reaction of the producing countries was immediate: in 1960, at a Baghdad meeting, OPEC was formed by Venezuela, Iran, Saudi Arabia, Iraq, and Kuwait, with the goal of defending oil prices. The foun-

dation of this new organization, whose members represented 80 percent of crude-oil exports, was the first collective act of sovereignty by the oil-exporting countries and the initial step toward state control of natural resources. In its first decade, OPEC did not cause much difficulty for the multinational oil companies. The reasons for this situation lie in the strong rivalries among the oil-producing states and the clever policy of the oil companies in negotiating with each producing country rather than with the new organization representing them.

By the early 1970s the oil order set up by the United States and Great Britain after World War II had changed. In fact, both powers were facing political problems: the United States was involved in a long and exhausting war in Vietnam (ended 1975), while Great Britain, going through a strong domestic economic crisis, had decided to withdraw from the Persian Gulf. In the meantime, world oil demand had steeply increased, negating the previous years' oil surplus and tightening the international oil market. Once again, a good part of the oil consumption increase was satisfied by Middle Eastern production. This new position of strength was cleverly exploited by the producing countries. Libya was the first to ask for and obtain an oil concession term revision. The 50–50 formula was replaced by a new agreement, giving the producing country the main profit share and the opportunity to negotiate the posted price with the company. The Libyan example was soon followed by Iran, Saudi Arabia, and the other oil-producing countries, who inserted the "sharing principle" in the new contracts, according to which the Middle Eastern countries purchased equity stakes of the oil companies. The Western governments, primarily the United States, accepted the new state of affairs, realizing the West's dependence on Middle East oil and the strategic importance the Middle East had achieved as a bastion against Soviet expansionism. The situation came to a head during 1973. OPEC asked for a general increase of oil prices, denied by the multinational oil companies. On the eve of the OPEC meeting, the third Arab-Israeli War (1973) broke out. Abandoning further agreements with the companies, OPEC increased the crude-oil price from $2.90 to $5.12 a barrel. Following the granting of American military aid for Israel during the Arab-Israeli War, OPEC decided on a selective oil embargo against Israel's friends and a production decrease by 5 percent per month. In the months following the conflict, oil prices increased fourfold, up to $11.65 a barrel. The golden age of the big multinational oil companies was coming to an end, and, at the same time, the postwar economic development slowed down. Although the oil crisis did not economically penalize the companies (1973 profits were

OIL PRODUCTION

up 60 percent on the previous year's figures), they were not able to avoid losing the most precious good: oil concessions. First in Kuwait (1974–1975) and then in Saudi Arabia (1974–1976), Arab governments decided to nationalize those companies holding the concession, thus the oil giants were obliged to accept the new balance of power. The relations between oil-producing countries and companies changed; the international oil order had been overthrown. The new protagonists were the producing countries, which, after decades of discussions and failed attempts, had successfully used the oil weapon and had managed not only to modify relations between oil producers and consumers but also to reshape the global economy—and transform Middle East geopolitics.

Thus in a few years OPEC oil-producing countries had gained a paramount position in global oil policy. During the 1970s they controlled more than 50 percent of the world crude-oil production. Through a method similar to that used by the Seven Sisters, the members of the organization regularly met in order to fix the oil price suitable to the current situation and the production quotas to maintain that price in the market. This price was inserted into oil-sale contracts between producers and international companies, but the lack of a long-term strategy in international oil policy did not contribute stability to the market. Responsibility for this oversight can be attributed to the unscrupulous policy pursued by the international oil companies and to that which was promoted by the U.S. government. The world press wondered what the role played by the United States and the companies was, and the U.S. Senate set up an inquiry in order to find out their role in the 1973 oil crisis. Although there was no mention of imperialism or hidden government actions, the inquiry outlined the intricacy of interactions between the U.S. government and the oil companies; but this relationship had prevented a clear, coherent, and, above all, long-term strategy from developing that would have stabilized the international oil industry. In fact, after initial support, the U.S. government abandoned the oil companies during hard times. Lacking an organic policy, the government and the companies were at the mercy of an ungovernable political and economic oil situation. So, as they had not been able to avoid the 1973 oil shock, likewise they could not avoid the second crisis in 1979–1980.

In 1979–1980 four important events shook the Middle East: the fall of the Shah because of the Iranian Revolution (February 1979); the occupation of the U.S. embassy in Iran by the revolutionaries (November 1979); the Soviet invasion of Afghanistan (December 1979); and the outbreak of the Iran-Iraq War (1980–1988).

For the United States the Iranian Revolution was a great loss. (Iran was the world's fourth-largest crude-oil producer—10 percent of global oil production—and the second largest oil exporter.) The country the United States had relied on to contain the Soviet Union was in Ruhollah Khomeini's hands, who incited Muslim peoples to rise up against the West, especially the "Great Satan," the United States. Furthermore, the Soviet Union, by invading Afghanistan, came dangerously close to the Persian Gulf, thus threatening more than 60 percent of world oil stockpiles. Finally, the Iran-Iraq War, dragging on for eight years and drastically reducing the oil production of both countries, contributed to general destabilization in the area. Speculations on oil, especially in the spot markets, drove the price per barrel of oil to $42. Fear soon turned into panic. Not only had the United States lost Iran, but its failed attempt to free the embassy hostages in April 1980 ended in tragedy for some U.S. soldiers. The international oil companies gave up their power in the oil market to the producing countries. Their struggle against great oil trusts had been won. OPEC definitively became an important protagonist in the international balance of power.

–VALENTINA VANTAGGIO,
UNIVERSITY OF LECCE

Viewpoint:
No. The multinational oil companies successfully introduced Middle Eastern oil into the world market without lowering prices or sparking corporate battles over market shares.

Western oil companies began production operations in the Middle East in the first decade of the twentieth century, starting with Royal Dutch Shell in Egypt and the Anglo-Iranian Oil Company (AIOC, later British Petroleum, BP) in Iran. These companies were also rivals for concessionary rights in Iraq, at that time part of the Ottoman Empire. As so often happened in the history of the international oil industry, corporate rivalry ended in corporate cooperation. BP and Shell joined forces in a multinational consortium, Turkish Petroleum Company (TPC), which included minority German interests as well.

That consortium was restructured after World War I (1914–1918). BP and Shell were joined by Standard Oil of New Jersey (later Exxon), Standard Oil of New York (Socony, later Mobil), and a fledgling French firm, Total, which took over the German share. In 1927 TPC's drillers struck oil in northern Iraq. In the following year TPC's member companies drew up an exclusionary agreement in which they undertook to work together to keep most of the Middle East between Egypt and Iran as their exclusive preserve. Armed with this so-called Red Line agreement, the consortium (now renamed Iraq Petroleum Company, IPC) moved to commercial production in Iraq by 1934 and won concessionary rights from other states in the region.

However, IPC failed to keep rivals out of the Middle East. Gulf Oil Corporation managed to obtain a concession in Kuwait, though BP used diplomatic leverage to persuade Gulf to admit it as senior partner in what became their joint venture, Kuwait Oil Company. Standard Oil of California (or Socal, later Chevron) also obtained footholds in the Middle East, first in Bahrain in 1930 and then in eastern Saudi Arabia in 1933. Chevron formed a marketing and production partnership with Texaco in 1936, and their joint venture (Casoc, later Aramco) went into export production by 1939.

In sum, all of the historic Seven Sisters plus tiny Total were active in the Middle East before World War II (1939–1945). Their investments included the largest refinery in the world (BP's Abadan complex in Iran), three important production fields, and two pipelines (one to the Persian Gulf, one to the eastern Mediterranean). That said, it is essential to understand that the Middle East was only a minor frontier area at this time. In 1939 output from the region amounted to less than 5 percent of total world production of crude oil. During World War II, Venezuela produced more oil than all areas of the Middle East combined.

That situation changed in the two decades following the war. Everette DeGolyer, the most prominent petroleum geologist of his generation, famously predicted in 1944 that the center of gravity of world oil production would soon shift to the Middle East. New estimates of hydrocarbon reserves made clear that the production potential of the region was tremendous. This new perception came at a time when business and government in the United States were warning of a severe oil shortage after the war. So the newly recognized oil potential of the Middle East was good news indeed.

Or was it? For the oil majors an air of déjà vu hung over this prospect. During the 1920s they had lived through a cycle of anticipated shortage followed by plentiful supply. They had learned the hard way that too much oil can be worse than not enough. They had turned to collusion (the "As-Is" agreement and "Gulf-plus"

pricing) and government-enforced regulation (prorationing, import quotas) to deal with the problems of oversupply. They now feared that bringing the Middle East onstream would leave them facing the same problems all over again.

These fears were not groundless. The companies correctly anticipated that the political authorities of the three main producing countries—Iran, Iraq, and Saudi Arabia—would want to maximize revenues, and hence production, as postwar reconstruction proceeded. These three countries would be joined by Kuwait, whose enormous Burgan field was about to be brought into commercial production. Oil multinationals operating in frontier regions preferred to "shut in" new production and lift only enough crude to match projected marketing needs—which, of course, they could meet from sources of supply on four continents, the fact that gave the companies so much negotiating leverage. This policy was precisely what the IPC consortium had done in Iraq in the 1930s.

Now each Middle Eastern host country could point to the levels of production and exports of its neighbors and demand that "its" oil companies match or surpass those levels—or else. The companies could make the cogent counterargument that the absorptive capacity of existing markets was insufficient to dispose of "too much" new production. This argument might make for conclusive logic in the boardrooms, but it would predictably cut little ice with host governments, who could abrogate the concessionary rights of companies that refused to raise output sufficiently. In short, the companies faced the prospect of "leap-frogging" increases in production levels in the Middle East, which would lead inevitably to "disorderly market conditions"—corporate code for lower prices and squeezed profit margins.

The multinationals understood that they had to contain this danger, and the American companies were the first to act. In 1946 Exxon and Mobil negotiated a deal to purchase 40 percent of Aramco, Chevron and Texaco's joint venture in Saudi Arabia, at a total cost of $469.2 million (about $3.7 billion today). Exxon and Mobil would provide new capital to develop Aramco's fields and construct a big, new pipeline to the Mediterranean. In return, Aramco's crude would be directed into the extensive marketing networks of the new partners. Chevron and Texaco would have no reason to cut retail prices in order to capture market share, so the threat of a future price war was dispelled. Exxon and Mobil would gain access to huge new crude reserves outside the Western Hemisphere without having to bore a single discovery well.

However, an impediment stood in the way of the Aramco deal: the Red Line agreement of

An American (left) and Saudi working on an Aramco drilling derrick in 1960

(Aramco)

1928. In that agreement the member firms of the IPC consortium—BP, Shell, Exxon, Mobil, and Total—had undertaken not to compete with each other throughout the Middle East. Clause 10 legally bound them to offer prorated shares of any new acquisition to their consortium partners—something that the American firms had no intention of doing with Aramco. Thus the Red Line restriction had to go before an all-American Aramco deal could succeed.

Beginning in September 1946, Exxon and Mobil launched a campaign to escape from the constraints of the Red Line. They argued that wartime legislation in Britain, where IPC was incorporated, had legally nullified the restrictive 1928 agreement. The details of their case need not concern us, for the American majors realized that legal arguments alone could never win the day. They understood that their IPC partners would have to be bought off, and that was exactly what Exxon and Mobil proceeded to do.

In December 1946 Exxon signed a contract to purchase 1.2 billion barrels of crude oil from BP over the next two decades. As a producer of crude, BP was a giant in the international oil industry, but its small retail network made it a giant with an Achilles heel, for it needed markets for the larger volumes of oil that inevitably would result from rising postwar production in Iraq and Kuwait. Exxon's offer furnished the revenue stream with which BP could finance the development of Kuwait's Burgan field, where BP and Gulf Oil Corporation held a joint concession. By providing a long-term future market at a known selling price, the sales agreement in effect allowed BP to pay for its investment in Kuwait at Exxon's expense.

More importantly, the deal with Exxon guaranteed that BP's existing output from Iran would not want for postwar markets, for the deal allowed BP to supply Exxon's off-takes from either Kuwait or Iran. Thus, BP could

OIL PRODUCTION

adjust the composition of its deliveries to Exxon so as to sustain Iranian production levels. This aspect was important because all industry analysts expected a marked postwar expansion of Arabian output, and BP was worried about the effect of this surge on Iran's position as the leading producer of the region—something that was bound to have ramifications for the security of BP's concession rights. The political benefits of assured crude sales to Exxon were even more attractive than the purely commercial aspects of the deal, which nevertheless were considerable, for the problems of market adjustment to increased Arabian output would now fall largely on the shoulders of the American companies—and Exxon would also defuse the "disorderly marketing" potential posed by increased Kuwaiti production. Just as BP received a guarantee against the disruptive effects of a postwar flood of Arabian crude, the long-term sales contract allowed Exxon to absorb the anticipated surge in Kuwaiti output. And, of course, the contract provided the requisite inducement to persuade BP not to block the Aramco deal by invoking clause 10 of the Group Agreement.

Meanwhile, Shell was negotiating a similar long-term purchase contract with Gulf, BP's partner in Kuwait—negotiations in which BP may well have played a brokerage role. The needs of the two companies were complementary. Shell found itself crude short after the war, but Gulf was crude long. Estimates of its Kuwaiti reserves ranged to more than 5 billion barrels, five times Gulf's reserves in the United States, but Gulf's existing distribution network could not absorb new output on this scale. Shell needed oil and Gulf needed markets, and this concordance of interests led to an arrangement signed in May 1947. Shell undertook to purchase 1.25 billion barrels of crude from Gulf from 1947 through 1969. Gulf got a secure outlet for at least a quarter of its Kuwaiti reserves, and Shell got guaranteed access to Gulf's underground assets in Kuwait and thus greatly increased the size of "its" reserves in the Middle East. This arrangement also gave Shell a reason not to contest the Americans' Aramco deal.

That left Total, the weakest company in the IPC consortium. Total regarded the American attack on the Red Line as a body blow to its ambitions to become a major player in the international industry. Its management launched a legal and diplomatic campaign to keep the Red Line restrictions valid and force Exxon and Mobil to accord it a prorated share of Aramco, but this struggle was unequal and Total was out of its depth. The American firms had carefully kept the Departments of State, Justice,

War, and Interior in the picture right from the start, and Washington now extended strong diplomatic support to the Aramco buy-in and the dissolution of the Red Line restrictions. Why was Washington so supportive? During the war different agencies of the federal bureaucracy had addressed the question of postwar petroleum supply, giving particular attention to Saudi Arabia. All government plans for a postwar foreign oil policy, however, had miscarried. Exxon and Mobil's private initiative put in place what government policy had failed to produce: a credible framework for the protection and development of Arabian oil reserves under American control.

Grasping how long the odds had become, Total quickly gave up on the goal of saving the Red Line and securing a share of Aramco. The French company was ready to come to the table if Exxon and Mobil would guarantee that the Aramco deal would not curb the expansion of the Iraq consortium's output. Exxon and Mobil proposed to increase IPC's total production and give Total the right to acquire a larger share of this increased output. That deal persuaded Total to trade its Arabian ambitions for an enhanced position in Iraq, and a settlement was reached on 14 May 1947. Three weeks later Exxon, Mobil, Shell, BP, and Total signed a new "Heads of Agreement" for the Iraq consortium. The Red Line regime was history; the Aramco deal was in the bag; and American paramountcy in Middle Eastern oil was in the offing.

A general lesson emerges from this story: every one of the multinational oil companies involved had a stake in the success of the Aramco deal. Aramco's joint owners, Chevron and Texaco, accounted for just 5 percent of world crude-oil sales in 1946, but these firms held enormous reserves in Arabia, where wellhead costs were estimated to be the lowest in the world. Chevron and Texaco would predictably try to increase their market share by selling Arabian crude at low prices, for low production costs gave them room to compress margins and still turn a handsome profit. In short, the other majors could see a price war in prospect if Arabian output were brought to market in this fashion. What they needed was a sure way to "discipline" Aramco so that the surge in Arabian production would not push down prices or precipitate disruptive struggles for market share.

The Aramco deal supplied that discipline, for it included a mechanism to control the pace of development in Arabia. As part of the deal, Chevron and Texaco signed an eighteen-year off-take schedule to supply Exxon and Mobil with a large portion of Aramco's future output. This schedule obliged Chevron and Texaco to

OIL PRODUCTION

accept a modest rate of growth for Aramco's production of just 3 percent per year. The Aramco deal thus accomplished two things. It regulated the rate of future production in Arabia and made sure Aramco's production would be channeled into the majors' existing distribution networks, thereby avoiding a price war. All of the majors understood that new production from Arabia and Kuwait had to find a market. The trick was to keep that output in what the majors called "safe hands"—in other words, their own—in order to protect the international petroleum trade against conditions of oversupply. The intercompany purchases and contracts of 1946–1947 fulfilled that objective.

The "great oil deals of 1947"—the phrase comes from *Fortune* magazine—were the cornerstone of corporate control of Middle Eastern oil development after World War II. Those deals were supplemented by the restructuring of the Iranian oil industry in 1953–1955, when the oil multinationals displayed the same systemwide concern as they repaired the mess resulting from BP's badly played hand in the Iranian nationalization (or Muhammad Musaddiq) crisis. Their objective was familiar: to reintegrate Iranian production into world oil markets without generating "disorderly market conditions." The American majors plus Shell joined with BP in a new consortium to make sure that Iran's revived output would be "safely" absorbed into their existing marketing channels.

Throughout the 1950s and into the 1960s, the multinational oil companies succeeded in balancing steady increases in Middle Eastern production with the growth of demand for hydrocarbon products in Europe, America, and Japan. The result was rising oil supply combined with long-run price stability. Plentiful and relatively cheap oil fueled the reconstruction of Europe and the prosperity of the "thirty glorious years." That account is not in dispute. The question is whether this pattern favored the consuming countries of the industrialized West at the expense of the producing countries of the Middle East.

Answering this question requires the presentation of a hypothetical but plausible alternative to the control of production and marketing by the oil multinationals during those years. For the sake of argument one can posit the nationalization of the multinationals' in-country subsidiaries (though it should be said that the companies' reaction to the Iranian nationalization attempt of 1950–1953 hardly makes that a realistic assumption). A nationalized enterprise could in the short run have retained more profits for the host country beyond the 50–50 revenue split that became generalized in the region in the 1950s. But the need for imports of spare parts,

rolled steel pipe, refinery equipment, drilling rigs, and much else would ineluctably have required a hypothetical "national" producer to bring its costs for expanding production back toward the average costs obtaining in the industry. (It could, of course, compress local labor costs; but that possibility contributes nothing to the idea of a "better" alternative to the development by oil multinationals!)

More important, the multinational oil companies controlled the international marketing of crude oil and refined products. What one cannot plausibly posit for our hypothetical nationalized producer is independent marketing channels capable of absorbing large-volume off-takes. Internationally marketed crude oil had to be sold to the majors at some point in its journey toward the end user. The majors could and did source their off-takes from several world regions—that, after all, is what made them "majors." At this time, the volume of oil produced in the Middle East, though growing, was still insufficient to "make" the price of internationally traded crude. Host countries in the Middle East, like crude producers everywhere, were price takers; the selling price of their output was governed by the world price, not their views of what was the right price to charge for the sale of a national resource. This constraint applied even after interlopers such as Aminoil and Pacific Western gained footholds in the Persian Gulf. They too had to pay world prices for their off-takes; they too could not go beyond 50–50 without squeezing their profits or losing retail market share.

In sum, in the two decades after World War II the Middle East went from minor frontier region to the largest oil-producing area outside the United States. This transformation happened under conditions controlled by the multinational oil companies—and it is hard to see how, realistically, it could have happened under alternative conditions. The companies' achievement was to bring about this transition without generating leap-frogging production increases, supply surges, and price instability. The industrialized world—and, of course, the oil companies themselves—benefited, but so too did the host countries. The 50–50 regime, which the oil companies reluctantly imported into the region from Venezuela, meant that Middle Eastern governments took in a revenue share that amounted to the best expectations of the day. To assert that a higher local "take" was possible is neither here nor there. The eventual movement beyond 50–50 was propelled by changed global conditions of supply and demand, a new pattern of production in states such as Libya, and a radicalized political landscape in key parts of the Middle East. In other

OIL PRODUCTION

words, the 1950s were not the 1970s, and realistic historical understanding is not served by pretending otherwise.

–E. PETER FITZGERALD,
CARLETON UNIVERSITY

References

Paul H. Frankel, *Essentials of Petroleum: A Key to Oil Economics* (London: Cass, 1969).

Anthony Sampson, *The Seven Sisters: The Great Oil Companies and the World They Shaped* (New York: Viking, 1975).

Benjamin Shwadran, *The Middle East, Oil, and the Great Powers,* revised edition (New York: Wiley, 1974).

Ian Skeet, *OPEC: Twenty-five Years of Prices and Politics* (Cambridge, U.K. & New York: Cambridge University Press, 1988).

Philip Terzian, *OPEC: The Inside Story* (London: Zed, 1985).

Louis Turner, *Oil Companies in the International System* (London: Royal Institute of International Affairs, 1978).

Daniel Yergin, *The Prize: The Epic Quest for Oil, Money, and Power* (New York: Simon & Schuster, 1990).

OIL PRODUCTION

OSLO ACCORDS

Were the Oslo accords signed by the Israelis and Palestinians in 1993 successful?

Viewpoint: Yes. The Oslo accords were a success because they established a process for Israeli and Palestinian negotiations and established a timetable for resolving their differences.

Viewpoint: No. The Oslo accords were a failure because they were based on a phased approach and did not properly establish a vision of a final peace.

With the end of the superpower Cold War and the Soviet Union having imploded by the end of 1991, the United States reigned supreme in the Middle East following the impressive military victory in the Persian Gulf War (1990–1991), initiating what many called a *Pax Americana*. Washington was apparently without rival. The Palestine Liberation Organization (PLO), for its part, had actually been greatly weakened by the Gulf crisis and war. PLO chairman Yasser Arafat had tacitly supported Iraqi president Saddam Hussein, thus losing most of the international sympathy in the West that the Palestinian *intifada* (uprising) had garnered to that point, and, more importantly, as he discovered following the war, the PLO also lost financing from the Arab states in the Persian Gulf, on which it depended to a significant degree.

The administration of George H. W. Bush exploited the new regional balance of power in the aftermath of the Gulf War to convene an international peace conference in Madrid (October 1991) with the objective of settling once and for all the Arab-Israeli conflict. The PLO was not officially represented, a concession to the hard-line Israeli Likud government of Prime Minister Yitzhak Shamir, although Palestinians from the West Bank and Gaza Strip who attended the conference and subsequent meetings as part of the Jordanian delegation acted in close consultation with PLO officials in Tunis. This arrangement was a clear indication of the weakened position of the PLO, especially as non-PLO Palestinian delegates received more of the limelight.

Other than the Jordanian track, which would eventually result in a peace treaty with Israel in 1994, the Madrid process bogged down, especially on Palestinian issues. From Arafat's perspective the talks had essentially ground to a halt, with an inversely proportional increase in the popularity of those Palestinian groups, such as Hamas (Islamic Resistance Movement), that had opposed participation in the Madrid process from the beginning. In Israel, meanwhile, the Labor Party came back to power in June 1992, with Yitzhak Rabin as prime minister and known peace activist Shimon Peres as foreign minister. The ruling coalition was composed of representatives from a variety of parties that advocated a peaceful settlement and territorial compromise. Against this background, an alternative channel for direct Israeli-Palestinian negotiations was opened up with Norwegian assistance during the summer of 1992. The catalysts to the Oslo talks were Yossi Beilin, a close ally of Peres and deputy foreign minister in the new Israeli government; Terje Rod Larsen, a Norwegian academic; and Ahmad Qurai, the PLO treasurer. The Clinton administration, coming to power in January 1993, was aware of the talks in general terms but did not know the nature of the discussions or the level of progress; indeed, the United States was intentionally kept largely out of the picture, even though both sides understood that Washington would play a crucial role as the guarantor of any agreement. The secrecy of the talks also insured against unwanted leaks to the media and unwarranted expectations and deadlines.

What finally resulted was the Oslo agreement, signed at the White House by Rabin and Arafat, with U.S. president Bill Clinton presiding, on 13 September 1993. It consisted of a Declaration of Principles as well as letters of mutual recognition. Overall, the agreement set in motion the establishment of a Palestinian self-governing authority, or what became known as the Palestinian Authority (PA), of which Arafat was eventually elected president. The PA was slated to have civil administration authority over the Gaza Strip as well as the city of Jericho in the West Bank, which was consummated in May 1994. In addition, the accords established a timetable of negotiations to enhance PA authority and eventually tackle what have been called the "final status" issues—in other words, the most intractable of all of the outstanding problems between Israel and the Palestinians, such as the nature of a Palestinian state, the status of Palestinian refugees, Israeli settlements, and whether Jerusalem remain the united capital of Israel or East Jerusalem, including the holy sites, should become the capital of an independent Palestinian state. However, the Oslo accords have all but been forgotten following the failed summit meeting at Camp David (July 2000) among Clinton, Arafat, and Israeli prime minister Ehud Barak—one seemingly last-gasp attempt to resolve the Israeli-Palestinian situation under the Oslo parameters—and the subsequent outbreak of the al-Aqsa intifada in September 2000.

Viewpoint:
Yes. The Oslo accords were a success because they established a process for Israeli and Palestinian negotiations and established a timetable for resolving their differences.

During the days that led up to and immediately followed the White House signing of the Oslo agreement by Palestinian and Israeli representatives in September 1993, world leaders were acutely aware of the importance of what had happened. "This declaration represents a historic and honorable compromise between two peoples who have been locked in a bloody struggle for almost a century," remarked President Bill Clinton in his statement at the White House on 10 September 1993. President Clinton also called the declaration "an extraordinary act." Israeli foreign minister Shimon Peres referred to the accords as "another genesis." U.S. secretary of state Warren Christopher believed that the Israelis and Palestinians had "broken through the barriers of hatred and fear . . . demonstrat[ing] extraordinary courage and statesmanship." Palestinian leader Yasser Arafat believed that the signing marked "the beginning of the end of a chapter of pain and suffering."

Initially, some observers were aware that there would be problems. Vice President Al Gore believed that there would be "obstacles and setbacks." Of course, some members within the Palestinian and Israeli communities denounced the agreement and threatened those who signed it. For example, Ahmed Jabril, a Syrian-based guerilla group, said that Arafat would "pay with

his life" for signing the accords and for recognizing the right of Israel to exist. Benjamin Netanyahu, the Likud Party leader, called the accords "a black day for Israel" and vowed to fight against the implementation of the agreement.

It is too easy to say that the Oslo accords failed because there today does not exist a just and lasting peace in the Middle East built upon the twin tenets of an Israeli state and a Palestinian state with recognized, defensible borders. An absence of finality does not mean an absence of success; it just means that the process has yet to reach its desired or anticipated end. In order to examine the possibility that the Oslo agreement is a success, one must not look at Oslo through the restrictive lens of the end (which has yet to manifest itself either in the form of a finalized peace plan or in the participants ringing its death knell) but rather through the wide lens of the process. In other words, until Oslo is declared dead by the participants or until Oslo reaches its anticipated goal, the process is not dead. The mortician has no body; thus, there can be no postmortem.

Some observers believe the accords benefited both sides. For example, in 1995 the *Jerusalem Post* reported that Oslo was successful because armed attacks against Israelis were carried out by a small number of radical Islamic organizations as opposed to members within the general Palestinian community or mainstream Palestinian organizations such as the Palestine Liberation Organization (PLO); support for Palestinian attacks inside the Green Line against Israeli civilians had dropped from 32 percent to 20 percent; and politics and society in Gaza was slowly normalizing as radical groups such as Hamas were loosening their grips of control over the mainstream Palestinians. Three years

OSLO ACCORDS

Israeli prime minister Yitzhak Rabin, U.S. president Bill Clinton, and PLO chairman Yasser Arafat (l.-r.) at the signing of the September 1993 peace accords in Washington, D.C.

(© AP/Wide World Photos)

later the British-based Palestinian Information Center reported that Oslo was a success, although more for Israelis than for Palestinians, because Israel was able to transfer some of the more costly aspects of government—such as health, education, and municipal services—to the Palestinian Authority (PA). Others, however, believed that the success of the Oslo accords was less tangible; for example, in 2002 scholar Neill Lochery surmised that Oslo forwarded aspects of Conflict Resolution theory such as the need for secret diplomacy, the benefits of interim staged agreements, and how to deal with opponents of peace.

The Oslo accords are a success for a variety of reasons. First, the Oslo accords brought the sides together in a way that they had been either unwilling or unable to meet in the past. Gore noted that there would be impasses and road-blocks to peace, yet he also argued that the agreement facilitated surmounting the obstacles. What the Oslo accords created, according to Gore, was "a framework within which Israelis and Palestinians can face these challenges together." This assertion is important yet rudimentary. Oslo can be viewed as a success because, unlike all previous attempts to bring about peace

between the Israelis and Palestinians that typically circumvented one side or the other, Oslo actually brought the parties together. For example, President Jimmy Carter's 1978 Camp David meetings between Egypt and Israel held discussions about the Palestinians but did not include a representative of the Palestinian people. President Gerald Ford had earlier promised the Israelis that the United States would never recognize the PLO until the PLO accepted United Nations (UN) Resolution 242 and renounced the use of terrorism. Even as late as 1991, when President George H. W. Bush convened the Madrid Conference, the Israelis refused to meet face-to-face with a "Palestinian" delegation. Instead, Palestinians were allowed to tag along with the Jordanian delegation.

Palestinians, Israelis, and others recognized this central importance to Oslo. Mahmoud Abbas, a PLO Executive Committee member, said that the Oslo accords "will enable us to overcome all obstacles." Secretary Christopher noted that the simple act of Palestinians and Israelis working together, which was symbolized by the historic handshake between Arafat and Rabin on the White House lawn, was "a mighty redemptive power that can help heal the wounds of this too-often-violent century." Another member of the State Department commented on how both inspiring it was and natural it seemed to see "Arab ambassadors going up to the foreign minister of Israel . . . and you have them shaking hands with . . . Rabin, you have an event of just extraordinary significance psychologically."

Of course, it was not just that Israelis and Palestinians first met face-to-face in 1993 and continued to meet after signing the accords, but also that Oslo can be viewed as a success because it facilitated major Arab-Israeli contacts. For example, besides representatives from Israel and the Palestinians, members from several Arab countries participated in bilateral and multilateral summit meetings as a result of Oslo. "This demonstrates that one of the underlying principles" of the Oslo accords, according to Edward P. Djerejian, assistant secretary for Near Eastern affairs, "is sound." Daniel C. Kurtzer, U.S. ambassador to Israel, said that the Oslo agreement "revolutionized" the way in which Americans thought of bringing peace to the Middle East because "it brought about direct Israeli-PLO recognition and negotiation."

Second, the Oslo declaration can be considered a success because it reversed decades of relegating either side to obscurity. It legitimized the plight and position of each side to the other. The agreement forced each side to examine its counterpart as human beings as opposed to vermin. It humanized, in other words, the situation. Rashid Khalidi noted that "the mere fact that any agreement has been reached is unquestionably significant, given the history of profound enmity between Israelis and Palestinians." Likewise, Israeli leaders Yossi Beilin and Shimon Peres reversed decades of animosity and enmity by seeking and maintaining contacts with Palestinians (even during heightened periods of attacks against Israeli civilians and a drop in Israeli support for the Oslo process) in order to establish a Palestinian state. Aaron David Miller, U.S. deputy special Middle East coordinator, noted that the humanizing factor of Oslo is important if peace is ever to be obtained: "Mutual recognition turned an existential conflict into a political conflict with the possibility of solution." Even conflict-resolution specialists applauded the Oslo accords for its humanizing factor and the step-by-step process, which was designed to increase personal contacts between the parties and thus build confidence and trust along the way. Political scientist Ian S. Lustick pointed out that the Casablanca conference (one of the many multilateral conferences that fell under the umbrella of the Oslo process) brought Arabs and Jews together to discuss such regionwide issues as terrorism and water resources. In addition, Oslo resulted in what Lustick calls "the new wel-

coming attitude displayed toward the Jewish state by so many previously hostile countries, the end of the Arab boycott, and an economy booming at the prospect of an explosion in the access of Israeli businessmen to worldwide markets."

Third, the Oslo agreement can be considered a success because it established a regimented formula or process for reaching goals and surmounting obstacles. This arrangement is important because prior to the Oslo accords both sides accepted only the military answer to the whole vexing question of how to impose or force one side's beliefs or goals upon the other. The Oslo accords shattered the illusion that the military option was viable and instead replaced it with the understanding that a just and lasting peace can only be obtained through political means laid out in a series of formulaic meetings and agreements that were designed to build confidence between the sides that would replace the decades-old feelings of animosity and mistrust.

The Declaration of Principles (DOP) was merely the first in a long series of agreements. In September 1995 Israelis and Palestinians signed the Interim Agreement on the West Bank and the Gaza Strip (known as Oslo II), which facilitated the initial transfer of administrative control from the Israelis to the Palestinians. In January 1997 the Israelis and Palestinians signed the Hebron Protocol. In October 1998 the parties signed the Wye River Agreement. In September 1999 the Israelis and Palestinians signed the Sharm el-Sheikh Memorandum. These agreements represented the bulk of the interim phase, in which Israeli troops began to be redeployed away from Palestinian-controlled areas. The PA was also established and was allowed to administer many of the day-to-day aspects of government such as education, trash collection, and internal security.

The leaders from both sides also frequently met, and formal and informal meetings continued throughout the 1990s. In what seemed to be a last-ditch effort to consummate a final agreement, they also met at Camp David in July 2000. Peace took a back seat, however, to political rhetoric, saber rattling, and violence with the outbreak of the al-Aqsa *intifada* in September 2000, but both sides still met in Taba, Egypt, in January 2001 in an attempt to return to the confidence-building measures called for in the Oslo accords.

Oslo can be considered a success because, unlike earlier attempts that merely supported unilateralism, it established a series of confidence-building measures geared to produce a political response to the conflict. For example, the DOP established several Palestinian-Israeli committees, task forces, and organizations that dealt with economic cooperation, water, electricity, trade, education, culture, health, social welfare, taxation, and tourism as well as political and security issues. Furthermore, Oslo also outlined specific goals that included, but were not limited to, withdrawing Israeli troops from Gaza and Jericho (originally to begin on 13 December 1993 and to be completed on 13 April 1994); transferring to the PA control over education, culture, health, social welfare, direct taxation, and tourism in most of the Gaza Strip and Jericho; and holding general elections for the Palestinians.

For decades Israeli leaders, most infamously Golda Meir, refused to acknowledge even the existence of the Palestinians. Oslo reversed that obsolete Israeli policy and replaced it with one that tacitly accepted Palestinians as a reality. Moreover, Oslo relegated the standing positions of the Likud and Labor Parties to the political trashcan by accepting a centralized Israeli government with legislative, executive, and judicial powers as well as a strong police force and by accepting the idea that peace will come through negotiation, not through the use of U.S.-made rifles, tanks, and helicopter gunships. Israel also accepted the principle that the Occupied Territories (West Bank, Gaza Strip, and Golan Heights) must remain an integral whole. Likewise, Palestinian leaders reversed their positions on the use of violence and intrigue to win independence for their people when Arafat first renounced terrorism in 1988 upon the insistence of President Ronald Reagan and Secretary of State George Shultz. The Oslo accords were thus a logical springboard to end the conflict, violence, and de facto colonial apartheid through a political process that was hung on the coatrack of face-to-face negotiations.

Overall, the Oslo accords were indeed successful. First, they brought the two sides together as legitimate and recognized representatives of their respective peoples. By working outside the construct of the UN and out from under American pressures, Israelis and Palestinians were allowed to meet, discuss, and acknowledge that they both wanted to seek a political end to the seemingly untenable situation. This situation does not necessarily mean that the talks always produced desired effects, because it is not easy to erase from any group's collective memory decades of abuse, misery, fear, and death. It is, however, a beginning. Second, it reversed decades of relegating the other side to obscurity—not that Israel has ceased its neocolonial, apartheid-like control and suppression of the Palestinians, nor did it end armed attacks by Palestinian militants against Jewish civilian targets. It is, however, a step in the right direction, and thus it is a success. Third, the Oslo accords established a mutually agreed-upon formula for achieving a just and lasting peace. As of this writing the formula has not been abandoned, nor have the goals (peace between an Israeli and a Palestinian state with mutually recognized borders). The Oslo accords are about the process because it established a mechanism that for the first time produced benefits.

If the Oslo accords are to realize their ultimate goals, the people intimately involved must adhere to the process. Some leaders on both sides, however, are simply not committed to peace through negotiations. Instead, some are determined to returning to a darker time when bombs were used instead of accords, guns were used instead of discussions, and armed assaults were the way to advance an agenda. For example, Israeli prime minister Benjamin Netanyahu tried to show Israeli dominance and control over Jerusalem when he decided to open a tourist tunnel near the al-Aqsa mosque in October 1996, a move that resulted in extensive material damage, increased misery for all, and heavy casualties on both sides. He also planned to establish a new settlement (Har Homa) on disputed land (Jabal Abu-Ghneim). That act "triggered a complete halt to negotiations, indefinite postponement of an Israeli Army redeployment, and a wave of terrorist attacks inside Jewish Jerusalem and Tel-Aviv." Netanyahu even allowed Jewish extremists to seize control of a small strip of land (Ras el-Amud) that Beilin and Abbas had identified as the future site of the Palestinian capital. Netanyahu's actions should come as no surprise because he wanted to end the peace process. According to Susan Sachs, Middle East correspondent for *Newsday,* "he vowed to fight the autonomy agreement."

Similarly, Knesset member and former military commander Ariel Sharon called the Oslo accords "humiliating" and said that Arafat should be "tried as a war criminal." He even said that when the Likud Party was returned to power by Israel's voters, the Oslo accords would not be honored. When Sharon became prime minister in February 2001, he initiated what some observers saw as a vendetta war against Arafat. Whenever Hamas attacked Israeli civilians through suicide bombings, Sharon answered by striking against the PA, its police and security force, and Arafat's personal security. Interestingly enough, Sharon had the Israeli Army invade nearly every major West Bank city but did not attack any Hamas-controlled or Hamas-supported towns in the Gaza Strip until international pressure forced the Israeli leader to order a withdrawal. Of course, the first Palestinian suicide bombings did not commence until two months after Israeli settler Baruch Goldstein opened fire on a group of Muslims praying at a mosque in Hebron on 25 February 1994. According to Lustick, "Oslo . . . could not be opposed in principle, but rather sabotaged in implementation." Problems with the peace process are human inspired.

Jan Egeland, the secretary of state for Norway who mediated much of the secret negotiations that resulted in the Oslo accords, believes the process is a success because they allowed Palestinian and Israeli leaders to honestly discuss their goals without external pressures from the media and/or opposition groups. Also, what was discussed between Palestinian and Israeli leaders was done divorced from public pressures, public opinions, or emotions. Palestinians for the first time since Israel's establishment (1948) actually control parts of the West Bank and Gaza Strip, and "the third far-reaching implication, is that both sides probably have realized even as they engage militarily with each other that there is not a military solution for this conflict."

Secretary Christopher said that "the historic reconciliation between the Israelis and the Palestinians confirms our belief that hope can eventually replace despair, cooperation can overcome conflict, and peace and freedom can triumph over war and tyranny." The Oslo accords established a process in which Palestinians and Israelis can cooperate and achieve peace and freedom. As scholar Sharon Burde noted, "Leaders signed the agreement, but the populace must implement it. Attitudinal change is slow." There is no reason to throw the baby out with the bathwater.

–JIM ROSS-NAZZAL,
MONTGOMERY COLLEGE

Viewpoint:
No. The Oslo accords were a failure because they were based on a phased approach and did not properly establish a vision of a final peace.

After nearly three years of vicious fighting between Israel and the Palestinians that began in September 2000, it is easy to note that the Oslo peace process failed. No debate exists about that fact. The real question is why Oslo failed. Why did that process, which began full of promise with the famous handshake on the White House lawn between Israeli prime minister Yitzhak Rabin and Palestine Liberation Organization (PLO) chairman Yasser Arafat, end in blood and despair?

The answer lies in the very structure of the peace process. Oslo was about interim steps and confidence-building measures in the absence of a grand vision of the final outcome, of where the interim steps were going to lead. All of the really big, important issues were put off to a future date—one that never came. The vast imbalance of power between Israel and the Palestinians made Oslo's failure virtually inevitable.

Trouble in the Palestinian-Israeli peace process could have been predicted at the outset in 1991 because of the conditions under which both parties entered negotiations. Israel came to the Madrid conference at the apex of its power. Its peace with Egypt (1979), while never warm, had stood the test of time. The only other Arab power militarily capable of giving Israel trouble—Iraq—had just been pummeled in the Persian Gulf War (1990–1991). Not only was Israel the unsurpassed and unchallenged military power in the region, it was economically far ahead of its immediate neighbors, a gap that was only to grow wider. Indeed, throughout the peace process of the 1990s Israel had one of the fastest growing economies in the world, spurred by a dynamic high-tech sector.

The PLO, by contrast, entered the peace process at the low ebb of its history. It had foolishly backed Iraq during the Gulf War, thereby alienating many countries around the world. Included among the angered were Kuwait and Saudi Arabia, the PLO's two biggest financial patrons. Thus, the PLO was isolated politically and bankrupt financially when the peace process threw the organization a lifeline. The price of organizational survival for the PLO was to accept terms and conditions from Israel it had always rejected in the past.

It was the PLO's acceptance of far-reaching concessions in private talks in Norway that convinced Rabin in 1993 to accept Oslo in place of the stalled Washington talks that had followed the Madrid conference. Arafat was willing to accept an interim agreement as opposed to a comprehensive settlement, to accept Jerusalem's exclusion from the interim arrangements, and to leave the settlements and refugee issues to a later date. These far-reaching concessions came out of the PLO's weakness, and Rabin, the old warrior, wisely seized them. The very weakness of the PLO that led to such short-term advantage for Israel, however, also helped guarantee the ultimate failure of Oslo.

A peace process between two relative equals tends to bear fruit as both parties have a self-interest in making relatively equal concessions. Peace born of a relative balance of power tends to be stable as well. Not so for a peace process so badly tilted in favor of the much stronger party. When there is such a vast imbalance of power, then instability and breakdown generally result. The temptation for the hegemonic party

DECLARATION OF PRINCIPLES ON INTERIM SELF-GOVERNMENT ARRANGEMENTS

September 13, 1993

The Government of the State of Israel and the P.L.O. team (in the Jordanian-Palestinian delegation to the Middle East Peace Conference) (the "Palestinian Delegation"), representing the Palestinian people, agree that it is time to put an end to decades of confrontation and conflict, recognize their mutual legitimate and political rights, and strive to live in peaceful coexistence and mutual dignity and security and achieve a just, lasting and comprehensive peace settlement and historic reconciliation through the agreed political process. Accordingly, the two sides agree to the following principles:

ARTICLE I: AIM OF THE NEGOTIATIONS

The aim of the Israeli-Palestinian negotiations within the current Middle East peace process is, among other things, to establish a Palestinian Interim Self-Government Authority, the elected Council (the "Council"), for the Palestinian people in the West Bank and the Gaza Strip, for a transitional period not exceeding five years, leading to a permanent settlement based on Security Council Resolutions 242 and 338.

It is understood that the interim arrangements are an integral part of the whole peace process and that the negotiations on the permanent status will lead to the implementation of Security Council Resolutions 242 and 338.

ARTICLE II: FRAMEWORK FOR THE INTERIM PERIOD

The agreed framework for the interim period is set forth in this Declaration of Principles.

ARTICLE III: ELECTIONS

In order that the Palestinian people in the West Bank and Gaza Strip may govern themselves according to democratic principles, direct, free and general political elections will be held for the Council under agreed supervision and international observation, while the Palestinian police will ensure public order.

An agreement will be concluded on the exact mode and conditions of the elections in accordance with the protocol attached as Annex I, with the goal of holding the elections not later than nine months after the entry into force of this Declaration of Principles.

These elections will constitute a significant interim preparatory step toward the realization of the legitimate rights of the Palestinian people and their just requirements.

ARTICLE IV: JURISDICTION

Jurisdiction of the Council will cover West Bank and Gaza Strip territory, except for issues that will be negotiated in the permanent status negotiations. The two sides view the West Bank and the Gaza Strip as a single territorial unit, whose integrity will be preserved during the interim period.

ARTICLE V: TRANSITIONAL PERIOD AND PERMANENT STATUS NEGOTIATIONS

The five-year transitional period will begin upon the withdrawal from the Gaza Strip and Jericho area. Permanent status negotiations will commence as soon as possible, but not later than the beginning of the third year of the interim period, between the Government of Israel and the Palestinian people's representatives.

It is understood that these negotiations shall cover remaining issues, including: Jerusalem, refugees, settlements, security arrangements, borders, relations and cooperation with other neighbors, and other issues of common interest.

The two parties agree that the outcome of the permanent status negotiations should not be prejudiced or preempted by agreements reached for the interim period.

ARTICLE VI: PREPARATORY TRANSFER OF POWERS AND RESPONSIBILITIES

Upon the entry into force of this Declaration of Principles and the withdrawal from the Gaza Strip and the Jericho area, a transfer of authority from the Israeli military government and its Civil Administration to the authorized Palestinians for this task, as detailed herein, will commence. This transfer of authority will be of a preparatory nature until the inauguration of the Council.

Immediately after the entry into force of this Declaration of Principles and the withdrawal from the Gaza Strip and Jericho area, with the view to promoting economic development in the West Bank and Gaza Strip, authority will be transferred to the Palestinians on the following spheres: education and culture, health, social welfare, direct taxation, and tourism. The Palestinian side will commence in building the Palestinian police force, as agreed upon. Pending the inauguration of the Council, the two parties may negotiate the transfer of additional powers and responsibilities, as agreed upon.

ARTICLE VII: INTERIM AGREEMENT

The Israeli and Palestinian delegations will negotiate an agreement on the interim period (the "Interim Agreement"). The Interim Agreement shall specify, among other things, the structure of the Council, the number of its members, and the transfer of powers and responsibilities from the Israeli military government and its Civil Administration to the Council. The Interim Agreement shall also specify the Council's executive authority, legislative authority in accordance with Article IX below, and the independent Palestinian judicial organs.

The Interim Agreement shall include arrangements, to be implemented upon the inauguration of the Council, for the assumption by the Council of all of the powers and responsibilities transferred previously in accordance with Article VI above.

In order to enable the Council to promote economic growth, upon its inauguration, the Council will establish, among other things, a Palestinian Electricity Authority, a Gaza Sea Port Authority, a Palestinian Development Bank, a Palestinian Export Promotion Board, a Palestinian Environmental Authority, a Palestinian Land Authority and a Palestinian Water Administration Authority, and any other Authorities agreed upon, in accordance with the Interim Agreement that will specify their powers and responsibilities.

After the inauguration of the Council, the Civil Administration will be dissolved, and the Israeli military government will be withdrawn.

ARTICLE VIII: PUBLIC ORDER AND SECURITY

In order to guarantee public order and internal security for the Palestinians of the West Bank and the Gaza Strip, the Council will establish a strong police force, while Israel will continue to carry the responsibility for defending against external threats, as well as the responsibility for overall security of Israelis for the purpose of safeguarding their internal security and public order.

ARTICLE IX: LAWS AND MILITARY ORDERS

The Council will be empowered to legislate, in accordance with the Interim Agreement, within all authorities transferred to it.

Both parties will review jointly laws and military orders presently in force in remaining spheres.

ARTICLE X: JOINT ISRAELI-PALESTINIAN LIAISON COMMITTEE

In order to provide for a smooth implementation of this Declaration of Principles and any subsequent agreements pertaining to the interim period, upon the entry into force of this Declaration of Principles, a Joint Israeli-Palestinian Liaison Committee will be established in order to deal with issues requiring coordination, other issues of common interest, and disputes.

ARTICLE XI: ISRAELI-PALESTINIAN COOPERATION IN ECONOMIC FIELDS

Recognizing the mutual benefit of cooperation in promoting the development of the West Bank, the Gaza Strip and Israel, upon the entry into force of this Declaration of Principles, an Israeli-Palestinian Economic Cooperation Committee will be established in order to develop and implement in a cooperative manner the programs identified in the protocols attached as Annex III and Annex IV.

ARTICLE XII: LIAISON AND COOPERATION WITH JORDAN AND EGYPT

The two parties will invite the Governments of Jordan and Egypt to participate in establishing further liaison and cooperation arrangements between the Government of Israel and the Palestinian representatives, on the one hand, and the Governments of Jordan and Egypt, on the other hand, to promote cooperation between them. These arrangements will include the constitution of a Continuing Committee that will decide by agreement on the modalities of admission of persons displaced from the West Bank and Gaza Strip in 1967, together with necessary measures to prevent disruption and disorder. Other matters of common concern will be dealt with by this Committee.

ARTICLE XIII: REDEPLOYMENT OF ISRAELI FORCES

After the entry into force of this Declaration of Principles, and not later than the eve of elections for the Council, a redeployment of Israeli military forces in the West Bank and the Gaza Strip will take place, in addition to withdrawal of Israeli forces carried out in accordance with Article XIV.

In redeploying its military forces, Israel will be guided by the principle that its military forces should be redeployed outside populated areas.

Further redeployments to specified locations will be gradually implemented commensurate with the assumption of responsibility for public order and internal security by the Palestinian police force pursuant to Article VIII above.

ARTICLE XIV: ISRAELI WITHDRAWAL FROM THE GAZA STRIP AND JERICHO AREA

Israel will withdraw from the Gaza Strip and Jericho area, as detailed in the protocol attached as Annex II.

ARTICLE XV: RESOLUTION OF DISPUTES

Disputes arising out of the application or interpretation of this Declaration of Principles, or any subsequent agreements pertaining to the interim period, shall be resolved by negotiations through the Joint Liaison Committee to be established pursuant to Article X above.

Disputes which cannot be settled by negotiations may be resolved by a mechanism of conciliation to be agreed upon by the parties.

The parties may agree to submit to arbitration disputes relating to the interim period, which cannot be settled through conciliation. To this end, upon the agreement of both parties, the parties will establish an Arbitration Committee.

ARTICLE XVI: ISRAELI-PALESTINIAN COOPERATION CONCERNING REGIONAL PROGRAMS

Both parties view the multilateral working groups as an appropriate instrument for promoting a "Marshall Plan," the regional programs and other programs, including special programs for the West Bank and Gaza Strip, as indicated in the protocol attached as Annex IV.

ARTICLE XVII: MISCELLANEOUS PROVISIONS

This Declaration of Principles will enter into force one month after its signing.

All protocols annexed to this Declaration of Principles and Agreed Minutes pertaining thereto shall be regarded as an integral part hereof.

Done at Washington, D.C., this thirteenth day of September, 1993.
For the Government of Israel
For the P.L.O.

Witnessed By:

The United States of America
The Russian Federation of Principles

Source: *"Declaration of Principles on Interim Self-government Arrangements, September 13, 1993," Israeli Ministry of Foreign Affairs <http:// www.mfa.gov.il/mfa/go.asp?MFAH00q00>.*

OSLO ACCORDS

to dictate terms is too great under such circumstances, and the resulting resentment and rage in the weaker party are too powerful to lead to a healthy peace.

The one-sidedness of the Oslo peace process was evident in all the major issues. First, there was the issue of a comprehensive settlement versus an interim settlement. The PLO (and the Arab world) had argued for years that a settlement with Israel should be comprehensive and immediate and not be characterized by a piecemeal approach. A comprehensive settlement of the Arab-Israeli conflict would, of course, maximize Arab leverage in the negotiations. It was on this basis that Arabs chastised other Arabs for making a "separate peace" with Israel. Only Egypt dared to cut its own deal with Israel, and it suffered years of isolation within the Arab world as a result.

The PLO in particular had strong reasons to maintain the Arab consensus for a comprehensive, not piecemeal, settlement with Israel. As the weakest of all Arab parties, the PLO had the most to lose by going it alone and forfeiting the leverage of a united Arab negotiating front. Palestinians historically had rejected the concept of an "interim approach" as little more than an Israeli trick to get all of the political advantages of reaching a settlement with the Palestinians without actually having to make significant concessions. What is more, the PLO knew that signing any separate agreement with Israel would open the door for other Arab countries to make their own peace deals. Of course, this situation is exactly what happened with Jordan, which could not politically "go first" with Israel—it had to have political cover from the PLO. Oslo gave Jordan the justification it needed to make that peace with Israel in 1994.

Israel, on the other hand, had always resisted a comprehensive settlement to the Arab-Israeli conflict. Israel preferred to engage in a series of separate peace treaties. From Israel's perspective this policy made good sense as it maximized its leverage against any one Arab country. Facing a united Arab front in peace negotiations would minimize Israel's leverage and result, it was believed, in a less-than-optimal peace agreement. Israel's strong preference was for a bilateral, not multilateral, approach to peacemaking.

Israel won a significant victory when Arafat agreed to enter into peace negotiations with Israel based entirely on an interim five-year agreement. None of the big issues was to be discussed for three years, and there was no road map or statement of principles about where the interim agreement was supposed to lead. Contrary to some popular perceptions, the Oslo accords did not promise Palestinians that an independent state in the West Bank and Gaza would come into being after the interim period ended. Indeed, not having an agreed-upon end goal was the major shortcoming of Oslo.

Israel's power and the PLO's weakness gave Israel a major victory in that its preference for an interim-only, bilateral (or separate) agreement with the Palestinians was fully realized. The PLO's only real leverage was lost as result. Israel could now normalize relations with other Arab states without actually having to make major, permanent concessions to the Palestinians. The major "final status" issues were put off for three years on paper (longer in reality). Four of the delayed final-status issues deserve special mention: Jerusalem, settlements, refugees, and borders. On each issue Israel's power won out over Palestine's justice.

Oslo dictated that the final status of Jerusalem would be resolved later, but no later than 1999 (in other words, five years after the establishment of the PA in the Gaza-Jericho agreement of May 1994). Needless to say, this resolution did not happen. Throughout the interim period Israel maintained full control over all of Jerusalem, a city holy to Jews, Christians, and Muslims. Checkpoints along the municipal boundaries of Jerusalem prevented most Palestinians from entering even Arab East Jerusalem. Jewish settlements in Palestinian neighborhoods of East Jerusalem continued unabated, including the enormous new settlement at Har Homa (a beautiful forested hilltop overlooking Bayt Sahur on land Palestinians call Jabal Abu Ghanim). In addition, Israel continued to compel Palestinians to leave East Jerusalem for the West Bank. During the peace process thousands of Palestinians lost their residency permits for Jerusalem in what was a clear attempt by Israel to administratively "cleanse" Jerusalem of as many Palestinians as possible.

Thus, while there was an Israeli promise to negotiate the future of Jerusalem at some point, the reality throughout the Oslo period was a tightening of Israeli control throughout the city. A weak and hapless Palestinian leadership could do little more than orally protest what Israeli power was changing on the ground in Jerusalem.

The issue for negotiation is not solely East Jerusalem, but all of Jerusalem. Because of the United Nations (UN) Partition Plan (1947), Jerusalem has always had a different status under international law than the surrounding lands. Because of the special status for the entirety of Jerusalem, few countries recognized Israel's claim of Jerusalem as its capital. Even Israel's closest international ally, the United States, does not recognize the Israeli claim and maintains its embassy in Tel Aviv. West Jerusalem is also to be negotiated—in theory—under Oslo. In addition to its special status under international law, Jerusalem has land ownership issues still to be negotiated. Specifically, on the eve of the Arab-Israeli War (1947–1949), Jews only owned about 30 percent of the land in West Jerusalem. Palestinians privately owned about 40 percent of West Jerusalem's land, while public lands (church and mosque lands primarily) made up the other 30 percent. These ownership claims have never been abrogated by the Palestinians. However, Israel's ability to dictate the conditions on the ground meant that Oslo only solidified Israel's control over Jerusalem and was not a viable process to reach a negotiated solution over Jerusalem.

Likewise, Oslo excluded from negotiation discussion of the illegal Jewish settlements built in the Occupied Territories (West Bank, Gaza Strip, and Golan Heights), excluding East Jerusalem. Settlements were not to be addressed until the final-status issues were sorted out. This exclusion once again reflected Israel's wish and power. It is also the single most important issue that soured Palestinians on the peace process. While leaders at international conferences were talking about making peace, most Palestinians saw a different reality on the ground: continuous land confiscations and settlement building. Indeed, settlements doubled in size over the course of the 1990s, from about 120,000 settlers when Rabin and Arafat had their famous handshake in 1993 to about 240,000 by 2003. All but about 7,000 settlers live in the West Bank.

Land confiscations and settlement building in a time of supposed peace were not limited to the housing structures alone. During this same period Palestinian land was also confiscated to build hundreds of kilometers of "bypass roads" that linked settlements to each other and to Israel, while bypassing Palestinian communities.

There is no real debate that the settlements are illegal under international law. The Fourth Geneva Convention (1949) is clear in prohibiting an occupying power from transferring its own civilian population to an occupied territory (as well as prohibiting a transfer of an indigenous population to outside the occupied territory). Periodic UN resolutions have reaffirmed the illegality of the settlements, with U.S. concurrence. Thus, it would have been relatively easy to freeze all settlement activity at the outset of Oslo. Again, the hegemonic nature of Oslo trumped legality and good sense. By ignoring, at Israel's insistence, the crucial issues of continued settlements and land confiscations, the Oslo process dug its own grave.

There are nearly four million Palestinian refugees registered with the UN living primarily in Jordan, Syria, Lebanon, and the West Bank/Gaza. Registered refugees are those Palestinians

and their descendants made homeless by the 1947–1949 war. In addition, there are hundreds of thousands of Palestinians who are considered "displaced persons" from the 1967 Arab-Israeli War. Not all Palestinians are registered refugees; indeed, a little less than half of the total Palestinian population of more than eight million are defined as refugees. The total world population of Palestinians is split evenly between Palestinians living in historic Palestine (Israel, West Bank, and Gaza Strip) and those living outside.

The refugee issue is the most important emotional and symbolic issue for Israelis and Palestinians. For Israelis the thought of allowing Palestinians to return to their homes in what is now Israel represents a threat to the existence of the Jewish state. Conversely, the Palestinian national story revolves around the injustice inflicted upon them in 1948. For Israelis the creation of the Palestinian refugee crisis should be blamed on the Arabs for fighting against Israel's independence. For Palestinians 1948 represents nothing less than the ethnic cleansing of almost an entire native population by Israel. Oslo put off discussion of the refugee issue until final-status negotiations. During the Oslo peace process no Palestinian was allowed to return to his or her home in Israel, and only a relative handful were allowed to return to the West Bank and Gaza.

For those who participated in Oslo, the use of the term *borders* as another final-status issue was something of a code word for Palestinian statehood. After all, if there was to be a border between Israel and Palestinian lands, did not that presuppose that a Palestinian state would be on the other side of that border? Too bad the Oslo framers could not have been more frank and open about where the process should be leading.

Borders meant more than possible statehood for Palestinians, however. It meant that the "green line" of 1967 was only to be a starting point for discussions of final borders. In other words, it opened the door to what eventually happened at the Camp David talks in July 2000: an Israeli gambit to annex parts of the West Bank that contained many illegal settlements. In addition, Israel planned to annex much of East Jerusalem and its environs as part of a final agreement, moving the border further eastward, northward, and southward.

The piecemeal and hegemonic nature of the Oslo process only alienated the Palestinians. Their reality on the ground was made worse under Oslo, not better. Not only was more and more land confiscated for settlements, but the remaining land was cut up into a jigsaw puzzle of control. Palestinians controlled small pockets of land, surrounded by much larger Israeli areas of control. At the high-water mark the PA controlled less than 20 percent of the West Bank, while Israel had full control of 60 percent of the West Bank; the remainder was jointly shared. Checkpoints arose everywhere as boundaries between these pockets of control were nearly infinite. The result was to effectively imprison most Palestinians in their own towns or villages.

While Oslo called for three subsequent Israeli withdrawals that would leave Palestinians with all of the West Bank and Gaza save settlements and Israeli military bases (in other words, Palestinians should have had control of about 85 percent of the West Bank and Gaza heading into the final-status negotiations), it never happened. In Oslo there were no consequences for parties failing to meet their commitments.

In sum, the interim and piecemeal nature of Oslo allowed for Israeli power to be expressed in many small ways. As a rational actor Israel naturally sought to maximize its advantage every step of the way. Given its vast edge in power, it could do so successfully. By making sure that each small tree was cut to its advantage, Israel ensured that the forest of possible peace was lost. The take-home lesson from Oslo's failure, however, is not to blame one party or the other. While certainly mistakes were made, in general each side acted rationally given its set of circumstances. Rather, the take-home lesson is that a peace process between two unequals cannot be piecemeal and devoid of a vision of a final peace. If it is, the power imbalance will be expressed throughout the process, alienating the weaker party and leading to failure. Locking in up front a grand vision of a just peace will tend to mitigate the logic and seduction of the use of power. The year 1993 represented a moment in history when such a grand vision could have been expressed and the Arab-Israeli conflict could have been settled. It was one of many missed opportunities in history.

–GLENN E. ROBINSON,
NAVAL POSTGRADUATE SCHOOL

References

George T. Abed, *The Economic Viability of a Palestinian State* (Washington, D.C.: Institute for Palestine Studies, 1990).

Ran Greenstein, *Geneologies of Conflict: Class, Identity, and State in Palestine/Israel and South Africa* (Hanover, N.H.: University Press of New England, 1995).

Muhammad Y. Muslih, *The Origins of Palestinian Nationalism* (New York: Columbia University Press, 1988).

William B. Quandt, *Peace Process: American Diplomacy and the Arab-Israeli Conflict since 1967,* revised edition (Berkeley: University of California Press, 2001).

Bernard Reich, ed., *Arab-Israeli Conflict and Conciliation* (Westport, Conn.: Praeger, 1995).

Glenn E. Robinson, *Building a Palestinian State: The Incomplete Revolution* (Bloomington: University of Indiana Press, 1997).

Edward W. Said, *The Politics of Dispossession* (New York: Pantheon, 1994).

OSLO ACCORDS

PALESTINE LIBERATION ORGANIZATION

Has the Palestine Liberation Organization been an effective representative of the Palestinian people?

Viewpoint: Yes. The PLO has been and is a legitimate, necessary, and largely successful representative of the Palestinian people that has gone far beyond its original mandate.

Viewpoint: No. The PLO was hastily formed, and it is inherently incapable of decisive action because of its splintered development and vulnerability to external influence.

The Palestine Liberation Organization (PLO) was formed by the League of Arab States during its January 1964 summit meeting in Cairo, Egypt. The new organization was created ostensibly to represent the Palestinian people and work for "the liberation of Palestine." It has often been said, however, that Egyptian president Gamal Abd al-Nasser acquiesced to the formation of the PLO in order to better control the actions of various Palestinian groups toward Israel. As such, Nasser could prevent the Palestinians from embroiling him in a war with Israel before the Arab world was ready; in addition, the creation of the PLO deflected criticism from Syria and other Arab countries that thought he was not doing enough to counter Israel, especially as Tel Aviv neared completion of its diversion of the headwaters of the Jordan River.

Ahmad al-Shuqayri was chosen as head of the PLO, although he was considered at the time to be an acolyte of Nasser who would establish nothing more than a facade of activism. As time passed, the PLO began to resemble the Palestinian diaspora; in other words, it was composed of several factions that tended to represent the views of their constituents and, more importantly, their benefactors—the countries where particular factions were allowed to reside and operate. Many would view this increasing fragmentation as both a strength and a weakness for the PLO as a whole, in that it would be difficult to eliminate it with one bold stroke, yet it would be equally difficult for the various factions to agree on policies proposed and/or enacted by the Palestine National Council (PNC), the Palestinian parliament in exile. The faction known as al-Fatah became the dominant element within the PLO, exemplified by the selection of its leader, Yasser Arafat, to become PLO chairman in 1969, a post he has held ever since. It was also during this time that the PLO inaugurated a more aggressive policy against Israel, launching what it called a "war of liberation" through sustained guerrilla activity.

In 1974, at an Arab League summit meeting in Rabat, Morocco, the PLO was declared the sole legitimate representative of the Palestinian people, giving the organization more regional leverage and international legitimacy. Since that time, in reaction to events in the Middle East as they transpired, it has wavered between political and military responses to achieve its often changing objectives. By the late 1980s it officially accepted the idea of a two-state solution to the Israeli-Palestinian problem, in other words, a Palestinian state, alongside Israel, presumably encompassing the Gaza Strip, the West Bank, and East Jerusalem (as its capital), a scenario that since then has been debated, negotiated, argued, and fought over, but not yet consummated.

Viewpoint:
Yes. The PLO has been and is a legitimate, necessary, and largely successful representative of the Palestinian people that has gone far beyond its original mandate.

To make the case that the Palestine Liberation Organization (PLO) has been a legitimate, necessary, and largely successful representative of the Palestinian people that has gone far beyond its original mandate requires that one qualify some key points. The first point is simply a matter of approach. Given that the seventh Arab Summit Conference at Rabat declared the PLO to be the "sole legitimate representative of the Palestinian people" on 28 October 1974, the Palestinians themselves should serve as the standard by which to evaluate the legitimacy, necessity, and success of the PLO's representation. That judgment should not be left to the capriciousness of other governments. Another point that requires clarification, particularly in the case of the Palestinians, is one's conceptualization of the term *representation*. For the PLO to act as a representative body, it must have a constituency. Given the fact that the Palestinians are dispersed as a population and do not reside within the formal boundaries of a Palestinian state, the representative role of the PLO takes on a different meaning than that traditionally associated with Western ideals of constituent representation. Palestinians reside in diverse geographic locations and exist under a variety of political circumstances, not all of which are wholly democratic. They live under Israeli military occupation and reside in refugee camps in the Occupied Territories (West Bank, Gaza Strip, and Golan Heights) and in neighboring states. They are essentially exiles. Consequently, it is not feasible for all Palestinians to exercise a procedural right as individual constituents and legitimize their choice of representation in an electoral manner, especially one that would capture the range of Palestinian viewpoints regarding the effectiveness of the PLO's representative role.

As an umbrella organization, the PLO has been responsible for representing all Palestinians in its endeavors at securing an independent homeland. Theoretically, that representation is embodied in the Palestine National Council (PNC), which is the highest policy-making body within the PLO and performs the legislative functions of a semiparliament that defines the PLO's official policies and guidelines. However, in the post-Oslo accords period that began after 1993, the PNC has convened only once. In 1996 the twenty-first PNC met in an extraordinary session in late April in the Gaza Strip, ostensibly to abrogate the sections of the PLO National Charter deemed as contrary to the exchange of letters between the PLO and the State of Israel that were signed on 13 September 1993.

Moreover, in the years following this last session, the PLO's inability to secure a viable Palestinian state and its neglect of constituent groups beyond the territorial reach of the Palestinian Authority (PA) has led to open challenges of the PLO's legitimacy by groups such as Hamas (Islamic Resistance Movement). Additionally, the ideological divisions among the PLO's rank-and-file secular groups, and their characteristic policy of boycotting participation in political institutions as an anti-peace-process tactic, further reduced the organization's ability to speak with a united representative voice. Even though the PLO's net gains are both challenged and arguable, that alone does not make it irrelevant or any less legitimate. What might be perceived as largely a function of semantics, Article 2 of the Rabat Resolution does "affirm the right of the Palestinian people to establish an independent national authority under the command of the PLO, the sole legitimate representative of the Palestinian people in any Palestinian territory that is liberated." In essence, the PLO still remains the legitimate representative of all the Palestinian people alongside the PA, which was established as the governing body to administer those areas of the West Bank and Gaza over which the Palestinians were permitted to exercise some autonomy. In practice, however, the PLO's legitimacy has exceeded its mandate partly because it has abrogated decision-making functions regarding the fate of all Palestinians to the institutional structures of the PA, which includes the Palestine Legislative Council (PLC), wholly at the expense of the PNC. The PLC's constituency resides in the Occupied Territories and functions as an electoral constituency. This constituency lives under the harsh realities of Israel's occupation, its expansive settlement building on Palestinian land, and its severe military retaliation aimed at crushing Palestinian aspirations for an end to the occupation. Further complicating the issue is the fact that Yasser Arafat still retains his position as chairman of the Executive Committee of the PLO, and he is also the elected president of the PA. Although the PNC has often acted as a rubber stamp for the policies of the chairman, it still remains a structural organ of the PLO that could reverse the current trend and restore the legitimacy of the PLO's representative role. However, such a feat would require a change of leadership at the top along with a substantial commitment to legislative reform and some means of democratic representation to ensure a full range of Palestinian political participation. To that end it is necessary to examine a few key PNC sessions that highlight the changing relationship between the PNC and the PLO leadership at particular points in the organization's history.

The PLO was formed in 1964 when a congress of 422 Palestinian representatives assembled in East Jerusalem for what became the first meeting of the PNC. At this meeting, delegates of Diaspora Palestinian groups proclaimed the liberation of Palestine as their primary objective. They also adopted two documents that hereafter formed the core of future PLO policy—the Palestine National Charter and the Basic Law. The Charter embodies the more substantive elements of PLO actions in that it contains the ideological manifesto of Palestinian beliefs. The Basic Law is more procedural in that it prescribes the legalistic framework within which the PLO functions. Over the years the PLO has restructured its political composition by annulling or amending articles in the Basic Law to allow for changes that included the expansion of the PNC and the creation of the Central Council (CC) to serve as an intermediary body between the PNC and the Executive Committee.

Unlike the Basic Law, the PNC has amended the National Charter only once since the founding of the PLO, which occurred at the fourth PNC (1968) in which the guerrilla organizations participated for the first time and drew up seven new articles that formed the core of the new National Charter that, inter alia, proclaimed the primacy of armed struggle, the total liberation of Palestine, and the identification of Israel as the enemy of the Palestinian people. The fourth PNC is also historic because it produced the Constitution of the PLO on 17 July 1968, which defines the relationship among the various organs of the PLO. Article 8 specifies that the PNC is the supreme authority of the PLO and that under certain circumstances it has the power to convene itself, while Article 32 specifies that "the National Assembly alone is entitled to co-opt new members." It has the power to create or

abolish any institution of the PLO, and it also elects the members who serve on the Executive Committee and the CC. Nevertheless, the PNC can only function if it is in session. In terms of its physical size, the PNC is somewhat elastic because membership is supposed to depend on the proportional representation of all Palestinians dispersed throughout the international community. Despite the formality of a constitution, over the years membership in the PNC has expanded at the behest of Arafat, who was elected chairman at the fifth PNC (1969).

At the eighth PNC (1971) in Cairo the non-Fatah guerrilla factions argued for a more equitable distribution of representation in the PNC. The proposed recommendation for reorganization was approved by the ninth PNC (1971) that met five months later, giving the guerrillas a total of 85 seats. However, the PNC also approved the Executive Committee's recommendation to add 41 seats for independent members with technical qualifications plus 25 more seats for members representing the unions, for a combined total of 151 seats. Additionally, the PNC approved a readjustment of leadership in the Executive Committee that enabled Fatah to secure a majority of votes in this executive body.

Initially, the PLO limited its involvement in the Occupied Territories to the dissemination of rhetorical support for Palestinian steadfastness under military occupation. By 1970 nationalist segments of the West Bank population searched for ways to give public character to their protest against the occupation in response to Israel's prohibition of any form of political mobilization. This quest led to the formation of organizations such as the Supreme Muslim Council and the Committee for National Unity, to institutionalize West Bank protest activities. Yet, these organizations clashed with the veteran West Bank traditional elite, who searched for ways to cooperate with the Israelis on practical matters. During this time the West Bank traditional elite attached themselves to the PLO for instrumental purposes only. In exchange for recognizing the PLO as their official spokesman regarding West Bank political aspirations, the PLO provided the traditional elite with a reason to exercise passive resistance rather than overt acts of civil disobedience that threatened their status. In late 1971 the Israeli government announced its plan to hold West Bank municipal elections in the spring of 1972 in the hopes that a more cooperative group of mayors and council members would be elected. The PLO's immediate reaction was to reject the call for elections fearing that they could result in the installment of nationalist candidates willing to accept a terri-

THE PALESTINIAN NATIONAL CHARTER

Resolutions of the Palestine National Council, July 1–17, 1968

Text of the Charter:

Article 1: Palestine is the homeland of the Arab Palestinian people; it is an indivisible part of the Arab homeland, and the Palestinian people are an integral part of the Arab nation.

Article 2: Palestine, with the boundaries it had during the British Mandate, is an indivisible territorial unit.

Article 3: The Palestinian Arab people possess the legal right to their homeland and have the right to determine their destiny after achieving the liberation of their country in accordance with their wishes and entirely of their own accord and will.

Article 4: The Palestinian identity is a genuine, essential, and inherent characteristic; it is transmitted from parents to children. The Zionist occupation and the dispersal of the Palestinian Arab people, through the disasters which befell them, do not make them lose their Palestinian identity and their membership in the Palestinian community, nor do they negate them.

Article 5: The Palestinians are those Arab nationals who, until 1947, normally resided in Palestine regardless of whether they were evicted from it or have stayed there. Anyone born, after that date, of a Palestinian father—whether inside Palestine or outside it—is also a Palestinian.

Article 6: The Jews who had normally resided in Palestine until the beginning of the Zionist invasion will be considered Palestinians.

Article 7: That there is a Palestinian community and that it has material, spiritual, and historical connection with Palestine are indisputable facts. It is a national duty to bring up individual Palestinians in an Arab revolutionary manner. All means of information and education must be adopted in order to acquaint the Palestinian with his country in the most profound manner, both spiritual and material, that is possible. He must be prepared for the armed struggle and ready to sacrifice his wealth and his life in order to win back his homeland and bring about its liberation.

Article 8: The phase in their history, through which the Palestinian people are now living, is that of national *(watani)* struggle for the liberation of Palestine. Thus the conflicts among the Palestinian national forces are secondary, and should be ended for the sake of the basic conflict that exists between the forces of Zionism and of imperialism on the one hand, and the Palestinian Arab people on the other. On this basis the Palestinian masses, regardless of whether they are residing in the national homeland or in diaspora *(mahajir)* constitute—both their organizations and the individuals—one national front working for the retrieval of Palestine and its liberation through armed struggle.

Article 9: Armed struggle is the only way to liberate Palestine. Thus it is the overall strategy, not merely a tactical phase. The Palestinian Arab people assert their absolute determination and firm resolution to continue their armed struggle and to work for an armed popular revolution for the liberation of their country and their return to it. They also assert their right to normal life in Palestine and to exercise their right to self-determination and sovereignty over it.

Article 10: Commando action constitutes the nucleus of the Palestinian popular liberation war. This requires its escalation, comprehensiveness, and the mobilization of all the Palestinian popular and educational efforts and their organization and involvement in the armed Palestinian revolution. It also requires the achieving of unity for the national *(watani)* struggle among the different groupings of the Palestinian people, and between the Palestinian people and the Arab masses, so as to secure the continuation of the revolution, its escalation, and victory.

Article 11: The Palestinians will have three mottoes: national *(wataniyya)* unity, national *(qawmiyya)* mobilization, and liberation.

Article 12: The Palestinian people believe in Arab unity. In order to contribute their share toward the attainment of that objective, however, they must, at the present stage of their struggle, safeguard their Palestinian identity and develop their consciousness of that identity, and oppose any plan that may dissolve or impair it.

Article 13: Arab unity and the liberation of Palestine are two complementary objectives, the attainment of either of which facilitates the attainment of the other. Thus, Arab unity leads to the liberation of Palestine, the liberation of Palestine leads to Arab unity; and work toward the realization of one objective proceeds side by side with work toward the realization of the other.

Article 14: The destiny of the Arab nation, and indeed Arab existence itself, depend upon the destiny of the Palestine cause. From this interdependence springs the Arab nation's pursuit of, and striving for, the liberation of Palestine. The people of Palestine play the role of the vanguard in the realization of this sacred *(qawmi)* goal.

Article 15: The liberation of Palestine, from an Arab viewpoint, is a national *(qawmi)* duty and it attempts to repel the Zionist and imperialist aggression against the Arab homeland, and aims at the elimination of Zionism in Palestine. Absolute responsibility for this falls upon the Arab nation—peoples and governments—with the Arab people of Palestine in the vanguard. Accordingly, the Arab nation must mobilize all its military, human, moral, and spiritual capabilities to participate actively with the Palestinian people in the liberation of Palestine. It must, particularly in the phase of the armed Palestinian revolution, offer and furnish the Palestinian people with all possible help, and material and human support, and make available to them the means and opportunities that will enable them to continue to carry out their leading role in the armed revolution, until they liberate their homeland.

Article 16: The liberation of Palestine, from a spiritual point of view, will provide the Holy Land with an atmosphere of safety and tranquility, which in turn will safeguard the country's religious sanctuaries and guarantee freedom of worship and of visit to all, without discrimination of race, color, language, or religion. Accordingly, the people of Palestine look to all spiritual forces in the world for support.

Article 17: The liberation of Palestine, from a human point of view, will restore to the Palestinian individual his dignity, pride, and freedom. Accordingly the Palestinian Arab people look forward to the support of all those who believe in the dignity of man and his freedom in the world.

Article 18: The liberation of Palestine, from an international point of view, is a defensive action necessitated by the demands of self-defense. Accordingly the Palestinian people, desirous as they are of the friendship of all people, look to freedom-loving, and peace-loving states for support in order to restore their legitimate rights in Palestine, to re-establish peace and security in the country, and to enable its people to exercise national sovereignty and freedom.

Article 19: The partition of Palestine in 1947 and the establishment of the state of Israel are entirely illegal, regardless of the passage of time, because they were contrary to the will of the Palestinian people and to their natural right in their homeland, and inconsistent with the principles embodied in the Charter of the United Nations, particularly the right to self-determination.

Article 20: The Balfour Declaration, the Mandate for Palestine, and everything that has been based upon them, are deemed null and void. Claims of historical or religious ties of Jews with Palestine are incompatible with the facts of history and the true conception of what constitutes statehood. Judaism, being a religion, is not an independent nationality. Nor do Jews constitute a single nation with an identity of its own; they are citizens of the states to which they belong.

Article 21: The Arab Palestinian people, expressing themselves by the armed Palestinian revolution, reject all solutions which are substitutes for the total liberation of Palestine and reject all proposals aiming at the liquidation of the Palestinian problem, or its internationalization.

Article 22: Zionism is a political movement organically associated with international imperialism and antagonistic to all action for liberation and to progressive movements in the world. It is racist and fanatic in its nature, aggressive, expansionist, and colonial in its aims, and fascist in its methods. Israel is the instrument of the Zionist movement, and geographical base for world imperialism placed strategically in the midst of the Arab homeland to combat the hopes of the Arab nation for liberation, unity, and progress. Israel is a constant source of threat vis-a-vis peace in the Middle East and the whole world. Since the liberation of Palestine will destroy the Zionist and imperialist presence and will contribute to the establishment of peace in the Middle East, the Palestinian people look for the support of all the progressive and peaceful forces and urge them all, irrespective of their affiliations and beliefs, to offer the Palestinian people all aid and support in their just struggle for the liberation of their homeland.

Article 23: The demand of security and peace, as well as the demand of right and justice, require all states to consider Zionism an illegitimate movement, to outlaw its existence, and to ban its operations, in order that friendly relations among peoples may be preserved, and the loyalty of citizens to their respective homelands safeguarded.

Article 24: The Palestinian people believe in the principles of justice, freedom, sovereignty, self-determination, human dignity, and in the right of all peoples to exercise them.

Article 25: For the realization of the goals of this Charter and its principles, the Palestine Liberation Organization will perform its role in the liberation of Palestine in accordance with the Constitution of this Organization.

Article 26: The Palestine Liberation Organization, representative of the Palestinian revolutionary forces, is responsible for the Palestinian Arab people's movement in its struggle—to retrieve its homeland, liberate and return to it and exercise the right to self-determination in it—in all military, political, and financial fields and also for whatever may be required by the Palestine case on the inter-Arab and international levels.

Article 27: The Palestine Liberation Organization shall cooperate with all Arab states, each according to its potentialities; and will adopt a neutral policy among them in the light of the requirements of the war of liberation; and on this basis it shall not interfere in the internal affairs of any Arab state.

Article 28: The Palestinian Arab people assert the genuineness and independence of their national *(wataniyya)* revolution and reject all forms of intervention, trusteeship, and subordination.

Article 29: The Palestinian people possess the fundamental and genuine legal right to liberate *and* retrieve their homeland. The Palestinian people determine their attitude toward all states and forces on the basis of the stands they adopt vis-a-vis to the Palestinian revolution to fulfill the aims of the Palestinian people.

Article 30: Fighters and carriers of arms in the war of liberation are the nucleus of the popular army which will be the protective force for the gains of the Palestinian Arab people.

Article 31: The Organization shall have a flag, an oath of allegiance, and an anthem. All this shall be decided upon in accordance with a special regulation.

Article 32: Regulations, which shall be known as the Constitution of the Palestinian Liberation Organization, shall be annexed to this Charter. It will lay down the manner in which the Organization, and its organs and institutions, shall be constituted; the respective competence of each; and the requirements of its obligation under the Charter.

Article 33: This Charter shall not be amended save by [vote of] a majority of two-thirds of the total membership of the National Congress of the Palestine Liberation Organization [taken] at a special session convened for that purpose.

Source: Leila S. Kadi, ed., Basic Political Documents of the Armed Palestinian Resistance Movement *(Beirut: Palestine Research Centre, 1969), pp. 137–141.*

torial solution short of total liberation. Additionally, the PLO leadership believed that elections threatened to create a local leadership that could challenge the PLO's claim to represent the Occupied Territories. Furthermore, on 15 March 1972 King Hussein of Jordan unveiled his United Arab Kingdom (UAK) plan, which was intended to halt the psychological disengagement by Palestinians of the West Bank from Jordan that began in September 1970 (as a result of the Jordanian Civil War, or Black September). Moreover, Hussein wanted to block any claim that might undermine Jordan's intent to represent the Palestinians and to regain the West Bank lost to Israel in the Arab-Israeli War of 1967. The PLO's reaction to the plan was vehement rejection.

To extricate itself from a situation in which the representational function of the PLO was being challenged, the PLO rallied around the theme of national unity. To foster that unity and legitimately assert its right to speak on behalf of the Palestinians, the PLO convened a Palestine People's Conference (PPC) in conjunction with the tenth meeting of the PNC in April 1972. Designed to create an impression of representation, the PLO leadership invited more than seven hundred Palestinians to participate in the PPC, of which approximately four hundred members attended. While the tenth PNC subsequently endorsed the PPC's recommendations, the Popular Front for the Liberation of Palestine (PFLP) and the Popular Democratic Front for the Liberation of Palestine (PDFLP) criticized Arafat for flooding the PPC with independents sympathetic to Fatah. This practice of flooding the PNC with loyal Arafat supporters persisted for years. The guerrillas' formation of the Rejection Front in 1974 and their boycott of subsequent PNC sessions over the direction in which Arafat was leading the PLO reduced the overall representative function of the organization.

The PLO leadership has also used membership in the PNC as a tactic to co-opt its opponents. In an attempt to break its diplomatic isolation following the Persian Gulf War (1990–1991), a meeting of the twentieth PNC (1991) convened to discuss the terms of Palestinian representation in the Madrid Peace Conference (1991). While Hamas was invited to attend a preparatory meeting in Tunis, they boycotted the meeting because they disagreed on the terms of membership in the PLO's legislative body. According to Hamas, representation in the PNC should be determined on the basis of elections and a system of patronage. Despite the Executive Committee's request to seek some form of accommodation with Hamas, Arafat could not accept their demands

for 40 percent of the PNC's seats as a precondition for participation. Consequently, the twentieth PNC convened in Algiers in September without the attendance of Hamas and many of the PLO's factions that opposed Palestinian participation in the peace process.

Despite the malapportionment of its representational makeup, throughout the late 1970s and 1980s, the PNC began to gradually endorse a more pragmatic solution to the Palestinian plight, and the PLO enjoyed the support of the Palestinian people. Following the Rabat declaration of October 1974, the United Nations (UN) granted the PLO observer status in November of the same year. In 1976 the Arab League accorded the organization full membership status, and by 1988 the PLO began to meet the conditions necessary for the beginning of dialogue with the United States following the nineteenth PNC's acceptance of UN Security Council Resolution 242 and its rejection of terrorism in all its forms. The task of achieving some measure of Palestinian statehood appeared on the horizon in September 1993 when the PLO and Israel signed the Declaration of Principles. However, since then, the necessity of the PLO, and more specifically the PNC, is conspicuously absent as a policy-making apparatus for securing a Palestinian homeland.

At the twenty-first PNC the delegates in attendance voted to annul several articles of the 1968 National Charter as a precondition for continuing the peace process with Israel. However, because no new charter has been presented to the PNC for its approval, the PLO is still functioning under the 1968 Charter despite Arafat's insistence that annulment alone should suffice and a gathering of the PNC is not needed. Although unlikely, should a Palestinian state emerge on any portion of West Bank territory in the near future, it will not serve as a state for all Palestinians nor will it reflect the achievements of the PLO. Rather, it will signify the political aspirations of Arafat, who can no longer claim to represent all Palestinians. Perhaps this sequence of events is what it will take to reconstitute the PLO as the legitimate, necessary, and representative organization for all the Palestinian people.

In conclusion, the PLO still remains the only legitimate and wholly representative organization of the Palestinian people. The excessive role of its leadership, which has steered the PLO beyond its mandate through its control over membership in the PNC and the contents of its resolutions, should not detract from its necessity.

–JOANN A. DIGEORGIO-LUTZ,
TEXAS A&M UNIVERSITY-COMMERCE

Viewpoint:
No. The PLO was hastily formed, and it is inherently incapable of decisive action because of its splintered development and vulnerability to external influence.

The Palestine Liberation Organization (PLO) was founded in Cairo in 1964 by the League of Arab States. Ahmad al-Shuqayri, a Palestinian lawyer, was chosen as its first chairman. He was generally considered a man of little substance who was controlled by Egyptian president Gamal Abd al-Nasser. Many believed that the new organization was designed to represent the interests of Egypt, not the interests of the Palestinian people. Nevertheless, the formation of the organization raised concerns in some quarters, especially Jordan. There, King Hussein ruled over a nation whose population was nearly 60 percent Palestinian. Hussein feared that the existence of the PLO might threaten his leadership. Hussein also controlled the West Bank and was concerned about the possible effects of PLO activity there.

Despite Hussein's fears, the PLO accomplished little during the first few years of its existence. This situation irritated the Syrians, who favored military action, and so they turned their support to a small organization known as al-Fatah, whose leaders were prepared to undertake offensive operations into Israel. Al-Fatah was formed sometime between 1959 and 1962, and it was led by a group of young Palestinians who had fled to Gaza when Israel was created. Among them was Yasser Arafat. They were dedicated to the proposition that the liberation of Palestine was of the utmost importance and could only be achieved by violent means. They were strongly influenced by the recent success of the Algerian revolt against France. Their strategy was to undertake operations to terrorize the Israeli population, which would arouse the Israeli military to action and, in turn, would bring about Arab unity to confront the threat. A united Arab world would then overpower Israel, and the result would be the liberation of Palestine.

As al-Fatah operations escalated after 1964 Israeli concerns were naturally aroused, and since most of the raids originated in Jordan, Hussein feared Israeli retaliations. Nasser also feared an outbreak of hostilities. He controlled the PLO but not al-Fatah. Only Syrian interests were served by these events because they were interested in toppling the Jordanian government. Thus, the world of Arab politics was dangerously fragmented, and the results contributed little to the welfare of the Palestinian people.

After the Arab-Israeli War of 1967 the situation in the region changed. The Israelis occupied the West Bank, and Hussein suspected that they intended to keep it. Thus, he became more interested in supporting Arafat and al-Fatah. At the same time, Arafat hoped to generate a revolt against Israeli occupation within the West Bank. His failure to instigate this revolution led to a marriage of convenience with Hussein, who now decided to permit military incursions into the West Bank from Jordan. Hussein hoped such actions would improve his standing with his Palestinian subjects and at the same time discourage Israel from retaining control of the land. The results were not what he expected.

Israel undertook retaliatory raids into Jordan, and al-Fatah began to take over the refugee camps in the country, thus removing them from Jordanian control. At the same time, however, splinter groups with leaders much more radical than Arafat began to fragment the resistance movement. Among these groups were the Popular Front for the Liberation of Palestine (PFLP) and the Popular Democratic Front for the Liberation of Palestine (PDFLP). The former was led by George Habash and the latter by Nayef Hawatmah. From this point on, factionalism became endemic in the Palestinian movement and has hampered its efforts ever since.

Late in 1967 Shuqayri was forced to resign as head of the PLO, and during a period of interim leadership it was decided to give the commando groups membership in the Palestinian National Council (PNC), the legislative branch of the PLO. Al-Fatah gained the most seats, and as a result Arafat was elected head of the PLO in 1969. He has retained power ever since, but he has never been able to thoroughly control all the factions.

From 1969 until 1974 Arafat's stated goal was the destruction of Israel. Thus, he rejected United Nations (UN) Security Council Resolution 242, the so-called land-for-peace resolution, which would have required the recognition of the right of Israel to exist. Hence, this period was marked by continual violence during which the Israelis became even more determined to protect themselves, while the Palestinians achieved only meager results.

Most of the events of this period were, in fact, damaging to the Palestinian cause. By 1970 the PLO had become so much like a state within a state in Jordan that Hussein had no alternative but to expel them by force. They moved their headquarters to Beirut, Lebanon. Meanwhile, splinter groups such as the PFLP, the PDFLP, and Black September continued their violent activities; but at the same time, sympathy for the rights of the Palestinian people to self-determination came to be more commonly recognized, and Palestinian nationalism emerged as a significant

new factor. The major question was whether or not Arafat and the PLO could effectively exploit these developments to the benefit of the people. In an effort to do so Arafat modified his position on the liberation of Palestine. The PLO Covenant called for armed struggle and many PLO resolutions called for the destruction of Israel, but in 1974 Arafat indicated a willingness to consider the creation of a Palestinian state in the West Bank and Gaza, thus taking a position that implied the continued existence of Israel. The splinter groups, of course, opposed this move and stepped up their terrorist actions. Arafat could not control them. Nevertheless, he was invited to address the UN General Assembly in November 1974. In a memorable speech he concluded by saying, "I have come bearing an olive branch and a freedom fighter's gun. Do not let the olive branch fall from my hand." The Israelis ignored this signal. Instead of looking for ways to open communications with the Palestinians, they stepped up the construction of settlements in the West Bank. Then, in 1977, when the Likud Party gained control of the government, its leader, Menachem Begin, made it clear that he had no intention of negotiating with the Palestinians on any issue whatsoever.

Under these conditions, terrorist attacks launched from Lebanon against Israel's northern region escalated and the Israelis responded. In 1978 and again in 1982 they launched invasions of Lebanon designed to crush the PLO. In the second attack Israeli forces drove north all the way to Beirut, and the PLO leadership was forced to flee—first to Syria, then for a short time back to northern Lebanon, and finally to Tunis. There Arafat and his inner circle remained for the next twelve years. By this time the PLO was badly weakened by dissension. Radicals blamed Arafat for the defeat in Lebanon and criticized him mercilessly with charges that he was more interested in diplomacy than war.

During the next few years conditions in the West Bank and Gaza deteriorated. By the mid 1980s an entire generation of Palestinians had grown up under Israeli occupation. Civil and human rights were curtailed, and the Palestinian economy was hostage to that of Israel. The people were disillusioned with the PLO and Arafat, who from their perspective had achieved nothing. Rage and frustration finally boiled over, and in December 1987 the first *intifada* (uprising) erupted.

Although Arafat had nothing to do directly with the outbreak of the *intifada,* he took credit for it and attempted to use it to his advantage. In July 1988 he authored a peace plan calling for the creation of a Palestinian state in the West Bank and Gaza, and in November he declared independence. He also formally rejected terrorism and accepted Resolution 242 as a basis for negotiation. Many nations granted diplomatic recognition to the PLO as the Palestinian government in exile, but Israel rejected Arafat's advances and so did Palestinian hard-liners.

In 1990 Iraq invaded Kuwait and the PLO made the monumental error of supporting the Iraqis. This move cost them credibility worldwide and also cost them considerable financial support from the Arab world. Nevertheless, the Persian Gulf War (1990–1991) led to the most sustained effort in history to bring peace to the Middle East through a resolution of the Palestinian question. This effort began with the Madrid Peace Conference (1991) that in turn led to the inauguration of bilateral and multilateral talks on Middle East issues, most notably the Israeli-Palestinian conflict. Although these talks led to a peace treaty between Israel and Jordan, they accomplished little else. Then the world was taken by surprise by the Oslo accords (1993) that were aimed, it appeared, at a final peace settlement. Thus began the so-called peace process. Unfortunately, it was a process that led not to peace but to disaster.

Under the original terms of the Oslo accords the PLO became the Palestinian National Authority (PNA) and was recognized as the government of Palestine. Israel transferred the Gaza Strip and the Jericho area in the West Bank to the Palestinians with the understanding that more land would be ceded later. Arafat and his entourage were allowed to return, and it was agreed that negotiations would proceed forthwith. It was also agreed that major issues such as settlements, refugees, the status of Jerusalem, and borders would be settled later, and by 1995 the existence of a Palestinian state would be recognized. Two major problems, however, posed obstacles to the success of this plan: the Israelis never intended for the peace process to be consummated, and the PNA played into their hands by squandering whatever advantage they had through incompetence and corruption in their efforts to govern. Arafat demonstrated that he had little administrative ability. Moreover, Arafat and his men failed to exert effective control over the various hard-line factions who did not want peace. The result was that the peace process dragged on with little success. Rage and frustration escalated, and at length the second, or al-Aqsa, *intifada* broke out in September 2000.

Since 2000 the possibility for an equitable peace has diminished. Israeli prime minister Ariel Sharon has been wary in his negotiations with Mahmoud Abbas, the first prime minister of the PA (elected in March 2003). As president of the PNA, Arafat has been unable to satisfy the needs of his people, control the various hard-line groups, such as Hizbollah (Party of God) and Hamas (Islamic Resistance Movement), or root out factionalism. Moreover, his administration has continued to be characterized by corruption and incompetence, he has made no effort to groom a successor, and he is known to be in ill health. The horrible truth is that, in Palestine, conditions have come full circle. The Palestinian people are no better off today than they were in 1947.

–KENNETH HENDRICKSON,
MIDWESTERN STATE UNIVERSITY

References

Jillian Becker, *The PLO: The Rise and Fall of the Palestine Liberation Organization* (New York: St. Martin's Press, 1984).

Helena Cobban, *The Palestine Liberation Organization: People, Power, and Politics* (Cambridge, U.K. & New York: Cambridge University Press, 1984).

Alain Gresh, *The PLO: The Struggle Within* (London: Zed, 1985).

David Makovsky, *Making Peace with the PLO: The Rabin Government's Road to the Oslo Accords* (Boulder, Colo.: Westview Press, 1996).

Shaul Mishal, *The PLO under Arafat: Between Gun and Olive Branch* (New Haven: Yale University Press, 1986).

William B. Quandt, Fuad Jabber, and Ann Mosely Lesch, *The Politics of Palestinian Nationalism* (Berkeley: University of California Press, 1973).

Barry Rubin, *Revolution until Victory? The Politics and History of the PLO* (Cambridge, Mass.: Harvard University Press, 1994).

Emile Sahliyeh, *In Search of Leadership: West Bank Politics* (Washington, D.C.: Brookings Institution, 1988).

Yezid Sayigh, "Struggle Within, Struggle Without: The Transformation of PLO Politics Since 1982," *International Affairs,* 65 (Fall 1989): 247–265.

Avraham Sela, *The PLO and Israel: From Armed Conflict to Political Solution, 1964–1994* (New York: St. Martin's Press, 1997).

PALESTINE LIBERATION ORGANIZATION

POINT FOUR PROGRAM

Did Harry S Truman's Point Four Program in the Middle East have a realistic chance of success?

Viewpoint: Yes. Point Four was a well-intended program that would have been successful in the Middle East if given the necessary support and time to develop.

Viewpoint: No. Point Four was a mismanaged and idealistic program that had little chance of succeeding amid the heightened tension of the Cold War and regional developments.

Following the end of World War II (1939–1945) and the onset of the Cold War with the Soviet Union, the United States attempted to promote stability in various regions so as not to allow communism to establish any more footholds. The Marshall Plan (1948) implemented in Europe became a linchpin of this overall development-based policy, in the process of promoting democratic, capitalist-based institutions that were synergistic with American political and economic interests. The Point Four Program (1950) of President Harry S Truman's administration (it was the fourth major point of Truman's inaugural address in 1949) was an attempt by the United States to broaden the Marshall Plan philosophy toward regions that would become the battleground of the emerging Cold War and would be loosely grouped together and termed the *Third World*. The Point Four Program was initiated to provide technical assistance to less-developed countries in an effort to prop them up economically in order to eliminate avenues for possible Soviet/communist influence. The Mutual Security Program, established by the Mutual Security Act (1951), similarly offered military and capital assistance and was an indication of the broadening needs and responsibilities of the Cold War.

The Point Four Program as applied in the Middle East essentially fizzled out by 1953, because it ran into many obstacles, such as Washington's role in the creation of, and its relationship with, Israel; indigenous regimes' fears of the domestic consequences of seemingly subordinating themselves to an external influence after having so recently jettisoned the last vestiges of European colonialism; the exigencies of the Cold War; and the typical bureaucratic and administrative problems of such an ambitious program. As the British Foreign Office concluded at the time, the program failed because the United States did not realize that it was "not possible with money and persuasion alone to bring a region in a short time to a stage of development at which American technical and administrative assistance is both palatable and capable of absorption by the national and social systems to which it is applied," and that the "long-run, indigenous developmental considerations were generally subordinated in U.S. aid policy to more immediate measures designed to insure the recipient against actual or anticipated Soviet influences."

Was the Point Four Program destined to fail in the manner it did? With time and better management could the well-intended program have succeeded? Or was it too much of an idealistic program that had little chance of success in practical terms considering the regional and international circumstances?

Viewpoint:
Yes. Point Four was a well-intended program that would have been successful in the Middle East if given the necessary support and time to develop.

The Point Four Program was the best example of the extent to which the U.S. executive and legislative powers could collaborate. According to Walter S. Salant, staff economist during the Truman administration, there were at least four versions of how the program originated: President Harry S Truman's, Clark M. Clifford's (the president's special adviser), State Department official Benjamin H. Hardy's, and Salant's own account. During a conversation in December 1948 with David D. Lloyd, an administrative assistant, Salant suggested that the United States should have given "aid to less developed countries on a continuing basis and that such aid should be devoted to a major role in our foreign policy."

"Point Four is not an aid program in the sense that the Marshall Plan and the Mutual Defense Program are. It is a plan to furnish 'know how' from our experience in the fabulous development of our own resources." This statement was Truman's definition of Point Four as it appeared in his autobiography, though Truman's memoirs seemed to merge the two essential components of technical assistance and capital. In his book *Present at the Creation: My Years in the State Department* (1969) Secretary of State Dean Acheson ascribed the origin of the program to Clifford. However, Clifford suggested that the foundation of Point Four was officially in a Department of State memorandum personally written by one of its officials, Hardy.

Hardy worked in the Office of Public Affairs as speechwriter and deputy to Acting Director Francis H. Russell. As Truman's White House Research Director Ken Hechler stated in his personal memoir of his White House years, Hardy's conception of U.S. foreign policy was "concentrated too heavily on wealthy and powerful leaders without helping the average people of other nations gain better lives for themselves." Both Robert A. Lovett, Undersecretary of State, and Paul H. Nitze, who headed the Policy Planning Staff, had rejected the plan twice—the first draft because of "relatively trivial administrative consideration" and the second "on the grounds that it was not timely." Hardy turned to Clifford and George M. Elsey, one of Truman's administrative aides. Both men were looking for a key topic for the president's inaugural address. In a short time a group of White House aides started promoting Hardy's idea: Lloyd and Charles S. Murphy,

administrative assistants, and David E. Bell, from the Budget Bureau.

Point Four was encompassed in the more complex Truman Doctrine policy of containment. In his address Truman, after having pointed out his administration's first three aims—support to and strengthening of the United Nations (UN) and related agencies, the continuous implementation of the Marshall Plan, and participation in the North Atlantic Treaty Organization (NATO)—stated that the United States had to "embark on a bold new program for making the benefits of our scientific advances and industrial progress available for the improvement and growth of underdeveloped areas."

The primary objective of Point Four was to make all underdeveloped countries self-sufficient by providing them with technical assistance in scientific and industrial areas. Once Truman introduced the final draft of the plan in his inaugural address (the American press dubbed it Point Four because of its location in the speech), it took him five months to ask Congress for Point Four legislation and an appropriation of $45 million for the first year of implementation. In May 1950 Congress passed the Point Four Program as the Act for International Development, and on 5 June it was signed into law by Truman. The new public law (PL 535) also established a Technical Cooperation Administration (TCA) within the Department of State whose goal was to administer the program. Congress authorized only $34.5 million for technical assistance, and by 6 September 1950 the appropriation decreased to $26.9 million. While Truman named Dr. Henry G. Bennett as first head of the TCA, Willard L. Thorp, Assistant Secretary of State for Economic Affairs, was appointed as the administrator responsible for developing the program.

As far as Truman was concerned it was important to win as many allies as possible in the Middle East, Africa, Asia, and Latin America. Supporting development in those countries represented a means of containing the Soviet Union in the Cold War and managing the decolonization process. By the end of March 1951 the U.S. government signed general agreements with twenty-two countries, and by the end of the year U.S. trainers and advisers worked in thirty-three countries. The deaths of Bennett and Hardy on 22 December 1951 in a plane crash had a devastating effect on the operations and spirit of the whole plan. Stanley Andrews, a former official in the Department of Agriculture, was named the new head of the TCA.

The application of an aid program such as Point Four to the Middle East came to the forefront of the Truman administration after the independence of Israel in May 1948. Considering the Tigris-Euphrates valley a modern Garden of Eden

U.S. president Harry S Truman (left) and the Shah of Iran at a state banquet in Washington, D.C., in 1949

(Photograph by Abbie Rowe)

and the future granary for the Near East, Truman dreamed of applying to the region one of his favorite models, the Tennessee Valley Authority (TVA). Though experts wanted Point Four appropriations to be used to obtain funds from the United Nations Relief and Work Agency for Palestine Refugees, Truman's administration pointed out that Point Four appropriations were not acceptable for that kind of investment. Thorp, talking with Egyptian ambassador Mohamed Kamil Abdul Rahim on 15 July 1949, underlined that Point Four "had been conceived as assistance in increasing the productivity of a country and thereby raising its standard of living."

A turning point in the program as far as the Arab states were concerned was the request advanced by Azzam Pasha, Secretary General of the Arab League, to provide Point Four aid to assist the League's socio-economic programs. Acheson made clear that "aid to [the] League would be in addition to Point 4 allotments to individual Arab States: [the] programs would operate simultaneously."

Reactions to Azzam Pasha's suggestion were diverse. On 4 December 1950 the American embassy in Cairo "advised that such aid would be most useful as a political gesture and might also stimulate the League's Economic Section which had been extremely weak." That same day the U.S. embassy in Tel Aviv stated that "political considerations made a program of this sort not desirable . . . the League was dedicated to perpetuating the antagonism between the Israelis and the Arabs

and to working against a peaceful settlement. . . . American funds would probably forestall the disintegration of the League . . . resuscitating the League in this way would contribute to instability in the area." While as far as the U.S. embassy in Jeddah, Saudi Arabia, was concerned, "the utilization of the Arab League as a vehicle for Point IV aid had a natural appeal," the American legation in Damascus "thought that current emphasis should be placed on constructive national plans, considering the limitations on available funds." On 15 December the American embassy in Baghdad quoted the opinion of the Undersecretary of the Iraqi Foreign Office, who said "better results would be achieved by allocating funds to individual governments."

In a subsequent telegram to diplomatic and consular offices in the Arab capitals and Tel Aviv, Acheson pointed out that the Department of State was considering the possibility of asking Congress for a $500 million grant-in-aid program for fiscal year 1952 "of which Asian states to receive greater proportion." Once again the administration had focused on "grass roots" projects.

At the end of 1950 the first agreement with Iran was negotiated and technical assistance contracts were entered into with Saudi Arabia, Israel, Jordan, Iraq, Egypt, Yemen, and Lebanon. Syria did not sign any agreement. Point Four projects put to an end the typhus epidemic in Iran and supplied Egypt with means of transport and technical personnel to transform millions of desert acres into tillable soil. Irrigation programs were introduced in Jordan, while a modern banking and monetary system was introduced in Saudi Arabia. When Truman left office in 1953, Point Four appropriations had reached the sum of $155.6 million. Notwithstanding this amount, as assessed by Howard M. Sachar in *A History of Israel: From the Rise of Zionism to Our Time* (1976), the program's goals were not fully carried out because of:

> Arabs' constant suspicion toward Israeli-American relations; the propaganda against American imperialism; the particular structure of the Arab society and rulers' wariness toward reforms for the poor; and overpopulation and water shortage.

With regard to the first problem, the Israeli-American relationship was beginning to become a special one. U.S. recognition of a Jewish state in Palestine was not a guarantee that the American government would have supported it under any circumstances. The Soviet Union had recognized Israel as well without provoking any panic in the Arab world, especially since the exigencies of the superpower Cold War had yet to push most Arab states toward Moscow. Moreover, one cannot ignore the general State Department attitude toward the idea of a Jewish state. Sachar points out that State Department officials "reflected a pro-Arab background and training, particularly those who had studied at the American University of Beirut and others who had accumulated years of consular or ministerial service in various Arab cities and capitals. Their acquaintance was limited for the most part to the Arab world and its mentality."

The propaganda against American imperialism could be expected; in fact, Sachar states that "American economic and strategic interests in the Middle East had grown dramatically since World War II." Air transport agreements with Egypt, Lebanon, and Syria on behalf of American airline companies and the U.S. ownership of approximately 42 percent of Middle Eastern oil supplies in Saudi Arabia, Kuwait, Bahrain, and Iraq could give nothing but the feeling that America was stretching its reach in the region too much. The Defense and State Departments, Sachar notes, together with the Joint Chiefs of Staff, "reminded Truman that access to Arab petroleum was a matter of critical national importance, one that would have to be evaluated in any governmental decision on the Palestine issue."

Finally, the total lack of social mobility had preserved the particular structure of Arab society and rulers' wariness toward reforms for the poor; the overpopulation problem compounded the situation. Sachar states that "The Arab hostility toward Israel could be defused, and the plight of the refugees mitigated, by an economic scheme that required the joint commitment of Arabs and Israelis alike." This economic scheme in the mind

of President Dwight D. Eisenhower's Secretary of State John Foster Dulles was a Jordan Valley Authority that would have permitted the exploitation and the allocation of waters of the Jordan River system among all the neighboring riparian states. Eric Johnston, the man chosen by Dulles to carry out this plan, only succeeded in working out an agreement that allocated to Israel 40 percent of the water and the rest of it to Jordan and Syria. The agreement remained only a tentative one, however, and was never implemented in full.

Truman's Point Four Program was well intended. First, U.S. involvement in two geopolitical and military organizations required as a counterpart American involvement in economic ones. The UN and NATO had been already counterbalanced by the Marshall Plan, but that plan exclusively focused on the reconstruction of Western Europe. What about world areas such as Latin America, Africa, the Middle East, and Asia? Second, the program was conceived above all as "one of teaching and demonstration and . . . it should attack such basic problems as hunger, illness, and illiteracy." Though regional circumstances limited its success, and though by 1953 TCA had merged into the military-oriented Mutual Security Agency (MSA), the spirit of technical assistance programs remained and influenced future assistance programs such as the Agency for International Development (AID, 1961), which has accomplished a tremendous amount during its history and generated a great deal of goodwill toward the United States.

—PAOLA OLIMPO,
UNIVERSITY OF LECCE

Viewpoint:
No. Point Four was a mismanaged and idealistic program that had little chance of succeeding amid the heightened tension of the Cold War and regional developments.

The Point Four Program was the first attempt by the United States at creating a global program to attack the root causes of "underdevelopment." The idea emerged from the fourth point of President Harry S Truman's inaugural address in 1949 in which he announced his intention of creating "a bold new program for making the benefits of our scientific advances and industrial progress available for the improvement and growth of underdeveloped areas." Embodied in the Act for International Development (AID, 1950) that called for the creation of the Technical Cooperation Agency (TCA), the

Point Four Program was established by the U.S. Congress on 5 June 1950. Despite the subsequent creation of the better-funded Mutual Security Agency (MSA) in 1951, which dwarfed the technical-assistance aspect of the U.S. overseas development initiative, the TCA remained an autonomous agency within the broader MSA umbrella throughout the 1950s. Dean Acheson, Secretary of State under Truman, referred to the Point Four Program in his memoirs as "the Cinderella of the foreign aid family."

Despite its limited budget, especially in relation to the MSA, the goals of the Point Four Program were ambitious, aimed at the development of modern societies and polities throughout the emerging postcolonial world. The approach was broad rather than targeted, designed to set in motion a modernization process that would eventually—though not necessarily immediately—improve people's lives and reduce poverty. At the roots of its diagnosis of the main source of underdevelopment was the absence of know-how and technology that discouraged the flow of domestic and overseas investment capital. It therefore focused on technical as opposed to capital assistance, believing that the beneficial effects of the former would catalyze the latter, and there was a particularly strong emphasis on the development of human capital through the provision of technical advice and equipment. Moreover, the approach was to be as comprehensive in scope as possible, targeting several economic and social sectors simultaneously through the inauguration of small-scale pilot projects in such fields as health, education, infrastructure, and agriculture. While the program also had hopes of countering the effects of Soviet-style propaganda—the first congressional hearings concerning Point Four were held shortly after the Communist victory in China (1950)—its time frame was essentially long-term, with some officials envisaging a life span of up to fifty years for the program. It was not, as one author stressed, necessarily designed to achieve "quick or dramatic results."

Before being passed by Congress in 1950, however, the Point Four Program was the subject of much congressional debate, the effects of which resulted in the stipulation of several restrictions on its scope. Of these, five stand out as being most important. First, Congress insisted that recipient nations pay for a fair share of the costs, in theory as a way of ensuring that successful projects would eventually be integrated into the recipient country's own development program. To facilitate this eventual administrative integration, Congress also recommended the establishment of field-level "cooperative departments" that would have American technicians working alongside their foreign counterparts.

Congress also insisted that the recipient country attempt to integrate the program into its overall technical cooperation program, designed in part to reduce the degree of overlap with programs being offered by other agencies, notably by Britain and the newly created United Nations Technical Assistance Agency (UNTAA). A further stipulation required that work only begin after the signing of both an overall country program agreement in addition to specific project agreements. Finally, Congress retained the right to terminate any program that was inconsistent with American foreign policy.

The first Point Four agreement was signed with the Jordanian government in 1950. This achievement was followed by Point Four agreements in Lebanon, Iran, Egypt, and Iraq. A Point Four agreement was never signed with Syria. The type of projects it became involved with were broad, ranging from feasibility studies for large capital-works projects such as dam and irrigation work on the Jordan and Litani Rivers, to many afforestation projects in Jordan and Iraq, to the design of land-settlement programs in Iraq and Iran, to the geological mapping and development of local water resources throughout the region, in addition to many grassroots community development projects in the fields of health and education. In the course of its work in the region, however, Point Four officials came under significant criticism from many sources, notably local government officials, nationalist elites, rival foreign development technicians, and American development and political officials in Washington. These criticisms revolved around three main issues—ones that bring into question the overall effectiveness of the Point Four Program: the excessive politicization of American aid programs; the unsustainable nature of Point Four's development approach, particularly with respect to questions of local administrative and financial capacity; and the hierarchical and Washington-centered nature of administrative mechanisms responsible for aid policy formulation and delivery.

President Truman's Point Four initiative coincided with the radicalization of politics within the Middle East. The creation of Israel after the defeat of the Arab armies in 1949, combined with the intensification of the Cold War, had a destabilizing effect on the politics of the region. Postcolonial Arab states now found themselves subject to intense pressures from emerging social forces that were espousing more-radical notions of Arab nationalism and more-ambitious projects of socio-economic development that threatened the bases of political power. In order to stave off pressures for significant social and economic reform, especially with respect to the redistribution of land, politicians in the region adopted more-radical nationalistic stances as a way of gaining local political legitimacy, a dynamic that created a spiraling effect in the region as a whole. Arab states, therefore, were extremely wary of entering into agreements with Western powers, evidenced by the destabilizing effects of treaty negotiations between Britain and its former colonial possessions Egypt and Iraq in the late 1940s. Although not a former colonial power, the United States—in part because of its role in the creation of Israel—was not immune from these anti-Western nationalist sentiments. Hence, the Middle East portion of the Point Four Program was launched in an unpropitious political environment.

However, two factors exacerbated political resistance to Point Four assistance in the region. The first was Congress's stipulation that Point Four enter into both general program and more technical project agreements before work on the ground could begin; the second was its insistence that development work receive widespread publicity within the recipient country. These conditions resulted in serious consequences for Point Four officials and technicians trying to push forward their work in the field. First, work on the ground was in some crucial instances delayed given the understandable reticence on the part of Arab technocrats and politicians to be seen signing formal agreements that would lead to the flooding of their countries with American technocrats just at a time when they were trying to reduce the visibility of Western officials. This problem was particularly the case with respect to American involvement in two key Middle East states, Syria and Iraq. The Point Four Program never reached an agreement with Syria, whereas in Iraq the program found its involvement in the crucial *Miri Sirf* land-settlement program, designed to help alleviate the plight of landless peasants flooding into Baghdad from the south, delayed for more than two years, despite its being targeted by American officials as a vital component of that country's efforts to promote social and economic reform. As this Point Four memo from Lebanon in 1951 indicated:

> In the Arab states there is a great hesitancy in signing any kind of general accord, probably because of suspicion that we are trying to tie them up to some hypothetical future arrangement and possibly because they read into a general accord the implications of a treaty alliance or other commitments which are not there and not intended by us. The attitude seems to be "We are friends. We can deal with every problem that comes up on an individual basis. Why do we need a general agreement?"

Congress's insistence that Point Four officials operate in more-formal and high-profile ways also inhibited their work once in the field.

During the process of negotiations concerning a general agreement in Iraq, for example, the American ambassador argued that while Iraq offered "a great opportunity to show Point IV working at its best, . . . it must be a low pressure program here with works speaking rather than words. . . . It must not (repeat not) be a big splash." However, given that the signing of a Point Four agreement often resulted in the arrival of large numbers of well-paid American technical experts, often concentrated in the capital city and complete with their "Point IV" cars, it was not surprising that local communities reached the not unwarranted conclusion that Point Four was spending more money on American goods and services than on Middle Eastern development needs. Indeed, this tendency has been a consistent feature of U.S. development assistance. One study, for example, estimated that as much as 70 percent of U.S. aid has been spent on its own experts and products. Combine this trend with the penchant for Point Four to spend for widespread publicity—in part motivated by the well-intentioned if naive desire to promote American values abroad—and one had a recipe for scapegoating and resentment. Branded as "a new imperialism by cowboys," Point Four personnel and installations often found themselves the targets of demonstrations and violence across the region, incidents that, at times, had serious repercussions for the continuity and effectiveness of their work.

Point Four officials hoped that the success of their development work would eventually overcome any lingering political suspicion of their intentions. They pinned their hopes on the successful demonstration of American technical know-how, expecting that the importation of new technologies such as water spreading that would make "the desert bloom" would spark a more widespread enthusiasm for Western-style modernization. The more widespread the introduction of technical innovations, the stronger the psychological effect. In that sense, Point Four officials were interested in effecting as much a "behavioral" revolution as a "technical" one.

American optimism, however, was quickly confronted by the administrative and fiscal realities of doing development work in the region. Projects with a high technological content, for example, often required local administrative expertise and financial resources that simply were not available. "The sky is not the limit on technical assistance," wrote the American ambassador in Jordan in stressing the limited carrying capacity of the Jordanian administration. "[I]t is up to Point IV to exercise some constraint." In short, the obstacles to development in the region (as in the rest of the underdeveloped world) were

A BOLD NEW PROGRAM

In his inaugural address given on 20 January 1949, Harry S Truman commented on U.S. foreign relations:

Fourth, we must embark on a bold new program for making the benefits of our scientific advances and industrial progress available for the improvement and growth of underdeveloped areas.

More than half the people of the world are living in conditions approaching misery. Their food is inadequate. They are victims of disease. Their economic life is primitive and stagnant. Their poverty is a handicap and a threat both to them and to more prosperous areas.

For the first time in history, humanity possesses the knowledge and the skill to relieve the suffering of these people.

The United States is pre-eminent among nations in the development of industrial and scientific techniques. The material resources which we can afford to use for the assistance of other peoples are limited. But our imponderable resources in technical knowledge are constantly growing and are inexhaustible.

I believe that we should make available to peace-loving peoples the benefits of our store of technical knowledge in order to help them realize their aspirations for a better life. And, in cooperation with other nations, we should foster capital investment in areas needing development.

Our aim should be to help the free peoples of the world, through their own efforts, to produce more food, more clothing, more materials for housing, and more mechanical power to lighten their burdens.

We invite other countries to pool their technological resources in this undertaking. Their contributions will be warmly welcomed. This should be a cooperative enterprise in which all nations work together through the United Nations and its specialized agencies wherever practicable. It must be a worldwide effort for the achievement of peace, plenty, and freedom.

With the cooperation of business, private capital, agriculture, and labor in this country, this program can greatly increase the industrial activity in other nations and can raise substantially their standards of living.

Such new economic developments must be devised and controlled to benefit the peoples of the areas in which they are established. Guarantees to the investor must be balanced by guarantees in the interest of the people whose resources and whose labor go into these developments.

The old imperialism—exploitation for foreign profit—has no place in our plans. What we envisage is a program of development based on the concepts of democratic fair-dealing.

All countries, including our own, will greatly benefit from a constructive program for the better use of the world's human and natural resources. Experience shows that our commerce with other countries expands as they progress industrially and economically.

Greater production is the key to prosperity and peace. And the key to greater production is a wider and more vigorous application of modern scientific and technical knowledge.

Only by helping the least fortunate of its members to help themselves can the human family achieve the decent, satisfying life that is the right of all people.

Democracy alone can supply the vitalizing force to stir the peoples of the world into triumphant action, not only against their human oppressors, but also against their ancient enemies—hunger, misery, and despair.

On the basis of these four major courses of action we hope to help create the conditions that will lead eventually to personal freedom and happiness for all mankind.

If we are to be successful in carrying out these policies, it is clear that we must have continued prosperity in this country and we must keep ourselves strong.

Slowly but surely we are weaving a world fabric of international security and growing prosperity.

We are aided by all who wish to live in freedom from fear—even by those who live today in fear under their own governments.

We are aided by all who want relief from the lies of propaganda—who desire truth and sincerity.

We are aided by all who desire self-government and a voice in deciding their own affairs.

We are aided by all who long for economic security—for the security and abundance that men in free societies can enjoy.

We are aided by all who desire freedom of speech, freedom of religion, and freedom to live their own lives for useful ends.

Our allies are the millions who hunger and thirst after righteousness.

In due time, as our stability becomes manifest, as more and more nations come to know the benefits of democracy and to participate in growing abundance, I believe that those countries which now oppose us will abandon their delusions and join with the free nations of the world in a just settlement of international differences.

Events have brought our American democracy to new influence and new responsibilities. They will test our courage, our devotion to duty, and our concept of liberty.

But I say to all men, what we have achieved in liberty, we will surpass in greater liberty.

Steadfast in our faith in the Almighty, we will advance toward a world where man's freedom is secure.

To that end we will devote our strength, our resources, and our firmness of resolve. With God's help, the future of mankind will be assured in a world of justice, harmony, and peace.

Source: "Inaugural Address of Harry S. Truman," The Avalon Project at Yale Law School <http://www.yale.edu/lawweb/avalon/presiden/inaug/truman.htm>.

as much "material" and "administrative" as "psychological." Yet, the Point Four Program failed to adjust to this reality, attested to by the burgeoning reports about many Point Four projects that began with spectacular success but ended with abandonment. In a particularly candid report published in 1954 by the Jordanian Department of Forestry, for example, the Point Four work in this field was criticized for being not only "excessively expensive" and, hence, unsustainable in the long term but also for crowding out much of the existing work of the Jordanian department itself. When Point Four assistance in the field of forestry was suddenly reduced in 1956 for political reasons, the Jordanian Department of Forestry suddenly found itself in utter disarray.

In theory, Point Four's policy of creating "cooperative departments" to work alongside their local administrative counterparts was designed to facilitate the process of project absorption. In reality, however, it had the opposite effect in many instances. The case of Jordan, again, provides a glaring example. Facilitated by the higher salaries offered by the Point Four Program, the cooperative departments in Jordan tended to grow by leaps and bounds, not only reaching unsustainable sizes but also pulling expertise away from, and hence weakening, the fledgling Jordanian administration. By 1954 the number of employees in Point Four's administrative apparatus in Jordan had reached in excess of 1,500 personnel. When the more nationalist Jordanian government elected in 1956 tried to check this trend and reintegrate these autonomous departments back into the existing Jordanian administration, however, American Point Four officials refused. The trend continued, and it was not until 1959 that the Americans, now confronted by many stories of corruption and waste, decided to dismantle their cooperative administrative structures altogether.

Why was Point Four assistance seemingly so blind to the limits of local capacities? Why was it unable to adapt to the realities of local conditions? This problem cannot be placed at the feet of individual American experts in the field exclusively, most of whom worked with the best of intentions. The problem was more systematic and relates to the overall administrative structure of the Point Four Program as a whole, one that saw experts, field administrators, and local policymakers ultimately beholden to officials in Washington.

American involvement in the *Miri Sirf* land-development program in Iraq provides perhaps the best case in point. Excited by what they saw as the "gargantuan" social and political opportunities provided by this application of American technical know-how in the creation of "planned communities of farmers," complete with newly reclaimed land, physical infrastructure, and social amenities, Point Four officials in Washington looked upon their involvement in this project as a top priority and went about drafting an agreement with the Iraqis. Yet, when the agreement was received in Baghdad, the Iraqis held back. In part, this hesitancy was the result of their reluctance to hand over such a politically sensitive area of their reform program to a foreign agency. They also worried that the American proposals were too technically ambitious. As the British member of Iraq's Development Board remarked, the technical work of Point Four on the *Miri Sirf* land-development program was "planned and designed as if the farmers, supervisors, and engineers were up to Californian standards and thick enough on the ground—which they aren't. [It] has no flexibility. . . . [and] presupposes a body of people to run it and people it with the skill and experience we just don't possess." The result was not only delay in signing the project agreement upon which American involvement in the program depended, it also resulted, perhaps appropriately, in a dramatic downscaling of U.S. involvement as a whole. So exasperated did the Point Four official appointed to head the American *Miri Sirf* land-development team become that he eventually resigned. Rather than target the Iraqis for blame, however, this official pointed his criticisms at "the entire confused travesty of programming" required by Washington. "The fundamental mistake of the Point IV idea," he wrote,

> was that it was controlled and planned by people in Washington who, although sincere in their motives, had no practical knowledge of the varying problems of foreign countries, and who thought that, because a particular kind of programme was 'fundamentally right', it could automatically be applied to all underdeveloped areas. This attitude, combined with the constitutional necessity for drawing up programmes some 18 months in advance in order to obtain money from Congress, led the Point IV authorities in Washington to draw up programmes of action which, when it came to the point, were quite impractical and were frequently also unacceptable to the local authorities.

The Point Four Program in the Middle East, as in other parts of the emerging postcolonial world, suffered from many problems that have become endemic within the field of international development. Assistance was not sensitive to the limitations of promoting growth and "modernization" and tended to ignore the constraints that local underdeveloped environments and administrations presented. This situation was, in part, caused by the operational nature in which such aid programs have been structured, characterized by hierarchical "aid chains" within donor agencies in which accountability flowed upward and outward toward the donor capital city rather than downward and inward toward the people whom aid is designed to assist. It was hampered as well by the broad political goals, with which Point Four assistance was associated, that mandated quick delivery and fast results based on the requirements of Washington rather than a more measured and careful approach sensitive to local conditions. Hence, while the Point Four Program was a good idea in theory, its initial promise was frustrated by the political and administrative manner in which it was implemented.

–PAUL W. T. KINGSTON,
UNIVERSITY OF TORONTO

References

Paul W. T. Kingston, "The Ambassador for the Arabs: The Locke Mission and the Unmaking of American Development Diplomacy in the Near East, 1952–1953," in *The Middle East and the United States: A Historical and Political Reassessment,* edited by David W. Lesch (Boulder, Colo.: Westview Press, 1996, 1999, 2003), pp. 29–50.

Kingston, *Britain and the Politics of Modernization in the Middle East, 1945–1958* (Cambridge & New York: Cambridge University Press, 1996).

Louis W. Koenig, ed., *The Truman Administration: Its Principles and Practice* (New York: New York University Press, 1956).

Vernon W. Ruttan, *United States Development Assistance Policy: The Domestic Politics of Foreign Economic Aid* (Baltimore: Johns Hopkins University Press, 1996).

Harry S Truman, *Memoirs: Years of Trial and Hope* (New York: Doubleday, 1956).

RESOLUTION 242

Did United Nations Security Council Resolution 242 create an effective framework for peace following the Arab-Israeli War of 1967?

Viewpoint: Yes. The fact that UN Security Council Resolution 242 is still operative today is a testimony to its effectiveness as a framework for peace between Israel and the Arab states.

Viewpoint: No. The ambiguous passages used in UN Security Council Resolution 242 have damaged the peace process by allowing the parties involved to interpret the document differently.

If not the most important, certainly United Nations (UN) Security Council Resolution 242 is the most visible of all the resolutions passed by the UN since the organization was formed. Resolution 242 was passed on 22 November 1967. Formulated and engineered primarily by the United States and the Soviet Union in the aftermath of the Arab-Israeli War of 1967 (Six-Day War or June War), the resolution represented an attempt by the superpowers to create a mechanism by which the warring parties might resolve the dispute—cynics would accuse Washington and Moscow of simply trying to isolate the problem so as to prevent the possibility of a superpower confrontation emerging from another regional conflagration.

The preamble spoke of "the inadmissibility of the acquisition of territory by war and the need to work for a just and lasting peace in which every state in the area can live in security." Some of the more important operative clauses include: withdrawal of Israel from territories occupied in the recent conflict; and termination of all claims or states of belligerency and respect for and acknowledgment of the sovereignty, territorial integrity, and political independence of every state in the area and their right to live in peace within secure and recognized boundaries free from threats of acts of force. The resolution, inter alia, also affirmed the necessity "for achieving a just settlement of the refugee problem," with obvious reference to the Palestinian situation.

In essence, Resolution 242 established the "land-for-peace" framework. In other words, in exchange for returning the territories obtained in the Six-Day War to the respective Arab states who lost them, Israel would sign peace treaties with its Arab combatants, and thereby the latter would be extending recognition to the Jewish state. The importance of Resolution 242 is clearly derived from the simple fact that it still remains the operative framework for peace negotiations in the Arab-Israeli arena, regardless of what many believe to be its inherent ambiguities.

Israeli soldier conducting a house census of Palestinians in the Gaza Strip after the 1967 War

(Topham)

Viewpoint:
Yes. The fact that UN Security Council Resolution 242 is still operative today is a testimony to its effectiveness as a framework for peace between Israel and the Arab states.

On 22 November 1967, several months after the end of the fighting in the Middle East, the United Nations (UN) Security Council adopted Resolution 242. Since then, this resolution has served as the cornerstone of every peace process in the region.

The secret of the effectiveness and relevance of this resolution is contained in two central issues. One was the link it created between the Arab demand for Israel's withdrawal from the territories it had occupied in the course of the Arab-Israeli War of 1967 (Six-Day War or June War) and the Israeli demand for achieving a peace agreement between Israel and the Arabs. The other was its "constructive" ambiguity, in other words, the lack of clarity of its articles that would allow this resolution to become a convenient framework for both sides in conducting peace negotiations.

For the first time the Arab demand for Israeli withdrawal from the territories it captured in 1967 was bound up with achieving a comprehensive peace between Israel and the Arabs. Whereas previous resolutions on the Israeli-Arab conflict did not provide any incentive to the sides to embark upon the road to peace, this one provided that incentive in the form of "land-for-peace." Thus, for example, after the Suez campaign of October 1956, in the course of which Israel gained control over Sinai as part of a joint Israeli-British-French military operation, Israel agreed to withdraw from Sinai without Egypt's having to commit itself to recognize the Jewish state's right to exist or to negotiate peace with it. However, in 1956 most of the world viewed Israel's attack as an act of aggression, and worse than that, as part of a British-French colonial plot. Moreover, Israel was asked to pay the price of an American effort to solve the crisis before it spiraled out of control and into an international crisis. Resolution 242 refrained from demanding that Israel withdraw unconditionally from the territories it occupied, thus recognizing, at least implicitly, the legitimacy of Israel's decision to go to war against its Arab neighbors.

There can be no doubt that this resolution encouraged the Arab states, although gradually, to adopt a diplomatic and peaceful resolution to the problem. These countries, or more correctly their leaders, understood that without negotiations or even the signing of a peace agreement in which the Arabs recognized Israel's right to exist they could not win back the territories that they lost in the 1967 conflict. In the wake of this war, the return of Egyptian, Jordanian, and Syrian territories that Israel occupied became the highest priority for the Arab countries involved, ranking higher than finding a solution to the Palestinian problem, as demanded in the past by the common Arab in the streets.

In response to public criticism directed at them, the Arab rulers felt it was imperative to regain the lost homeland territories—the Sinai Peninsula, the Golan Heights, and, in the case of Jordan, the West Bank (instead of the Palestinian lands that had been lost in the 1948 Arab-Israeli War). Until that time Arab rulers refused to recognize the State of Israel and to negotiate with it for peace. They took this stand because they had neither incentives nor constraints that might lead them to negotiate with Israel. On the contrary, the leaders were concerned with their personal safety and the stability of their regimes in view of the possible reaction of the Arab public should they adopt a moderate policy toward Israel. This time, however, in the wake of the Six-Day War, an incentive had been created; in addition, with the strengthening of the Arab territorial states, the leaders were now able to appear before their public with a policy that promoted their own political concerns before pan-Arab interests. The result was that the Arab states adopted a more moderate approach toward the Arab-Israeli conflict that ultimately led to the recognition of Israel and even to a readiness to sign a peace treaty. The fact is that even the Arab-Israeli War of 1973, which

was an important Arab achievement, and certainly a morale-enhancing one, did not bring the Arabs any closer to regaining territories they had lost in the Six-Day War, and thus proved that exclusively military means would not motivate Israel to return these lands to them—this end could be achieved only through peaceful means.

The first country to realize this fact was Egypt, which as soon as the fighting ceased in 1973 entered into negotiations with Israel and in 1979 signed a peace agreement with it. Other countries gradually joined Egypt in diplomatic entreaties to the Israelis. Even Syria, which had initially opposed Resolution 242 precisely because it included making Israel's withdrawal from the Arab territories conditional on reaching a peace agreement, found itself throughout the 1990s engaged in negotiations with Israel designed to regain the Golan Heights.

It should be emphasized that Resolution 242 states in clear terms that in return for peace with the Arabs, Israel will have to pay a price—withdrawal from territories captured in the Six-Day War. This concession became complicated because of the settlement activity that Israel has promoted since the mid 1970s. Israeli settlements fundamentally changed the map in the West Bank and even in the Gaza Strip. Nevertheless, Resolution 242 requires Israel to withdrawal from these territories, although in return Israel is entitled to demand peace agreements with its Arab neighbors.

However, a contradiction exists between the English and French texts of the resolution. The English text relates to Israel's withdrawal from territories captured in the Six-Day War, while the French one states that Israel must withdraw from all the territories to the 4 June 1967 lines. This vague wording has allowed Israel to argue that the resolution does not require it to withdraw to the 4 June borders, which Israeli foreign minister Abba Eban defined as "Auschwitz" borders. Thus, the Israeli position is that the resolution allows Israel to demand that changes be made in the 1967 lines. Yitzhak Shamir, Israeli prime minister at the time of the Madrid peace conference (1991), even contended that the contents of this resolution do not require total Israeli withdrawal on all fronts and that the fact that Israel withdrew from Sinai, which formed 90 percent of all territory captured in 1967, allows Israel to claim that it had met the requirements of the resolution.

This argument could ostensibly serve as an indication that the multifaceted text of the resolution lends itself to many interpretations; however, it appears that the advantages of its obscure wording outweigh its disadvantages. The resolution does not determine what mechanism is to be used in resolving the conflict. For example, no detailed

RESOLUTION 242

schedules have been determined for beginning negotiations and maintaining them, nor does the text lay out the steps that the sides must take in order to promote them. Moreover, the resolution does not interpret or provide details on the vision of the future peace agreement—what the borders are to be, as well as solutions to such issues as Palestinian refugees and Jerusalem.

The importance of this ambiguity has to do with the fact that at the time the resolution was adopted not only was it impossible to reach an Israeli-Arab peace agreement, it was impossible to even begin negotiations on peace. While the Israeli government expressed its readiness on 19 June 1967 to withdraw from all territories captured in the Six-Day War in return for peace, the Arab states did not pick up the gauntlet and—at the Arab League summit meeting in Khartoum, Sudan, on 29 August—announced the three well-known "no's" regarding Israel: no recognition of, no negotiations with, and no reconciliation with Israel. Thus, the Arab world was not prepared to consider the possibility of reaching a peace agreement with Israel; what they desired was a return to the cease-fire arrangement that had been in effect since 1949. The change in the Arab position was, therefore, gradual and did not ripen until the end of the 1970s and then only in the Egyptian context. In October 1967, in view of the lack of a positive Arab response, Israel retracted its offer to withdraw from all the territories it had captured during the Six-Day War. There were later additional changes in Israel's attitude toward the Occupied Territories, which it had originally viewed as adding to its security, ultimately reaching the point where it refused to withdraw from the West Bank and Gaza Strip, and under the Likud government in the 1980s even made efforts to ensure Israeli rule in these territories in perpetuity.

Thus, the secret of the effectiveness of Resolution 242 was not in an attempt to force a clearly defined, unrealistic, and inapplicable plan unacceptable to all sides, thus destined to find its way into the wastebasket as had many other plans. Instead, Resolution 242 created and determined in general terms the way in which a peace settlement could be attained, terms that to this day have remained the only ones acceptable to all sides.

On the basis of this resolution, and with none of the sides feeling that it had given in to or had been demeaned by the other, it was possible to enter into negotiations, and it is only through the dynamics of the negotiating process that any breakthrough can be made along the path to peace. This fact is even clearer in the Israeli domestic context, since conventional wisdom holds that the Israeli public can be persuaded to make territorial concessions as part of the negoti-

ating process and not as part of an imposed solution. This conclusion has been proven true regarding the Egyptian-Israeli case following Anwar Sadat's historic visit to Israel in November 1977. In the wake of that visit a dramatic change occurred within the Israeli public, expressed mainly in its readiness to withdraw from Sinai, whereas the majority of Israelis had previously been opposed to such a move.

Syrian president Hafiz al-Asad said on more than one occasion in the 1970s and 1980s that he was opposed to Syria joining a peace process whose outcome it did not know in advance. Asad went on to explain that a process of that kind had its own dynamic—the sides that join it know what their opening positions are, but cannot know for certain where the process will lead them. Therefore, Syria refused from the outset to accept Resolution 242 since the Salah Jadid regime, which preceded Asad, recognized that bound up with the resolution was Arab recognition of Israel, which Syria was not prepared to accept even in return for regaining the Golan Heights. It was only in 1971, shortly after Asad came to power, that Syria was prepared to accept Resolution 242, albeit with some reservation. Twenty years later Syria joined the peace process that led it and, incidentally, Israel as well, to the brink of signing a peace treaty.

UN Security Council Resolution 242 created a convenient framework of action that serves as the basis for the initiation, operation, and even agreement in principle of peace negotiations. Of course, this resolution was not enough to achieve peace, but it was the maximum that could be attained in 1967, and it is still relevant, certainly as a basis for the renewal of Israeli-Arab negotiations. Over the years the resolution has gained the support of both sides despite their initial reservations, and they have even sanctified it and made it a necessary cornerstone without which no peace process in the region is possible.

—EYAL ZISSER,
TEL AVIV UNIVERSITY

Viewpoint:
No. The ambiguous passages used in UN Security Council Resolution 242 have damaged the peace process by allowing the parties involved to interpret the document differently.

The end of the Arab-Israeli War of 1967 (Six-Day War or June War) brought with it a diplomatic debate that has lasted to this day. Diplomacy had been active since the beginning of the war, with four United Nations (UN) Security Council cease-fire resolutions, "crowned with success" by the final one on 22 November 1967. The cease-fire resolutions that preceded Resolution 242 were Resolution 233 (6 June 1967); Resolution 234 (7 June 1967); Resolution 235 (9 June 1967); and Resolution 236 (11 June 1967).

The framework of Resolution 242 essentially resulted from two events: U.S. president Lyndon B. Johnson's Five Principles speech (19 June 1967) and the summit conference of the Arab leaders that took place in Khartoum, Sudan, in late August, known as the "three no's" conference. President Johnson decided not to go in person to the United Nations; instead, he gave his speech on television. After referring briefly to the Vietnam conflict (ended 1975) he immediately started to talk about the Middle Eastern situation and what was necessary to resolve it. He addressed five principles: the recognized right to national life; justice for the (Palestinian) refugees; innocent maritime passage; limits on the wasteful and destructive arms race; and political independence and territorial integrity for all. The second event, the Khartoum summit, turned out to be a sort of antithesis to Johnson's plan for the Middle East. As William B. Quandt states in *Peace Process: American Diplomacy and the Arab-Israeli Conflict since 1967* (2001), the final guidelines (to which Egypt and Jordan agreed only reluctantly) called for no peace with Israel, no recognition of the Jewish state, and no negotiations (the author adds, no abandonment of Palestinian rights as well).

Problems arose immediately because the purposes of the two declarations contradicted each other. When the UN General Assembly convened on 19 June 1967, Soviet premier Alexei Kosygin called for "a condemnation of Israel, for total Israeli withdrawal from occupied Arab territory, and for financial restitution to the Arab countries." This proposal was supported by the Arab delegates, most of the other Muslim ambassadors, and ambassadors from the Communist bloc. It avoided the danger of a Yugoslavian proposal, supported by sixteen nonaligned states, that asked for the "immediate and unconditional withdrawal of Israeli forces to positions prior to June 5." After two meetings between Johnson and Kosygin on 23 June 1967, at Glassboro, New Jersey, a Washington-backed Latin American resolution was presented on 26 June. The new proposition called for "universal recognition of Israel . . . full rights of Israeli passage through international waterways" but also stated that "the problem of refugees had to be confronted, together with a recognition that alteration of boundaries by force was inadmissible."

When the twenty-second UN General Assembly session convened on 19 September, Austria, Finland, and Sweden submitted their proposal, the main focus of which was to make the UN reconsider the Middle East problem. The situation was turned over to the Security Council, where India, Mali, and Nigeria presented a resolution that asked Israel "to withdraw from all the lands occupied as a result of the recent conflict." This resolution was supported by the Arabs and the Soviets but rejected by the United States. Finally, on 22 November 1967, Resolution 242, sponsored by Great Britain, was passed unanimously. Lord Caradon's version (S/8247) kept the India-Mali-Nigeria sentence referring to the "inadmissibility of the acquisition of territory by war," and, as to the Israeli withdrawal from territories conquered during the conflict, it stated: "Withdrawal of Israeli armed forces from territories of recent conflict, but not from all such territories."

This last sentence became in the final version "withdrawal of the Israeli armed forces from territories occupied in the recent conflict" and in the French version "retrait des forces armeés israéliennes des territoires occupés lors du récent conflict." As scholar Prosper Weil explained, Lord Caradon's text turned out to be a mixture of the India-Mali-Nigeria version with the American draft resolution presented soon after Johnson's speech on 20 June that called for, among other things, "recognized boundaries."

While English and French are both working languages of the Security Council, the English version of the resolution turned out to be ambiguous as far as Israeli withdrawal was concerned. Grammatically speaking, the wording of the resolution left little room for misunderstandings because if in the first part "withdrawal of Israeli armed force from (the) territories occupied"—the definite article "the" was absent (while it was present in the French and Spanish versions), it was present in the second part—"in the recent conflict." Consequently, Israel was asked to withdraw from the Golan Heights, Sinai Peninsula, Gaza Strip, West Bank, and East Jerusalem. Paradoxically, the ambiguities were placed elsewhere in the resolution. Starting from the beginning, the Security Council's "continuing concern with the grave situation in the Middle East" had only been an apparent one. Each country involved, with probably the exception of China, had acted in order to bring grist to its own mill. As to "the inadmissibility of the acquisition of territory by war," one found oneself in a ridiculous, if not awkward, situation. When on earth did war not produce as a result the conquest of lands? What about the commitment undertaken by all member states "to act in accordance with Article 2 of the Charter"? Israel had not under-

LA RÉSOLUTION 242

Conseil de sécurité des Nations unies 22 novembre 1967

Le Conseil de sécurité,

Exprimant l'inquiétude que continue de lui causer la grave situation au Moyen-Orient;

Soulignant *l'inadmissibilité de l'acquisition de territoire par la guerre* et la nécessité d'œuvrer pour une paix juste et durable permettant à chaque Etat de la région de vivre en sécurité;

Soulignant en outre que tous les Etats membres, en acceptant la Charte des Nations unies, ont contracté l'engagement d'agir conformément à l'article 2 de la Charte.

1. Affirme que l'accomplissement des principes de la Charte exige l'instauration d'une paix juste et durable au Moyen-Orient qui devrait comprendre l'application des deux principes suivants:

    (i) *Retrait des forces armées israéliennes des territoires occupés lors du récent conflit;*

    (ii) Cessation de toutes assertions de belligérance ou de tous états de belligérance et respect et reconnaissance de la souveraineté, de l'intégrité territoriale et de l'indépendance politique de chaque État de la région et leur droit de vivre en paix à l'intérieur de *frontières sûres et reconnues* à l'abri de menaces ou d'actes de force.

2. Affirme en outre la nécessité:

    (a) De garantir la liberté de navigation sur les voies d'eau internationales de la région;

    (b) De réaliser un juste règlement du problème des réfugiés;

    (c) De garantir l'inviolabilité territoriale et l'indépendance politique de chaque État de la région, par des mesures comprenant la création de zones démilitarisées.

3. *Prie le secrétaire général de désigner un représentant spécial pour se rendre au Moyen-Orient afin d'y établir et d'y maintenir des rapports avec les États intéressés en vue de favoriser un accord et de seconder les efforts tendant à aboutir à un règlement pacifique et accepté, conformément aux dispositions et aux principes de la présente résolution.*

4. Prie le secrétaire général de présenter aussitôt que possible au Conseil de sécurité un rapport d'activité sur les efforts du représentant spécial.

Source: <www.monde-diplomatique.fr/cahier/proche-orient/reso242-fr> (emphasis added).

---

gone an armed attack by Syria, Egypt, Jordan, and Iraq, but considering the circumstances, were not the actions by Egypt and other Arab combatants prior to the outbreak of war a gross violation, not to say a threat to Israel's existence? In this case was not Israel's action plausibly in accordance with Article 51 of the UN Charter regarding legitimate self-defense? One could object only to one point, that is, the absence in the area of a regional defensive alliance, a necessary clause meant to justify the intervention of a third party, but there could be no doubt that Israel was going to be attacked and that its call for help was implicit.

Finally, what can one say about the "secure and recognized boundaries"? How can one talk about boundaries if in the Arab mind there was not even the idea of a Jewish state? The fact is that after the Rhodes armistice agreements (1949), Israel had applied for membership in the UN, which was approved by the Security Council on 11 March 1949 and became reality in May. Was not Israel's right to exist ratified by the most important world body?

So, while Egypt, Jordan, and Israel accepted Resolution 242 (only reluctantly), Syria, Iraq, Algeria, and the Palestine Liberation Organization (PLO) initially rejected it. Moreover, the third point of the resolution had potential to create problems. In that passage, the Security Council called for the appointment of a UN special representative in order "to provide the UN emissary . . . with terms of reference" and "to reach some international consensus on principles that would help to moderate the conflict and guide it toward a settlement," according to Saadia Touval

RESOLUTION 242

UN Security Council 22 November 1967

The Security Council,

Expressing its continuing concern with the grave situation in the Middle East;

Emphasizing **the inadmissibility of the acquisition of territory by war** and the need to work for a just and lasting peace in which every State in the area can live in security;

Emphasizing further that all Member States in their acceptance of the Charter of the United Nations have undertaken a commitment to act in accordance with Article 2 of the Charter.

1. Affirms that the fulfillment of Charter principles requires the establishment of a just and lasting peace in the Middle East which should include the application of both the following principles:

    (i) **Withdrawal of Israeli armed forces from territories occupied in the recent conflict;**

    (ii) Termination of all claims or states of belligerency and respect for and acknowledgment of the sovereignty, territorial integrity and political independence of every State in the area and their right to live in peace within **secure and recog-** **nized boundaries** free from threats or acts of force;

2. Affirms further the necessity:

    (a) For guaranteeing freedom of navigation through international waterways in the area;

    (b) For achieving a just settlement of the refugee problem;

    (c) For guaranteeing the territorial inviolability and political independence of every State in the area, through measures including the establishment of demilitarized zones.

3. **Requests the Secretary General to designate a Special Representative to proceed to the Middle East to establish and maintain contacts with the States concerned in order to promote agreement and assist efforts to achieve a peaceful and accepted settlement in accordance with the provisions and principles in this resolution**.

4. Requests the Secretary-General to report to the Security Council on the progress of the efforts of the Special Representative as soon as possible.

Source: George J. Tomeh, ed., United Nations Resolutions on Palestine and the Arab-Israeli Conflict, 1947–1974, volume 1 (Washington, D.C.: Institute for Palestine Studies, 1975), p. 143 (emphasis added).

---

in *The Peace Brokers: Mediators in the Arab-Israeli Conflict, 1948–1979* (1982). Since the existing boundaries were based on the armistice agreement(s) of 1949, the Arabs wanted Israel to withdraw to positions held prior to 5 June, the start of the war, and Israel would finally be recognized as a state by the Arabs in order to negotiate peace directly. UN secretary-general U Thant appointed Gunnar V. Jarring, who at that moment was serving as Swedish ambassador in Moscow, as the special representative. Touval describes the Jarring mission as divided into two time phases: the first from 1967 to 1969 and the second from 1970 to 1971.

Jarring adopted what Israeli foreign minister Abba Eban called "shuttle diplomacy," later to become more famous with U. S. secretary of state Henry Kissinger. The Swedish emissary had his headquarters in Cyprus and from there began his mission to Cairo, Amman, Jerusalem, Beirut, and New York. Unfortunately, the only thing that resulted from the Jarring mission was the application of a new procedure in order to solve the embarrassing stalemate. As U Thant stated, "any plan initiated by the U.S. or the U.S.S.R. must first get the endorsement of both and then be presented to Britain and France. After all four powers agreed to it, the plan would be transmitted to me for transmission to Mr. Jarring for negotiation with Israel and the Arab states." The diplomatic impasse showed the extent to which there were difficulties for both Israel and the Arab states to divest themselves of the great powers, and it also gave the opportunity to Egyptian president Gamal Abd al-Nasser to confirm the "three no's" policy that materialized in the conflict known as the War of Attrition.

The fact that the War of Attrition broke out within a year and a half of the passage of Resolution 242 and that the much more costly and dangerous Arab-Israeli War of 1973 occurred so soon after the 1967 conflagration overtly attests to its failure to establish sufficiently the parameters for a successful peace process. Resolution 242 is, indeed, a masterpiece of ambiguity, as most UN resolutions are, especially those that were cosponsored by rival superpowers during the height of the Cold War. It established the overall "land-for-peace" framework, but the lack of any timetables or mechanisms to implement its design and the vague passages that have been interpreted and reinterpreted by all parties to the conflict in a variety of ways have undermined its effectiveness.

—PAOLA OLIMPO,
UNIVERSITY OF LECCE

References

Herbert Druks, *The Uncertain Alliance: The U.S. and Israel from Kennedy to the Peace Process* (Westport, Conn.: Greenwood Press, 2001).

Abba Eban, *Abba Eban: An Autobiography* (London: Weidenfeld & Nicolson, 1977).

Fred J. Khouri, *The Arab-Israeli Dilemma* (Syracuse, N.Y.: Syracuse University Press, 1985).

William B. Quandt, *Peace Process: American Diplomacy and the Arab-Israeli Conflict Since 1967,* revised edition (Berkeley: University of California Press, 2001).

George J. Tomeh, ed., *United Nations Resolutions on Palestine and the Arab-Israeli Conflict: 1947–1974,* volume 1 (Washington, D.C.: Institute for Palestine Studies, 1975).

Saadia Touval, *The Peace Brokers: Mediators in the Arab-Israeli Conflict, 1948–1979* (Princeton: Princeton University Press, 1982).

RESOLUTION 242

SADAT'S TRIP TO ISRAEL

Was Egyptian president Anwar Sadat's trip to Israel in 1977 his "greatest triumph," as he proclaimed?

Viewpoint: Yes. Sadat's trip to Israel was a necessary strategic move that helped reactivate the peace process.

Viewpoint: Yes. However, the full significance of Sadat's trip to Israel can only be properly understood in the context of his 1973 decision to go to war with Israel.

Viewpoint: No. Sadat's trip to Israel was a desperate gamble that placed the Egyptian leader immediately in a vulnerable bargaining position.

Following the 1967 Arab-Israeli War (also known as the Six-Day War or the June War), a bargaining situation existed between Israel and the Arab states; however, it was an asymmetrical one—Israel held all of the land captured in the war (the Sinai Peninsula and Gaza Strip from Egypt; the Golan Heights from Syria; and the West Bank, including East Jerusalem, from Jordan). Egyptian president Gamal Abd al-Nasser had attempted through the War of Attrition to strengthen the Egyptian bargaining position through low-level conflict with Israel. Nasser's successor, Anwar Sadat, came to power in Egypt in October 1970, and for economic and political reasons was determined to regain the Sinai Peninsula either through diplomacy or, if necessary, war. After exhausting the diplomatic option with little to show for it, in October 1973 he (along with Syrian president Hafiz al-Asad) chose the war option.

The outcome of the 1973 Arab-Israeli War (also known as the October War, the Yom Kippur War, or the Ramadan War) essentially led to the Camp David accords (1978) and the subsequent Egyptian-Israeli peace treaty (1979). In addition, the war also led to the closest confrontation between the the United States and the Soviet Union since the Cuban Missile Crisis (1962), and it precipitated an oil crisis that revolutionized the oil industry by quadrupling the price per barrel by January 1974 because of the Organization of Petroleum Exporting Countries (OPEC, actually OAPEC or the Organization of Arab Petroleum Exporters, in other words, the Arab members of OPEC) oil embargo launched during the October War.

The course of the war itself, as well as the military situation upon the cessation of hostilities, combined with U.S. diplomacy to produce a more favorable environment for Arab-Israeli negotiations. Disengagement agreements resulted between Egypt and Israel in January 1974 (also known as Sinai I) and Syria and Israel the following May, both of which included mutual withdrawals accompanied by the insertion of United Nations (UN) observer forces to monitor the newly created buffer zones. Egypt and Israel went on to conclude another partial withdrawal agreement in September 1975 (which became known as Sinai II).

Following Sinai II, there seemed to be some momentum toward a comprehensive Arab-Israeli accord. In January 1977 the new U.S. president Jimmy Carter made the Middle East his highest foreign policy priority. The near-nuclear confrontation and the oil embargo in 1973, as well as the potential destructiveness of the "next" all-out Arab-Israeli conflagration, compelled Washington to seek a resolution to the conflict. In Israel, however, in May 1977, the right-wing Likud Party came to power for the first time in Israeli history, with Menachem Begin as prime minister. As expected, he immediately adopted a more hawkish position regarding the Arab-Israeli situation. As a result, another diplomatic stalemate ensued, and as he did in 1973, Sadat undertook another bold gamble to reactivate diplomacy. In 1973 he chose war; in November 1977 he engaged in a no-less-dramatic gesture: he traveled to Israel and spoke before the Knesset (Israeli parliament), becoming the first Arab leader ever to officially visit the Jewish state and, in effect, to recognize Israel. It was a decision that was hailed in some quarters and vehemently opposed in others.

Viewpoint:
Yes. Sadat's trip to Israel was a necessary strategic move that helped reactivate the peace process.

In order to analyze the importance of Anwar Sadat's trip to Jerusalem on 19–21 November 1977 and his subsequent speech to the Knesset (Israeli parliament) on 20 November, one must examine events that occurred seven years earlier. On 28 September 1970 Egyptian president Gamal Abd al-Nasser died of a heart attack at age fifty-two, and Sadat succeeded him. Sadat had taken part in the Free Officers Revolution (1952). The new Egyptian president was as different from his predecessor as his objectives were. Sadat did not seem interested in radical pan-Arab nationalism. Convinced that part of his strength was in the Egyptian Army, he also believed that Egypt needed to change its priorities to concentrate on the national economy. Thus, Sadat inaugurated a ten-year development plan in order to attract foreign investors. Certainly, progress at home did not mean that relations with the other Arab states had to change. Sadat fostered good relations with Syrian president Hafiz al-Asad, King Faisal of Saudi Arabia, and King Hussein of Jordan, while in 1972 he expelled from Egypt about fifteen thousand Soviet advisers. Syria took advantage of this last move and obtained an unprecedented amount of military equipment from the Soviet Union. Sadat's behavior toward the Soviets did not, however, according to scholar Howard M. Sachar, prevent them from providing Egypt with "the latest antiaircraft missiles . . . from the highly mobile SAM-6s to shoulder-carried SAM-7s (Strelas), as well as a limited number of SCUD and Frog ground-to-ground missiles."

This military buildup resulted in the 1973 Arab-Israeli War (also known as the October War, the Yom Kippur War, or the Ramadan War) that lasted from 6 October to 24 October. The war took the Israelis by surprise even though their military readiness was at an appropriate level. As Sachar has pointed out, "all of Israel's military

preparations had been oriented to a swift counterpunch," but "its ground forces no longer could function effectively by placing disproportionate reliance upon the air force and armor." Two United Nations (UN) Security Council resolutions were necessary to implement a cease-fire proposed by both the Soviets and the Americans. The first one, Resolution 338, passed on 22 October 1973, called for a cease-fire and for the implementation of Resolution 242 in all of its parts and was adopted unanimously (China did not participate in the voting). On 23 October, Resolution 339 confirmed Resolution 338 but further requested the dispatch of UN observers to supervise the cease-fire.

The Egyptian economy was negatively impacted by the October War. The first step toward economic revitalization was to organize a Middle East peace conference to carry out separate agreements between Egypt and Israel, as well as between Syria and Israel. The conference was held in Geneva on 21 December 1973 and resulted in a formal gathering of nations such as Israel, Egypt, Jordan, the United States, and the Soviet Union. The far-reaching impact was the beginning of direct negotiations between Israel and Egypt, with Henry Kissinger, President Richard M. Nixon's Secretary of State and National Security Adviser, acting as the mediator.

Jimmy Carter, with little background in foreign policy, became president of the United States in 1977. It was probably his lack of preparedness in foreign affairs that led the Democratic administration to rely heavily on the 1975 report on the Middle East situation by the Brookings Institution think tank in Washington, D.C. (Members of the Study Group included Professor Zbigniew Brzezinski, later to become Carter's National Security Adviser.) That report stated that "Israel would pledge in advance to withdraw from the occupied territories, and the Arabs (including representatives of the PLO) would agree in advance to sign a formal peace treaty with the Jewish state."

The new administration responded with the formal publication of the U.S.-Soviet communiqué, on 1 October 1977, in which the superpowers announced the agreement that should have

IN THE SPIRIT OF PEACE

In her autobiography, Jehan Sadat remembers some of the details of her husband's historic 1977 trip to Jerusalem:

"Anwar, please, will you wear a bullet-proof vest in Jerusalem?" I pleaded with him.

He refused. "There has been too much suspicion between Egypt and the Israelis for years," he said. "A soldier may enter the home of his enemy prepared to be attacked, but I am entering Israel in the spirit of peace."

Not for the first time was I frustrated by Anwar's serenity. He knew as well as I did that there were those who were as vehemently against such a peace as he was for it. The Zionists could kill him. Islamic fundamentalists could kill him. The Palestinians could kill him. I was convinced my husband would not return from Jerusalem alive. . . .

Now Sherif and I watch Anwar's plane draw to a stop on the runway, watch as an El Al ramp is wheeled to the forward door. Sitting on my lap, Sherif still cries from discomfort. My own tears are those of fear and disbelief. My husband in Israel. It cannot be.

Trumpets strike a fanfare. The door of the plane opens. There he is! My heart pounds as I watch him walk down the steps. He looks so serene and confident. What must he be feeling underneath? "I felt that God had sent me on this mission of peace," he will tell me later. "When I first set foot on Israeli soil I felt I was not of this world but as if I were flying." Watching him, I too feel I am dreaming, but on the brink of a nightmare. How I wish my eyes were television cameras so that I could scan the crowds for suspicious characters, so that I could spot the bulge of a revolver or the gleam of a gun barrel before it is too late. Anwar is well protected, of course. Extra security men had flown to Israel the day before to double-check the arrangements. . . .

I cannot believe my eyes. Anwar is shaking hands with Ephriam Katzir, the President of Israel, with Premier Menachem Begin. There they are on the same television screen, the leaders of two enemy countries for whom tens of thousands have given their lives. I hear the familiar strains of our national song, "Biladi, Biladi," My Country, My Country, being played by an Israeli military band, see Egyptian flags waving side by side with the Israeli Star of David. How can this be? . . . As our anthem draws to a close in Jerusalem, shots ring out. I knew it! Anwar! I grip Sherif so tightly that momentarily he is distracted from the pain in his lip. My eyes must be boring holes in the television screen. But my husband does not fall and I realize that the shots are coming from a twenty-one-gun salute. I begin to count the segments of time my husband has survived. He has made it through the first ten minutes. . . .

Moshe Dayan. Ariel Sharon. Golda Meir. Mordechai Gur. There they are, all of them, in the receiving line of government officials, past and present, at the airport. Anwar is moving toward them, shaking their hands, laughing. Laughing! I strain to read his lips and theirs. What are they saying to each other? They seem to be greeting each other like the oldest of friends. If war is absurd, then this scene of peace makes it even more so. . . .

On the television screen I see Anwar holding Mrs. Meir's hand, see her listening intently to him. My ears burn with tension and curiosity. Suddenly her face creases into a huge smile. Instinctively, I smile also.

"You are very well known in our country, Mrs. Meir," Anwar later reported their conversation to me. "Do you know what you are called?"

"No. What?" she had asked.

"The strongest man in Israel," my husband had said. It was then that Mrs. Meir had smiled. "I take that as a compliment, Mr. President," she had replied.

Source: Jehan Sadat, A Woman of Egypt *(New York: Simon & Schuster, 1987), pp. 374–378.*

led to the resumption of the Geneva conference. An excerpt in the communiqué stated:

> The United States and the Soviet Union believe that, within the framework of a comprehensive settlement of the Middle East problem, all specific questions of the settlement should be resolved, including such key issues as withdrawal of Israeli Armed Forces from territories occupied in the 1967 conflict; the resolution of the Palestinian question, including insuring the legitimate rights of the Palestinian people; termination of the state of war and establishment of normal peaceful relations on the mutual recognition of the principles of sovereignty, territorial integrity and political independence.

It could be argued that the U.S.-Soviet declaration gave Sadat the necessary boldness to undertake his trip to Jerusalem. The Carter administration's "high priority to the settlement of the Arab-Israeli conflict" and its aim at favoring the establishment of a "homeland for the Palestinians . . . in the West Bank and Gaza" balanced against Israeli prime minister Menachem Begin's resistance to enter into negotiations. The right-wing Likud Party in Israel won the general elections on 17 May 1977, and one of the main obstacles to negotiations was that the Israeli government would not negotiate with the Palestine Liberation Organization (PLO), because to do so would have meant the acceptance of a Palestinian entity in the West Bank and granting legitimacy to the PLO.

Only a grand gesture could save the situation, and Sadat seized the day. On 9 November 1977 he announced to the People's Assembly of the Egyptian parliament his intention: "Israel would be astonished when they hear me say this. But I say it. I am ready to go even to their home . . . to the Knesset and discuss peace with them if need be." As Sachar has reported, "the impact of the declaration was stunning. Foreign Minister Ismail Fahmi . . . resigned. . . . Jimmy Carter was confused and silent. . . . Begin was hardly less astounded." It was the American ambassador to Israel, Samuel W. Lewis, who officially asked the Israeli prime minister to extend an invitation to Sadat, which he did on 15 November. The Egyptian president accepted, but before going to Jerusalem he decided to go to Syria in order to gain the support of President Hafiz al-Asad. He did not succeed. On Saturday, 19 November 1977, Sadat left for Israel and the following day he delivered his speech to the Knesset.

The speech lasted forty minutes. After an explanatory introduction Sadat pointed out that he had not come "for a separate agreement between Egypt and Israel . . . or between any Arab confrontation state and Israel." Such an interim peace would not bring permanent peace "in the absence of a just solution of the Palestinian problem." Sadat was not looking for a third disengagement agreement such as Sinai I and Sinai II:

> In all sincerity I tell you we welcome you among us with full security and safety. This in itself is a tremendous turning point, one of the landmarks of a decisive historical change. We used to reject you. We had our reasons and our fears . . . I have announced on more than one occasion that Israel has become a fait accompli, recognized by the world, and that the two superpowers have undertaken the responsibility for its security and the defense of its existence. . . . What is peace for Israel? It means that Israel lives in the region with her Arab neighbors in security and safety. . . . It means that Israel lives within its borders, secure against any aggression. . . . It means that Israel obtains all kinds of guarantees that will ensure these two factors.

Israel had waited more than twenty years to hear such words, and Sadat spoke them, but he was firmly convinced that there were "Arab territories that Israel has occupied and still occupies by force. We insist on complete withdrawal from these territories, including Arab Jerusalem" that "should be a free and open city for all believers." As far as the Palestinian question was concerned, Sadat underlined that "even the United States of America . . . has opted to face up to reality and admit that the Palestinian people are entitled to legitimate rights and that the Palestine problem is the cause and essence of the conflict and that so long as it continues to be unresolved, the conflict will continue to aggravate, reaching new dimensions." There could be no peace without the Palestinians. Begin's reply to Sadat was aimed at ending the state of war, signing a peace treaty with Egypt, and meeting with Asad and Hussein as well as "genuine representatives of the Arabs of Eretz Yisra'el."

From that moment on the diplomatic events followed one after the other at a frantic pace. If on the one hand Sadat considered his trip to Jerusalem "his greatest triumph" and that, through it, he had broken "the psychological barrier, " according to Herbert Druks, on the other hand "he found himself in the following months increasingly isolated." Syria, Libya, Iraq, Algeria, and South Yemen did not support Sadat's grand gesture, and when on 14 December 1977 he summoned a conference in Cairo to unify the Arab front, neither the Arab countries nor the Soviet Union attended. Even the meeting on 25 December at Ismailiya, Egypt, with Begin, Dayan, Minister of Defense Ezer Weizman, and Attorney General Ahron Barak, ended in an impasse. During their talks, Sadat accepted Begin's request to establish two separate committees in order to discuss political and military issues. The former also agreed that the political committee would meet in Jerusalem, thus de facto recognizing the Holy City as Israel's capital. Unfortunately the stalemate remained, on which President Carter reaffirmed his position in his Aswan Declaration (4 January 1978), talking about "a resolution of the Palestinian problem in all its aspects." Recognizing the necessity for Israel to live in peace with its neighbors and within secure borders, Sadat viewed Israel as a geopolitical reality. However, reaffirming Egypt's position with regard to Israel's withdrawal from territories "conquered" during the 1967 Arab-Israeli War and the establishment of Jerusalem as a free and open city, so reviving the 1947 UN partition plan, did not protect him from other Arab countries' criticism and blame.

The lack of support from Syria should have warned him of the impossibility of sharing his dream with countries whose hatred of Israel was so deep-rooted. Sadat was probably blinded by his grand design, and he did not envisage its effects in the long run. He conceived it, however, and he carried it out, although he never saw the final return of the Sinai Peninsula (April 1982), for he was assassinated on 6 October 1981 by Islamic extremists opposed to the peace treaty with Israel.

Egypt and Israel were on the right track to the Camp David accords and the final Egyptian-Israeli peace treaty, though it was an uphill battle. Whatever one may think of the 1979 peace treaty, and there are certainly more than a few detractors, Sadat's goal in traveling to Israel was to reactivate the peace process, which was amply achieved by convincing skeptical Israelis that he was serious about peace, thus providing Begin with the political cover necessary in order to engage in negotiations. Sadat may have sacrificed some diplomatic leverage with his visit by de facto recognizing the State of Israel prior to direct negotiations, but it is equally clear that the peace process would have remained stalled and moribund without his dramatic gesture.

−PAOLA OLIMPO,
UNIVERSITY OF LECCE

Viewpoint:
Yes. However, the full significance of Sadat's trip to Israel can only be properly understood in the context of his 1973 decision to go to war with Israel.

Upon succeeding Gamal Abd al-Nasser in 1970, Anwar Sadat confronted the task of leading an impoverished, war-weary, and depressed Egypt. Long derided as "Mr. Yes," Sadat was vul-

nerable to Nasserists, communists, and other leftists early in his presidency. He knew that Egypt needed to realign with the West. Only the United States, the European states, and their allies could offer Egypt the sort of assistance it needed to improve its economy and pressure Israel into making the sorts of territorial concessions the Egyptian leadership needed to justify a peace treaty. In this light, Sadat's decision to go to war is at once confusing and strange. In ordinary circumstances, war is the last thing a besieged, vulnerable leader needs. Yet, Sadat needed the war for the sake of establishing legitimacy and to make the United States aware that Egypt was a country whose interests and concerns could not simply be disregarded.

His decision to wage war against Israel in 1973 was informed by several factors. First, his attempts to attract Western attention had failed; he had expelled his Soviet advisers in July 1972 in an attempt to gain favor with the West, without avail. Second, he had remade the Egyptian Army into a more professional force, thereby increasing his risks of a coup d'état. He needed to use the Egyptian Army before it overthrew him. Third, his preparations for war had the natural consequence of draining the already depleted Egyptian treasury; every training exercise cost money. This investment had to yield political results, and war was the harvest. Fourth, October 1973 marked the overlap of Jewish and Muslim holidays, making it an unexpected time to start a war. Sadat differed from Nasser, but the world chose not to notice. He had renamed the country the "Arab Republic of Egypt" instead of Nasser's "United Arab Republic." This was a signal to the rest of the world that his concerns were primarily centered around Egypt rather than on a pan-Arab project.

Like the rest of his signals, the West disregarded the name change. Sadat continued his attempts to attract the attention of Western powers by asking the Soviet military mission to leave Egypt. This demand meant the departure of twenty thousand Soviet military advisers, including pilots, paratroopers, and technicians. These Soviet troops had insured that the Israelis faced the risk of direct confrontation with the Union of Soviet Socialist Republics (U.S.S.R.) should they choose to cross the Suez Canal without the absolute guarantee of United States assistance. By asking the Soviets to leave, Sadat sent several messages. The most striking message was sent to the Israelis: Egypt did not fear confrontation and did not need the Soviet Union to guarantee its survival. Israel, then under the leadership of Golda Meir, believed that Sadat was bluffing. Sadat had promised to make 1971 "the year of decision," but it had come and gone without a war. Sadat had offered Israel a peace treaty in

exchange for the return of the Sinai Peninsula, but Israel chose not to respond. Israeli intelligence did not take Sadat seriously and neither apparently did Western intelligence services. For two years Sadat threatened war with Israel, forcing it to conduct costly partial mobilizations. He wanted a reputation for crying wolf, and he acquired it. His message to the West was simpler: Egypt is an independent actor in international relations and not a Soviet satellite. The mix of events in 1972 worked against U.S. and Western comprehension and against Sadat's overture to the West. Not only did the Palestinian murder of eleven Israeli athletes at the Munich Olympics (5 September) take Western attention away from Egypt, the event made the Arab cause less palatable to Western public opinion as a whole. Rapprochement with the leading Arab state became more problematic and harder to sell to Western voters. Sadat had probably hoped to use the zero-sum dynamic of the Cold War to his advantage. Expelling Soviet advisers was often seen as a sign of forthcoming realignment during the Cold War. He probably believed that the United States would make a gesture in response. Such a gesture could have been an offer of economic aid or an offer to mediate the Egyptian-Israeli dispute. It would have obviously taken time to materialize, so waiting a year after expelling the Soviets would have made sense, but no American overtures mate-

rialized by June 1973. By that time Sadat faced two options: wait patiently or go to war.

Sadat had changed the Egyptian military in many ways. Egyptian military objectives were altered. Limited war against Israel was more likely to yield the results Sadat had hoped for: "I used to tell Nasser that if we could recapture 4 inches of Sinai territory (by which I meant a foothold, pure and simple), and establish ourselves so firmly that no power on earth could dislodge us, then the whole situation would change—east, west, all over."

This change meant a reprofessionalization of the Egyptian military. Sadat attempted to bring back a measure of initiative at the unit level and to improve relations between officers and their men. Although these changes would be natural for any country wishing to win a war, they entailed a great deal of risk-taking in Egypt, because the military constantly intervened in politics. Military structures in Egypt and other Arab countries are intentionally duplicated and rendered ineffective in order to protect ruling regimes from coups. The Egyptian Army was checked and balanced by the Central Security Forces. Sadat could release the military from these political straitjackets for a short period of time. These reforms could not be permanent, and this situation meant that the war needed to take place as soon as the Egyptian Army was ready and the timing was right.

Time is often equated with money. This aphorism is especially true in military affairs. Sadat spent a great deal of money preparing for the war, and Egypt's treasury could not sustain these expenditures permanently. He also had to spend money preparing for possible defeat, and his plans included transforming Egyptian territory from Alexandria to Aswan into a partisan-filled region for the Israeli Army. He had to train his soldiers and use their skills before they mustered out of the military, which meant that he had the use of only one conscription cycle. He could not expect Soviet support and funding, so he probably calculated that he needed to wage the war within eighteen to twenty-four months of the expulsion of the Soviets. All these circumstances dictated that the war needed to take place toward the end of 1973, but the actual date was to be selected on a combination of religious, political, and environmental factors.

The water in the Suez Canal was often calm during October, and the temperature in the Sinai was moderate. Snow was not yet present on the Golan Heights, thus enabling Egypt's Syrian allies to make some movement toward Israeli positions there. A full moon illuminated the night of 5 October, enabling Egyptian and Syrian troops to move comfortably. From an environmental perspective, October was the correct month to begin the war. In addition, a combination of several factors improved Egypt's chances of a successful surprise attack. Yom Kippur, the Jewish high holiday, fell on a Saturday that coincided with the tenth day of Ramadan—the Muslim holy month. Ramadan is often marked with reduced commercial and physical activity, given the burdens of fasting. Israel did not expect an attack during Ramadan, especially when most Israelis were at home for the Yom Kippur holiday. In addition, Israeli elections were planned for 28 October. Election day could also serve as a psychological deadline for the Israeli leadership, who would almost certainly face blame for not predicting the war. In short, the day marked the overlap of many factors that favored Egyptian and Syrian plans.

With hindsight, it is difficult to imagine Egypt striking at Israel any other day in 1973. Sadat willfully undermined this logic for the previous two years through a deliberate strategy of crying wolf. By expelling his Soviet advisers and refusing to wait for replacement weapons from the U.S.S.R., he gave the impression that Egypt was a great deal weaker than it actually was. He also faced a closing window of opportunity. His funds were limited, and his retrained Egyptian Army posed a coup threat as long as it did not face the political procedures and checks that rendered it intentionally ineffective. Sadat's Egypt was a landscape of broken hopes, smashed dreams, and poverty. It was bedeviled by Nasser's strategy of "no war, no peace" and the bloody legacy of the War of Attrition with the Jewish state (1967–1970). Everything, rather than something, had to change. At worst, Sadat faced a defeat, and Egypt's defeat was a victory that Israel could not afford, as the Camp David accords (1978) later proved.

Sadat went to war not to defeat Israel—the 1967 War indicated this goal was well-nigh impossible—but to reactivate diplomacy and improve Egypt's bargaining position in any negotiations by bloodying the Jewish state as well as establishing a presence in the then Israeli-controlled Sinai Peninsula. The Israelis were caught off guard primarily because they assumed Sadat would not go to war if he could not win, but the Egyptian president did so with only limited objectives in mind. The destructiveness of the war combined with the oil embargo launched by the Arab members of the Organization of Petroleum Exporting Countries (OPEC) during the conflagration and the near super-power confrontation during the closing moments of the war indicated to all concerned, especially the United States and Israel, that some air needed to be let out of the inflating balloon of rising tensions on the Arab-Israeli front. As such, the diplomatic will as well as the new military reality brought Egypt and Israel to the path toward eventual peace. In different ways, Sadat's tactics in the Arab-Israeli War of 1973 and his visit to Israel in 1977 were two bookends to the same journey, and they were equally dramatic and necessary to culminating an Egyptian-Israeli peace.

–JACK KALPAKIAN,
AL-AKHAWAYN UNIVERSITY

Viewpoint:
No. Sadat's trip to Israel was a desperate gamble that placed the Egyptian leader immediately in a vulnerable bargaining position.

In May 1967 Egyptian president Gamal Abd al-Nasser ordered the United Nations Emergency Forces (UNEF) to withdraw from its Sinai positions held since the end of the Suez War (1956) to guarantee the free passage of Israeli vessels through the Strait of Tiran. UN secretary-general U Thant consented to the

UNEF withdrawal. Israel, feeling threatened, decided to strike before the Egyptians moved first. After six days of intense fighting, Israel conquered the Sinai Peninsula and Gaza Strip from Egypt; the Golan Heights from Syria; and the West Bank, including East Jerusalem, from Jordan. One of the fastest and most lopsided military campaigns in history ended with Israel almost doubling its territory.

After this war the Arab states realized that it was impossible to destroy the Jewish state even though they maintained their position of no peace with Israel, no recognition of Israel, and no negotiations with Israel. The international community, however, working with the UN, established principles that would govern eventual negotiations. Security Council Resolution 242 (November 1967) became the framework for future negotiations. Above all, Resolution 242 called for the sovereignty, independence, and territorial integrity of all states in the Middle East; sought a solution to the growing Palestinian refugee problem; and declared the inadmissibility of acquiring land and territory through war.

In September 1970, Nasser died suddenly, and his close aide Anwar Sadat took power, becoming the new Egyptian president. Sadat tried to alter Nasser's priorities and change Egypt's political orientation, lessening its dependence on the Soviet Union and turning more toward the United States. Foremost, however, Sadat was committed to regaining the Sinai. First, Sadat tried to entice American diplomats to pressure an Israeli withdrawal from Sinai, but he failed.

It was time for a gamble. In October 1973, after having coordinated his plans with Syria, Sadat, without warning, surprised Israel with war during the holiest day of the Jewish religion, Yom Kippur. It was clear that Sadat did not expect to destroy Israel, because he was well aware of its military strength, and he also thought that the United States would not allow Israel's destruction. What he wanted was to reactivate negotiations and, above all, to improve his bargaining position vis-à-vis Israel. U.S. secretary of state Henry Kissinger was involved in secret negotiations, and following the war he initiated his step-by-step diplomacy. In short, after the Yom Kippur War, Sadat gave the Nixon administration and Israel what they never had before: a viable Arab negotiating partner who wanted a diplomatic resolution of the Arab-Israeli conflict.

For Sadat, making peace with Israel would be a collateral by-product in the process of securing full American support for his objective of reorienting Egyptian policy. A new diplomatic process was thus initiated: the United States replaced the Soviet Union as Egypt's patron and dominated the diplomatic process. Step-by-step negotiations succeeded in the phased separation of Israeli and Arab military forces in the Sinai I (1974) and Sinai II (1975) agreements. Israel exchanged "land-for-peace," which entailed a promise of peaceful relations with its neighbors.

The steps taken between 1973 and 1977 prepared the ground for one of the most dramatic acts in Middle East diplomatic history. Jimmy Carter, who became U.S. president in 1977, was consumed with finding the right formula for convening a Middle East peace conference. At the same time, and for the first time in Israeli history, a party from the Right took power. In May 1977 the right-wing Likud Party candidate Menachem Begin became the new prime minister of Israel. Begin believed that the best strategic course was to separate Egypt from the larger pan-Arab conflict with Israel. It was the same policy pursued by the first Israeli prime minister, David Ben-Gurion, when the young Free Officers took power in Cairo (1952). Even then, Ben-Gurion's idea was that a new, democratic, and reformist Egypt could be helpful in finding a real solution to the Arab-Israeli conflict, although nothing came of it for a host of reasons during the 1950s.

Sadat and Begin began testing each other in secret negotiations. They found that, in fact, each would be better off dealing with one another directly and not adopting Washington's preferred method of comprehensive peace negotiations at an international conference. Furthermore, Sadat and Begin realized they shared a common goal: that an agreement between them would serve their respective national interests. It is unequivocally accepted that Sadat's historic trip to Jerusalem broke psychological barriers, which, like his launching of the Yom Kippur War, restarted the stalled diplomatic negotiating processes, even if it was not clear where they might go. Sadat, however, was angered that Begin did not reciprocate his momentous trip to Israel, such as by immediately withdrawing all Israeli troops from the Sinai Peninsula. Sadat's impatience and Begin's weak response led to another stalemate. Many differences remained between Sadat and Begin, and the personal intervention of President Carter was necessary to bring together the two sides at Camp David in September 1978.

Sadat's trip to Israel demonstrated, once again after the October War, that the Egyptian president was a showman, maybe a statesman, but certainly a daring risk taker. He did what no other Arab leader had done in almost thirty years: he broke the Arab psychological barrier by recognizing the existence and legitimacy of the Jewish state. He did not believe Zionism was the path to righteousness and fulfillment. Sadat did not want to go to Jerusalem, but he needed to go in order to get the Sinai Peninsula back with all of its economic and political benefits. His ego, chauvinism, and personal flamboyance, as well as the dilly-dallying of the other players in a stagnating diplomatic environment, all forced Sadat to make the dramatic visit. In catalyzing a moribund negotiating process, he enraged his Arab counterparts, and they in return punished Egypt with isolation for abandoning the Arab fold. He quickly attempted to blunt Arab criticism by telling all who would listen what he had said in public before his trip: he did not go to Israel to sign a separate peace agreement. Nonetheless, after his visit, every Arab leader and media outlet brutalized him for speaking to the Israelis directly and in public. A constant barrage of verbal abuse was hurled at him; its level of intensity peaked in the immediate aftermath of the Jerusalem journey, the signing of the Camp David accords (1978), and the signing of the Egyptian-Israeli peace treaty (1979). His Arab contemporaries labeled him an "honorary Zionist" and characterized his visit to Jerusalem as a day of humiliation and submission to Zionism. Given Syrian leader Hafiz al-Asad's opposition to the Jerusalem journey and his unwavering commitment to Arab solidarity, Arab leaders flew to Damascus to persuade him to confront Sadat's objective.

Sadat expected a grand Israeli gesture equivalent in significance to his Jerusalem trip. He did not get it. He really believed that his visit would lead to an agreement within a week, but his brave journey placed him in a weakened negotiating position. Moreover, an unintended result of Sadat's visit was to push Begin to center stage, where he relished the opportunistic spotlight and grabbed the diplomatic offensive. Thus, rather than the United States responding to Sadat's initiative, Washington was forced to respond to Begin's reply. Sadat was now in a vulnerable bargaining position because Begin's response was the outline of a two-part Egyptian-Israeli agreement: the return of Sinai in exchange for a peace treaty and some self-rule or autonomy for the Palestinian people—but Israel would keep the West Bank, including all of Jerusalem. Begin wanted an agreement with Egypt but not at any price. Judea and Samaria (the West Bank) were not on the negotiating table. As Sadat soon realized these facts, the emotional luster of his visit quickly drifted off into hard realities. Sadat was growing impatient, even exasperated, with the slowness of Begin's response. One imposing problem was that Begin still did not trust Sadat, and when they met personally, there was little chemistry between them.

The mistrust between Sadat and Begin was balanced by the direct involvement of President Carter. Thanks to his intervention, the vulnerable bargaining position of Sadat was offset by some concessions by Begin; for example, notwithstanding the initial refusal to dismantle the Israeli settlements in Sinai, Jerusalem formally conceded this point. Furthermore, possible self-rule of the Palestinians proposed by Begin was removed from the agenda.

Historians really do not know if Sadat had fears about his personal safety as a consequence of his trip to Jerusalem—he never showed it. It should be said that, for a decade, Sadat's accommodation with Israel made Egypt a pariah among the Arab states. Along the way he put his political and personal life on the line; he was assassinated on 6 October 1981. Even so, by April 1982 all of the Sinai had been returned to Egyptian sovereignty, and by the end of the decade, Egypt had climbed its way back into the key position in inter-Arab politics. In the end, however, Sadat had signed a separate peace agreement in Israel that did not adequately deal with other serious problems in the Arab-Israeli arena, especially the Palestinian situation.

–DANIELE DE LUCA,
UNIVERSITY OF LECCE

References

George W. Ball and Douglas B. Ball, *The Passionate Attachment: America's Involvement with Israel, 1947 to the Present* (New York: Norton, 1992).

William Cleveland, *A History of the Modern Middle East* (Boulder, Colo.: Westview Press, 1999).

Golda Meir, *My Life* (New York: Putnam, 1975).

William B. Quandt, *Peace Process: American Diplomacy and the Arab-Israeli Conflict since 1967*, revised edition (Berkeley: University of California Press, 2001).

Anwar el-Sadat, *In Seach of Identity: An Autobiography* (New York: Harper & Row, 1978).

Saad el-Shazly, *The Crossing of the Suez* (San Francisco: American Mideast Research, 1980).

Charles D. Smith, *Palestine and the Arab-Israeli Conflict* (New York: St. Martin's Press, 2001).

Kenneth W. Stein, *Heroic Diplomacy: Sadat, Kissinger, Carter, Begin, and the Quest for Arab-Israeli Peace* (New York: Routledge, 1999).

Saadia Touval, *The Peace Brokers: Mediators in the Arab-Israeli Conflict, 1948–1979* (Princeton: Princeton University Press, 1982).

SADAT'S TRIP TO ISRAEL

SHAH OF IRAN

Could the Shah of Iran have forestalled the Iranian Revolution of 1977–1979?

Viewpoint: Yes. The Shah of Iran could have stayed in power had he won the support of the *bazaaris* (small merchants) and the clergy and promoted democratization.

Viewpoint: No. The Shah of Iran's ouster was inevitable because of his ambivalent policy toward protesters and the charisma of Ayatollah Ruhollah Khomeini.

The term *revolution* has been used often to describe changes of regime in various lands and countries throughout history, but few are actually true revolutions in the modern sense—most are simply coups d'état, in other words, a change of regime essentially within the ruling class. A revolution denotes something much more dramatic, including a change of power from one class to another and the adoption of an entirely new political ideology. Most revolutionary movements, especially the successful ones, are marked by much death and destruction from years of sustained guerrilla warfare by the opposition in its attempt to overthrow the existing regime and uproot its political, economic, and sociocultural structures and representations. Governments tend to fight back, oftentimes with brutal efficiency, in an attempt to remain in power and crush the opposition.

Unlike other twentieth-century revolutions in China, Cuba, Vietnam, or Nicaragua, there was no systematic guerrilla offensive against the government in the Iranian Revolution (1977–1979). Blood was, indeed, spilled, and some violence occurred during the revolutionary period, but it was episodic and usually the result of unplanned encounters and even misunderstandings between opposition and government forces. The revolutionary movement typically manifested itself in strikes, demonstrations, and protests; mobilization was made primarily through the mosques as it developed. As such, some of the questions remain regarding the Iranian Revolution. Could the ruler of Iran, Muhammad Reza Pahlavi, have used the formidable repressive apparatus at his disposal, the U.S.-supplied and -trained military and security services, more effectively in order to repress the opposition movement and stay in power? Did the nature of the movement itself, in combination with the fact that the Shah of Iran was terminally ill, obviate the apparent necessity and willingness to unleash the repressive structures of the state against the revolutionary forces marshaled by Ayatollah Ruhollah Khomeini? Would it have made a difference in terms of the final outcome had the Shah acted more forcefully?

Viewpoint:
Yes. The Shah of Iran could have stayed in power had he won the support of the *bazaaris* (small merchants) and the clergy and promoted democratization.

In early 1978 Muhammad Reza Pahlavi, the Shah of Iran, was regarded as one of the richest and most powerful monarchs in the world. Since 1941 he had ruled an oil-rich country that was also strategically important. Since the first National Development Plan (1949) the Shah committed himself to developing Iran's economy and changing its social and cultural foundations. Nationalism and modernization characterized his kingdom: in fact, during World War II (1939–1945) the Shah had committed himself to oppose secessionist attempts in the north of the country and face down the communist threat. He tried to reduce Iran's economic dependence on Great Britain and to limit British supremacy in the oil sector. In order to achieve this goal, he asked for a third power's help, the United States, in an attempt to balance Anglo-Soviet influence in his country. He also tried to transform Iran into a modern country, a regional power with a strong industry and a powerful military, relying once again on American help. His reform program in the early 1960s, known as the "White Revolution," embodied agrarian and cultural reform as well as modernization. Together with his unparalleled buildup of the military, it was ultimately a self-defeating effort that undermined the Shah's power. On 17 January 1979 he was obliged to flee his country. His repressive policy, starting in the 1970s, from industrialization to pseudodemocratization, resulted in the Iranian Revolution, led by Ayatollah Ruhollah Khomeini. The Ayatollah had returned to Iran after a fourteen-year exile, having managed to coalesce the diverse opposition to the Shah.

In the second half of the 1950s, thanks to the nationalization of the oil industry and subsequent oil-export income, there had been tremendous economic growth, although it was uneven. This process was changing Iranian society, still organized in a feudal way, especially in the countryside. A new Iranian middle class—professionals and skilled technicians who had studied economics and management abroad—was created. There were also plenty of foreign professionals, particularly Americans. These conditions had already caused an increase in tension within the country and represented a threat to the political stability of the monarchy. The situation worsened in the early 1960s when the Iranian economy was in a state of recession, inflation was high, and the level of productivity was decreasing. This downturn was the result of both an anachronistic power structure and a corrupt administration, which was partially responsible for the deteriorating socio-economic situation. The political realm was not any better—institutions of the Iranian system had not developed or had been turned by the Shah into mere instruments of the regime. In order to improve conditions, it was necessary to carry out a series of structural economic, social, and political reforms, assuring rational and orderly economic development.

On 26 January 1963 the Shah launched the White Revolution. He wanted to use the philosophy of revolution and the reform program as an instrument for the transformation of Iran from a poor, socially feudal-driven, and politically corrupt country into a progressive, industrialized, independent country, following the Western example. In implementing this kind of system, the Shah asserted that "as a nation we must demand steady progress, but we must also realize that the achievement of political, economic and social democracy perforce takes time. It requires education and psychological development, the reconciliation of individual wishes with social responsibility, the rethinking of moral values and individual and social loyalties, and learning to work in co-operation more than ever before." However, Westernization, according to the Shah, had to be "selective and judicious" and had to "help us [Iranians] towards the goal of democracy and shared prosperity" without abandoning "our great heritage."

In this context the Shah became the guardian of Iran's great tradition, the identity of a sovereign nation with a glorious past and a rich cultural heritage. The Shah's reference to pre-Islamic Persia and the spread of a pro-West culture provoked tenacious opposition by the Iranian clergy. In 1971 impressive celebrations in Persepolis honoring the 2,500th anniversary of the Persian Empire were particularly criticized when the Shah "linked himself directly to Cyrus the Great." The Shah urged the population to pray for "our Noble Land" and for him, who had been elected by God as "Custodian of the Land of Iran." Despite his rhetoric, however, the population had grown restless and felt ignored.

The White Revolution program included land reform, nationalization of forests, public sale of state-owned factories, profit sharing in industry, electoral power for women, and the formation of a literacy corps. It was a project designed within the political elite to change radically the face of Iran, turning it into a powerful, modern, and Western-type state.

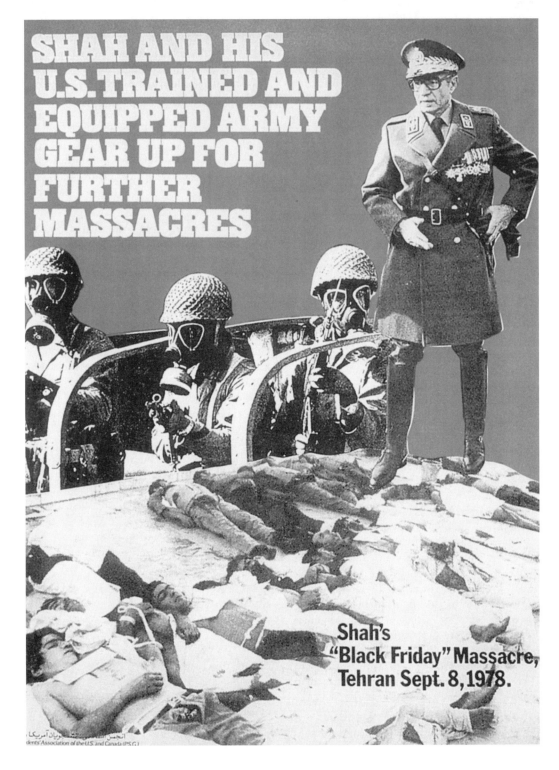

SHAH AND HIS U.S. TRAINED AND EQUIPPED ARMY GEAR UP FOR FURTHER MASSACRES

Shah's "Black Friday" Massacre, Tehran Sept. 8, 1978.

SHAH OF IRAN

Iran, however, was structurally almost entirely feudal. Most of its population was dependent on agriculture and lived in isolated small villages. It was at the mercy of its landowners and had little political consciousness. Among the projects planned by the Shah, land reform was the most significant. He was intent on changing the feudal structure of society, redistributing land, and encouraging landowners' investment in the industrial sector. The landowners were powerful; indeed, in the 1960s, 56 percent of the land was owned by 1 percent of the population. The reform limited the ownership of land in each village; surplus land was to be sold to the state to be, in turn, resold to the peasants. By eliminating large landed estates, the power of important social classes, such as the *bazaaris* (small merchants) and the clergy, who were powerful opponents of the reform policy of the monarchy, was circumscribed. In fact, according to the Shah, *bazaaris* represented a backward-looking social class, and their fanatic resistance to any kind of change in creating a modern country had to be eliminated. With regard to the clergy, the Shah decided to wage a frontal attack on its institutions. Besides severely penalizing them financially, the Shah also tried to deprive them of their religious role. In fact, in 1971 he ordered the formation of the *Sepa-e Din* (Religious Corps) and the Religious Propagandists with the task of spreading a conservative and nonpolitical version of Shiism, showing the compatibility of the monarchy with Shiite religion and testifying to the commitment of the state to religion. Not requesting the bazaar merchants' cooperation and his unsuccessful frontal attack on the clergy were two of the Shah's major political mistakes. In fact, *bazaaris* and the clergy represented two important protagonists of the Iranian social reality: they were the main constitutional actors dating back to the Constitutional Revolution (1906), and in the 1970s they still played an important role as interpreters of the needs of the Iranian population as a whole. They became the mouthpieces of the working class following the industrialization program imposed by the Shah.

The industrialization process brought an alteration to class structure, rapid urban sprawl, and a decline of the agrarian sector. With the growing industrialization and urbanization, a significant working class emerged, initially in three main Iranian towns: Teheran, Isfahan, and Tabriz. It was a fragmented and heterogeneous class, which had not developed a class consciousness yet, and consequently, at first it did not threaten the Shah and his regime at all. The fact that it had spread only to three towns made it easily controllable by the secret police (SAVAK or *Sazeman-e Ettela' at va Amniyat-e Keshivar*). Most of this new middle class were young immigrants coming from the countryside who, attracted by the towns, were catapulted into a situation quite different from that which the Shah promised. They often suffered under terrible living conditions, packed in unauthorized and rundown boroughs of towns. For them, as for the *bazaaris,* the modern and earthly ideology promoted by the regime was incomprehensible. They understood the world and their role within society through religious categories. The mosque remained their bedrock, representing at the same time a place of cultural identification and reinforcement.

Undoubtedly, the most significant result of the industrialization process was the development of a new kind of middle class, formed by skilled technicians, bureaucrats, and professionals who had studied and graduated mostly in Europe and had the task of implementing the economic and industrial growth promoted by the Shah. So, there was a close alliance among this new Iranian industrial middle class, the state (represented by the court, the armed forces, SAVAK, and state bureaucracy), and foreign investors, most of whom were American, which only added to the alienation of traditional Iranian social classes. These elite elements benefited most from the reform plan imposed by the Shah, as opposed to the majority of the population.

The Shah tried to modernize the economy and the society without changing the nature of the Persian political system. Although in 1961 he had declared that "if ever I felt that Persia's monarchy had outlived its usefulness, I would be happy to resign as King and would even join in helping to abolish our monarchical institution," he affirmed, at that particular moment, that Western-type democracy was not a good fit for Iran. He distinguished between "apparent" and "true" democracy and highlighted that the latter required education and intellectual maturity. In fact, the Shah was mainly interested in legitimizing the monarchical institution and the Pahlavi dynasty. The concept of modernism was often confused and replaced with that of "Pahlavism," his vision of political, social, and economic progress. The Shah wanted to become a democratic, progressive, and benevolent monarch—to guarantee a certain well-being for most Iranians—as well as be a revolutionary monarch, to represent left-wing nationalism and the leftist National Front.

During the Shah's reign the political system, state machinery, and politics in general strictly remained under his personal supervision and control. Basic civil freedoms, necessary for a gradual democratization, were denied to the Iranian people. After the dissolution of the *Majlis* (Iranian parliament) in 1961, the Shah ruled through decrees until 1963. In order to gain the largest popular consensus, he reintroduced the plebiscitary system. A referendum was sponsored in order to enact his White Revolution (the Shah gained 99 percent of support for his program), but above all, it highlighted the fact that the monarchy was the supreme authority. He did not hesitate to use his repressive apparatus, the powerful home-security organization SAVAK, in order to assure the implementation of his program: not only were protest marches put down harshly, but any kind of criticism and opposition was also forbidden. Since 1964 the two-party parliamentary system had been abolished in favor of a one-party system, *Iran-e Novin* (New Iran), the composition of which was supposed to represent the spirit of the White Revolution. The lack of a democratization process in Iran was

THE NEWS FROM IRAN

Writer V. S. Naipaul, a Trinidadian-born writer of Indian descent, visited Iran after the Revolution and made the following observations:

In August of 1979, six months after the overthrow of the Shah, the news from Iran was still of executions. The official Iranian news agency kept count, and regularly gave a new grand total. The most recent executions had been of prostitutes and brothel-managers; the Islamic revolution had taken that wicked turn. The Ayatollah Khomeini was reported to have outlawed music. And Islamic rules about women were being enforced again. Mixed bathing had been banned; Revolutionary Guards watched the beaches at the Caspian Sea resorts and separated the sexes. . . .

After all that I had heard about the Shah's big ideas for his country, the airport building at Tehran was a disappointment. The arrival hall was like a big shed. Blank rectangular patches edged with reddish dust—ghost pictures in ghostly frames—showed where, no doubt, there had been photographs of the Shah and his family or his monuments. Revolutionary leaflets and caricatures were taped down on walls and pillars; and—also taped down: sticky paper and handwritten notices giving a curious informality to great events—there were colored photographs of the Ayatollah Khomeini, as hard-eyed and sensual and unreliable and roguish-looking as any enemy might have portrayed him.

The airport branch of the Melli Bank—rough tables, three clerks, a lot of paper, a littered floor—was like an Indian bazaar stall. A handwritten notice on the counter said: *Dear Guests. God is the Greatest. Welcome to the Islamic Republic of Iran.* Bits of sticky brown paper dotted the customs notice boards that advised passengers of their allowances. The brown paper did away with the liquor allowance; it was part of the Islamic welcome. . . .

In the pavement kiosks there were magazines of the revolution. The cover of one had a composite photograph of the Shah as a bathing beauty: the head of the Shah attached to the body of a woman in a bikini—but the bikini had been brushed over with a broad stroke of black, not to offend modesty. In another caricature the Shah, jacketed, his tie slackened, sat on a lavatory seat with his trousers down, and with a tommy gun in his hand. A suitcase beside him was labeled *To Israel* and *Bahama;* an open canvas bag showed a bottle of whiskey and a copy of *Time* magazine. . . .

Khomeini received and preached and blessed; Khalkhalli hanged. He was Khomeini's hanging judge. It was Khalkhalli who had conducted many of those swift Islamic trials that had ended in executions, with official before-and-after photographs: men shown before they were killed, and then shown dead, naked on the sliding mortuary slabs.

Khalkhalli had recently been giving interviews, emphasizing his activities as judge, and a story in Tehran was that he had fallen out of favor and was trying through these interviews to keep his reputation alive. He told the Tehran *Times* that he had "probably" sentenced four hundred people to death in Tehran: "On some nights, he said, bodies of 30 or more people would be sent out in trucks from the prison. He claimed he had also signed the death warrants of a large num-

ber of people in Khuzistan Province." Khuzistan was the Arab province in the southwest, where the oil was. . . .

On Revolution Avenue, formerly Shah Reza, opposite the big iron-railed block of Tehran University, were the publishers (mingled with men's shops) and the pavement book-sellers and cassette-sellers and print-sellers. The cassettes were of speeches by Khomeini and other ayatollahs; they were also—in spite of Khomeini's ban on music—of popular Persian and Indian songs. Some booksellers had books in Persian about the revolution, its ideologues and its martyrs. Some had solid piles of communist literature—Persian paperbacks, and hardback sets of Lenin or Marx in English, from Russia. One revolution appeared to flow into the other.

And there were photograph albums of the revolution. The emphasis in these albums was on death, blood, and revenge. There were photographs of people killed during the Shah's time; photographs of the uprising: blood in the streets, bodies in the morgues, with slogans daubed in blood on the white tiles; galleries of people executed after the revolution, and shown dead, page after page, corpse upon corpse. One corpse was that of Hoveyda, the Shah's prime minister: the black bullet hole in Hoveyda's old man's neck was clear in the photograph.

All the buildings in the university block—founded by the Shah's father—were disfigured with slogans. The university was the great meeting place of Tehran, and even on a day like this, a day without any scheduled event, it was full of discussion groups. Behzad said, "It goes on all the time." What did they talk about? He said, "The same things. Islam, communism, the revolution." It looked a pacific campus scene; it was hard to associate these young men in jeans and pretty shirts with the bloodiness celebrated in the books and albums across the road.

But violence was in the air, and just after we came out through the main gate we saw this incident. A student in a white shirt, small and with glasses, inexpertly and with some comic effort taped a leaflet onto the iron rails of the gate. The leaflet was a protest about the closing down of *Ayandegan,* the paper of the left. A workman near a food stall at the edge of the pavement walked slowly over, drew a red hammer and sickle on the leaflet, crossed the whole sheet with an X, slapped the student twice, in the middle of the pavement crowd; and then, without hurry, taped up the defaced leaflet more securely.

The student had ducked to save his glasses and his eyes. No one moved to help him. Even Behzad did nothing. He only said, as though appealing to me for justice, "Did you see that? Did you see that?"

The two revolutions appeared to flow together, the revolution of Khomeini, and what Behzad would have seen as the true revolution of the people. But they were distinct. The previous weekend Behzad and some of his group had gone to a village to do "constructive" work. They had run into trouble with the Revolutionary Guards: every village had its *komiteh,* young men with guns who were now the law in parts of Iran. The Guards, Moslems, didn't want communists in the village.

Source: *V. S. Naipaul, "Among the Believers," Atlantic Monthly, 250 (July 1981): 28–48.*

SHAH OF IRAN

another political mistake committed by the Shah. Therefore, the opposition was forced to adopt revolutionary struggle.

The complete lack of freedom of expression in Iran obstructed the spread of a democratic culture within the middle class, particularly among liberal and social intellectuals. This democratic void favored the development of radical political doctrines, such as Marxism and socialist Shiism, especially among university students. Many young intellectuals were drawn to Islam, interpreted from a revolutionary point of view and the peculiar Messianic expectations of Marxism. This socialist Shiism, in its most radical form, found expression in the mujahideen (holy warriors) who, together with the *fedayeen* (guerrillas), launched an armed struggle against the Shah. They criticized the modernization program, contested the authoritarian features of the monarchy, and exposed the excesses of SAVAK, which forbade any kind of political debate. In June 1963 Ayatollah Ruhollah Khomeini was arrested and exiled for having criticized land reform, women's emancipation, and the announcement of immunity for U.S. personnel based in Iran. Khomeini's anger focused on this latter point, believing that this serious question, together with the coup organized against Muhammad Mussadiq by the Central Intelligence Agency (CIA) in 1953 in order to restore the Shah's power, highlighted the contradictions in the Iranian sovereign's reform program.

The recession in the second half of the 1970s caused economic and social tensions. Protests against the Shah's policy arose in the main Iranian towns. The urban working class and bazaar merchants were the protagonists of these protests, as they were clearly penalized by measures the Iranian state took in order to deal with the economic crisis. Broad popular unrest, spreading all over the country within a few years, was cleverly organized and led by Iranian clergy. In fact, the lack of success in modernizing the country could be seen in the miserable economic and social conditions of most Iranians. A large part of the population, oppressed and outcast, found in religion the answer to its problems. Hence, Islam increasingly became the only effective mouthpiece of the people's frustration. The Shah did not offer a valid ideological alternative to that proffered by Shiite clergy. He also could not limit the mullahs' activities and did not gain the support of any other Iranian religious faction.

The Shah could have successfully remained in power had he pursued cooperation with the bazaar merchants and the clergy, recognizing the former's important economic role and the

latter's undeniable social role. Together with them he could have successfully implemented the complex socio-economic processes in Iran, thus giving voice to a real Persian identity. Moreover, had he managed to promote more democratization, thus allowing the political opposition to express its dissent, he would have prevented the spread of popular unrest, which later became the mainstay of the revolution's success. In this case, the protest would have been absorbed within the political system, and the population could have been represented in the monarchy's institutions. However, the Shah's policies were a total failure, and he fled Teheran: his monarchy collapsed, and by February the Islamic Republic of Iran was born.

–VALENTINA VANTAGGIO,
UNIVERSITY OF LECCE

**Viewpoint:
No. The Shah of Iran's ouster was inevitable because of his ambivalent policy toward protesters and the charisma of Ayatollah Ruhollah Khomeini.**

In the second half of the 1970s the growing intensity of the protest movement left Muhammad Reza Pahlavi, the Shah of Iran, in a difficult political situation. The government had managed neither to quell the riots nor to reach a compromise with moderate factions of the opposition. In the last two years of his reign (1977–1979) the Shah showed himself to be more confused, hesitant, and weak than ever: his strategy vacillated between a reconciliation policy and forceful repression of riots. The protest movement against the Shah's regime was becoming stronger and more widespread among the Iranian people. Under influence from the Americans, in 1977 the Shah initiated a liberalization program by promising to create "a free political atmosphere," assure free elections, end censorship, and allow greater political freedom. This new situation engendered the growth of the popular protest movement that emerged with a reformist, anti-violent focus, backed by lay intellectuals and students. The Shah's attitude was ambivalent toward these protests: on one hand, the popular movement was legitimated when he promised Iranians he would "hear the voice of your Revolution" and "not repeat the past mistakes," such as "lawlessness, oppression and corruption"; on the other hand, the Shah had no scruples about ordering the army to repress protests, introducing martial law, and virtually forbidding demonstrations. In fact, although there never was a real improvement in the political atmosphere, the Shah was not willing to share his authority with anyone else, least of all with the opposition. In November 1978 the Shah, in a desperate attempt to save his crown, formed a military government, thus entrusting his destiny to the armed forces, the only loyal ally upon which he believed he could rely.

However, the situation became irreparable after the bloody riots of 8 September, known as "Black Friday." Thousands of demonstrators, not realizing martial law was in force, had gathered in Teheran, and, following their refusal to disperse, soldiers opened fire and killed hundreds of people. The rioting turned into a battle between the demonstrators, who put up barricades and burned buildings, and the police, who responded with tanks. The entire country was in disarray: oil workers went on strike; opposition guerrilla groups threatened government officials; students knocked down a statue of the Shah in front of the University of Teheran; and opposition forces stormed the British embassy, as well as offices of several U.S. companies. These protests expanded to include the middle class, professionals, and civil servants. The popular movement had changed, becoming more organized and violent, and it spread to major Iranian towns. The Iranian clergy became involved by putting religion at the forefront of the political struggle. Mosques, theology schools, and all Islamic centers became vital points of mass mobilization, and the use of Shiite symbols and rituals gave the political struggle a sense of sacredness against the Shah's blasphemous and profane regime. This mass mobilization undoubtedly led to the success of the Revolution.

In early December 1978 Ayatollah Ruhollah Khomeini, from his Parisian exile, ordered the population to demonstrate against the Shah's regime on the occasion of the holy representations and processions in honor of Ali's son, Husayn, the fourth Imam of the Twelver Shiites, during the Islamic month of Muharram. These celebrations commemorated Husayn's martyrdom. Some people, ignoring the curfew, paraded through towns wearing white clothes, a symbol of martyrdom, while others yelled slogans against the Shah. It was a brilliant manipulation of the Shiite religion for a political purpose. Imam Husayn seemed to lead them into battle on the day of his commemoration, and Khomeini seemed to lead them from afar, like a kind of hidden imam. One of the crucial elements for Khomeini's seizure of power was, as Nikki R. Keddie states, the revival of the "ideological Shi'i tradition that contained elements

that he could rework so as to legitimize revolution, republicanism, and rule by a top clerical leader." Khomeini emerged as the sole leader of the Iranian Revolution (1977–1979) and the only alternative to the Shah. The entire opposition rallied around the clergy and Khomeini: liberals, laity, religious liberals, left-wingers, and guerrillas. Huge differences among them were overcome in the name of the only element they had in common: opposition to the Shah. The extreme diversity of the movement, comprising nearly the entire population, also contributed to the success of the Revolution. Men and women from every walk of life, young and old, intellectuals and illiterates, students and professors, professionals and civil servants, workers and *bazaaris* (small merchants), all proclaimed the end of the Shah's regime and the formation of a just government that respected Islam's precepts. The clergy, headed by Khomeini, believed an open confrontation with the government was necessary even if repression and a bloodbath were inevitable. This stance was supposed to highlight the atrocities of the Shah's regime, leading to the consequent radicalization of the movement.

Actually, the Shah had two alternatives: to pursue an iron-fist policy or to submit to the opposition and leave the country, thus favoring a political solution of the crisis. The former alternative, which was not supported by the Americans, would play into Khomeini's hands. The latter possibility seemed more realistic. Because of U.S. support over the years, the Shah believed that the Americans would intervene and save his regime, as it had in 1953, but this time his fall was inevitable. In January 1979, while trying to reach a belated agreement with the opposition, the Shah proposed that Shahpour Bakhtiar, leader of the National Front, form a new government, and he agreed to leave the country until a solution to the crisis was found. Believing that his absence would be "no more than a matter of days but of hours," the Shah was overwhelmed by the revolutionary forces and could not return to Iran. At the same time, Khomeini, "in accordance with the rights conferred by the law of Islam and the basis of the vote of confidence given me by the overwhelming majority of the Iranian people," announced the formation of a Council of the Islamic Republic, with the task of coordinating activities of the opposition to the Shah. In the meantime, Bakhtiar was trying to calm the revolution: he released political prisoners, dismantled SAVAK (secret police), reduced military expenses, and refused to sell oil to Israel. It was, however, too late. People clamored for Khomeini's homecoming and invited him to become Iran's new leader. Acknowledging the people's will, on 1 February 1979, the

Bakhtiar government allowed the Ayatollah to return to Iran. His comeback was triumphant. A poem written for the event by Taha Hijazi well interprets the widespread popular mood and the hope for his return to mark the beginning of a new and just society: "this broken, wounded mother / will be liberated forever / from the shackles of tyranny and ignorance / and from the chains of plunder, torture and prison."

Like Ali, Husayn, and other imams of Shiism, Khomeini had been oppressed by an unjust sovereign, forced into exile, and from there obliged to fight with all his strength against a tyrant. He had not accepted any compromise with the "satanic tyrant," and, like most Iranians, he lived an austere life, in contrast to the politicians who were corrupt and living in luxury. He seemed sincere, defiant, and, above all, incorruptible. He was a "man of God," not interested in achieving power but rather being the highest spiritual authority. He promised to liberate the country from foreign domination, grant participation to political parties, safeguard the rights of religious minorities, and guarantee social justice—particularly to *bazaaris,* intellectuals, farmers, and, more generally, to the *mostazafin* (deprived masses).

In Iran the bond between politics and religion is of paramount importance, and to realize this bond allows one to understand the social and political changes characterizing the history of this country. In fact, the Iranian Revolution was not only political. Certainly, the Shah's tyrannical and repressive regime and the serious economic crisis contributed to incite the uprising. It was also, above all, a religious revolution. Iranians rose up against the secular ethos imposed from above and against their will that attempted to exclude religion from their lives. The Shah had often talked about the greatness of pre-Islamic Iran, and he lavishly celebrated the 2,500th anniversary of the founding of the Persian Empire, changing the starting date of the Iranian calendar from the Prophet's *hijra* (migration) to the foundation of the pre-Islamic monarchy.

According to most Iranians, the Shah's strength basically derived from unconditional U.S. support. Additionally, the United States brought to Iran its political culture of strictly separating religion and state. This concept was incomprehensible to most Iranians. For them, living a hedonistic and materialistic life was inconceivable. Similarly, it was untenable for U.S. president Jimmy Carter, a defender of human rights, to continue to support the Shah, who had started killing his own people. In a series of wall paintings, Khomeini was portrayed as Moses, the Shah as the Pharaoh, while Carter was portrayed as the idol whom the Pharaoh worshiped. America had corrupted the Shah, and Khomeini represented the only religious alternative to the profane dictatorship. According to the clergy, the unsuccessful attempts at modernizing the country, industrialization, and consequent mass urbanization had led to economic and social misery with growing inequalities. The attempted imposition of Western ideology and culture pushed the population toward Islam, which became, in their eyes, the only possible solution to their problems. Hence, ayatollahs, opposed to cultural and political models imported from outside, became the voice of the Iranian people's frustrations. In the Revolution, the enemy was certainly the Shah, as a bearer of Westernization and a culture of lay and secular elements at the expense of Islam and Iranian traditions, and he was seen as a servant of Western governments. Khomeini argued that Islam and politics were two sides of the same coin: the Prophet Muhammad was at the same time head of the state, commander of the army, and spiritual leader of the community. After his death, according to Shiite Islam, these responsibilities were conveyed to his cousin and son-in-law, Ali, and from him to his descendants. With the death of the twelfth Imam, the Imamate's cycle was over, and until his return, according to Khomeini, the clergy bore responsibility for leading the community. The Shiite *ulema* (clergy), economically and politically independent, played a crucial role in the Revolution.

Another pivotal factor for the success of the Revolution was undoubtedly represented by the charismatic personality of Khomeini. He had been the only true antagonist to the Shah, a persistent opponent of monarchy and of foreign cultural influence and domination. He was certainly wise to gather around himself the whole revolutionary movement and impose his absolutist and fundamentalist conception of Islam. His Manichaean vision of the world, divided between oppressed Muslims and oppressor Westerners, also found a receptive audience among left-wing secular elements and the Shiite socialists in the revolutionary movement. As Keddie observes, "the fusion of modern, secular Manichaeism, traditional Islam, and uncompromising hostility to monarchy, dependence, and imperialism created a revolutionary ideology that distinguished the revolutionaries from Western and westernized oppressors." It was a true ideology of mobilization, gathering, under the aegis of Khomeini, *bazaaris* and the lower classes, yearning for the creation of an ideal society following the Prophet Muhammad's and

Imam Ali's community. This ideology had a tremendous influence on the Iranian population, and Khomeini convinced the masses of his righteous path. In fact, he gained almost total popular support. The middle class regarded him as a defender of private property, as a backer of its business interests, and as the only one able to abolish the monarchy and put an end to the excessive foreign influence in the country. The working class and peasantry backed him, since they were attracted by his commitment to social justice, agrarian reform, and the construction of schools and public works. The Iranian masses, relying only on their religion, overthrew the Shah's dictatorial regime without the aid of weapons. Instead of paralyzing the Iranian population, the Shah's repression caused the opposite effect, inciting people to riot. After years of terror and repression, through the Revolution the Iranian population gained control of their own country's political life—and there was nothing the Shah could have done about it.

–GALIA VITALI,
TARANTO, ITALY

References

Ervand Abrahamian, *Iran between Two Revolutions* (Princeton: Princeton University Press, 1982).

Shahrough Akhavi, *Religion and Politics in Contemporary Iran: Clergy-State Relations in the Pahlavi Period* (Albany: State University of New York Press, 1980).

James Bill, *The Politics of Iran: Groups, Classes and Modernization* (Columbus, Ohio: Merrill, 1972).

Nikki R. Keddie, *Iran and the Muslim World: Resistance and Revolution* (New York: New York University Press, 1995).

Mohsen M. Milani, *The Making of Iran's Islamic Revolution: From Monarchy to Islamic Republic* (Boulder, Colo.: Westview Press, 1988).

Muhammad Reza Pahlavi, *Answer to History* (New York: Stein & Day, 1980).

Amin Saikal, *The Rise and Fall of the Shah* (Princeton: Princeton University Press, 1980).

SINAI I AND II

Did the disengagement agreements known as Sinai I (1974) and Sinai II (1975) facilitate the Arab-Israeli peace process?

Viewpoint: Yes. The step-by-step approach that led to Sinai I and Sinai II was the correct diplomatic methodology at the time, because it gave incentives to the Arabs and the Israelis to continue the peace process.

Viewpoint: No. Sinai I and Sinai II were interim agreements that failed to deal comprehensively with the larger Arab-Israeli dispute.

From a negotiating standpoint, the problem in the aftermath of the 1967 Arab-Israeli War was that Israel held all of the territory acquired in the conflict; therefore, it was an asymmetrical bargaining situation, and the Arab states were not going to negotiate from such a position of glaring weakness. The 1973 Arab-Israeli War restored some symmetry to the bargaining equation between Israel and the Arab states, as the latter, for the first time, had bloodied Israel in battle and actually, by the end of the war, held some territory in the Sinai Peninsula that had been under Israeli control. In addition, the destructiveness of the war itself; the near direct confrontation between the two superpowers toward the end of the conflict, as both Washington and Moscow supported their respective client states; and the oil embargo implemented by the Arab members of the Organization of Petroleum Exporting Countries against supporters of Israel (primarily the United States) compelled almost all involved to seek a negotiated solution before there was another all-out Arab-Israeli war.

U.S. secretary of state Henry Kissinger realized even before the 1973 War that limited agreements in the Arab-Israeli arena might be the best way to begin the negotiation process, eventually leading toward a comprehensive resolution. If some of the more intractable problems in the conflict, especially those concerning the Palestinian issue or the question of Israeli withdrawal from territories it captured in the 1967 War, were discussed at the start of negotiations, the whole process may never have gotten off the ground. Kissinger recognized that the outcome of the war and the disposition of forces were conducive to a series of disengagement agreements that might act as building blocks toward a comprehensive Arab-Israeli peace. As such, he almost immediately engaged in his famous shuttle diplomacy between Cairo, Jerusalem, and Damascus, implementing the step-by-step approach of limited agreements. In January 1974 Egypt and Israel agreed to disengage forces, with Israeli forces withdrawing across the Suez Canal to the Sinai Peninsula—this agreement became known as Sinai I (there was also a disengagement agreement between Syria and Israel in May 1974 along the Golan Heights). In September 1975 another disengagement agreement between Israel and Egypt was consummated, known as Sinai II, with Israeli forces withdrawing about halfway across the Sinai, and with United Nations observer forces and monitoring stations emplaced between the two sides to ensure compliance.

Viewpoint:
Yes. The step-by-step approach that led to Sinai I and Sinai II was the correct diplomatic methodology at the time, because it gave incentives to the Arabs and the Israelis to continue the peace process.

In June 1992 Yitzhak Rabin was elected prime minister of Israel. Rabin granted in the early stages of his tenure first priority to peace negotiations between Israel and Syria. He felt, however, that in view of the huge gaps between the two sides, negotiations had to be promoted gradually. Therefore, Rabin proposed that instead of expending efforts to reach a comprehensive Israeli-Syrian peace agreement, a task that was clearly beyond the ability of either side to achieve at that time, it would be preferable for the United States and the two sides involved to channel these efforts into reaching an interim agreement. It was Rabin's hope that such an agreement would assist in breaking down the wall of distrust between Syria and Israel and would ultimately lead the sides toward the much desired peace accord.

However, Syrian president Hafiz al-Asad rejected Rabin's proposal out-of-hand. Asad, it seemed, believed that Rabin's proposed interim agreement was designed to assist Israel in preserving the status quo between the two countries. This compact would allow Israel to "buy" Syria's agreement to its continued and prolonged presence on the Golan Heights for the proverbial "mess of pottage." Asad was afraid that the time that Israel would "buy" would be used to entrench its presence there, for instance, in establishing new settlements, thus making the entire idea of Israeli withdrawal from the Heights impracticable—Syria would be committed, through the interim agreement, to ensuring quiet along Israel's northern border. Thus, Asad viewed any interim agreement with Israel as a stumbling block or barrier, or even as potentially hindering negotiations between the two countries rather than promoting them.

Both Rabin and Asad had good reasons for adopting opposing positions regarding an interim agreement as a means of promoting the path of peace. The model to which each side related was undoubtedly the interim agreements reached between Israel, Egypt, and Syria following the October 1973 Arab-Israeli War. Although the Israeli-Syrian agreement did not result in a breakthrough toward peace, and relations between them remained hostile (although in the Golan Heights quiet continued along their common border), the first and second Sinai agreements between Israel and Egypt, especially the second one, during Rabin's first term as prime minister (1974–1977), undoubtedly paved the way toward the Egyptian-Israeli peace agreement. Thus, if Asad's rejection of an interim agreement with Israel is understandable, Rabin's position is also understandable and justified, since, from the historical standpoint, one may argue that the Sinai agreements laid the groundwork for achieving the Israeli-Egyptian peace agreement (1979).

This reluctance ostensibly begs the question of why was it necessary from the start to require the interim agreements instead of attempting to reach an Israeli-Egyptian peace agreement directly. After all, in the long-term view, it seems that the journey made by Israel and Egypt along the path toward peace was obvious and inevitable. In retrospect there are even those who argue that Egyptian president Anwar Sadat had already decided to pursue a peace agreement with Israel when he rose to power in Cairo in September 1970 following the death of his predecessor, Gamal Abd al-Nasser.

There are those, incidentally, who claim that in the early 1970s the Israeli government, headed by Golda Meir, had missed the opportunity to reach an Israeli-Egyptian peace agreement that might have prevented the outbreak of the October 1973 war. As soon as he rose to power, Sadat began sending out feelers toward Israel with the aim of promoting security and political arrangements, even if not a peace agreement. Sadat proposed, for instance, that in exchange for Israel's withdrawal from the Suez Canal and the deployment of Egyptian policemen on both its banks, Egypt would open the Canal to all shipping. This proposal was rejected by an Israeli government that did not consider Sadat trustworthy and viewed him as a weak leader incapable of pursuing a serious political process. In addition, the Israelis felt no military or political pressures to agree to the proposal, which they viewed as minimal (since it did not offer a comprehensive peace agreement) in return for substantial Israeli territorial concessions. It is quite possible that Israeli reaction pushed Sadat to decide to go to war.

One must, however, admit that claims Israel had missed an opportunity to reach a peace agreement at the beginning of the 1970s embody a kind of historical anachronism. It is not at all clear that Sadat would have been able to offer Israel in 1973, and certainly not immediately after his rise to power, a signed peace agree-

ment, which he was able to do clearly, unequivocally, and publicly by 1977 when he made his historic trip to Israel. Even those who argue that Sadat was determined to reach an Israeli-Egyptian peace agreement immediately after his rise to power are unable to provide any substantial support for this view. Before his visit to Jerusalem, Sadat tended to express himself cautiously and never said, absolutely and unequivocally, anything about bringing an end to the Israeli-Egyptian conflict. For instance, he never proposed a comprehensive peace agreement with Israel that would include recognition of its right to exist, and he appeared still to be committed to the resolutions of the Arab League summit meeting in Khartoum, Sudan, in August 1967. These resolutions recognized the need to pursue political means in retrieving Arab lands captured by Israel in 1967. However, at the same time, they rejected any direct negotiations with it or the recognition of its right to exist.

Moreover, one must bear in mind that when Sadat rose to power, he was considered in Israel, the United States, and even Egypt as a colorless, uncharismatic leader who lacked public support and certainly not as a partner capable of making difficult decisions on the issue of war and peace with Israel. Even after the 1973 War, it is difficult to imagine the possibility of a breakthrough on the road to peace in view of the ill feelings following the bitter and bloody battles between Israel and the Arab states.

At the same time, it is not at all clear whether Israel could have, immediately after the end of the 1973 War, agreed to a complete withdrawal from the Sinai Peninsula and the evacuation of all Israeli settlements that had been established there, a move to which Israeli prime minister Menachem Begin finally agreed in the course of the Israeli-Egyptian negotiations at Camp David in the summer of 1978—and that only after some strenuous arm-twisting by the Americans. Finally, it is also worth bearing in mind that the United States, which had been an important player in the efforts to achieve an Israeli-Egyptian peace agreement, had little influence over Egypt at the beginning of the 1970s. Its relations with Cairo were in their earliest stages and needed some time to develop and ripen to the extent of a strategic alliance in which the existence of peaceful relations served as a basic and necessary component.

In view of the chasm that divided their positions, the two countries, as orchestrated by the chief arbiter of the Israeli-Egyptian peace process, U.S. secretary of state Henry Kissinger, had no choice but to pursue a gradual process. Even this incremental approach produced opposition. In Israel there were mass demonstrations against withdrawal from Israeli-held territories in Sinai as part of Sinai I and II. There were even those who claimed that the Rabin government was endangering the security of Israel. Even the Rabin government had initially rejected the pro-

Posters in English and Hebrew, July 1975, urging Israel to continue its occupation of the Sinai Peninsula

(© CORBIS/David Rubinger)

posal that Kissinger made designed to promote the Israeli-Egyptian interim agreement (Sinai II) claiming that the concessions demanded of Israel posed a threat to its security. This position prompted the U.S. administration to announce a reassessment of relations between the two countries, a sharp and unprecedented step in Israeli-American relations, which ultimately led to the Israeli government's adoption of a more flexible position. Sadat was also the object of severe criticism in the Arab world following the signing of Sinai I and II for what was considered a betrayal and a "liquidation sale" of the rights of Arabs. These agreements marked the beginning of Egypt's estrangement from its Arab friends, especially Syria, together with whom Egypt had gone to war in 1973.

Worth mentioning in this connection is the influence of the Cold War on the chances of promoting a comprehensive Middle East peace process. In view of the U.S.-Soviet rivalry, there can be no doubt that a step-by-step policy, even if it was only on the Egyptian front, was the only way of progressing toward peace, since it may be assumed that any attempt to achieve comprehensive Arab-Israeli peace would have been thwarted because of superpower rivalry. In addition, the fact that the Soviet Union was ready to side with the Arabs and that the United States supported the Israelis was in itself a deterrent to any incentive for either side to choose an accelerated path toward peace. Such incentives were created, at least for most of the Arab world, only following the collapse of the Soviet Union at the end of the 1980s.

Thus, Sinai I and II provided the opportunity for a separation of forces and the construction of a buffer zone between the armies of Israel and Egypt and, most important, the opening of the Suez Canal to navigation and the rehabilitation of cities along the Canal. This arrangement provided something of an important incentive for Egypt to continue negotiations and also proof for Israel that Egypt was serious and determined in its efforts toward economic rehabilitation and development. Thus, it was the necessary mechanism toward establishing peace, with no commitment involved. Also, the deployment of a U.S. force at the early warning station in Sinai, which enabled the Americans to observe moves by the two sides as a means of establishing mutual trust, made Washington a key player in connecting, mediating, and reaching compromises. In any case, forging closer ties between Washington and Cairo completed Sadat's initial tack toward the United States, begun when Egypt separated from the Soviet Union and expelled Soviet advisers in July

1972. All of these factors served to create the mechanism, or more accurately the dynamics, that led the two sides to a peace agreement.

These interim agreements clarified for the two sides the advantages offered by progress toward peace. Egypt was able to understand that it would regain the Sinai Peninsula, and proof of this fact was Israel's gradual withdrawal, mainly from the Suez Canal area. Furthermore, America's generous assistance to Israel made it clear that Israel would improve its security in return for territorial concessions.

Asad's reservations in accepting interim steps demonstrate the importance of the context within which the two Sinai agreements were signed. For example, Sadat adopted the idea of the peace option as soon as he rose to power, and while he hesitated and found it difficult to pursue the path of peace, ultimately in November 1977, on his own initiative he took the decisive step. The will was there, and the Sinai agreements assisted, rather than hindered, his desire to see his goal achieved. In other words, the agreements were not forced on one or both sides. Interim agreements that are not accompanied by true readiness and determination to achieve peace will not necessarily assist in promoting a peace process, as borne out by the cases of Syria and the Palestinians. However, from the beginning the Egyptian case was different. It was a combination of desire anchored in a vision of peace: Sadat's vision that was shared in November 1977 by Begin. At the same time, desire was anchored in political ability and was based on the strength of the Egyptian state, which had emerged victorious in its own eyes in the October 1973 War. Kissinger identified the propitious moment and exploited it to the fullest extent in a step-by-step approach leading to the interim agreements.

–EYAL ZISSER,
TEL AVIV UNIVERSITY

Viewpoint:
No. Sinai I and Sinai II were interim agreements that failed to deal comprehensively with the larger Arab-Israeli dispute.

In April 1974 U.S. secretary of state Henry Kissinger arrived in Damascus, where he met with Syrian president Hafiz al-Asad. This visit was another station in Kissinger's shuttle diplomacy and was designed to achieve the signing of a viable disengagement agreement between Israel and Syria following the October 1973

Arab-Israeli War. A bloody War of Attrition had raged on the front between Israel and Syria long after the war had ended. Before his arrival in Damascus, Kissinger had successfully brokered a disengagement agreement separating Israeli and Egyptian forces. Now he was trying his hand at achieving the same thing in Syria.

While Asad had, according to Kissinger, shown real interest in reaching an arrangement that would end fighting on the Golan Heights, he was apparently interested in more than that. Indeed, when Kissinger informed Asad that he had succeeded in getting Israel to agree to the Syrians' demand to determine a cease-fire line and a separation of forces that would be more advantageous to the Syrians, transferring to Syria several meters of territory held by Israel in the Golan Heights, Asad interrupted him, asking Kissinger where all this information was leading. In other words, was this process leading toward the return of the entire Golan Heights to the Syrians? Asad did not tell Kissinger what he was prepared to give in return for regaining the Golan Heights, but it may be assumed that he understood that he would have to pay a price and may even be forced to reach a settlement with Israel. Nonetheless, Asad continued to express his interest in promoting the idea of a comprehensive settlement over Kissinger's preference for a partial, segmented agreement.

Kissinger preferred to ignore Asad's position since he had nothing that he could offer the Syrian president. He apparently assessed that the time was not yet ripe for a move of that kind. First, it was not at all clear whether Asad had reached the point of signing a full and comprehensive peace agreement with Israel, Jerusalem's unequivocal condition for progressing toward a territorial settlement on the Golan Heights. Asad had indeed created the impression that he was prepared to enter into a far-reaching settlement, but at that time he had given no clear and significant indication of this stance, and he certainly had refrained from unequivocal statements to this effect. Second, it may be assumed that Kissinger had assessed that Syria would have difficulty in getting Israel to agree to a withdrawal from all, or even most, of the Golan Heights. After all, Israel, still reeling from the October 1973 War, was finding it difficult to place any faith in the Arabs' intentions. For instance, Israeli prime minister Golda Meir had difficulty in discussing and later accepting the idea of Israeli withdrawal from the eastern shore of the Suez Canal. One can easily imagine how she would have reacted to a proposal to withdraw from the Golan Heights. Finally, Kissinger decided to grant priority to his efforts to reach a breakthrough in the Egyptian-Israeli front where chances for success seemed better and not to

dilute his efforts and energy on two fronts. In any event, on 31 May 1974, Kissinger succeeded in bringing Israel and Syria to an agreement on the separation of forces, which ensured quiet along the Golan Heights front for many years.

In June 1974, about two months after his meeting with Kissinger, Asad held a similar conversation with U.S. president Richard M. Nixon, who had arrived in Damascus as part of his historic visit to the Middle East with the objective of moving the Arab-Israeli peace process forward—and perhaps of escaping the shadow of the Watergate scandal that had been hounding him in the American domestic arena and that forced his resignation several weeks after his return from the Middle East. However, Kissinger interrupted this conversation when the two leaders began discussing how to promote a comprehensive peace settlement in the region and how to force Israel to withdraw from the Golan Heights. Kissinger reminded Nixon that he had to rush to his plane and move on to another stop on his Middle East tour, thus ending the dialogue.

According to accounts of this meeting, in Kissinger's memoirs and in statements by others involved, it seems that it could have been possible, in the wake of the October 1973 War, to reach a breakthrough in Syrian-Israeli negotiations at least on the part of the Syrians, whose aim was to regain the Golan Heights. Of course, it is not certain whether Asad was prepared at this stage to reach a peace agreement with Israel; nevertheless, one cannot rule out the possibility that he, and the Israelis as well, could have been motivated to do this. The war had substantially increased Israel's dependence on the United States, thus providing Washington with bargaining chips in its dialogue with Israel. However, the approach of step-by-step and interim agreements, arising mainly because Kissinger did not believe that the sides could ultimately reach a peace agreement, prompted him to make the erroneous decision to abandon the comprehensive approach and to adopt the idea of promoting interim agreements in its stead, concentrating first of all on the Egyptian-Israeli front. For this decision, the Middle East was destined to pay with continued regional conflict.

There can be no doubt that the step-by-step policy ultimately brought an Israeli-Egyptian peace agreement (1979). Nevertheless, it is not clear whether a different policy would have yielded the same results much sooner. After all, immediately after Sadat rose to power in Egypt, there were indications of willingness on his part to reach a peace agreement with Israel. Sadat came out with a peace initiative of his own on the eve of the October 1973 War that Israel rejected because it refused to believe the sincerity

SEPARATION OF FORCES AGREEMENT

EGYPTIAN-ISRAELI AGREEMENT ON DISENGAGE-MENT OF FORCES IN PURSUANCE OF THE GENEVA PEACE CONFERENCE

A. Egypt and Israel will scrupulously observe the cease-fire on land, sea, and air called for by the UN Security Council and will refrain from the time of the signing of this document from all military or para-military actions against each other.

B. The military forces of Egypt and Israel will be separated in accordance with the following principles:

1. All Egyptian forces on the east side of the Canal will be deployed west of the line designated as Line A on the attached map. All Israeli forces, including those west of the Suez Canal and the Bitter Lakes, will be deployed east of the line designated as Line B on the attached map.

2. The area between the Egyptian and Israeli lines will be a zone of disengagement in which the United Nations Emergency Force (UNEF) will be stationed. The UNEF will continue to consist of units from countries that are not permanent members of the Security Council.

3. The area between the Egyptian line and the Suez Canal will be limited in armament and forces.

4. The area between the Israeli line (Line B on the attached map) and the line designated as Line C on the attached map, which runs along the western base of the mountains where the Gidi and Mitla Passes are located, will be limited in armament and forces.

5. The limitations referred to in paragraphs 3 and 4 will be inspected by UNEF. Existing procedures of the UNEF, including the attaching of Egyptian and Israeli liaison officers to UNEF, will be continued.

6. Air forces of the two sides will be permitted to operate up to their respective lines without interference from the other side.

C. The detailed implementation of the disengagement of forces will be worked out by military representatives of Egypt and Israel, who will agree on the stages of this process. These representatives will meet no later than 48 hours after the signature of this agreement at Kilometre 101 under the aegis of the United Nations for this purpose. They will complete this task within five days. Disengagement will begin within 48 hours after the completion of the work of the military representatives and in no event later than seven days after the signature of this agreement. The process of disengagement will be completed not later than 40 days after it begins.

D. This agreement is not regarded by Egypt and Israel as a final peace agreement. It constitutes a first step toward a final, just and durable peace according to the provisions of Security Council Resolution 338 and within the framework of the Geneva Conference.

For Egypt General Abdul Gani al Garnasy

For Israel David Elazar, Lt. Gen., Chief of Staff of I.D.F.

Source: *"Separation of Forces Agreement (January 18, 1974)," Jewish Virtual Library <http:// www.us-israel.org/jsource/Peace/sepforce.html>.*

---

of his intentions. Instead it wanted the territorial status quo that had existed since the 1967 Six-Day War. In any event, what is clear is that step-by-step and interim agreements destroyed the chances of a comprehensive peace in the region for generations to come. Kissinger may have been right that the road was strewn with obstacles, but that is not reason enough to abandon the goal of a comprehensive peace. When one examines the price that has been paid by the countries because of the absence of peace, it is clear that it was far too high. Not only was the region bloodied and vulnerable to new waves of violence, which indeed broke out with ever increasing frequency, but suspicion and distrust

between Israel and the Arab states have also grown with the passage of time. Furthermore, the removal of Egypt from the Arab fold with the Egyptian-Israeli peace treaty destabilized the region and hardened Israel's position on remaining in the Occupied Territories (West Bank, Gaza Strip, and Golan Heights).

Thus, for instance, the question of the Israeli settlements in the Occupied Territories became a major obstacle on the road to peace. In the early 1970s Israel still viewed the West Bank and Gaza Strip (and even the Golan Heights) as temporary collateral that it would return in exchange for a full and comprehensive peace settlement. However, the attachment to these territories increased to the point where Israel, or at least important segments of the Israeli public, began viewing them as an inseparable part of the homeland. Beginning in 1977 Israel began establishing settlements that created demographic realities that every Israeli government since has found difficult to deal with. Therefore, it is no wonder that the Arab distrust of Israel increased, and they began to believe that Israel had no honest intentions of withdrawing from the territories captured in the Six-Day War. On the other side, there were few in the Arab camp calling for peace. Many Israelis began to think that the Arab demand for the territories that had been captured in 1967 was just one stage in their plan for the gradual annihilation of Israel. The result is that the states in the region moved step-by-step along the road to peace—but backwards.

One should also bear in mind that the American decision to adopt the step-by-step policy in finding a solution to the Middle East conflict was based to a considerable degree on the need to promote U.S. interests in the region and not only the need to progress toward an Israeli-Arab peace agreement. Thus, progress along this road proceeded slowly and mainly in keeping with the readiness of the states involved—Egypt and Syria—to form closer relations with the United States and, of course, to break away from the Soviet Union. Egypt was ready for such a move, and in fact began it in July 1972 with the expulsion of Soviet advisers. Syria, however, hesitated to change sides and thus became a pariah in the eyes of the United States. While Kissinger claims in his memoirs that the Soviet Union was an obstacle to peace, it is not clear whether he really believed that. His policy may have been designed to exclude the Soviet Union from any future regional settlement as part of superpower rivalry, even at the expense of chances to achieve a comprehensive peace settlement. It would appear that this approach was somewhat shortsighted, since in the end there was nothing in it that would serve America's long-range interests. The establishment of Israeli-Egyptian peace by means of interim agreements was important to America in drawing Egypt to its side, but at the same time they lost Syria and the Palestinians as well as the chance to bring comprehensive peace to the region, which might in retrospect have served their regional and global interests far better.

It would appear that with the end of the fighting in October 1973, the sides were ready, even if it was not readily apparent, to make an historic breakthrough. If the Americans had only invested efforts in an attempt to solve the overall problems through a long-range view, they might have succeeded in achieving a comprehensive regional peace agreement. They chose the easier path, however, which ultimately condemned the region to bloody conflict for many years to come.

–JAMES STONE,
LONDON

References

Henry Kissinger, *Years of Upheaval* (Boston: Little, Brown, 1982).

Richard M. Nixon, *The Memoirs of Richard Nixon* (New York: Grosset & Dunlap, 1978).

William B. Quandt, *Decade of Decisions: American Policy toward the Arab-Israeli Conflict, 1967–1976* (Berkeley: University of California Press, 1977).

Quandt, *Peace Process: American Diplomacy and the Arab-Israeli Conflict since 1967,* revised edition (Berkeley: University of California Press, 2001).

Nadav Safran, *Israel: The Embattled Ally* (Cambridge, Mass.: Belknap Press, 1978).

Patrick Seale, *Asad of Syria: The Struggle for the Middle East* (London: I. B. Tauris, 1988).

SINAI I AND II

SUEZ WAR

Was the Eisenhower administration justified in opposing the tripartite invasion of Egypt in 1956?

Viewpoint: Yes. By opposing the tripartite invasion, the United States avoided appearing imperialistic and preserved its influential position in the Arab world.

Viewpoint: No. The United States should have been supportive of the tripartite invasion, since it served to undermine Egyptian leader Gamal Abd al-Nasser.

Contrary to expectations, in the years immediately following the 1947–1949 Arab-Israeli War, the regional environment was less propitious for another eruption between Israel and the Arab states. The reasons for this relative calmness included the following: the Tripartite Declaration (1950), in which the United States, Great Britain, and France pledged to control the flow of arms to the region and prevent an arms race from developing; the July revolution in Egypt (1952) that removed for the time being the most powerful and populous Arab country from the military equation as the new regime in Cairo concentrated on consolidating its position in power and enacting domestic reform; and the Anglo-Egyptian accord (1954) that finally arranged for the evacuation of British troops from the Suez Canal base, thus at one and the same time ameliorating a festering sore between Egypt and the West and prying open the door to a possible Arab-Israeli settlement.

As often happens in the Middle East, however, the political and strategic winds can change rather quickly and dramatically. Tension began to build in the Arab-Israeli arena by early 1955 that had a chain effect leading directly to the Suez War (1956). The infamous Gaza raid carried out by Israeli forces in February 1955 (in which scores of Egyptian soldiers were killed), combined with the Baghdad Pact in March, compelled Egyptian president Gamal Abd al-Nasser to search for an alternative source of military aid when he failed to obtain it from the United States. That supplier turned out to be the Soviet Union in September 1955. This decision transformed Nasser into an all-Arab hero overnight, because an Arab state finally had the potential wherewithal to confront Israel while not bowing down to the traditional Western powers. Nasser leveraged this popularity to combat the Baghdad Pact and isolate its lone Arab member, Iraq, while Egypt also undermined what was left of the British position in the Middle East. The French, for their part, were concerned lest Egypt send its obsolete weapons to the Algerian rebels, whom Nasser had vociferously supported. Israel, with the two most powerful Arab countries receiving and/or having access to military aid from the superpowers, felt increasingly hemmed in and threatened, and it wanted to act against Nasser if given the opportunity before Egypt could assimilate Russian arms into its military.

While obviously concerned with the Soviet-Egyptian arms deal, the United States in late 1955 attempted to wean Nasser from Moscow's embrace by offering to provide the bulk of the funding for the Aswan High Dam project that was important for Nasser's domestic political and economic program. There were several lobbying groups in the United States that did not support the funding offer, including the pro-Israeli and Cotton (since the dam would increase Egypt's cotton yield) lobbies. When Nasser recognized the People's Republic of China in the spring of 1956 (thus adding the "China bloc" to the anti-Nasser list), the combination of domestic pressures conspired to force Secretary of State John Foster Dulles to withdraw the U.S. offer to fund the dam. In reaction to this reversal, on the anniversary of the July revolution in 1956, Nasser nationalized the Suez Canal Company, which operated the strategically important Canal and whose largest shareholders were Great Britain and France.

The nationalization was the last straw for Britain, France, and Israel, all of whom had increasingly seen Nasser as an ominous threat and were looking for just such an opportunity to either cut him down to size or get rid of him altogether. Despite diplomatic attempts to resolve the crisis throughout the summer and fall of 1956, officials from London, Paris, and Tel Aviv secretly conspired to launch an invasion of Egypt, activating dormant clauses in previous Anglo-Egyptian agreements that ostensibly allowed Britain to "protect" Egypt in case it were attacked by a third party (Israel). In late October, the Israelis launched a two-pronged invasion of the Sinai Peninsula, one heading toward the Canal and the other thrusting toward the town of Sharm al-Shaykh at the tip of the peninsula and overlooking the strategic Strait of Tiran. As previously arranged, this assault gave the British and the French the opportunity to launch an amphibious invasion of Port Said, at the northern mouth of the Canal, to secure the Suez waterway—and deal a severe blow to Nasser.

The Eisenhower administration was caught largely unawares, because its erstwhile friends deliberately excluded it from the planning. While not necessarily disagreeing with the ultimate objective of the tripartite invasion, it thoroughly disagreed with the means, as it felt the aggression smacked of nineteenth-century European gunboat diplomacy, undermined the West's position in the area, and allowed the Soviets to escape the negative publicity of their military intervention in Hungary a short while after the Suez invasion began. As such, the Eisenhower administration pressured the British and the French to withdraw their forces, and by early 1957 it eventually forced the Israelis to evacuate the Sinai.

Viewpoint:
Yes. By opposing the tripartite invasion, the United States avoided appearing imperialistic and preserved its influential position in the Arab world.

Washington's opposition to the Israeli, British, and French invasion of Egypt in 1956 following President Gamal Abd al-Nasser's nationalization of the Suez Canal Company (SCC)—as well as its demand that the aggressors withdraw unconditionally and immediately from the territories they occupied—stands out as one of the few high points of its policy in the Middle East since 1945. U.S. president Dwight D. Eisenhower's rhetorical question in February 1957, as Israel resisted demands for leaving conquered areas, best epitomized the issue: "Should a nation which attacks and occupies foreign territory . . . be allowed to impose conditions on its own withdrawal?" It was Washington's otherwise persistent hostility to legitimate Arab nationalist aspirations, notably its recurrently illegal behavior before, during, and after the crisis of 1956 (for example, its attempts to overthrow Syria's parliamentary government that hardly were less egregious than the tripartite aggression), that canceled out the moral, legal, and political credit it earned.

The Israeli, French, and British attack on Egypt constituted a serious violation of the United Nations (UN) Charter. The basic legal norm applicable since 1945 is Article 2(4) of the Charter, which bans the use—or even the threat—of force in international relations, the exceptions being actions taken by the Security Council and, as stated in Article 51, "individual or collective self-defense if an armed attack occurs." Even if Egypt had violated the legal rights of any state (other than by carrying out an armed attack), the use of force to rectify the wrong would consequently have been illegal. U.S. support for such behavior by its allies, while opposing the Soviet invasion of Hungary, would have been utterly hypocritical.

Furthermore, for Britain and France to join Israel in an attack on Egypt was to defy the Tripartite Declaration (1950). This statement of policy was issued by the two European powers and the United States, committing them not only to maintain a balance in the arms supply between the parties to the Arab-Israeli conflict but also to oppose any aggression in violation of the 1949 armistice lines. For the aggressors to deceive Washington about their plans also meant that to go along with them later would constitute a classic case of a big power being dragged along by smaller allies.

The conspiratorial nature of the way the three aggressors waged war made their behavior particularly reprehensible. Israel attacked first;

Scuttled ships in the Suez Canal, 1956

(© CORBIS/BBC Hulton Picture Library)

Britain and France, feigning to be merely concerned with the safety of the Canal, issued a bogus ultimatum intended to be so unreasonable that Egypt could not possibly accept it. As planned in advance at a meeting in Sevres, near Paris, a week earlier, the ultimatum called on both sides to withdraw ten miles from the waterway. If the parties to the conflict did not cease and desist, Britain and France declared that they would occupy the Canal. Since Israeli forces had not penetrated nearly that far, it was Egypt that, in effect, was being called on to withdraw from its own territory on both sides of the waterway while allowing Israel to continue the invasion.

The three aggressors had no legitimate legal grievance against Egypt. As the United States fully realized, the nationalization of the SCC was completely within Egypt's rights under international law, which imposes only the obligation to provide compensation in such cases. In fact, Egypt's nationalization decree specifi-

cally provided that the shareholders would be paid on the basis of their stock's value at the close of the Paris Bourse (French Stock Exchange) the previous day. Indeed, Egypt eventually fully paid the shareholders in accordance with an agreement reached with them in 1958. From the beginning it was clear that even if Egypt had wanted to avoid paying compensation it would not have been able to do so, as the Egyptian sterling accounts that were frozen by Britain were more than sufficient to compensate the shareholders. Although President Nasser's action in July 1956 represented a dramatic assertion of his country's independence and dignity and a drastic blow to the imperial order, from a legal point of view it was no different from, say, the British government's previous nationalization of its own steel industry.

The way Egypt's enemies pejoratively referred to the "seizure of the Canal" was completely misleading. What happened was the nationalization of foreign-owned property within Egyptian sovereignty, not the "seizure" of foreign territory. There was nothing in the case of Suez comparable to the Panama Canal Zone, which was separated by treaty from Panama and in effect a part of the territory of the United States. Notwithstanding the nature of the Suez Canal as a remnant of colonialism, the company that ran it was always Egyptian, incorporated under the law of Egypt. For that matter, the right to nationalize the company's assets within Egypt (with compensation) would have been no less valid if, hypothetically, it had been incorporated elsewhere. In fact, Egypt's legal case was so sound on this issue as to frustrate its critics, who were looking for a pretext to attack, and to cause them to obfuscate the issues.

The Constantinople Convention (1888) often was invoked, typically by paraphrasing its provisions in terms of establishing the Canal as an "international waterway." What the Convention provided was that the waterway would "always be free and open" to vessels of all nationalities. It said nothing about ownership. The SCC's concession was scheduled to end in 1968 in any case, but it would not have affected the continuing validity of the provisions of the Convention. When British prime minister Anthony Eden's legal advisers told him that Nasser had not violated international law, he responded angrily and dismissed such reasoning as "legal quibbles."

Following nationalization, Egypt continued to keep the Canal open to international shipping as before, and it repeatedly assured the world of its intention to do so in the future in conformity with the Constantinople Convention, the binding nature of which it accepted. Its own economic interests—that is, the importance of tolls as a source of revenue—reinforced the likelihood that it would never change this policy. It went overboard in its respect for the right of passage by allowing vessels to go through the waterway even if they refused to pay tolls to the new Suez Canal Authority. Far from showing inflexibility, Egyptian foreign minister Mahmoud Fawzi accepted the Six Principles for settlement proposed by British foreign secretary Selwyn Lloyd in private talks convened by UN secretary general Dag Hammarskjold that the UN Security Council adopted 13 October 1956 as the aggressive plot was being hatched. The idea of some people in the West that Egyptians were incapable of operating the Canal was soon proved wrong, as a few new pilots were able to perform their operation more efficiently than had the SCC. The only threat to navigation came from Egypt's enemies, as Britain and France—in an attempt to disrupt navigation and thus provide the pretext they wanted—ordered the SCC

to dismiss its non-Egyptian pilots (and to threaten any employees with loss of pensions if they continued to work for the nationalized enterprise). Finally, the tripartite attack, rather than safeguarding navigation, was what finally brought about its temporary closure.

The invaders had a variety of motives apart from the issue of nationalization. The main motivation for France's tacit alliance with Israel that began in 1954 was the false belief—a kind of self-deception—that Egyptian support was at the heart of the Algerian revolt against French colonialism. In fact, Egypt might more appropriately be blamed for the near absence of anything more than verbal support for this just cause. Britain was concerned about the broader erosion of its colonial position in the area of which Suez was only one part. Eden, whose irrationality apparently had medical causes, had an exaggerated notion of Nasser's role in this movement, notably in Jordanian king Hussein's dismissal of Sir John Bagot Glubb, the British commander of his army, a few months earlier.

For Israel, nationalization provided a convenient opportunity for it to engage in the kind of aggression it had long contemplated. Aside from engaging in a "preventive war" before Egypt could become stronger militarily (especially following its momentous arms deal with the Soviet bloc in September 1955), it aimed at ending the closure of the Canal and also the Strait of Tiran (entrance to the Gulf of Aqaba) to Israeli vessels and cargo that predated the events of 1956. In the case of the Canal, the provision of the Constantinople Convention allowing Egypt to take measures for its defense, the precedent set during previous wars when Britain closed the Canal to its enemies, and the fact that no treaty ending the state of war had followed the Egyptian-Israeli Armistice Agreement (1949) undermined the Israeli claim that its legal rights were being violated. Egypt was so confident in the soundness of its case regarding the Canal that in 1957 it recognized the jurisdiction of the International Court of Justice in cases relating to it. While under today's international law (as reflected in the UN Convention [of 1982] on the Law of the Sea) the closure of the Strait of Tiran would be illegal, the rules at that time relating to passage through straits that were parts of a state's territorial waters but connected the high seas with the territorial waters of other states, as in this case, were debatable. According to Eugene Rostow, President Lyndon B. Johnson's fervently pro-Israeli undersecretary of state, Washington feared shortly before the 1967 Arab-Israeli War that Egypt would propose submitting the issue to the International Court of Justice and win its case.

TRIPARTITE DECLARATION (1950)

The Governments of the United Kingdom, France, and the United States, having had occasion during the recent Foreign Ministers meeting in London to review certain questions affecting the peace and stability of the Arab states and of Israel, and particularly that of the supply of arms and war material to these states, have resolved to make the following statements:

1. The three Governments recognize that the Arab states and Israel all need to maintain a certain level of armed forces for the purposes of assuring their internal security and their legitimate self defense and to permit them to play their part in the defense of the area as a whole. All applications for arms or war material for these countries will be considered in the light of these principles. In this connection the three Governments wish to recall and reaffirm the terms of the statements made by their representatives on the Security Council on August 4, 1949, in which they declared their opposition to the development of an arms race between the Arab states and Israel.

2. The three Governments declare that assurances have been received from all the states in question, to which they permit arms to be supplied from their countries, that the purchasing state does not intend to undertake any act of aggression against any other state. Similar assurances will be requested from any other state in the area to which they permit arms to be supplied in the future.

3. The three Governments take this opportunity of declaring their deep interest in and their desire to promote the establishment and maintenance of peace and stability in the area and their unalterable opposition to the use of force or threat of force between any of the states in that area. The three Governments, should they find that any of these states was preparing to violate frontiers or armistice lines, would, consistently with their obligations as members of the United Nations, immediately take action, both within and outside the United Nations, to prevent such violation.

Source: *"Tripartite Declaration Regarding the Armistice Borders: Statement by the Governments of the United States, The United Kingdom, and France, May 25, 1950," The Avalon Project at Yale Law School <http://www.yale.edu/lawweb/avalon/mideast/mid001.htm>.*

Even if it were determined that Egypt's closure of the Canal and the Strait of Tiran to Israeli shipping was illegal, one would have to see this act in the context of more serious violations by Israel. Sporadic acts of Israeli state terrorism, such as the October 1953 massacre of Palestinians in the village of Qibya by Ariel Sharon's Unit 101 and violations of demilita-

rized zones, are cases in point. Both the Mixed Armistice Commissions and the Security Council repeatedly condemned Israeli acts. On its Egyptian front in particular, Israel gradually took over the al-Auja demilitarized area and militarized it during the years preceding the October 1956 aggression. Some groups within the Israeli government—apparently Israeli prime minister David Ben-Gurion's supporters at a time he was not in office—went so far as to organize clumsy terrorist operations in Egypt directed against the United States and Great Britain in 1954, as was later revealed in Israel in the so-called Lavon Affair.

Israel could not justify its invasion as a response to continuing Palestinian *fedayeen* (guerrilla) attacks organized by Egypt, as Israel bore the main responsibility for violations of the cease-fire on the Egyptian front during the previous two years. The *fedayeen* activities began as a response to a series of major attacks launched by Israel, starting with the bloody raid on Gaza in February 1955 that ended the relative quiet that had prevailed on the Egypt-Israel frontier. It is well known that the post-1952 Egyptian leaders had little interest in the conflict with Israel (or in building up their military strength) before the Gaza raid and were receptive to proposals for peaceful settlement. There is evidence that Israeli raids sometimes were designed to thwart moves in this direction. Israeli prime minister Moshe Sharret's diaries demonstrate how Ben-Gurion (who became minister of defense shortly before the Gaza raid and later took the helm again as prime minister) conspired to start an expansionist war. Ben-Gurion's resistance to calls for withdrawal from the occupied territories and his frankness about plans to annex the Gaza Strip and part of Sinai continued until President Eisenhower threatened to cut off economic aid and propose UN sanctions, all of which confirms Israel's expansionist intent.

Although information about these acts did not come to light until much later, and apparently the events were on a smaller scale than in the 1967 war, Israel committed serious war crimes during its invasion of Egypt. Hundreds of Egyptian prisoners of war were murdered (in at least one case the victim was forced to dig his own grave), according to revelations made in 1995 by Israeli army officers who either committed the crimes themselves or saw other Israelis do so. Egyptians discovered mass graves of the victims in the same year. Israelis also committed atrocities against Palestinians in Gaza, and there is evidence of plans to expel most of them, while several hundred people were expelled from the Syrian-Israeli demilitarized zone and their homes destroyed. Even Palestinian citizens of Israel were victims of a massacre by Israeli border police in the village of Kafr Qasim at the beginning of the Sinai campaign. The French also committed atrocities in Port Said.

The relative quiet in the Arab-Israeli conflict that followed the implementation of Washington's demand that Israel withdraw contrasts with the unending turmoil resulting from its acceptance a decade later of the idea that occupation could be used as leverage to force concessions from the Arab world. Surviving the tripartite aggression bolstered President Nasser's position as a hero in the Arab world, but if the fundamental interest of the United States was containment of Soviet (or communist) expansion, a strengthened Nasser as a non-aligned Arab nationalist leader was not inconsistent with such a goal and might indeed have been more effective for that purpose than was reliance on unpopular client regimes.

Nasser consistently opposed communism in Egypt and throughout the Arab world. At first he accepted Soviet military aid reluctantly after the new series of aggressive attacks by Israel in 1955 demonstrated his military impotence and after his attempt to purchase arms from the United States failed. His eventual acceptance of Soviet aid in building the Aswan High Dam occurred only after the United States reneged on its own offer in July 1956. When accepting Soviet aid, he attempted to balance it with aid from the United States. Furthermore, he gave the Soviets nothing in return. It is significant that only in the desperate situation created by the defeat in 1967 in which Washington reversed its policy in the Suez War by refusing to call for immediate withdrawal that the Soviets gained access to naval facilities in Egyptian harbors and began to gain a foothold as military advisers. If the misguided U.S. policy in 1967 threatened momentarily to bring Egypt under Soviet control, it ultimately was thwarted by the unwillingness of Nasser and his successor to allow such to happen. By contrast, in 1956 Washington rightly recognized that support for the tripartite aggression would be conducive to the growth of Soviet influence in the region.

Only if the main purpose of the United States were to protect its Arab client regimes from the popular opposition that Nasser inspired—even at the risk of Soviet domination of Egypt and Syria—did the reversal of Washington's Suez policy a decade later make sense, and then not in the long run. Thus, while Washington's policy in 1956 resulted in the strengthening of Arab nationalism and of Nasser as its spokesman, its policy in 1967 made way for both to be deflated and for conservative monarchies that emphasized Islam instead of Arab

nationalism, particularly the Saudi royal family, to obtain a new lease on life. The conservative, establishment Islam of the Saudi regime eventually made way for radical Islamism to replace Arab nationalism as the primary mode of protest against Western domination. It is clear that the emergence of such leaders as Osama bin Laden represents, in part, blowback from Washington's eventual reversal of the principled policy it pursued in the Suez crisis. Thus, one sees demonstrated not only the moral and legal rectitude but also the long-term political wisdom of President Eisenhower's position.

–GLENN E. PERRY,
INDIANA STATE UNIVERSITY

Viewpoint:
No. The United States should have been supportive of the tripartite invasion, since it served to undermine Egyptian leader Gamal Abd al-Nasser.

It is commonly accepted that the Suez War (1956) was a real turning point in modern Middle East history. It is still, however, difficult to understand completely why the United States left France, Great Britain, and Israel to fight alone in a war that the Eisenhower administration supported in principle.

The United States had been indifferent toward the new Egyptian regime since its inception. It is true that Washington hoped for a different regime than that of King Farouk and that the U.S. intelligence community helped, after the Free Officers Revolution (1952), to build a new intelligence structure in Egypt to support the military junta in the hope of establishing an important strategic ally in the Middle East. After U.S. secretary of state John Foster Dulles's trip to the region in late spring 1953, however, it was quite clear that the new regime in Cairo was not the one the Eisenhower administration desired. In fact, both President Muhammad Neguib and strongman Gamal Abd al-Nasser stressed it was not the Soviet Union that was dangerous in the Middle East but rather the British presence and its colonialist policies. In particular, during his talk with Dulles, Nasser was extremely clear when he said that Egypt was moving toward a policy of neutrality. Notwithstanding this shift in policy, Egypt was ready to do business with the United States. In fact, because of a persistent feeling of inse-

SUEZ WAR

curity, the Egyptian government was ready to buy a healthy amount of heavy arms.

The United States was still bound to the Tripartite Declaration (1950), which forbade the selling of arms to countries involved in the Arab-Israeli conflict, but, above all, Dulles and President Dwight D. Eisenhower were upset by several of Nasser's political moves. First of all was his neutralist position in the Cold War. As a consequence, Nasser decided to participate and become one of the most important leaders of the Bandung conference (April 1955) that initiated the nonaligned movement. The decision to recognize communist China in the spring of 1956 hit at the deep anticommunist feelings of Dulles. In addition, the Soviet-Egyptian arms deal in 1955 greatly upset the Eisenhower administration. Moreover, there was deep disillusionment in Washington caused by the Egyptian refusal to accept the so-called Alpha Plan for a definitive (even if complicated) solution to the Arab-Israeli problem.

Trying to convince Nasser to accept the Alpha Plan, mute Egyptian condemnation of the Baghdad Pact (1955), and wean Egypt away from the Soviet Union following the arms deal, Great Britain and the United States decided to support Nasser's important economic and social initiative: the construction of the Aswan High Dam. This dam could be used to generate hydroelectric power and expand the amount of land that could be used for agricultural purposes. The continuing rejection of the Baghdad Pact and the recognition of communist China compelled Washington and London to withdraw the economic assistance for the construction of the dam.

Seven days after the withdrawal of economic assistance, on 26 July 1956, Nasser decided to nationalize the Suez Canal Company (SCC) to collect the necessary money for the Aswan Dam. Since the end of the nineteenth century the Suez Canal had been managed by a French- and British-owned company, although the contract was going to expire in 1968. In one simple move, Nasser struck at Western interests in the Middle East and gave a strong signal to the masses that he was the real leader of the Arab world.

Another country in the Middle East was worried by Nasser's actions: Israel. Since 1950 the Strait of Tiran was closed to Israeli shipping and any ship headed to the Israeli port of Eilat at the northern shore of the Gulf of Aqaba. Now, with the SCC completely in Egyptian hands, Jerusalem had no hope to have free access to the Canal. Moreover, after the large amount of Soviet arms bought by Nasser, Israel felt particularly insecure.

Above all, France and Great Britain had real motives and reasons to oppose Nasser. The Egyptian leader was supporting rebels in Algeria against the French, and Nasser, through the Anglo-Egyptian agreement (1954), brought about the withdrawal of British forces from their military base on the Suez Canal. Now, finally, France and Great Britain were losing the last symbol of their colonial power and position in the heartland of the Middle East.

For all of these reasons, Great Britain, France, and Israel were determined to go to war with Egypt. Even Eisenhower administration officials, in private talks with their French and British counterparts, recognized that Nasser had to be cut down to size. Notwithstanding these private declarations, neither Eisenhower nor Dulles supported in public the use of force. The United States attempted to resolve the situation with what turned out to be two useless conferences in London that only angered France and Great Britain. The United States could not present themselves in the Middle East as an ally and, at the same time, support a military action against an Arab country. Yet, in doing so the administration was leaving its most faithful allies on their own.

In fact, when the war broke out, Washington decided to abandon their allies and, for the first time in history, the U.S. delegate voted with his Soviet counterpart against France and Great Britain in the United Nations Security Council. Then the Eisenhower administration decided to demand, using economic pressure, a complete withdrawal of French and British forces from Egypt. Even if the United States shared the same Anglo-French concerns about Egypt and the Middle East, perhaps the Eisenhower administration understood that France and Great Britain were in their last days of empire and tried to push them aside without giving the impression of replacing them.

It is difficult to understand the administration's moves because its actions following the war produced less than satisfactory results. In fact, if during the war Washington separated itself from Paris and London in an attempt to present itself as far removed from colonialism, in 1957, after the complete withdrawal of the Anglo-French forces, the Eisenhower administration announced a new doctrine to fill the vacuum of power created by the Anglo-French retreat from the Middle East. The so-called Eisenhower Doctrine—in clear Eisenhower-Dulles style—pronounced that the Soviet Union and communism were the only dangers in the region. Only one Arab country (Lebanon) officially accepted the Eisenhower Doctrine and only two asked for its application. In neither case (Jordan [1957] nor Lebanon [1958]), was the Soviet Union or "international communism" the cause for the revolts that occurred in these two countries. The United States did not hesitate to invade Lebanon to oppose "communist penetration," but no communist was involved in the revolt—it was just a civil war caused by internal political and religious dynamics.

So what was the difference between the Anglo-French action in Egypt and the U.S. invasion of Lebanon? In Egypt, the Anglo-French forces were defending Western interests in the Middle East. What about the U.S. action in Lebanon? U.S. Marines, landing on Beirut's beaches, were defending the interests of a leader who was trying to stay in power by ignoring the Lebanese constitution. The U.S. action was anachronistic and useless; the administration lost most of the goodwill it had gained in the Suez War. The Jordanian and Lebanese crises were caused by nationalist movements. Thanks to the U.S. decision to stop the Anglo-French-Israeli action, this same nationalist movement—Nasserism—was responsible for the coup d'état that caused the overthrow of the moderate Iraqi regime (1958) and the extermination of the royal family and its aides. Once again, the Eisenhower administration was unable to comprehend the intraregional dynamics of the Middle East to the detriment of Washington's long-term interest in the region.

–DANIELE DE LUCA,
UNIVERSITY OF LECCE

References

Mordechai Bar-On, *The Gates of Gaza: Israel's Road to Suez and Back, 1955–1957* (New York: St. Martin's Press, 1994).

Robert R. Bowie, *Suez 1956* (New York: Oxford University Press, 1974).

Mohamed H. Heikal, *Cutting the Lion's Tail: Suez through Egyptian Eyes* (London: Deutsch, 1986).

Diane B. Kunz, *The Economic Diplomacy of the Suez Crisis* (Chapel Hill: University of North Carolina Press, 1991).

Wm. Roger Louis and Roger Owen, eds., *Suez 1956: The Crisis and Its Consequences* (Oxford: Clarendon Press, 1989).

Kenneth Love, *Suez: The Twice-Fought War, A History* (New York: McGraw-Hill, 1969).

Donald Neff, *Warriors at Suez: Eisenhower Takes America into the Middle East* (New York: Simon & Schuster, 1981).

Hugh Thomas, *Suez* (New York: Harper & Row, 1967).

Selwin Ilan Troen and Moshe Shemesh, eds., *The Suez-Sinai Crisis 1956: Retrospective and Reappraisal* (New York: Columbia University Press, 1990).

SUPERPOWER COLD WAR

Did the superpowers inflame regional conflict in the Middle East during the Cold War?

Viewpoint: Yes. The United States and the Soviet Union contributed to heightened tensions in the Middle East by supporting competing sides with military and economic aid.

Viewpoint: No. The Cold War actually dampened regional conflict in the Middle East as the opposing influences of the United States and the Soviet Union served to create a balance of power that often stabilized the area.

Although many historians place the beginning of the Cold War toward the end of World War II with the breakdown of the wartime alliance between the Soviet Union and the United States, the effectual start of the ideologically based conflict between East and West, communism and capitalism, occurred soon after the war ended. The diplomatic struggle between Moscow and Washington, D.C., regarding the removal of Soviet troops from Iran in 1946 was often pinpointed as the launching pad for the Cold War. The fact that this first incident in the Cold War occurred in the Middle East presaged what would be the frequent appearance of the region on the battleground stage of the superpower confrontation.

As each superpower built up its respective nuclear arsenal during the 1950s, it became more and more unthinkable that the two sides would engage in a direct confrontation that could lead to nuclear annihilation, which is why the "war" soon acquired the sobriquet of "cold" rather than "hot." As such, the superpowers attempted to expand their influence by proxy in areas adjacent to themselves and to each other in what was generally referred to as the Third World. In both Washington and Moscow allies gained by one side were seen as proportionate losses for the other.

From the beginning of the Cold War the Middle East was important to each superpower. Not only did the region contain two-thirds of the world's proven oil reserves at a time when the global economy became increasingly dependent on energy derived from oil, but located as it was at the crossroads between East and West along the underbelly of both Europe and the Soviet Union, it was also of tremendous strategic value. The United States and its allies attempted to construct a system of defense alliances drawn around the Soviet Union (as well as the People's Republic of China) in order to contain what they perceived to be Soviet/communist expansionism. As a result the Middle East almost immediately became a vital component in this strategy and inevitably inspired Soviet attempts to counter it.

Looking back upon the Cold War era and the rivalry that superimposed itself on the Middle East, some see it as a consistently destabilizing element in the region, with the possibility of a regional conflict leading to a direct superpower standoff replete with the potential of a nuclear conflagration (as in the Arab-Israeli War of 1973). Others, however, especially in light of the instability and conflict still prevalent in the Middle East in the aftermath of the effective end of the Cold War by the late 1980s, have asserted that the Cold War actually served to dampen tension and conflict more often than not.

Viewpoint:
Yes. The United States and the Soviet Union contributed to heightened tensions in the Middle East by supporting competing sides with military and economic aid.

It has sometimes been argued that the world in general, and the Middle East in particular, were more "under control" during, rather than after, the Cold War because each of the superpowers, the United States and the Soviet Union, kept their respective clients in check. This assertion, however, has not been the case, as several wars erupted during the Cold War, in the Middle East as well as elsewhere, irrespective of the wishes of the superpowers. While it is true that in some cases, such as the Suez War (1956)—for which Moscow was indirectly responsible by arming Egypt—the superpowers worked together to end the war, their motives were different and in any case the cooperation was the exception, not the rule. Indeed, in both the 1967 and 1973 Arab-Israeli Wars, the Union of Soviet Socialist Republics (U.S.S.R.) either helped instigate the conflict (1967) or did nothing to prevent it (1973)—in both cases hoping to profit from the outcome of the war.

By contrast, in the Iran-Iraq War (1980–1988), Moscow proved unable to either prevent the Iraqi invasion or stop it once it had begun, despite the fact that Iraq was a Soviet client, and despite the negative effect the war had on Soviet Middle East interests. Only in 1990, when the Cold War was nearly over, did the world witness renewed superpower cooperation in the Middle East as they worked together against the Iraqi invasion of Kuwait. In sum, the Cold War neither restrained the U.S.S.R. nor its clients, and through most of the struggle the Russians were often the major contributor to Middle East instability.

In the immediate aftermath of World War II (1939–1945), Moscow exerted heavy pressure on both Turkey and Iran in what appeared to be another case of Soviet premier Joseph Stalin's efforts to expand the Soviet Union's area of territorial control, as occurred in Eastern Europe. Stalin demanded Soviet bases in the Turkish straits as well as Turkish territory in the Caucasus and was only prevented from succeeding in his efforts by strong U.S. backing for Turkey. Similarly, despite an agreement with Britain to withdraw its troops from Iran six months after

the end of World War II, the U.S.S.R. actually intensified its control of northern Iran and was only induced to withdraw its forces by a combination of U.S. pressure and deft Iranian diplomacy. Only in the case of the Arab-Israeli War of 1947–1949 did Moscow play, at least from the Israeli perspective, a more positive role, first backing the partition of Palestine into Jewish and Arab states at the United Nations (UN) and then supporting Israel in its war against five invading Arab armies. While Stalin's motives in helping Israel remain open to debate, the available archival evidence indicates that the primary Soviet motivation was an effort to create a neutral Jewish state in a region that was perceived by Moscow to be controlled by Britain.

In the latter days of Stalin's rule, however, because of Israeli support for the United States over the Korean War (1950–1953) and growing anti-Semitism in the U.S.S.R., Soviet-Israeli relations chilled, and diplomatic relations were broken in 1952. Following the death of Stalin, while Soviet-Israeli diplomatic relations were restored, Moscow increasingly moved to take a pro-Arab position in the Arab-Israeli conflict. Nikita Khrushchev, who became the dominant leader in Moscow in 1955, saw the Arab world as part of the Third World that could be won over to the side of the communists through Soviet military, economic, and diplomatic assistance.

The first major Middle Eastern example of this policy was the Soviet arms deal to Egypt in 1955 that provided Cairo with long-range bombers along with heavy tanks and other military equipment. The fact that this arms deal exacerbated the Arab-Israeli conflict, and helped motivate Israel to join Britain and France in a tripartite attack on Egypt in October 1956, did not appear to be a matter of concern for Khrushchev; rather it was a matter of increasing Soviet influence in the Arab world in what Moscow saw as a zero-sum-game struggle for influence with the United States. Soviet nuclear threats against Britain, France, and Israel during the 1956 war, while coming late in the conflict, after the United States had pressured Britain and France (if not yet Israel) to withdraw, were nonetheless irresponsible.

Following the 1956 war, both the United States and the Soviet Union became involved in other conflict areas (Berlin, Cuba, Vietnam, and so on) and became less active in the Middle East. Moscow was, however, to play yet another negative role in Middle Eastern regional stability by helping to precipitate the 1967 Arab-Israeli War (also known as the Six-Day War or the June

War). In 1966 Moscow urged the Arabs to join in "anti-imperialist" unity, aimed against what Moscow called the "linchpin" of American imperialism in the Middle East (Israel); one result of the Soviet effort was the November 1966 treaty between Syria and Egypt, hitherto Arab rivals. Then, in May 1967, Moscow provided false information to Egypt that Israel was about to attack Syria, thus prompting President Gamal Abd al-Nasser to send Egyptian forces into the Sinai and force the UN Expeditionary Force (UNEF) from its positions on the Egyptian-Israeli border and from the Strait of Tiran. This act was followed by Jordan's joining the Syrian-Egyptian alliance, which was aimed at Israel's destruction, as Nasser's speeches clearly indicated. The end result was that Israel, after trying to avert a war through three weeks of diplomacy, including an offer to take the Soviet ambassador to the Israeli-Syrian border to show him that there was no Israeli buildup (a trip the Soviet ambassador refused to take, further demonstrating Moscow's irresponsibility during much of the Cold War), went to war against Egypt, Syria, and Jordan.

During the 1967 war, unlike the 1956 war, Moscow kept a low profile, with its only substantive action being the breaking of diplomatic relations with Israel. Following the war, however, Moscow was able to exploit Arab weaknesses by agreeing to resupply weaponry to such countries as Egypt and Syria in return for access to naval bases and, in the case of Egypt in 1970, control over air bases as well. Moscow then helped to sabotage the U.S.-arranged cease-fire between Israel and Egypt in July 1970 by helping Egypt to sneak surface-to-air missiles up to the Suez

Canal. These missiles were to give the Egyptian army protection from Israeli aircraft when Egypt attacked Israel in the 1973 Arab-Israeli War (Yom Kippur War).

Unlike the 1967 war, Moscow was far more active in the 1973 war, supplying Syria and Egypt with replacement weaponry, cheering on the Arab oil embargo against the United States, and, at the end of the war when Israel had gone on the offensive, threatening to intervene if the United States did not stop Israeli attacks on Egypt (the Israeli army was 101 kilometers from Cairo at this time). All of these actions contributed to instability in the region.

Unfortunately for Moscow, however, its active intervention in the 1973 Arab-Israeli War did not pay any diplomatic dividends in Egypt. The new Egyptian leader, Anwar Sadat, who had come to power after Nasser's death in 1970, changed his country's foreign-policy orientation from Moscow to Washington, as the United States mediated a series of agreements between Israel and Egypt leading to their 1979 peace treaty. While Moscow sought to undermine this process through such actions as promoting the 1975 "Zionism is Racism" resolution in the UN General Assembly and denouncing the Israeli-Egyptian peace treaty, it proved unable to do so. These Cold War actions helped to inflame the region rather than to calm it.

The most egregious actions taken by the Soviet Union in the Middle East occurred in 1979. In November of that year, perhaps hoping to drive a permanent wedge between the United States and the new Islamic regime in Iran, Moscow warmly praised the Iranians who stormed the U.S. embassy in Tehran and held its occupants hostage. Six weeks later the U.S.S.R. invaded Afghanistan, the first Soviet invasion of a Middle Eastern state since 1941 when the U.S.S.R. and Britain jointly invaded Iran. Needless to say, the Soviet invasion, another negative action by Moscow during the Cold War, served to destabilize the Middle East. However, the invasion divided the Arab and Muslim worlds—with only Syria, Libya, South Yemen, and the Palestine Liberation Organization (PLO) supporting the Soviet action—and it undermined Soviet attempts at recreating the "anti-imperialist" Arab unity that it had sought following the signing of the Egyptian-Israeli peace treaty. Moscow suffered a second blow to its Middle Eastern position in 1980, when Iraq invaded Iran, further dividing the Arab world. Soviet foreign policy alternately supported both sides in the conflict and ultimately proved ineffective in stopping it.

Another turning point came in 1982 when Israel invaded Lebanon. A sick Leonid Brezhnev, leading an isolated Soviet Union once again in a full-scale Cold War with the United States, exercised little influence during that conflict as it was the United States that intervened to save the Soviet-supported PLO leader Yasser Arafat, by organizing his departure to Tunis. While Brezhnev's successor, Yuri Andropov, sought to regain some influence for Moscow by sending advanced surface-to-air missiles to Syria, he too soon died, as did his successor, Konstantin Chernenko.

Soviet policy toward the Middle East began to take a more positive turn, as far as regional security and stability were concerned, following the accession of Mikhail Gorbachev as leader of the U.S.S.R. in March 1985, albeit not immediately. For the first year and a half of his rule, Soviet policy continued in its old direction, as Moscow's military efforts intensified in Afghanistan and Gorbachev approved a major military sale to Libya at a time when U.S.-Libyan relations were extremely tense. By 1987, however, it was clear that Soviet policy had changed, both domestically and internationally, especially toward the Middle East. In the Arab-Israeli conflict Gorbachev admonished both Syrian leader Hafiz al-Asad and Arafat to resolve their conflicts with Israel politically. Moscow also began the process of restoring full diplomatic relations with Israel, which was completed in 1991. By 1988 Gorbachev announced the withdrawal of Soviet troops from Afghanistan, a development that was concluded in 1989, thus reinforcing the new spirit of détente that had begun to characterize U.S.-Russian relations, helping to restabilize the Middle East. It was, however, the Iraqi invasion of Kuwait in August 1990 that was to symbolize the new era of superpower cooperation in the Middle East, as the U.S.S.R. not only joined

the United States in condemning the invasion but also supported a series of UN Security Council resolutions imposing sanctions against Iraq. While Soviet foreign minister Eduard Shevardnadze, who took the lead in cooperating with the United States, was forced to resign in December 1990 because of a rightward turn in Soviet politics, Gorbachev sought, albeit unsuccessfully, to mediate between the United States and Iraq as he sought almost to "plea bargain" for Saddam Hussein; on balance the U.S.S.R. played a positive role during the crisis, in marked contrast to its position during the 1956, 1967, 1973, and 1982 Middle East wars.

Unfortunately for Gorbachev, less than a year after the end of the Persian Gulf War (1990–1991), the Soviet Union collapsed, and he was out of a job. Nonetheless, he can be credited with turning Soviet policy in the Middle East from a zero-sum competition for influence with the United States to one of active superpower cooperation. However, during the bulk of the Cold War the U.S.S.R. was a source of instability, not stability, and there is little evidence that the dynamics of the Cold War made the Middle East a safer or more secure region.

–ROBERT O. FREEDMAN,
BALTIMORE HEBREW UNIVERSITY

Viewpoint:
No. The Cold War actually dampened regional conflict in the Middle East as the opposing influences of the United States and the Soviet Union served to create a balance of power that often stabilized the area.

There can be no doubt that the Cold War rivalry between the United States and the Soviet Union had a dramatic effect on Third World regional conflicts, especially in the Middle East. The superpowers—each for its own reasons—contributed to tensions in the region. Yet, the counterargument that superpower involvement tamped down regional conflict can also be made. There were limits to how far the superpowers were willing to let things go before they intervened to manage the several conflicts in the region. Indeed, there are multiple examples of the superpowers cooperating to manage crises that their involvement had inflamed.

There is little question that the Soviet Union set off the chain of events that led to the 1967 Arab-Israeli War (also known as the Six-Day War or the June War) by forwarding

AN UNPARALLELED OPPORTUNITY

In 1953 U.S. chargé d'affaires Philip W. Ireland described efforts to counter communist activities among Iraqi students:

The realization that recent student disturbances in Iraq have been to a large measure Communist-inspired has led the Ministry of Education to embark officially on a program of anti-Communist activities among the students. This program has presented the Embassy, through USIS, with an unparalleled opportunity to reach a priority target audience through Government channels. Accordingly, USIS has proposed to the Minister of Education four lines of action. Departmental cooperation in making possible the realization of these proposals will give USIS a unique opportunity to be effective in assisting in the solution of one of the most critical political problems in Iraq. . . .

The suggestions were:

1) *That the Ministry consider the establishment of an Institute of International Affairs.* It was suggested to the Minister that such an Institute, affiliated with a college, could conduct courses in international affairs and, at the same time, could arrange and sponsor extra-curricular activities designed to channel the students' political interests into constructive discussion groups, lectures and organizations. It was suggested that a professor of Soviet Affairs could be on the staff of such an Institute and could assist in demonstrating to the students the nature of international Communism. As the Embassy indicated in its telegram number 1184 of March 30, a first step has been taken in this direction by the Ministry's agreement to the Fulbright grant to Mr. Albert Parry to study and lecture on this subject in Iraq. It is possible that the Minister may wish to pursue this subject further and to seek still another professor in the field of international relations.

2) *That positive anti-Communist instruction be undertaken among the students presently in jail.* It appears to be a fact that students jailed after the recent disturbances are subject to the strong influences of hardcore Communists jailed for long periods, who are prepared to indoctrinate newcomers with libraries, pamphlets and other materials smuggled in to them by outside comrades. The Public Affairs Officer has brought this fact to the attention of the Minister of Education and had suggested that if his Ministry or any of the other appropriate ministries wish to choose three or four thoroughly reliable people, USIS would undertake to indoctrinate these people and give them material which they could use in personal interviews, conferences and lectures with the jailed students. The Minister plans to discuss this matter with the Ministers of Interior and Social Affairs and to advise USIS as to whether such cooperation may be possible.

3) *That Fulbright provide an advisor on extra-curricular activities.* A part of the student problem stems from the fact that there are almost no extra-curricular activities in Baghdad's colleges. As a result, students flock to coffee houses, political centers, and other places where the only recreation is political agitation. The Minister readily agreed to this suggestion and asked first that Fulbright provide someone who could develop a well-rounded athletic program among the colleges. This request will be formalized by the United States Educational Foundation and forwarded in a separate communication.

4) *That the Ministry undertake the dissemination of anti-Communist material among students.* The Minister has agreed to this and has requested that the Public Affairs Officer forward to him material which is either suitable or can be adapted for this purpose. The Minister's interest, already reported to the Department, in having Arabic translations made of articles in the IPS publication "Problems of Communism" is a beginning in this direction.

Source: *United States Embassy, Iraq, Dispatch from Philip W. Ireland to the Department of State, "Opportunities for Anti-communist Activities among Students" [Includes Memorandum of Conversation], 30 March 1953, National Archives, Record Group 59, Records of the Department of State. Decimal Files, 1950–1954, The National Security Archive <http://www.gwu.edu/~nsarchiv/NSAEBB/NSAEBB78/propaganda092.pdf>.*

false reports of Israeli mobilization on the Syrian border. Scholar Michael B. Oren offers multiple explanations of Moscow's intentions but claims that there was in reality little new in the intelligence report. However, once the war broke out, the two superpowers worked to prevent escalation of the conflict: Moscow moved to impose a cease-fire when an Israeli victory seemed imminent; and the Kremlin severed diplomatic relations with Tel Aviv and sent a note to U.S. president Lyndon B. Johnson threatening military action when it appeared that Israeli troops would advance on Damascus. The Johnson administration signaled to the Soviet Union not to intervene by sending U.S. ships toward Syria. This round of crisis management culminated with United Nations (UN) Security Council Resolution 242. In their conversations at Glassboro, New Jersey, the Soviet premier and the U.S. president praised their communication during the war and concurred that they had achieved "some measure of success in bringing about a cease-fire."

Superpower relations entered the era of détente in 1972 with the signing of the Strategic Arms Limitation Agreement, the Basic Principles Agreement, and the Agreement on the Prevention of Nuclear War. Yet, in retrospect, it is clear that each side held tenaciously to its view of the "enemy," and each operated on diametrically opposite assumptions about the way détente was supposed to work. President Richard M. Nixon and Secretary of State Henry Kissinger saw détente as a way to entangle Moscow in a series of links with the West, while the Soviets used détente to uncouple the central U.S.-Soviet relationship from their activities in the Third World. Despite these contradictory assumptions, superpower behavior before and during the 1973 Arab-Israeli War (Yom Kippur War) illustrates the attempt of each side to control the ongoing Arab-Israeli conflict.

In the prewar period, the Soviet Union proved unwilling to condone another Middle East war, despite Egyptian president Anwar Sadat's proclamation of 1971 as the "Year of Decision." In 1972 Sadat expelled twenty thousand Soviet advisers, but by 1973 the Brezhnev regime, fearing that Sadat would turn to the United States, seemingly relented and accelerated arms deliveries to the Egyptians. Richard Ned Lebow and Janice Gross Stein argue that although the arms were supplied, the Soviet leadership privately urged Sadat to seek a diplomatic solution. That the Soviets were intent on reining in their clients and hopefully preventing war may be seen in the several warnings they issued to the United States. When in May 1973 Kissinger went to Moscow to prepare for the upcoming Nixon-Brezhnev summit, Communist Party of the Soviet Union (CPSU) leader Leonid Brezhnev told him of the growing likelihood of war and hinted at the difficulties they were experiencing in restraining their allies. Then in June, in a late-night meeting with President Nixon at San Clemente, Brezhnev suggested that a solution to the Middle East conflict was needed or he "could not guarantee that war would not resume." It would seem that at this point the U.S.S.R. was indeed dampening the potential conflict, but the United States missed the signals.

Once war erupted, Moscow sought a cease-fire while the Arabs were still winning, because a "victorious" cease-fire would have avoided any escalatory potential. Both the Syrians and the Egyptians rejected the proposal. The outbreak of the war also triggered conflict management on the part of the United States. On 10 October, Kissinger proposed that the Soviets curtail their airlift to the Arabs in exchange for American restraint in supplying Israel. This suggestion in its turn was rejected by the Politburo.

The asymmetries in timing changed only later during the war. As the tide turned against the Arabs, Brezhnev invited Kissinger to Moscow to negotiate what became UN Security Council Resolution 338. In the face of what was becoming a rout of his army, Sadat urgently requested a cease-fire. Lebow and Stein argue that the two superpowers could only agree to a minimalist resolution, one that referred to a cease-fire, to Resolution 242, and used the phrase "under appropriate auspices." Tacit crisis management threatened to break down when the Israelis violated the cease-fire resolution and moved to surround the Egyptian Third Army. In order to protect its client, the U.S.S.R. put its troops in the southern military district on alert and proposed to the United States a joint force to intervene in the conflict. In a note to President Nixon, Brezhnev wrote, as quoted by Galia Golan:

> I will say it straight that if you find it impossible to act jointly with us in this matter, we should be faced with the necessity urgently to consider the question of taking appropriate steps unilaterally. We cannot allow arbitrariness on the part of Israel.

According to Viktor Israelyan, the Kremlin felt that the message accomplished three things: first, the threat would force Washington to pressure Israel; second, it would be applauded by the Arabs; and third, by urging joint intervention, Brezhnev also apparently thought he was promoting détente. Evidence to support the Soviet threat was seen in the temporary halt in the airlift of equipment to Egypt. It seems, however, that the U.S.S.R. never intended to introduce troops into the region. Raymond Garthoff asserts that the airlift was stopped to signal

Soviet willingness to cooperate with the United States in implementing the cease-fire. In his memoirs former Soviet first deputy foreign minister Georgi Kornienko adds further weight to this more benign interpretation. He writes that in order to give the warning greater credibility "certain Soviet divisions were put on alert." But he asserts that there was no "predetermination regarding the sending of our troops to Egypt." As a result, U.S. troops in Europe were put on a defense readiness condition III alert. The immediate crisis was defused when the Soviet Union chose not to respond to the U.S. alert, and the United States pressured Israel to allow the resupply of the Egyptian Third Army trapped by the Israelis at Suez City.

The examples of the 1967 and 1973 wars illustrate successful and unsuccessful attempts at crisis management. Where the superpowers were unsuccessful, it was because they were caught between maintaining relations with their clients in the region and managing their own relationship. One of the lessons of the 1973 war, according to Alexander George, would seem to be that "in order to remove the other superpower's incentive to intervene . . . each superpower shall accept responsibility for pressuring its regional ally to stop short of inflicting such a defeat on its local opponent."

In 1977 the Soviet Union and the United States turned their attention to conflict resolution. Transcripts of high-level meetings between U.S. and Soviet officials reveal that Moscow was intensely interested in collaboration on Middle East issues. In two sessions at the Kremlin on 29 March 1977 Foreign Minister Andrei Gromyko criticized U.S. unilateralist approaches to the Middle East conflict and proposed that the superpowers not only coordinate their activities but also act as guarantors of future peace in the region. By mid September the Soviets presented a draft statement to the United States that seemed balanced. Given the stalemate in the region, U.S. secretary of state Cyrus Vance saw this draft as an opportunity to move forward on Middle East peace and, equally important, to ameliorate relations with the U.S.S.R. In all, the 1 October declaration was about procedures and principles and not an imposed peace. However, within days, the Carter administration backed away from the statement because of pressures from Israel, from American supporters of Israel, and from those who objected that President Jimmy Carter in effect had undone what Kissinger had worked so hard to accomplish—the eviction of the Soviet Union from a major role in the Middle East.

The failure of this effort can be attributed to domestic politics on both sides and not necessarily to the rivalry per se between the United States and the U.S.S.R. The episode of the October 1977 memorandum shows that the inherent duality of détente was magnified by internal divisions on both sides. Thus, for example, pressures from Israel and from the pro-Israel lobby played into the hands of those who opposed collaboration with the Soviet Union. Within the Politburo, the collapse of cooperation in 1977 confirmed the opinion of those who saw U.S. policies as designed to exclude the U.S.S.R. from the Middle East.

In order to illustrate how rigid bipolarity helped to dampen the conflict in the Arab-Israeli arena, it is useful to draw a comparison with the Persian Gulf War (1990–1991). Iraqi president Saddam Hussein made the decision to invade Kuwait at a time in which Soviet leader Mikhail Gorbachev's "new political thinking" weakened bipolarity and facilitated cooperation between the United States and the U.S.S.R. It would seem that Saddam calculated that, given the lessening of Soviet support for and the attenuation of relations with radical clients, the attack on Kuwait would not evoke U.S. countermeasures. Further, had the old rules of the game prevailed, Moscow would have, at the least, attempted to rein in its client so as to forestall any U.S. reaction.

One could look as well at the Persian Gulf War as an example of newfound cooperation between the United States and the then-collapsing Soviet Union. Details of the negotiations between Moscow and Washington are beyond the scope of this article. Nonetheless, it should be noted that at the 9 September 1990 Helsinki meeting between President Gorbachev and President George H. W. Bush, the two leaders indicated that if the UN Security Council resolutions passed to that point were not sufficient, then further actions would be necessary. Gorbachev clearly hoped to avoid a U.S.-led war and dispatched Yevgeny Primakov to attempt to persuade Saddam to back down. Unable to convince Saddam to withdraw, a reluctant U.S.S.R. voted for Security Council Resolution 678 in December 1990, authorizing the use of "all necessary means" to liberate Kuwait. For its part, the United States used a combination of cajoling and arm-twisting to assemble the coalition and to secure the necessary votes in the UN Security Council. Simultaneously, the Bush administration worked to minimize any resulting tensions with Moscow. On one hand, the administration was sensitive to the opposition facing Gorbachev and his foreign minister, Eduard Shevardnadze. On the other hand, although Bush did not want to precipitate a major disagreement with Moscow, it was clear that he was not going to be deterred from confronting Saddam.

In the end, though, given recent history, one could make the argument that the Gulf War was but the first of many new types of conflicts in the Middle East. During the Cold War the Soviet-American competition helped to fuel the Israeli-Arab arms race; but the superpowers worked to impose balanced limits between the combatants. The inherent risks of escalation of Middle East conflicts were ultimately contained by the superpowers conflict-management initiatives. As a corollary, one could also argue that the new era has seen new arms races in the region. By the late 1980s other suppliers increased their shares of the arms market, making control far more difficult. Since the demise of the Cold War, Iraq has threatened its neighbors more than once, there has been a proliferation of weapons of mass destruction (WMD), and al-Qaida attacked the United States on 11 September 2001. At least during the Cold War, the rules of the game were generally well understood.

–CAROL R. SAIVETZ,
DAVIS CENTER
FOR RUSSIAN STUDIES

References

Robert O. Freedman, *Soviet Policy toward the Middle East since 1970* (New York: Praeger, 1982).

Raymond Garthoff, *Détente and Confrontation: American-Soviet Relations from Nixon to Reagan,* revised edition (Washington, D.C.: Brookings Institution, 1994).

Viktor Israelyan, *Inside the Kremlin during the Yom Kippur War* (University Park: Pennsylvania State University Press, 1995).

Richard Ned Lebow and Janice Gross Stein, *We All Lost the Cold War* (Princeton: Princeton University Press, 1994).

Georgiy Mirsky, "The Soviet Perception of the U.S. Threat," in *The Middle East and the United States: A Historical and Political Reassessment,* edited by David W. Lesch (Boulder, Colo.: Westview Press, 1996, 1999, 2003), pp. 397–405.

Michael B. Oren, *Six Days of War: June 1967 and the Making of the Modern Middle East* (Oxford & New York: Oxford University Press, 2002).

William B. Quandt, *Peace Process: American Diplomacy and the Arab-Israeli Conflict since 1967,* revised edition (Berkeley: University of California Press, 2001).

Carol Saivetz, "The Superpowers in the Middle East: Cold War and Post–Cold War Policies," in *The Fall of Great Powers: Peace, Stability and Legitimacy,* edited by Geir Lundestad (New York: Oxford University Press, 1994).

SYRIAN-ISRAELI NEGOTIATIONS

Did the Syrian-Israeli peace negotiations in the 1990s have a chance of producing a peace agreement?

Viewpoint: Yes. The Syrian-Israeli negotiations in the 1990s could have produced a peace agreement if the Israelis had adhered to a consistent policy and the Syrians had been more flexible on procedural issues.

Viewpoint: No. Although some progress was made on the technical details of a peace agreement, the Syrians and Israelis were doomed to failure by their mutual suspicion and animosity.

With the reordering of the balance of power in the Middle East as a result of the end of the Cold War (symbolically hailed by the dismantling of the Berlin Wall in 1989, the implosion of the Soviet Union by late 1991, and the unusual panoply of allies that joined the United States in the Persian Gulf Crisis and War in 1990–1991), the political environment in the region seemed much more propitious for a peaceful resolution of the Arab-Israeli conflict. No longer could Arab countries opposed to Israel look to the Soviet Union for political, economic, and military support. This situation was one of the main reasons Syria, traditionally at the forefront in the Arab world in terms of its anti-Israeli actions and rhetoric, joined the U.S.-led Gulf War coalition and actually sent troops to assist in the expulsion of Iraq from Kuwait.

With his country mired in a decade-long economic malaise, Syrian president Hafiz al-Asad, as he did in the 1980s when he supported non-Arab Iran over Iraq in the Iran-Iraq War (1980–1988), chose the pragmatic rather than the ideological course of action. He knew he needed to open up to the West, particularly the United States, while attempting to earn the gratitude of the Gulf Arab states for helping to turn back the Iraqi regional hegemonic threat. He took advantage of the opportunity presented him and in the process weakened his Baathist rival Saddam Hussein in Baghdad. Even though Israel was not officially part of the Gulf War coalition, Syria's participation was crucial in two ways: Damascus was essentially on the same side as Israel, thus breaking at least the psychological barrier of cooperation; and the inclusion of Syria made the coalition appear to be broadly constituted within the Arab world, and not just composed of the usual pro-West array of nations.

It was within this political milieu that the administration of President George H. W. Bush sought to leverage newfound U.S. influence in the region in the immediate post–Gulf War environment. Along with the Soviet Union (which restored diplomatic relations with Israel shortly beforehand) as an official cosponsor, the United States convened the Madrid Peace Conference in October 1991, where for the first time Israel publicly sat across the table from its Arab combatants, Syria, Lebanon, and a joint Jordanian-Palestinian delegation—those countries bordering the Jewish state that were still officially at war with it. A series of multilateral talks were held contemporaneous with these proceedings at a variety of venues where several Arab states, Israel, and the major international actors discussed such issues as water sharing, arms control, and ways to enhance regional economic development. After the initial meeting in Madrid, the conference split into a series of panels in which

Israeli teams of negotiators met separately with their Arab counterparts (Syrians, Lebanese, and the joint Jordanian-Palestinian delegation).

While progress on the Israeli-Palestinian track ebbed and flowed throughout the remainder of the decade, the Israeli-Syrian track also was revived from time to time, especially in 1995–1996 as well as in 1999–2000. Although still complex in their own right, the Israeli-Syrian negotiations were generally more straightforward and less intertwined with other obfuscating issues than was the Israeli-Palestinian track. The primary issue is the return to Syria of the Golan Heights, which Israel obtained during the 1967 Arab-Israeli War. The negotiations targeted such issues as the extent and the timing of a supposed Israeli withdrawal, related security concerns by both sides, and the normalization of relations. Israeli-Syrian negotiations, however, have never restarted since they were broken off after a last-gasp attempt at an agreement in the spring of 2000, only a couple of months before the long-serving Asad died.

Viewpoint:
Yes. The Syrian-Israeli negotiations in the 1990s could have produced a peace agreement if the Israelis had adhered to a consistent policy and the Syrians had been more flexible on procedural issues.

Syria and Israel were close to reaching a peace agreement on several occasions before the eruption of the al-Aqsa *intifada* (uprising) in September 2000. They had achieved substantial progress on principal issues and delved into the complexity of issues where disagreement remained. At the heart of Syrian-Israeli negotiations is Israeli withdrawal from the Golan Heights, which Israel has occupied since the 1967 Arab-Israeli War (also known as the Six-Day War and June War). From the inauguration of the Madrid Peace Conference in October 1991 until January 2000 both sides held several rounds of negotiations and achieved significant progress on the four major issues: withdrawal, normalization, security, and the timetable of fulfillment. Other issues, such as regional economic cooperation, water, and settlers, were discussed as well. The negotiations of August 1993, July 1994, January 1996, and January 2000 constituted four crucial breakthroughs.

Movement toward the Madrid Peace Conference was riddled with difficulties. Right after Israeli occupation of Syrian territory in June 1967, a state of "no peace/no war" prevailed. To break the stalemate, Syria joined Egypt in launching a surprise attack against Israeli forces in the occupied areas of the Golan Heights and Sinai Peninsula on 6 October 1973. While the 1973 Arab-Israeli War (also known as the October War, Yom Kippur War, and Ramadan War) did not lead to a clear-cut military victory for either side, the advances made by Syrian and Egyptian forces in the first few days of the war against the supposedly invincible Israeli Defense Forces (IDF) raised morale and was heralded as a "victory" in those countries. It also showed these countries' resolve to recover their lost territory by any means.

In the aftermath of the October War, United Nations (UN) Security Council Resolution 338 reaffirmed Resolution 242, which demanded Israel's withdrawal from "occupied territories" in return for "termination of all claims or state of belligerency and respect for and acknowledgment of every state in the area." Resolution 242 established the principle of "land for peace." Israeli withdrawal from the Occupied Territories (West Bank, Gaza Strip, and the Golan Heights), as well as the Sinai, would be traded for recognition by the Arab states of the sovereignty of the state of Israel in its pre-1967 border. As early as 1974, Syria accepted Resolutions 338 and 242.

Diplomatic efforts in the aftermath of the 1973 war did not accomplish much beyond the "Agreement on Disengagement Between Syria and Israel," signed in 1974. Despite Syria's readiness to negotiate for the recovery of its occupied territory (the Golan Heights), Israel opted for peace with Egypt. The latter two countries signed a peace treaty in 1979. Syrian president Hafiz al-Asad was critical of Egyptian president Anwar Sadat's "unilateral" quest for peace, judging that by acting alone, Sadat had undercut both his own bargaining position and that of all the other Arab parties. Asad's fears came true in the 1980s. Israel claimed that it had fulfilled UN resolutions by withdrawing from "occupied territories" and refused to offer any meaningful solution to the Palestinians or to Syria. Moreover, the Likud government of Menachem Begin ordered an occupation of South Lebanon in 1978 to secure Israel's northern borders from Palestinian attacks, and it carried out a full invasion of that country in 1982. No progress was made on the peace front, and Egypt was isolated and expelled from the League of Arab States.

On the Syrian front, the Knesset (Israeli parliament) extended, on 14 December 1981, the application of its laws to the Golan Heights, a step seen as de facto annexation of Syrian terri-

MADRID PEACE CONFERENCE

On 30 October 1991 the United States and the Soviet Union formally invited Israel, Syria, Lebanon, Jordan, and the Palestinians to the Madrid Peace Conference:

After extensive consultations with Arab states, Israel and the Palestinians, the United States and the Soviet Union believe that an historic opportunity exists to advance the prospects for genuine peace throughout the region. The United States and the Soviet Union are prepared to assist the parties to achieve a just, lasting and comprehensive peace settlement, through direct negotiations along two tracks, between Israel and the Arab states, and between Israel and the Palestinians, based on United Nations Security Council Resolutions 242 and 338. The objective of this process is real peace.

Toward that end, the president of the U.S. and the president of the USSR invite you to a peace conference, which their countries will co-sponsor, followed immediately by direct negotiations. The conference will be convened in Madrid on October 30, 1991.

President Bush and President Gorbachev request your acceptance of this invitation no later than 6 P.M. Washington time, October 23, 1991, in order to ensure proper organization and preparation of the conference.

Direct bilateral negotiations will begin four days after the opening of the conference. Those parties who wish to attend multilateral negotiations will convene two weeks after the opening of the conference to organize those negotiations. The co-sponsors believe that those negotiations should focus on region-wide issues of water, refugee issues, environment, economic development, and other subjects of mutual interest.

The co-sponsors will chair the conference which will be held at ministerial level. Governments to be invited include Israel, Syria, Lebanon and Jordan. Palestinians will be invited and attend as part of a joint Jordanian-Palestinian delegation. Egypt will be invited to the conference as a participant. The European Community will be a participant in the conference, alongside the United States and the Soviet Union and will be represented by its presidency. The Gulf Cooperation Council will be invited to send its secretary-general to the conference as an observer, and GCC member states will be invited to participate in organizing the negotiations on multilateral issues. The United Nations will be invited to send an observer, representing the secretary-general.

The conference will have no power to impose solutions on the parties or veto agreements reached by them. It will have no authority to make decisions for the parties and no ability to vote on issues of results. The conference can reconvene only with the consent of all the parties.

With respect to negotiations between Israel and Palestinians who are part of the joint Jordanian-Palestinian delegation, negotiations will be conducted in phases, beginning with talks on interim self-government arrangements. These talks will be conducted with the objective of reaching agreement within one year. Once agreed, the interim self-government arrangements will last for a period of five years; beginning the third year of the period of interim self-government arrangements, negotiations will take place on permanent status. These permanent status negotiations, and the negotiations between Israel and the Arab states, will take place on the basis of Resolutions 242 and 338.

It is understood that the co-sponsors are committed to making this process succeed. It is their intention to convene the conference and negotiations with those parties who agree to attend.

The co-sponsors believe that this process offers the promise of ending decades of confrontation and conflict and the hope of a lasting peace.

Thus, the co-sponsors hope that the parties will approach these negotiations in a spirit of good will and mutual respect. In this way, the peace process can begin to break down the mutual suspicions and mistrust that perpetuate the conflict and allow the parties to begin to resolve their differences. Indeed, only through such a process can real peace and reconciliation among the Arab states, Israel and the Palestinians be achieved. And only through this process can the peoples of the Middle East attain the peace and security they richly deserve.

Source: *"Letter of Invitation to Madrid Peace Conference, October 30, 1991," United States Embassy, Israel <http://usembassy-israel.org.il/publish/peace/madrid.htm>.*

SYRIAN-ISRAELI NEGOTIATIONS

tory. The UN Security Council, acting in response to a complaint from the Syrian government, issued Resolution 497 on 17 December 1981, declaring Israel's decision to impose its jurisdiction on the Golan Heights "null and void and without international legal effect." This resolution was crucial because it reasserted the principle of the "inadmissibility of the acquisition of territory by force," as did previous resolutions 242 and 338, and hence, stressed Syria's legal right to the Golan Heights.

The beginning of the 1990s witnessed two major challenges for Syria: the collapse of the former Soviet Union (1991) and the Iraqi invasion of Kuwait (1990). Asad understood that the collapse of the Soviet Union, Syria's main backer in the Cold War, was a setback to his country's ability to reach strategic parity with Israel. To recover from losing a major ally, but also to grab a seat in the new world order, Asad made two skillful moves. First, he joined the American-led coalition against Iraq during the Persian Gulf War (1990–1991), contributing to the coalition's credibility in Arab public opinion. The second strategic move was to attend the Madrid Peace Conference in October 1991.

The basis of the Madrid Conference was the principle of "land for peace," as indicated in UN Resolutions 242 and 338. Syria's position was in line with the letters of invitation sent by the Bush administration to the participants. Syria was ready to offer peace to Israel in exchange for Israel's full withdrawal from the Golan Heights and South Lebanon, and a solution to the Palestinian problem, either through the establishment of a Palestinian state in the West Bank and Gaza Strip or by the formation of a Jordanian-Palestinian confederation.

Negotiations after Madrid reflected the preference of Israel for breaking down the discussion into separate tracks, whereby Israeli representatives would meet separate Jordanian, Syrian, Lebanese, and later Palestinian delegations in order to solve the contentious issues with each country separately. No progress was made during the tenure of the Likud government of Yitzhak Shamir, who insisted that Syria offer Israel recognition and end the state of war before Israel would reciprocate with any commitment to "territorial compromise" in the Golan Heights.

The election of Prime Minister Yitzhak Rabin, head of the Labor Party, in June 1992 created an opening for progress in the Syrian-Israeli peace negotiations. According to Itamar Rabinovich, who headed the Israeli delegation under Rabin in negotiations with Syria, the "turning point" for Rabin's change of mind about the Syrian track came after a visit by U.S. secretary of state James Baker to Israel in July 1992. During that visit Baker assured Rabin of Asad's willingness to offer Israel genuine peace and of Baker's commitment to undertaking serious efforts on that track. In the first round of negotiation between the new Israeli delegation and Syria in August 1992, Rabinovich indicated to the Syrians that the Rabin government accepted the "applicability of the territorial element" in Resolution 242 to the Golan Heights.

The first substantive accomplishment in negotiations between Syria and Israel took place on 3 August 1993. Rabin asked U.S. secretary of state Warren Christopher to convey the following message to the Syrian leader: "Prime Minister Rabin has asked me to tell you that Israel is ready for full withdrawal from the Golan provided its requirements on security and normalization are met." The head of the Syrian delegation to the peace talks, Walid al-Moualem, said that it took the two delegations almost a year to reach an agreement on the full withdrawal to the 4 June 1967 lines. Again, the clarification about what was meant by "full withdrawal" was made as another commitment from Rabin to Asad through Christopher in July 1994.

Israel having fulfilled the basic Syrian demand for full withdrawal to the June 1967 lines, it was Syria's turn to compromise over the other issues of security, normalization, and a timetable for finalizing a peace treaty. While the Syrian leadership began preparing its people to accept full peace with Israel—defined in terms of normal relations, an end to the state of war, and the exchange of ambassadors—the Israelis created a long list of demands to be included under the other three issues: security, normalization, and time frame. Under "security," Israel wanted to maintain an early-warning station on the Golan, even after withdrawal. Israel also insisted on cutting substantially the size of the Syrian armed forces and creating a demilitarized zone reaching just south of Damascus. Under "normalization," Israel was interested in open borders, an open market for its products, and Israeli tourism to Syria. Finally, Rabin wanted a period of five years for Israel to withdraw from the Golan, during which time Syria had to agree to open borders, diplomatic relations, and elaborate security arrangements.

The two countries turned their attention to the question of security during negotiations from April 1995 to Rabin's assassination in November 1995. Because of the wide gap on the issues of early-warning stations and the size of the demilitarized zones, much work focused on the objectives of any security arrangements. With the help of the United States, the two countries reached an agreement on 24 May 1995 in a document entitled "Aims and Principles of Security Arrangements." The document stated that the aims were to reduce the risk of surprise attack and minimize daily friction. As for the principles, the document indicated that since security was a legitimate need for both sides, security arrangements should be equal, mutual, and reciprocal; that security arrangements should be arrived at through mutual agreement; and that such arrangements should be confined to the relevant areas on both sides. While this document did not solve all the security issues, it was an agreeable framework in which to hammer out the differences.

This agreement was followed by a second conference of the Chiefs of Staff of both sides in July 1995 (COS II). At the end of COS II, the American mediator, Dennis Ross, prepared a fifteen-page summary of the points of agreement and disagreement. Both the document on security arrangements and the summary of COS II, while they did not solve all disagreements over security, made considerable headway in the negotiating process.

The assassination of Rabin on 4 November 1995 constituted an abrupt setback for peace talks between Syria and Israel. Shortly after becoming prime minister, Shimon Peres conveyed to Asad, through President Bill Clinton and Ross, his endorsement of Rabin's commitment and his desire to hold a summit meeting with Asad. Peres, however, presented a new set of concerns, namely the issues of regional economic cooperation and water security as well as the urgency of reaching a peace agreement before a new election was called in Israel. Three rounds of negotiations, known as the Wye Plantation talks, took place between 27 December 1995 and 29 February 1996.

All sources agree that enormous progress was made during the Wye Plantation talks on all issues. Ross, the chief U.S. negotiator, expressed his satisfaction at the end of the first round, stating that more had been achieved in six days than in the four years of negotiations between the two sides. Syrian chief negotiator al-Moualem said that the participants completed 75 percent of the work on negotiating an agreement. He also told Middle East specialist and author Helena Cobban of progress made in all the areas related to security, especially the early-warning system and demilitarized areas; and the Syrian side agreed to nine of the fifteen points related to normalization. In another interview, al-Moualem, reaffirming the progress made during the Wye talks, added, "Uri Savir, Dennis Ross, and I, as the heads of the delegations, decided that we would hold continuous talks to finalize the structure of an agreement on all issues. We set a deadline for ourselves, agreeing to close the remaining gaps and finalize all the elements of an agreement by June 1996."

On the Israeli side Savir, who replaced Rabinovich as head of the Israeli delegation, was more forthcoming about what was achieved than Rabinovich (who remained on the delegation). Savir affirmed in his memoir, *The Process: 1,100 Days that Changed the Middle East* (1998), that achievement and progress were made in all areas during the Wye talks, including economic development, the nature of peace, security arrangements, the depth of withdrawal, the U.S. role in the negotiations, and the methodology for future progress.

Peres's authorization of the assassination of Yahya Ayyash, leading figure of the military wing of Hamas, and who had been inactive for more than a year, set in motion the deterioration of peace talks between Syria and Israel. Ayyash's assassination on 5 January 1995 was followed by a series of suicide bombings in revenge. In addition, Peres announced that he would call for an early election in May instead of its due date in October. This decision was disappointing to Asad, who felt that Peres had closed the window of opportunity for finalizing a peace agreement. When a fourth suicide bomber struck in Tel Aviv on 4 March, Peres suspended the peace negotiations and recalled the Israeli delegation from Washington, D.C. The second most important opportunity for a peace treaty between Israel and Syria thus ended.

Clashes between Israel and Hizbollah (Party of God) contributed to increased mistrust between Asad and Peres. In an effort to show his toughness Peres launched the Grapes of Wrath operation in South Lebanon in April 1996. The operation turned out to be disastrous, as became evident in the brutal massacre at Qana in which Israeli forces killed more than one hundred civilian Lebanese. All these developments cost Peres the election. Israelis elected Likud hardliner Benjamin Netanyahu as their new leader on 26 May 1996. During Netanyahu's tenure, no further negotiations took place between Syria and Israel. Even worse was the new leader's effort to change the frame of reference by calling for negotiations based on the principle of "peace for peace," implying that he would not honor the commitments made by his predecessors about full withdrawal from the Golan Heights; in other words, land-for-peace.

The third "near miss" of a Syria-Israel peace agreement was during the January 2000 negotiations. Even here, progress was made. Following the election of Labor leader Ehud Barak as prime minister on 17 May 1999, Asad and Barak traded public compliments, mainly through British journalist Patrick Seale. But it would take about six months for the two sides to resume talks. On 8 December 1999 President Clinton announced that Israel and Syria had agreed to resume negotiations "from the point at which they left off," a Syrian demand, and with "no preconditions," an Israeli demand. This compromise allowed each side to interpret the talks in its own way.

Preliminaries began on 15 December 1999, with a high-level formal meeting held between Barak and Syrian foreign minister Farouk al-Shara at Shepherdstown, West Virginia; it was mediated by President Clinton. The two sides agreed to resume talks on 3–9 January 2000. The Clinton administration convinced the two sides to set up four technical committees to discuss simultaneously the issues of borders/withdrawal, security arrangements, normalization of relations, and water. The simultaneity of these four "legs" of the negotiating table was a solution to the dilemma posed by the fact that each side insisted on prioritizing different issues. Syria wanted to discuss Israeli withdrawal before talking about anything else, while Israel refused to talk about withdrawal before security and normalization had been conceded by Syria. Convening all four committees at the same time ended this chicken-and-egg quandary. The State Department confirmed that talks touched on demilitarized zones between the two nations and on high-tech early-warning stations that would be "left on the Golan." Syria complained that Israel was refusing to convene the border and water committees, so it suspended its participation in the normalization and security committees.

On 7 January 2000 the United States presented Barak and Shara with a draft for an Israeli-Syrian core agreement. The State Department described the document as "a summary of the issues to be decided and the differences between the parties." The summarizing of all relevant issues in one comprehensive document was yet another positive development. This accomplishment may seem a minor point, but history shows that it is in fact important. Israeli negotiators, even during Rabin's tenure, kept their commitments verbal, secret, and ambiguous. Syria had pressed before for written confirmations of progress made during negotiations but had not received them, although Ross had begun taking notes and getting them approved by both sides. The creation of a public document that defined all issues in a manner acceptable to both sides, a document both Syria and Israel could own, was indeed an achievement, one that further talks could build upon. The teams adjourned for consultations with their respective capitals and agreed to open the second round on 19 January.

Unfortunately, it was during this interlude that the talks fell apart. There were reports that both governments leaked to the media certain documents favorable to them. Syria is believed to have leaked an old document to the Arabic daily *al-Hayat* on 9 January 2000, which outlined Syr-

ian and Israeli positions in a way that implied Israeli consent to a withdrawal but revealed no Syrian concessions. Israel retaliated by leaking the full text of the U.S. working paper to *Ha'aretz*, which published it on 12 January. This document was more favorable to Israel: it contained no Israeli acceptance of full withdrawal and revealed Syrian acceptance of early-warning ground stations in the Golan. Syria was embarrassed by the asymmetry of concessions indicated by the leak. The Syrian delegation was also disturbed by Israeli attempts to evade discussions of withdrawal during the Shepherdstown talks. On 16 January, Shara called U.S. secretary of state Madeleine Albright to say Syria could not participate in further negotiations unless Israeli withdrawal from the Golan topped the agenda and there was a reasonable chance of progress. Again, by the end of January, there was deterioration in the security situation in Lebanon. Barak decided to shift his focus to Lebanon in the next few months, and Israeli forces withdrew unilaterally from South Lebanon by the end of May 2000.

The last attempt to revive the Syrian track was the summit between President Clinton and Asad on 26 March 2000. Asad was told that Clinton had "good news" from Barak. Asad thought that the American president finally got Barak's endorsement of the Rabin/Peres commitment for full withdrawal. Instead, Clinton conveyed a new proposal from Barak, which would recognize Syria's rights to the Golan up to Lake Tiberias, but Syria would "forgo" access to the lake. In practical terms, the new suggestion would allow Israel to maintain a small portion of the Golan, hence depriving Syria access to water. Asad rejected the offer outright.

If the two sides were so close—on at least three occasions—to reaching a peace treaty, how to explain their failure? Leaving aside the tendency of each side to blame the other for not taking the process to fruition, the fact is that the two sides plus the United States, which was present throughout the negotiations, are responsible to varying degrees for the failure. Seale, who studied and carried messages back and forth between the two leaderships, describes the 1992–1996 talks as "a tale of political deception, of saying one thing and meaning another, of missed opportunities and bitter disappointments."

On the Israeli side, there have been three Likud and three Labor cabinets since Madrid. No progress whatsoever was made during any of the Likud governments, two of which were elected with a platform emphasizing security, not peace. Shamir was the last prime minister to accept the U.S. invitation to attend the Madrid Conference. After the talks broke into separate tracks, Shamir's government demonstrated no willingness to make any serious territorial compromise in accordance with Resolutions 242 and 338. When Netanyahu become prime minister in May 1996, he refused to recognize the progress made through four years of negotiations and wanted to set a new basis for negotiations, one inconsistent with UN resolutions. Netanyahu deserves some credit for the deterioration of the Palestinian track as well. Finally, Sharon was elected to put an end to the al-Aqsa *intifada* and bring security to the Israeli people. With no political solution included in his "vision," more Israeli civilians had been killed under Sharon than any previous government.

All progress between Syria and Israel was achieved under Labor leaders, yet no agreement was reached under any of them. Available published records reveal that Rabin, despite his commitment to withdrawal, was not ready to sign a peace treaty during his first term. His assassination killed the possibility for a peace agreement for which he could take credit. Peres brought new hope and another missed opportunity to finalize a peace treaty with Syria. Yet, his lack of credibility—compared with Rabin—and his attempts to prove his toughness against Hamas and Hizbollah backfired. His call for an early election closed the window of opportunity to finalize a peace treaty. Barak's first few months in office revived the expectations of the Syrian leadership and the United States. Asad went out of his way to praise the Israeli leader. While there are not as many details about why the January 2000 negotiations broke down, there is enough evidence to suggest that Barak was more interested in fulfilling his promise to find a way out of the Lebanese "quagmire" and to concentrate on the Palestinian track. Barak told this author, during a visit to the University of Arkansas on 24 October 2002, that he felt Shara was not authorized to finalize a deal during the Shepherdstown talks and that Asad was more focused on setting the stage for succession by his son than on reaching a peace treaty with Israel.

On the Syrian side, Asad's insistence on observing the rituals of "steadfastness" may have contributed to missed opportunities. According to Rabinovich, had Asad been more forthcoming in assuring the Israeli public or shown more flexibility on procedural issues, there would have been better prospects for peace. "At any given point during the four-year negotiation a decision by Asad to come to a meeting with President Clinton and the prime minister of Israel would have produced an agreement based on a compromise," Rabinovitch claims. Al-Moualem's response to Rabinovich is that it was not the job of the Syrian leadership to prepare the Israeli public for peace. The Syrian government had enough on its plate in preparing its own public to swallow normalization and open borders with a country that has been portrayed for forty years as a Zionist and racist enemy "entity." Moreover, the Syrians have always argued that a premature summit between Asad and any Israeli prime minister is likely to backfire. In retrospect, the Camp David summit between Palestine Liberation Organization (PLO) chairman Yasser Arafat and Barak could be cited as a parallel example.

Underneath the mutual finger-pointing between Syrian and Israel are two realities. First is the issue of mutual mistrust and misunderstanding between the two leaderships, and second is the mutual unwillingness to seize the moment by taking risks. For instance, while Israelis expected Asad to follow in the footsteps of Sadat, King Hussein of Jordan, and Arafat, the Syrian leader—though ready to make an historic compromise with Israel—was not about to imitate those men. He wanted peace with more dignity and strength than he saw them as having. Syrians and Arabs at large have, it is true, admired Asad's will to recover every inch of Syrian territory without being forced to toady up to Israel or make major concessions, such as opening his country to Israeli products. They appreciated his steadfastness compared to other Arab leaders, who are seen as having made peace on Israeli terms. While these leaders were lauded in the West for signing peace agreements with Israel, images of these Arab leaders hugging and kissing Israeli leaders in public and giving Israel trade concessions and other advantages before legitimate Arab rights had been restored lowered these men's standing in Arab public opinion. Asad's refusal to allow even his foreign minister to shake hands with the Israeli prime minister before Syrian lands were restored touched a sympathetic nerve with the Arab public.

Both Syria and Israel have hesitated to take risks in reaching a peace agreement. Asad and Rabin were cautious in making their compromises public and, as the assassination of Rabin proved, for good reason. Unlike the Palestinian and even the Lebanese tracks in which the status quo was too risky to maintain, in the Syrian case, "there was a sense among both delegations that, if necessary, we could live without peace." Finally, the American role in the negotiations, while accepted by both sides, was not assertive in pushing either side, especially Israel, to build on what had been agreed upon. How can a country that is a strategic ally of Israel and classifies Syria as a "terrorist" country act as an "honest" broker? Was the United States ever ready to exert pressure on Israel to comply with Resolutions 242 and 338? The negative answers to these questions are relevant to the failed outcome.

The failure to reach a peace treaty between Syria and Israel does not mean progress has not been achieved. Even Rabinovich, whose entire book intended to downplay the progress made during the four-year period, identifies the following four achievements: both sides became thoroughly familiar with each other's positions; the general contours of a prospective settlement were sketched, and several important barriers were crossed; two Israeli prime ministers have indicated to the Israeli public their willingness to make massive concessions; and Asad publicly agreed to make full peace and to offer normalization with Israel. Any future leadership, on either side, interested in pursuing peace is likely to acknowledge and benefit from these accomplishments. The only reason not to call what has been achieved "progress" is to ignore the hard work of making peace.

—NAJIB GHADBIAN,
UNIVERSITY OF ARKANSAS

Viewpoint:
No. Although some progress was made on the technical details of a peace agreement, the Syrians and Israelis were doomed to failure by their mutual suspicion and animosity.

On 8 December 1999 U.S. president Bill Clinton announced the renewal of Syrian-Israeli peace negotiations, this time with the participation of Israeli prime minister Ehud Barak and Syrian foreign minister Farouk al-Shara. The renewal of these negotiations at such a senior level, and in essence the first at the political level, aroused considerable optimism about an expected breakthrough and a possible Israeli-Syrian peace settlement within a few months.

However, no such breakthrough occurred. The renewal of talks in Washington, D.C., and later in Shepherdstown, West Virginia, yielded no results. The talks ended shortly after they had begun, and the Syrian-Israeli peace negotiations once again reached an impasse. It also appeared that the already existing psychological barriers between the two countries—of suspicion, distrust, and animosity—intensified in the wake of the failed negotiations. The peace process, at least on the Syrian and Lebanese tracks, was buried following the failed summit between President Clinton and Syrian president Hafiz al-Asad in Geneva in March 2000. The optimistic assessments regarding an immediate Syrian-Israeli peace agreement were quickly replaced by pessimism and even the possibility that hostilities might break out between the two countries against the background of the eruption of the al-Aqsa *intifada* and the renewed Hizbollah

(Party of God) attacks on Israeli positions along its northern border.

Syrian-Israeli peace negotiations were initiated in October 1991 with the convening of the Madrid Peace Conference. President Asad's readiness to join the American-initiated peace process indicated a true volte-face in his traditional policy vis-à-vis Israel. Asad was now prepared to consider the possibility of establishing peace with Israel, which he had considered until then the eternal enemy against which the Arab world, under Syrian leadership, was engaged in a life-or-death battle. This change in Asad's attitude regarding the conflict with Israel must be understood against the background of the weakening of Syria's standing in the regional and international arenas following the collapse of the Soviet Union and Iraq's defeat in the Persian Gulf War (1990–1991) as well as the growing moderation in the Arab world regarding Israel. A similar change took place in Israel's position under Yitzhak Rabin, who had replaced Yitzhak Shamir as prime minister following the 1992 general elections in Israel. This change was mainly in Rabin's readiness to consider the possibility of withdrawal from the entire Golan Heights to the border between Israel and Syria prior to the start of the 1967 Arab-Israeli War (also known as the Six-Day War or June War).

However, despite progress that had been made in Israeli-Syrian negotiations during the leadership of Rabin (1992–1995) and his successor Shimon Peres in early 1996 as well as when Ehud Barak served as prime minister (1999–2000), both countries failed in their attempts to achieve a breakthrough and reach a peace agreement. The failure marked the end of the Syrian-Israeli negotiations, at least in the form in which they were held throughout the 1990s. While Israel and Syria arrived at the brink of peace, in the end they failed to achieve the desired goal. Despite the fact that throughout the decade the two sides managed to overcome most of the issues that separated them, a final peace settlement was ultimately beyond their reach.

What ostensibly separated Syria and Israel were differences concerning a narrow strip of land, several hundred meters along the northeastern shore of the Sea of Galilee, which was seen in Damascus as an issue in principle involving national honor and pride; this strip separated peace with honor that Asad desired and peace with surrender that the Syrians absolutely refused to accept. From Israel's point of view, this land also became an issue of principle, having to do not only with the question of the allocation of water in the region but also with Israeli national pride. Syria's intransigence regarding the reacquisition of all of the Golan Heights, including the strip of land that had originally been part of mandatory

Palestine and was captured by the Syrians in 1948 (along the Sea of Galilee), often was accompanied by grim, if not hostile, Syrian attitudes directed toward Israel. This stand was viewed by many in Israel as an insult to national pride and a sign of a lack of any true desire for peace. Israeli public opinion polls showed that Syria's insistence that Israel withdraw to the 4 June 1967 border deterred many Israelis from supporting the proposed peace agreement between the two countries. It has also been claimed in retrospect that the results of these polls deterred Barak from reaching an agreement with Asad in the early months of 2000.

However, it would appear that this rather simplistic approach, which blames the failure of the Syrian-Israeli negotiations on differences amounting to a couple of hundred isolated meters, tends to ignore the fact that this failure had exposed a lack of maturity on both sides—the leaders and the public in Syria as well as in Israel—regarding the readiness to pay the price for peace. The Syrians refused to adopt a "policy of peace"; in other words, to send a message of peace to the public in Israel, a message that was the sine qua non for creating wide public support in Israel for the painful concession it would

be required to make in order to achieve a peace agreement. Without such explicit intentions, any Israeli government, including that of Barak, would find it difficult to recruit public support for a withdrawal from the entire Golan Heights. The Israeli government refused, primarily because of strong opposition within Israel to comply with the Syrian demand for withdrawal to the 4 June borders, which would have meant the return of the Syrians to the northeastern shore of the Sea of Galilee. It should be mentioned that the Israeli public's affinity for the Golan Heights, a preferred tourist area whose strategic importance cannot be overestimated, is stronger than its affinity for the West Bank and Gaza Strip, regions heavily populated by hostile and rebellious Palestinians. Only a small number of Syrians have remained in the Golan Heights, and since the 1973 Arab-Israeli War (also known as the October War, Yom Kippur War, and Ramadan War) it has enjoyed peace and tranquility. The Israeli government found it difficult to sway public opinion in Israel without public diplomacy in Damascus as well.

Damascus failed to embolden the peace camp in Israel that would have put pressure on Israeli governments to make concessions on the issue of the Golan Heights and assist an Israeli government in convincing the Israeli public to support concessions. There were many in Israel who compared Asad to Anwar Sadat. While the Egyptian president's historic visit to Jerusalem in November 1977 brought in its wake the creation of a peace camp in Israel that would assist him in conducting negotiations with Israel, Asad used Hizbollah in South Lebanon as an instrument of pressure designed to make Israel accept Syria's positions. Asad's utilization of Hizbollah caused some Israelis to support withdrawal from the Golan Heights because of their desire to stop the constant bloodshed inflicted on Israeli forces in Lebanon. Nevertheless, Asad's scheme had its limitations in that it aroused doubts in Israel as to Damascus's real intentions.

The Syrian-Israeli case bore witness more than anything else to the huge gap between the concept of peace in Israel and that which existed on the Syrian side. The Israeli public wanted peace with Syria to be a "warm peace," based on broad and deep normalization of relations, including trade relations, tourism, and cultural exchanges. The establishment of peace with its neighboring Arab countries is viewed by the Israeli public as crucial. Since the peace process must involve painful territorial concessions, the Israeli public wanted to be convinced that the Syrians sincerely wanted peace. Syria, for its part, did want a peace settlement with Israel. The Syrian regime wanted a formal and even technical peace, which was to be no more than a nonbelligerency pact with formal diplomatic relations. Syria was opposed to the idea of a "warm peace," and it was deeply apprehensive about the possibility of genuine and deep normalization of relations with Israel that would allow the latter to gain economic and political control of the region, exploiting its economic superiority. This position apparently had its roots in the fact that the basic Arab concept regarding Israel had not undergone any substantial change. Israel is still viewed as an enemy and, worse than that, as an alien entity lacking any legitimacy in the region, the price of whose creation has been paid by the Arabs, especially the Palestinians.

The Syrians accused Israel of not being sufficiently prepared to pursue a practical and not emotionally charged policy guided by the yearnings of the Israeli public. The Syrians found it difficult to understand the request that they assist the Rabin government, and later that of Barak, in persuading Israeli public opinion to support the concessions necessary for achieving peace, assistance that meant engaging in public diplomacy or, as the Syrians viewed it, Syria bending down on its knees for the benefit of Israel. According to the Syrian view, each of the sides had to convince its own public of the necessity of these moves and not rely on help from the other side.

Under these conditions, it seems that hopes of a breakthrough in the Syrian-Israeli negotiations have been too optimistic and that the road to peace is longer than had been thought. In the final analysis, the obstacle was not necessarily several hundred meters one way or the other; it was rooted in the question of the basic concepts each side had regarding a future peace settlement between them. Despite the fact that progress had been made on the technical details of a peace agreement, there was almost no progress on the basic problems at the root of the Syrian-Israeli conflict. To sum up, the long-drawn-out negotiations between Israel and Syria throughout most of the 1990s brought the two sides closer to achieving a peace agreement, but much of that progress had been imagined and was more like constructing a building without first laying its foundation. Thus, the two countries must fundamentally change their perspectives on peace before an agreement can be reached.

–EYAL ZISSER,
TEL AVIV UNIVERSITY

References

Helena Cobban, *The Israeli-Syrian Peace Talks: 1991–96 and Beyond* (Washington, D.C.: U.S. Institute of Peace Press, 1999).

Alasdair Drysdale and Raymond Hinnebusch, *Syria and the Middle East Peace Process* (New York: Council on Foreign Relations Press, 1991).

Najib Ghadbian, "The New Asad: Dynamics of Continuity and Change in Syria," *Middle East Journal*, 55 (Autumn 2001): 625–641.

Frederic C. Hof, *Line of Battle, Border of Peace? The Line of June 4, 1967* (Washington, D.C.: Middle East Insight, 1999).

Moshe Maoz, *Syria and Israel: From War to Peacemaking* (Oxford & New York: Oxford University Press, 1995).

Itamar Rabinovich, *The Brink of Peace: The Israeli-Syrian Negotiations* (Princeton: Princeton University Press, 1998).

Uri Savir, *The Process: 1,100 Days that Changed the Middle East* (New York: Random House, 1998).

Patrick Seale, "The Syrian-Israel Negotiations: Who Is Telling the Truth?" *Journal of Palestine Studies*, 29 (Winter 2000): 65–77.

Eyal Zisser, *Asad's Legacy: Syria in Transition* (London: C. Hurst, 2000).

SYRIAN-ISRAELI NEGOTIATIONS

UNITED ARAB REPUBLIC

Did the United Arab Republic (1958–1961) fail because of mistakes by Gamal Abd al-Nasser?

Viewpoint: Yes. Egyptian president Gamal Abd al-Nasser's reluctance to share power undermined popular support for the United Arab Republic.

Viewpoint: No. The failure of the United Arab Republic was largely the result of the unrealistic expectations of Arab nationalists.

By early 1958 the calls for integral pan-Arab unity had reached a crescendo in the Middle East. Egyptian president Gamal Abd al-Nasser's popularity in the Arab world was at its height following the Suez War (1956); in addition, he had expertly maneuvered Egypt into an advantageous position in Syria during the American-Syrian Crisis (1957), when the United States attempted to overthrow in Damascus what it viewed as a pro-Soviet regime. The resulting American failure resulted in Nasser's enhanced prestige in the area and a bolstering of pro-Nasserist elements in Syria, particularly the Arab nationalist Baath Party.

Led by the Baath Party, Arab nationalist elements in Syria clamored for union with Egypt, the acknowledged leader of the Arab world. Despite the rhetoric proclaiming otherwise, Nasser was actually reluctant to enter into formal union with Syria. As scholar George Lenczowski put it, "it was one thing to propagate the idea of Arab unity in a broad sense of political solidarity, military coordination, and revolutionary progress, and another to give it a concrete political form and assume the responsibility of government." In addition, little political, economic, or institutional commonality existed between the two systems, making convergence all the more difficult.

In the end, however, Nasser succumbed to the momentum he had created, and both the Egyptian Assembly and Syrian Parliament approved the union of the two countries into the United Arab Republic (UAR) on 1 February 1958—Nasser was, naturally, selected as president. Throughout the Arab world, this event was heralded as the beginning of attaining the ultimate objective of Arab nationalism; in other words, a union of the Arab peoples from the Atlantic Ocean to the Persian Gulf. In March, Yemen joined in a federal union with the UAR, forming the United Arab States, which was a much less integral confederation than that which was entered into by Egypt and Syria. Reacting to the formation of the UAR, in what was really a convulsive defensive gesture by the pro-West conservative Arab monarchies, Jordan and Iraq on 14 February 1958 merged into the Arab Union, an organization that was abrogated by the Iraqi Revolution, which occurred five months later.

By 1961 there were many disaffected elements in Syria. Nasser's socialist decrees in July, including the nationalization of a host of industries and enterprises, seemed to be the last straw for Syrians, especially the business community, who were opposed to continuing the union. The literal coup de grace came in September, when a group of army officers took power in Damascus and quickly announced Syria's secession from the UAR. The federation with Yemen was terminated the following December.

Viewpoint:
Yes. Egyptian president Gamal Abd al-Nasser's reluctance to share power undermined popular support for the United Arab Republic.

Dear Mr. President: Our conference is drawing to a close in an atmosphere dominated by concern over the union of Syria with Egypt. It is the unanimous view of the Middle East members that this is an unhappy development that can presage much trouble. It does not seem to be entirely clear whether it is promoted by the Communists or whether the Communists are going along with Nasser's ambition to unify the Arab world under his leadership. Under either contingency the development is viewed with lively concern.

So stated U.S. secretary of state John Foster Dulles in a telegram to a meeting of U.S. ambassadors to the Middle East. The conference that Dulles was talking about was the Baghdad Pact Ministerial Meeting, and the union so openly feared was proclaimed on 1 February 1958.

One must, however, digress back a year to the Eisenhower Doctrine, which was passed as a joint resolution by the U.S. Congress on 9 March 1957. The effect of this policy during the Cold War era set the Western powers against the Soviets. Concurrently, a contrary position was adopted in the Arab world. Two mutually antagonistic camps—the radicals (Egypt, Syria, Iraq, Yemen, and Algeria) and the conservatives (Saudi Arabia, Jordan, Kuwait, Libya, and Morocco)—were engaged in the so-called Arab Cold War. Because of the U.S. promise to intervene economically as well as militarily wherever communism posed a threat, President Dwight D. Eisenhower decided to explore the intentions of fifteen Middle East countries by sending former Democratic congressman and chairman of the House Foreign Affairs Committee James P. Richards as his special assistant, "with the personal rank of Ambassador to advise and assist the President and the Secretary of State on problems of the Middle Eastern area."

Ambassador Richards's trip to the Middle East began on 12 March 1957 and lasted almost a month. With his special group made up of personnel from the Departments of State and Defense plus International Cooperation Administration officials, the ambassador visited Lebanon, Libya, Turkey, Iran, Pakistan, Afghanistan, Iraq, Saudi Arabia, Yemen, Ethiopia, Sudan, Greece, Israel, Tunisia, and Morocco. The mission did not visit Syria, Egypt, or Jordan because, as scholar Bonnie F. Saunders states, "the first two countries' lack of an invitation, and Jordan's acknowledgment of Communism's dangers."

The Eisenhower Doctrine was not welcomed by all of the Middle East countries. Iraq, Lebanon, and Libya hailed it with "enthusiastic statements," but King Saud of Saudi Arabia only "reluctantly endorsed" it. Shortly afterward, the Jordanian Crisis brought into question the implementation of the doctrine and, in August, what David W. Lesch calls the American-Syrian Crisis severely tested the Eisenhower administration's containment policy.

In the second half of the 1950s Syria's two major political entities—the People's Party and the National Party—were losing ground to the more ideological and leftist Baath Socialist Party, the Communist Party, and the right-wing Syrian Nationalist Popular Party, as well as the Moslem Brotherhood. The Baath (founded by Michel Aflaq, a Christian, and Salah al-Din al-Bitar, a Muslim) became a formal party in 1946 and in 1953 merged with the Arab Socialist Party (ASP), founded by Akram Hawrani in 1945, to become the Arab Socialist Resurrection Party (ASRP). The Syrian Social Nationalist Party became the Baath's strongest opponent by advocating the creation of a Greater Syria and fostering Syrian nationalism against its pan-Arabism. The Baath Party effectively came to power in early 1957, and on 13 August 1957 the American-Syrian Crisis broke out. The Syrian government's discovery of a coup d'état organized by the Central Intelligence Agency (CIA) and dissident Syrians led to the expulsion of three officials of the American embassy in Damascus. The U.S. response to this action was prompt: Syrian ambassador Farid Zeineddine and the second secretary of the embassy in Washington, Yassin Zakaria, were expelled.

The Eisenhower administration's attempt to protect the Middle East from Soviet influence had the opposite effect: the previous Anglo-Iraqi plot of 24 November 1956, known as Operation Straggle, warned the Syrians of the possibility of a Western-bloc initiative against the perceived communist menace. Now it was Syria's neighboring countries' turn to worry about a Syrian response. Lebanon, Jordan, and Turkey started to mass troops on their Syrian borders. The Kremlin warned Turkey not to intervene in Syria, and by mid September 1957 the crisis dissipated.

UNITED ARAB REPUBLIC

What had happened to the Arab moderate states? Since the outbreak of the crisis, pro-Western countries such as Saudi Arabia and Iraq refused to assume leadership in the Middle East for primarily one reason: Nasser's power and influence as a leader of radical pan-Arab nationalism. The Egyptian president acted promptly and on 13 October sent troops to Latakia, a city on the Syrian coast. Considering the number of soldiers deployed—about two thousand—it was obvious that Nasser's aim was not to wage war against the Western bloc but rather to reassert his supremacy in the region, especially over King Saud of Saudi Arabia. The outcome was the creation on 1 February 1958 of the United Arab Republic (UAR).

This geopolitical union did not come about by happenstance. In October 1955 the two countries signed a mutual defense treaty in order to counterbalance the Baghdad Pact (1955) among Iran, Iraq, Pakistan, Turkey, and Great Britain. Syria helped Egypt during the Suez War (1956) and, in turn, was supported by Egypt during the crisis with the United States. The meeting in Cairo between Nasser and Syrian president Shukri al-Quwatli, therefore, represented the logical conclusion of this collaboration from the perspective of the Syrian government. Conversely, the nature of the agreement seemed to be somewhat different to Nasser, who immediately pointed out the characteristics of the union. It became evident that a union on a federal basis was not possible. Nasser was not the kind of leader to share his power readily with someone else; he dissolved all of Egypt's political parties but his own National Union Party. The Syrian people were represented in the UAR Parliament in Cairo while Syrian military officers served in the UAR army under Egyptian command. Plebiscites in both countries ratified the union on 21 February 1958, and Nasser was proclaimed its first president. The Eisenhower administration's recognition of the UAR was immediate.

The UAR's establishment triggered a chain reaction, the conclusion of which was not Arab unity. On 14 February Jordan and Iraq merged into the Arab Union. In order to make the union even stronger, Iraqi crown prince Abd al-Ilah wanted to incorporate Kuwait. As scholar Malik Mufti states, "the matter became moot on July 14, 1958, when Iraqi military leader Abd al-Karim Qassim overthrew the Iraqi government in a coup and slaughtered its Hashemite leadership."

Qassim's coup took place in the midst of the Lebanese Crisis. This last event involved the United States, which sent fifteen thousand Marines to protect the country from falling under the control of pro-Nasser forces. What was still not evident to the Eisenhower administration was Qassim's desire to play a leadership role in the region apart from Nasser. In fact, after having enjoyed the support of the Iraqi Communist Party in order to counterbalance the Iraqi Baath's plan to merge the country with the UAR, Qassim turned against it and established a virtual dictatorship. Moreover, he formally withdrew from the Baghdad Pact on 24 March 1959, thus isolating his country, and proclaimed it the "Eternal Iraqi Republic."

The UAR therefore seemed the only stable entity in the Middle East, adding the state of Yemen in March 1958. The honeymoon was short-lived. Syria's defection from the UAR on 28 September 1961 and Yemen's defection in December confirmed that Nasser's dream of a pan-Arab union was not feasible. Each Middle Eastern country had its own concept of Arab nationalism. Syria, after Nasser's abolition of its political parties, "the dismissal of Syrian officers, and the forced introduction of a modified version of the Egyptian land reform laws," according to William L. Cleveland, decided to be independent once again. In a certain way the UAR turned out to be one of the lowest points of Nasser's career. To unify the Arab world under the aegis of pan-Arabism had been child's play. After all, both radical and conservative Arab countries recognized each other's role in the Middle Eastern puzzle. However, the creation of a union between Egypt and Syria turned out to be anything but child's play—indeed, it was counterproductive.

Each Arab state aimed at playing an independent role in the international arena, fearing that the Syrian-Egyptian axis would have been a starting point for the establishment of a third geopolitical pole in the superpower bipolar world. A regional organization already existed—the Arab League, established in March 1945—and paradoxically, though the UAR found support throughout much of the Arab world, it essentially included only Egypt and Syria.

What probably did not work in Nasser's favor to constitute a union with Syria was the timing. What more could the Egyptian leader do after the victory at Suez? He had succumbed to his own rhetoric and popularity. Even though the UAR ultimately failed by 1961, as George Lenczowski concludes in *American Presidents and the Middle East* (1990), the United States could have exploited Nasser's failure, but it did not. The Kennedy administration could have "joined its voice to those who claimed with derision that the U.A.R. was a misnomer because it was neither 'united' (but ruled by Cairo) nor 'Arab' (but overwhelmingly Egyptian, that is, Nilotic-African)," but it overlooked this definition and continued to recognize the pretense of Egypt as the UAR.

–PAOLA OLIMPO,
UNIVERSITY OF LECCE

Viewpoint:
No. The failure of the United Arab Republic was largely the result of the unrealistic expectations of Arab nationalists.

The United Arab Republic (UAR), formed in February 1958 and terminated forty-four months later, was a serious setback for Arab nationalism and for its major hero, Egyptian president Gamal Abd al-Nasser. Although the failure of this ill-fated union of Egypt and Syria is commonly attributed to Nasser's ambitions and mistakes, it was the latter country that spearheaded both its inception and its demise. Arab nationalism has played a leading role in Syrian political thought; it has usually been secondary to or absent from the drama of clashing ideologies in Egypt. Syria's Baath (Renaissance) Party championed Arab unity; it later bore Nasser's censure for the collapse of the UAR. Nasser, by contrast, never visited an independent Arab country before he consented to Syria's offer to unite with Egypt under his lead-

THE QUESTION OF RECOGNITION

Memorandum From the Secretary of State to the President

Washington, February 8, 1958

Subject

Recognition of United Arab Republic

It is expected that a plebiscite will be held in Egypt and Syria on February 21 to vote on the union of those two countries into the "United Arab Republic" and on the election of Gamal Abdel Nasser as President. Nasser will apparently assume the Presidency on or about February 22 or 23. At that time the United Arab Republic will officially come into existence and Egypt and Syria will cease to exist as international entities. Chiefs of diplomatic missions in Damascus will have no status as of that date and all political questions with foreign governments will be dealt with by the Foreign Office of the new republic in Cairo. The United States will then be faced with the question of recognition of the new republic and the accreditation of an Ambassador.

We have been in close consultation with Iraq, Jordan, Lebanon and Saudi Arabia which are deeply concerned by the implications of the creation of the new republic. We have advised those governments that we should be glad to give active consideration to supporting any feasible common plan they might be able to devise to thwart or otherwise oppose the union of Egypt and Syria. So far we have received little or no evidence that our Arab friends are able or willing to formulate common action. On the contrary, there is increasing evidence that one or more of these governments may recognize the United Arab Republic.

We believe that if our Arab friends cannot formulate common action which we could feasibly and appropriately support and particularly if one or more of them recognize, we could not justifiably withhold our recognition of the United Arab Republic without renouncing our traditional policy on Arab unity and without giving offense to the popular appeal of Arab nationalism.

Thus, in the likely event that our Arab friends do not devise a common plan of action which we can appropriately support and especially if one or more of them recognize the United Arab Republic, your authority is sought for the United States to extend recognition to the new republic as soon as such a step is appropriate following the proclamation of the republic.

Your approval is also sought for the designation of Raymond Arthur Hare, now Ambassador to Egypt, to be Ambassador to the United Arab Republic.

Source: "Memorandum From the Secretary of State to the President," 8 February 1958, in Foreign Relations of the United States, 1958–1960, *volume 13:* Arab-Israeli Dispute; United Arab Republic; North Africa *(Washington, D.C.: U.S. Government Printing Office, 1992), pp. 421–422.*

ership, and he admitted at the time that he knew at most half a dozen Syrians personally.

The idea of Arab nationalism emerged in the late nineteenth century among Syrians, mainly the Orthodox Christian minority, who opposed the Ottoman Empire, which was strengthening its control over remote provinces such as Syria. Although most Syrians and other Arabic-speaking subjects of the Ottoman Empire remained loyal to Sultan Abd al-Hamid II (who reigned from 1876 to 1909) and hailed the restoration of its long-suspended constitution in 1908 under the Young Turks, many Christians longed for greater autonomy, and some Muslims hoped to form an Arab caliph-

ate. When the World War I (1914–1918) Allies, aided by the Arab revolt, took Syria (including Palestine) from the Ottoman Turks, Syrian leaders saw an opportunity to declare an independent Arab state with its capital in Damascus and a member of the Hashimite family (descendants of Muhammad) as its king. This Arab kingdom lasted less than two years. The British let the French occupy the Mediterranean coast; French forces seized Damascus in July 1920; and the Arab kingdom came to an end.

For many Syrian Arab nationalists, their history since 1920 has been dominated by their desire to re-create that united state. They have debated whether its borders would encompass one of four territorial options: what are now Syria and Lebanon; those republics plus present-day Israel and its Occupied Territories, and the Hashimite Kingdom of Jordan; the Fertile Crescent (thus adding Iraq); or every country in which speakers of Arabic form the majority (from the Atlantic Ocean to the Persian Gulf). The fourth and most extreme option became the basis for the formation of the Baath Party, founded in 1940 by two teachers, one of them Christian, the other Muslim. Until the Baath became popular, Syrian politicians were divided between those who favored a union of Fertile Crescent countries and those who wanted Syria to work closely with Saudi Arabia and Egypt in opposition to such a union, which Iraq would have dominated. Up to 1946, however, politically conscious Syrians focused on getting rid of the French mandate.

Egypt has had its own nationalist movements since the late 1870s, but their focus has been on insuring the independence of the Nile Valley from European, especially British, control. Its popular leaders—Ahmad Urabi, Mustafa Kamil, Muhammad Farid, and Sa'd Zaghlul—believed in "Egypt for the Egyptians" and were indifferent, if not hostile, to the Arab nationalism of the Syrians. Zaghlul's successor as leader of the Wafd Party, Mustafa al-Nahhas, took an interest in Arab issues when he was prime minister (1942–1944, 1950–1952), but he did so mainly to support the creation of the Arab League as an effort to block Iraq's Fertile Crescent unity plan and to secure Egypt's place as the leader of the Arabic-speaking peoples. The military coup against the monarchy in 1952 had strongly nationalist motives, but the nation in question was Egypt, and neither Muhammad Naguib nor Nasser spoke of their movement as an Arab one in its early stages. Arab nationalism entered the Egyptian government's discourse during and after the Suez Crisis (1956) as a result of the decline of British and French rule in the Middle East and North Africa, the rising saliency of the Arab-Israeli conflict, and the Cold War. At no time have most Egyptians willingly identified themselves as *Arabs,* a term they commonly applied to desert Bedouin. By education and culture Egyptians knew about and identified with Europe and North America and viewed the eastern Arab countries as client states or markets for their cultural and industrial output. Few Egyptians went to Syria or other Arab states as tourists; they went as teachers, entertainers, or entrepreneurs. The triumph of Arab nationalism in 1958 took both Egypt's rulers and citizens by surprise.

Arab nationalism was stronger in Syria, partly because its citizens had good reason to feel that their country had been deprived of lands as well as dignity by the policies and actions of France, Britain, Turkey, and the United States. France's abortive attempt to create separate republics of Damascus, Aleppo, Jebel Druze, and Latakia to dissipate Syrian political unity; its successful excision of lands around Tripoli, Beirut, and Sidon to create a greater Lebanon; and the separation of Hatay (Alexandretta) and its award to Turkey (1939) all angered the Syrians. British support for the Hashimite Kingdom of Jordan and American backing for Israel likewise distressed Syrian nationalists. The frequent military coups of 1949 and the country's political instability in the 1950s were embarrassments, and the rise of the Baath Party with its slogans of "Unity, Freedom, and Socialism" and "One Arab nation with an immortal mission" won support among Syrian intellectuals and students. Its spread to Jordan and Iraq suggested that the Baath's commitment to Arab nationalism would increase Syrian influence in the Arab world. Between 1955 and 1958 the Baath made substantial gains in Syria (possibly aided by the Egyptians, who wanted to counter Iraq's influence), and it won several cabinet posts in the government late in 1956. It had to share power with both leftists (some of whom may have been Communists) and rightists (some of whom may have been Muslim Brothers) and to weather serious crises with the Americans and the Turks during 1957. They saw Nasser as the one Arab leader who could help them surmount all these threats.

As Syria weathered a crisis in its relations with the United States and nearly had a border war with Turkey, Baathist deputies, ministers, and officers trekked to Cairo in autumn 1957 to petition Nasser for a union between Syria and Egypt. Nasser hesitated. He favored gradual federation over an organic union, partly because he distrusted Syria's highly politicized officer corps, but his public proclamations of Arabism, combined with his growing popularity among the Arab masses, made it impossible to spurn the Syrians. At Nasser's insistence, President Shukri al-Quwatli came to Cairo to finalize the agreement to form the UAR. He became "the first citizen of the republic." Nasser became its president.

The formal announcement of the union on 1 February 1958 led to joyful demonstrations throughout the Arab world, and even Arab governments that feared Nasser's influence made haste to congratulate him on this event. Syrians were ecstatic; only later did they see that they had surrendered their sovereignty to Egypt. They had to abolish their political parties, even the Baath, which was represented by a ceremonial vice president and three ministers in the new UAR cabinet. There continued to be cabinets for the "southern region" (Egypt) and the "northern region" (Syria). The two regions were separated by Lebanon, Israel, and the Mediterranean Sea. Arab nationalists hoped that other states would join this new republic, but only Yemen did so, and only in a federation that enabled it to remain a hereditary imamate with its traditional institutions. Jordan and Iraq formed an Arab Union that lasted only five months, until an officers' revolution in Baghdad ended both the Iraqi kingdom and the royal union, which had little popular backing. A civil war broke out in Lebanon, and some foreigners assumed that Nasser had stirred up Arab nationalist sentiment to undermine its government, but the truth was that the Lebanese president, who had rigged the 1957 parliamentary elections, was trying to secure himself a second term in office, contrary to the constitution. Neither the army coup in Iraq nor a later one in Sudan produced new recruits for the UAR in 1958.

Understandably, many Syrians began wondering why they were in a union that brought floods of Egyptian officers and officials into their land, increased the bureaucracy and paperwork of government, and led to land reform by presidential decree and to fears that the least inhabited parts of Syria would soon be overrun by landless Egyptian *fellahin* (peasants). Why were they in the UAR whereas Iraq, Jordan, and Lebanon were not? Although Nasser remained popular in Syria, the heavy-handed Egyptian bureaucrats were resented by the Syrians, who had retained a strong tradition of individual enterprise. Severe restraints on freedom of expression were enforced by Abd al-Hamid Sarraj, a Syrian Arab nationalist, but Nasser's appointment of Field Marshal Abd al-Hakim Amir as his personal representative (or viceroy) smacked of Egyptian imperialism. Because Nasser was still acclaimed by crowds whenever he visited Syria, he did not realize that his government was losing Syrian support.

A group of Syrian army officers backed by civilian politicians initiated the revolt on 28 September 1961 that ended the UAR. Amir tried to talk the rebels into submission, but he was sent home the following day. The Egyptians and a few Syrian troops tried to resist the secession, but the tide of opinion overwhelmed them. It was a huge defeat for Nasser, one that he accepted as soon as it was clear that preserving the union would have led to a bloodbath. Naturally, he and other Egyptians attributed Syria's secession to the machinations of Israel, foreign imperialism, and Arab reactionaries. There followed eighteen months of bitter recriminations between Egypt (which would go on calling itself the "United Arab Republic" until 1971) and Syria. When Baathists took control of both Iraq and Syria in military coups early in 1963, the new leaders entered into "unity talks" with Nasser to revive the UAR, but the negotiations ultimately failed. Efforts to unite two or more Arab states have occurred since 1963, but none has worked, except the unification of the Yemen Arab Republic with the People's Democratic Republic of Yemen.

Although foreign experts have repeatedly dismissed Arab nationalism as a failure, and the beacon of Islamic unity has often beamed brighter since the Iranian Revolution (1977–1979), the pan-Arab idea has an attractive logic. There are now about twenty Arabic-speaking countries that have various assets, land areas, and populations. Their divisions have often muffled their ability to defend their interests, win respect, pool their material resources, and concert their policies against outside interference and, of course, Israel. The Arab League has preserved their differences, serving at best as a forum for them to come together and argue. A genuine economic and political union would release Arab energies that have been wasted on internal debates and quarrels, but such a union must be backed by both governments and peoples.

The UAR was formed in haste. Nasser would have preferred a gradual and federal approach, but the Syrian Baathists felt threatened by the Turks, Americans, and their own extremists. Syria and Egypt were not contiguous. Syria saw itself as the rump of what should have been a larger Arab state. Egypt had only recently adopted Arabism. Syria had a variety of religious minorities, both Christian and Muslim, that were politically active. Egypt was about 90 percent Sunni Muslim; its Coptic Christians had no desire to secede or to seize power. Syria had a vibrant capitalist class, while Egypt was in the process of repudiating capitalism in favor of socialism. Syria's Baath Party had developed a coherent ideology of democratic socialism over the course of its existence; Egypt's Nasser had long prided himself on not subscribing to any one of Egypt's competing ideologies. Syria had undeveloped agricultural land, whereas Egypt's peasantry was crowded into the valley and delta of the Nile. They could unite against Zionism (Israel), imperialism (the United States), and Arab reactionaries (Jordan and Saudi Arabia), but what could they unite for? This inability to find common positive ground was the fundamental weakness of the UAR.

–ARTHUR GOLDSCHMIDT, PENNSYLVANIA STATE UNIVERSITY

References

Kamel Abu Jaber, *The Arab Ba`th Socialist Party: History, Ideology, and Organization* (Syracuse, N.Y.: Syracuse University Press, 1966).

Michael Ionides, *Divide and Lose: The Arab Revolt of 1955-1958* (London: G. Bles, 1960).

James Jankowski, *Nasser's Egypt: Arab Nationalism, and the United Arab Republic* (Boulder, Colo.: Lynne Rienner, 2001).

Malcolm Kerr, *The Arab Cold War: Gamal Abd al-Nasir and His Rivals, 1958-1970* (London & New York: Oxford University Press, 1971).

Eberhard Kienle, "Arab Unity Schemes Revisited: Interest, Identity, and Policy in Syria and Egypt," *International Journal of Middle East Studies,* 27 (1995): 53-71.

David W. Lesch, "The 1957 American-Syrian Crisis: Globalist Policy in a Regional Reality," in *The Middle East and the United States: A Historical and Political Reassessment,* edited by Lesch (Boulder, Colo.: Westview Press, 1996, 1999, 2003), pp. 131-146.

Malik Mufti, *Sovereign Creations: Pan-Arabism and Political Order in Syria and Iraq* (Ithaca, N.Y.: Cornell University Press, 1996).

Mufti, "The United States and Nasserist Pan-Arabism," in *The Middle East and the United States: A Historical and Political Reassessment,* edited by Lesch (Boulder, Colo.: Westview Press, 1996, 1999, 2003), pp. 167-186.

Elie Podeh, *The Decline of Arab Unity: The Rise and Fall of the United Arab Republic* (Brighton, U.K. & Portland, Ore.: Sussex Academic Press, 1999).

APPENDIX

Selected UN Security Council Resolutions on Iraq from 1990 to 2003

EDITOR'S NOTE

The situation in Iraq, a country containing the second-largest proven oil reserves in the world, has been an important international concern for more than a decade. While the international community, led by the United States, went to war in 1991 to remove Iraqi forces from Kuwait, this event would only mark the beginning of a long and tortuous relationship between the Iraqi regime of Saddam Hussein and the United Nations (UN). The UN became the conduit through which the international community, primarily the United States, defined and monitored the parameters of post–Gulf War Iraq up to and through the 2003 American-led invasion that toppled Saddam's regime. As such, the multitude of UN resolutions dealing with Iraq since it invaded Kuwait in August 1990 is, in effect, an outline of this story, starting with the UN response to the Iraqi invasion, the postwar conditions imposed on Baghdad, the establishment of UN inspections and sanctions, and the 2003 American occupation.

The following resolution condemned Iraq's invasion of Kuwait and demanded the immediate withdrawal of its troops.

RESOLUTION 660 (1990)

Adopted by the Security Council at its 2932nd meeting, on 2 August 1990

The Security Council,

Alarmed by the invasion of Kuwait on 2 August 1990 by the military forces of Iraq,

Determining that there exists a breach of international peace and security as regards the Iraqi invasion of Kuwait,

Acting under Articles 39 and 40 of the Charter of the United Nations,

1. Condemns the Iraqi invasion of Kuwait;

2. Demands that Iraq withdraw immediately and unconditionally all its forces to the positions in which they were located on 1 August 1990;

3. Calls upon Iraq and Kuwait to begin immediately intensive negotiations for the resolution of their differences and supports all efforts in this regard, and especially those of the League of Arab States;

4. Decides to meet again as necessary to consider further steps with which to ensure compliance with the present resolution.

This resolution reaffirmed Resolution 660 and placed economic sanctions on Iraq.

RESOLUTION 661 (1990)

Adopted by the Security Council at its 2933rd meeting on 6 August 1990

The Security Council,

Reaffirming its resolution 660 (1990) of 2 August 1990,

Deeply concerned that that resolution has not been implemented and that the invasion by Iraq of Kuwait continues with further loss of human life and material destruction,

Determined to bring the invasion and occupation of Kuwait by Iraq to an end and to restore the sovereignty, independence and territorial integrity of Kuwait,

Noting that the legitimate Government of Kuwait has expressed its readiness to comply with resolution 660 (1990),

Mindful of its responsibilities under the Charter of the United Nations for the maintenance of international peace and security,

Affirming the inherent right of individual or collective self-defence, in response to the armed attack by Iraq against Kuwait, in accordance with Article 51 of the Charter,

Acting under Chapter VII of the Charter of the United Nations,

1. Determines that Iraq so far has failed to comply with paragraph 2 of resolution 660 (1990) and has usurped the authority of the legitimate Government of Kuwait;

2. Decides, as a consequence, to take the following measures to secure compliance of Iraq with paragraph 2 of resolution 660 (1990) and to restore the authority of the legitimate Government of Kuwait;

3. Decides that all States shall prevent:

(a) The import into their territories of all commodities and products originating in Iraq or Kuwait exported therefrom after the date of the present resolution;

(b) Any activities by their nationals or in their territories which would promote or are calculated to promote the export or trans-shipment of any commodities or products from Iraq or Kuwait; and any dealings by their nationals or their flag vessels or in their territories in any commodities or products originating in Iraq or Kuwait and exported therefrom after the date of the present resolution, including in particular any transfer of funds to Iraq or Kuwait for the purposes of such activities or dealings;

(c) The sale or supply by their nationals or from their territories or using their flag vessels of any commodities or products, including weapons or any other military equipment, whether or not originating in their territories but not including supplies intended strictly for medical purposes, and, in humanitarian circumstances, foodstuffs, to any person or body in Iraq or Kuwait or to any person or body for the purposes of any business carried on in or operated from Iraq or Kuwait, and any activities by their nationals or in their territories which promote or are calculated to promote such sale or supply of such commodities or products;

4. Decides that all States shall not make available to the Government of Iraq or to any commercial, industrial or public utility undertaking in Iraq or Kuwait, any funds or any other financial or economic resources and shall prevent their nationals and any persons within their territories from removing from their territories or otherwise making available to that Government or to any such undertaking any such funds or resources and from remitting any other funds to persons or bodies within Iraq or Kuwait, except payments exclusively for strictly medical or humanitarian purposes and, in humanitarian circumstances, foodstuffs;

5. Calls upon all States, including States non-members of the United Nations, to act strictly in accordance with the provisions of the present resolution notwithstanding any contract entered into or licence granted before the date of the present resolution;

6. Decides to establish, in accordance with rule 28 of the provisional rules of procedure of the Security Council, a Committee of the Security Council consisting of all the members of the Council, to undertake the following tasks and to report on its work to the Council with its observations and recommendations:

(a) To examine the reports on the progress of the implementation of the present resolution which will be submitted by the Secretary-General;

(b) To seek from all States further information regarding the action taken by them concerning the effective implementation of the provisions laid down in the present resolution;

7. Calls upon all States to co-operate fully with the Committee in the fulfilment of its task, including supplying such information as may be sought by the Committee in pursuance of the present resolution;

8. Requests the Secretary-General to provide all necessary assistance to the Committee and to make the necessary arrangements in the Secretariat for the purpose;

9. Decides that, notwithstanding paragraphs 4 through 8 above, nothing in the present resolution shall prohibit assistance to the legitimate Government of Kuwait, and calls upon all States:

(a) To take appropriate measures to protect assets of the legitimate Government of Kuwait and its agencies;

(b) Not to recognize any regime set up by the occupying Power;

10. Requests the Secretary-General to report to the Council on the progress of the implementation of the present resolution, the first report to be submitted within thirty days;

11. Decides to keep this item on its agenda and to continue its efforts to put an early end to the invasion by Iraq.

The following document concerned the protection and safety of third State nationals as well as diplomatic and consular personnel in Kuwait during the Iraqi occupation. It also demanded that Iraq provide food, water, and basic services to the Kuwaiti population.

RESOLUTION 674 (1990)

Adopted by the Security Council at its 2951st meeting on 29 October 1990

The Security Council,

Recalling its resolutions 660 (1990), 661 (1990), 662 (1990), 664 (1990), 665 (1990), 666 (1990), 667 (1990) and 670 (1990),

Stressing the urgent need for the immediate and unconditional withdrawal of all Iraqi forces from Kuwait, for the restoration of Kuwait's sovereignty, independence and territorial integrity, and of the authority of its legitimate Government,

Condemning the actions by the Iraqi authorities and occupying forces to take third State nationals hostage and to mistreat and oppress Kuwaiti and third State nationals, and the other actions reported to the Council such as the destruction of Kuwaiti demographic records, forced departure of Kuwaitis, and relocation of population in Kuwait and the unlawful destruction and seizure of public and private property in Kuwait including hospital supplies and equipment, in violation of the decisions of this Council, the Charter of the United Nations, the Fourth Geneva Convention, the Vienna Conventions on Diplomatic and Consular Relations and international law,

Expressing grave alarm over the situation of nationals of third States in Kuwait and Iraq, including the personnel of the diplomatic and consular missions of such States,

Reaffirming that the Fourth Geneva Convention applies to Kuwait and that as a High Contracting Party to the Convention Iraq is bound to comply fully with all its terms and, in particular is liable under the Convention in respect of the grave breaches committed by it, as are individuals who commit or order the commission of grave breaches,

Recalling the efforts of the Secretary-General concerning the safety and well-being of third State nationals in Iraq and Kuwait,

Deeply concerned at the economic cost, and at the loss and suffering caused to individuals in Kuwait and Iraq as a result of the invasion and occupation of Kuwait by Iraq,

Acting under Chapter VII of the United Nations Charter,

Reaffirming the goal of the international community of maintaining international peace and security by seeking to resolve international disputes and conflicts through peaceful means,

Recalling also the important role that the United Nations and its Secretary-General have played in the peaceful solution of disputes and conflicts in conformity with the provisions of the United Nations Charter,

Alarmed by the dangers of the present crisis caused by the Iraqi invasion and occupation of Kuwait, directly threatening international peace and security, and seeking to avoid any further worsening of the situation,

Calling upon Iraq to comply with the relevant resolutions of the Security Council, in particular resolutions 660 (1990), 662 (1990) and 664 (1990),

Reaffirming its determination to ensure compliance by Iraq with the Security Council resolutions by maximum use of political and diplomatic means,

A.

1. Demands that the Iraqi authorities and occupying forces immediately cease and desist from taking third State nationals hostage, and mistreating and oppressing Kuwaiti and third State nationals, and from any other actions such as those reported to the Council and described above, violating the decisions of this Council, the Charter of the United Nations, the Fourth Geneva Convention, the Vienna Conventions on Diplomatic and Consular Relations and international law;

2. Invites States to collate substantiated information in their possession or submitted to them on the grave breaches by Iraq as per paragraph 1 above and to make this information available to the Council;

3. Reaffirms its demand that Iraq immediately fulfil its obligations to third State nationals in Kuwait and Iraq, including the personnel of diplomatic and consular missions, under the Charter, the Fourth Geneva Convention, the Vienna Conventions on Diplomatic and Consular Relations, general principles of international law and the relevant resolutions of the Council;

4. Reaffirms further its demand that Iraq permit and facilitate the immediate departure from Kuwait and Iraq of those third State nationals, including diplomatic and consular personnel, who wish to leave;

5. Demands that Iraq ensure the immediate access to food, water and basic services necessary to the protection and well-being of Kuwaiti nationals and of nationals of third States in Kuwait and Iraq, including the personnel of diplomatic and consular missions in Kuwait;

6. Reaffirms its demand that Iraq immediately protect the safety and well-being of diplomatic and consular personnel and premises in Kuwait and in Iraq, take no action to hinder these diplomatic and consular missions in the performance of their functions, including access to their nationals and the protection of their person and interest and rescind its orders for the closure of diplomatic and consular missions in Kuwait and the withdrawal of the immunity of their personnel;

7. Requests the Secretary-General, in the context of the continued exercise of his good offices concerning the safety and well being of third State nationals in Iraq and Kuwait, to seek to achieve the objectives of paragraphs 4, 5 and 6 and, in particular, the provision of food, water and basic services to Kuwaiti nationals and to the diplomatic and consular missions in Kuwait and the evacuation of third State nationals;

8. Reminds Iraq that under international law it is liable for any loss, damage or injury arising in regard to Kuwait and third States, and their nationals and corporations, as a result of the invasion and illegal occupation of Kuwait by Iraq;

9. Invites States to collect relevant information regarding their claims, and those of their nationals and corporations, for restitution or financial compensation by Iraq with a view to such arrangements as may be established in accordance with international law;

10. Requires that Iraq comply with the provisions of the present resolution and its previous resolutions, failing which the Council will need to take further measures under the Charter;

11. Decides to remain actively and permanently seized of the matter until Kuwait has regained its independence and peace has been restored in conformity with the relevant resolutions of the Security Council;

B.

12. Reposes its trust in the Secretary-General to make available his good offices and, as he considers appropriate, to pursue them and undertake diplomatic efforts in order to reach a peaceful solution to the crisis caused by the Iraqi invasion and occupation of Kuwait on the basis of Security Council resolutions 660 (1990), 662 (1990) and 664 (1990), and calls on all States, both those in the region and others, to pursue on this basis their efforts to this end, in conformity with the Charter, in order to improve the situation and restore peace, security and stability;

13. Requests the Secretary-General to report to the Security Council on the results of his good offices and diplomatic efforts.

This operative resolution authorized the use of force against Iraq in the Persian Gulf War.

RESOLUTION 678 (1990)

Adopted by the Security Council at its 2963rd meeting on 29 November 1990

The Security Council,

Recalling, and reaffirming its resolutions 660 (1990) of 2 August 1990, 661 (1990) of 6 August 1990, 662 (1990) of 9 August 1990, 664 (1990) of 18 August 1990, 665 (1990) of 25 August 1990, 666 (1990) of 13 September 1990, 667 (1990) of 16 September 1990, 669 (1990) of 24 September 1990, 670 (1990) of 25 September 1990, 674 (1990) of 29 October 1990 and 677 (1990) of 28 November 1990.

Noting that, despite all efforts by the United Nations, Iraq refuses to comply with its obligation to implement resolution 660 (1990) and the above-mentioned subsequent relevant resolutions, in flagrant contempt of the Security Council,

Mindful of its duties and responsibilities under the Charter of the United Nations for the maintenance and preservation of international peace and security,

Determined to secure full compliance with its decisions,

Acting under Chapter VII of the Charter,

1. Demands that Iraq comply fully with resolution 660 (1990) and all subsequent relevant resolutions, and decides, while maintaining all its decisions, to allow Iraq one final opportunity, as a pause of goodwill, to do so;

2. Authorizes Member States co-operating with the Government of Kuwait, unless Iraq on or before 15 January 1991 fully implements, as set forth in paragraph 1 above, the foregoing resolutions, to use all necessary means to uphold and implement resolution 660 (1990) and all subsequent relevant resolutions and to restore international peace and security in the area;

3. Requests all States to provide appropriate support for the actions undertaken in pursuance of paragraph 2 of the present resolution;

4. Requests the States concerned to keep the Security Council regularly informed on the progress of actions undertaken pursuant to paragraphs 2 and 3 of the present resolution;

5. Decides to remain seized of the matter.

This resolution detailed UN demands on Iraq following the suspension of U.S. and Coalition offensive operations in the Persian Gulf War.

RESOLUTION 686 (1991)

Adopted by the Security Council at its 2978th meeting on 2 March 1991

The Security Council,

Recalling and reaffirming its resolutions 660 (1990), 661 (1990), 662 (1990), 664 (1990), 665 (1990), 666 (1990), 667 (1990), 669 (1990), 670 (1990), 674 (1990), 677 (1990), and 678 (1990),

Recalling the obligations of Member States under Article 25 of the Charter,

Recalling paragraph 9 of resolution 661 (1990) regarding assistance to the Government of Kuwait and paragraph 3 (c) of that resolution regarding supplies strictly for medical purposes and, in humanitarian circumstances, foodstuffs,

Taking note of the letters of the Foreign Minister of Iraq confirming Iraq's agreement to comply fully with all of the resolutions noted above (S/22275), and stating its intention to release prisoners of war immediately (S/22273),

Taking note of the suspension of offensive combat operations by the forces of Kuwait and the Member States cooperating with Kuwait pursuant to resolution 678 (1990),

Bearing in mind the need to be assured of Iraq's peaceful intentions, and the objective in resolution 678 (1990) of restoring international peace and security in the region,

Underlining the importance of Iraq taking the necessary measures which would permit a definitive end to the hostilities,

Affirming the commitment of all Member States to the independence, sovereignty and territorial integrity of Iraq and Kuwait, and noting the intention expressed by the Member States cooperating under paragraph 2 of Security Council resolution 678 (1990) to bring their military presence in Iraq to an end as soon as possible consistent with achieving the objectives of the resolution,

Acting under Chapter VII of the Charter,

1. Affirms that all twelve resolutions noted above continue to have full force and effect;

2. Demands that Iraq implement its acceptance of all twelve resolutions noted above and in particular that Iraq:

(a) Rescind immediately its actions purporting to annex Kuwait;

(b) Accept in principle its liability for any loss, damage, or injury arising in regard to Kuwait and third States, and their nationals and corporations, as a result of the invasion and illegal occupation of Kuwait by Iraq;

(c) Under international law immediately release under the auspices of the International Committee of the Red Cross, Red Cross Societies, or Red Crescent Societies, all Kuwaiti and third country nationals detained by Iraq and return the remains of any deceased Kuwaiti and third country nationals so detained; and

(d) Immediately begin to return all Kuwaiti property seized by Iraq, to be completed in the shortest possible period;

3. Further demands that Iraq:

(a) Cease hostile or provocative actions by its forces against all Member States including missile attacks and flights of combat aircraft;

(b) Designate military commanders to meet with counterparts from the forces of Kuwait and the Member States cooperating with Kuwait pursuant to resolution 678 (1990) to arrange for the military aspects of a cessation of hostilities at the earliest possible time;

(c) Arrange for immediate access to and release of all prisoners of war under the auspices of the International Committee of the Red Cross and return the remains of any deceased personnel of the forces of Kuwait and the Member States cooperating with Kuwait pursuant to resolution 678 (1990); and

(d) Provide all information and assistance in identifying Iraqi mines, booby traps and other explosives as well as any chemical and biological weapons and material in Kuwait, in areas of Iraq where forces of Member States cooperating with Kuwait pursuant to resolution 678 (1990) are present temporarily, and in adjacent waters;

4. Recognizes that during the period required for Iraq to comply with paragraphs 2 and 3 above, the provisions of paragraph 2 of resolution 678 (1990) remain valid;

5. Welcomes the decision of Kuwait and the Member States cooperating with Kuwait pursuant to resolution 678 (1990) to provide access to and to commence immediately the release of Iraqi prisoners of war as required by the terms of the Third Geneva Convention of 1949, under the auspices of the International Committee of the Red Cross;

6. Requests all Member States, as well as the United Nations, the specialized agencies and other international organizations in the United Nations system, to take all appropriate action to cooperate with the Government and people of Kuwait in the reconstruction of their country;

7. Decides that Iraq shall notify the Secretary-General and the Security Council when it has taken the actions set out above;

8. Decides that in order to secure the rapid establishment of a definitive end to the hostilities, the Security Council remains actively seized of the matter.

The resolution below established a cease-fire and provided the conditions essential to the restoration of peace and security in Kuwait following the Persian Gulf War. Stipulations placed upon Iraq included the destruction of all chemical and biological weapons (section 8a) and inspection of nuclear capability sites (section 13).

RESOLUTION 687 (1991)

Adopted by the Security Council at its 2981st meeting, on 3 April 1991

The Security Council,

Recalling its resolutions 660 (1990) of 2 August 1990, 661 (1990) of 6 August 1990, 662

(1990) of 9 August 1990, 664 (1990) of 18 August 1990, 665 (1990) of 25 August 1990, 666 (1990) of 13 September 1990, 667 (1990) of 16 September 1990, 669 (1990) of 24 September 1990, 670 (1990) of 25 September 1990, 674 (1990) of 29 October 1990, 677 (1990) of 28 November 1990, 678 (1990) of 29 November 1990 and 686 (1991) of 2 March 1991,

Welcoming the restoration to Kuwait of its sovereignty, independence and territorial integrity and the return of its legitimate Government,

Affirming the commitment of all Member States to the sovereignty, territorial integrity and political independence of Kuwait and Iraq, and noting the intention expressed by the Member States cooperating with Kuwait under paragraph 2 of resolution 678 (1990) to bring their military presence in Iraq to an end as soon as possible consistent with paragraph 8 of resolution 686 (1991),

Reaffirming the need to be assured of Iraq's peaceful intentions in the light of its unlawful invasion and occupation of Kuwait,

Taking note of the letter sent by the Minister for Foreign Affairs of Iraq on 27 February 1991 and those sent pursuant to resolution 686 (1991),

Noting that Iraq and Kuwait, as independent sovereign States, signed at Baghdad on 4 October 1963 "Agreed Minutes Between the State of Kuwait and the Republic of Iraq Regarding the Restoration of Friendly Relations, Recognition and Related Matters", thereby recognizing formally the boundary between Iraq and Kuwait and the allocation of islands, which were registered with the United Nations in accordance with Article 102 of the Charter of the United Nations and in which Iraq recognized the independence and complete sovereignty of the State of Kuwait within its borders as specified and accepted in the letter of the Prime Minister of Iraq dated 21 July 1932, and as accepted by the Ruler of Kuwait in his letter dated 10 August 1932,

Conscious of the need for demarcation of the said boundary,

Conscious also of the statements by Iraq threatening to use weapons in violation of its obligations under the Geneva Protocol for the Prohibition of the Use in War of Asphyxiating, Poisonous or Other Gases, and of Bacteriological Methods of Warfare, signed at Geneva on 17 June 1925, and of its prior use of chemical weapons and affirming that grave consequences would follow any further use by Iraq of such weapons,

Recalling that Iraq has subscribed to the Declaration adopted by all States participating in the Conference of States Parties to the 1925

Geneva Protocol and Other Interested States, held in Paris from 7 to 11 January 1989, establishing the objective of universal elimination of chemical and biological weapons,

Recalling also that Iraq has signed the Convention on the Prohibition of the Development, Production and Stockpiling of Bacteriological (Biological) and Toxin Weapons and on Their Destruction, of 10 April 1972,

Noting the importance of Iraq ratifying this Convention,

Noting moreover the importance of all States adhering to this Convention and encouraging its forthcoming Review Conference to reinforce the authority, efficiency and universal scope of the convention,

Stressing the importance of an early conclusion by the Conference on Disarmament of its work on a Convention on the Universal Prohibition of Chemical Weapons and of universal adherence thereto,

Aware of the use by Iraq of ballistic missiles in unprovoked attacks and therefore of the need to take specific measures in regard to such missiles located in Iraq,

Concerned by the reports in the hands of Member States that Iraq has attempted to acquire materials for a nuclear-weapons programme contrary to its obligations under the Treaty on the Non-Proliferation of Nuclear Weapons of 1 July 1968,

Recalling the objective of the establishment of a nuclear-weapons-free zone in the region of the Middle East,

Conscious of the threat that all weapons of mass destruction pose to peace and security in the area and of the need to work towards the establishment in the Middle East of a zone free of such weapons,

Conscious also of the objective of achieving balanced and comprehensive control of armaments in the region,

Conscious further of the importance of achieving the objectives noted above using all available means, including a dialogue among the States of the region,

Noting that resolution 686 (1991) marked the lifting of the measures imposed by resolution 661 (1990) in so far as they applied to Kuwait,

Noting that despite the progress being made in fulfilling the obligations of resolution 686 (1991), many Kuwaiti and third country nationals are still not accounted for and property remains unreturned,

Recalling the International Convention against the Taking of Hostages, opened for signature at New York on 18 December 1979,

which categorizes all acts of taking hostages as manifestations of international terrorism,

Deploring threats made by Iraq during the recent conflict to make use of terrorism against targets outside Iraq and the taking of hostages by Iraq,

Taking note with grave concern of the reports of the Secretary-General of 20 March 1991 and 28 March 1991, and conscious of the necessity to meet urgently the humanitarian needs in Kuwait and Iraq,

Bearing in mind its objective of restoring international peace and security in the area as set out in recent resolutions of the Security Council,

Conscious of the need to take the following measures acting under Chapter VII of the Charter,

1. Affirms all thirteen resolutions noted above, except as expressly changed below to achieve the goals of this resolution, including a formal cease-fire;

A.

2. Demands that Iraq and Kuwait respect the inviolability of the international boundary and the allocation of islands set out in the "Agreed Minutes Between the State of Kuwait and the Republic of Iraq Regarding the Restoration of Friendly Relations, Recognition and Related Matters", signed by them in the exercise of their sovereignty at Baghdad on 4 October 1963 and registered with the United Nations and published by the United Nations in document 7063, United Nations, Treaty Series, 1964;

3. Calls upon the Secretary-General to lend his assistance to make arrangements with Iraq and Kuwait to demarcate the boundary between Iraq and Kuwait, drawing on appropriate material, including the map transmitted by Security Council document S/22412 and to report back to the Security Council within one month;

4. Decides to guarantee the inviolability of the above-mentioned international boundary and to take as appropriate all necessary measures to that end in accordance with the Charter of the United Nations;

B.

5. Requests the Secretary-General, after consulting with Iraq and Kuwait, to submit within three days to the Security Council for its approval a plan for the immediate deployment of a United Nations observer unit to monitor the Khor Abdullah and a demilitarized

zone, which is hereby established, extending ten kilometres into Iraq and five kilometres into Kuwait from the boundary referred to in the "Agreed Minutes Between the State of Kuwait and the Republic of Iraq Regarding the Restoration of Friendly Relations, Recognition and Related Matters" of 4 October 1963; to deter violations of the boundary through its presence in and surveillance of the demilitarized zone; to observe any hostile or potentially hostile action mounted from the territory of one State to the other; and for the Secretary-General to report regularly to the Security Council on the operations of the unit, and immediately if there are serious violations of the zone or potential threats to peace;

6. Notes that as soon as the Secretary-General notifies the Security Council of the completion of the deployment of the United Nations observer unit, the conditions will be established for the Member States cooperating with Kuwait in accordance with resolution 678 (1990) to bring their military presence in Iraq to an end consistent with resolution 686 (1991);

C.

7. Invites Iraq to reaffirm unconditionally its obligations under the Geneva Protocol for the Prohibition of the Use in War of Asphyxiating, Poisonous or Other Gases, and of Bacteriological Methods of Warfare, signed at Geneva on 17 June 1925, and to ratify the Convention on the Prohibition of the Development, Production and Stockpiling of Bacteriological (Biological) and Toxin Weapons and on Their Destruction, of 10 April 1972;

8. Decides that Iraq shall unconditionally accept the destruction, removal, or rendering harmless, under international supervision, of:

(a) All chemical and biological weapons and all stocks of agents and all related subsystems and components and all research, development, support and manufacturing facilities;

(b) All ballistic missiles with a range greater than 150 kilometres and related major parts, and repair and production facilities;

9. Decides, for the implementation of paragraph 8 above, the following:

(a) Iraq shall submit to the Secretary-General, within fifteen days of the adoption of the present resolution, a declaration of the locations, amounts and types of all items specified in paragraph 8 and agree to urgent, on-site inspection as specified below;

(b) The Secretary-General, in consultation with the appropriate Governments and, where appropriate, with the Director-General of the World Health Organization, within forty-five days of the passage of the present resolution, shall develop, and submit to the Council for approval, a plan calling for the completion of the following acts within forty-five days of such approval:

(i) The forming of a Special Commission, which shall carry out immediate on-site inspection of Iraq's biological, chemical and missile capabilities, based on Iraq's declarations and the designation of any additional locations by the Special Commission itself;

(ii) The yielding by Iraq of possession to the Special Commission for destruction, removal or rendering harmless, taking into account the requirements of public safety, of all items specified under paragraph 8 (a) above, including items at the additional locations designated by the Special Commission under paragraph 9 (b) (i) above and the destruction by Iraq, under the supervision of the Special Commission, of all its missile capabilities, including launchers, as specified under paragraph 8 (b) above;

(iii) The provision by the Special Commission of the assistance and cooperation to the Director-General of the International Atomic Energy Agency required in paragraphs 12 and 13 below;

10. Decides that Iraq shall unconditionally undertake not to use, develop, construct or acquire any of the items specified in paragraphs 8 and 9 above and requests the Secretary-General, in consultation with the Special Commission, to develop a plan for the future ongoing monitoring and verification of Iraq's compliance with this paragraph, to be submitted to the Security Council for approval within one hundred and twenty days of the passage of this resolution;

11. Invites Iraq to reaffirm unconditionally its obligations under the Treaty on the Non-Proliferation of Nuclear Weapons of 1 July 1968;

12. Decides that Iraq shall unconditionally agree not to acquire or develop nuclear weapons or nuclear-weapons-usable material or any subsystems or components or any research, development, support or manufacturing facilities related to the above; to submit to the Secretary-General and the Director-General of the International Atomic Energy Agency within fifteen days of

the adoption of the present resolution a declaration of the locations, amounts, and types of all items specified above; to place all of its nuclear-weapons-usable materials under the exclusive control, for custody and removal, of the International Atomic Energy Agency, with the assistance and cooperation of the Special Commission as provided for in the plan of the Secretary-General discussed in paragraph 9 (b) above; to accept, in accordance with the arrangements provided for in paragraph 13 below, urgent on-site inspection and the destruction, removal or rendering harmless as appropriate of all items specified above; and to accept the plan discussed in paragraph 13 below for the future ongoing monitoring and verification of its compliance with these undertakings;

13. Requests the Director-General of the International Atomic Energy Agency, through the Secretary-General, with the assistance and cooperation of the Special Commission as provided for in the plan of the Secretary-General in paragraph 9 (b) above, to carry out immediate on-site inspection of Iraq's nuclear capabilities based on Iraq's declarations and the designation of any additional locations by the Special Commission; to develop a plan for submission to the Security Council within forty-five days calling for the destruction, removal, or rendering harmless as appropriate of all items listed in paragraph 12 above; to carry out the plan within forty-five days following approval by the Security Council; and to develop a plan, taking into account the rights and obligations of Iraq under the Treaty on the Non-Proliferation of Nuclear Weapons of 1 July 1968, for the future ongoing monitoring and verification of Iraq's compliance with paragraph 12 above, including an inventory of all nuclear material in Iraq subject to the Agency's verification and inspections to confirm that Agency safeguards cover all relevant nuclear activities in Iraq, to be submitted to the Security Council for approval within one hundred and twenty days of the passage of the present resolution;

14. Takes note that the actions to be taken by Iraq in paragraphs 8, 9, 10, 11, 12 and 13 of the present resolution represent steps towards the goal of establishing in the Middle East a zone free from weapons of mass destruction and all missiles for their delivery and the objective of a global ban on chemical weapons;

D.

15. Requests the Secretary-General to report to the Security Council on the steps taken to facilitate the return of all Kuwaiti property seized by Iraq, including a list of any property that Kuwait claims has not been returned or which has not been returned intact;

E.

16. Reaffirms that Iraq, without prejudice to the debts and obligations of Iraq arising prior to 2 August 1990, which will be addressed through the normal mechanisms, is liable under international law for any direct loss, damage, including environmental damage and the depletion of natural resources, or injury to foreign Governments, nationals and corporations, as a result of Iraq's unlawful invasion and occupation of Kuwait;

17. Decides that all Iraqi statements made since 2 August 1990 repudiating its foreign debt are null and void, and demands that Iraq adhere scrupulously to all of its obligations concerning servicing and repayment of its foreign debt;

18. Decides also to create a fund to pay compensation for claims that fall within paragraph 16 above and to establish a Commission that will administer the fund;

19. Directs the Secretary-General to develop and present to the Security Council for decision, no later than thirty days following the adoption of the present resolution, recommendations for the fund to meet the requirement for the payment of claims established in accordance with paragraph 18 above and for a programme to implement the decisions in paragraphs 16, 17 and 18 above, including: administration of the fund; mechanisms for determining the appropriate level of Iraq's contribution to the fund based on a percentage of the value of the exports of petroleum and petroleum products from Iraq not to exceed a figure to be suggested to the Council by the Secretary-General, taking into account the requirements of the people of Iraq, Iraq's payment capacity as assessed in conjunction with the international financial institutions taking into consideration external

debt service, and the needs of the Iraqi economy; arrangements for ensuring that payments are made to the fund; the process by which funds will be allocated and claims paid; appropriate procedures for evaluating losses, listing claims and verifying their validity and resolving disputed claims in respect of Iraq's liability as specified in paragraph 16 above; and the composition of the Commission designated above;

F.

20. Decides, effective immediately, that the prohibitions against the sale or supply to Iraq of commodities or products, other than medicine and health supplies, and prohibitions against financial transactions related thereto contained in resolution 661 (1990) shall not apply to foodstuffs notified to the Security Council Committee established by resolution 661 (1990) concerning the situation between Iraq and Kuwait or, with the approval of that Committee, under the simplified and accelerated "no-objection" procedure, to materials and supplies for essential civilian needs as identified in the report of the Secretary-General dated 20 March 1991, and in any further findings of humanitarian need by the Committee;

21. Decides that the Security Council shall review the provisions of paragraph 20 above every sixty days in the light of the policies and practices of the Government of Iraq, including the implementation of all relevant resolutions of the Security Council, for the purpose of determining whether to reduce or lift the prohibitions referred to therein;

22. Decides that upon the approval by the Security Council of the programme called for in paragraph 19 above and upon Council agreement that Iraq has completed all actions contemplated in paragraphs 8, 9, 10, 11, 12 and 13 above, the prohibitions against the import of commodities and products originating in Iraq and the prohibitions against financial transactions related thereto contained in resolution 661 (1990) shall have no further force or effect;

23. Decides that, pending action by the Security Council under paragraph 22 above, the Security Council Committee established by resolution 661 (1990) shall be empowered to approve, when

required to assure adequate financial resources on the part of Iraq to carry out the activities under paragraph 20 above, exceptions to the prohibition against the import of commodities and products originating in Iraq;

24. Decides that, in accordance with resolution 661 (1990) and subsequent related resolutions and until a further decision is taken by the Security Council, all States shall continue to prevent the sale or supply, or the promotion or facilitation of such sale or supply, to Iraq by their nationals, or from their territories or using their flag vessels or aircraft, of:

(a) Arms and related materiel of all types, specifically including the sale or transfer through other means of all forms of conventional military equipment, including for paramilitary forces, and spare parts and components and their means of production, for such equipment;

(b) Items specified and defined in paragraphs 8 and 12 above not otherwise covered above;

(c) Technology under licensing or other transfer arrangements used in the production, utilization or stockpiling of items specified in subparagraphs (a) and (b) above;

(d) Personnel or materials for training or technical support services relating to the design, development, manufacture, use, maintenance or support of items specified in subparagraphs (a) and (b) above;

25. Calls upon all States and international organizations to act strictly in accordance with paragraph 24 above, notwithstanding the existence of any contracts, agreements, licences or any other arrangements;

26. Requests the Secretary-General, in consultation with appropriate Governments, to develop within sixty days, for the approval of the Security Council, guidelines to facilitate full international implementation of paragraphs 24 and 25 above and paragraph 27 below, and to make them available to all States and to establish a procedure for updating these guidelines periodically;

27. Calls upon all States to maintain such national controls and procedures and to take such other actions consistent with the guidelines to be established by the Security Council under

paragraph 26 above as may be necessary to ensure compliance with the terms of paragraph 24 above, and calls upon international organizations to take all appropriate steps to assist in ensuring such full compliance;

28. Agrees to review its decisions in paragraphs 22, 23, 24 and 25 above, except for the items specified and defined in paragraphs 8 and 12 above, on a regular basis and in any case one hundred and twenty days following passage of the present resolution, taking into account Iraq's compliance with the resolution and general progress towards the control of armaments in the region;

29. Decides that all States, including Iraq, shall take the necessary measures to ensure that no claim shall lie at the instance of the Government of Iraq, or of any person or body in Iraq, or of any person claiming through or for the benefit of any such person or body, in connection with any contract or other transaction where its performance was affected by reason of the measures taken by the Security Council in resolution 661 (1990) and related resolutions;

G.

30. Decides that, in furtherance of its commitment to facilitate the repatriation of all Kuwaiti and third country nationals, Iraq shall extend all necessary cooperation to the International Committee of the Red Cross, providing lists of such persons, facilitating the access of the International Committee of the Red Cross to all such persons wherever located or detained and facilitating the search by the International Committee of the Red Cross for those Kuwaiti and third country nationals still unaccounted for;

31. Invites the International Committee of the Red Cross to keep the Secretary-General apprised as appropriate of all activities undertaken in connection with facilitating the repatriation or return of all Kuwaiti and third country nationals or their remains present in Iraq on or after 2 August 1990;

H.

32. Requires Iraq to inform the Security Council that it will not commit or support any act of international terrorism or allow any organization directed towards commission of such acts to operate within its territory and to con-

demn unequivocally and renounce all acts, methods and practices of terrorism;

33. Declares that, upon official notification by Iraq to the Secretary-General and to the Security Council of its acceptance of the provisions above, a formal cease-fire is effective between Iraq and Kuwait and the Member States cooperating with Kuwait in accordance with resolution 678 (1990);

34. Decides to remain seized of the matter and to take such further steps as may be required for the implementation of the present resolution and to secure peace and security in the region.

The resolution below condemned the repression of the Iraqi civilian population, especially the Kurds.

RESOLUTION 688 (1991)

Adopted by the Security Council at its 2982nd meeting on 5 April 1991

The Security Council,

Mindful of its duties and its responsibilities under the Charter of the United Nations for the maintenance of international peace and security,

Recalling Article 2, paragraph 7, of the Charter of the United Nations,

Gravely concerned by the repression of the Iraqi civilian population in many parts of Iraq, including most recently in Kurdish populated areas, which led to a massive flow of refugees towards and across international frontiers and to cross-border incursions, which threaten international peace and security in the region,

Deeply disturbed by the magnitude of the human suffering involved,

Taking note of the letters sent by the representatives of Turkey and France to the United Nations dated 2 April 1991 and 4 April 1991, respectively (S/22435 and S/22442),

Taking note also of the letters sent by the Permanent Representative of the Islamic Republic of Iran to the United Nations dated 3 and 4 April 1991, respectively (S/22436 and S/22447),

Reaffirming the commitment of all Member States to the sovereignty, territorial integrity and political independence of Iraq and of all States in the area,

Bearing in mind the Secretary-General's report of 20 March 1991 (S/22366),

1. Condemns the repression of the Iraqi civilian population in many parts of Iraq, including most recently in Kurdish populated areas, the consequences of which threaten international peace and security in the region;

2. Demands that Iraq, as a contribution to remove the threat to international peace and security in the region, immediately end this repression and express the hope in the same context that an open dialogue will take place to ensure that the human and political rights of all Iraqi citizens are respected;

3. Insists that Iraq allow immediate access by international humanitarian organizations to all those in need of assistance in all parts of Iraq and to make available all necessary facilities for their operations;

4. Requests the Secretary-General to pursue his humanitarian efforts in Iraq and to report forthwith, if appropriate on the basis of a further mission to the region, on the plight of the Iraqi civilian population, and in particular the Kurdish population, suffering from the repression in all its forms inflicted by the Iraqi authorities;

5. Requests further the Secretary-General to use all the resources at his disposal, including those of the relevant United Nations agencies, to address urgently the critical needs of the refugees and displaced Iraqi population;

6. Appeals to all Member States and to all humanitarian organizations to contribute to these humanitarian relief efforts.

The next four documents (707, 1134, 1284, and 1441) urged Iraq to comply with Resolution 687. The UN specifically wanted Iraq to make a full disclosure of its weapons of mass destruction and long-range missile programs.

RESOLUTION 707 (1991)

Adopted by the Security Council at its 3004th meeting, on 15 August 1991

The Security Council,

Recalling its resolution 687 (1991), and its other resolutions on this matter,

Recalling the letter of 11 April 1991 from the President of the Security Council to the Permanent Representative of Iraq to the United Nations (S/22485) noting that on the basis of Iraq's written agreement (S/22456) to implement fully resolution 687 (1991) the preconditions established in paragraph 33 of that resolution for a cease-fire had been met,

Noting with grave concern the letters dated 26 June 1991 (S/22739), 28 June 1991 (S/22743) and 4 July 1991 (S/22761) from the Secretary-General, conveying information obtained from the Executive Chairman of the Special Commission and the Director-General of the IAEA which establishes Iraq's failure to comply with its obligations under resolution 687 (1991),

Recalling further the statement issued by the President of the Security Council on 28 June 1991 (S/22746) requesting that a high-level mission consisting of the Chairman of the Special Commission, the Director-General of the IAEA, and the Under-Secretary-General for Disarmament Affairs be dispatched to meet with officials at the highest levels of the Government of Iraq at the earliest opportunity to obtain written assurance that Iraq will fully and immediately cooperate in the inspection of the locations identified by the Special Commission and present for immediate inspection any of those items that may have been transported from those locations,

Dismayed by the report of the high-level mission to the Secretary-General (S/22761) on the results of its meetings with the highest levels of the Iraqi Government,

Gravely concerned by the information provided to the Council by the Special Commission and the IAEA on 15 July 1991 (S/22788) and 25 July 1991 (S/22837) regarding the actions of the Government of Iraq in flagrant violation of resolution 687 (1991),

Gravely concerned also by the evidence in the letter of 7 July 1991 from the Minister of Foreign Affairs of Iraq to the Secretary-General and in subsequent statements and findings that Iraq's notifications of 18 and 28 April were incomplete and that it had concealed activities, which both constituted material breaches of its obligations under resolution 687 (1991),

Noting also from the letters dated 26 June 1991 (S/22739), 28 June 1991 (S/22743) and 4 July 1991 (S/22761) from the Secretary-General that Iraq has not fully complied with all of its undertakings relating to the privileges, immunities and facilities to be accorded to the Special Commission and the IAEA inspection teams mandated under resolution 687 (1991),

Affirming that in order for the Special Commission to carry out its mandate under paragraph 9 (b) (i), (ii) and (iii) of resolution 687 (1991) to inspect Iraq's chemical and biological weapons and ballistic missile capabilities and to take possession of them for destruction, removal or rendering harmless, full disclosure on the part of Iraq as required in paragraph 9 (a) of resolution 687 (1991) is essential,

Affirming that in order for the IAEA with the assistance and cooperation of the Special Commission, to determine what nuclear-weapons-usable material or any subsystems or components or any research, development, support or manufacturing facilities related to them need, in accordance with paragraph 13 of resolution 687 (1991), to be destroyed, removed or rendered harmless, Iraq is required to make a declaration of all its nuclear programmes including any which it claims are for purposes not related to nuclear-weapons-usable material,

Affirming that the aforementioned failures of Iraq to act in strict conformity with its obligations under resolution 687 (1991) constitutes a material breach of its acceptance of the relevant provisions of resolution 687 (1991) which established a cease-fire and provided the conditions essential to the restoration of peace and security in the region,

Affirming further that Iraq's failure to comply with its safeguards agreement with the International Atomic Energy Agency, concluded pursuant to the Treaty on the Non-Proliferation of Nuclear Weapons of 1 July 1968, as established by the resolution of the Board of Governors of the IAEA of 18 July 1991 (GOV/2531), constitutes a breach of its international obligations,

Determined to ensure full compliance with resolution 687 (1991) and in particular its section C,

Acting under Chapter VII of the Charter,

1. Condemns Iraq's serious violation of a number of its obligations under section C of resolution 687 (1991) and of its undertakings to cooperate with the Special Commission and the IAEA, which constitutes a material breach of the relevant provisions of resolution 687 which established a cease-fire and provided the conditions essential to the restoration of peace and security in the region,

2. Further condemns non-compliance by the Government of Iraq with its obligations under its safeguards agreement with the International Atomic Energy Agency, as established by the resolution of the Board of Governors of 18 July, which constitutes a violation of its commitments as a party to the Treaty on the Non-Proliferation of Nuclear Weapons of 1 July 1968,

3. Demands that Iraq

(i) provide full, final and complete disclosure, as required by resolution 687 (1991), of all aspects of its programmes to develop weapons of mass destruction and ballistic missiles with a range greater than 150 kilometres, and of all holdings of such weapons, their components and production facilities and locations, as well as all other nuclear programmes, including any which it claims are for purposes not related to nuclear-weapons-usable material, without further delay,

(ii) allow the Special Commission, the IAEA and their Inspection Teams immediate, unconditional and unrestricted access to any and all areas, facilities, equipment, records and means of transportation which they wish to inspect,

(iii) cease immediately any attempt to conceal, or any movement or destruction of any material or equipment relating to its nuclear, chemical or biological weapons or ballistic missile programmes, or material or equipment relating to its other nuclear activities without notification to and prior consent of the Special Commission,

(iv) make available immediately to the Special Commission, the IAEA and their Inspection Teams any items to which they were previously denied access,

(v) allow the Special Commission, the IAEA and their Inspection Teams to conduct both fixed wing and helicopter flights throughout Iraq for all relevant purposes including inspection, surveillance, aerial surveys, transportation and logistics without interference of any kind and upon such terms and conditions as may be determined by the Special Commission, and to make full use of their own aircraft and such airfields in Iraq as they may determine are most appropriate for the work of the Commission,

(vi) halt all nuclear activities of any kind, except for use of isotopes for medical, agricultural or industrial purposes until the Security Council determines that Iraq is in full compliance with this resolution and paragraphs 12 and 13 of resolution 687 (1991), and the IAEA determines that Iraq is in full compliance with its safeguards agreement with that Agency,

(vii) ensure the complete implementation of the privileges, immunities and facilities of the representatives of the Special Commission and the IAEA in accordance with its previous undertakings and their complete safety and freedom of movement,

(viii) immediately provide or facilitate the provision of any transportation, medical or logistical support requested by the Special Commission, the IAEA and their Inspection Teams,

(ix) respond fully, completely and promptly to any questions or requests from the Special Commission, the IAEA and their Inspection Teams,

4. Determines that Iraq retains no ownership interest in items to be destroyed, removed or rendered harmless pursuant to paragraph 12 of resolution 687 (1991),

5. Requires that the Government of Iraq forthwith comply fully and without delay with all its international obligations, including those set out in the present resolution, in resolution 687 (1991), in the Treaty on the Non-Proliferation of Nuclear Weapons of 1 July 1968 and its safeguards agreement with the IAEA.

6. Decides to remain seized of this matter.

RESOLUTION 1134 (1997)

Adopted by the Security Council at its 3826th meeting, on 23 October 1997

The Security Council,

Recalling all its previous relevant resolutions, and in particular its resolutions 687 (1991) of 3 April 1991, 707 (1991) of 15 August 1991, 715 (1991) of 11 October 1991, 1060 (1996) of 12 June 1996, and 1115 (1997) of 21 June 1997,

Having considered the report of the Executive Chairman of the Special Commission dated 6 October 1997 (S/1997/774),

Expressing grave concern at the report of additional incidents since the adoption of resolution 1115 (1997) in which access by the Special Commission inspection teams to sites in Iraq designated for inspection by the Commission was again denied by the Iraqi authorities,

Stressing the unacceptability of any attempts by Iraq to deny access to such sites,

Taking note of the progress nevertheless achieved by the Special Commission, as set out in the report of the Executive Chairman, towards the elimination of Iraq's programme of weapons of mass destruction,

Reaffirming its determination to ensure full compliance by Iraq with all its obligations under all previous relevant resolutions and reiterating its demand that Iraq allow immediate, unconditional and unrestricted access to the Special Commission to any site which the Commission wishes to inspect, and in particular allow the Special Commission and its inspection teams to conduct both fixed wing and helicopter flights throughout Iraq for all relevant purposes including inspection, surveillance, aerial surveys, transportation and logistics without interferences of any kind and upon such terms and conditions as may be determined by the Special Commission, and to make use of their own aircraft and such airfields in Iraq as they may determine are most appropriate for the work of the Commission,

Recalling that resolution 1115 (1997) expresses the Council's firm intention, unless the Special Commission has advised the Council that Iraq is in substantial compliance with paragraphs 2 and 3 of that resolution, to impose additional measures on those categories of Iraqi officials responsible for the non-compliance,

Reiterating the commitment of all Member States to the sovereignty, territorial integrity and political independence of Kuwait and Iraq,

Acting under Chapter VII of the Charter of the United Nations,

1. Condemns the repeated refusal of the Iraqi authorities, as detailed in the report of the Executive Chairman of the Special Commission, to allow access to sites designated by the Special Commission, and especially Iraqi actions endangering the safety of Special Commission personnel, the removal and destruction of documents of inter-est to the Special Commission and interference with the freedom of movement of Special Commission personnel;

2. Decides that such refusals to cooperate constitute a flagrant violation of Security Council resolutions 687 (1991), 707 (1991), 715 (1991) and 1060 (1996), and notes that the Special Commission in the report of the Executive Chairman was unable to advise that Iraq was in substantial compliance with paragraphs 2 and 3 of resolution 1115 (1997);

3. Demands that Iraq cooperate fully with the Special Commission in accordance with the relevant resolutions, which constitute the governing standard of Iraqi compliance;

4. Demands in particular that Iraq without delay allow the Special Commission inspection teams immediate, unconditional and unrestricted access to any and all areas, facilities, equipment, records and means of transportation which they wish to inspect in accordance with the mandate of the Special Commission, as well as to officials and other persons under the authority of the Iraqi Government whom the Special Commission wishes to interview so that the Special Commission may fully discharge its mandate;

5. Requests the Chairman of the Special Commission to include in all future consolidated progress reports prepared under resolution 1051 (1996) an annex evaluating Iraq's compliance with paragraphs 2 and 3 of resolution 1115 (1997);

6. Expresses the firm intention—if the Special Commission reports that Iraq is not in compliance with paragraphs 2 and 3 of resolution 1115 (1997) or if the Special Commission does not advise the Council in the report of the Executive Chairman due on 11 April 1998 that Iraq is in compliance with paragraphs 2 and 3 of resolution 1115 (1997)—to adopt measures which would oblige all States to prevent without delay the entry into or transit through their territories of all Iraqi officials and members of the Iraqi armed forces who are responsible for or participate in instances of non-compliance with paragraphs 2 and 3 of resolution 1115 (1997), provided that the entry of a person into a particular State on a

specified date may be authorized by the Committee established by resolution 661 (1990), and provided that nothing in this paragraph shall oblige a State to refuse entry into its own territory to its own nationals or persons carrying out bona fide diplomatic assignments or missions;

7. Decides further, on the basis of all incidents related to the implementation of paragraphs 2 and 3 of resolution 1115 (1997), to begin to designate, in consultation with the Special Commission, individuals whose entry or transit would be prevented upon implementation of the measures set out in paragraph 6 above;

8. Decides not to conduct the reviews provided for in paragraphs 21 and 28 of resolution 687 (1991) until after the next consolidated progress report of the Special Commission, due on 11 April 1998, after which those reviews will resume in accordance with resolution 687 (1991), beginning on 26 April 1998;

9. Reaffirms its full support for the authority of the Special Commission under its Executive Chairman to ensure the implementation of its mandate under the relevant resolutions of the Council;

10. Decides to remain seized of the matter.

RESOLUTION 1284 (1999)

Adopted by the Security Council at its 4084th meeting, on 17 December 1999

The Security Council,

Recalling its previous relevant resolutions, including its resolutions 661 (1990) of 6 August 1990, 687 (1991) of 3 April 1991, 699 (1991) of 17 June 1991, 707 (1991) of 15 August 1991, 715 (1991) of 11 October 1991, 986 (1995) of 14 April 1995, 1051 (1996) of 27 March 1996, 1153 (1998) of 20 February 1998, 1175 (1998) of 19 June 1998, 1242 (1999) of 21 May 1999 and 1266 (1999) of 4 October 1999,

Recalling the approval by the Council in its resolution 715 (1991) of the plans for future ongoing monitoring and verification submitted by the Secretary-General and the Director General of the International Atomic Energy Agency (IAEA) in pursuance of paragraphs 10 and 13 of resolution 687 (1991),

Welcoming the reports of the three panels on Iraq (S/1999/356), and having held a comprehensive consideration of them and the recommendations contained in them,

Stressing the importance of a comprehensive approach to the full implementation of all relevant Security Council resolutions regarding Iraq and the need for Iraqi compliance with these resolutions,

Recalling the goal of establishing in the Middle East a zone free from weapons of mass destruction and all missiles for their delivery and the objective of a global ban on chemical weapons as referred to in paragraph 14 of resolution 687 (1991),

Concerned at the humanitarian situation in Iraq, and determined to improve that situation,

Recalling with concern that the repatriation and return of all Kuwaiti and third country nationals or their remains, present in Iraq on or after 2 August 1990, pursuant to paragraph 2 (c) of resolution 686 (1991) of 2 March 1991 and paragraph 30 of resolution 687 (1991), have not yet been fully carried out by Iraq,

Recalling that in its resolutions 686 (1991) and 687 (1991) the Council demanded that Iraq return in the shortest possible time all Kuwaiti property it had seized, and noting with regret that Iraq has still not complied fully with this demand,

Acknowledging the progress made by Iraq towards compliance with the provisions of resolution 687 (1991), but noting that, as a result of its failure to implement the relevant Council resolutions fully, the conditions do not exist which would enable the Council to take a decision pursuant to resolution 687 (1991) to lift the prohibitions referred to in that resolution,

Reiterating the commitment of all Member States to the sovereignty, territorial integrity and political independence of Kuwait, Iraq and the neighboring States,

Acting under Chapter VII of the Charter of the United Nations, and taking into account that operative provisions of this resolution relate to previous resolutions adopted under Chapter VII of the Charter,

A.

1. Decides to establish, as a subsidiary body of the Council, the United Nations Monitoring, Verification and Inspection Commission (UNMOVIC) which replaces the Special Commission established pursuant to paragraph 9 (b) of resolution 687 (1991);

2. Decides also that UNMOVIC will undertake the responsibilities mandated to the Special Commission by the Council with regard to the verification of compliance by Iraq with its obligations under paragraphs 8, 9 and 10 of

resolution 687 (1991) and other related resolutions, that UNMOVIC will establish and operate, as was recommended by the panel on disarmament and current and future ongoing monitoring and verification issues, a reinforced system of ongoing monitoring and verification, which will implement the plan approved by the Council in resolution 715 (1991) and address unresolved disarmament issues, and that UNMOVIC will identify, as necessary in accordance with its mandate, additional sites in Iraq to be covered by the reinforced system of ongoing monitoring and verification;

3. Reaffirms the provisions of the relevant resolutions with regard to the role of the IAEA in addressing compliance by Iraq with paragraphs 12 and 13 of resolution 687 (1991) and other related resolutions, and requests the Director General of the IAEA to maintain this role with the assistance and cooperation of UNMOVIC;

4. Reaffirms its resolutions 687 (1991), 699 (1991), 707 (1991), 715 (1991), 1051 (1996), 1154 (1998) and all other relevant resolutions and statements of its President, which establish the criteria for Iraqi compliance, affirms that the obligations of Iraq referred to in those resolutions and statements with regard to cooperation with the Special Commission, unrestricted access and provision of information will apply in respect of UNMOVIC, and decides in particular that Iraq shall allow UNMOVIC teams immediate, unconditional and unrestricted access to any and all areas, facilities, equipment, records and means of transport which they wish to inspect in accordance with the mandate of UNMOVIC, as well as to all officials and other persons under the authority of the Iraqi Government whom UNMOVIC wishes to interview so that UNMOVIC may fully discharge its mandate;

5. Requests the Secretary-General, within 30 days of the adoption of this resolution, to appoint, after consultation with and subject to the approval of the Council, an Executive Chairman of UNMOVIC who will take up his mandated tasks as soon as possible, and, in consultation with the Executive Chairman and the Council members, to appoint suitably qualified experts as a College of Commissioners for UNMOVIC which will

meet regularly to review the implementation of this and other relevant resolutions and provide professional advice and guidance to the Executive Chairman, including on significant policy decisions and on written reports to be submitted to the Council through the Secretary-General;

6. Requests the Executive Chairman of UNMOVIC, within 45 days of his appointment, to submit to the Council, in consultation with and through the Secretary-General, for its approval an organizational plan for UNMOVIC, including its structure, staffing requirements, management guidelines, recruitment and training procedures, incorporating as appropriate the recommendations of the panel on disarmament and current and future ongoing monitoring and verification issues, and recognizing in particular the need for an effective, cooperative management structure for the new organization, for staffing with suitably qualified and experienced personnel, who would be regarded as international civil servants subject to Article 100 of the Charter of the United Nations, drawn from the broadest possible geographical base, including as he deems necessary from international arms control organizations, and for the provision of high quality technical and cultural training;

7. Decides that UNMOVIC and the IAEA, not later than 60 days after they have both started work in Iraq, will each draw up, for approval by the Council, a work programme for the discharge of their mandates, which will include both the implementation of the reinforced system of ongoing monitoring and verification, and the key remaining disarmament tasks to be completed by Iraq pursuant to its obligations to comply with the disarmament requirements of resolution 687 (1991) and other related resolutions, which constitute the governing standard of Iraqi compliance, and further decides that what is required of Iraq for the implementation of each task shall be clearly defined and precise;

8. Requests the Executive Chairman of UNMOVIC and the Director General of the IAEA, drawing on the expertise of other international organizations as appropriate, to establish a unit which will have the responsibilities of the joint unit constituted by the Special

Commission and the Director General of the IAEA under paragraph 16 of the export/import mechanism approved by resolution 1051 (1996), and also requests the Executive Chairman of UNMOVIC, in consultation with the Director General of the IAEA, to resume the revision and updating of the lists of items and technology to which the mechanism applies;

9. Decides that the Government of Iraq shall be liable for the full costs of UNMOVIC and the IAEA in relation to their work under this and other related resolutions on Iraq;

10. Requests Member States to give full cooperation to UNMOVIC and the IAEA in the discharge of their mandates;

11. Decides that UNMOVIC shall take over all assets, liabilities and archives of the Special Commission, and that it shall assume the Special Commission's part in agreements existing between the Special Commission and Iraq and between the United Nations and Iraq, and affirms that the Executive Chairman, the Commissioners and the personnel serving with UNMOVIC shall have the rights, privileges, facilities and immunities of the Special Commission;

12. Requests the Executive Chairman of UNMOVIC to report, through the Secretary-General, to the Council, following consultation with the Commissioners, every three months on the work of UNMOVIC, pending submission of the first reports referred to in paragraph 33 below, and to report immediately when the reinforced system of ongoing monitoring and verification is fully operational in Iraq;

B.

13. Reiterates the obligation of Iraq, in furtherance of its commitment to facilitate the repatriation of all Kuwaiti and third country nationals referred to in paragraph 30 of resolution 687 (1991), to extend all necessary cooperation to the International Committee of the Red Cross, and calls upon the Government of Iraq to resume cooperation with the Tripartite Commission and Technical Subcommittee established to facilitate work on this issue;

14. Requests the Secretary-General to report to the Council every four months on compliance by Iraq with its obligations regarding the repatriation or return of all Kuwaiti and third country nationals or their remains, to report every six months on the return of all Kuwaiti property, including archives, seized by Iraq, and to appoint a high-level coordinator for these issues;

C.

15. Authorizes States, notwithstanding the provisions of paragraphs 3 (a), 3 (b) and 4 of resolution 661 (1990) and subsequent relevant resolutions, to permit the import of any volume of petroleum and petroleum products originating in Iraq, including financial and other essential transactions directly relating thereto, as required for the purposes and on the conditions set out in paragraph 1 (a) and (b) and subsequent provisions of resolution 986 (1995) and related resolutions;

16. Underlines, in this context, its intention to take further action, including permitting the use of additional export routes for petroleum and petroleum products, under appropriate conditions otherwise consistent with the purpose and provisions of resolution 986 (1995) and related resolutions;

17. Directs the Committee established by resolution 661 (1990) to approve, on the basis of proposals from the Secretary-General, lists of humanitarian items, including foodstuffs, pharmaceutical and medical supplies, as well as basic or standard medical and agricultural equipment and basic or standard educational items; decides, notwithstanding paragraph 3 of resolution 661 (1990) and paragraph 20 of resolution 687 (1991), that supplies of these items will not be submitted for approval of that Committee, except for items subject to the provisions of resolution 1051 (1996), and will be notified to the Secretary-General and financed in accordance with the provisions of paragraph 8 (a) and 8 (b) of resolution 986 (1995); and requests the Secretary-General to inform the Committee in a timely manner of all such notifications received and actions taken;

18. Requests the Committee established by resolution 661 (1990) to appoint, in accordance with resolutions 1175 (1998) and 1210 (1998), a group of experts, including independent inspection agents appointed by the Secretary-General in accordance with paragraph 6 of resolution 986 (1995), decides that this group will be mandated to approve

speedily contracts for the parts and the equipments necessary to enable Iraq to increase its exports of petroleum and petroleum products, according to lists of parts and equipments approved by that Committee for each individual project, and requests the Secretary-General to continue to provide for the monitoring of these parts and equipments inside Iraq;

19. Encourages Member States and international organizations to provide supplementary humanitarian assistance to Iraq and published material of an educational character to Iraq;

20. Decides to suspend, for an initial period of six months from the date of the adoption of this resolution and subject to review, the implementation of paragraph 8 (g) of resolution 986 (1995);

21. Requests the Secretary-General to take steps to maximize, drawing as necessary on the advice of specialists, including representatives of international humanitarian organizations, the effectiveness of the arrangements set out in resolution 986 (1995) and related resolutions including the humanitarian benefit to the Iraqi population in all areas of the country, and further requests the Secretary-General to continue to enhance as necessary the United Nations observation process in Iraq, ensuring that all supplies under the humanitarian programme are utilized as authorized, to bring to the attention of the Council any circumstances preventing or impeding effective and equitable distribution and to keep the Council informed of the steps taken towards the implementation of this paragraph;

22. Requests also the Secretary-General to minimize the cost of the United Nations activities associated with the implementation of resolution 986 (1995) as well as the cost of the independent inspection agents and the certified public accountants appointed by him, in accordance with paragraphs 6 and 7 of resolution 986 (1995);

23. Requests further the Secretary-General to provide Iraq and the Committee established by resolution 661 (1990) with a daily statement of the status of the escrow account established by paragraph 7 of resolution 986 (1995);

24. Requests the Secretary-General to make the necessary arrangements, subject to Security Council approval, to allow funds deposited in the escrow account established by resolution 986 (1995) to be used for the purchase of locally produced goods and to meet the local cost for essential civilian needs which have been funded in accordance with the provisions of resolution 986 (1995) and related resolutions, including, where appropriate, the cost of installation and training services;

25. Directs the Committee established by resolution 661 (1990) to make a decision on all applications in respect of humanitarian and essential civilian needs within a target of two working days of receipt of these applications from the Secretary-General, and to ensure that all approval and notification letters issued by the Committee stipulate delivery within a specified time, according to the nature of the items to be supplied, and requests the Secretary-General to notify the Committee of all applications for humanitarian items which are included in the list to which the export/import mechanism approved by resolution 1051 (1996) applies;

26. Decides that Hajj pilgrimage flights which do not transport cargo into or out of Iraq are exempt from the provisions of paragraph 3 of resolution 661 (1990) and resolution 670 (1990), provided timely notification of each flight is made to the Committee established by resolution 661 (1990), and requests the Secretary-General to make the necessary arrangements, for approval by the Security Council, to provide for reasonable expenses related to the Hajj pilgrimage to be met by funds in the escrow account established by resolution 986 (1995);

27. Calls upon the Government of Iraq:

   (i) to take all steps to ensure the timely and equitable distribution of all humanitarian goods, in particular medical supplies, and to remove and avoid delays at its warehouses;

   (ii) to address effectively the needs of vulnerable groups, including children, pregnant women, the disabled, the elderly and the mentally ill among others, and to allow freer access, without any discrimination, including on the basis of religion or nationality, by United Nations agencies and humanitarian organizations to all areas and sections of the population for evaluation of their nutritional and humanitarian condition;

   (iii) to prioritize applications for humanitarian goods under the arrangements set out in resolution 986 (1995) and related resolutions;

    (iv) to ensure that those involuntarily displaced receive humanitarian assistance without the need to demonstrate that they have resided for six months in their places of temporary residence;

    (v) to extend full cooperation to the United Nations Office for Project Services mine-clearance programme in the three northern Governorates of Iraq and to consider the initiation of the demining efforts in other Governorates;

28. Requests the Secretary-General to report on the progress made in meeting the humanitarian needs of the Iraqi people and on the revenues necessary to meet those needs, including recommendations on necessary additions to the current allocation for oil spare parts and equipment, on the basis of a comprehensive survey of the condition of the Iraqi oil production sector, not later than 60 days from the date of the adoption of this resolution and updated thereafter as necessary;

29. Expresses its readiness to authorize additions to the current allocation for oil spare parts and equipment, on the basis of the report and recommendations requested in paragraph 28 above, in order to meet the humanitarian purposes set out in resolution 986 (1995) and related resolutions;

30. Requests the Secretary-General to establish a group of experts, including oil industry experts, to report within 100 days of the date of adoption of this resolution on Iraq's existing petroleum production and export capacity and to make recommendations, to be updated as necessary, on alternatives for increasing Iraq's petroleum production and export capacity in a manner consistent with the purposes of relevant resolutions, and on the options for involving foreign oil companies in Iraq's oil sector, including investments, subject to appropriate monitoring and controls;

31. Notes that in the event of the Council acting as provided for in paragraph 33 of this resolution to suspend the prohibitions referred to in that paragraph, appropriate arrangements and procedures will need, subject to paragraph 35 below, to be agreed by the Council in good time beforehand, including suspension of provisions of resolution 986 (1995) and related resolutions;

32. Requests the Secretary-General to report to the Council on the implementation of paragraphs 15 to 30 of this resolution within 30 days of the adoption of this resolution;

D.

33. Expresses its intention, upon receipt of reports from the Executive Chairman of UNMOVIC and from the Director General of the IAEA that Iraq has cooperated in all respects with UNMOVIC and the IAEA in particular in fulfilling the work programmes in all the aspects referred to in paragraph 7 above, for a period of 120 days after the date on which the Council is in receipt of reports from both UNMOVIC and the IAEA that the reinforced system of ongoing monitoring and verification is fully operational, to suspend with the fundamental objective of improving the humanitarian situation in Iraq and securing the implementation of the Council's resolutions, for a period of 120 days renewable by the Council, and subject to the elaboration of effective financial and other operational measures to ensure that Iraq does not acquire prohibited items, prohibitions against the import of commodities and products originating in Iraq, and prohibitions against the sale, supply and delivery to Iraq of civilian commodities and products other than those referred to in paragraph 24 of resolution 687 (1991) or those to which the mechanism established by resolution 1051 (1996) applies;

34. Decides that in reporting to the Council for the purposes of paragraph 33 above, the Executive Chairman of UNMOVIC will include as a basis for his assessment the progress made in completing the tasks referred to in paragraph 7 above;

35. Decides that if at any time the Executive Chairman of UNMOVIC or the Director General of the IAEA reports that Iraq is not cooperating in all respects with UNMOVIC or the IAEA or if Iraq is in the process of acquiring any prohibited items, the suspension of the prohibitions referred to in paragraph 33 above shall terminate on the fifth working day following the report, unless the Council decides to the contrary;

36. Expresses its intention to approve arrangements for effective financial and other operational measures, including on the delivery of and payment for authorized civilian commodities and

products to be sold or supplied to Iraq, in order to ensure that Iraq does not acquire prohibited items in the event of suspension of the prohibitions referred to in paragraph 33 above, to begin the elaboration of such measures not later than the date of the receipt of the initial reports referred to in paragraph 33 above, and to approve such arrangements before the Council decision in accordance with that paragraph;

37. Further expresses its intention to take steps, based on the report and recommendations requested in paragraph 30 above, and consistent with the purpose of resolution 986 (1995) and related resolutions, to enable Iraq to increase its petroleum production and export capacity, upon receipt of the reports relating to the cooperation in all respects with UNMOVIC and the IAEA referred to in paragraph 33 above;

38. Reaffirms its intention to act in accordance with the relevant provisions of resolution 687 (1991) on the termination of prohibitions referred to in that resolution;

39. Decides to remain actively seized of the matter and expresses its intention to consider action in accordance with paragraph 33 above no later than 12 months from the date of the adoption of this resolution provided the conditions set out in paragraph 33 above have been satisfied by Iraq.

RESOLUTION 1441 (2002)

Adopted by the Security Council at its 4644th meeting, on 8 November 2002

The Security Council,

Recalling all its previous relevant resolutions, in particular its resolutions 661 (1990) of 6 August 1990, 678 (1990) of 29 November 1990, 686 (1991) of 2 March 1991, 687 (1991) of 3 April 1991, 688 (1991) of 5 April 1991, 707 (1991) of 15 August 1991, 715 (1991) of 11 October 1991, 986 (1995) of 14 April 1995, and 1284 (1999) of 17 December 1999, and all the relevant statements of its President,

Recalling also its resolution 1382 (2001) of 29 November 2001 and its intention to implement it fully,

Recognizing the threat Iraq's non-compliance with Council resolutions and proliferation of weapons of mass destruction and long-range missiles poses to international peace and security,

Recalling that its resolution 678 (1990) authorized Member States to use all necessary means to uphold and implement its resolution 660 (1990) of 2 August 1990 and all relevant resolutions subsequent to resolution 660 (1990) and to restore international peace and security in the area,

Further recalling that its resolution 687 (1991) imposed obligations on Iraq as a necessary step for achievement of its stated objective of restoring international peace and security in the area,

Deploring the fact that Iraq has not provided an accurate, full, final, and complete disclosure, as required by resolution 687 (1991), of all aspects of its programmes to develop weapons of mass destruction and ballistic missiles with a range greater than one hundred and fifty kilometres, and of all holdings of such weapons, their components and production facilities and locations, as well as all other nuclear programmes, including any which it claims are for purposes not related to nuclear-weapons-usable material,

Deploring further that Iraq repeatedly obstructed immediate, unconditional, and unrestricted access to sites designated by the United Nations Special Commission (UNSCOM) and the International Atomic Energy Agency (IAEA), failed to cooperate fully and unconditionally with UNSCOM and IAEA weapons inspectors, as required by resolution 687 (1991), and ultimately ceased all cooperation with UNSCOM and the IAEA in 1998,

Deploring the absence, since December 1998, in Iraq of international monitoring, inspection, and verification, as required by relevant resolutions, of weapons of mass destruction and ballistic missiles, in spite of the Council's repeated demands that Iraq provide immediate, unconditional, and unrestricted access to the United Nations Monitoring, Verification and Inspection Commission (UNMOVIC), established in resolution 1284 (1999) as the successor organization to UNSCOM, and the IAEA, and regretting the consequent prolonging of the crisis in the region and the suffering of the Iraqi people,

Deploring also that the Government of Iraq has failed to comply with its commitments pursuant to resolution 687 (1991) with regard to terrorism, pursuant to resolution 688 (1991) to end repression of its civilian population and to provide access by international humanitarian organizations to all those in need of assistance in Iraq, and pursuant to resolutions 686 (1991), 687 (1991), and 1284 (1999) to return or cooperate in accounting for Kuwaiti and third country nationals wrongfully detained by Iraq, or to return Kuwaiti property wrongfully seized by Iraq,

Recalling that in its resolution 687 (1991) the Council declared that a cease-fire would be based on acceptance by Iraq of the provisions of that resolution, including the obligations on Iraq contained therein,

Determined to ensure full and immediate compliance by Iraq without conditions or restrictions with its obligations under resolution 687 (1991) and other relevant resolutions and recalling that the resolutions of the Council constitute the governing standard of Iraqi compliance,

Recalling that the effective operation of UNMOVIC, as the successor organization to the Special Commission, and the IAEA is essential for the implementation of resolution 687 (1991) and other relevant resolutions,

Noting that the letter dated 16 September 2002 from the Minister for Foreign Affairs of Iraq addressed to the Secretary-General is a necessary first step toward rectifying Iraq's continued failure to comply with relevant Council resolutions,

Noting further the letter dated 8 October 2002 from the Executive Chairman of UNMOVIC and the Director-General of the IAEA to General Al-Saadi of the Government of Iraq laying out the practical arrangements, as a follow-up to their meeting in Vienna, that are prerequisites for the resumption of inspections in Iraq by UNMOVIC and the IAEA, and expressing the gravest concern at the continued failure by the Government of Iraq to provide confirmation of the arrangements as laid out in that letter,

Reaffirming the commitment of all Member States to the sovereignty and territorial integrity of Iraq, Kuwait, and the neighbouring States,

Commending the Secretary-General and members of the League of Arab States and its Secretary-General for their efforts in this regard,

Determined to secure full compliance with its decisions,

Acting under Chapter VII of the Charter of the United Nations,

1. Decides that Iraq has been and remains in material breach of its obligations under relevant resolutions, including resolution 687 (1991), in particular through Iraq's failure to cooperate with United Nations inspectors and the IAEA, and to complete the actions required under paragraphs 8 to 13 of resolution 687 (1991);

2. Decides, while acknowledging paragraph 1 above, to afford Iraq, by this resolution, a final opportunity to comply with its disarmament obligations under relevant resolutions of the Coun-

cil; and accordingly decides to set up an enhanced inspection regime with the aim of bringing to full and verified completion the disarmament process established by resolution 687 (1991) and subsequent resolutions of the Council;

3. Decides that, in order to begin to comply with its disarmament obligations, in addition to submitting the required biannual declarations, the Government of Iraq shall provide to UNMOVIC, the IAEA, and the Council, not later than 30 days from the date of this resolution, a currently accurate, full, and complete declaration of all aspects of its programmes to develop chemical, biological, and nuclear weapons, ballistic missiles, and other delivery systems such as unmanned aerial vehicles and dispersal systems designed for use on aircraft, including any holdings and precise locations of such weapons, components, subcomponents, stocks of agents, and related material and equipment, the locations and work of its research, development and production facilities, as well as all other chemical, biological, and nuclear programmes, including any which it claims are for purposes not related to weapon production or material;

4. Decides that false statements or omissions in the declarations submitted by Iraq pursuant to this resolution and failure by Iraq at any time to comply with, and cooperate fully in the implementation of, this resolution shall constitute a further material breach of Iraq's obligations and will be reported to the Council for assessment in accordance with paragraphs 11 and 12 below;

5. Decides that Iraq shall provide UNMOVIC and the IAEA immediate, unimpeded, unconditional, and unrestricted access to any and all, including underground, areas, facilities, buildings, equipment, records, and means of transport which they wish to inspect, as well as immediate, unimpeded, unrestricted, and private access to all officials and other persons whom UNMOVIC or the IAEA wish to interview in the mode or location of UNMOVIC's or the IAEA's choice pursuant to any aspect of their mandates; further decides that UNMOVIC and the IAEA may at their discretion conduct interviews inside or outside of Iraq, may facilitate the travel of those interviewed

and family members outside of Iraq, and that, at the sole discretion of UNMOVIC and the IAEA, such interviews may occur without the presence of observers from the Iraqi Government; and instructs UNMOVIC and requests the IAEA to resume inspections no later than 45 days following adoption of this resolution and to update the Council 60 days thereafter;

6. Endorses the 8 October 2002 letter from the Executive Chairman of UNMOVIC and the Director-General of the IAEA to General Al-Saadi of the Government of Iraq, which is annexed hereto, and decides that the contents of the letter shall be binding upon Iraq;

7. Decides further that, in view of the prolonged interruption by Iraq of the presence of UNMOVIC and the IAEA and in order for them to accomplish the tasks set forth in this resolution and all previous relevant resolutions and notwithstanding prior understandings, the Council hereby establishes the following revised or additional authorities, which shall be binding upon Iraq, to facilitate their work in Iraq:

–UNMOVIC and the IAEA shall determine the composition of their inspection teams and ensure that these teams are composed of the most qualified and experienced experts available;

–All UNMOVIC and IAEA personnel shall enjoy the privileges and immunities, corresponding to those of experts on mission, provided in the Convention on Privileges and Immunities of the United Nations and the Agreement on the Privileges and Immunities of the IAEA;

–UNMOVIC and the IAEA shall have unrestricted rights of entry into and out of Iraq, the right to free, unrestricted, and immediate movement to and from inspection sites, and the right to inspect any sites and buildings, including immediate, unimpeded, unconditional, and unrestricted access to Presidential Sites equal to that at other sites, notwithstanding the provisions of resolution 1154 (1998) of 2 March 1998;

–UNMOVIC and the IAEA shall have the right to be provided by Iraq the names of all personnel currently and formerly associated with Iraq's chemical, biological, nuclear, and ballistic missile programmes and the associated research, development, and production facilities;

–Security of UNMOVIC and IAEA facilities shall be ensured by sufficient United Nations security guards;

–UNMOVIC and the IAEA shall have the right to declare, for the purposes of freezing a site to be inspected, exclusion zones, including surrounding areas and transit corridors, in which Iraq will suspend ground and aerial movement so that nothing is changed in or taken out of a site being inspected;

–UNMOVIC and the IAEA shall have the free and unrestricted use and landing of fixed- and rotary-winged aircraft, including manned and unmanned reconnaissance vehicles;

–UNMOVIC and the IAEA shall have the right at their sole discretion verifiably to remove, destroy, or render harmless all prohibited weapons, subsystems, components, records, materials, and other related items, and the right to impound or close any facilities or equipment for the production thereof; and

–UNMOVIC and the IAEA shall have the right to free import and use of equipment or materials for inspections and to seize and export any equipment, materials, or documents taken during inspections, without search of UNMOVIC or IAEA personnel or official or personal baggage;

8. Decides further that Iraq shall not take or threaten hostile acts directed against any representative or personnel of the United Nations or the IAEA or of any Member State taking action to uphold any Council resolution;

9. Requests the Secretary-General immediately to notify Iraq of this resolution, which is binding on Iraq; demands that Iraq confirm within seven days of that notification its intention to comply fully with this resolution; and demands further that Iraq cooperate immediately, unconditionally, and actively with UNMOVIC and the IAEA;

10. Requests all Member States to give full support to UNMOVIC and the IAEA in the discharge of their mandates, including by providing any information related to prohibited programmes or other aspects of their mandates, including on Iraqi attempts since 1998 to acquire prohibited items, and by recommending sites to be inspected, persons to be interviewed, conditions of such interviews, and data to be collected, the results of which shall be reported to the Council by UNMOVIC and the IAEA;

11. Directs the Executive Chairman of UNMOVIC and the Director-General of the IAEA to report immediately to the Council any interference by Iraq with inspection activities, as well as any failure by Iraq to comply with its disarmament obligations, including its obligations regarding inspections under this resolution;

12. Decides to convene immediately upon receipt of a report in accordance with paragraphs 4 or 11 above, in order to consider the situation and the need for full compliance with all of the relevant Council resolutions in order to secure international peace and security;

13. Recalls, in that context, that the Council has repeatedly warned Iraq

that it will face serious consequences as a result of its continued violations of its obligations;

14. Decides to remain seized of the matter.

Annex

Text of Blix/El-Baradei letter

United Nations Monitoring, Verification and Inspection Commission

The Executive Chairman

International Atomic Energy Agency

The Director General

8 October 2002

Dear General Al-Saadi,

During our recent meeting in Vienna, we discussed practical arrangements that are prerequisites for the resumption of inspections in Iraq by UNMOVIC and the IAEA. As you recall, at the end of our meeting in Vienna we agreed on a statement which listed some of the principal results achieved, particularly Iraq's acceptance of all the rights of inspection provided for in all of the relevant Security Council resolutions. This acceptance was stated to be without any conditions attached.

During our 3 October 2002 briefing to the Security Council, members of the Council suggested that we prepare a written document on all of the conclusions we reached in Vienna. This letter lists those conclusions and seeks your confirmation thereof. We shall report accordingly to the Security Council.

In the statement at the end of the meeting, it was clarified that UNMOVIC and the IAEA will be granted immediate, unconditional and unrestricted access to sites, including what was termed "sensitive sites" in the past. As we noted, however, eight presidential sites have been the subject of special procedures under a Memorandum of Understanding of 1998. Should these sites be subject, as all other sites, to immediate, unconditional and unrestricted access, UNMOVIC and the IAEA would conduct inspections there with the same professionalism.

H.E. General Amir H. Al-Saadi

Advisor

Presidential Office

Baghdad

Iraq

We confirm our understanding that UNMOVIC and the IAEA have the right to determine the number of inspectors required for access to any particular site. This determination will be made on the basis of the size and complexity of the site being inspected. We also con-

firm that Iraq will be informed of the designation of additional sites, i.e. sites not declared by Iraq or previously inspected by either UNSCOM or the IAEA, through a Notification of Inspection (NIS) provided upon arrival of the inspectors at such sites.

Iraq will ensure that no proscribed material, equipment, records or other relevant items will be destroyed except in the presence of UNMOVIC and/or IAEA inspectors, as appropriate, and at their request.

UNMOVIC and the IAEA may conduct interviews with any person in Iraq whom they believe may have information relevant to their mandate. Iraq will facilitate such interviews. It is for UNMOVIC and the IAEA to choose the mode and location for interviews.

The National Monitoring Directorate (NMD) will, as in the past, serve as the Iraqi counterpart for the inspectors. The Baghdad Ongoing Monitoring and Verification Centre (BOMVIC) will be maintained on the same premises and under the same conditions as was the former Baghdad Monitoring and Verification Centre. The NMD will make available services as before, cost free, for the refurbishment of the premises.

The NMD will provide free of cost: (a) escorts to facilitate access to sites to be inspected and communication with personnel to be interviewed; (b) a hotline for BOMVIC which will be staffed by an English speaking person on a 24 hour a day/seven days a week basis; (c) support in terms of personnel and ground transportation within the country, as requested; and (d) assistance in the movement of materials and equipment at inspectors' request (construction, excavation equipment, etc.). NMD will also ensure that escorts are available in the event of inspections outside normal working hours, including at night and on holidays.

Regional UNMOVIC/IAEA offices may be established, for example, in Basra and Mosul, for the use of their inspectors. For this purpose, Iraq will provide, without cost, adequate office buildings, staff accommodation, and appropriate escort personnel.

UNMOVIC and the IAEA may use any type of voice or data transmission, including satellite and/or inland networks, with or without encryption capability. UNMOVIC and the IAEA may also install equipment in the field with the capability for transmission of data directly to the BOMVIC, New York and Vienna (e.g. sensors, surveillance cameras). This will be facilitated by Iraq and there will be no interference by Iraq with UNMOVIC or IAEA communications.

Iraq will provide, without cost, physical protection of all surveillance equipment, and construct antennae for remote transmission of data, at the request of UNMOVIC and the IAEA. Upon request by UNMOVIC through the NMD, Iraq will allocate frequencies for communications equipment.

Iraq will provide security for all UNMOVIC and IAEA personnel. Secure and suitable accommodations will be designated at normal rates by Iraq for these personnel. For their part, UNMOVIC and the IAEA will require that their staff not stay at any accommodation other than those identified in consultation with Iraq.

On the use of fixed-wing aircraft for transport of personnel and equipment and for inspection purposes, it was clarified that aircraft used by UNMOVIC and IAEA staff arriving in Baghdad may land at Saddam International Airport. The points of departure of incoming aircraft will be decided by UNMOVIC. The Rasheed airbase will continue to be used for UNMOVIC and IAEA helicopter operations. UNMOVIC and Iraq will establish air liaison offices at the airbase. At both Saddam International Airport and Rasheed airbase, Iraq will provide the necessary support premises and facilities. Aircraft fuel will be provided by Iraq, as before, free of charge.

On the wider issue of air operations in Iraq, both fixed-wing and rotary, Iraq will guarantee the safety of air operations in its air space outside the no-fly zones. With regard to air operations in the no-fly zones, Iraq will take all steps within its control to ensure the safety of such operations.

Helicopter flights may be used, as needed, during inspections and for technical activities, such as gamma detection, without limitation in all parts of Iraq and without any area excluded. Helicopters may also be used for medical evacuation.

On the question of aerial imagery, UNMOVIC may wish to resume the use of U-2 or Mirage overflights. The relevant practical arrangements would be similar to those implemented in the past.

As before, visas for all arriving staff will be issued at the point of entry on the basis of the UN Laissez-Passer or UN Certificate; no other entry or exit formalities will be required. The aircraft passenger manifest will be provided one hour in advance of the arrival of the aircraft in Baghdad. There will be no searching of UNMOVIC or IAEA personnel or of official or personal baggage. UNMOVIC and the IAEA will ensure that their personnel respect the laws of Iraq restricting the export of certain items, for example, those related to Iraq's national cultural heritage. UNMOVIC and the IAEA may bring into, and remove from, Iraq all of the items and materials they require, including satellite phones and other equipment. With respect to samples, UNMOVIC and IAEA will, where feasible, split samples so that Iraq may receive a portion while another portion is kept for reference purposes. Where appropriate, the organizations will send the samples to more than one laboratory for analysis.

We would appreciate your confirmation of the above as a correct reflection of our talks in Vienna.

Naturally, we may need other practical arrangements when proceeding with inspections. We would expect in such matters, as with the above, Iraq's co-operation in all respects.

Yours sincerely,
Hans Blix,
Executive Chairman
United Nations Monitoring,
Verification and Inspection Commission
Mohamed ElBaradei,
Director General
International Atomic Energy Agency

This resolution addressed the need for humanitarian aid for the Iraqi people following the U.S. invasion in March 2003.

RESOLUTION 1472 (2003)

Adopted by the Security Council at its 4732nd meeting, on 28 March 2003

The Security Council,

Noting that under the provisions of Article 55 of the Fourth Geneva Convention (Geneva Convention Relative to the Protection of Civilian Persons in Time of War of August 12, 1949), to the fullest extent of the means available to it, the Occupying Power has the duty of ensuring the food and medical supplies of the population; it should, in particular, bring in the necessary foodstuffs, medical stores and other articles if the resources of the occupied territory are inadequate,

Convinced of the urgent need to continue to provide humanitarian relief to the people of Iraq throughout the country on an equitable basis, and of the need to extend such humanitarian relief measures to the people of Iraq who leave the country as a result of hostilities,

Recalling its previous relevant resolutions, and in particular resolutions 661 (1990) of 6 August 1990, 986 (1995) of 14 April 1995, 1409 (2002) of 14 May 2002, and 1454 (2002) of 30 December 2002, as they provide humanitarian relief to the people of Iraq,

Noting the decision made by the Secretary-General on 17 March 2003 to withdraw all United Nations and international staff tasked with the implementation of the "Oil-for-Food" Programme (hereinafter "the Programme") established under resolution 986 (1995),

Stressing the necessity to make every effort to sustain the operation of the present national food basket distribution network,

Stressing also the need for consideration of a further reassessment of the Programme during and after the emergency phase,

Reaffirming the respect for the right of the people of Iraq to determine their own political future and to control their own natural resources,

Reaffirming the commitment of all Member States to the sovereignty and territorial integrity of Iraq,

Acting under Chapter VII of the Charter of the United Nations,

1. Requests all parties concerned to strictly abide by their obligations under international law, in particular the Geneva Conventions and the Hague Regulations, including those relating to the essential civilian needs of the people of Iraq, both inside and outside Iraq;

2. Calls on the international community also to provide immediate humanitarian assistance to the people of Iraq, both inside and outside Iraq in consultation with relevant States, and in particular to respond immediately to any future humanitarian appeal of the United Nations, and supports the activities of the International Committee of the Red Cross and of other international humanitarian organizations;

3. Recognizes that additionally, in view of the exceptional circumstances prevailing currently in Iraq, on an interim and exceptional basis, technical and temporary adjustments should be made to the Programme so as to ensure the implementation of the approved funded and non-funded contracts concluded by the Government of Iraq for the humanitarian relief of the people of Iraq, including to meet the needs of refugees and internally displaced persons, in accordance with this resolution;

4. Authorizes the Secretary-General and representatives designated by him to undertake as an urgent first step, and with the necessary coordination, the following measures:

(a) to establish alternative locations, both inside and outside Iraq, in consultation with the respective governments, for the delivery, inspection and authenticated confirmation of humanitarian supplies and equipment provided under the Programme, as well as to re-direct shipments of goods to those locations, as necessary;

(b) to review, as a matter of urgency, the approved funded and non-funded contracts concluded by the Government of Iraq to determine the relative

priorities of the need for adequate medicine, health supplies, foodstuffs and other materials and supplies for essential civilian needs represented in these contracts which can be shipped within the period of this mandate, to proceed with these contracts in accordance with such priorities;

(c) to contact suppliers of these contracts to determine the precise location of contracted goods and, when necessary, to require suppliers to delay, accelerate or divert shipments;

(d) to negotiate and agree on necessary adjustments in the terms or conditions of these contracts and their respective letters of credit and to implement the measures referred to in paragraph 4 (a), (b) and (c), notwithstanding distribution plans approved under the Programme;

(e) to negotiate and execute new contracts for essential medical items under the Programme and to authorize issuance of the relevant letters of credit, notwithstanding approved distribution plans, provided that such items cannot be delivered in execution of contracts pursuant to paragraph 4 (b) and subject to the approval of the Committee established pursuant to resolution 661 (1990);

(f) to transfer unencumbered funds between the accounts created pursuant to paragraphs 8 (a) and 8 (b) of resolution 986 (1995) on an exceptional and reimbursable basis as necessary to ensure the delivery of essential humanitarian supplies to the people of Iraq and to use the funds in the escrow accounts referred to in paragraphs 8 (a) and (b) of resolution 986 (1995) to implement the Programme as provided for in this resolution, irrespective of the phase in which such funds entered the escrow accounts or the phase to which those funds may have been allocated;

(g) to use, subject to procedures to be decided by the Committee established by resolution 661 (1990) prior to the end of the period set out in paragraph 10 below and based on recommendations provided by the Office of the Iraq Programme, funds deposited in the accounts created pursuant to paragraphs 8 (a) and (b) of resolution 986 (1995), as necessary and appropriate, to compensate suppliers and shippers for agreed additional shipping, transportation and storage costs incurred as a result of diverting and delaying shipments as directed by him according to the provisions of paragraph 4 (a), (b) and (c) in order to perform his functions set out in paragraph 4 (d);

(h) to meet additional operational and administrative costs resulting from the implementation of the temporarily modified Programme by the funds in the escrow account established pursuant to paragraph 8 (d) of resolution 986 (1995) in the same manner as costs arising from those activities set forth in paragraph 8 (d) of resolution 986 (1995) in order to perform his functions set out in (d);

(i) to use funds deposited in the escrow accounts established pursuant to paragraphs 8 (a) and 8 (b) of resolution 986 (1995) for the purchase of locally produced goods and to meet the local cost for essential civilian needs which have been funded in accordance with the provisions of resolution 986 (1995) and related resolutions, including, where appropriate, the costs of milling, transportation and other costs necessary to facilitate the delivery of essential humanitarian supplies to the people of Iraq;

5. Expresses its readiness as a second step to authorize the Secretary-General to perform additional functions with the necessary coordination as soon as the situation permits as activities of the Programme in Iraq resume;

6. Expresses further its readiness to consider making additional funds available, including from the account created pursuant to paragraph 8 (c) of resolution 986 (1995), on an exceptional and reimbursable basis, to meet further the humanitarian needs of the people of Iraq;

7. Decides that, notwithstanding the provisions of resolution 661 (1990) and resolution 687 (1991) and for the duration of the present resolution, all applications outside the Oil-for-Food Programme submitted by the United Nations agencies, programmes and funds, other international organizations and non-governmental organizations (NGOs) for distribution or use in Iraq of emergency humanitarian supplies and equipment, other than medicines, health supplies and foodstuffs, shall be reviewed by the Committee established pursuant to resolution 661

(1990), under a 24-hour no-objection procedure;

8. Urges all parties concerned, consistent with the Geneva Conventions and the Hague Regulations, to allow full unimpeded access by international humanitarian organizations to all people of Iraq in need of assistance and to make available all necessary facilities for their operations and to promote the safety, security and freedom of movement of United Nations and associated personnel and their assets, as well as personnel of humanitarian organizations in Iraq in meeting such needs;

9. Directs the Committee established pursuant to resolution 661 (1990) to monitor closely the implementation of the provisions in paragraph 4 above and, in that regard, requests the Secretary-General to update the Committee on the measures as they are being taken and to consult with the Committee on prioritization of contracts for shipments of goods, other than foodstuffs, medicines, health and water sanitation related supplies;

10. Decides that the provisions contained in paragraph 4 of this resolution shall remain in force for a period of 45 days following the date of adoption of this resolution and may be subject to further renewal by the Council;

11. Requests the Secretary-General to take all measures required for the implementation of the present resolution and to report to the Security Council prior to the termination of the period defined in paragraph 10;

12. Decides to remain seized of the matter.

The document below reaffirmed the UN commitment to humanitarian aid and the reconstruction of Iraq following the U.S. invasion.

RESOLUTION 1483 (2003)

Adopted by the Security Council at its 4761st meeting, on 22 May 2003

The Security Council,

Recalling all its previous relevant resolutions,

Reaffirming the sovereignty and territorial integrity of Iraq,

Reaffirming also the importance of the disarmament of Iraqi weapons of mass destruction and of eventual confirmation of the disarmament of Iraq,

Stressing the right of the Iraqi people freely to determine their own political future and control their own natural resources, welcoming the commitment of all parties concerned to support the creation of an environment in which they may do so as soon as possible, and expressing resolve that the day when Iraqis govern themselves must come quickly,

Encouraging efforts by the people of Iraq to form a representative government based on the rule of law that affords equal rights and justice to all Iraqi citizens without regard to ethnicity, religion, or gender, and, in this connection, recalls resolution 1325 (2000) of 31 October 2000,

Welcoming the first steps of the Iraqi people in this regard, and noting in this connection the 15 April 2003 Nasiriyah statement and the 28 April 2003 Baghdad statement,

Resolved that the United Nations should play a vital role in humanitarian relief, the reconstruction of Iraq, and the restoration and establishment of national and local institutions for representative governance,

Noting the statement of 12 April 2003 by the Ministers of Finance and Central Bank Governors of the Group of Seven Industrialized Nations in which the members recognized the need for a multilateral effort to help rebuild and develop Iraq and for the need for assistance from the International Monetary Fund and the World Bank in these efforts,

Welcoming also the resumption of humanitarian assistance and the continuing efforts of the Secretary-General and the specialized agencies to provide food and medicine to the people of Iraq,

Welcoming the appointment by the Secretary-General of his Special Adviser on Iraq,

Affirming the need for accountability for crimes and atrocities committed by the previous Iraqi regime,

Stressing the need for respect for the archaeological, historical, cultural, and religious heritage of Iraq, and for the continued protection of archaeological, historical, cultural, and religious sites, museums, libraries, and monuments,

Noting the letter of 8 May 2003 from the Permanent Representatives of the United States of America and the United Kingdom of Great Britain and Northern Ireland to the President of the Security Council (S/2003/538) and recognizing the specific authorities, responsibilities, and obligations under applicable international law of these states as occupying powers under unified command (the "Authority"),

Noting further that other States that are not occupying powers are working now or in the future may work under the Authority,

Welcoming further the willingness of Member States to contribute to stability and security in Iraq by contributing personnel, equipment, and other resources under the Authority,

Concerned that many Kuwaitis and Third-State Nationals still are not accounted for since 2 August 1990,

Determining that the situation in Iraq, although improved, continues to constitute a threat to international peace and security,

Acting under Chapter VII of the Charter of the United Nations,

1. Appeals to Member States and concerned organizations to assist the people of Iraq in their efforts to reform their institutions and rebuild their country, and to contribute to conditions of stability and security in Iraq in accordance with this resolution;

2. Calls upon all Member States in a position to do so to respond immediately to the humanitarian appeals of the United Nations and other international organizations for Iraq and to help meet the humanitarian and other needs of the Iraqi people by providing food, medical supplies, and resources necessary for reconstruction and rehabilitation of Iraq's economic infrastructure;

3. Appeals to Member States to deny safe haven to those members of the previous Iraqi regime who are alleged to be responsible for crimes and atrocities and to support actions to bring them to justice;

4. Calls upon the Authority, consistent with the Charter of the United Nations and other relevant international law, to promote the welfare of the Iraqi people through the effective administration of the territory, including in particular working towards the restoration of conditions of security and stability and the creation of conditions in which the Iraqi people can freely determine their own political future;

5. Calls upon all concerned to comply fully with their obligations under international law including in particular the Geneva Conventions of 1949 and the Hague Regulations of 1907;

6. Calls upon the Authority and relevant organizations and individuals to continue efforts to locate, identify, and repatriate all Kuwaiti and Third-State Nationals or the remains of those present in Iraq on or after 2 August 1990, as well as the Kuwaiti archives, that the previous Iraqi regime failed to

undertake, and, in this regard, directs the High-Level Coordinator, in consultation with the International Committee of the Red Cross and the Tripartite Commission and with the appropriate support of the people of Iraq and in coordination with the Authority, to take steps to fulfil his mandate with respect to the fate of Kuwaiti and Third-State National missing persons and property;

7. Decides that all Member States shall take appropriate steps to facilitate the safe return to Iraqi institutions of Iraqi cultural property and other items of archaeological, historical, cultural, rare scientific, and religious importance illegally removed from the Iraq National Museum, the National Library, and other locations in Iraq since the adoption of resolution 661 (1990) of 6 August 1990, including by establishing a prohibition on trade in or transfer of such items and items with respect to which reasonable suspicion exists that they have been illegally removed, and calls upon the United Nations Educational, Scientific, and Cultural Organization, Interpol, and other international organizations, as appropriate, to assist in the implementation of this paragraph;

8. Requests the Secretary-General to appoint a Special Representative for Iraq whose independent responsibilities shall involve reporting regularly to the Council on his activities under this resolution, coordinating activities of the United Nations in post-conflict processes in Iraq, coordinating among United Nations and international agencies engaged in humanitarian assistance and reconstruction activities in Iraq, and, in coordination with the Authority, assisting the people of Iraq through:

(a) coordinating humanitarian and reconstruction assistance by United Nations agencies and between United Nations agencies and non-governmental organizations;

(b) promoting the safe, orderly, and voluntary return of refugees and displaced persons;

(c) working intensively with the Authority, the people of Iraq, and others concerned to advance efforts to restore and establish national and local institutions for representative governance, including by working together to facilitate a process leading to an internationally recognized, representative government of Iraq;

(d) facilitating the reconstruction of key infrastructure, in cooperation with other international organizations;

(e) promoting economic reconstruction and the conditions for sustainable development, including through coordination with national and regional organizations, as appropriate, civil society, donors, and the international financial institutions;

(f) encouraging international efforts to contribute to basic civilian administration functions;

(g) promoting the protection of human rights;

(h) encouraging international efforts to rebuild the capacity of the Iraqi civilian police force; and

(i) encouraging international efforts to promote legal and judicial reform;

9. Supports the formation, by the people of Iraq with the help of the Authority and working with the Special Representative, of an Iraqi interim administration as a transitional administration run by Iraqis, until an internationally recognized, representative government is established by the people of Iraq and assumes the responsibilities of the Authority;

10. Decides that, with the exception of prohibitions related to the sale or supply to Iraq of arms and related materiel other than those arms and related materiel required by the Authority to serve the purposes of this and other related resolutions, all prohibitions related to trade with Iraq and the provision of financial or economic resources to Iraq established by resolution 661 (1990) and subsequent relevant resolutions, including resolution 778 (1992) of 2 October 1992, shall no longer apply;

11. Reaffirms that Iraq must meet its disarmament obligations, encourages the United Kingdom of Great Britain and Northern Ireland and the United States of America to keep the Council informed of their activities in this regard, and underlines the intention of the Council to revisit the mandates of the United Nations Monitoring, Verification, and Inspection Commission and the International Atomic Energy Agency as set forth in resolutions 687 (1991) of 3 April 1991, 1284 (1999) of

17 December 1999, and 1441 (2002) of 8 November 2002;

12. Notes the establishment of a Development Fund for Iraq to be held by the Central Bank of Iraq and to be audited by independent public accountants approved by the International Advisory and Monitoring Board of the Development Fund for Iraq and looks forward to the early meeting of that International Advisory and Monitoring Board, whose members shall include duly qualified representatives of the Secretary-General, of the Managing Director of the International Monetary Fund, of the Director-General of the Arab Fund for Social and Economic Development, and of the President of the World Bank;

13. Notes further that the funds in the Development Fund for Iraq shall be disbursed at the direction of the Authority, in consultation with the Iraqi interim administration, for the purposes set out in paragraph 14 below;

14. Underlines that the Development Fund for Iraq shall be used in a transparent manner to meet the humanitarian needs of the Iraqi people, for the economic reconstruction and repair of Iraq's infrastructure, for the continued disarmament of Iraq, and for the costs of Iraqi civilian administration, and for other purposes benefiting the people of Iraq;

15. Calls upon the international financial institutions to assist the people of Iraq in the reconstruction and development of their economy and to facilitate assistance by the broader donor community, and welcomes the readiness of creditors, including those of the Paris Club, to seek a solution to Iraq's sovereign debt problems;

16. Requests also that the Secretary-General, in coordination with the Authority, continue the exercise of his responsibilities under Security Council resolution 1472 (2003) of 28 March 2003 and 1476 (2003) of 24 April 2003, for a period of six months following the adoption of this resolution, and terminate within this time period, in the most cost effective manner, the ongoing operations of the "Oil-for-Food" Programme (the "Programme"), both at headquarters level and in the field, transferring responsibility for the administration of any remaining activity under the Programme to the Authority, including by taking the following necessary measures:

(a) to facilitate as soon as possible the shipment and authenticated delivery of priority civilian goods as identified by the Secretary-General and representatives designated by him, in coordination with the Authority and the Iraqi interim administration, under approved and funded contracts previously concluded by the previous Government of Iraq, for the humanitarian relief of the people of Iraq, including, as necessary, negotiating adjustments in the terms or conditions of these contracts and respective letters of credit as set forth in paragraph 4 (d) of resolution 1472 (2003);

(b) to review, in light of changed circumstances, in coordination with the Authority and the Iraqi interim administration, the relative utility of each approved and funded contract with a view to determining whether such contracts contain items required to meet the needs of the people of Iraq both now and during reconstruction, and to postpone action on those contracts determined to be of questionable utility and the respective letters of credit until an internationally recognized, representative government of Iraq is in a position to make its own determination as to whether such contracts shall be fulfilled;

(c) to provide the Security Council within 21 days following the adoption of this resolution, for the Security Council's review and consideration, an estimated operating budget based on funds already set aside in the account established pursuant to paragraph 8 (d) of resolution 986 (1995) of 14 April 1995, identifying:

(i) all known and projected costs to the United Nations required to ensure the continued functioning of the activities associated with implementation of the present resolution, including operating and administrative expenses associated with the relevant United Nations agencies and programmes responsible for the implementation of the Programme both at Headquarters and in the field;

(ii) all known and projected costs associated with termination of the Programme;

(iii) all known and projected costs associated with restoring Government of Iraq funds that were provided by Member States to the Secretary-General as requested in paragraph 1 of resolution 778 (1992); and

(iv) all known and projected costs associated with the Special Representative and the qualified representative of the Secretary-General identified to serve on the International Advisory and Monitoring Board, for the six month time period defined above, following which these costs shall be borne by the United Nations;

(d) to consolidate into a single fund the accounts established pursuant to paragraphs 8 (a) and 8 (b) of resolution 986 (1995);

(e) to fulfil all remaining obligations related to the termination of the Programme, including negotiating, in the most cost effective manner, any necessary settlement payments, which shall be made from the escrow accounts established pursuant to paragraphs 8 (a) and 8 (b) of resolution 986 (1995), with those parties that previously have entered into contractual obligations with the Secretary-General under the Programme, and to determine, in coordination with the Authority and the Iraqi interim administration, the future status of contracts undertaken by the United Nations and related United Nations agencies under the accounts established pursuant to paragraphs 8 (b) and 8 (d) of resolution 986 (1995);

(f) to provide the Security Council, 30 days prior to the termination of the Programme, with a comprehensive strategy developed in close coordination with the Authority and the Iraqi interim administration that would lead to the delivery of all relevant documentation and the transfer of all operational responsibility of the Programme to the Authority;

17. Requests further that the Secretary-General transfer as soon as possible to the Development Fund for Iraq 1 billion United States dollars from unencumbered funds in the accounts established pursuant to paragraphs 8 (a) and 8 (b) of resolution 986 (1995), restore Government of Iraq funds that were provided by Member States to the Secretary-General as requested in paragraph 1 of resolution 778 (1992), and decides that, after deducting all relevant United Nations expenses associated with the shipment of authorized contracts and costs to the Programme outlined in paragraph 16 (c) above, including residual obligations, all surplus funds in the escrow accounts established pursuant to paragraphs 8 (a), 8 (b), 8 (d), and 8 (f) of resolution 986 (1995) shall be transferred at the earliest possible time to the Development Fund for Iraq;

18. Decides to terminate effective on the adoption of this resolution the functions related to the observation and monitoring activities undertaken by the Secretary-General under the Programme, including the monitoring of the export of petroleum and petroleum products from Iraq;

19. Decides to terminate the Committee established pursuant to paragraph 6 of resolution 661 (1990) at the conclusion of the six month period called for in paragraph 16 above and further decides that the Committee shall identify individuals and entities referred to in paragraph 23 below;

20. Decides that all export sales of petroleum, petroleum products, and natural gas from Iraq following the date of the adoption of this resolution shall be made consistent with prevailing international market best practices, to be audited by independent public accountants reporting to the International Advisory and Monitoring Board referred to in paragraph 12 above in order to ensure transparency, and decides further that, except as provided in paragraph 21 below, all proceeds from such sales shall be deposited into the Development Fund for Iraq until such time as an internationally recognized, representative government of Iraq is properly constituted;

21. Decides further that 5 per cent of the proceeds referred to in paragraph 20 above shall be deposited into the Compensation Fund established in accordance with resolution 687 (1991) and subsequent relevant resolutions and that, unless an internationally recognized, representative government of Iraq and the Governing Council of the United Nations Compensation Commission, in the exercise of its authority over methods of ensuring that payments are made into the Compensation Fund, decide otherwise, this requirement shall be binding on a properly constituted, internationally recognized, representative government of Iraq and any successor thereto;

22. Noting the relevance of the establishment of an internationally recognized, representative government of Iraq and the desirability of prompt completion of the restructuring of Iraq's debt as referred to in paragraph 15 above, further decides that, until December 31, 2007, unless the Council

decides otherwise, petroleum, petroleum products, and natural gas originating in Iraq shall be immune, until title passes to the initial purchaser from legal proceedings against them and not be subject to any form of attachment, garnishment, or execution, and that all States shall take any steps that may be necessary under their respective domestic legal systems to assure this protection, and that proceeds and obligations arising from sales thereof, as well as the Development Fund for Iraq, shall enjoy privileges and immunities equivalent to those enjoyed by the United Nations except that the abovementioned privileges and immunities will not apply with respect to any legal proceeding in which recourse to such proceeds or obligations is necessary to satisfy liability for damages assessed in connection with an ecological accident, including an oil spill, that occurs after the date of adoption of this resolution;

23. Decides that all Member States in which there are:

(a) funds or other financial assets or economic resources of the previous Government of Iraq or its state bodies, corporations, or agencies, located outside Iraq as of the date of this resolution, or

(b) funds or other financial assets or economic resources that have been removed from Iraq, or acquired, by Saddam Hussein or other senior officials of the former Iraqi regime and their immediate family members, including entities owned or controlled, directly or indirectly, by them or by persons acting on their behalf or at their direction, shall freeze without delay those funds or other financial assets or economic resources and, unless these funds or other financial assets or economic resources are themselves the subject of a prior judicial, administrative, or arbitral lien or judgement, immediately shall cause their transfer to the Development Fund for Iraq, it being understood that, unless otherwise addressed, claims made by private individuals or non-government entities on those transferred funds or other financial assets may be presented to the internationally recognized, representative government of Iraq; and decides further that all such funds or other financial assets or economic resources shall enjoy the same privileges, immunities, and protections as provided under paragraph 22;

24. Requests the Secretary-General to report to the Council at regular intervals on the work of the Special Representative with respect to the implementation of this resolution and on the work of the International Advisory and Monitoring Board and encourages the United Kingdom of Great Britain and Northern Ireland and the United States of America to inform the Council at regular intervals of their efforts under this resolution;

25. Decides to review the implementation of this resolution within twelve months of adoption and to consider further steps that might be necessary;

26. Calls upon Member States and international and regional organizations to contribute to the implementation of this resolution;

27. Decides to remain seized of this matter.

Source: *"Security Council Resolutions Regarding Iraq"*
<http://achilles.net/~sal/un-resolutions.html>.

APPENDIX

REFERENCES

1. GENERAL

Arkoun, Mohammed. *Rethinking Islam: Common Questions, Uncommon Answers.* Translated and edited by Robert D. Lee. Boulder, Colo.: Westview Press, 1994.

Bennis, Phyllis and Michel Moushabeck, eds. *Altered States: A Reader in the New World Order.* New York: Olive Branch Press, 1993.

Cleveland, William. *A History of the Modern Middle East.* Boulder, Colo.: Westview Press, 1999.

Copeland, Miles. *The Game of Nations.* London: Weidenfeld & Nicolson, 1970.

Danzer, Gerald A. *An Atlas of World History.* Ann Arbor, Mich.: Borders, 2000.

Fay, Mary Ann, ed. *Auto/Biography and the Construction of Identity and Community in the Middle East.* New York: Palgrave, 2002.

Freedman, Robert O. *Soviet Policy toward the Middle East since 1970.* New York: Praeger, 1982.

Freedman, ed. *The Middle East Enters the Twenty-first Century.* Gainesville: University Press of Florida, 2003.

Goldschmidt, Arthur, Jr. *A Concise History of the Middle East.* Sixth edition. Boulder, Colo.: Westview Press, 1999.

Hinnebusch, Raymond and Anoushiravan Ehteshami, eds. *The Foreign Policies of Middle East States.* Boulder, Colo.: Lynne Rienner, 2002.

Kingston, Paul W. T. *Britain and the Politics of Modernization in the Middle East, 1945–1958.* Cambridge & New York: Cambridge University Press, 1996.

Lesch, David W. *1979: The Year that Shaped the Modern Middle East.* Boulder, Colo.: Westview Press, 2001.

Lewis, Bernard. *What Went Wrong? Western Impact and Middle Eastern Response.* New York: Oxford University Press, 2002.

Louis, William Roger and Roger Owen, eds. *A Revolutionary Year: The Middle East in 1958.* Washington, D.C.: Woodrow Wilson Center Press, 2002.

Murden, Simon W. *Islam, the Middle East, and the New Global Hegemony.* Boulder, Colo.: Lynne Rienner, 2002.

Nolte, Richard H., ed. *The Modern Middle East.* New York: Atherton, 1963.

Potter, Lawrence G. and Gary G. Sick, eds. *Security in the Persian Gulf: Origins, Obstacles, and the Search for Consensus.* New York: Palgrave, 2002.

2. ALGERIA

Aussaresses, Paul. *The Battle of the Casbah: Terrorism and Counter-Terrorism in Algeria 1955-1957.* Translated by Robert L. Miller. New York: Enigma, 2002.

Courriere, Yves. *Les Fils de la Toussanit: La Guerre d'Algerie.* Paris: Fayard, 1968.

Courriere. *L'heure des Colonels: La Guerre d'Algerie.* Paris: Fayard, 1970.

Courriere. *Les temps des Leopards: La Guerre d'Algerie.* Paris: Fayard, 1969.

Entelis, John P. and Phillip C. Naylor, eds. *State and Society in Algeria.* Boulder, Colo.: Westview Press, 1992.

Horne, Alistair. *A Savage War of Peace: Algeria, 1954–1962.* New York: Viking, 1977.

Le Mire, Henri. *Histoire militaire de la guerre d'Algerie.* Paris: A. Michel, 1982.

Martinez, Luis. *The Algerian Civil War, 1990–1998.* New York: Columbia University Press, 2000.

Quandt, William B. *Between Ballots and Bullets: Algeria's Transition from Authoritarianism.* Washington, D.C.: Brookings Institution, 1998.

Ruedy, John. *Modern Algeria: The Origins and Development of a Nation.* Bloomington: University of Indiana Press, 1992.

Stora, Benjamin. *Algeria, 1830–2000: A Short History.* Ithaca, N.Y.: Cornell University Press, 2001.

Talbott, John. *The War without a Name: France in Algeria, 1954–1962.* New York: Knopf, 1980.

Thomas, Martin. *The French North African Crisis: Colonial Breakdown and Anglo-French Relations, 1954–1962.* New York: St. Martin's Press, 2000.

Wall, Irwin M. *France, the United States, and the Algerian War.* Berkeley: University of California Press, 2001.

Willis, Michael. *The Islamist Challenge in Algeria: A Political History.* Washington Square, N.Y.: New York University Press, 1997.

3. ARAB-ISRAELI CONFLICT

Abu-Lughod, Ibrahim, ed. *The Arab-Israeli Confrontation of June 1967: An Arab Perspective.* Evanston, Ill.: Northwestern University Press, 1970.

Bar-On, Mordechai. *The Gates of Gaza: Israel's Road to Suez and Back, 1955–1957.* New York: St. Martin's Press, 1994.

Bowie, Robert R. *Suez 1956.* New York: Oxford University Press, 1974.

Cobban, Helena. *The Israeli-Syrian Peace Talks: 1991–96 and Beyond.* Washington, D.C.: U.S. Institute of Peace Press, 1999.

Eisenberg, Laura Zitrain and Neil Caplan. *Negotiating Arab-Israeli Peace: Patterns, Problems, Possibilities.* Bloomington: University of Indiana Press, 1998.

Hof, Frederic C. *Line of Battle, Border of Peace? The Line of June 4, 1967.* Washington, D.C.: Middle East Insight, 1999.

Israelyan, Viktor. *Inside the Kremlin during the Yom Kippur War.* University Park: Pennsylvania State University Press, 1995.

Khouri, Fred J. *The Arab-Israeli Dilemma.* Syracuse, N.Y.: Syracuse University Press, 1985.

Louis, Wm. Roger and Roger Owen, eds. *Suez 1956: The Crisis and Its Consequences.* Oxford: Clarendon Press, 1989.

Love, Kenneth. *Suez: The Twice-Fought War, A History.* New York: McGraw-Hill, 1969.

Maoz, Moshe. *Syria and Israel: From War to Peacemaking.* Oxford & New York: Oxford University Press, 1995.

Moskin, Robert J. *Among Lions: The Battle for Jerusalem, June 5–7, 1967.* New York: Arbor House, 1982.

Neff, Donald. *Warriors for Jerusalem: The Six Days that Changed the Middle East.* New York: Linden/Simon & Schuster, 1984.

Oren, Michael B. *Six Days of War: June 1967 and the Making of the Modern Middle East.* New York & Oxford: Oxford University Press, 2002.

Pappe, Ilan. *The Making of the Arab-Israeli Conflict 1947–1951.* London & New York: I. B. Tauris, 1992.

Quandt, William B. *Peace Process: American Diplomacy and the Arab-Israeli Conflict since 1967.* Revised edition. Berkeley: University of California Press, 2001.

Rabinovich, Itamar. *The Brink of Peace: The Israeli-Syrian Negotiations.* Princeton: Princeton University Press, 1998.

Savir, Uri. *The Process: 1,100 Days that Changed the Middle East.* New York: Random House, 1998.

Shazly, Saad el-. *The Crossing of the Suez.* San Francisco: American Mideast Research, 1980.

Smith, Charles D. *Palestine and the Arab-Israeli Conflict.* New York: St. Martin's Press, 2001.

Stein, Kenneth W. *Heroic Diplomacy: Sadat, Kissinger, Carter, Begin, and the Quest for Arab-Israeli Peace.* New York: Routledge, 1999.

Thomas, Hugh. *Suez.* New York: Harper & Row, 1967.

Tomeh, George J., ed. *United Nations Resolutions on Palestine and the Arab-Israeli Conflict: 1947–1974.* Volume 1. Revised edition. Washington, D.C.: Institute for Palestine Studies, 1987.

Touval, Saadia. *The Peace Brokers: Mediators in the Arab-Israeli Conflict, 1948–1979.* Princeton: Princeton University Press, 1982.

Troen, Selwin Ilan and Moshe Shemesh, eds. *The Suez-Sinai Crisis 1956: Retrospective and Reappraisal.* New York: Columbia University Press, 1990.

4. ECONOMICS

Chaudhry, Kiren Aziz. *The Price of Wealth: Economies and Institutions in the Middle East.* Ithaca, N.Y.: Cornell University Press, 1997.

El-Ghonemy, M. Riad. *Affluence and Poverty in the Middle East.* New York: Routledge, 1998.

Friedman, Thomas. *The Lexus and the Olive Tree: Understanding Globalization.* New York: Anchor, 2000.

Harik, Iliya and Denis J. Sullivan, eds. *Privatization and Liberalization in the Middle East.* Bloomington: Indiana University Press, 1992.

Hirst, Paul and Graham Thompson. *Globalization in Question: The International Economy and the Possibilities of Governance.* Cambridge, Mass.: Polity, 1996.

Hudson, Michael, ed. *Middle East Dilemma: The Politics and Economics of Arab Integration.* New York: Columbia University Press, 1999.

Hutton, Will and Anthony Giddens, eds. *On the Edge: Living with Global Capitalism.* London: Cape, 2000.

Kavoossi, Masoud. *The Globalization of Business and the Middle East: Opportunities and Constraints.* Westport, Conn.: Quorom, 2000.

Kunz, Diane B. *The Economic Diplomacy of the Suez Crisis.* Chapel Hill: University of North Carolina Press, 1991.

Maitra, Priyatosh. *The Globalization of Capitalism in Third World Countries.* Westport, Conn.: Praeger, 1996.

Niblock, Tim and Emma Murphy. *Economic and Political Liberalization in the Middle East.* London: British Academic Press, 1993.

Owen, Roger and Sevket Pamuk. *A History of Middle East Economies in the Twentieth Century.* Cambridge, Mass.: Harvard University Press, 1999.

Richards, Alan and John Waterbury. *A Political Economy of the Middle East.* Boulder, Colo.: Westview Press, 1996.

Rivlin, Paul. *Economic Policy and Performance in the Arab World.* Boulder, Colo.: Lynne Reinner, 2001.

Shafik, Nemat. *Globalization, Regionalism and Growth: Economic Prospects for the Middle East and North Africa.* Turin, Italy: Fondazione Giovanni Agnelli, 1996.

Wilson, Rodney. *Economic Development in the Middle East.* London: Routledge, 1995.

5. EGYPT

Abdel-Malek, Anouar. *Egypt: Military Society.* New York: Random House, 1968.

Beattie, Kirk J. *Egypt during the Nasser Years: Ideology, Politics, and Civil Society.* Boulder, Colo.: Westview Press, 1994.

Boutros-Ghali, Boutros. *Egypt's Road to Jerusalem: A Diplomat's Story of the Struggle for Peace in the Middle East.* New York: Random House, 1997.

Gershoni, Israel and James Jankowski. *Redefining the Egyptian Nation, 1930–1945.* Cambridge & New York: Cambridge University Press, 1995.

Goldschmidt, Arthur. *Modern Egypt: The Formation of a Nation-State.* Boulder, Colo.: Westview Press, 1988.

Gordon, Joel. *Nasser's Blessed Movement: Egypt's Free Officers and the July Revolution.* New York: Oxford University Press, 1992.

Heikal, Mohamed H. *Cutting the Lion's Tail: Suez through Egyptian Eyes.* London: Deutsch, 1986.

Hopwood, Derek. *Egypt: Politics and Society 1945–1990.* London & New York: Routledge, 1993.

Jankowski. *Nasser's Egypt: Arab Nationalism, and the United Arab Republic.* Boulder, Colo.: Lynne Rienner, 2001.

Mansfield, Peter. *Nasser's Egypt.* Baltimore: Penguin, 1965.

Podeh, Elie. *The Decline of Arab Unity: The Rise and Fall of the United Arab Republic.* Brighton, U.K. & Portland, Ore.: Sussex Academic Press, 1999.

Vatikiotis, P. J. *Nasser and His Generation.* New York: St. Martin's Press, 1978.

Woodward, Peter. *Nasser.* London & New York: Longman, 1992.

6. IRAN & IRAQ

Abrahamian, Ervand. *Iran Between Two Revolutions.* Princeton: Princeton University Press, 1982.

Akhavi, Shahrough. *Religion and Politics in Contemporary Iran: Clergy-State Relations in the Pahlavi Period*. Albany: State University of New York Press, 1980.

Amjad, Mohammed. *Iran: From Royal Dictatorship to Theocracy*. New York & London: Greenwood Press, 1989.

Arjomand, Said Amir. *The Turban for the Crown: The Islamic Revolution in Iran*. New York: Oxford University Press, 1988.

Batatu, Hanna. *The Old Social Classes and the Revolutionary Movements of Iraq*. Princeton: Princeton University Press, 1978.

Bill, James A. *The Eagle and the Lion: The Tragedy of American-Iranian Relations*. New Haven: Yale University Press, 1988.

Bill. *The Politics of Iran: Groups, Classes and Modernization*. Columbus, Ohio: Merrill, 1972.

Boroujerdi, Mehrzad. *Iranian Intellectuals and the West: The Tormented Triumph of Nativism*. Syracuse, N.Y.: Syracuse University Press, 1996.

Calabrese, John, ed. *The Future of Iraq*. Washington, D.C.: Middle East Institute, 1997.

Dann, Uriel. *Iraq under Qassem: A Political History 1958-1963*. New York: Praeger, 1969.

Diba, Farhad. *Mohammad Mossadegh: A Political Biography*. London & Dover, N.H.: Croom Helm, 1986.

Farouk-Sluglett, Marion and Peter Sluglett. *Iraq Since 1958: From Revolution to Dictatorship*. London & New York: KPI, 1987.

Goode, James. *The United States and Iran: In the Shadow of Musaddiq*. London: Macmillan, 1997.

Haj, Samira. *The Making of Iraq, 1900-1963: Capital, Power and Ideology*. New York: State University of New York Press, 1997.

Helms, Christine Moss. *Iraq: Eastern Flank of the Arab World*. Washington, D.C.: Brookings Institution, 1984.

Hooglund, Eric, ed. *Twenty Years of Islamic Revolution: Political and Social Transition in Iran since 1979*. Syracuse, N.Y.: Syracuse University Press, 2002.

Katouzian, Homa. *Musaddiq and the Struggle for Power in Iran*. London & New York: I.B. Tauris, 1990.

Katouzian. *The Political Economy of Modern Iran: Despotism and Pseudo-Modernism, 1926-1979*. London: Macmillan, 1981.

Keddie, Nikki R. *Iran and the Muslim World: Resistance and Revolution*. New York: New York University Press, 1995.

Keddie. *Roots of Revolution: An Interpretive History of Modern Iran*. New Haven: Yale University Press, 1981.

Khadduri, Majid. *Republican Iraq: A Study in Iraqi Politics since the Revolution of 1958*. London: Oxford University Press, 1969.

Lenczowski, George, ed. *Iran under the Pahlavis*. Stanford, Cal.: Hoover Institution Press, 1979.

Marr, Phebe. *The Modern History of Iraq*. Boulder, Colo.: Westview Press, 1985.

Menashri, David. *Post-Revolutionary Politics in Iran: Religion, Society and Power*. London & Portland, Ore.: Frank Cass, 2001.

Milani, Mohsen M. *The Making of Iran's Islamic Revolution: From Monarchy to Islamic Republic*. Boulder, Colo.: Westview Press, 1988.

Nonneman, Gerd. *Iraq, the Gulf States, and the War: A Changing Relationship, 1980-1986 and Beyond*. London & Atlantic Highlands, N.J.: Ithaca Press, 1986.

Rajaee, Farhang, ed. *The Iran-Iraq War: The Politics of Aggression*. Gainesville: University Press of Florida, 1993.

Ramazani, R. K., ed. *Iran's Revolution: The Search for Consensus*. Bloomington: Indiana University Press, 1990.

Roosevelt, Kermit. *Countercoup: The Struggle for the Control of Iran*. New York: McGraw-Hill, 1979.

Saikal, Amin. *The Rise and Fall of the Shah*. Princeton: Princeton University Press, 1980.

Sick, Gary. *All Fall Down: America's Tragic Encounter with Iran*. New York: Random House, 1985.

7. ISRAEL

Barnavi, Eli. *Une Histoire Moderne D'Israel*. Paris: Flammarion, 1988.

Cohen, Avner. *Israel and the Bomb*. New York: Columbia University Press, 1998.

Drake, Laura. *Israel's Nuclear Development and Strategy: Future Ramifications for the Middle East Regional Balance*. League of Arab States Occasional Paper. No. 1. February 1996.

Druks, Herbert. *The Uncertain Alliance: The U.S. and Israel from Kennedy to the Peace Process*. Westport, Conn.: Greenwood Press, 2001.

Evron, Yair. *Israel's Nuclear Dilemma*. London: Routledge, 1994.

Feldman, Shai. *Israeli Nuclear Deterrence: A Strategy for the 1980s*. New York: Columbia University Press, 1982.

Feldman. *Nuclear Weapons and Arms Control in the Middle East*. Cambridge, Mass.: MIT Press, 1997.

Gaffney, Mark. *Dimona, The Third Temple?: The Story Behind the Vanunu Revelation*. Brattleboro, Vt.: Amana, 1989.

Garfinkle, Adam. *Politics and Society in Modern Israel: Myths and Realities*. London: M.E. Sharpe, 2000.

Halsell, Grace. *Journey to Jerusalem*. New York: Macmillan, 1981.

Kimmerling, Baruch. *The Invention and Decline of Israeliness: State, Society, and the Military*. Berkeley: University of California Press, 2001.

Reich, Bernard and Gershon R. Kieval, eds. *Israeli Politics in the 1990s: Key Domestic and Foreign Policy Factors*. New York: Greenwood Press, 1991.

Rubenberg, Cheryl A. *Israel and the American National Interest: A Critical Examination*. Urbana: University of Illinois Press, 1986.

Sachar, Howard. *A History of Israel: From the Rise of Zionism to Our Time*. New York: Knopf, 1996.

Safran, Nadav. *Israel: The Embattled Ally*. Cambridge, Mass.: Belknap Press, 1981.

Sandler, Shmuel. *The State of Israel, the Land of Israel: The Statist and Ethnonational Dimensions of Foreign Policy*. Westport, Conn.: Greenwood Press, 1993.

Schiff, Zeev and Ehud Yaari. *Israel's Lebanon War*. New York: Simon & Schuster, 1984.

Schulze, Kirsten E. *Israel's Covert Diplomacy in Lebanon*. New York: St. Martin's Press, 1998.

Segev, Tom. *1949: The First Israelis*. New York: Free Press, 1986.

Shapira, Anita. *Land and Power: The Zionist Resort to Force, 1881-1948*. Translated by William Templar. New York: Oxford University Press, 1992.

Sprinzak, Ehud. *The Ascendance of Israel's Radical Right*. New York: Oxford University Press, 1991.

Sternhell, Zeev. *The Founding Myths of Israel: Nationalism, Socialism, and the Making of the Jewish State*. Translated by David Maisel. Princeton: Princeton University Press, 1998.

REFERENCES

Viorst, Milton. *What Shall I Do With These People? Jews and the Fractious Politics of Judaism.* New York: Free Press, 2002.

8. ISRAELI-PALESTINIAN CONFLICT

Abed, George T. *The Economic Viability of a Palestinian State.* Washington, D.C.: Institute for Palestine Studies, 1990.

Abu-Sitta, Salman H. *The Palestinian Nakba, 1948: The Register of Depopulated Localities in Palestine.* Second revised edition. London: Palestinian Return Centre, 2000.

Aronson, Geoffrey. *Settlements and the Israel-Palestinian Negotiations: An Overview.* Washington, D.C.: Institute for Palestine Studies, 1996.

Bar-Simon-Tov, Yaacov. *Israel and the Peace Process, 1977–1982: In Search of Legitimacy for Peace.* Albany: State University of New York Press, 1994.

Becker, Jillian. *The PLO: The Rise and Fall of the Palestine Liberation Organization.* New York: St. Martin's Press, 1984.

Cobban, Helena. *The Palestine Liberation Organization: People, Power, and Politics.* Cambridge & New York: Cambridge University Press, 1984.

Dumper, Michael. *The Politics of Sacred Space: The Old City of Jerusalem in the Middle East Conflict.* Boulder, Colo.: Lynne Rienner, 2002.

Finkelstein, Norman G. *Image and Reality of the Israel-Palestine Conflict.* London: Verso, 1995.

Freedman, Robert O., ed. *The Intifada: Its Impact on Israel, the Arab World, and the Superpowers.* Miami: Florida International University Press, 1991.

Greenstein, Ran. *Geneologies of Conflict: Class, Identity, and State in Palestine/Israel and South Africa.* Hanover, N.H.: University Press of New England, 1995.

Gresh, Alain. *The PLO: The Struggle Within.* London: Zed, 1985.

Hass, Amira. *Drinking the Sea at Gaza: Days and Nights in a Land under Siege.* New York: Metropolitan, 1999.

Israeli, Raphael. *Jerusalem Divided: The Armistice Regime, 1947–1967.* Portland, Ore.: Frank Cass, 2002.

Kimmerling, Baruch and Joel S. Migdal. *Palestinians: The Making of a People.* New York: Free Press, 1993.

Kozodoy, Neal, ed. *The Mideast Peace Process: An Autopsy.* San Francisco: Encounter Books, 2002.

Lapidoth, Ruth and Moshe Hirsch, eds. *The Jerusalem Question and Its Resolution: Selected Documents.* Boston: M. Nijhoff, 1994.

Lockman, Zachary and Joel Beinin, eds. *Intifada: The Palestinian Uprising against Israeli Occupation.* Boston: South End, 1989.

Makovsky, David. *Making Peace with the PLO: The Rabin Government's Road to the Oslo Accords.* Boulder, Colo.: Westview Press, 1996.

Masalha, Nur. *Expulsion of the Palestinians: The Concept of "Transfer" in Zionist Political Thought, 1882–1948.* Washington, D.C.: Institute for Palestinian Studies, 1992.

Mishal, Shaul. *The PLO under Arafat: Between Gun and Olive Branch.* New Haven: Yale University Press, 1986.

Morris, Benny. *The Birth of the Palestinian Refugee Problem, 1947–1949.* Cambridge & New York: Cambridge University Press, 1987.

Morris. *1948 and After: Israel and the Palestinians.* New York: Oxford University Press, 1990.

Muslih, Muhammad Y. *The Origins of Palestinian Nationalism.* New York: Columbia University Press, 1988.

Oren, Michael B. *Six Days of War: June 1967 and the Making of the Modern Middle East.* Oxford & New York: Oxford University Press, 2002.

Ovendale, Ritchie. *Britain, the United States, and the End of the Palestine Mandate, 1942–1948.* London: Royal Historical Society, 1989.

Pappe, Ilan, ed. *The Israel/Palestine Question.* New York: Routledge, 1999.

Pemberton, Danny. *The People of Nowhere: The Palestinian Vision of Home.* New York: Times, 1991.

Peretz, Don. *Palestinians, Refugees, and the Middle East Peace Process.* Washington, D.C.: United States Institute of Peace Press, 1993.

Quandt, William B., Fuad Jabber, and Ann Mosely Lesch. *The Politics of Palestinian Nationalism.* Berkeley: University of California Press, 1973.

Reich, Bernard, ed. *Arab-Israeli Conflict and Conciliation.* Westport, Conn.: Praeger, 1995.

Robinson, Glenn E. *Building a Palestinian State: The Incomplete Revolution.* Bloomington: University of Indiana Press, 1997.

Rogan, Eugene L. and Avi Shlaim, eds. *The War for Palestine: Rewriting the History of 1948.* New York: Cambridge University Press, 2001.

Rubin, Barry. *Revolution until Victory? The Politics and History of the PLO.* Cambridge, Mass.: Harvard University Press, 1994.

Sahliyeh, Emile. *In Search of Leadership: West Bank Politics.* Washington, D.C.: Brookings Institution, 1988.

Said, Edward W. *The Politics of Dispossession.* New York: Pantheon, 1994.

Sayigh, Yezid. *Armed Struggle and the Search for State: The Palestinian National Movement 1949–1993.* New York: Oxford University Press, 1997.

Schiff, Zeev and Ehud Yaari. *Intifada: The Palestinian Uprising–Israel's Third Front.* New York: Simon & Schuster, 1990.

Sela, Avraham. *The PLO and Israel: From Armed Conflict to Political Solution, 1964–1994.* New York: St. Martin's Press, 1997.

Shah, Samira. *The By-pass Road Network in the West Bank: An Analysis of the Effects of the Network on the Palestinian Territories.* Ramallah, Palestine: al-Haq, 1997.

Watson, Geoffrey R. *The Oslo Accords: International Law and the Israeli-Palestinian Peace Agreements.* Oxford & New York: Oxford University Press, 2000.

9. JORDAN, LEBANON & SYRIA

Abu Odeh, Adnan. *Jordanians, Palestinians and the Hashemite Kingdom in the Middle East Peace Process.* Washington, D.C.: United States Institute of Peace Press, 1999.

Bailey, Clinton. *Jordan's Palestinian Challenge, 1948–1983: A Political History.* Boulder, Colo.: Westview Press, 1984.

Dann, Uriel. *King Hussein and the Challenge of Arab Radicalism: Jordan, 1955–1967.* New York: Oxford University Press, 1989.

Drysdale, Alasdair and Raymond Hinnebusch. *Syria and the Middle East Peace Process.* New York: Council on Foreign Relations Press, 1991.

Dupuy, Trevor N. and Paul Martell. *Flawed Victory: The Arab-Israeli Conflict and the 1982 War in Lebanon.* Fairfax, Va.: Hero, 1986.

Fisk, Robert. *Pity the Nation: Lebanon at War.* Oxford: Oxford University Press, 1991.

Joffe, George, ed. *Jordan in Transition*. New York: Palgrave, 2002.

Khalidi, Walid. *Conflict and Violence in Lebanon: A Confrontation in the Middle East*. Cambridge, Mass.: Harvard University Center for International Affairs, 1979.

Lynch, Marc. *State Interests and Public Spheres: The International Politics of Jordan's Identity*. New York: Columbia University Press, 1999.

Mackinlay, John. *The Peacekeepers: An Assessment of Peacekeeping Operations at the Arab-Israeli Interface*. London & Boston: Unwin Hyman, 1989.

Massad, Joseph A. *Colonial Effects: The Making of National Identity in Jordan*. New York: Columbia University Press, 2001.

McDermott, Anthony and Kjell Skjelsbaek, eds. *The Multinational Force in Beirut, 1982–1984*. Miami: Florida International University Press, 1991.

Perthes, Volker. *The Political Economy of Syria under Asad*. London: I. B. Tauris, 1995.

Picard, Elizabeth. *The Lebanese Shi`a and Political Violence*. Geneva: United Nations Research Institute for Social Development, 1993.

Pogany, Istvan S. *The Arab League and Peacekeeping in the Lebanon*. New York: St. Martin's Press, 1987.

Rabinovich, Itamar. *The War for Lebanon, 1970–1985*. Ithaca, N.Y.: Cornell University Press, 1985.

Ryan, Curtis R. *Jordan in Transition: From Hussein to Abdullah*. Boulder, Colo.: Lynne Rienner, 2002.

Salibi, Kamal. *A House of Many Mansions: The History of Lebanon Reconsidered*. Berkeley: University of California Press, 1988.

Salibi. *The Modern History of Jordan*. London & New York: I. B. Tauris, 1993.

Seale, Patrick. *Asad of Syria: The Struggle for the Middle East*. London: I. B. Tauris, 1988.

Thakur, Ramesh C. *International Peacekeeping in Lebanon: United Nations Authority and Multinational Force*. Boulder, Colo.: Westview Press, 1987.

Winckler, Onn. *Demographic Developments and Population Policies in Ba`thist Syria*. Brighton, U.K.: Sussex Academic Press, 1999.

Zisser, Eyal. *Asad's Legacy: Syria in Transition*. London: C. Hurst, 2000.

10. MEMOIRS, AUTOBIOGRAPHIES & PRIMARY DOCUMENTS

Baker, James A., III. *The Politics of Diplomacy: Revolution, War, and Peace, 1989–1992*. New York: Putnam, 1995.

Dayan, Moshe. *Moshe Dayan: Story of My Life*. New York: Morrow, 1976.

Eban, Abba. *Abba Eban: An Autobiography*. London: Weidenfeld & Nicolson, 1977.

Eisenhower, Dwight D. *Waging Peace, 1956–1961*. Garden City, N.Y.: Doubleday, 1965.

Falle, Sir Samuel. *My Lucky Life in War, Revolution, Peace and Diplomacy*. Sussex: Book Guild, 1996.

Khomeini, Ayatollah Ruhollah. *Islam and Revolution: Writings and Declarations of Imam Khomeini*. Translated and annotated by Hamid Algar. London: KPI, 1981.

Kissinger, Henry. *Years of Upheaval*. Boston: Little, Brown, 1982.

Macmillan, Harold. *Riding the Storm, 1956–1959*. New York: Harper & Row, 1971.

Meir, Golda. *My Life*. New York: Putnam, 1975.

Mohi El Din, Khaled. *Memories of a Revolution: Egypt, 1952*. Cairo: American University in Cairo Press, 1995.

Murphy, Robert. *Diplomat among the Warriors*. Garden City, N.Y.: Doubleday, 1964.

Nasser, Gamal Abdel. *Egypt's Liberation: The Philosophy of the Revolution*. Cairo: Information Department, 1954.

Neguib, Mohammed. *Egypt's Destiny: A Personal Statement*. Garden City, N.Y.: Doubleday, 1955.

Nixon, Richard M. *The Memoirs of Richard Nixon*. New York: Grosset & Dunlap, 1978.

Pahlavi, Muhammad Reza. *Answer to History*. New York: Stein & Day, 1980.

Sadat, Anwar el-. *In Search of Identity: An Autobiography*. New York: Harper & Row, 1978.

Sadat. *Revolt on the Nile*. New York: John Day, 1957.

Truman, Harry S. *Memoirs: Years of Trial and Hope*. New York: Doubleday, 1956.

11. OIL

Alnasrawi, Abbas. *OPEC in a Changing World Economy*. Baltimore: Johns Hopkins University Press, 1985.

Amuzegar, Jahangir. *Managing the Oil Wealth: OPEC's Windfalls and Pitfalls*. London: I. B. Tauris, 1999.

Elm, Mostafa. *Oil, Power, and Principle: Iran's Oil Nationalization and Its Aftermath*. Syracuse, N.Y.: Syracuse University Press, 1992.

Frankel, Paul H. *Essentials of Petroleum: A Key to Oil Economics*. London: Cass, 1969.

Ghanem, Shukri. *OPEC: The Rise and Fall of an Exclusive Club*. New York: KPI, 1986.

Sampson, Anthony. *The Seven Sisters: The Great Oil Companies and the World They Shaped*. New York: Viking, 1975.

Shwadran, Benjamin. *The Middle East, Oil, and the Great Powers*. Revised edition. New York: Wiley, 1974.

Skeet, Ian. *OPEC: Twenty-five Years of Prices and Politics*. Cambridge & New York: Cambridge University Press, 1988.

Terzian, Philip. *OPEC: The Inside Story*. London: Zed, 1985.

Turner, Louis. *Oil Companies in the International System*. London: Royal Institute of International Affairs, 1978.

Yergin, Daniel. *The Prize: The Epic Quest for Oil, Money, and Power*. New York: Simon & Schuster, 1990.

12. PERSIAN GULF WAR (1990–1991)

Atkinson, Rick. *Crusade: The Untold Story of the Persian Gulf War*. New York: Houghton Mifflin, 1993.

Freedman, Lawrence and Efraim Karsh. *The Gulf Conflict, 1990–1991: Diplomacy and War in the New World Order*. Princeton: Princeton University Press, 1993.

Gordon, Michael and General Bernard E. Trainer. *The Generals' War: The Inside Story of the Conflict in the Gulf*. Boston: Little, Brown, 1995.

Khadduri, Majid and Edmund Ghareeb. *War in the Gulf, 1990–1991: The Iraq-Kuwait Conflict and Its Implications*. New York: Oxford University Press, 1997.

Sifry, Micah L. and Christopher Cerf, eds. *The Gulf War Reader*. New York: Times Books, 1991.

U.S. News & World Report. *Triumph Without Victory: The History of the Persian Gulf War*. New York: Times Books, 1993.

13. POLITICAL ENVIRONMENT

Abootalebi, Ali R. *Islam and Democracy: State-Society Relations in Developing Countries, 1980–1994*. New York: Garland, 2000.

Ajami, Fouad. *The Dream Palace of the Arabs: A Generation's Odyssey*. New York: Pantheon, 1998.

Ayubi, Nazih N. *Political Islam: Religion and Politics in the Arab World.* London & New York: Routledge, 1991.

Beinin, Joel and Joe Stork, eds. *Political Islam: Essays from Middle East Report.* Berkeley: University of California Press, 1997.

Bill, James A. and Robert Springborg. *Politics in the Middle East.* New York: HarperCollins, 1994.

Brynen, Rex, Bahgat Korany, and Paul Noble, eds. *Political Liberalization and Democratization in the Arab World.* 2 volumes. Boulder, Colo.: Lynne Rienner, 1995, 1998.

Casanova, Jose. *Public Religions in the Modern World.* Chicago: University of Chicago Press, 1994.

Eickelman, Dale F. and James P. Piscatori. *Muslim Politics.* Princeton: Princeton University Press, 1996.

El-Nawawy, Mohammed and Adel Iskandar. *Al-Jazeera: How the Free Arab News Network Scooped the World and Changed the Middle East.* Boulder, Colo.: Westview Press, 2002.

Esposito, John L. *The Islamic Threat: Myth or Reality.* New York: Oxford University Press, 1992.

Esposito and John O. Voll. *Islam and Democracy.* Oxford & New York: Oxford University Press, 1996.

Gerges, Fawaz A. *The Superpowers and the Middle East: Regional and International Politics, 1955–1967.* Boulder, Colo.: Westview Press, 1994.

Halliday, Fred. *Islam and the Myth of Confrontation: Religion and Politics in the Middle East.* New York: I. B. Tauris, 1995.

Jaber, Kamel Abu. *The Arab Ba`th Socialist Party: History, Ideology, and Organization.* Syracuse: Syracuse University Press, 1966.

Norton, Augustus Richard, ed. *Civil Society in the Middle East.* 2 volumes. New York: Brill, 1995, 1996.

Ovendale, Ritchie. *Britain, the United States and the Transfer of Power in the Middle East, 1945–1962.* London & New York: Leicester University Press, 1996.

Owen, Roger. *State, Power and Politics in the Making of the Modern Middle East.* London & New York: Routledge, 1992.

Parker, Richard B. *The Politics of Miscalculation in the Middle East.* Bloomington: Indiana University Press, 1993.

Sakr, Naomi. *Satellite Realms: Transnational Television, Globalization & the Middle East.* London: I.B. Tauris, 2001.

Sisk, Timothy D. *Islam and Democracy: Religion, Politics, and Power in the Middle East.* Washington, D.C.: United States Institute of Peace, 1992.

Soroush, Abdolkarim. *Reason, Freedom and Democracy in Islam.* New York: Oxford University Press, 2000.

Tibi, Bassam. *The Challenge of Fundamentalism: Political Islam and the New World Disorder.* Berkeley: University of California Press, 1998.

Tibi. *Islam between Culture and Politics.* New York: Palgrave, 2001.

Zubaida, Sami. *Islam, the People, and the State: Political Ideas and Movements in the Middle East.* Revised edition. New York: I. B. Tauris, 1993.

14. REGIONAL RELATIONS

Cohen, Michael. *Fighting World War Three from the Middle East: Allied Contingency Plans, 1945–1954.* London & Portland, Ore.: Frank Cass, 1997.

Gomaa, Ahmed M. *The Foundation of the League of Arab States: Wartime Diplomacy and Inter-Arab Politics, 1941 to 1945.* London & New York: Longman, 1977.

Ionides, Michael. *Divide and Lose: The Arab Revolt of 1955–1958.* London: G. Bles, 1960.

Kerr, Malcolm. *The Arab Cold War: Gamal Abd al-Nasir and His Rivals, 1958–1970.* London & New York: Oxford University Press, 1971.

MacDonald, Robert W. *The League of Arab States: A Study in the Dynamics of Regional Organization.* Princeton: Princeton University Press, 1965.

Maddy-Weitzman, Bruce. *The Crystallization of the Arab State System, 1945–1954.* Syracuse, N.Y.: Syracuse University Press, 1993.

Mufti, Malik. *Sovereign Creations: Pan-Arabism and Political Order in Syria and Iraq.* Ithaca, N.Y.: Cornell University Press, 1996.

Persson, Magnus. *Great Britain, the United States, and the Security of the Middle East: The Formation of the Baghdad Pact.* Lund, Sweden: Lund University Press, 1998.

Podeh, Elie. *The Quest for Hegemony in the Arab World: The Struggle over the Baghdad Pact.* Leiden & New York: Brill, 1995.

Yeshoshua, Porath. *In Search of Arab Unity, 1930–1945.* London: Frank Cass, 1986.

15. SAUDI ARABIA

Aburish, Said K. *The Rise, Corruption and Coming Fall of the House of Saud.* London: Bloomsbury, 1994.

Champion, Daryl. *The Paradoxical Kingdom: Saudi Arabia and the Momentum of Reform.* New York: Columbia University Press, 2002.

Fandy, Mamoun. *Saudi Arabia and the Politics of Dissent.* New York: St. Martin's Press, 1999.

Gause, F. Gregory. *Oil Monarchies: Domestic and Security Challenges in the Arab Gulf States.* New York: Council on Foreign Relations, 1994.

Kechichian, Joseph A. *Succession in Saudi Arabia.* New York: Palgrave, 2001.

Long, David E. *The Kingdom of Saudi Arabia.* Gainesville: University Press of Florida, 1997.

Peterson, J. E. *Saudi Arabia and the Illusion of Security.* London: Oxford University Press, 2002.

Rasheed, Madawi al-. *A History of Saudi Arabia.* New York: Cambridge University Press, 2002.

16. UNITED STATES
& THE MIDDLE EAST

Alin, Erika. *The United States and the 1958 Lebanon Crisis: American Intervention in the Middle East.* Lanham, Md.: University Press of America, 1994.

Aruri, Naseer. *The Obstruction of Peace: The United States, Israel and the Palestinians.* Monroe, Me.: Common Courage, 1995.

Ball, George W. and Douglas B. Ball. *The Passionate Attachment: America's Involvement with Israel, 1947 to the Present.* New York: Norton, 1992.

Dockrill, Saki. *Eisenhower's New-Look National Security Policy, 1953–1961.* New York: St. Martin's Press, 1996.

Freiberger, Steven Z. *Dawn over Suez: The Rise of American Power in the Middle East, 1953–1957.* Chicago: I. R. Dee, 1992.

Frum, David. *The Right Man: The Surprise Presidency of George W. Bush.* New York: Random House, 2003.

Hahn, Peter L. *The United States, Great Britain, and Egypt, 1945–1956: Strategy and Diplomacy in the Early Cold War.* Chapel Hill: University of North Carolina Press, 1991.

Hooshang, Amirahmadi and Eric Hoogland. *US-Iran Relations: Areas of Tension and Mutual Interest.* Washington, D.C.: Middle East Institute, 1994.

REFERENCES

Kaufman, Burton I. *The Arab Middle East and the United States: Inter-Arab Rivalry and Superpower Diplomacy.* New York: Twayne, 1996.

Kemp, Geoffrey. *Forever Enemies: American Policy and the Islamic Republic of Iran.* Washington, D.C.: Carnegie Endowment for International Peace, 1994.

Klare, Michael. *Rogue States and Nuclear Outlaws: America's Search for a New Foreign Policy.* New York: Hill & Wang, 1995.

Koenig, Louis W., ed. *The Truman Administration: Its Principles and Practice.* New York: New York University Press, 1956.

Lenczowski, George. *American Presidents and the Middle East.* Durham, N.C.: Duke University Press, 1990.

Lesch, David W. *Syria and the United States: Eisenhower's Cold War in the Middle East.* Boulder, Colo.: Westview Press, 1992.

Lesch, ed. *The Middle East and the United States: A Historical and Political Reassessment.* Boulder, Colo.: Westview Press, 1996, 1999, 2003.

McGhee, George. *The US-Turkish-NATO Middle East Connection: How the Truman Doctrine Contained the Soviets in the Middle East.* New York: St. Martin's Press, 1990.

Meyer, Cord. *Facing Reality: From World Federalism to the CIA.* New York: Harper & Row, 1980.

Neff, Donald. *Warriors at Suez: Eisenhower Takes America into the Middle East.* New York: Simon & Schuster, 1981.

Nielson, Jonathan M., ed. *Paths Not Taken: Speculations on American Foreign Policy and Diplomatic History, Interests, Ideals, and Power.* Westport, Conn.: Praeger, 2000.

Pach, Chester J. and Elmo Richardson. *The Presidency of Dwight D. Eisenhower.* Lawrence: University Press of Kansas, 1991.

Quandt, William B. *Decade of Decisions: American Policy toward the Arab-Israeli Conflict, 1967–1976.* Berkeley: University of California Press, 1977.

Ruttan, Vernon W. *United States Development Assistance Policy: The Domestic Politics of Foreign Economic Aid.* Baltimore: Johns Hopkins University Press, 1996.

Safty, Adel. *From Camp David to the Gulf: Negotiations, Language & Propaganda, and War.* New York: Black Rose Books, 1992.

Satloff, Robert. *Devising a Public Diplomacy Campaign toward the Middle East.* Washington, D.C.: Washington Institute for Near East Policy, 2001.

Stanik, Joseph T. *El Dorado Canyon: Reagan's Undeclared War with Qaddafi.* Annapolis, Md.: Naval Institute Press, 2003.

Telhami, Shibley. *The Stakes: America and the Middle East: The Consequences of Power and the Choice for Peace.* Boulder, Colo.: Westview Press, 2002.

Wittkopf, Eugene R., ed. *The Domestic Sources of American Foreign Policy: Insights and Evidence.* Second edition. New York: St. Martin's Press, 1994.

Woodward, Bob. *Bush at War.* New York: Simon & Schuster, 2002.

REFERENCES

CONTRIBUTORS

ABOOTALEBI, Ali R.: Associate Professor of Middle Eastern and International Studies at the University of Wisconsin–Eau Claire; author of *Islam and Democracy: State-Society Relations in Developing Countries, 1980–1994* (2000).

DE LUCA, Daniele: Associate Professor of the History of International Relations at the University of Lecce in Italy; author of *Fuochi sul Canale: La crisi di Suez, gli Statie Uniti e la ricerca di una nuova politica in Medio Oriente, 1955–1958* (1999) and *La difficile amicizia: Alle radici dell'alleanza israelo-americana, 1956–1963* (2001).

DIGEORGIO-LUTZ, JoAnn A.: Associate Professor of Political Science at the University of Texas A&M-Commerce; author of "The U.S.-PLO Relationship: From Dialogue to the White House Lawn," in *The Middle East and the United States: A Historical and Political Reassessment*, edited by David W. Lesch (1996).

DILLMAN, Bradford: Assistant Professor in the School of International Service and the School of Public Affairs at American University; author of *State and Private Sector in Algeria: The Politics of Rent-Seeking and Failed Development* (2000).

DONNO, Antonio: Professor of North American History at the University of Lecce, Italy; among his books are *Gli Stati Uniti, il sionismo e Israele, 1938–1956* [The United States, Zionism, and Israel, 1938–1956] (1992) and *Ombre di guerra fredda: Gli Stati Uniti nel Medio Oriente durante gli anni di Eisenhower, 1953–1961* [Cold War Shadows: The United States in the Middle East During the Eisenhower Years] (1998).

FALLE, Sir Sam: Served as a British diplomat in Iran from 1949 to 1952, in Lebanon from 1952 to 1955, on the Middle East oil desk in London from 1955 to 1957, and in Iraq from 1957 to 1961; ambassador to Kuwait in 1969 to 1970, and ambassador to Sweden and high commissioner to Singapore and Nigeria; wrote autobiography titled *My Lucky Life in War, Revolution, Peace and Diplomacy* (1996).

FITZGERALD, E. Peter: Associate Professor and Chair of the Department of History at Carleton University, Ottawa, Canada; published several works on oil diplomacy and the activities of the major oil companies in the Middle East.

FREEDMAN, Robert O.: Peggy Meyerhoff Pearlstone Professor of Political Science at the Baltimore Hebrew University; among his publications are *Moscow and the Middle East* (1991), *Israel Under Rabin* (1995), and *The Middle East Enters the Twenty-first Century* (2002).

GHADBIAN, Najib: Assistant Professor of Political Science and Middle East Studies at the University of Arkansas; among his publications is *Democratization and the Islamist Challenge* (1997); contributes political commentaries for al-Jazeera and other Middle Eastern media.

GOLDSCHMIDT, Arthur: Professor Emeritus of Middle East History at Pennsylvania State University; among his many publications are *A Concise History of the Middle East*, seventh edition (2002), *Modern Egypt: The Formation of a Nation State* (1988), and *Historical Dictionary of Egypt* (1994).

GOODE, James: Professor of History and Coordinator of Middle East Studies at Grand Valley State University, Michigan; included among his publications is *The United States and Iran: In the Shadow of Musaddiq* (1997).

HANISH, Shak: Assistant Professor of Political Science—teaching courses in the politics, history, and society of the Middle East—at the National University, San Diego campus.

HENDRICKSON, Kenneth: Hardin Distinguished Professor of American History and Chairman of the Department of History at Midwestern State University, Wichita Falls, Texas; his publications include *Profiles in Power: Twentieth-Century Texans in Washington* (1993) and *The Chief Executives of Texas* (1995).

KALPAKIAN, Jack: Assistant Professor of International Studies at Al-Akhawayn University in Ifrane, Morocco, where he specializes in security, international political economy, and Middle East affairs.

KINGSTON, Paul W. T.: Associate Professor of Political Science at the University of Toronto, Scarborough College; author of *Debating Development: Britain and the Politics of Modernization in the Middle East, 1945–1958* (1996).

LESCH, David W.: Professor of Middle East History and Director of the Middle East Concentration in the International Studies Program at Trinity University (San Antonio); publications include *Syria and the United States: Eisenhower's Cold War in the Middle East* (1992), *The Middle East and the United States: A Historical and Political Reassessment* (1996, 1999, 2003), and *1979: The Year that Shaped the Modern Middle East* (2001).

MEHDI, Abbas: Professor of Organization and Sociology at St. Cloud University in Minnesota; founder and chairman of the Union of Independent Iraqis, an international organization promoting democracy and the replacement of the Saddam Hussein regime in Iraq; born in Iraq, he is a consultant on the Middle East for several American and European organizations.

MOHAMAD, Husam: Assistant Professor of Political Science at the University of Central Oklahoma; has published articles on nationalist and religious movements and conflicts in the Middle East.

NAYLOR, Phillip C.: Associate Professor of History at Marquette University; author of *France and Algeria: A History of Decolonization and Transformation* (2000).

OLIMPO, Paola: Teaches North American History and is a Ph.D. candidate at the University of Lecce, Italy; currently working on U.S. policy during the Six-Day War (1967).

PAPPE, Ilan: Professor of Middle East History at Haifa University, Israel; publications include *The Israel/Palestine Question* (1999), *A History of Modern Palestine and Israel* (1997), and *The Making of the Arab-Israeli Conflict, 1947–1951* (1994).

PERRY, Glenn E.: Professor of Political Science at Indiana State University; author of *The Middle East: Fourteen Islamic Centuries* (1997).

PEYRON, Michael: A longtime resident of North Africa, he served as a junior lieutenant with an infantry unit in French Army operations in Algeria during the revolution in the Colomb Bechar and Oran regions, 1957–1959; author of *Algerie a l'anglaise: From British Public School to North African Djebel* (2000).

PODEH, Elie: Senior Lecturer at the Hebrew University of Jerusalem and head of the Middle East Unit at the Harry S Truman Research Institute for the Advancement of Peace; publications include *The Decline of Arab Unity: The Rise and Fall of the United Arab Republic* (1999) and *The Quest for Hegemony in the Arab World: The Struggle Over the Baghdad Pact* (1995).

ROBINSON, Glenn E.: Associate Professor of Defense Analysis at the Naval Postgraduate School in Monterey, California, and Research Associate at the Center for Middle East Studies at the University of California, Berkeley; author of *Building a Palestinian State: The Incomplete Revolution* (1997).

ROSS-NAZZAL, Jim: Assistant Professor of History at Montgomery College in Houston, Texas; specializes in the Arab-Israeli conflict and U.S. foreign policy in the Middle East.

SAIVETZ, Carol R.: Research Associate at the Davis Center for Russian Studies, Harvard University, and Executive Director of the American Association for the Advancement of Slavic Studies; among her publications is "The Superpowers in the Middle East: Cold War and Post-Cold War Policies," in *The Fall of Great Powers, Peace, Stability, and Legitimacy,* edited by Geir Lundestad (1994).

STEINBERG, Gerald: Professor of Political Science and Director of the Program on Conflict Management and Negotiation at Bar Ilan University in Israel; has published many works on the Middle East peace process and Israeli elections in a variety of forums; member of the United Nations University research group on democratic peace.

STONE, James: An independent scholar from London, England.

VANDENBERG, Jeffrey A.: Assistant Professor of Political Science and Chairman of the Department of History and Political Science at Drury University; publications include an upcoming co-edited volume on Jordan under King Abdullah II.

VANDERLIPPE, John M.: Associate Professor of History at the State University of New York at New Paltz; author of several works on Turkish-American relations and the role of cultural stereotypes in foreign policy.

VANTAGGIO, Valentina: Teaches in the Department of History and International Relations at the University of Lecce, Italy; her publications include works on U.S.-Iranian relations and U.S. oil interests in the Middle East.

VITALI, Galia: An independent scholar from Taranto, Italy.

ZISSER, Eyal: Senior Research Fellow at the Moshe Dayan Center for Middle Eastern Studies and Head of the Middle Eastern Studies program at Tel Aviv University; author of *Asad's Legacy: Syria in Transition* (2000) and *Lebanon: The Challenge of Independence* (2000).

CONTRIBUTORS

INDEX

British military strategy XII 267–275
British Southern strategy XII 39
British West Indies XII 310–316
Canada XII 43–49, 86, 268
causes XII 50–55
Continental Army XII 85–91
Conway Cabal XII 92–98
culpability of George III XII 136–144
Franco-American alliance XII 39, 41, 101, 103, 181–182, 186, 255, 306, 308
French participation in XII 100–107
guerilla warfare XII 27, 33
Hessian deserters XII 89
impact of Great Awakening upon XII 145–153
impact on Great Britain XII 27–35, 164–172
influence on French Revolution XII 127–134
Loyalists XII 25, 30, 37, 39, 41, 82, 86, 139, 158, 160, 167, 169, 181–194, 218–219, 260, 268, 306, 316
mercantilism as cause of XII 196–203
mob action in XII 214–215
nationalism in XII 204–212
Native Americans XII 37, 44, 49, 173–180, 217, 268
naval warfare XII 77–83
Newburgh Conspiracy XII 221–229
Parliamentary policies XII 230–237
Parliamentary supremacy XII 239–245
philisophical influences upon Founding Fathers XII 118–125
popular support in Great Britain XII 248–256
possibility of British victory in XII 36–41
privateers XII 77–78, 81, 83, 106
role of the elite XII 213–219
slavery XII 37, 293–300; XIII 17–24
women in XII 217, 317–324
American River VII 29
American-Syrian Crisis (1957) XV 270–271
American System XIII 283
American Telephone and Telegraph IX 21
American Type Culture Collection XV 78
American University of Beirut XV 205
Amery, Julian XV 15, 161
Amin, Hafizullah I 10–12, 15; VI 165–166
Amin, Idi VI 83; XI 71; XIV 197
Amnesty International I 146
Amphibians VII 216–217
Amphictionic Confederacy (circa sixteenth century B.C.E.) XII 19
Anabaptist Germans XII 235
Anarchism VIII 254
Anarcho-Syndicalism VIII 254
Anatolia VIII 189, 211–214; X 280, 282; XIV 168, 261
Christians in VIII 211
Greeks evacuated from IX 206
Islamic rule in VIII 211
Anatolian Plain VII 10
Anderson, Sherwood III 177
André, John XII 11
Andre, Louis VIII 151
Andrew II X 89
Andrew of Strumi X 229
Andronicus II Palaeologus X 30
Andropov, Yuri I 13; II 60; VI 111, 116, 226, 239; XV 255
domestic programs I 197
foreign policy I 186
views on Afghan war I 13
Angell, Norman IX 228
Angleton, James Jesus I 66
Anglican Church
American Revolution XII 148, 167, 314
World War I VIII 202
Anglo-American Corporation VII 5
Anglo-American Financial Agreement (1945) VI 79
Anglo-American Mutual Aid Agreement (1942) VI 78
Anglo-Boer War (1899–1902) VIII 34, 73, 103, 200, 272

opposition to VIII 77
Anglo-Egyptian accord (1954) XV 244, 255
Anglo-Egyptian Treaty (1936) XV 66
Anglo-French rivalry XII 252
Anglo-German naval rivalry VIII 29–36
Anglo-Iranian Oil Company (AIOC) I 69; VI 255; XV 108, 156, 160, 173, 176
Anglo-Iraqi Treaty (1930) XV 117
Anglo-Irish Treaty (1921) VIII 158, 160
Anglo-Irish War (1916–1921) IX 93
Anglo-Japanese Alliance (1902) IX 167
Anglo-Persian Oil Company XIV 211–212
Angola I 95, 105, 152; II 56; VI 7, 44, 50, 65–66, 83, 87, 165, 178, 188, 194, 221–222, 241, 256, 261, 265; VII 236, 239; XIII 11, 272
Cuban troops in VI 41, 43
female agricultural practices XIII 40
Portuguese immigration to VII 237
slave trade XIII 35, 130, 134
Soviet support I 185
withdrawal of Cuban troops VI 7
Annan, Kofi XIV 199, 280–282
Annapolis Convention (1786) XII 287, 289, 291
Anne (Queen) XII 141
Annie Hamilton Brown Wild Life Sanctuary VII 277
Anno of Cologne X 284
Anschluss (political union, 1938) IV 19–20, 126, 191, 224; V 293; XI 14 , 149
European reactions to IV 127
Anselm II of Lucca X 81, 85
Anthony, Susan B. II 74; III 199
Anti-Ballistic Missile (ABM) Treaty (1972) I 199, 200, 227, 231; II 61, 171; VI 18, 30, 35, 43; XIV 17
anti-ballistic missiles (ABMs) VI 17
anti-Catholicism XII 149
Anti-Comintern Pact (1936) V 115, 229
anticommunism V 114
concensus builder II 211
domestic II 211
impact on labor movement II 189
influence on foreign policy II 205
legislation II 131
propaganda II 130
Antifederalists XII 19, 21–22, 73–75, 121–122, 277–279, 281, 288, 291
Antigua XII 311–314
antinuclear weapons protests VI 15, 22
impact on Soviet policy VI 17
Antioch X 25, 27, 35, 46–48, 52, 128, 138, 155, 187, 191, 201, 247–248, 251, 254, 256, 259, 282; XI 20
Antipodes XII 168
Anti-Saloon League III 262
anti-Semitism III 252, 254; IV 137, 139; VI 88; VIII 61; X 20, 62; XI 2, 5, 17–24, 33, 55–56, 77, 81, 87, 90, 111–112, 114, 120, 160–161, 181, 183, 185, 189, 243, 264–266, 268, 271; XIV 14; XV 37
impact on Nazi collaboration IV 131
policy of Nazi Party XI 103
Soviet Union XV 253
Anti-Submarine Detection Investigation Committee VIII 196
Anti-Tactical Ballistic Missiles (ATBM) I 195
Anti-Tank Guided Missiles (ATGMs) VI 172
antiwar movement II 159, 161
demonstrations II 3
impact on American politics II 3
Apache helicopter VI 173
apartheid II 20, 100; VI 6; VII 5, 7; XI 167; XIV 221
Apollo 8 (1968) II 257–258
Apollo 11 (1969) II 258
Apollo 12 (1969) II 259
Apollo Theatre III 188
Appalachian Mountains XII 199, 230
settlers banned from crossing XII 53
appeasement I 300; IV 16–21; XI 14

Asmal, Kader VII 9
Aspinall, Wayne Norviel VII 114
Asquith, Herbert VIII 77–78, 81–82, 103–104, 106, 155, 161–162; IX 55, 58, 100
Assad, Hafiz al- I 163, 314
Assassins X 184, 258; XIV 286
Association of Professional NGOs for Social Assistance in Baia Mare (ASSOC) VII 252
Association of South-East Asian Nations (ASEAN) VI 271
Assyria XI 125, 169
Astoria, Oregon VII 53
Aswan Dam (Egypt) II 146, 148; VII 3; XV 21, 62, 70, 244, 249–250
Aswan Declaration (1978) XV 223
Ataturk, Mustafa Kemal VIII 118, 211–214; XIV 134, 168, 261; XV 108
Ataturk Dam (Turkey) VII 82
Atchafalaya River VII 161
Atlanta Exposition (1895) III 268, 271
Atlantic Charter (1941) I 301; II 99; V 45, 146–149; VI 9, 78–79; IX 250; XI 110
Atlantic Ocean IX 77, 79, 140, 142, 181, 245; XI 174; XII 78, 198, 202; XIII 42, 129, 133–134, 164, 167; XIV 75, 192, 276; XV 275
Atlantic slave trade XII 7
Atlas Mountains XIV 206, 209
atmospheric nuclear testing VI 16
atomic bomb II 228; III 10, 16; V 48–55; VI 20, 57, 136, 154, 254–255; VIII 195
    American I 260, 262–263
    Anglo-American cooperation on VI 10
    data passed to Soviet Union II 231
    development V 44
    Hiroshima and Nagasaki III 10
    impact on World War II II 268; III 11
    introduction I 4
    Soviet development of II 229
    "Stockholm Appeal" II 47
Atomic Energy Act (1946) I 220–221
Atomic Energy Act (1954) VII 175
Atomic Energy Commission (AEC) I 27, 29–31, 214, 220; II 82; VII 174–175, 178
Atoms for Peace I 216–217, 221; II 51
Atta, Muhammad XV 54
Attila the Hun XI 71
Attlee, Clement VI 11, 250
Attorney General's List I 76
Auchinleck, Sir Claude John Eyre V 76, 172
Auden, Wystan VIII 191
Audubon Society VII 31, 258
Aufmarschplan I (Deployment Plan I) VIII 247
Aufmarschplan II (Deployment Plan II) VIII 247–248
August Revolution (1945) V 146
Augustine of Hippo, Saint X 20, 80–81, 84–85, 103–104, 117, 135, 212, 229, 277; XI 19–20, 23, 169; XIII 31; XIV 205
Aum Shinrikyo XIV 262
Aurul SA cyanide spill (Romania) VII 248–250, 252–255
Auschwitz (concentration camp) I 138; III 253–254, 256; V 54, 56–57, 60, 158, 160–163, 219; VIII 94; XI 2, 4, 9, 11, 16, 45, 50, 69–70, 79, 102–104, 111, 114, 131, 148, 180, 186, 188, 206, 213–214, 217–221, 224, 227–228, 230–231, 235–237, 239–240, 250
    theories of formation V 156
Ausgleich agreement (1867) IX 137
Aussaresses, Paul XV 13, 19
Australia VI 136; VIII 33, 133, 137, 160–161, 208; IX 76, 173; XI 62, 93, 96; XII 165, 169; XIV 166; XV 39
    Aborigines XI 57
    British convicts in XII 167
    British immigration to XII 168
    grain reserves VIII 290
    immigrants XI 57, 59, 62
    Japanese immigration to IX 162

    motivation of soldiers VIII
    represented at Evian Conference XI 55
    World War I VIII 54, 117–123, 220
Australia (Australian ship) VIII 137
Australia Light Horse IX 72
Australia Mounted Division IX 67
Australian and New Zealand Army Corps (ANZAC) VIII 121–122
Austria I 253, 293; VI 136; VIII 18, 82, 106, 251–252, 266, 281; IX 49, 82, 93, 120, 158, 225–226; XI 14, 36, 56, 59, 88, 110, 123, 167, 175, 179, 211; XII 105; XIV 171; XV 215
    alliance with Germany (1879) VIII 35
    Central European Model I 108
    contribution of Jews in VIII 167
    customs union with Germany forbidden VIII 283
    dam agreement with Hungary VII 101
    dams in VII 101
    East German emigration through VI 118, 121
    Jehovah's Witnesses in XI 129
    Jews in XI 55, 60, 93
    occupation of I 108
    pre–World War I alliances VIII 225–231
    Socialists in VIII 260
    supports Slovak anti-nuclear activists VII 103
    union with Nazi Germany VIII 284
Austria-Hungary VIII 76, 95, 98, 104, 172, 178, 226, 228, 230, 266–267, 280, 299; IX 30, 64–65, 99, 102, 140, 154, 192–193, 204, 206, 225, 227, 248, 266–272
    army VIII 69; IX 134, 158
    collapse of VIII 216–217; IX 81
    invades Poland VIII 72
    invades Serbia VIII 72
    relations with Germany concerning Slavic lands VIII 94
    Socialists in VIII 257, 261
    U.S. trade with IX 22
    World War I VIII 11, 43–49; IX 133–138
        aircraft IX 13
        casualties VIII 125, 268
        defense budget VIII 44
        Jews in VIII 164
        mobilization in VIII 125
        motivation of soldiers VIII 266
        war against the United States VII 11
Austrian Refugee Foundation XI 62
Austrian War of Succession (1740–1748) XII 131
Auténtico Party I 91
automobile
    impact on interstate highway development II 106
    impact on United States II 109
    recreation II 108
Axis I 3; V 62–67
    defeat in Tunisia IV 144
    North African campaign V 66
    parallel war theory V 63–65
"axis of evil" XIV 37, 41, 126, 193
Ayyubids X 48–49, 139, 183, 185, 187–188, 274
Azerbaijan VI 255; VIII 96, 216; X 183, 187; XIV 231

B

B-1 bomber I 191; II 57
B-1B "Lancer" supersonic nuclear bomber VI 109, 234
B-17 bomber V 4, 5, 6, 98
B-17C bomber V 5
B-17E bomber V 5
B-24 bomber V 7, 98
B-26 bomber V 5
B-29 bomber V 3, 7, 49, 52,
B-36 bomber I 3–8
B-52 I 189, 193
B-58 I 193
Baath Party XIV 65, 253; XV 41, 100–101, 104, 117, 144, 260
Babbitt (1922) II 109; III 177

Baby Boomers VI 24–25
Baby M II 80
Babylon XI 125; XIV 159
Babylonian Captivity X 210; XIV 153
Bach, Johann Sebastian XI 2
Back to Africa movement III 121
Backfire bomber VI 259
Bacon, Francis VI 195
Bacon, Roger X 53, 65, 67, 69, 79, 181, 235
Bacon's Rebellion (1676) XIII 164–165, 249
Badeni crisis (1897) IX 138
Badoglio, Marshall Pietro V 178
 Italian campaign IV 144
Baghdad X 48, 52, 77, 172, 193
Baghdad Pact (1955) I 161, 277; II 146; XV 26–32,
  58–59, 61, 62, 116–117, 120, 170, 244, 250,
  271–273
 Iraq I 277
 Turkey I 277
Baghdad Railway VIII 212
Bahai XIV 140
Bahamas XII 81
Bahrain XIV 31, 52, 55, 60–62, 64–65, 79, 81, 88, 115,
  177, 179, 181, 211, 229, 247; XV 104, 205
 closes al-Jazeera office XIV 65
 democratization XIV 67
 National Charter (2001) XIV 67
 oil XV 177
 parliamentary elections XIV 64
 political parties illegal in XIV 65
 Shi'a Muslims in XIV 67
 Sunni Muslims in XIV 67
 water XIV 269
 women XIV 64, 287
Baia Mare, Romania VII 247, 249, 253, 255
Baia Mare Environmental Protection Agency VII 248,
  253
Baia Mare Task Force VII 248, 252, 254
Baker, James XIV 96, 276, 280–282, 284; XV 81, 84,
  263
Baker, Newton VIII 17–18; IX 2
Baker v. Carr (1962) II 139, 281–282, 286
Bakhtiar, Shahpour XV 100, 158, 234
Bakunin, Mikhail Aleksandrovich VI 179
Bakuninist anarchists VI 178
balance of power VI 45
Balcones Escarpment VII 70
Baldric of Bourgueil X 105
Baldric of Dol X 105
Baldwin IV X 51
Baldwin of Boulogne X 73, 119
Baldwin, James II 90–91; III 82
Baldwin, Stanley V 120; VIII 168, 190
Balfour, Arthur VIII 16, 168
Balfour Declaration (1917) VIII 37, 41, 163, 166, 168,
  208; XI 121, 126; XIV 153; XV 33–34, 52,
  121
Balkan League VIII 212
Balkan Wars VIII 39, 43–45, 117, 211, 214, 230; IX 226
Balkans I 289; V 68–78; VI 50, 272; VII 82; VIII 76,
  80, 95, 106, 226, 228, 252; IX 27, 133, 203,
  224–226, 266–272; X 281, 285; XI 193; XIV
  175, 180, 261; XV 16
 as second front V 75–76
 Christians in VIII 211
 genocide in VI 216
 Islamic rule in VIII 211
 Soviet influence I 304
 World War I VII 43–49
Ballistic Missile Defense (BMD) I 186, 195–203, 225
 technological problems I 199–200
Baltic Sea VII 18, 148; VIII 75; IX 144, 181; X 66, 69
 German control of IX 194
 salmon populations in VII 90
 submarines in VIII 292
Baltic States VI 133, 218, 251; X 270, 294, 296–297
Bandung Conference (1955) VI 267, 269; XV 68, 120,
  167, 250

Bangladesh XIV 171, 190
Bank for International Settlements (BIS) XI 178
Bank of England XI 179
Bank of North America XII 25
Bank of the United States XIII 281
Banking Act (1935) III 59
Bao Dai I 290; V 146, 148; VI 98
Baptist War XIII 159
Baptists XII 62–63, 148, 150, 205, 216, 254, 263
 slave religion XIII 186
Barada River VII 81
Barak, Ehud XIV 19–20, 22, 25, 95, 99, 131, 146, 155,
  166, 224, 253, 258; XV 133, 183, 265–268
Barbados XII 171, 310–314; XIII 64, 66
 Quaker slaveholders in XIII 31
 slave revolts XIII 91, 154–155, 157, 231
Barbary states XII 73; XIV 192
Barber, Daniel XII 149
Barbie, Klaus XI 173
Barbot, Jean XIII 134, 136
Barbusse, Henri VIII 59, 188; IX 212
Barcelona Convention VII 143–145
Barghouti, Marwan XIV 26, 63
Bargi Project (India) VII 132
Barmen Confession XI 30–31
Barmen Declaration (1934) IV 189
Barnes, Michael D. VI 193
Barré, Issac XII 53, 57
Barth, Karl XI 29, 32
Baruch, Bernard I 27, 29–30, 220; VIII 296; IX 23
Baruch Plan (1946) I 27–32, 216, 220, 258
Basic Principles Agreement (1972) XV 257
Basic Principles of Relations (U.S.-Soviet) VI 43
Basie, Count II 214
Basques X 244
Basri, Driss XIV 68, 284
Basutoland VII 237, 241
Bataan Death March (1942) V 152, 183
Batista y Zaldívar, Fulgencio I 49, 91–92, 121, 275; II
  266; III 51; VI 63, 141
Battles—
 —Adowa (1896) IX 175
 —Alexandria (1882) IX 49
 —Algiers (1956) XV 15–16, 18
 —Al-Mansurah (1250) X 66, 92, 139
 —Al-Manurah (1250) X 141
 —Amiens (1918) VIII 54, 56–57, 194; IX 122
 —Antietam (1862) VIII 67
 —Antioch (1098) X 25–26, 262, 282
 —Anzio (1944) VIII 223
 —Argonne Forest (1918) VIII 10, 20, 25; IX 26, 31
 —Arras (1917) VIII 223
 —Artois (1915) VIII 110
 —Atlanta (1864) VIII 68
 —the Atlantic (1939-1945) IV 261; V 46, 79–82,
  131, 176, 180; V 85
 —Austerlitz (1805) VIII 67
 —Avranches (1944) V 125
 —Ayn Jalut (1260) X 48, 183, 185, 187
 —Beaumont (1870) IX 14
 —Beersheba (1917) IX 72
 —Belleau Wood (1918) VIII 27; IX 28
 —Bemis Heights (1777) XII 15, 86, 179, 270, 274
 —Benevento (1266) X 67, 142
 —Bennington (1777) XII 86, 181, 270
 —Bolimov (1915) VIII 242
 —Bouvines (1214) X 89
 —Brandywine (1777) XII 97, 106, 160, 274, 305,
  307
 —Breed's Hill (1775) XII 307
 —Britain (1940) IV 168; V 4, 80, 106, 124, 135,
  152, 176, 261; V 96
 —Broodseinde (1917) VIII 220
 —Bulge, the (1944-1945) IV 44, 51, 64, 184; V 2,
  13, 21–23, 129; XI 260
 —Bull Run, First (1861) XIII 5
 —Bunker Hill (1775) XII 37, 44, 54, 86, 160

—Cambrai (1917) VIII 52–53, 56, 112–113, 221;
IX 16, 27, 33, 72, 129
—Cannae (216 B.C.E.) VIII 72, 179, 249
—Cantigny (1918) VIII 15
—Caporetto (1917) VIII 52, 221; IX 104–105, 107,
127, 129, 235
—Caucasia (1914) VIII 216
—Champagne (1915) VIII 110
—Charles Town (1776) XII 86
—Charles Town (1780) XII 41, 181, 184, 186
—Chateau-Thierry (1918) IX 28
—Chemin des Dames (1917) VIII 104, 149; IX
115, 235
—Chesapeake Capes (1781) XII 80
—Chickamauga (1863) XI 169
—Civitate (1053) X 122, 228–229, 284
—Cold Harbor (1864) VIII 67
—Concord (1775) XII 14, 40, 44, 54, 101, 149,
175, 255, 282; XIII 19
—Coral Sea (1942) IV 2, 6
—Coronel (1914) VIII 133, 135, 137; IX 141
–Cowpens (1781) XII 86
—Cuito Cuanavale (1987) I 96; VI 7
—Culloden (1746) XII 188
—Dardanelles (1915) IX 105
—Dien Bien Phu (1954) I 70; II 266; VI 106,
136; IX 260
—Dogger Bank (1915) IX 142, 177, 179
—Dorylaeum (1097) X 74, 262, 282
—Dunkirk (1940) IX 51; XI 14
—El Alamein (1943) IV 180; V 176, 179, 181
—Eutaw Springs (1781) XII 86
—Falkland Islands (1914) VIII 133, 137; IX 141
—Field of Blood (1119) X 67
—Flanders (1914) IX 50
—Flanders Offensive (1917) VIII 77; IX 212
—France (1940) IV 176
—Franklin (1864) VIII 60
—Fredericksburg (1862) VIII 77
—Freeman's Farm (1777) XII 86, 179, 274
—Froschwiller (1870) IX 14
—Gallipoli (1915) VIII 38, 40, 104, 106, 117–123,
162, 166, 213, 216, 264; IX 50–51, 53, 108,
207
—Germantown (1777) XII 97, 103, 106, 274, 305,
307
—Gettysburg (1863) VIII 67–68; XI 169
—Gorlice (1915) IX 61, 64, 127
—Guadalcanal (1942–1943) V 132, 196, 199
—Guilford Court House (1781) XII 184, 187
—Gumbinnen (1914) IX 155
—Hamel (1918) VIII 57
—Haw River (1781) XII 187
—Heligoland Bight (1914) IX 142
—Hillsborough (1781) XII 185
—Homs (1281) X 183, 185–186
—Horns of Hattin (1187) X 27, 33, 46, 51–52, 67,
130, 153–154, 170, 186–188, 247–252, 255,
257, 259, 261, 306
—Isandhlwana (1879) VIII 200
—Isonzo (1915–1917) VIII 113, 125, 264
—Iwo Jima V 52, 199; VIII 60
—Jutland (1916) VIII 72, 289, 292; IX 50, 75, 142,
177–178, 180, 188
—Karamah (1968) XV 47
—Kasserine Pass (1942) V 124
—Kettle Creek (1779) XII 184, 187
—Khalkin Gol (1938) V 136
—King's Mountain (1780) XII 86, 89, 187
—Kip's Bay (1776) XII 307
—Koniggratz (1866) IX 99
—Kut-al-Amara (1916) VIII 216
—La Forbie (1244) X 67, 143, 188
—Lake Naroch (1916) IX 128, 131
—Le Cateau (1914) VIII 252; IX 52
—Lemberg (1914) IX 155
—Lepanto (1571) X 174

—Lexington (1775) XII 10, 14, 40–41, 44, 54–55,
101, 149, 175, 189, 255, 282; XIII 19
—Long Island (1776) XII 38, 155, 157, 161, 307
—Loos (1915) VIII 239, 243, 272, 276
—Lorraine (1914) VIII 179–185, 274
—Ludendorff Offensive (1918) VIII 55, 112
—Malvern Hill (1862) VIII 67
—Manzikert (1071) X 24, 26, 29, 118, 127, 138,
213, 218, 280, 288–289; XIV 261
—Marengo (1800) VIII 67
—Marne (1914) VIII 20, 114, 180, 182, 184, 199,
246, 253; IX 38, 50, 52, 70, 111, 117, 124,
212, 263
—Mars-la-Tour (1870) VIII 75
—Masurian Lakes (1914) VIII 114, 252, 268; IX
160, 242
—Meggido (1918) VIII 41, 216
—Menin Road (1917) VIII 219
—Messines (1917) VIII 219
—Metz (1870) VIII 71
—Meuse-Argonne (1918) VIII 17, 19, 23, 25, 27,
114, 301; IX 7
—Michael (1918) IX 11
—Midway (1942) IV 2, 6; V 5, 132, 196
—Minden (1759) XII 47
—Monmouth Court House (1778) XII 305
—Mons (1914) VIII 252; IX 35, 52, 72, 212
—Moore's Creek Bridge (1776) XII 182, 187
—Moscow (1941–1942) VI 40
—Mukden (1905) VIII 75
—Neuve-Chapelle (1915) VIII 110, 242, 272, 276
—New York City (1776) XII 106, 304
—Nile (1250) X 30
—Nivelle Offensive (1917) VIII 107, 114, 218, 223,
269
—North Africa (1940–1943) V 80
—Okinawa (1945) V 52; VIII 60
—Oriskany (1777) XII 175, 177, 179
—Papua, New Guinea V 199
—Passchendaele (1917) VIII 80, 102, 104, 104,
111, 186, 218–224; IX 27, 33, 48, 104, 212,
253
—Pearl Harbor (1941) XI 14, 174
—Penobscot Bay (1779) XII 82, 83
—Petersburg (1864) VIII 23, 68
—Philippines, the V 199
—Polygon Wood (1917) VIII 219
—Princeton (1777) XII 38, 46, 103, 158, 182, 272,
304
—Quebec (1759) XII 159–160
—Quebec (1775) XII 9–11, 15, 43–44
—Riga (1917) VIII 52, 112; IX 127–129, 131
—Saipan V 52
—Salonika (1918) VIII 104, 149, 212, 216; IX 105,
203–206, 270
—Saratoga (1777) XII 9–12, 39, 78, 80, 89, 95–96,
100–106, 129, 158, 224, 255–256, 267–268,
271, 275
—Sarikamish (1914) VIII 216
—Savannah (1778) XII 181, 184
—Second Aisne (1917) VIII 114
—Second Marne (1918) IX 28, 118
—Second Ypres (1915) VIII 200
—Sedan (1870) VIII 67; IX 30, 99
—Soissons (1918) VIII 17, 27, 54–55; IX 16, 28
—Somme (1916) VIII 14, 19, 52, 56, 61, 67, 78, 80,
103, 106, 111, 113–114, 125, 128–129, 143,
158, 186–187, 200, 203, 218, 223–224, 239,
266, 268, 271–276, 289; IX 10–11, 26, 30,
34, 36, 39, 48, 56, 59, 72, 104, 107–108, 117,
121–122, 129, 210, 212, 232, 235, 252–253;
XI 169
—Spichern (1870) IX 14
—Spring Offensive (1918) VIII 201, 241, 244, 266;
IX 16, 105, 127, 131, 193
—St. Mihiel (1918) VIII 17, 19, 25; IX 11, 31, 107
—Stalingrad (1942–1943) V 132, 179; VIII 139
—Suez Canal (1915) VIII 213, 216

Bhakhra Dam (India) VII 130
Bhopal, India (1984) II 86
Bible X 82, 212, 273; XIV 184, 188
    slavery XIII 187
    view of blacks XIII 182-183
Bidault, Georges I 175, 273; VI 101
Biddle, Francis V 187-188, 224; XI 258
Big Bend Dam (United States) VII 31
Big Brother and the Holding Company II 219
Bight of Benin XIII 35
    slave trade XIII 39
Bill of Rights (1791) XII 61, 76, 108, 113, 120-122,
        131, 276-283, 290
Billboard II 217
      charts II 214
      classifications of music II 214
      music categories II 218
Biltmore Conference (1942) II 145; XV 34
Binding, Karl XI 247
Bingham, William XII 79
bioengineering II 83-85
bipartisanship II 195
    vs. concensus II 205
bipolarity VI 213
birds—
      bald eagle VII 215, 220, 234
      Black Capped Vireo VII 72
      brown-headed cowbird VII 216
      ducks VII 277
      European Starling VII 216
      Golden Cheeked Warbler VII 72
      in the Pacific flyway VII 151
      in the Atlantic flyway VII 277
      kingfisher VII 205
      southwestern willow flycatcher VII 211, 216
      spotted owl VII 226
      western yellow-billed cuckoo VII 215
      white-tailed sea eagle VII 252-253
      Yuma clapper rail VII 215
Birkenau (concentration camp) XI 70, 102, 240
birth control pill II 224-240
Birzeit University XV 94
Biscayne Bay VII 266
Bismarck, Otto von VI 9; VIII 35, 137, 207, 226, 249;
        IX 98-99, 101, 224, 226; XI 168; XIV 173;
        XV 101
Bizonia VI 101
Black, Hugo II 280, 284; III 105
Black and Tans IX 93
Black Codes XIII 5, 50, 53-55
Black Death (1347-1351) VIII 61, 189; XI 24; XIII
        161, 165, 181
Black Hand IX 102
Black Manhattan (1930) III 122
black nationalism II 89, 93; III 120
Black Panthers II 89, 165, 197
      demonstration at the California State Assembly
        (1967) II 94
      Party for Self-Defense II 94
Black Power II 24, 93-95, 162; III 120
Black Power conference (1966) II 93, 95
Black Sea VII 104, 148, 204-205, 210, 247; IX 181,
        205; X 53, 187; XIII 167
    submarines in VIII 292
    time needed to flush pollution from VII 142
    Turkish control of IX 194
Black Sea Fleet VIII 33, 280
Black September XIV 198; XV 49, 149, 198-199
Black Sharecroppers Union II 197
Black Student Union II 94
Black Tom Island IX 21
Blackboard Jungle (1955) II 214, 219
Blackman, Harry A. II 221, 225
Blackstone, William XII 263, 278
Blair, Tony VI 8; XIV 10
Blanco River, Texas VII 72
Blanquistes VI 178
Blatnik, John Anton VII 258, 268

Bledsoe, Albert Taylor XIII 27, 96, 270
Bletchley Park IV 261, 263
Blitzkrieg (lightning war) IV 23-32, 54, 56, 100, 105,
        167, 282; V 102, 118, 228; XI 83, 108
Bloody Sunday (1920) IX 93
Bloomer, Amelia III 167
Blue Gold Report VII 285
Blunden, Edmund IX 212
Blunt, Anthony VI 11
Board of Admiralty (U.S.) XII 81
Boer War (1899-1902) IX 55, 92
Bohemia IX 93, 136; XI 60
Bohemond I X 128, 191, 215-216
Bohemond VII X 185, 187
Bohemond of Taranto X 73-74, 175
Bohr, Niels
    Soviet nuclear spying I 241-242, 247-248
Bokassa, Jean Bédel VI 83
Boland, Edward Patrick VI 61
Boland Amendments I 54; VI 58, 61, 193, 195, 231
Boldt, George VII 199
Bolingbroke, Viscount XII 122, 124
Bolivia I 21, 95, 125-126; VI 50, 178
Bolling v. *Sharpe* (1950) II 137
Bolshevik Revolution (1917) I 73; VIII 82, 98, 223; IX
        87
Bolsheviks VI 244, 247; VIII 95, 171, 173, 175-176,
        178, 255, 258, 260-261, 269, 278; IX 27,
        195-202
Bolshevism VIII 209, 295
Bomber gap I 188-189, 191, 193; VI 35
bomber offensive V 86-92
      Battle of Hamburg (1943) V 87-88
      Dresden raids (1945) V 92
      Pacific theater V 89, 91-92
Bonaparte, Napoleon I 167; VIII 30, 47, 49, 66-67, 71,
        132, 194, 196, 199, 233-234, 237, 266; IX
        30, 45, 49, 105, 134, 159, 259; XI 169; XII
        134, 167, 209, 251, 302, 308; XIII 160, 210,
        213, 215
    reinstates slavery in French colonies XIII 1, 209
Bonhoeffer, Dietrich XI 29, 33, 35, 135
Bonhomme Richard (U.S. ship) XII 77, 83
Boniface VIII X 207, 223, 226, 266
Bonizo of Sutri X 85, 227-228
Bonneville Dam (United States) VII 29, 31, 53, 57, 60,
        198
Bonneville Power Administration VII 55, 202, 223
Bonomel, Ricaut X 66
Book of Maccabees XIV 153
bore-hole technology VII 34, 62-68
Bormann, Martin XI 257
Bosch, Hieronymus VIII 204
Bosch Gavíño, Juan I 24, 71
Bosnia VI 51, 53, 213, 217, 225; VIII 11, 44, 230; IX
        226-227; X 6; XIV 92
    lack of environmental control in VII 145
Bosnia-Herzegovina IX 99, 267-268
Bosnian Crisis (1908) VIII 43-45, 226, 228; IX 99
Bosporus Straits VI 255; VIII 214, 216; X 29, 74
Bossert, Wayne VII 187
Boston VII 256, 261-262; XII 44, 78, 303-304, 306
Boston Massacre (1770) XII 31, 59, 140, 237, 316
Boston Tea Party (1773) III 219; XII 51, 54-55, 140-
        141, 197, 234, 237, 253, 260
Botswana VI 83; VII 236, 243
    fences in VII 33-39
Botswana Meat Commission (BMC) VII 33
Boukman XIII 209-210
Boulanger, Georges VIII 147, 152
Boulder Dam (United States) VII 28-29, 109
Boumedienne, Houari XIV 82; XV 6
Boundary Waters Treaty (1909) VII 116-117, 120
Bourbon dynasty XII 189
Bourguiba, Habib XIV 197, 253; XV 136
Bouteflika, Abdelaziz XV 5, 9
Boutros-Ghali, Boutros XIV 278
Bowdoin, James XII 285

INDEX

Bowker, W. K. VII 158

Bowman, Isaiah VII 47

Boxer Rebellion (1900) III 136; VIII 87; IX 96

Boy Scouts IX 147

Brackenridge, Hugh Henry XII 208

Bradley, Omar N. I 6; V 15, 21, 23, 102, 125–126, 129, 136

Bradley armored personnel carrier VI 241

Brandeis, Justice Louis D. II 280; III 25–27, 207

Brandenburg, slave trade XIII 270

Brandenberg v. *Ohio* (1969) II 281

Brandon v. *Planters' and Merchants' Bank of Huntsville* XIII 102

Brandt, Willy I 35; VI 59, 206–208, 210–211
  treaty with Soviets I 185
  visit to Moscow VI 207, 211

Brant, Joseph XII 175–176, 178–179

Brattle, Thomas XII 194

Brauchitsch, Walter von V 127, 143

Brazil I 15, 20, 25, 125, 143, 219, 223; VI 215, 266; XIII 44; XIV 71, 79
  abolishes slavery XIII 36, 198
  abolitionism in XIII 2
  British relations with XII 167
  Catholic Church in XIII 192
  maroons in XIII 104–105, 107–108, 110
  religious syncretism in XIII 192
  slave rebellions XIII 154, 192, 193, 231
  slave trade XIII 38
  slavery in XIII 62–63, 65, 94, 129, 131, 134, 212, 233, 269, 272

Brazzaville Conference (1944) V 171

Brecht, Berthold VI 229; IX 84

Breckenridge, Henry VIII 301

Bredehoeft, John VII 182

Brennan, William II 221, 282

Bretton Woods Conference (1944) VI 78, 144

Bretton Woods finance system VI 204

Brezhnev, Leonid I 104, 151, 153, 197; II 69, 169; VI 21, 43, 68, 75, 111, 116, 163, 184, 226, 239; XIV 2; XV 255, 257

Brezhnev Doctrine I 10–11; VI 43, 118; XIV 2, 6

Brezhnev-Nixon summit (1972) II 170

Briand, Aristide VIII 255; IX 207

Bridge Canyon Dam (United States) VII 30, 109

Brissenden, Richard B. VII 158

Bristol Bay, Alaska VII 197

British and Foreign Anti-Slavery Society XIII 131

British Army XII 29, 38, 88, 105, 260, 302, 305, 316
  punishments in XII 304

British Broadcasting Corporation (BBC) XIV 28, 30, 34
  Arab Service XIV 29

British Cavalry Division IX 69

British Colonial Office XIV 176

British Empire XII 32, 34, 50, 52, 164–165, 167–169, 210, 231, 233; XIII 1
  administration of XII 139
  emancipation of slaves XIII 22, 65, 154–155, 160
  slave rebellions XIII 231

British Expeditionary Force (BEF) VIII 71, 77, 79, 102–103, 106, 110, 219–224, 252, 265, 271–276; IX 26, 48–53, 55, 69, 72, 104, 108, 230, 245, 260
  chaplains in VIII 203
  command structure IX 33–40
  use of tanks VIII 51–58

British Guiana I 15, 24, 125; VI 96
  slavery in XIII 233

British Honduras (Belize) XII 167

British Isles IX 140

British Legion XII 32, 186

British Navy XII 260

British North America Act (Constitution Act, 1867) VII 117

British Petroleum XIV 211–212; XV 108, 156, 172–173, 176, 178–179

British Royal Flying Corps IX 217, 220

British South Sea Company XIII 272

British-United States Agreement (BRUSA) VI 11

British West Indies XII 290, 295, 310–316
  slavery in XII 311

Brittain, Vera VIII 266

Broadcasting Board of Governors XIV 233, 235

Brodie, Bernard I 165; II 65

Brodsky, Joseph XIV 233

Brooke, Alan Francis V 43, 76

Brooke, Rupert VIII 188; IX 149

Brookings Institution XV 220

Brooks, John XII 222–224

Brooks, William K. VII 40, 43, 46–47

Broom and Whisk Makers Union II 191

Brotherhood of Sleeping Car Porters II 189, 217–218

Brower, David Ross VII 110, 112

Brown, Harold VI 42–43

Brown, John XII 11; XIII 4

Brown v. *Board of Education of Topeka, Kansas* (1954) II 20, 23–24, 26, 45, 80, 90–91, 136–143, 270, 280, 286, 293, 295; III 27, 185

Brown Synod (1933) XI 27

Brown University XIII 31, 198

Bruchmuller, Georg IX 127–129

Brusilov, Aleksey VIII 266; IX 60–66, 193, 242

Brusilov Offensive (1916) IX 72, 137, 155, 193, 243, 252

Brussels Treaty (1954) I 208; VI 101

Bryan, Samuel XII 76

Bryan, William Jennings III 32, 34, 36–37; VIII 204; IX 19, 21, 246
  Scopes Trial III 33

Brzezinski, Zbigniew I 135, 143, 146; VI 42, 166, 256, 263; XIV 8; XV 220

Buchanan, James XIII 195, 278

Buchenwald (concentration camp) V 57; XI 45, 236, 245
  German people's reaction V 215

Buck v. *Bell* (1927) III 18, 21

Buddhist monks, immolation of VI 23

Bukovina IX 136

Bulganin, Nikolai A. VI 135

Bulgaria I 107, 294; II 39, 153; VI 251–252, 261, 274, 276, 280; VIII 11, 14, 44, 46, 95, 212, 216–217, 230; IX 120, 171, 203–206, 270, 272; XI 214, 220; XIV 176, 178; XV 120
  ally of Germany VIII 278
  U.S. push for greater freedoms I 110
  U.S. recognizes communist government I 303

Bulgars X 29

Bull, William XII 215

Bull Moose Party III 243

Bund Deutscher Mädel (German Girls' Organization) IV 191

Bund Naturschutz in Bayern (BUND) VII 206, 210

Bundestag (Federal Diet) VI 102

Bundy, McGeorge I 29, 294; II 6
  flexible response I 120
  use of nuclear weapons policy I 171

Bureau of Indian Affairs (BIA) III 141, 143; VII 55–56, 59, 166–167, 169, 172

Burger, Justice Warren E. II 182, 221, 284; XII 283

Burgess, Guy I 243, 245; VI 11

Burgh, James XII 278

Burgoyne, John XII 10, 15, 39, 45–47, 80, 95–96, 100, 103, 155, 158, 162, 181, 267–274, 305

Burke, Edmund XII 29–30, 139, 143, 166

Burke, Thomas XII 185

Burma VIII 35; XII 33; XIV 177; XV 14
  fall of V 197
  opium trade I 15

Burns, William XIV 100, 107

Burundi II 101, 155

Bush, George H. W. VI 28, 51, 58, 61, 191, 195, 205, 226, 229, 242, 257; X 56; XIV 97, 100, 198, 247; XV 102, 182, 258, 260
  Africa policy VI 7
  civil war in Somalia II 155
  foreign policy "balance of power" II 155

international political experience II 152
Iraq XV 73–79
Madrid Conference XV 184
New World Order II 152–158; XV 81
nuclear nonproliferation policy I 224
Panama intervention II 155
Persian Gulf crisis II 153
Persian Gulf War XV 80–87
relationship with former Yugoslavia II 155
role of United States II 155
U.S. spying on Soviet Union I 191
unilateral U.S. foreign policy II 156
Bush (George H. W.) administration II 100; VI 120;
        XIV 199
arms-control agreements VI 20
defense spending VI 224
envision of New World Order II 155
Iraq XV 73–79, 81, 84, 86
nuclear-nonproliferation policy I 217
policy on Afgahnistan I 14–16
Bush, George W. VII 224; XIV 13–15, 33, 37–38, 41,
        43, 88, 112, 168, 193, 228–229, 239, 247,
        267; XV 78
governor of Texas XIV 103
Iraq XV 80, 87
Middle East XIV 95–108
on terrorism XIV 126
Bush (George W.) administration XIV 109, 193, 231,
        247, 238, 239
Bush Doctrine XIV 14, 17, 43, 237, 239–240
conservative ideology XIV 16
Middle East XIV 95–108
response to World Trade Center attack XIV 228
terrorism XIV 10, 13, 17
view on Hizbollah XIV 126
Bushido code III 13
Butler, Justice Pierce III 25
Butler, Pierce XII 296
Butler, Smedley, IX 96
Butterfield, Herbert X 278, 304
Buxton, Thomas Fowell XIII 131, 159
Byrd II, William XIII 150–151, 207
Byrnes, James F. I 28, 31, 263, 304; II 206; V 51, 53;
        XI 256
Byzantine Empire X 33, 73, 88, 92, 107–108, 110, 112,
        118–119, 121, 128, 138, 150–151, 156, 172–
        174, 188, 205, 208–209, 215, 238–239, 249–
        250, 262, 269, 280, 282, 284, 287; XIII 167;
        XIV 261
Crusades X 15, 24–31
relations with the West X 24–31

C

Cable News Network (CNN) XIV 29, 34, 61, 66
Cabora Bassa Dam (Mozambique) VII 237, 239, 240
Cadwalader, John XII 98
Caesar, Julius XII 302
cahiers des doleances (notebooks of grievances) XII 129,
        133
Cairncross, John VI 11
Soviet nuclear spying I 243–245
Cairnes, John E. XIII 174, 240, 242
Cairo X 76–77, 89, 170, 172, 185, 192, 262
Cairo Agreement XV 48–49
Cairo Conference (1943) VI 146
Cairo Declaration (2000) XIV 282
Calais XII 242
Calhoun, John XIII 48
California VII 180, 201; X 8; XI 124; XIV 162
dams in VII 27, 29
Department of Fish and Game VII 178
environmental activism in VII 174
flood control in VII 273
legislation on Holocaust reparations XI 216
pollution control in VII 264
receives federal swamplands VII 272
water policy in VII 153

California Aqueduct VII 179
California Coastal Commission VII 175, 179
California Development Company (CDC) 155
Calloway, Cab IX 4
Calonne, Charles-Alexandre de XII 131–132
Calueque Dam (Angola) VII 239
Calvin's Case (1607) XII 42
Calvinism XII 149–150; XIII 31
Cambodia I 40–47, 145, 289, 299; II 6, 177; VI 4, 44,
        60, 63, 65, 68, 83, 93, 188, 194, 203, 221;
        XII 33; XV 133
colony of France I 290
genocide in XI 71, 79, 166–167 169
Khmer Rouge movement I 15; VI 271
spread of communism I 297
supply lines through VI 60
U.S. bombing of I 183, 291; VI 86
U.S. invasion of I 291; VI 23, 26, 165, 284
Vietnam invasion of VI 44
Cambon, Paul IX 44
Cambridge University IX 172
Camp David XV 51–53, 57, 104, 226, 266
Camp David agreement (1978) I 159; XIV 96; XV 219,
        223, 225, 227, 239
Camp David summit (2000) XIV 19–20, 22, 24–25, 98,
        100, 166, 258; XV 183, 185, 191
Camp Gordon, Georgia VIII 23, 299
Campbell, Alexander XII 313
Campbell, Archibald XII 184
Canada I 30–31; VI 101, 136; VII 182; VIII 33, 83,
        160–161, 208; IX 122, 173; XI 62;. XII 10,
        12, 15, 39, 98, 109, 165, 171, 199, 267–268,
        272–274, 316; XIII 120; XIV 135, 225; XV
        14, 135
American Revolution XII 43–49
Atomic Energy Act I 221
British immigration to XII 168
charter member of NATO I 208
criticism of Libertad Act I 98
Cuban investment I 97
discussion of nuclear weapons I 28
escaped slaves XIII 124
fish hatcheries in VII 202
fishing rights in VIII 35
French desire to regain territory in XII 104
grain reserves VIII 290
Loyalists in XII 167, 189, 192, 194
motivation of World War I soldiers VIII 266
Native Americans XII 174, 176–177, 180
Nazi gold in XI 179
oil XV 173
policy on cleaning Great Lakes VII 116–124
production of WWI materials IX 23
Rebel attack upon XII 161
relations with United States VII 116–124
seized by Great Britain XII 55
social programs in VI 187
World War I VIII 220
Canada Water Bill (1969) VII 119–120
Canada-Ontario Agreement (COA) VII 120
Canary Islands
slavery in XIII 161, 167
slaves from XIII 167
Candide (1759) IX 207
Candomble XIII 192
Capuano, Peter X 149
Cape Colony VIII
Cape Fear River XII 182, 184, 187
Cape of Good Hope XIII 136
capitalism II 30–31, 34, 56–57, 60; III 63, 191, 194–195
capitalist encirclement II 39
capitalist system III 190
Card, Andrew H. Jr. XIV 97, 100
Cárdenas, Lazaro VII 155
expropriates lands of Colorado River Land
        Company VII 152
pushes against agricultural production VII 153
Cardozo, Justice Benjamin III 25, 28

Index

Central Committee of the French Communist Party VII
97
Central Europe
impact of anticanal protest VII 206
Rhine-Main-Danube Canal VII 204–210
Central High School, Little Rock, Arkansas II 20, 52
Central Intelligence Agency (CIA) I 49, 64–71, 92, 94,
119, 191, 211, 263; II 5, 52, 54, 57, 63, 69,
103, 115, 152, 178, 260; VI 6, 24, 57, 61, 64,
96, 133, 151, 188, 231, 260; XIV 4, 6, 17, 37–
38, 41, 97, 103, 230, 233; XV 61, 87, 108,
158, 163, 175, 233, 271
anti-Sandanista forces I 54
assessment of Soviet military strength VI 257,
259
covert operations in British Guiana I 24
covert operations in Chile I 124, 131; VI 86–87
covert operations in Guatemala I 123, 131; XV
157
covert operations in Latin America I 26
Cuba XV 157
Musaddiq, overthrow of XV 157–158, 160
Operation Mongoose II 120
origins I 64, 74
plot to overthrow Castro I 275
Rosenberg records II 230
supply of Angolan rebels VI 1
support of contras VI 237
training of anti-Castro Cubans in Guatemala VI
141
Central Powers VI 176; VIII 18, 22, 117, 133. 172–
173, 221, 242, 251, 278, 290, 295; IX 60, 63,
99, 154–155, 203, 205, 207–208, 238, 247–
249, 266; X 59, 62
collapse of VIII 267
motivation of World War I soldiers VIII 266
U.S. trade with IX 22
Central Treaty Organization (CENTO) XV 27, 29, 120
Central Utah Project (CUP) VII 31
Central Valley Project VII 29
Ceyhan River VII 79
Chaco War (1932–1935) I 125
Chad XIV 198, 200
Chagall, Marc VIII 191
Challe, Maurice XV 12, 18
Chamberlain, Neville IV 17, 20, 125; V 117, 169; XII
33
appeasement policy IV 18
Ten Year Rule IV 21
Chambers, Whittaker II 130; III 34; VI 123–129
Chamorro, Violeta Barrios de VI 191, 195
Chamoun, Camille XV 61, 63, 169
Chandelier Workers Union II 191
Channing, William Ellery XIII 29, 33
Charlemagne X 24, 26, 65, 81, 127, 177, 212, 269, 287;
XI 80
Charles I XIII 63
Charles II XII 209; XIII 62
Charles V X 8
Charles of Anjou X 30, 66, 139, 142–146, 226
Charles Town XII 41, 182, 190, 192
Charter 77 movement VI 237
Chasseurs d'Afrique IX 116
Chauncy, Charles XII 148, 150
Chechnya XIV 12, 93, 180, 230
Soviet operations in VI 169, 218
Chelmno (concentration camp) XI 220
Chemical warfare V 101–107
World War I VIII 239–244; IX 38
Cheney, Dick XIV 97, 101, 103, 105; XV 78
Chernenko, Konstantin I 197; II 60; VI 111, 226; XV
255
succeeded by Gorbachev I 14
Chernobyl (1986) II 86; VII 18, 20, 22, 247
Chesapeake (region) XII 169, 205
slavery in XIII 85, 151, 179, 247
trade restrictions on tobacco XII 201
Chesapeake Bay XII 33, 172, 271; XIII 60

oysters in VII 40–50
Chesapeake Bay 2000 Agreement VII 49
Chesapeake Biological Laboratory VII 47–48
Chesnut, Mary Boykin XIII 123, 205, 218, 229, 238
Chetniks VI 275, 277
Chevron (Standard Oil of California, or Socal) XIV
211–212; XV 172–173, 177, 179
Chiang Kai-shek I 40, 58, 61, 86, 265–266, 268, 275,
303–304; II 133, 211; V 191, 194–196; VI
38, 146, 158, 254
Chicago VII 116, 122, 262; IX 3, 7
water supply system in VII 283
Chicago Daily News IX 4
Chicano Power II 94
Chief Joseph Dam (United States) VII 53
Childers, Robert IX 93
Chile I 123–128, 140, 152; VI 64, 87, 194, 265–266;
XI 88; XIV 23
access to Import-Export Bank I 53
Allende government I 26
CIA activites in VI 86–87
coup of 1960s I 26
human rights record I 143
U.S. intervention (early 1970s) I 15, 123–133
China I 41, 44, 54, 59, 86–91, 141, 277, 287–288, 292;
II 4, 9, 36, 39–40, 47, 119, 168, 171; VI 10,
35, 42, 49, 53, 56, 59, 90, 107, 121, 136, 147,
154, 175, 178, 181, 199, 201, 203, 213–214,
243, 265, 271; IX 91, 96, 162, 164–165,
167–168, 174–175, 246; X 186, 305; XII 29,
171; XIV 2–3, 12, 46, 88, 143, 176–177, 239;
XV 49, 68, 81, 120, 167, 215, 220, 228, 245,
250, 252
accuses Soviets of aiding Vietnam VI 44
attacks on Quemoy and Matsu I 265–270, 275
attacks Vietnam VI 43
balance to U.S.S.R VI 201
blue-water navy of VI 53
bombing of embassy in Belgrade VI 54
border clashes with Soviet Union VI 40, 43
communist victory in XV 206
condemns terrorism XIV 16
Cultural Revolution XI 166–167
defense spending of VI 54
economy VI 53, 219
German interests in VIII 31, 137
human rights in VI 219
influence on North Vietnam I 296–297
Korean War I 273–275; XIV 147
meeting with United States in Warsaw (1969) VI
43
Nationalists I 61
nuclear espionage of VI 219
Nuclear Non-Proliferation Treaty I 218
nuclear proliferation I 222–224
nuclear weapons development I 222, 239
purchase of Western military hardware VI 42
rapprochement with the United States VI 38–45
relations with Russia VI 53
relations with Soviet Union VI 38, 113, 203
Russian threat to British interests in VIII 33
Shantung province siezed IX 163
Soviet role in postwar VI 254
support for Afghan resistance VI 166
support for FNLA and UNITA VI 1
Taiwan-U.S. mutual-security treaty I 268
Tiananmen Square Massacre (1989) VI 54, 113,
121
U.N. Security Council membership I 300
U.S. intelligence sites in VI 43
U.S. Ping-Pong team trip VI 43
U.S. relations with VI 4, 88
China Hands I 58–63; VI 158
Chinese Civil War VI 150
Chinese Communist Party (CCP) VI 181
Chinese Cultural Revolution (1966–1976) VI 40
Chinese Revolution (1949) VI 177; IX 168
Chirac, Jacques XIV 241

73, 81, 83, 116, 139, 148, 152, 157, 173, 175,
182, 202–203, 206, 218, 224, 240, 250, 260,
263, 271, 275
casualties in VI 50
causes of VI 252
conclusion of VI 47–51, 213–216
dam building in VII 29
effect of nuclear weapons I 250–257
end of VI 150, 214
impact on development of space programs II 241
impact on federal highway development II 107
impact on U.S. space program development II
257
late 1970s intensification II 172
Middle East XV 252–259
military buildup II 43
mutual assured destruction (MAD) I 251–252
origins of I 258–264; II 30
Reagan's role in ending VI 221–241
Stalin's role in starting VI 250–252
vindicationist interpretation VI 155
Colden, Cadwallader XII 214
Cole (U.S. ship), attack on (2000) XIV 16, 190
Cole v. *Young* I 80
Collier, John (Commissioner of Indian Affairs) III
141–142
Collins, J. Lawton I 6; V 122
Colombia XIII 104; XV 79
colonialism X 55–56, 63; XIV 171; XV 35
Colorado VII 10, 13, 112, 181, 182
farmers' use of water in VII 13
production of crops on irrigated land in VII 11
Colorado River VII 27, 31, 151–153, 155, 168, 211, 214
dams on VII 108–115, 152
Colorado River Compact (CRC) VII 152–153
Colorado River Irrigation District VII 157
Colorado River Land Company VII 152
Colorado River Storage Project (CRSP) VII 27, 112
Columbia Basin VII 29
dams in VII 196
Columbia Basin Project VII 202
Columbia River VII 25, 27–28, 31, 51–61, 197, 199,
202, 219–220, 222, 225, 227
first major navigation project on VII 52
hydroelectric dams on VII 198
salmon producer VII 53
Columbia River Fisherman's Protective Union VII 53
Columbia River Highway VII 57
Columbia River Inter-Tribal Fish Commission VII 61
Columbia River Packers Association VII 53
Columbia University XIII 198
Columbus, Christopher X 7–8, 304; XIII 147, 210
Comal River VII 70
combat effectiveness
Germany V 282, 284
Japan V 281–282
Leyte campaign V 281
Normandy invasion V 282
psychological limits IV 47–52
United States V 278–286
Combined Bomber Offensive IX 223
Combined Chiefs of Staff (CCS) V 20, 23, 25, 38, 42–
45
Commission on Polish Affairs VIII 281
Commission on Presidential Debates II 196, 199
Committee for National Unity XV 195
Committee on Political Refugees XI 60
Committee on Public Information (CPI) VIII 296; IX
78
Commission on Sustainable Development XIV 268
Committee on the Present Danger VI 256, 262
Committee to Re-Elect the President (CREEP) II 177;
VI 24
Common Sense (1776) XII 54, 110, 121, 143, 153
Commonwealth of Independent States (CIS) VI 54
Commonwealth of Nations VI 13
The Commonwealth of Oceana (1656) XII 123
Commonwealth v. *Turner* (1827) XIII 102

communism I 148–155; II 31–32, 56–57, 160; VI 49;
IX 83
atheism of VI 176
attraction for women VI 49
China II 267e
collapse of II 153
global II 130
ideology I 258–262; VI 49
infiltration of federal government II 133
world domination VI 175–182
Communist Control Act (1954) I 74, 77
Communist Information Bureau (Cominform) I 36–
113; VI 179, 246
Communist International (Comintern) I 113; III 224,
226; IV 80; VI 178, 254, 277
Communist Manifesto (1848) VI 178; XIII 69
Communist Party I 74; III 182, 221; XIV 181
in Chile I 124
in Guatemala I 123
of the Soviet Union III 224; VI 179, 276; XV
257
of Yugoslavia (CPY) VI 273–278, 280–281
Communist Party of the United States of America
(CPUSA) II 46–48; III 237; VI 123, 154,
157
Federation of Architects, Engineers, Chemists and
Technicians II 228
history of III 224
organization of Southern Tenant Farmers
Unions II 189
1932 presidential candidate III 182
Community Action Programs (CAP) II 270–276
Community Development Corporation XIII 200
Community Reinvestment Act (1977) XIII 200
Comnena, Anna X 211, 215
Comoros XIV 55, 181; XV 141
Compañía de Terrenos y Aguas de la Baja California,
S.A. VII 155
Comprehensive Immigration Law (1924) III 233
Comprehensive Test Ban Treaty (CTBT) I 224; VI 58
Comprehensive Wetlands Management and
Conservation Act VII 274
Concert of Europe VI 203
Confederate Army, Zouave units in IX 116
Confederate Congress XIII 153, 277
Confederate Constitution XIII 274, 277
Confederate States of America XIII 5, 45, 195
use of symbols from XIII 269–278
Confederation Congress XII 293, 299
Conference of the States (1995) XIV 150
Conference on Environmental Economics at Hyvinkää
(1998) VII 89
Confessing Church XI 27–35, 135
Confiscation Plan XIII 51
Congo IX 226; XIII 11
slave trade XIII 35, 40
Congregational Church VIII 204; XII 148, 150, 216,
254, 263
Congress of African People (1970) II 95; III 193, 195
Congress of Berlin IX 99
Congress of Industrial Organizations (CIO) II 188,
197; III 183–184, 191, 195
Congress of Vienna (1815) IX 45, 226
Congress of Racial Equality (CORE) II 161; III 219;
XIII 256
Congressional Black Caucus XIII 198
Connally, John VI 257
Connecticut XII 10–12, 15, 66, 70, 205, 209, 215
gradual emancipation in XIII 19
impact of Shays's Rebellion in XII 287
prohibits importation of slaves XIII 18
religion in XII 148, 150, 263
slave uprising in XIII 235
Connolly, Thomas T. II 208; III 31; VI 151
Conrad X 48, 286
Conrad III X 128, 294
Conrad of Montferrat X 256, 258

Index

INDEX

166, 170–176, 178, 180, 183, 185–188, 190–196, 247–248, 254–259, 275, 294, 296–297, 300–306

cultural interaction in X 197–203
importance of maritime traffic X 152
treatment of Muslims in X 190–196
Crusaders, motivations of X 143
Crusades XIV 159, 161
Albigensian X 112, 210, 226, 236, 239, 270
Children's X 32–38, 88, 231, 234–235, 239
Christian ethics X 79–86
class structure of X 32–38
cost of X 145
cultural interaction during X 197–203
definition of X 123–131
disillusionment with X 64–70
economic motives X 71–78
Markward of Anweiler X 225
Western imperialism X 300–306
Fifth X 64, 87–96, 112, 130, 139, 144, 167, 170, 173, 177–178, 189, 239, 255, 262, 294
First X 13–23, 25–26, 29, 33, 35–36, 51, 60, 65, 71–72, 75, 81, 88, 97–106, 117–119, 122, 125, 127–129, 135, 137, 143, 148–150, 153, 158, 163–164, 168, 171, 173–174, 177, 190–191, 194–200, 208–221, 224, 231–233, 236, 238–239, 255–256, 263, 265, 267, 272, 274, 279–292, 295–298; XIV 187
First Crusade of Louis IX X 64, 69, 112, 139–147, 167, 170, 173
Fourth X 24, 26–30, 33, 87–88, 92, 107–114, 126, 128, 130, 148–149, 156, 167, 209, 239, 255, 262, 291, 297
impact of ribats X 158–166
impact on modern world X 55–63
impact on the papacy X 204–210
Jews in X 13–23
Military Orders X 158–166
military strategy X 167–175
missionay activity X 176–181
Mongols X 112, 182–189
motivation X 71–78, 97–106
of 1101 X 112
of 1128 X 112
of Frederick II X 112
of Pope Boniface VIII X 266
of the Poor X 38
origins of X 115–122
Peasants' X 213, 219
People's X 13, 19, 101–102, 112, 234
Political X 223–229
Popular X 32–38, 100, 231–240
Second X 13, 16–17, 24, 33, 48, 74, 92, 128, 130, 150, 167–168, 174, 179, 207, 225, 255–256, 265, 294, 296–297; XI 20
Second Crusade of Louis IX X 66, 68, 112, 139–147
Seventh X 64, 69
Shepherds' X 14, 32–38, 141–142, 231, 233, 239
Sixth X 112
Spain X 241–246
Third X 16–17, 24, 26–29, 47, 52, 57, 59, 77, 88, 107, 116, 127, 141, 144, 151, 153, 168, 174, 195, 249, 251, 252, 254–263, 277, 294, 297
traditionalsit-pluralist debate X 223, 236, 264–271
treatment of Jews by X 238
vow redemption X 291–299
CSX Corporation XIII 197–198
Cuba I 51, 53, 68, 89, 91, 94, 96, 98, 125, 292; VI 35, 50, 63–68, 77, 141–142, 182, 188, 213, 246, 249, 261, 271; IX 96; XIII 104; XIV 40, 193, 250; XV 49, 81, 228, 253
Bay of Pigs invasion (1961) I 66, 70, 89, 92, 94, 129; II 115, 247, 266; VI 131
blockade of VI 72
Castro takeover I 17
CIA plot XV 157
emancipation in XIII 36

exiles VI 64
exports to Soviet Union VI 249
imperialism I 151
Jewish refugees XI 4, 93
maroons in XIII 105, 108, 110
nuclear missiles in VI 70–71
policy in Angola VI 165
receives aid from Soviet Union I 275
relations with the United States VI 70–76
revolution of 1959 I 18, 20, 125; VI 63
slave revolts XIII 91, 154
slave trade XIII 272–273
slavery in XIII 90, 94, 269
Soviet subsidies VI 249
Soviet troops in VI 70
support for MPLA VI 1
support for revolutions VI 64
support for Third World VI 63
threat to stability in Central America I 49
troops in Africa VI 2, 4, 249
troops in Angola VI 1, 7, 41, 43
troops in Ethiopia VI 41
troops in Grenada VI 221
troops overseas VI 65
U.S. intervention (1898) I 125
Cuban Communist Party I 91–93
Cuban Liberty and Democratic Solidarity (Libertad) Act
See Helms-Burton bill
Cuban Missile Crisis (1962) I 49, 92–94, 98, 102, 125, 131, 168, 183–184, 230, 294; II 66, 117, 120, 257, 265; VI 30–31, 36, 42, 50, 64, 66, 70–76, 101–104, 139, 142, 174, 262; XV 219
Cuito Canavale, battle of (1987) VI 7
Cullen, Countee III 79, 234–236
Cumming v. *County Board of Education* (1899) XIII 53
Cunene River VII 236–237, 239, 240, 242
Curagh Mutiny (1914) VIII 161
Currency Act (1764) XII 232, 236
Currie, Arthur IX 33
Curzon, George (Marquis Curzon of Kedleston) IX 83
Cuyahoga River VII 116, 118, 123, 265
cyanide, effects of VII 247, 253
Cyprus VI 135; X 30, 67, 140–141, 146, 256; XIV 235, 265; XV 79, 217
Jewish refugees XI 124
sugar cane in XIII 167
Czech Republic VI 217
Czechoslovakia I 109–110, 112, 277, 293–294, 303; II 9; VI 103, 110, 119, 131, 133, 165–166, 178, 217, 227, 237, 246, 249, 251–252, 261, 274, 276; IX 93, 136, 272; XI 14–15, 56, 68, 86, 110, 167, 178–179, 207; XV 68, 70, 120
appeal of Marshall Plan I 178
arms shipment to Guatemala (1954) I 49, 123, 126
attempted alliance with France VI 255
dams in VII 100
frontiers recognized VIII 283
Germany annexes border districts VIII 284
human rights abuses I 146
Munich Agreement (1938) I 300
occupation of VIII 284
political changes in VII 101
Soviet coup (1948) I 173, 182, 185
Soviet invasion (1968) I 11–12, 218; VI 43, 116, 182, 249; XIV 2
Czerniakow, Adam XI 139–142

D

Dachau (concentration camp) XI 13, 45, 148, 151–152, 170, 213, 220, 222, 224, 232, 236, 255–256, 260
Dahomey XIII 11
famine in XIII 38
slave trade XIII 39, 40
Daladier, Edouard V 116
appeasement policy IV 20

Dalmatia IX 136, 208
   enslavement of Dalmatians XIII 167
Damascus VIII 39, 41; IX 72; X 51, 77, 167, 172, 196,
   305; XV 275
Damietta X 60, 87, 90, 92, 95, 139–140, 145–146, 262
Damodar Valley VII 130, 132
Damodar Valley Corporation VII 127, 132
Dams VII 1–9, 14, 25–32, 51–61, 100–107, 125–134,
   196, 236–246
   benefits of VII 1, 28
   breaching of VII 31, 221, 224, 226
   fish VII 53, 196–203
   hydroelectric energy VII 226
   political economy of VII 129
Danbury Baptist Association XII 62
Dandalo, Enrico X 107, 149, 152
Danish West India Company XIII 274
Dante XI 129; XIII 262
Danube River VII 100, 101–104, 106, 204–207, 209–
   210, 247, 250, 253, 255
Danzig VIII 280–281; XI 179
Dardanelles VIII 38, 80, 117–123, 212, 214, 216; IX
   114, 207; X 15
Darrow, Clarence III 32–34, 37–39
   relationship with NAACP III 186
   Scopes Trial III 33
Darwin, Charles III 32–33; VIII 93; XI 17–18
Davenport, James XII 148
Davidic dynasty (tenth century B.C.E.) XIV 163
Davidiz, Sisnando X 2, 41
Davies, John Paton VI 158
Davis, Jefferson XIII 270, 274, 277
Davis Sr., Benjamin O. IX 7
Dawes, Charles VIII 285
Dawes Plan (1924) IV 270; V 119; VIII 298; IX 92,
   171
Dawes Severalty Act (1887) III 140–143; VII 166, 167,
   168, 171
Day, Nathaniel XII 48
Dayan, Moshe XV 23–24, 136, 221–222
Dayton Accords (1995) II 100, 154
D-Day (6 June 1944) VI 168, 251
Deane, Silas XII 79, 100, 102–103, 105–106
De Bow, J. D. B. XIII 28, 101
De Bow's Review XIII 86
Debs, Eugene V. II 196; III 151, 175, 208, 222–223,
   234
Declaration of Independence (1776) VI 9; XII 18, 32,
   34, 46, 54–55, 69, 71, 108–116, 118, 120,
   129–131, 134, 136–137, 140, 143, 171, 191,
   215, 235, 261–262, 265, 277, 282, 293, 314;
   XIII 18–19, 23, 147, 156, 272
Declaration of Paris (1856) VIII 136
Declaration of Punta del Este (1961) I 17
Declaration of St. James XI 261
Declaration of the Rights of Man and Citizen
   (1789) XII 130, 131, 265; XIII 156
Declaratory Act (1720) XII 246
Declaratory Act (1766) XII 57, 141, 233, 237, 239–240
Decolonization VI 264
   effects of on Third World VI 83
Defense Intelligence Agency (DIA) XV 86
   NIE reports VI 257
   Soviet military strength VI 259
Defense of the Realm Act (1914) VIII 158; IX 58
Defense Policy Board XIV 97
Defense Readiness Condition (DEFCON) VI 163
Deism XII 151
Delaware XII 70, 78, 175–176, 306
   ratification of Constitution XII 74
Delaware River XII 271
Delbo, Charlotte XI 222–223
Demerara (Guyana) XIII 190
   slave revolts XIII 154, 159, 231
Democratic Front for the Liberation of Palestine
   (DFLP) XIV 195; XV 95
Democratic National Committee (DNC)
   headquarters broken into VI 24

Democratic National Convention
   (1964) II 28, 161–163
   (1968) II 162, 180; VI 25
Democratic Party II 49, 162–165, 180, 194–195, 198,
   257; III 191–195; XIII 21, 56, 222, 276,
   281–283
   association with labor movement II 187–192
   Mississippi Freedom Democratic Party II 28, 161,
   197
   relationship with African Americans III 118
Democratic Republic of Vietnam. *See* North Vietnam
Deng Xiaoping VI 4, 42, 44, 204
   visits United States VI 43
Denmark VIII 280, 283–284; IX 171, 225; XI 176;
   XIV 31
   Iceland's secession from XIV 171
   Jewish rescue in WWII XI 175
   slave trade XIII 270
Dennis v. *United States* I 78–79
deoxyribonucleic acid (DNA) II 82–85
Department of Commerce and Labor, Bureau of
   Corporations III 242
Department of Defense I 74, 83
Department of Energy VI 257
Department of State I 83
Der Ewige Jude (The Eternal Jew, 1940) XI 269
Der Hauptmann von Kopenick (The Captain from
   Kopenick, 1930) IX 84
Der Rosenkavalier (1911) IX 84
Der Stürmer XI 24, 185, 254
Derby Scheme IX 58
Desert Storm (1991) VI 28
Dessalines, Jean-Jacques XIII 209–210, 213
   assassinated XIII 213
d'Estaing, Valéry Giscard VI 104
Destouches, Louis-Ferdinand (Louis-Ferdinand Celine)
   IX 84
détente I 11, 52, 101–106, 140–143; II 56, 60, 63, 118,
   168, 170–174; VI 2, 21, 32–33, 35, 41, 65,
   68, 88, 103, 112, 116, 164–166, 202–204,
   209, 229, 232, 237–238, 256–257, 270; XIV
   2
deterrence theory VI 31
Detroit riots VI 141
Dew, Thomas Roderick XIII 71, 73
Dewey, Thomas E. I 60, 272; II 280
DeWitt, John L. III 103, 106, 109; V 184, 187
Diablo Canyon VII 178
Diagne, Blaise IX 113
Diamond Necklace Affair (1785) XII 131
Diary of Anne Frank, The (1959) XI 155, 158
Díaz, Porfirio III 125, 127
Diaz de Vivar, Rodrigo (el Cid) X 2, 41, 245
dichlorodiphenyltrichloroethane (DDT) VII 147, 234
Dickey, James IX 234
Dickinson, Goldsworthy IX 172
Dickinson, John XII 54, 70, 95, 113, 214, 233
Diderot, Denis X 80
Dies, Martin Jr. XI 57
Dietrich, Marlene XI 158
Dimitrov, Georgi Mikhailovich VI 275, 280
Dinosaur National Monument, Colorado VII 27, 29,
   112
Dinwiddie, Robert XII 199
Directive 21 XI 82
Dismal Swamp XIII 104, 107, 157
Displaced Persons (DPs) XI 122–124, 126
Disqualifying Act XII 291
Disraeli, Benjamin VIII 168; IX 98–99, 112; X 57, 59
Dissenters XII 235
District of Columbia
   signs the Chesapeake Bay 2000 Agreement VII 49
Dixiecrats VI 142
Djibouti XIV 55
Djilas, Milovan VI 275, 278, 280–281
Dobruja IX 205
Dobrynin, Anatoly VI 41, 163
Doctors' Trial (1946–1949) XI 147–148

Doctrine of World Empires IX 112
Dodacanese Islands VIII 212
Dodd, Christopher J. VI 194
Dodd, Thomas XII 29
Dole, Robert XV 78
Dome of the Rock XIV 19, 22, 159, 165
Dominica XII 311, 313–314
    maroons in XII 314
Dominican Republic I 15, 24, 71, 91, 94, 125; III 247;
    VI 66, 140, 266; IX 96
    rumored coup in VI 140
    U.S. troops in (1965) VI 140, 165–166
Dominicans X 65; XI 23
domino theory I 130, 266–267, 295–299; II 119, 266–
    267
Donatism X 17
Dongamusi area, Zimbabwe VII 64
Dönitz, Karl V 3, 79–85, 143, 256–257, 262; XI 254,
    258, 262
Donzère-Mondragon Dam (France) VII 93, 95
Doolittle, James C. "Jimmy" V 92, 98–99
Doolittle Raid (1942) V 3
Dornier, Claudius IX 218
Dorsey, Tommy IX 4
Dos Passos, John III 182, 234–237; IX 4
Dostoyevsky, Fyodor XI 75
Douglas, Stephen A. XIII 18, 173
Douglas, William O. II 284; III 105; XII 64
Douglass, Frederick XIII 3, 9, 83, 113, 116, 124, 204,
    234
Douhet, Giulio IX 220, 223
Doullens Conference (1918) IX 108
Downey, Sheridan VII 153, 156
Down's Syndrome XI 17
*Dr. Strangelove or How I Learned to Stop Worrying and
    Love the Bomb* (1964) I 236; VI 31
draft resistance movement II 4, 6
Drakensburg Mountains VII 236
Drayton, William Henry XII 68
Dreadnought (British ship) IX 141, 179
Dred Scott v. *Sandford* (1857) II 280; III 28; XII 263;
    XIII 57, 95, 100
Dresden, bombing of V 5, 54, 88, 221
Dresden (German ship) VIII 133, 137
Dresdner Bank VII 250
Drexil Institute IX 21
Dreyfus, Alfred VIII 68, 147, 149, 168
Dreyfus Affair (1894–1898) VI 136; VIII 68, 146–147,
    149, 151–152, 164
Du Bois, W. E. B. II 44, 46, 137; III 84, 117–118, 120–
    123, 182, 267–274; IX 2–3, 5; XIII 54, 95,
    202, 204
Dual Alliance VIII 73
Dual Monarchy VIII 43–47, 76; IX 133–134, 136
Dubai XIV 34
Dubcek, Alexander VI 119
Duhamel, Georges IX 212
Dulany, Daniel XII 58, 139
Dulles, Allen I 71, 130; II 50; XV 61, 158
    ties to United Fruit Company I 126
Dulles, John Foster I 49, 69, 130, 149, 267–274, 278,
    282; II 50–51, 135, 168, 208; VI 130, 153,
    221, 268; XIV 177; XV 14, 26, 30–31, 58–64,
    158, 168, 205, 245, 249, 271
    "massive retaliation" policy I 192, 211, 213
    New Look policy I 117, 211, 214
    Northern Tier approach XV 26, 31, 59
    U.S. policies in Europe I 208
Dunkirk evacuation (1940) V 123
Dunkirk Treaty (1947) I 208; VI 210
Du Pont Corporation IX 22
Duportail, Louis Lebègue de Presle XII 106
Durance River VII 98
Dust Bowl VII 181, 183, 185
Dutch East Indies VIII 137
Dutch Middleburg Company XIII 136, 269, 274
Dutch Reformers XII 235
Dutch West India Company XIII 274

Duvalier, François "Papa Doc" XI 167
Duwamish River VII 189, 191
Dyer, Reginald IX 93
Dyer Bill IX 4
Dzhugashvili, Iosef IX 197

E

Eaker, Ira C. V 5, 98
Earl of Sandwich XII 36
Earth Day VII 123, 265
East Africa VIII 193
    bombing of U.S. embassies in (1998) XIV 12
East Germany I 107, 274; VI 110–111, 115–122, 141,
    178, 182, 206–212, 217, 246, 249, 251, 261,
    276; XI 214
    defectors VI 170
    dissidents in VI 117, 121, 211
    Dulles acceptance of Soviet influence I 273
    flight of citizens VI 141
    political parties in VI 121
    reforms I 154
    relations with Soviet Union I 253
    revolt against totalitarianism (1953) I 254
    shift in leadership VI 117
    Soviet suspicion of I 185
    strategic importance I 109
East India Company XII 197, 200, 234, 237; XIII 271
East Jerusalem XIV 19, 154, 157, 160, 162–163; XV 20–
    21, 42, 79, 134, 136, 183, 190–191, 194–195,
    215, 219, 226
East Prussia VIII 249, 252, 280; IX 15, 158
East St. Louis, riot IX 7
East Timor, Indonesian invasion of VI 270
Easter Rising (1916) VIII 154–162, 209; IV 21
Eastern Europe VI 116, 120, 131, 148, 181, 201, 207–
    208, 221, 224, 226, 236, 251, 267, 281; VII
    250; IV 81, 83; X 62, 67, 130, 178, 180–182,
    206, 265, 301; XIV 2, 6, 82, 110, 112; XV 33,
    253
    collapse of communist regimes in VII 101
    collapse of Soviet control in VI 216
    Crusades in X 66, 128, 270
    democracies in XV 82
    dissident movements in VI 229
    environmental crisis in VII 17–24
    German occupation (World War I) VIII 91–101,
    176
    German occupation (World War II) VIII 91–101
    NATO expansion in VI 54
    political repression in VII 18
    removal of Soviet forces VI 110
    Soviets block Marshall Plan to VI 255
    Soviets in VI 244–245, 250, 252
    treatment of refuges VI 251
    U.S. support of dissidents in VI 3
    voter apathy on environmental issues VII 20
Eastern Orthodox Church VIII 207; X 25, 190, 208
Easton, James XII 11
Eban, Abba XV 135, 213, 217
Ebert, Friedrich VIII 257, 280; IX 32
Ebro River VII 147
Echo Park Dam (United States) VII 27, 29, 30–31
Economic Commission for Latin America (ECLA) I
    20–22
Economic Market of the Southern Cone
    (Mercosur) XIV 71
Economic Opportunity Act (1964) II 276
Economic Opportunity Act (1965) II 272
Ecuador XIII 104; XIV 212, 217
Eden, Anthony I 272, 280; V 41, 290, 312; VI 11; XV
    160, 247
    "Mansion Speech" (1941) XV 146
Edessa X 48, 74, 92, 129–130, 167, 191, 270, 296–297
Edison, Thomas Alva VIII 197
Edmondson, W. T. VII 189, 192
Edward I X 189
Edward VII X 57

INDEX

Edwards, Jonathan XII 147–149

Edwards Aquifer VII 69–75

Egypt I 308–312, 273, 283; II 53; VI 11, 83, 137, 162–
164, 172, 246, 271–27; VII 29, 82, 135, 149;
VIII 31–32, 38, 168, 213; IX 96; X 24, 30,
46–51, 56, 60, 64, 66, 78, 89, 95, 107, 109,
139–142, 144–148, 155–156, 167, 170, 173–
174, 182, 185, 187, 193, 239, 248, 251, 255–
258, 273, 277, 282, 287, 292; XII 165, 168;
XIV 7, 23, 31, 34, 52, 55–56, 61, 68, 79, 81–
83, 85, 88, 105, 114, 116, 134, 141, 143, 146–
149, 154, 176–183, 186, 190, 193–195, 197–
201, 206, 217, 220, 225, 228, 235, 242, 252,
255, 282; XV 12, 14, 19–23, 27, 30–34, 40,
42, 45, 51–57, 58–59, 61–62, 73, 79, 81, 100–
101, 116, 127, 134–137, 141–146, 150, 166,
168–169, 176, 184–185, 199, 204, 206–207,
213, 216, 219–220, 223, 226–227, 238–241,
254, 257, 261, 275

    Arab-Israeli War (1967) II 150

    Arab Republic of Egypt XV 223

    Arab Socialist Union XV 70

    arms XV 68

    Aswan Dam II 146, 148; VII 3

    attack on Israel VI 10, 161, 163

    attacks on tourists XIV 191

    boycotts XIV 50

    Central Security Forces XV 224

    conflict with Israel I 159

    Coptic Christians XV 276

    corruption in XIV 48

    cotton and textile exports XIV 45

    deportation of Jews VIII 166

    economy XIV 47, 51, 54

    education XIV 52

    environmental control in VII 145

    expels Soviet advisers XV 220, 223, 240

    Free Officers' regime II 148; XIV 193

    Free Officers Revolution (1952) XV 59, 63, 65–
70, 101, 119, 220, 226, 244, 249

    Great Britain in VIII 35

    Hadeto (Democratic Movement for National
Liberation) XV 69

    Jewish spying in XIV 129

    July Laws (1961) XV 70

    Kafara Dam VII 3

    labor XIV 52

    Marxists in XV 69

    National Assembly XV 56, 222

    National Union Party XV 273

    nuclear weapons development I 219

    relations with United States XIV 16

    Revolutionary Command Council (RCC) XV 66,
68, 70

    Soviet alliance I 161; II 146; VI 43, 81

    Soviet arms XV 40, 253

    Soviet-Egyptian Pact (1955) I 162

    Suez Canal I 308, 316

    Suez Crisis I 289; VI 135, 270

    Suez War I 277, 280; XV 244–251, 253

    Sunni Muslims XV 276

    United Arab Republic (UAR) XV 70, 147, 270–
276

    U.S. resistance to return of Soviet troops VI 163

    U.S. support for authoritarian regime XIV 14

    Wafd Party XV 69

    water XIV 269–271

    weapons XIV 144

    Western Desert Project VII 2

    women XIV 116, 119, 121, 287, 291

    World War I VIII 37–42

    Young Egypt XV 70

Egyptian Center for Women Rights XIV 116

Egyptian Communist Party XV 69

Egyptian Space Channel (ESC) XIV 29

Egyptian-Israeli Armistice Agreement (1949) XV 247

Egyptian-Israeli peace treaty (1979) XIV 19, 116, 125,
145, 154; XV 20, 51–57, 104, 127, 130, 133,
149, 187, 219, 227, 238, 241, 255

Ehrlichman, John D. VI 24

Eichmann, Adolf XI 36–43, 51, 75, 103, 158, 211, 227,
233

Einsatzgruppen (mobile killing units) IV 88, 131, 134,
141; V 161; XI 14, 86, 90–91, 102, 108, 171,
250

Einstein, Albert VIII 167; IX 87

Eisenhower, Dwight D. I 35, 64, 71, 92, 102, 210–215,
274, 292, 297, 306; II 38, 45, 49–55, 64, 67,
105–106, 112, 135, 137, 200, 229, 232, 260,
280; IV 183; V 314, 92, 69, 281, 284; VI
11, 17, 35, 64, 86, 96, 130, 133, 136, 139,
153, 155, 231; IX 108–109; XI 123–124,
252, 257; XII 31, 303; XIV 177; XV 26, 30–
31, 135, 137, 165, 167–169, 245, 249–250,
271

    appeal to Soviets VI 135

    Atoms for Peace I 216–217; II 49, 53

    Battle of the Bulge IV 64

    Bay of Pigs invasion II 52, 54, 115

    Berlin crisis I 69

    "Chance for Peace" speech II 53

    dealings with de Gaulle VI 105

    Eisenhower Doctrine (1957) I 280–282; II 148;
XIV 177; XV 14, 58–64, 166, 168–169, 250,
271

    foreign policy of VI 141

    Interstate Highway Act II 105

    Korea VI 146

    military career IV 65

    NATO commander-general I 208

    1952 presidential campaign I 274

    Open Skies policy II 51, 54; VI 20, 35

    planning D-Day invasion IV 68

    restraint in use of nuclear weapons I 236–237

    rollback policy I 72

    sends envoy to mediate Middle East water dispute
VII 138

    space program II 242, 260

    Suez Crisis VI 80

    summit with Macmillan VI 10

    support of U.S. involvement in Korea II 211

    Supreme Allied Commander II 50

    System of Interstate and Defense Highways II
109

    Taiwan policy I 68

    vetos rivers-and-harbors legislation VII 259

    WWI service VIII 192

    WWII strategy in Germany VI 169

Eisenhower administration I 49, 66, 94, 110, 117, 281;
VI 30, 56, 81, 92, 95, 139, 149, 238; VII
259

    "atomic diplomacy" I 211, 213, 267

    Atoms for Peace policy I 216

    concern over Soviet Middle East policy VI 239

    containment policy I 184

    defense spending VI 144

    Dulles, John Foster I 278

    East Germany policy I 271

    Eisenhower Doctrine I 282; XV 14, 166, 168–169,
250, 271

    Hungarian uprising VI 13

    Iran XV 108, 157

    Middle East policy I 161; XV 30, 58–64, 68, 156,
165–170, 271, 273

    military spending I 69, 192

    New Look policy I 210–215, 266; XV 26

    Nixon as vice president VI 203

    policy on Cuba VI 141

    refuses to recognize Castro VI 64

    rejection of arms control I 230

    "rollback" strategy VI 221

    Social Progress Trust Fund I 20

    Suez Crisis VI 11; XV 244–251

    Taiwan policy I 266, 268, 270

INDEX

INDEX

Groupe Islamique Armee (Armed Islamic Group, GIA) XV 2, 5
Groves, Leslie I 28, 235, 247
Guadeloupe IX 111
Guantanamo Bay VI 64
Guatemala I 54–56, 70, 89, 94, 122–133; II 40, 103; VI 21, 131, 194, 266
    Agrarian Reform Law (1952) I 123, 126
    CIA involvement I 211; XV 157
    CIA trained anti-Castro Cubans in VI 141
    coup of 1954 I 123
    human rights violations in VI 241
    Marxist guerrillas in VI 193
    military coup of 1963 I 24
    1954 coup I 128
    United Fruit Company I 70
    U.S. intervention (1954) I 15, 123–133
Guderian, Heinz W. IV 282; V 123–127
Guevara, Ernesto "Che" I 93; II 160, 215; VI 70; XV 49
    death I 126
    role in communist revolution in Bolivia I 126
Guibert of Nogent X 72, 97–98, 100, 103, 128, 164, 212–213, 234, 281
Guigo de Castro X 162–163
Guiscard, Robert X 73, 121–122, 220, 228, 269, 284–285
gulag archipelago VI 250
Gulf Cooperation Council (GCC) XIV 114, 180, 247; XV 141, 147
Gulf of Aqaba XV 20–21, 135, 137, 170, 247, 250
Gulf of Sidra VI 165, 234; XIV 198
Gulf of Tonkin incident (1964) I 291; VI 144
Gulf of Tonkin Resolution (1964) I 91; II 7; VI 139, 284, 287; XII 31
Gulf Oil Company XIV 211–212; XV 172–173, 177, 178
gunboat diplomacy VI 166
Gurion, David Ben I 216
Guy of Lusignan X 52, 251, 256, 259
Guyana. *See* British Guiana
Gypsies, murder of VIII 94–95; XI 66, 71, 73, 147, 149, 153, 171, 186, 190, 242–243, 247, 257

H

Haas, Richard XIV 97, 100
Habash, George XV 41, 90, 199
Habeas Corpus VI 9
Haber, Fritz VIII 241–242
Habib, Philip Charles VI 229; XV 132, 153
Habitat Patch Connectivity Project VII 232
Habsburg Empire VI 217; VIII 43, 257, 281; IX 133–138, 206, 225, 266–267; XII 189
Hachani, Abdelkader XV 4–5, 8
Hadid, Muhammad XV 122–123, 124
Hadrian XI 19
Hafiz El Assad II 146
Hafsids X 66, 146
Hague Conference (1911–1912) III 137; VIII 240
Hague Conventions (1907) V 222, 264; VIII 244; XI 258; XV 79
Haig, Alexander M. I 56; II 179; VI 44, 225, 229, 231; XIV 198
Haig, Douglas VIII 52, 56, 77, 79, 103–104, 106, 108, 114, 218–221, 223, 26, 271–273; IX 34–39, 107–108, 110, 120, 123, 211
Hainburg Dam Project (Austria) VII 105
Haiti I 51, 125; II 100; III 50; VI 58, 194, 213, 217, 283; IX 96; XII 169; XIII 156, 209–216
Haitian Revolution XIII 209–216
Haldane Reforms (1906) IX 51
Haldeman, Harry R. VI 24
Halder, Franz V 126–127, 227
Ha-Levi, Yehuda ben Shemuel X 273, 275
Hallstein Doctrine VI 208, 210
Halsey Jr., William F. IV 173
Hamad XIV 61–63

Haman Act VII 47
Hamas XIV 24, 41, 93, 103, 105, 107, 127, 148, 184, 230; XV 90, 182, 186, 194, 201, 264
Hamilton, Alexander XII 34, 58, 65, 68, 70, 73, 97, 114, 119–122, 127, 162, 222–224, 228–229, 258, 279, 289–291, 296; XIII 281
Hamilton, Ian VIII 118–119, 122
Hammarskjold, Dag XV 247
Hammond, James Henry XIII 27, 48, 81, 83, 87, 218–219, 240, 264–265
Hampton, Wade XIII 155, 233, 235
Hancock, John XII 110, 291; XIII 48
Hankey, Maurice VIII 79
Hannibal VIII 179, 249
Hanoi I 41–47
Hanoverians XII 136
Haram al-Sharif 19, 22–23, 159–160, 165–167
Hardin, Garrett VII 47, 70, 72–73
Harding, Warren G. III 25, 69, 175–178; IX 92; XI 56
Harding administration IX 171
Harkin, Thomas R. VI 194
Harlan, John Marshall II 23, 282–283; XIII 57
Harlem Renaissance III 78–84, 118–120, 184; IX 1, 4
Harper, William XIII 70, 73–74, 165, 217, 267
Harper's Ferry (1859) XIII 4
Harriman, W. Averell I 306; II 264; V 312; XV 160
Harrington, James XII 119, 122–123, 209
Harris, Sir Arthur "Bomber" V 87, 91
Harrison, Earl G. XI 122–124
Harrison Act (1914) III 133, 137
    narcotics legislation III 137
Hart, Sir Basil Henry Liddell V 23, 102
Harvard University VI 90, 129, 199, 203, 258; XIII 198; XIV 14
Hashemite Arabs VIII 40–41; XIV 245
Hashemite Kingdom XIV 160, 166; XV 32, 34, 41–42, 44–45, 116, 121, 142, 146, 273, 275
Hassan II XIV 74, 209, 278, 282–283; XV 44
Hat Act (1732) XII 198, 202, 243
Hatch Act (1939) III 11
Hauptmann, Bruno III 110–116
Hausner, Gideon XI 38–41
Hawaii IX 96
Hawatmah, Nayef XV 41, 90, 199
Hayden, Carl Trumbull VII 109, 112, 154–155
Hayes, James Allison VII 274
Hays, Mary Ludwig (Molly Pitcher) XII 263
Hazen, Moses XII 12
Heady, Earl O. VII 187
Hebrew University XIV 225
Hebron massacre (1994) XV 187
Hebron Protocol (1997) XV 185
Heeringen, Josias von VIII 180, 184
Hegel, Georg XIV 77, 84
Heights of Abraham XII 160
Heine, Heinrich VI 121
Hells Canyon Dam (United States) VII 55
Helms, Richard M. VI 24
Helms-Burton Bill I 97–98
Helper, Hinton Rowan XIII 46, 69
Helsinki Accords VI 200
Helsinki Conference (1975) I 142
Hemingway, Ernest VIII 186, 188, 191; IX 4
Henderson, Loy XV 158–159, 161–162
Hendrix, Jimi II 219
Henry II X 260; XI 88
Henry III X 66, 143, 284
Henry IV X 15, 85, 115, 117–119, 121, 205, 216, 219–220, 224, 227–229, 284–285; XI 80
Henry VIII, founds Royal Navy VIII 30
Henry of Le Mans X 215–216
Henry, Patrick XII 76, 97, 110, 113–114, 139, 205, 241, 263, 279, 281; XIII 18–19, 48
Hepburn Act (1906) III 243, III 245
Herder, Johann Gottfried XII 61
Herero/Nama Rebellion (1904) VIII 87
Herod the Great XIV 159
Herzl, Theodor XI 120, 126; XIV 163, 258; XV 33

Hopkins, Esek XII 77, 81
Hopkins, Harry L. I 306; V 196; VI 155
Hopkins, Joseph XII 287
Hopkins, Samuel XII 58
Hopkins, Stephen XII 152
Hopkinson, Francis XII 307
horizontal escalation VI 221
Horn of Africa VI 42, 164, 256; XIV 180
Hortobagy National Park VII 253
Hospitallers X 30, 49, 75, 90, 158, 174
Höss, Rudolf XI 131, 186
Hostiensis X 57, 178, 226, 236
House, Edward VIII 228
House of Burgesses XII 148, 241
House Un-American Activities Committee (HUAC) I
        77, 79, 306; II 130–134, 207; VI 124, 127,
        129, 178
Houston, Charles Hamilton II 19, 22, 137–138
Houston Accords (1997) XIV 279–280, 284
How the Other Half Lives (Riis) III 260
Howard University XIII 254
Howard v. *Howard* (1858) XIII 101
Howe, George Augustus XII 156, 159
Howe, Richard XII 37, 106, 155–158
Howe, William XII 30, 37, 39, 40, 44–45, 47–48, 94,
        146, 155–158, 181–182, 267–268, 270–271,
        273–274, 304–307
Hoxha, Enver VI 181
Hoyos Mission (1914) VIII 47
Huck, Christian XII 186
Hudson Bay XII 171
Hudson Bay Company XII 200
Hudson Motor Car Company IX 21
Hudson River VII 256, 261; XII 10, 39, 43–44, 98,
        162, 177, 267, 269–271, 304
Hudson River Valley XII 46
Hugh of Peccator X 161, 163, 165
Hughes, Justice Charles Evans III 25–27, 179; V 205
Hughes, Henry XIII 48, 221
Hughes, Langston III 79, 83, 182; IX 4
Hulegu X 183, 185–187
Hull, Cordell III 47, 50; V 264, 312; VI 78–79 ; XI 60
Human Development Index (HDI) XIV 55–56
human rights I 140–146; II 97–102; VI 51, 208
        influence on U.S. foreign policy II 101
        U.S. history II 98
Humbert of Romans X 33, 65–66, 69
Humbert of Silva X 209, 284
Humboldt, Alexander von XIII 272
Hume, David X 80, 98; XII 121
Humphrey, Hubert H. II 162, 177, 197; VI 85–86
Hundred Years' War (1337–1453) XI 80
Hungarian Revolutionary Committee VI 134
Hungarian uprising (1956) VI 130–137
Hungary I 109, 112, 119, 152, 274, 294; II 36, 52; VI
        8, 103, 110, 116, 118, 165, 178, 181, 217, 246,
        249, 251, 261, 274; VII 247–249, 253–254;
        IX 134, 225; IX 134, 225; XI 24, 60, 175,
        177, 214; XIV 265; XV 120
        attempted coup against communists (1956) I 276;
        VI 130, 270
        Crusaders X 15–16, 182
        dams in VII 100–107
        East German emigration through VI 118, 121
        environmental groups in VII 103
        Jews in XI 202, 213
        Ministry for Environmental Protection VII 247–
        248, 250
        Ministry of Water and T transportation VII 250
        Soviet invasion of VI 182; XV 245
Hunt, E. Howard VI 24
Huntington, Samuel P. VI 198
Hurston, Zora Neale II 137; III 78–82, 184; IX 4
Husayn XV 234–235
Husayn ibn 'Ali (King Hussein) VIII 37–40
Hussein (King of Jordan) I 156, 314, 317; II 147; VI
        201; XIV 64, 66, 68; XV 22–23, 25, 40–50,

        61–63, 136–137, 169, 198–199, 220, 247,
        266
        visits United States XV 44
Hussein, Saddam I 159, 163, 224; II 153, 156; VI 54,
        58, 61, 217, 225; X 56; XI 166; XIV 29, 31,
        36, 61, 88, 96, 102, 109, 146, 170, 173, 191,
        215, 237–243, 270; XV 72–82, 84, 86–87, 90,
        98, 100–101, 104–105, 112, 120, 182, 255,
        258, 260
Hutchinson, Thomas XII 192, 214
Hutier, Oskar von VIII 112, 240; IX 129
Hutt Committee XIII 136
Huxley, Aldous IX 84

I

I. G. Farben XI 205, 221
Ibadite movement XIV 206
Iberian Peninsula X 2, 219, 287
Ibn al-Athir X 47, 192, 248
ibn al-Saabah, Hassan X 183–184, 258
Ibn Jubayr X 47, 193–196, 198
ibn Munqidh, Usamah X 192, 198–200
Ibn Saud X 61
Ice Harbor Dam (United States) VII 31, 55
Iceland, secession from Denmark XIV 171
"Ichi-Go Offensive" (1944) V 151
Ickes, Harold L. II 211; III 150
Idaho VII 201, 220, 224
        dams in VII 26, 29
        salmon in VII 196
Idaho Fish and Game Department VII 53
Idaho Rivers United VII 221
Idrissid monarchy (789–926) XIV 206
Ilkhans X 60, 182, 185–186, 189
Illinois XI 124
        Native Americans in XII 176
Illyria IX 270
Immigration Act (1924) III 22, 229
Immigration and Nationality Act (1952) I 77
Imperial Economic Conference (1932) VI 78
Imperial Guard Cavalry IX 116
Imperial Irrigation District (IID) VII 152, 154–155
Imperial Valley VII 151, 154–155
Imperial Presidency VI 56–57
Imperialism XIV 178; XV 22, 58, 101
        during the Crusades X 55–56, 63
        end of IX 91–97
Import-Export Bank I 53; III 47
import-substituting industrialization (ISI) XV 106
Incidents at Sea Agreement (1972) VI 31
indentured servitude XIII 164
Independence Party II 199
Independent Air Force IX 11
India I 151, 277; II 85, 117; VI 50, 53, 79, 136, 188,
        214–215, 219, 271; VII 125; VIII 32–33, 83,
        103, 133, 168, 208; IX 93, 112, 225–226; X
        305; XII 33, 165, 168, 171, 252; XIV 88,
        144, 147, 176–177, 260; XV 68, 167, 215
        agriculture in VII 130, 133
        Army VIII 38
        British rule in VI 161; VII 125
        Central Ministry of Environment and Forests VII
        133
        dams in VII 9, 125–134
        Hindutva XIV 141
        Ministry of Environment and Forests VII 128
        Moghul canals in VII 125
        National Congress IX 93
        nuclear test (1974) I 216, 223
        nuclear weapons development I 219–223, 228; VI
        53; XIV 40
        policy toward Soviet Union VI 81
        slaves in XIII 37
        World War I VIII 216
        motivation of soldiers in VIII 266
Indian Ocean VIII 137; XII 39, 198; XIII 129
        Dutch traders in XII 198

Western interest in VI 255
Westernization XV 229
White Revolution XV 229, 231
women XIV 121, 123, 140, 231
Iran-Contra Affair VI 3, 57–58, 191–196, 231–232; XV 98, 102
Iran-Iraq War (1980–1988) I 54; VI 162, 271; XIV 36, 38, 41, 89, 173, 248; XV 72, 74, 78–79, 89, 91, 97–105, 109, 112, 126, 176, 253, 260
Iranian Revolution (1979) XIV 2, 36–37, 41, 89, 121, 123, 125–126, 131, 140, 186, 217; XV 29, 53, 97, 102, 104, 106–115, 149, 176, 228, 234–235, 276
Iraq I 202; II 144, 153; 54, 58, 107, 162–163, 213, 215, 217, 219, 261, 268, 271; IX 92, 96, 206; X 56, 60, 89, 185–186, 278, 288; XIV 31, 37–38, 40–41, 50, 55–56, 61, 79, 87, 95–96, 101, 106–107, 109–110, 112, 125–126, 143–144, 146, 176–177, 179–181, 190, 211–212, 215, 219–220, 230–231, 237–243, 250, 262, 265, 267; XV 20, 22–23, 26–27, 29, 31–32, 34, 41, 44–45, 48, 57, 59, 62, 75, 141–142, 144–146, 169, 187, 201, 204, 206, 209, 216, 222, 251, 263, 267, 270–272, 275
    ancient irrigation in VII 11
    Anfal campaign (1988–1989) XIV 169; XV 79
    Baath Party XIV 82, 253; XV 80, 117, 124, 273, 275
    biological weapons XV 78
    chemical weapons XV 74, 78–79
    Communist Party XV 117, 273
    Free Officers Movement XV 117–118
    Gulf War I 163; VI 72–79, 80–88, 225
    Halabja massacre (1998) XIV 169
    Highway of Death XV 85–86
    Independence Party XV 117
    Interim Constitution XV 117
    invasion of Kuwait I 289; XIV 215, 218; XV 89, 98, 147, 255
    Iran-Iraq War XV 97–105
    Iraqi Revolution XV 116–125
    Jews forced from XIV 221
    Kurds VI 54, 61, 217; XIV 168–174; XV 87, 98, 100, 102
    Kurds, massacres of XI 166
    Mosul Revolt XV 124
    National Democratic Party XV 117–118, 123
    National Union Front XV 117
    no-flight zone XV 87
    nuclear program XV 74
    oil XV 175, 177–178
    oil companies in XV 177
    Osirak nuclear facility VI 106; XIV 149
    overthrow of Faisal II (1958) I 282
    Pan-Arab campaign I 281
    Revolution (1958) XV 166, 168, 270
    Shiites in VI 61, 217; XV 102
    Sunnis in 98, 102
    U.S. invasion of (2003) XIV 14, 68, 89, 96, 191, 277
    U.S. propaganda in XV 256
    water policy in VII 135–141; XIV 269–270, 273; XV 206
    women XV 119
Iraq Liberation Act (1998) XIV 240, 243
Iraqi Atomic Energy Commission XV 78
Iraqi National Oil Company XV 119
Iraq Petroleum Company XV 119, 177
Ireland VIII 83; IX 93; XII 34, 166
    British rule in VIII 154–162
    Catholic condemnation of Easter Rising VIII 209
    Council of Bishops VIII 209
    Easter Rising VIII 154–162, 209; IX 21
    famine in VIII 189; XII 166
    Home Rule VIII 154–162
    immigrants to America XII 279
    uprising in (1798) XII 189
    World War I

conscription in VIII 158
    impact upon country VIII 154–162
    religion in VIII 208
    "Wild Geese" soldiers IX 116
Irish Citizen Army VIII 158
Irish Parliamentary Party VIII 155–156
Irish Republican Army VIII 158; IX 93; XIV 195, 198
Irish Republican Brotherhood VIII 155–156
Irish Sea XII 79
Irish Unionists VIII 161
Irish Volunteers VIII 158, 161
Iron Act (1750) XII 202, 243
Iron Curtain VI 49, 118, 173, 206
Iron Curtain speech (1946) VI 250
Iroquoia XII 174, 177, 179
Irving, Washington XII 259
Isaac II Angelus X 26, 29, 250
Isaacson, Judith XI 69, 223
Isabella X 2, 22
Isadore of Seville X 242
Islam X 4, 65, 100, 199, 201; XIV 19, 55, 81, 93, 159, 176, 180–181, 201, 205, 230–231, 235, 244, 250, 261, 291; XV 31
    democracy XIV 133–142
    disenfranchisement of women XIV 140
    movements XIV 79, 252
    political Islam XIV 136–137, 139
    radicalism XIV 61
    United States seen as enemy of XIV 87
    violence in XIV 182–191
Islamic fundamentalism XIV 7, 182, 231
    women XIV 121
Islamic Jihad XIV 24, 93, 103, 186, 230; XV 90
Islamic Salvation Army (AIS) XV 5
Islamism XIV 7, 182
Isle of Man XII 242
Isma'il, Hafiz I 309–312
Israel I 56, 162–164, 278, 283, 309, 316–317; VI 43, 83, 164, 172, 188, 200–201, 215, 246, 261, 271; X 55–56, 60, 63, 272, 305; XI 228; XIV 16, 30–32, 41, 55–56, 63, 76–77, 79, 87, 89, 95–108, 126, 129, 153, 159, 177, 179–180, 184, 198, 205, 217, 238–242, 246, 248; XV 19–21, 23, 30–31, 40, 42, 46–47, 51–58, 62–63, 69–70, 75, 78–79, 83, 91, 101, 121, 134–140, 142, 149–150, 152–153, 155, 167–168, 170, 193–194, 198–200, 202, 204, 213–216, 237–241, 271, 275–276
    Agudat Yisrael Party XIV 252, 256, 258–259
    Arab economic boycott of XIV 44, 50
    Arab invasion (1948) XIV 144
    Arab opposition to VI 160; XIV 125
    Arab population in XIV 258
    attacked by Egypt and Syria VI 163
    attacks Iraqi nuclear facility XIV 148–149
    Basic Law 256
    boundaries XV 33–39
    Central Religious Camp XIV 256
    control of Jerusalem XIV 159–167
    criticism of XIV 14
    Degel Torah XIV 256
    democratic army in XII 305
    Eichmann trial XI 36–43
    founding of IV 160
    Gahal (Gush Herut-Liberalim, or Freedom Liberal Bloc) XV 136
    Gaza raid (1955) XV 244, 248
    Gush Emunim (Bloc of the Faithful) XIV 256, 258; XV 139
    Herut Party XV 23
    impact of Holocaust on development of XI 120–127
    Internal Security Services XIV 225
    intifada in XIV 19–27; XV 89–96
    invasion of Lebanon I 196; XIV 126, 131, 270; XV 126–133, 255
    Iraqi bombing of I 195

INDEX

support of U.S. I 158; XIV 14
water XIV 269; XV 205
West Bank captured by Israel I 156
women XIV 116, 123–124, 287–288
Jordan River XIV 268–271; XV 20, 24, 34, 193, 205–
206
Jordan River Basin VII 137–138
Jordan Valley Authority XV 205
Jordanian-Israeli treaty (1994) XIV 116
Joyce, James VIII 191
Jud Süss (1940) XI 90, 185
Judaism XIV 19, 22, 81, 159, 183, 187, 191, 253
Judea XIV 151, 259
Judgment at Nuremberg (1961) XI 158
Jugurtha XIV 206
Jünger, Ernst VIII 59, 64, 263; IX 131, 149, 212
Jupiter missiles VI 71
Justin Martyr XI 20
Justinian I X 228

K

Kádár, János VI 130, 134
Kafara Dam (Egypt) VII 3
Kafue Dam (Zambia) VII 137, 240
Kafue River VII 2, 5, 137
Kahn, Agha Mohammad Yahya VI 88
Kalahari Desert VII 33–34, 36–37, 236
lack of surface water in VII 38
Kalb, Johann de XII 101
kamikaze VIII 60
Kampuchia VI 165
Kansas VII 10–11, 13, 181–182, 185, 187
alfalfa production in VII 13
sugar-beet production in VII 13
violence in XIII 5
water diverted from VII 13
water policy in VII 185
wheat sales XV 78
Kant, Immanuel XI 75
Kapp Putsch (1920) IV 271
Kardelj, Edvard VI 281
Karen Liberation Army XV 14
Kariba Dam VII 1, 4–5, 8, 239, 242–243
Kariba George VII 1, 237, 239, 245
Karine A (ship) XIV 101, 105
Karl I VIII 257
Karmal, Babrak I 10–15; VI 238
Kashmir XIV 88, 93, 147
Katse Dam (Lesotho) VII 7, 237, 241, 244
Kattenburg, Paul VI 96
Katyn Forest massacre (1940) XI 169, 258, 260, 262
Kaufman, Irving R. II 131, 230, 232
Kazakhstan VI 109, 215; XIV 180, 228
Keating, Kenneth B. VI 73
Keitel, Wilhelm V 3, 127, 142–143, 223–224
Kelheim VII 204, 209
Kellogg, James L. VII 49
Kellogg-Briand Pact (1928) III 179; V 115; VIII 298;
XI 258
Kemble, Frances Anne XIII 83, 88, 189, 226
Keneally, Thomas XI 202, 205–206
Kennan, George F. I 22, 31, 75, 82, 138, 148, 150, 154,
159, 284–285, 288; II 8, 60, 267; VI 188
containment policy I 110, 274
domino theory I 266
later view of containment I 183
"Long Telegram" I 261; II 34, 205, 264; VI 9
Marshall Plan I 176
Mr. X II 206
rules for handling relations with the Soviet
Union I 186
Kennedy, John F. I 23, 64, 68, 89, 92, 94, 119–121,
130, 257, 291–292; II 8, 45, 52, 67–68, 93,
114–120, 160; III 48; VI 64, 66, 70, 73, 93,
96, 102–103, 138–145, 188; XI 129; XII 33;
XV 19, 137, 168
Alliance for Progress I 17, 20, 23; II 115

assasssination I 18; II 180; VI 138, 142
Bay of Pigs I 71; II 115, 119
Camelot mystique II 117
Cold War policies II 117
compared with Franklin D. Roosevelt II 115
criticism of Eisenhower administration I 193; VI
141
critiques of performance in Cuban Missile
Crisis VI 73
Cuban Missile Crisis II 116, 120, 265
decolonization policy VI 81
Food for Peace II 116
foreign policy II 117
Inauguration Address I 23
Jimmy Hoffa II 190
Johnson as vice president running mate VI 142
limited-nuclear-war doctrines I 169
Nuclear Test Ban Treaty (1963) II 118
Peace Corps II 116
plot to overthrow Castro I 276
presidential campaign I 17
promotion of space program II 260
Roman Catholicism of VI 142
State of the Union address (1961) VI 140
strategy in Southeast Asia VI 95
support of British VI 11
supports coup against Diem VI 98
United Nations II 115
Vietnam policy I 183
Kennedy, Robert F. II 9; VI 75, 96; XIII 277
assassination of II 162, 180
civil-rights issues II 22
Cuban Missile Crisis VI 70–76
nuclear disarmament in Turkey I 121
U.S. Attorney General II 22
War on Poverty involvement II 272
Kennedy administration VI 26, 56, 72, 92, 99, 138–
145, 238
Alliance for Progress I 17–26
and civil rights II 26
attempts to overthrow Fidel Castro I 24
Berlin Wall Crisis I 119–120
Cuban Missile Crisis I 120
Cuban policy I 67
"flexible response" I 115, 214
Iran XV 158
Latin America policy I 17–26
liberal activism of VII 123
limited-nuclear-war doctrines I 171
policy on Berlin VI 141
policy on Castro VI 71
responsibility for Vietnam War VI 99
scraps Skybolt missile VI 11
Vietnam policy I 293–294
Kent State University VI 23; XII 31
Kentucky, slavery in XII 297; XIII 222, 233
Kentucky Resolution XII 125
Kenya VI 188; XIV 176, 190, 197, 230; XV 33
attack on U.S. embassy (1998) XIV 16
Kepler, Johannes X 131
Keppel, Augustus XII 251
Kerensky, Aleksandr VIII 170–178, 223, 258; IX 200
Kern County Water Agency VII 179
Kerouac, Jack II 74, 160
Kerr Dam (Unted States) VII 169
Key West Agreement I 5–8
Keynes, John Maynard III 54–55; VIII 191; IX 84
Khan, Genghis VI 40
Kharijite movement XIV 206
Khariton, Yuly Borisovich
Soviet nuclear weapons development I 244–248
Khartoum summit (1967) XV 144
Kharzai, Hamid XIV 10
Khatami, Muhammad XIV 36, 38, 42, 137–138
Khmer Rouge I 15, 41, 44, 46, 295; VI 271
Khobar Towers bombing XIV 16, 251
Khomeini, Ayatollah Ruhollah I 11, 141, 158; VI 165,
268, 270; XIV 7, 36–37, 41, 125, 134, 141,

INDEX

Lennon, John II 216
Leo III X 26
Leo IV X 122
Leo IX X 121–122, 224, 228–229, 269, 284
Leopold II IX 42, 44
Leopold of Austria X 89–90
Leopold, Aldo VII 226, 278
Lesbians, during the Holocaust XI 245
Lesotho (Africa) VII 2, 4, 7, 236, 241, 243
Lesotho Highlands Development Authority (LHDA)
        VII 1–2, 4, 237, 243
Lesser Tunbs XIV 217
L'Etoile, Isaac X 162–163
Letters from a Farmer in Pennsylvania (1767–1768) XII
        233
Lettow-Vorbeck, Paul von VIII 84–90
the Levant VI 103; X 47, 66, 142, 180–181, 191–192,
        251, 261, 270, 301; XIV 177, 179
Levi, Primo XI 52, 111, 114, 164, 214, 217–219, 221,
        223, 228–229, 233, 238, 240
Levi-Strauss, Claude IX 84; X 161
Levitt, Abraham II 110, 252
Levitt, William II 110
Levittown, N.Y. II 110, 249
Lewis, C. S. VIII 61
Lewis, John L. II 22, 90–91, 161; III 192
Lewis, Meriwether XIII 48
Liberator, The XIII 8
Liberia IX 96; XIV 199–200
Libertad Act. *See* Helms-Burton bill
Liberty Bonds VIII 204, 296; IX 57
Liberty Union Party II 197
Libya I 152, 159, 28; VI 54, 107, 163, 165, 217, 271;
        VIII 39; IX 96; XIV 31, 55–56, 61, 68–70,
        72, 76, 79, 85, 110, 131, 144, 146, 176–177,
        179–180, 190, 192, 202–203, 205, 212, 215,
        217, 219, 230, 262; XV 23, 45, 57, 75, 142,
        222, 255, 271
    airliner crash (1973) XIV 129
    expels Tunisian workers XIV 197
    General People's Congress (GPC) XIV 194
    Great Man-Made River XIV 195
    Green March (1975) XIV 284
    Imperialism I 151
    Italian invasion of VIII 212
    Jews forced from XIV 221
    Jews in XIV 193
    Kufrah aquifer XIV 270
    lack of environmental control in VII 145
    nuclear weapons development I 219
    oil XV 175, 180
    revolution I 158
    Revolutionary Command Council XIV 193, 197
    support for Corsican and Basque separatists XIV
        198
    U.S. air strikes on VI 107, 222, 234
    water XIV 269–270
Liddell Hart, B. H. VIII 71, 196; IX 48
Lieber, Frances XIII 95
Lieberthal, Kenneth VI 41
Likens, Gene E. VII 262
Lilienthal, David E. I 27–31
Liman von Sanders, Otto VIII 120–121
Limited Nuclear Test Ban Treaty (1963) VI 18, 33
Limited-nuclear-war doctrines I 165–172
Limpopo River VII 33
Lincoln, Abraham VI 57; IX 6; XII 62, 110; XIII 5,
        18–19, 33, 153, 270, 274, 278, 283
    first inaugural speech XIII 276
Lincoln, Benjamin XII 229, 285
Lindbergh, Charles A. III 110–116; V 135; IX 87
Lindbergh kidnapping III 110–116
Lippmann, Walter II 8, 59; III 34, 207; VI 75
Litani River XV 206
Lithuania VI 178; VIII 93–94, 96, 283–284; IX 93; X
        179; XI 175, 260
Little Goose Dam (United States) VII 31
Livingston, William XII 207

Livingstone, David XII 167
Livonia VIII 97; X 179
Ljubljana Gap V 72–74
Lloyd George, David III 99; VIII 11, 20, 57, 77–83,
        102–108, 155–156, 219–223, 278, 280, 282–
        283; IX 54–59, 76, 83, 104, 108, 172–173,
        222, 226, 250
    industrial mobilization by VIII 78
    Minister of Munitions VIII 78
    Minister of War VIII 78
    thoughts on Germany VIII 81
Locarno Pact (1925) VIII 284
Lochner v. *New York* (1905) II 280–281
Locke, John XII 2, 34, 109–110, 114, 118–119, 121–
        122, 209, 259, 261, 302; XIII 17, 40, 195
Lockerbie (Pan Am) attack (1988) XIV 196, 197, 199,
        217
Lodge, Henry Cabot I 290, 298, 306; II 208; III 247;
        VI 95–96, 196; XIII 57
Lodz Ghetto XI 138, 140–141, 143–144, 224
Log College XII 148
Lombard League X 286
Lombardy X 26, 95, 221, 229
Lomé Convention (1975) VII 33
London Charter (1945) V 222
London Conference (1930) V 204; IX 227
London Conference (1945) XI 261
London Missionary Society XIII 159
London Naval Conference (1930) V 207
London Recommendations (1 June 1948) VI 101
London Suppliers' Group I 219, 223
Long, Huey III 28, 86–94, 210
Long Parliament XII 246
Lopez, Aaron XIII 270, 273
Los Alamos I 242–243
Los Angeles Department of Water and Power (LADWP)
        VII 178
Los Angeles Olympics (1984) VI 242
Louis IX X 30, 38, 59, 64–70, 139–147, 156, 173, 189,
        199–200, 235, 239, 255, 303
Louis XIV VIII 81, 278; XII 131; XIII 40
Louis XV XII 131
Louis XVI XII 39, 101, 103, 105, 127, 129, 131–134
Louisiana
    disfranchisement of blacks XIII 56
    grandfather clause XIII 56
    maroons in XIII 108, 111
    Reconstruction, end of XIII 55
    slave revolt XIII 91, 155, 156, 233, 235
    slavery in XIII 92, 97, 195, 221, 232, 240
Louisiana Purchase XII 125
Louisiana Stream Control Commission VII 161, 165
Louisiana Territory XIII 210
    U.S. purchase spurred by Haiti slave revolt XIII
        160
Lovejoy, Elijah P. XIII 8
Lovell, James XII 93, 98
Lovett, Robert XV 158, 203
Loving v. *Virginia* (1967) II 139
Lower Granite Dam (United States) VII 31
Lower Monumental Dam (United States) VII 31
low-intensity conflicts (LIC) VI 3, 131, 229
Loyettes project (France) VII 93
Luce, Clare Booth VI 257
Ludendorff, Erich V 157; VIII 12, 49, 54–55, 91, 93–
        97, 100, 114–115, 140, 143, 220, 240, 252,
        257, 266; IX 9, 12, 29–30, 65, 120, 122, 124,
        128, 131, 159
Ludendorff Offensive IX 30
Ludwig Canal VII 204–205
Luftwaffe (German Air Force) IV 6, 14, 19, 107, 125,
        163–169, 264, 282; V 1–2, 4–5, 7, 14, 60, 69,
        72, 93, 95, 96, 123, 133, 179, 181, 223, 230,
        231–233, 257
Lusitania (British ship), sinking of VIII 204, 288, 292;
        IX 21, 74, 181, 247
Luther, Martin VIII 204; XI 20–21, 23–24, 31–32
Lutheran Church XII 150, 205

INDEX

Index

racism XIII 179, 180
slave rebellions XIII 231–238
slavery in XIII 59–66
North Atlantic Regional Study (NARS) VII 261
North Atlantic Treaty Organization (NATO) I 35, 107,
120, 124, 151, 154, 160, 168, 170, 175, 182,
196, 198, 213, 222, 254, 277, 283, 296; II
50, 61, 100, 146, 152, 264, 267; IV 30; V 42,
149; VI 8–9, 11, 18–19, 50, 53, 80, 100–102;
105–106, 115, 131, 134–136, 173, 188, 199,
206–207, 209, 215, 217, 267, 271; VII 83; XI
188, 256; XIV 2, 228, 261–262, 264, 270;
XV 12, 14, 19, 26–27, 31, 139, 148, 203, 205
creation of I 204–209
involvement in Bosnian conflict II 154
military strategy in Europe VI 168–174
nuclear crisis XIV 239
withdrawal of France VI 145
North Carolina XII 19, 70, 122, 205, 209, 216, 264;
XIII 104, 107, 157
Act of 1791 XIII 98
grandfather clause XIII 56
gun laws XII 279
Loyalists in XII 182, 184–185, 192
oyster management in VII 49
panic over slave unrest XIII 238
Reconstruction, end of XIII 55
Scots in XII 187
slave laws XII 4
slavery in XIII 64, 87, 97–98, 101–102, 172, 227,
262, 265
state legislature XII 22
North Dakota VII 31
dams in VII 29
Native Americans in VII 29
North Eastern Water Supply Study (NEWS) VII 261
North Korea I 41, 293; II 37; VI 50, 54, 102, 147,
149–150, 178, 215–217, 219, 252, 261; XV 75
cease-fire with U.S. I 275
invasion of South Korea (1950) I 87, 208; VI 28;
XIV 147
nuclear weapons development I 217, 219, 224,
239
North Sea VII 104, 204–205, 210, 230; IX 77–78,
140, 144, 181, 186, 257
time needed to flush pollution from VII 142
World War I VIII 29, 35, 122, 135
North Vietnam I 40–42, 44–46, 290–299; II 4–8, 263;
VI 28, 50, 96–97, 178, 201, 203, 285; XII 30,
34
conquers South Vietnam (1975) I 142; VI 24
declares independence I 290
Gulf of Tonkin incident I 291
peace agreement signed I 291
Soviet support VI 246
U.S. bombing VI 59, 165
Northam, William E. VII 43
Northern Buffalo Fence (NBF) VII 35
Northern Rhodesia VII 237
Northey, Edward VIII 86, 89
Northup, Solomon XIII 79, 92
Northwest Kansas Groundwater Management
District VII 185, 187
Northwest Ordinance (1787) XII 22, 65–66, 293, 300;
XIII 19
Northwest Territory, prohibition of slavery in XIII 18
Norway IX 78, 171; XI 62, 102, 176; XV 187
oil XIV 218
Notes on the State of Virginia (1781) XII 125, 296
Noto v. U.S. I 81
Nova Scotia XII 23, 171, 186, 304, 307
Loyalists in XII 169, 189, 194
Novikov, Nikolai I 178
"Novikov Telegram" II 35
Nuclear Nonproliferation Act (1978) I 223
Nuclear Nonproliferation Treaty (NPT) I 216, 217–
219, 222, 224; VI 30, 33, 104, 106; XIV 40,
143–147, 149; XV 75

Nuclear-power plants, regulation of VII 174–180
Nuclear spying I 239, 241–249, 261
Nuclear Test Ban Treaty (1963) II 117–118
Nuclear weapons I 117, 154, 163, 165–172, 216–224,
225–233, 234–241, 249–257
arms control VI 30–36
carried by bombers I 4, 6, 8
debate in House Armed Servies Committee
hearings of 1949 I 8
introduction I 4
safety of VI 214
U.S. monopoly I 27–28
Nueces River VII 70
Nur al-Din X 24, 48–49, 51, 251
Nuremberg Charter XV 79
Nuremberg Code of 1947 XI 151
Nuremberg Laws (1936) III 251; IV 137, 140–141; V
117–118; XI 5, 7, 32–33, 59, 90, 184, 247
Nuremberg Party Rally (1935) V 140
Nuremberg war-crimes trials (1945–1946) IV 88; V
225; XI 37, 39, 43, 45, 103, 115, 148, 152,
167, 252–262
Nyae Nyae conservancy, Namibia VII 38
Nyasaland VII 237
Nye Commission VIII 284

O

Oahe Dam (United States) VII 29, 31
Objectives for Boundary Water Quality (1951) VII 117,
120
Ocalan, Abdullah VII 79; XIV 173, 265
Occupied Territories (West Bank, Gaza Strip, and Golan
Heights) XIV 129, 151–153, 180, 220; XV
20, 78, 89–91, 93, 95, 132–134, 139, 186,
191, 194–195, 198, 214, 242, 261
O'Conner, Sandra Day XIV 115
Odendaal Commission into South-West African
Affairs VII 239
Office of the Coordinator for Counterterrorism
(U.S.) XIV 130
Office of Equal Opportunity (OEO) II 270–276
Office of Military Government for Germany, United
States (OMGUS) XI 255
Office of Minority Business Enterprise (OMBE) II 183
Office of Strategic Services (OSS) V 146–147
Ogallala Aquifer VII 181–187
Ogletree, Charles XIII 197–198
Ohio VII 265; XII 22
Ohio River XII 174, 234, 300
Ohio River Valley VII 256
oil
industry XIV 211–219
pollution VII 147, 265
production XV 172–176
shale VII 22–23
Okavango Delta VII 33, 236
Okavango River VII 236
Oklahoma VII 10, 181–182, 185
grandfather clause XIII 56
Oklahoma City, terrorist attack (1995) XIV 16
slavery in XIII 206
Oklahoma Water Resources Board VII 185
Okuma Shigenobu IX 163–164
Old Contemptibles IX 49, 51
Old Lights XII 145, 148, 150
Old Man of the Mountain X 183–184
Olive Branch Petition (1775) XII 95, 140, 143
Oliver, Peter XII 150, 208
Olmsted, Frederick Law XIII 42, 45, 121, 203, 205,
240
Oman XIV 55, 79, 177, 179, 247; XV 100, 109, 120
water XIV 269
women XIV 121
Omar, Muhammad XIV 11–12
Omnibus Rivers and Harbors Act (1965) VII 261
On the Road (Kerouac) II 109
On the Waterfront (movie) II 190

INDEX

Rhodes, Cecil XII 33; XV 15
Rhodes, James A. VII 265
Rhodes armistice agreements (1949) XV 216
Rhodesia VII 239; VIII 86; XI 268
    British immigration to VII 237
    colonialists in VII 7
Rhodesian Unilateral Declaration of Independence VII 240
Rhône River VII 92–95, 147
Rhône River Authority VII 93, 96
Ribbentrop, Joachim von V 134; XI 59, 62, 179, 254
Ribbentrop-Molotov Non-Aggression Pact (1939) V 28, 30, 32
Rice, Condoleezza XIV 101, 103, 129
Rich, Willis VII 201
Richard I, the Lion-Hearted X 30, 33, 48, 57, 59, 143–144, 151, 175, 247–253, 297, 304, 254–261
Richardson, Robert V. XIII 51, 53
Richtofen, Manfred von IX 38
Rift Valley VII 229
Righteous Among the Nations XI 161, 202, 206
Riis, Jacob August III 260
Rio Grande River VII 152
Rio Treaty I 93
riparian ecosystems in the U.S. Southwest VII 211–218
Rivers, Eugene XIII 253, 256
Rivers and Harbors Act (1899) VII 266
Rivers and Harbors Act (1925) VII 52
Roan Selection Trust VII 5
Robarts, John P. VII 118
Robert of Artois X 139, 141, 143, 145
Robert the Monk X 213, 215, 281, 283
Roberto, Holden VI 1, 165
Roberts, Justice Owen III 25, 28, 30; V 188
Robertson, William VIII 77, 102–108, 221
Robespierre, Maximillian XII 134
Robinson, Bestor VII 112
Robinson, James H. II 44
Robinson, Randall XIII 195, 197–198
Rochambeau, Comte de XII 33, 306, 308
Rock and Roll II 213–219
    "British invasion" II 216
    commercial aspects II 219
    form of rebellion II 219
    liberating force II 213
    mass marketing of II 216
    origin of term II 214
    punk trends II 216
    revolutionary force II 214
    unifying force II 216
Rock Around the Clock (1956) II 219
Rock Oil Company XV 172
Rockefeller, John D. III 271; XV 172
Rockefeller, Nelson A. III 48; VII 264
Rocky Boy's Reservation VII 172
Rocky Ford VII 15
Rocky Ford Ditch Company VII 13
Rocky Mountains VII 151, 181, 197
Roderigue Hortalez & Cie XII 101, 106
Roe v. *Wade* (1973) II 78, 220–226, 280, 284
Roger II (Sicily) X 198, 285, 289
Rogers, William XV 40, 135
Rogers Initiative (1970) XV 40, 42, 44–49
Rogue River VII 31, 223
Röhm, Ernst XI 243
Roland X 65, 103
Roman Empire X 24–25, 29, 88, 124, 167, 305
Romania I 110, 294; II 36, 39, 172; V 64; VI 51, 88, 175, 206, 210, 217, 245, 249, 252, 261, 265, 274, 276; VII 248–250, 252–254; VIII 43–44, 46, 93–97, 163, 216, 230, 278; IX 60–61, 66, 127, 193, 205, 207; X 65, 70; XI 15, 60, 142, 214, 220; XV 120
    chemical spill in VII 247–255
    Department of Waters, Forests, and Environmental Protection VII 248
    Environmental Protection Agency VII 248
    forest clear-cutting in VII 254

    relationship with Soviets I 253
    Soviet Domination I 107
    U.S. recognizes communist government I 303
Romanian Waters Authority VII 248
Rome XIII 274, 278; XIV 159, 161, 163
    slavery in XIII 165
    terrorism XIV 16
Rommel, Erwin V 123–126, 129, 135, 143, 176, 181, 226; VIII 111
    legend V 175
Roosevelt, Eleanor III 150, 217, 219
Roosevelt, Franklin D. II 32, 39, 50, 52, 165, 197, 203, 280; III 10–11, 14, 45, 48, 86, 89, 109, 147, 190, 193; IV 173, 210; V 58, 236, 249; VI 8–9, 20, 36, 56–57, 78, 104, 123, 146–147, 158, 205, 254, 267; VII 28, 97, 152, 202; XI 4, 10–12, 55–57, 60, 64, 110, 121, 168, 174, 252, 261; XV 163
    arsenal of democracy III 64
    Asia policy IV 254
    attitude toward Soviet Union III 13
    belief in a cooperative relationship with the Soviet Union I 101
    Brain Trust II 210
    Casablanca conference (1943) V 252
    Court packing scheme XI 168
    election of VII 27
    Executive Order 8802 (1941) III 219
    Executive Order 9066 (1942) III 103–104
    Fireside chats III 148, 152
    Four Freedoms V 250
    Good Neighbor Policy I 125; III 47
    Great Depression III 54–60
    Inaugural Address (1932) III 152
    isolationism V 289–294
    Lend Lease Act IV 160
    Native American policies III 141–142
    New Deal II 47, 271; III 193, 263
    New Deal programs III 62–63
    Operation Torch (1942) V 251
    opinion of Second Front IV 213
    presidential campaign (1932) III 148
    previous war experience V 253
    relationship with George C. Marshall V 251
    Roosevelt Court II 281
    Scottsboro case III 188
    Selective Service Act (1940) V 250
    State of the Union Address (1941) II 99
    support of Great Britain V 250
    support of highway building II 106
    support of naval reorganization IV 3
    Supreme Court III 24
    unconditional surrender policy V 270–276
    western irrigation VII 25
    World War II strategy V 251, 253
    Yalta conference V 252, 309–315
Roosevelt, Theodore I 306; II 195, 199, 271–272; III 208, 211, 240–247, 177; VIII 18, 22, 129, 205; IX 5, 168, 246; XIV 175
    appreciation of public image III 242
    Bull Moose Party III 243
    conservation efforts III 243
    Dominican Republic III 247
    establishes federal refuges VII 271, 273
    First Children III 242
    labor disputes III 243
    New Nationalism III 211
    Nobel Peace Prize II 99, 243
    racial prejudices III 246
    role as a family man III 242
    Rough Riders III 241
    signs Newlands Reclamation Act VII 25
    Spanish-American War (1898) III 245
    supports western reclamation VII 26
    Teddy bears III 242
    views on Latin America I 132
Roosevelt (FDR) administration III 46; VI 154; XI 123

INDEX

Sierra Nevada Mountains VII 112, 272
Sigismund Chapel, Wawel Cathedral, Poland VII 18
Silent Spring (Carson) II 183; III 7; VII 86, 160, 162
Silent Valley Project (India) VII 127
Silesia IX 136, 171; XI 270
Silvermaster, Nathan VI 126
Simms, William Gilmore XIII 48, 73, 205
Simpson, Alan XV 78
Sims, William IX 75, 184
Simsboro Aquifer VII 75
Sinai I (1974) XV 51, 219, 226, 237–243
Sinai II (1975) XV 51, 219, 226, 237–243
Sinai Peninsula I 308–309, 311–312, 316–317; VII 2,
     135; XI 125; XIV 144; XV 20–21, 23–24, 42,
     51, 56, 63, 93, 127, 134, 136–137, 213–215,
     219, 223–227, 237, 240, 245, 261
    demilitarization I 314
    Israeli forces I 313
    Israeli settlements destroyed XIV 154
Singapore XIV 171, 175
Sinn Féin VIII 156, 158–159, 161–162
Sino-French War (1884–1885) IX 101
Sisco, Joseph XV 44
Sister Carrie (Dreiser) II 239
Sit-in movement (1960s) II 27, 160; VI 25
Six-Day War (*See* Arab-Israeli War, 1967)
Skagit River VII 223
Skawina Aluminum Works VII 18–19
Skoropadsky, Pavlo VIII 99–100
Slave Carrying Act (1799) XIII 273
Slave Codes XIII 97, 99
slave trade XIII 35–42, 47, 129–137, 179, 269–275
slavery XII 1–8, 71, 134, 167, 263, 293–300, 311
    abolitionists XIII 1–9
    Act of 1791 XIII 97
    American Revolution XII 1–8; XIII 17–24
    as cause of Civil War XIII 276–283
    black care providers XIII 83
    child mortality XIII 80
    Christianity XIII 101, 186–193, 265
    compared to Nazi concentration camps XIII 138,
      142
    comparison between English and Spanish/
      Portuguese colonies XIII 59–66
    comparison with northern free labor XIII 113
    complicity of Africans in slave trade XIII 35–40,
      195
    control of pace of work XIII 202–208
    development of African-American culture XIII
      138–145
    diet of slaves XIII 77–83, 113, 136
    economic impact of XIII 42–48
    economic return XIII 47
    enslavement of Africans XIII 161–168
    forms of resistance XIII 172
    gang system XIII 172
    health of slaves XIII 65, 77–83
    Hebrew slavery XIII 27
    house servants and drivers XIII 85–92
    humanity of slaves XIII 95
    impact of emancipation on African
      Americans XIII 50–57
    in English law XIII 99
    infantilization of slaves (Elkins thesis) XIII 59
    intellectual assessment of XIII 146–153
    interracial female relations XIII 224–230
    justifications for use of Africans XIII 164
    laws pertaining to XIII 60, 61, 62
    legal definiton of status XIII 94–103
    life expectancy XIII 79, 80
    maroon communities XIII 104–111
    medical care XIII 77, 81
    Middle Passage XIII 129–137
    mortality rates XIII 77–78, 81
    murder of slaves XIII 98
    paternalism XIII 60, 112, 117–119, 172, 203,
      205, 232
    prices of slaves XIII 172, 174

    profitability of XIII 169–176
    profitability of transatlantic slave trade XIII 269–
      274
    proslavery ideology XIII 68–75, 96
    punishments XIII 62, 64
    racism as cause of XIII 178–184
    rebellions XIII 154–160, 231–238
    reparations XIII 194–201
    resistance to XIII 120–128, 203, 267
    retention of African culture XIII 10–15, 138–145
    revolts XIII 127
    sexual exploitation of slave women XIII 217–223
    singing XIII 204
    sinking of slave ships XIII 133
    slave codes XIII 115, 176
    slave religion XIII 186–193
    slaveholders as capitalists XIII 239–245
    stability of slave marriages XIII 261–267
    stereotypes XIII 115
    task system XIII 172
    treatment of slaves XIII 112–119
    use of Christianity to justify XIII 26–34
    use of slaves in industry XIII 48
Slim, William V 3, 122, 198
Slovak Green Party VII 103
Slovak Union of Nature and Landscape Protectors VII
    103
Slovakia VII 248, 250, 252; XI 195
    dams in VII 100–107
    environmentalists in VII 103
    importance of Gabcikovo dam VII 103
    nuclear reactor at Jaslovské Bohunice VII 103
    nuclear-power plant at Mochovce VII 103
    symbolic importance of Danube VII 102
Slovenia IX 136, 266–272
Smith, Adam IX 54–55; XII 118, 119, 120, 121, 122,
    164; XIII 173, 246
Smith, Bessie III 79, III 82
Smith, Holland M. "Howlin' Mad" V 297, 299
Smith, Howard Alexander II 208
Smith, Ian VI 2, 83
Smith Act (Alien Registration Act of 1940) I 77, 79, 81;
    III 11
Smith v. *Allwright*, 1944 II 141
Smuts, Jan VIII 85–86, 89; IX 13, 222
Smyrna VIII 214, 217; IX 208
Smyth, Henry De Wolf I 247–248
Smyth Report I 248
Smythe, William A. VII 151
Snake River 27, 29, 31, 53–54, 196–197, 220, 221, 223–
    225, 227
    dams on VII 219–228
Sobibor (concentration camp) XI 220, 236
Social Darwinism III 260; IV 86, 123; VIII 60, 299;
    IX 99, 112, 209, 224, 228; XI 82, 115
Social Democratic Party I 255; VI 20, 207
Social Ecological Movement VII 20
Social Security Act (1935) III 63, 149
Socialism II 34, 60, 160; VIII 254–262; IX 83
Socialist convention (1913) III 223
Socialist Labor Party II 42
Socialist Party II 196, 199; III 222–223
    Debs, Eugene V. III 221
Socialist People's Libyan Arab Jamahuriyya XIV 192
Socialist Unity Party (SED) VII 118, 121
Society for the Abolition of the Slave Trade XIII 1
Society for the Propagation of the Gospel in Foreign
    Parts (SPG) XII 148
Society of Jesus XIV 233
Soil Conservation and Domestic Allotment Act
    (1936) III 157
Solidarity VI 110, 237; VII 17, 19, 20
Solomon XIV 159
Solzhenitsyn, Aleksandr VI 200; XIV 233
Somalia II 100, 155–156; VI 164, 271; XIV 55, 190,
    198, 282
    claim to Ogaden VI 165
    Ethiopian conflict VI 165

INDEX

imperialism I 151
  relations with the Soviet Union VI 165
  U.S. troops in (1993) XIV 16
  water XIV 269
Somalilands XIV 176
Somerset case (1772) XIII 1
Somoza Debayle, Anastasio I 48– 49, 54, 126, 141; III
      51; VI 190–191
Somocistas VI 64, 191
Sonoran Desert VII 151–152
  agriculture in VII 152
Sons of Liberty XII 152, 214, 218, 261
Sontag, Susan XI 42
Sophie's Choice (1982) XI 158
Sorensen, Ted II 275
Sorenson, Theodore C. II 117
South (American) XIII 233, 256
  adaptibility of slaves to environment in XIII 11
  African-inspired architectural design XIII 141
  antebellum women in XIII 224–230
  black population in XII 299
  Civil War, slavery as cause of XIII 276
  clock ownership XIII 202–208
  cotton as single crop XIII 43
  economic impact of slavery upon XIII 42–48
  economy of XIII 169–170, 175, 243
  firearms in XIII 233
  impact of Revolution on economy of XII 264
  Ku Klux Klan XIII 55
  Loyalists in XII 181–182, 186
  power of slaveholding elite XIII 69
  Reconstruction, end of XIII 55
  religion in XIII 186–190
  segregation in XIII 57
  sexual exploitation of slave women in XIII 217–
      223
  slave codes XIII 176
  slave laws XIII 94, 96, 97, 261
  slave rebellions XIII 231
  slaveholders as capitalists XIII 239–245
  slavery in XIII 85, 86–92, 98, 101–102, 112–128,
      169–172, 175, 178–179, 231, 247–248, 262,
      264–267
  trade with New England XIII 195
  violence against blacks and Republicans in XIII
      55
  wealth of XIII 43
  women, interracial relations XIII 224–230
South Africa I 51; VI 1, 2, 4, 6, 50, 54, 87, 136, 178,
      215; VII 2, 5, 67, 236–237, 239–241; VIII
      31, 160–161, 208; XI 43, 167; XII 33, 169;
      XIV 199, 221; XV 39
  apartheid VI 13
  Bill of Rights VII 287
  British immigration to VII 237
  inequalities of water supply in VII 284
  intervention in Angola VI 7
  intervention in Mozambique VI 6
  nuclear weapons development I 219–223
  rinderpest epidemic VII 34
  use of water by upper class VII 7
  water policy in VII 286, 287
South African National Defense Force VII 7
South African War (1899–1902) IX 68
South America XIV 187
  corruption in XIV 48
  death squads in XI 166
  introduction of species to the United States
      from VII 217
  slavery in XIII 175
South Carolina XII 1, 39, 41, 68, 70, 75, 184–185, 205,
      209, 213, 218–219, 263, 314; XIII 53, 66, 71,
      73
  African Americans in XII 89
  anti-Loyalist activities in XII 190, 192
  Black Codes XIII 54
  cattle raising XIII 11
  clock ownership XIII 205

  dispute over Confederate flag XIII 270
  laws on rice dams and flooding VII 272
  Loyalists in XII 184, 187
  maroons in XIII 108, 111
  massacre of Rebels in XII 186
  mob action in American Revolution XII 215
  property qualifications to vote XIII 56
  prosecution of Thomas Powell XII 233
  Reconstruction, end of XIII 55
  religion in XII 263
  rice cultivation VII 272; XIII 11
  secession XIII 272, 276
  slave rebellions XIII 156, 210, 231, 235–236
  slavery in VII 272; XII 3–4, 295, 297, 299; XIII
      11, 61, 81, 83, 87, 98–99, 102, 140, 204, 218,
      232, 235, 240, 244, 248, 265, 267
  use of Confederate symbols XIII 277
  women in XII 319
South Carolina College XIII 28
South Carolina Declaration of the Causes of Secession
      (1860) XIII 270, 276
South Carolina Red Shirts XIII 55
South Dakota VII 181
  dams in VII 29
South East Asia Treaty Organization (SEATO) II 52,
      264
South Korea I 86–87, 288, 293; II 37; VI 102, 147–
      149, 217, 263; XIV 79, 147
  domino theory I 266
  invaded by North Korea (1950) I 208; VI 28
  invasion of I 184
  nuclear weapons development I 216, 219, 223
  U.S. intervention I 158
South Lebanon Army XV 127, 132
South Sea Company XIII 40
South Vietnam I 40–46, 290, 293–299; II 5–8, 263,
      266; VI 58–60, 92–99, 101, 138, 140, 201,
      203, 284; XII 30, 34; XIV 147
  aid received from United States I 158; VI 2, 66,
      142, 144
  conquered by North Vietnam I 142; VI 222
  declares independence I 290
  Soviet support I 185
South Yemen XV 57, 222, 255
Southeast Asia XII 28–29, 33–34
Southeast Asia Treaty Organization (SEATO) I 277;
      VI 203, 287; XV 26
Southeastern Anatolia Project VII 77, 83
Southern African Hearings for Communities affected by
      Large Dams VII 242
Southern Baptist Convention III 38
Southern Charibbee Islands XII 313
Southern Christian Leadership Conference (SCLC) II
      22, 26, 28, 89
Southern Economic Association XIII 174
Southern Okavango Integrated Water Development
      Project VII 243
Southern Pacific Railroad VII 151, 155
Southern Rhodesia VII 237, 239
Southern Tenant Farmers' Union (STFU) II 189; III
      159
South-West Africa VII 237, 239
South-West African People's Organization
      (SWAPO) VII 239
Southwest Kansas Groundwater Management
      District VII 185
Soviet expansionism I 262; II 34–35, 208, 264, 267;
      III 10
  U.S. fear of II 129, 207
Soviet intervention
  Hungary I 278, 281
  Middle East I 277
Soviet Union I 77, 91; II 9, 56–62, 64–71, 168, 171;
      III 10; VI 9, 16, 20–21, 32, 35, 49, 106, 115–
      116, 147, 149, 161, 201, 206, 208, 236, 250–
      255, 260, 264; VII 55; VIII 94, 97, 99, 277,
      285; X 55, 63; XI 9–10, 14–15, 83, 110, 175,
      252–253, 261–262; XII 33; XIV 40, 82, 143,

175, 178, 181, 192, 223, 238, 261–262; XV 23–24, 27, 30–31, 61–63, 68, 74–75, 81, 119, 139, 160, 165–166, 170, 182, 202–203, 205, 219, 223, 226, 240, 243–244, 250, 252, 258, 260, 263, 267

aging leadership VI 111
aid to China V 198
aid to Mozambique VI 2
Angola policy VI 41, 43, 165
annexes Estonia VII 22
"Aviation Day" I 192
bomber fleet I 6; VI 50
casualties in Afghanistan (1979–1989) I 12
Central Committee II 59
Central Committee Plenum II 60
challenge to U.S. dominance in Latin America I 125
collapse I 11; VI 47, 50, 58, 108, 213, 224, 227, 235, 237; VII 17, 207; VIII 139; XIV 6, 171; XV 82
Cominform I 178
Communist Party VI 244, 247
cooperation with Nationalist Chinese government I 304
coup (1991) VI 114
Cuban Missile Crisis II 116; VI 70–76
Czechoslovakia (1948) II 130, 133
defense spending I 197; VI 54; VI 116, 120, 226
demographics VI 242
demokratizatiia I 152
development of wartime economy IV 233
diplomatic work I 289
domination of eastern Europe I 258, 260
domination of other countries I 271
drain on resources by war in Afghanistan I 13
East Germany policy VI 115–122, 211
Eastern Europe as defensive barrier I 303
economy I 184; II 57, 59; VI 109, 111, 214, 242
Egypt, sells weapons to XV 40
empire VI 243–249
entry into war against Japan I 301
espionage network II 130
Estonian contribution to VII 22
fear of the West I 181
first Soviet atomic bomb test I 244
forces in Afghanistan I 13
foreign aid VI 54, 254
gains control of Eastern Europe I 302
German invasion of XI 104, 106, 117, 211
glasnost I 152; VI 108–114
government suspicion of citizens I 185
Great Purges XI 15, 166
Gross National Product II 60
human rights record II 104; VI 35, 85, 109, 200, 244
Hungarian uprising I 276
ICBM buildup I 190
ICBM development I 189–194
ideology in foreign policy I 148–154
industrialization ideology VII 104
influence in postwar Europe I 174
invasion of Afghanistan (1979) VI 2, 30, 35, 42–44, 66, 68, 116, 162, 165, 237, 241, 246; XIV 1–9
invasion of Chechnya (1990s) VI 169
invasion of Czechoslovakia (1968) I 11–12; VI 43
invasion of Hungary (1956) I 12
invasion of Manchuria III 15
Iran policy I 11
Jewish emigration VI 43, 200, 257
Jews in XI 14, 102
komitet gosudarstvennoy bezopasnosti (KGB) II 59
leaders I 262
League of Nations IX 170, 174
Middle East policy I 160; VI 160–167, 268
military balance VI 168–174
military capabilities II 30, 64
military expenditures I 125

"Molotov Plan" I 178
New Course I 184, 192
New Economic Policy (NEP) VI 113
nonaggression pact with Germany (1939) II 32
nuclear buildup I 230
nuclear capabilities I 213; II 130, 133; VI 35, 215
nuclear testing I 212; VI 49, 173, 177
nuclear weapons development I 184, 241–249; VI 31, 109, 144
nuclear weapons espionage I 239, 241–249
objections to Marshall Plan I 175, 178
occupies Iranian Azerbaijan XV 160
oil XV 173, 175
overthrow of Shah of Iran XIV 37
participation in war against Japan I 301
perestroika I 152; VI 108–114
Poland V 3
Iran policy I 11
post–Cold War VI 47–55, 219
post–World War II military budgets I 192
post–World War II war-crimes trial XI 260
postwar foreign policy I 238
postwar recovery I 177; VI 49, 175
Red Army I 181; VI 130–131, 136, 158, 221, 273, 275–276
relationship with China II 169; VI 40, 43–44, 113, 203
relationship with Cuba VI 63–66, 249
relationship with Great Britain V 28–33
relationship with United States V 28–33; VI 55
response to Marshall Plan I 238
response to Strategic Defense Initiative (SDI) I 186
response to U.S. defense spending I 197
response to West Germany admission to NATO I 206
rift with China I 141
role in postwar Poland I 301
Rosenbergs II 227
satellite states II 58
security interests in Eastern Europe II 36
scale of killings in XI 167
social problems VI 112
Soviet-friendly countries II 103
space program II 64–70
sphere of influence III 11; V 311, 314
Suez Crisis (1956) VI 246
supports Chinese over Quemoy and Matsu I 265
suspicion of the West II 31
technological deficiencies in weaponry I 196
Third World activities I 11; VI 81, 188
threat to Western allies I 4
troops in Afghanistan, narcotic use I 13
U.N. Security Council membership I 300
views of Marshall Plan I 177
war with Finland IV 57
Winter War (1939–1940) V 28
women in World War II V 304, 306
World War II losses II 267
Yalta Agreement (1945) I 300–301
Zond program II 258
Soviet-Egyptian Pact (1955) I 162
Soweto, South Africa VII 7–8
Spaatz, Carl A. "Tooey" V 7, 92; XI 12
use of bombing V 98–99
Spain VII 149; VIII 18, 277; IX 49, 84, 140 ; XI 2, 174–175, 178–179; XII 37, 105, 167, 248, 251–252, 255, 290; XIV 58, 73, 111
abolishes forced labor XIII 63
allies with Americans in American Revolution XII 39
beach closings in VII 147
Catholic movement XIV 256
Catholic orders in XI 23
Christian-Muslim relations X 40–45, 190
control of Mississippi River XII 25, 290
cost of Med plan to VII 146
free workers from XIII 168

Index

INDEX

Thompson, Dorothy XI 60
Thompson, Tommy VII 57–59
Thornwell, James Henley XIII 28–29, 48, 68, 183, 248
Three Emperors' League VIII 225–227
Three Mile Island (1979) II 86
Three-Staged Plan for Optimum, Equitable, and
    Reasonable Utilization of the Transboundary
    Watercourses of the Tigris-Euphrates
    Basin VII 79
Thucydides XV 53
Tibbets, Paul W. V 50
Tignes, France, riots at VII 99
Tigris River VII 77
    Turkish dams XIV 270
Tigris-Euphrates river system XIV 268–269, 271; XV
    72, 121, 203
Tijuana River VII 152
Timrod, Henry XIII 153
Tirailleurs Senegalais IX 113–115
Tirpitz, Alfred von VIII 29, 31, 34–35, 249; IX 101,
    140, 142–143, 221
Tisza Club VII 252
Tisza River, chemical spill on VII 247–255
Title IX (1972) II 77
Tito, Josip Broz I 36, 59, 86, 108–110, 113, 273, 277,
    283; VI 134, 136, 182, 217, 254, 265, 268,
    271, 273–281; VIII 192; IX 268; XV 68, 167
Tobago XII 311, 313–314; XIII 270
Tocqueville, Alexis de XII 260, 265; XIII 161–162,
    165, 201, 251
Togo XIII 11
Tojo, Hideki I 134; IV 7; V 49, 194, 264
Toledo X 2, 289
Tonga (Batonka) people VII 5, 239, 242, 245
    effect of dam onVII 4
Torah XIV 184, 188, 259
Tortola XII 311, 314
Tokyo trials (1945–1948) V 263–269
    comparison with Nuremberg trials V 266–267
    dissent of Radhabinod Pal V 267
    International Military Tribunal for the Far East
    (IMTFE) V 266
Torah X 44, 273
Torrey Canyon accident (1967) VII 143
Total (oil company) XV 177–179
Total Strategy White Paper VII 240
Totally Equal Americans VII 172
Toussaint L'Ouverture, Francois Dominque XIII 209–
    216
Tower of London XIII 229
Townshend, Charles XII 53, 139–141, 233, 237
Townsend, Charles Wendell VII 277
Townshend Acts (Townsend duties, 1767) XII 51, 141,
    149, 207, 214, 233, 237
    repeal of XII 55
Tracy, Spencer XI 158
Trading with the Enemy Act (1917) III 223
"Tragedy of the Commons" VII 47, 48, 70, 73
Trans-Jordan VII 81; VIII 166, 214; IX 96; XIV 67,
    176; XV 34, 44, 46, 142, 144, 146
Transparency International XIV 48
Treaties–
    –Brest-Litovsk (1918) VIII 95–97, 141, 173, 278;
    IX 27
    –Bucharest (1918) VIII 95
    –Dunkirk (1948) I 204
    –Frankfurt (1871) VIII 278
    –Lausanne (1923) VIII 214; XIV 168
    –Locarno (1925) V 116–120
    –London (1913) VIII 212
    –Moscow I 107
    –Ouchy (1912) VIII 212
    –Paris (1763) XII 52, 235
    –Paris (1783) XII 23, 25, 169, 174, 286
    –Peace and Friendship With Tripoli (1796) XII
    66
    –Ryswick (1695) XIII 210
    –Sevres (1920) VIII 214, 217; XIV 168

    –Turko-Bulgarian (1914) IX 204
    –Versailles (1919). *See* Versailles Treaty
    –Washington (1922) IX 168
    –Westphalia (1648) XIV 240
Treblinka (concentration camp) I 138; V 54, 57, 158,
    161; XI 52, 220
Tredegar Iron Works, Richmond, Virginia XIII 48
Trees
    cottonwoods VII 12, 212, 214, 215
    elms VII 232
    mesquites VII 212
    oaks VII 212, 232
    riparian importance of VII 215
    salt-cedars VII 12, 215, 217
    willows VII 212, 214, 215, 232
Trelawney, Edward XIII 108, 110
Trenchard, Hugh IX 10–11, 222
Trenchard, John XII 128, 147
Tribal Grazing Lands Policy (TGLP) VII 34
Trident Conference (1943) V 236
Trinidad XIII 147, 270
Trinity River VII 223
Tripartite Declaration (1950) XV 30, 244–245, 248,
    250
Tripartite Pact (1940) V 294
Triple Alliance VIII 44, 46, 226, 229
Triple Entente VIII 35, 45; IX 226
Tripoli X 27, 49, 151, 156, 191, 247–248, 251, 254, 256;
    XII 66
Tripoli Program (1962) XV 6
Tripolitan War XIV 192
Triumph des Willens (Triumph of the Will) XI 167
Trotsky, Leon VI 179, 274–275; VIII 167
Trout Unlimited VII 31, 213
Trudeau, Pierre E., signs Great Lakes Water Quality
    Agreement VII 120
Truitt, Reginald V. VII 43–44, 47
Truman, Harry S I 28, 35, 65, 69, 109, 113, 148, 159,
    257, 285; II 39, 42, 44, 49–50, 197, 199,
    203–204, 207–208, 280; III 10–14, 62; V
    46, 98, 106; VI 20, 56, 144, 146–148, 153,
    205, 231, 250, 284; IX 7; XI 121, 123–124,
    214, 253; XII 28; XV 30, 137, 167
    acceptance of a divided Europe I 264
    adoption of containment policy I 262
    anticommunism VI 155
    appointment of Baruch I 27
    approval of NSC-68 I 182
    atomic bombing of Japan I 239
    attitude toward Stalin I 259, 261–263
    containment policy I 274
    Executive Order 10241 II 131
    foreign policy I 58; II 205
    foreign policy links to domestic ideology II 209
    Interim Committee III 15
    Marshall Plan I 176
    Point Four Program XV 202–210
    Potsdam Conference I 263
    response to communism II 130
    restraint in use of nuclear weapons I 235
    service in World War I VIII 192
    Truman Doctrine II 145; XV 61, 203
    unconditional surrender policy V 275
    veto of Taft-Hartley Act II 188
    views on postwar role of military I 5
Truman administration I 30, 59, 74; II 36; VI 59, 101,
    147, 150, 155, 224; XI 123, 253, 255; XV 30
    acceptence of Soviet nuclear program I 237
    accused of abandoning China to communism I 59
    aid to China I 60
    aid to Taiwan I 266
    Baruch Plan I 31
    CIA, creation of I 64
    Cold War policy I 266
    concern about communist influence in Europe I
    174, 176
    concern about trade imbalances in Europe I 175

INDEX

U

151, 158, 234, 261; VII 2, 65, 79, 81, 240,
245; VIII 11; IX 171; XI 37, 121, 124; XIV
12, 14, 17, 55, 85, 96, 103, 106, 144, 146,
149, 159–160, 173, 180, 192, 195, 199, 219,
225, 228, 231, 237, 247, 265, 277, 282, 287;
XV 15, 21, 24, 34, 74, 80–81, 84, 91, 97, 100,
102, 120, 141, 153, 198, 203, 205, 219, 237,
253
adopts TVA model VII 1
agencies working in Latin America I 22
Atomic Energy Commission I 27, 29
censure of Soviet Union for invasion of
Afghanistan I 12
Charter XV 245
China seat VI 44, 148
Convention on the Law of the Sea (1982) XV 247
Council for Namibia VII 241
creation of II 100, 208
Decade for the Rights of Indigenous Peoples XIV
207
Declaration of Human Rights XV 79
Declaration on the Granting of Independence of
Colonial Countries and Peoples (1960) XIV
277
Economic Commission for Latin America
(ECLA) I 20
Economic Commission for the Middle East XIV
177
Fourth Committee on Decolonization XIV 277
General Assembly XIV 277; XV 34, 200, 254
human rights I 146
Hungarian uprising (1956) VI 270
Interim Force in Lebanon (UNIFIL) XV 153
International Law Commission XIV 274
intervention in the Congo II 115
Korea VI 146
Mission for the Referendum in Western Sahara
(MINURSO) XIV 278
nuclear weapons I 28
Observation Group in Lebanon (UNOGIL) XV
61
Palestinian refugees XIV 179
Panel on Water VII 286
Partition of Palestine XIV 163; XV 190
Persian Gulf War XV 73–79
Relief and Works Agency for Palestine Refugees in
the Near East XIV 179; XV 204
Resolution 181 XIV 152, 165; XV 181 37, 38
Resolution 194 XIV 221, 225
Resolution 338 VI 163
Resolution 339 VI 163
Resolution 340 VI 163
response to invasion of South Korea II 37
Security Council II 100; VI 11, 13, 163, 284; XIV
179, 228, 239, 278, 280, 284 ; XV 23, 81,
148, 150, 245, 247, 250, 258
Security Council Resolution 242 XIV 162; XV 40,
42, 46, 89, 134–135, 184, 198–199, 211–218,
220, 226, 257, 261, 263
Security Council Resolution 339 XV 220
Security Council Resolution 497 XV 263
Security Council Resolution 678 XV 81, 258
Security Council Resolution 687 XIV 75, 237
Security Council Resolution 1397 XIV 100, 105
Security Council Resolution 1441 XIV 239, 240
sets tone on water policy VII 286
Special Commission (UNSCOM) XV 75
Special Committee on Palestine (UNSCOP) XI
126
status of Taiwan I 269
Suez Crisis (1956) VI 80, 270
Technical Assistance Agency (UNTAA) XV 206
water studies XIV 269
Watercourses Convention (1997) XIV 274
Western Sahara XIV 276
United Nations Charter II 102
United Nations Development Programm (UNDP) VII
7; XIV 55, 110, 113, 115

United Nations Educational, Scientific and Cultural
Organization (UNESCO) VII 143
United Nations Emergency Force (UNEF) XV 20, 135,
225
United Nations Environmental Program (UNEP) VII
143, 248
United Nations Food and Agricultural Organization
(FAO) VII 143
United Nations Relief and Works Agency
(UNRWA) XIV 220
United Nations Special Commission (UNSCOM) I
239; XIV 241
United Nations War Crimes Commission V 264
United States
abolishes slave trade XIII 65
abolitionism in XIII 1–9
advisers in Vietnam I 291
African slave trade XIII 195
aid to China V 198
Air Force II 65–66
alliance with Israel I 156
Alpha Plan XV 68
Animal and Plant Health Inspection Service VII
217
anti-German feelings during World War I VIII
296
antinuclear protests VI 16
antiwar movement VI 23–29
Arab oil embargo I 162
arms control VI 30
Army IV 9–12; VI 126, 140, 149, 153, 171; VII
166; VIII 10–17, 20–25, 27, 67, 206, 269
Army Corps of Engineers VII 13, 26–27, 29, 52,
54–55, 57, 59–60, 202, 214, 220–224, 259,
261, 263, 266
Army War College VIII 16
as superpower XIV 88
Asia policy IV 253–259
backs Zionist settlements in Israel VII 136
bans African slave trade XII 300
Barbary pirates XIV 192
Bill of Rights II 98, 101; VII 170
bipartisanship II 203–212
bombing of Cambodia I 45
bore-hole drilling in VII 66
British immigration to XII 165, 168, 171
Bureau of the Budget II 271
Bureau of Land Management VII 216
Bureau of Near Eastern Affairs (BNEA) XIV 179
Bureau of Reclamation VII 13, 27–29, 110, 112,
202, 216, 259
capitalist economic system of I 184
Children's Bureau, Division of Juvenile
Delinquency Service 1960 report II 273
Christian roots of XII 60–66
Cold War ideology I 148–154; VI 47–55, 213–
220
Committee for Refugees XIV 284
communist activities in VI 126, 129
Congress VI 56–62, 194, 222, 224, 285–286; VII
59, 175; IX 21, 250; XII 7, 17, 21, 25, 31, 101,
121, 297; XIII 282; XIV 229, 240; XV 81,
173, 203, 206; allies of
environmentalists VII 123; appropriated
money for dams VII 55; approves
Chesapeake Bay oyster-restoration VII 49;
approves Flood Control Act of 1944 VII 29;
authorizes Hetch Hetchy Dam VII 112;
authorizes TVA VII 28; cedes swamplands
to states VII 272; creates flood plan VII
273; environmental concerns of VII 256;
environmental policy of VII 257; Fourteen
Points VIII 281; gag rule XIII 8; funds
regional wastewater systems planning VII
262; Indian policy VII 167–168; thermal
pollution VII 175; passes Central Arizona
Project bill VII 114; passes laws to promote
western settlement VII 26

ISBN 1-55862-478-3

90000

9 781558 624788